Christina Rossetti
A Descriptive Bibliography

Christina Rossetti

(By Dante Gabriel Rossetti, circa 1866.)

Christina Rossetti
A Descriptive Bibliography

Maura Ives

Oak Knoll Press

2011

o°o *for John* o°o

First Edition 2011

Published by
Oak Knoll Press
310 Delaware Street
New Castle, DE 19720
www.oakknoll.com

© 2011 Maura Ives

ISBN: 978-1-58456-291-7

Publishing Director: Laura R. Williams
Design & typography: Matthew McLennan Young

♾ Printed in the United States of America on acid-free paper meeting
the requirements of ANSI/NISO Z39.48–1992 (Permanence of Paper)

Library of Congress Cataloging-in-Publication Data

Ives, Maura C., 1960-
Christina Rossetti : a descriptive bibliography / Maura Ives. – 1st ed.
     p. cm.
Summary: "Bibliography of English poet Christina Rossetti covering 1862
through 1900. Examines anthologies, periodicals, hymnals, musical settings,
selected translations, ephemera, and other Rossettiana with bibliographical
details such as title page, collation, pagination, typography, papers,
bindings, illustrations, and supplementary notes. Illustrated
and indexed" – Provided by publisher.
 Includes bibliographical references and indexes.
 ISBN 978-1-58456-291-7 (alk. paper)
 1. Rossetti, Christina Georgina, 1830-1894--Bibliography. I. Title.

Z8759.75.I94 2011
[PR5238]
016.821'8--dc22

                                      2011002796

CONTENTS

ACKNOWLEDGMENTS

The initial work on this project was carried out in Princeton's Rare Book and Manuscript Library, and was made possible by a fellowship from the Bibliographical Society of America and a Library Research Grant from the Friends of the Princeton University Library. Various travel and research awards from Texas A&M University enabled me to visit other important collections in England and Canada over several years, and faculty development leave supported the focused writing and research time necessary to complete the manuscript. Through the Department of English's Undergraduate Research Opportunity Program, I have also had the pleasure of working with several outstanding Texas A&M English majors, including Janna Smartt, Sarah Walch, and Sharleen Mondal. I have also benefitted from the assistance of excellent graduate research assistants, including Christina Weston, Youngjoo Kim, Jungsun Choi, Kohei Furuya and Cory Lehman.

In my years at Texas A&M, it has been my good fortune to rely upon the advice, support, and friendship of Valerie Balester, Candace Benefiel, Amy Earhart, Jim Harner, Craig Kallendorf, Wendi Arant Kaspar, M. Jimmie Killingsworth, Janet McCann, J. Lawrence Mitchell, Paul Parrish, and Gary Stringer. Many other colleagues and collectors have answered questions, read drafts, and shared information about their books. At various points in my work I have consulted David Vander Meulen, whose expertise is matched only by the patience with which he has responded to my numerous queries. I am thankful for Ann Hawkins's sharp editorial eye and for her advice on various aspects of this project. William Baker's careful reading of the completed manuscript made this a much better book. My friends Mark Samuels Lasner and Margaret Stetz have supported and encouraged my work for many years; it is a special pleasure to acknowledge Mark's generosity in allowing access to his collection of Pre-Raphaelite materials (now housed at the University of Delaware). The late William (Dick) Fredeman invited me to work with his collection as well. No one who experienced the hospitality of Dick and his wife Betty could ever forget it. Leonard Roberts has readily shared his considerable knowledge of Victorian and Pre-Raphaelite bibliography. I must also offer special thanks to Mary Ann Stringer for help with questions about Rossetti's musical settings, and to Mary Louise VanDyke, of the Dictionary of American Hymnology Project at Oberlin College Library, for her help in sorting out Christina Rossetti's appearances in American hymnals. John Handford, former archivist at Macmillan UK, provided invaluable access to the company's records at Basingstoke.

The task of thanking the libraries and librarians who have assisted me over the years is daunting but welcome: this book would not exist without their help. The faculty and staff of the Texas A&M University Libraries have contributed in countless ways to my work; special thanks are due to the department of Document Delivery and Interlibrary Services, and to the current and former staff of the Cushing Memorial Library and Archives, especially Todd Samuelson and Cait Coker, who have graciously accommodated last minute requests for assistance. I am also very much indebted to the Department of Rare Books and Manuscripts at Princeton University, including Margaret Sherry Rich, Stephen Ferguson, Anna Lee Pauls, John Logan and Jennifer Meyer, as well as to Eric L. Pumroy, Marianne Hansen and Cheryl Klimaszewski in the Special Collections at Bryn Mawr. Several trips to work with the Angeli-Dennis and Colbeck collections at the Department of Rare Books and Manuscripts, University of British Columbia were made easier by the assistance of George Brandak. Sarena Fletcher and Rachael DiEleuterio of the Helen Farr Sloane Library, Delaware Art Museum, and Timothy Murray and Iris Snyder in the Special Collections department of the University of Delaware facilitated my work with the materials in their respective collections. For their help with various questions about musical settings held in the British Library, I must thank Robert Balchin, Christopher Scobie, and Fiona McHenry; and, for research assistance beyond what the library staff could provide, I thank Robert Parker.

In addition, I would like to thank Barbara J. Dalbach and Jennifer McClure at the University of Alabama; Marilyn Wurzburger at Arizona State University; Cynthia A. Burgess at the Armstrong Browning Library, Baylor University; Peter Ward Jones at the Bodleian Library; Stuart T. Walker and Eric P. Frazier at the Boston Public Library; David Day at Brigham Young University; Rosemary L. Cullen at Brown University; Mary Ann Williard at Bucknell University; Will Hepfer at the University of Buffalo; Apollonia Lang Steele at the University of Calgary; A. Iris Donovan and Dean Smith at the University of California, Berkeley; Tony Gardner at California State University, Northridge; Maggie Libby at Colby College; Eric Harbeson at the University of Colorado at Boulder; Judith Gray at the Concord Free Public Library; Erica Foden-Lenahan at the Courtauld Institute of Art; Mara Kaufman at Duke University; Beverly B. Allen at Emory University; Rita Smith at the University of Florida; Burt Altman at Florida State University; Peter Ross at the Guildhall Library; Alan Jutzi at the Huntington Library; Alvan Bregman at the University of Illinois at Urbana-Champaign; Jennifer Laherty at Indiana University; Julie Ramwell at the John Rylands University Library of Manchester; Tammy J. Eschedor Voelker at Kent State University; Peter Henderson at The King's School; Clark Evans and Margaret Kieckhefer at the Library of Congress; Maggie Valdez at the Los Angeles Public Library; Betsy Park at the University of Memphis Libraries; Kristen Castellana at the University of Michigan; Alicia Mavong at the National Library of Scotland; Roger Flury at the National Library of New Zealand; Lisa Schoblasky at the Newberry Library; Laura K. O'Keefe at The New York Public Library; Mike Kelly at New York University; Helen Black at Oberlin College Library; Jennifer Burr, Nazareth College of Rochester; Randy Miller, Norfolk Public Library; Scott Krafft at Northwestern University Library; David Kuzma at Rutgers University; Patrick Scott at the University of South Carolina; Erika Ripley at Southern Methodist University; Sundi Rutledge at Southwestern Baptist Theological Seminary; Polly Armstrong at Stanford University; Jonathan Jackson at Syracuse University Library; Christopher Densmore at Swarthmore College; Molly Schwartzburg and Margaret Tufts Tenney at the Harry Ransom Humanities Research Center, University of Texas at Austin; Helen Beaney and Isolde Harpur at Trinity College Library, Dublin; Danielle Russell at the University of Victoria; Gayle Cooper at the University of Virginia; Christine Bachman and Wilma R. Slaight at Wellesley College Library; and Colleen Brown and Ellen R. Cordes at Yale University.

It was a pleasure to work with the editorial staff at Oak Knoll Books, especially Laura Williams, and the creativity and attention of designer Matthew Young made this book better in every way. Above all, I am indebted to my husband Gary, both for lending me his time, energy, and expertise as a professional librarian, and for shouldering many day to day burdens so that I could have the luxury of working nights and weekends. And I especially thank my son John, whose frequent inquiries about the progress of "that book" kept me going when nothing else could. It is only fitting that this book be dedicated to him.

INTRODUCTION

[T]he new poetry seemed to have achieved no progress in the eye of the public since the experiment of The Germ *in 1850. Then at last came Christina Rossetti with her brilliant, fantastic, and profoundly original volume of* Goblin Market *in 1862, and achieved the earliest popular success for Pre-Raphaelite poetry. Swinburne never failed to recognize the priority of Christina; he used to call her the Jael who led their host to victory.*[1]

Literary scholars and the reading public have long appreciated Christina Rossetti's "brilliant, fantastic, and profoundly original" poetry. Over the last twenty-five years, renewed interest in women writers and in the Pre-Raphaelite movement has spurred a full-scale reassessment of Rossetti's work that has firmly established her status as a major Victorian poet. Rossetti's writing in other genres including short fiction, essays, and devotional writing has also attracted considerable scholarly attention. The reevaluation of Rossetti's work has yielded an abundance of new and important scholarship, including a critical edition of Rossetti's poems by Rebecca Crump (1979-1990), biographies by Georgina Battiscombe (1981), Kathleen Jones (1991), and Jan Marsh (1995), numerous critical studies including David A. Kent's early essay collection *The Achievement of Christina Rossetti* (1988), and an edition of Rossetti's letters by Antony Harrison (1997-2004). Scholarly efforts to understand Christina Rossetti within her contemporary context have also flourished, including any number of critical and biographical studies of the Rossetti family (and of Christina's role and relationships within it), as well as wider considerations of Christina's place within the Pre-Raphaelite movement, Victorian women's writing, writing for children, and Victorian religious and devotional literature.

Far less attention has been paid to the production and circulation of Rossetti's published work within (and beyond) the varied material and cultural contexts of Victorian print culture. Although interest in Rossetti's printing and publishing history is growing, as can be seen in books such as Lorraine Janzen Kooistra's groundbreaking *Christina Rossetti and Illustration* (2002), purely bibliographical study of Christina Rossetti's work has scarcely advanced beyond the enumerative list compiled by J. P. Anderson and included within Mackenzie Bell's 1898 biography, *Christina Rossetti: A Biographical and Critical Study*. The few bibliographical sources currently available to Rossetti scholars—including the bibliography in Lona Mosk Packer's *Christina Rossetti* (1963), William Fredeman's landmark *Pre-Raphaelitism: A Bibliocritical Study* (1965), *A Bookman's Catalogue: The Norman Colbeck Collection* (1987), and *Christina Rossetti in the Maser Collection* (1991)—are neither comprehensive in their listing of Rossetti's works nor fully descriptive, and do not provide an adequate foundation for scholarship. It is high time for a scholarly bibliography of the Pre-Raphaelites' Jael.

The contribution of a descriptive bibliography is different in kind from other forms of scholarship, which—if they treat printing and publishing history at all—either treat a small group of works in detail, or provide an overarching narrative that sacrifices detail in order to provide an

---

1. Edmund Gosse, *The Life of Algernon Charles Swinburne* (London: Macmillan, 1917): 136-137.

interpretive overview. Still, all scholarship that takes up printing and publishing history, including descriptive bibliography, shares a common goal: to document, and (in varying degrees) to interpret, the transformation of one—or many—clusters of words and images, by various people and through various technical, institutional, and social processes, into published artifacts. What is distinctive about bibliographical scholarship is its tendency to take up the stories of books and other printed artifacts from a different angle that is at once more widely and more narrowly focused than that of other scholarly modes. The wide angle of this descriptive bibliography thus takes into account not only Christina Rossetti's books, but the publication of her works in anthologies, in periodicals, in hymnals and in musical settings, and even on postcards, enameled boxes, and tea canisters. Item by item, detail by detail, this book's primary goal is to document, as fully as it can, the shape and range of Christina Rossetti's impact upon Victorian print culture, so as to offer a comprehensive (if not definitive) record of the primary sources that are crucial to scholarship on the production, reception and circulation of Rossetti's work.

One of the joys of bibliographical research is discovery, pure and simple. No one completes a work such as this one without uncovering more publications than one expected or imagined; for Victorian writers especially, advances in printing technology and the expansion of publishing genres and reading audiences make the discovery of new publications, sometimes in unlikely or unusual places, a virtual certainty, and the larger field of printed materials that ultimately emerges from bibliographical research can also change what we think we know about publications we discovered years before. The bibliography appended to Mackenzie Bell's biography of Rossetti included some 74 periodical publications and twelve appearances in anthologies (excluding hymnals and translations); in this bibliography, each of those categories includes over 100 entries, as well as eleven hymnals published within Rossetti's lifetime and nearly 200 musical settings published before 1900. The examination of multiple copies of Rossetti's works has also yielded new insight into the extent of her revisions and corrections. I discuss some of those discoveries in the first part of this introduction; still others are presented in my notes to various entries.

Readers unfamiliar with descriptive bibliography will find it helpful to consult the second part of this introduction, in which the format and content of entries are explained in some detail.

Overview

Section A: Separate Works

As is fitting for a writer known primarily as a poet, Christina Rossetti's career both began and ended with books titled *Verses*. The first *Verses*, privately printed in 1847 by her grandfather Gaetano Polidori when Christina was sixteen, would become a prize for collectors even during her lifetime[2]; the second, an 1893 collection of poems culled from her devotional writings published by the Society for Promoting Christian Knowledge, remained in print for over 30 years, with a "new edition" published in 1925. While the latter *Verses* confirmed Rossetti's emergence as one of the century's leading writers of religious poetry, 1893 also marked a different milestone in Rossetti's career with the first separate publication of her most celebrated poem, *Goblin Market*, illustrated by Laurence Housman. Here too, the close of Rossetti's career hearkened back to its beginning: her first published volumes, *Goblin Market and Other Poems* (1862) and *The Prince's Progress and Other Poems* (1866), for which Dante Rossetti provided both illustrations and binding designs, brought critical acclaim and served as the basis for collected volumes in Britain

---

2. In 1882, a copy was advertised in a bookseller's catalogue for 5 guineas (*The Letters of Christina Rossetti* 3: 16; henceforth *Letters*).

and America. After *The Prince's Progress*, Rossetti would not produce another new book of poems until 1881, with *A Pageant and Other Poems*; in the meantime, however, she published fiction (*Commonplace and Other Stories*, 1870; *Speaking Likenesses*, 1874) and three of her seven volumes of devotional poetry and prose (*Annus Domini*, 1874; *Seek and Find*, 1879; and *Called to Be Saints*, 1881). The last two decades of Rossetti's life saw the publication of three more devotional volumes (*Letter and Spirit*, 1883; *Time Flies*, 1885; and *The Face of the Deep*, 1892) and the 1893 *Verses*. In England, Rossetti's publishers included Macmillan, the Society for the Promotion of Christian Knowledge, F. S. Ellis, and Routledge; in the United States, her publisher was Roberts Brothers. Posthumous editions of her work were published by Thomas Mosher, Eragny Press, and others.

This section of the bibliography attempts to provide a comprehensive list of separate works wholly or primarily by Christina Rossetti through 1900, and selected separate publications after that date. Nearly 40 editions and subeditions are described, including William Michael Rossetti's important editions of Christina Rossetti's writings: the *Poetical Works* and his selection of Christina's *Poems* for Macmillan's Golden Treasury series (both published in 1904), as well as his edition of Christina's *Family Letters* (1908). Later collections of Christina Rossetti's poems by other editors are not included, with the notable exception of Rebecca Crump's exemplary variorum edition of the poems. Also excluded are a great many publications of Rossetti's works in the early 20th century (and beyond) that deserve more attention than could be given within this volume, the most obvious being the further history of "Goblin Market." However, most works first published before 1900 that remained in print in the early twentieth century, such as the Little, Brown reprintings of the Roberts Brothers editions of Rossetti's poetry, and the Society for Promoting Christian Knowledge's reprintings of several of Christina Rossetti's devotional works, are noted.

Rossetti's 1847 *Verses* provides a particularly compelling example of the Rossetti family's collaborative writing and publishing process, and of the value of examining multiple copies of Christina Rossetti's books. In 1981, Mark Samuels Lasner discovered several copies of *Verses* which contained hand corrections and annotations.[3] Half of the twenty copies of *Verses* I examined for this bibliography (and five additional copies identified via surveys of libraries with copies of the book) turned out to have at least one hand correction; many had more than one. Even within the same copy, the corrections often appear in several different hands, sometimes in pen and sometimes in pencil, which suggests that the books were marked by different people, at different times. Clearly "the dear G. P. booklet," as Christina fondly termed it (*Letters* 4: 224) held a special place within the Rossetti family. It represented Christina's first collection in print; it also represented the combined talents and collaborative efforts of the entire family: grandfather Polidori's press work, Christina's text and (in one copy, now lost)[4] illustrations, and various critical and aesthetic responses of other family members, including Dante, who also illustrated a copy of the book (now held at the Harry Ransom Humanities Research Center at the University of Texas at Austin) with pencil designs, including a frontispiece portrait of Christina.

This bibliography also provides some new insight into the nature and scope of Rossetti's corrections and revisions to her published works. In 1962, Lona Mosk Packer drew attention to hand corrections made by Macmillan on page 71 in some copies of *The Prince's Progress and*

3.   See his comments in "Christina Rossetti's 'Common Looking Booklet': A New Letter About Her Verses of 1847," *Notes and Queries* (October 1981): 420-421. Another corrected copy was recently described by William Baker ("Christina Rossetti: An Unpublished Letter and an Unrecorded Copy of *Verses*," *Notes and Queries* (June 2010): 221-223).

4.   William Michael Rossetti describes Christina's illustrations in his notes to the *Verses* poems included in his edition of Christina's *Poetical Works* (1904).

Other Poems (1866), but Macmillan's hand-corrections are actually more extensive than Packer realized.[5] The Boston Public Library holds a presentation copy of the book from Christina Rossetti to Philip Bourke Marston; this book, probably an author's proof, contains manuscript corrections, presumably by Christina Rossetti, on pages 37, 55, 71 and 89.[6] In examining published copies of the book, I found not only the hand corrections noted by Packer, but also the additional corrections present in the Boston Public Library copy. Another significant instance of revision in a Macmillan book occurred after Christina's death, in William Michael Rossetti's *Poetical Works*, a valuable collection of nearly all of Christina's published poetry. Scholars still consult the 1904 first printing of *Poetical Works*, unaware that the 1906 printing includes a variety of corrections requested by William, primarily (but not exclusively) in his editorial comments.

Rossetti's devotional works provide further examples of previously unnoticed authorial corrections and revisions, including some corrections that never appeared in printed texts. In one of Princeton's copies of Rossetti's first devotional volume, *Annus Domini* (1874), Rossetti has written several corrections, including a stanza added to the poem "Alas my lord"; none of the corrections appear in the British printing, and only one appears in Roberts Brothers' American printing.[7] Unfortunately, this was the usual course of events with Rossetti's later devotional books, all published by the Society for Promoting Christian Knowledge (SPCK). The various notations present in copies owned or presented by Rossetti show that she often discovered errors or had ideas for revisions after a volume had gone to press, but comparison with the later printings shows that she rarely succeeded in incorporating the changes into the printed text.

Rossetti's corrections for *Letter and Spirit* (1883), found in a copy of the book now owned by the Delaware Art Museum,[8] may not have been incorporated simply because later printings were not called for; Rossetti had slightly better luck with two later volumes, *Time Flies* (1885) and *The Face of the Deep* (1892), both of which were frequently reprinted. Rossetti's annotations to *Time Flies*, a devotional calendar within which her family relationships and personal associations figure prominently, reveal how deeply she cared about this book, testimony both to her devout religious faith, and to the treasured network of family and friends within which that faith was expressed and nurtured. Several extant corrected and annotated copies of the book bear witness to the personal relevance of the entries. Copies with annotations and hand corrections by Christina Rossetti are held at the British Library, the Delaware Art Museum, and the Harry Ransom Humanities Research Center at the University of Texas at Austin; another copy, with annotations by William Michael Rossetti, is owned by Mark Samuels Lasner.[9] In the Delaware and Texas copies, Rossetti's notes identify many of the people and events referred to in the book. The personal significance of the copies is evident in the inscriptions and mementos within them: the Delaware copy, which Christina had given to her mother Frances Rossetti in 1885, also includes a small paper pocket in which Rossetti placed two trefoils given to her by her friend Lisa Wilson. The Texas copy, the most heavily annotated of Christina's copies, once held a pressed flower, explained in a note Christina wrote beside the entry for 8 April: "1886. Dearest Mamma died. The flower opposite was one placed in her room after death." These copies of the book were cherished artifacts, within which Rossetti commemorated the most important past and present events of her life; they were

5. See Packer, "Christina Rossetti's "Songs in a Cornfield": A Misprint Uncorrected," *Notes and Queries* n.s. 9 (March 1962): 97-100.
6. I wish to thank Stuart T. Walker of the Boston Public Library for alerting me to this copy.
7. Department of Rare Books and Manuscripts, Princeton University Library, 5866.786, Ex copy 1.
8. Delaware Art Museum, Helen Farr Sloan Library and Archives, Bancroft PR5237 .L5.
9. British Library, shelfmark 12357.bb.36; Delaware Art Museum, Helen Farr Sloan Library and Archives, Bancroft PR5237 .T4; Harry Ransom Humanities Research Center, University of Texas at Austin, BV 4832 R74 1885.

also works in progress, which Rossetti continued to correct and revise. All three of the copies corrected by Christina indicate that she wished to change a passage within the entry for April 25; in the Texas copy, Rossetti has crossed out the portion of the text she wished to alter and has inserted a slip of paper with the revised passage. In this instance, the revisions were incorporated into the next printing of the book. However, further corrections which Christina had marked in the Delaware Art Museum and University of Texas copies were not made, and as late as 1893, Rossetti was still engaged with this text, writing revised entries for January 18 and February 3 on the back of an account statement from Macmillan.[10]

Rossetti's most successful experience in revising her later works occurred with *The Face of the Deep*, her last prose volume. Shortly after the book was published, Rossetti discovered a number of errors. In this instance, the Society for Promoting Christian Knowledge issued an errata slip and made corrections in the text of the second edition. Unfortunately, as Rossetti explained to her brother William, the list of mistakes she found "was so long I omitted trivial printer's errors" (*Letters* 4: 279); once again, some, but not all, of Rossetti's corrections made it into the printed text. A surviving presentation copy from Christina Rossetti to Henrietta Rintoul, now held at Princeton, contains handwritten corrections in pencil and ink; of these corrections, six do not appear in the printed errata slip or in the corrected text of the book.

Other aspects of Rossetti's relations with the Society for Promoting Christian Knowledge call out for further study. Rossetti's third devotional volume, *Called to Be Saints* (1881), includes a number of botanical illustrations of plants mentioned by Rossetti in the text. According to Lorraine Kooistra, these images transform Rossetti's text into a Victorian emblem book, in which text and image are interdependent (149-153). But the SPCK did not, as Kooistra suggests, hire an artist to illustrate Rossetti's book. Sixteen of the twenty-one drawings were previously published in botanical books by the Rev. Charles Alexander Johns, and were doubtless the work of his illustrator, Emily Stackhouse.[11] Of the five remaining illustrations, one bears Emily Stackhouse's initials, and two derive from Anne Pratt's *Wild Flowers*, leaving only two illustrations in Rossetti's book unidentified. Both Johns's and Pratt's books were widely circulated, as were the drawings they contained; one can assume that many readers of Rossetti's book would find them familiar, and that their response to Rossetti's text would be conditioned by that familiarity. Interestingly, although *Called to be Saints* was in production as early as December 1880, it was not published until December 1881. Could Rossetti have been asked to adapt her text to conform more closely to the illustrations that the SPCK supplied? In considering this possibility, one is led to consider another instance in which Rossetti's text underwent revision before publication by the Society. Scholars who have examined Rossetti's holograph manuscript of *Seek and Find*—presumably the printer's copy, as it bears "indications of which sections are italicized, or alterations that were made, or where pagination occurred"—have noted "verbal differences . . . of such a character that one must assume authorial intervention and revision" (Kent and Stanwood, 220). One can only wonder to what extent, and to what ends, Rossetti's revisions were prompted by the editorial requirements of the Society for Promoting Christian Knowledge.

The history of Rossetti's publications with Roberts Brothers in the United States seems at first glance to be relatively straightforward. Roberts Brothers' policy towards its collections of Rossetti's

10. Notes for a new edition of Time Flies, Janet Camp Troxell Collection of Rossetti Manuscripts, Box 1, Folder 27; Department of Rare Books and Special Collections, Princeton University Library.

11. On Stackhouse, see Clifford Evans, "A Botanist Who Painted: Emily Stackhouse" (in Deirdre Dare and Melissa Hardie, *A Passion for Nature*, Cornwall: Hypatia Press, 2008: 173-185), and Melissa Hardie-Budden's entry on Stackhouse in the *Oxford Dictionary of National Biography*.

poems was conservative and economical: the initial typesetting was plated and retained, with as few changes as possible, for the life of the firm, and beyond; Little, Brown continued to reprint from Roberts Brothers plates well into the twentieth century. From a bibliographical perspective, there was only one American edition of Rossetti's poems: the 1866 typesetting, which was partially revised in 1876, and offered in an expanded version sometime after 1888. But from the perspective of publishing and marketing history, the story is more complicated, and worthy of more attention than it has hitherto been granted. The publication of a new edition by Macmillan generally prompted Roberts Brothers to produce a new printing that combined existing plates with varying (but usually small) amounts of newly-set material. In situations such as this, the arrangement of a bibliography inevitably favors either printing or publishing history, but cannot give equal attention to both. In the arrangement of this bibliography, I have chosen to treat later printings from plates as subeditions, and to place them in separate listings, so as to clarify the relationship of the later subeditions to the Roberts Brothers parent edition as well as the Macmillan editions.

The texts of the Roberts Brothers printings of Rossetti's works rarely varied from the Macmillan printings, but the visual and material content of the American books differed, sometimes substantially, from their British counterparts. Roberts Brothers marketed Rossetti's poetry by emphasizing its similarity to that of Jean Ingelow both in content and in book design. Advertisements for Roberts Brothers' inaugural volume of Rossetti's *Poems* (1866) promised that it would be "bound to match" Ingelow's books.[12] Although a few clustered rings on the American book's spine echoed Dante Rossetti's distinctive binding designs for his sister's early Macmillan volumes, most of the Roberts Brothers books appeared in standard trade bindings. The illustrations that had appeared in Rossetti's British volumes were reused by Roberts Brothers, but they were often repositioned and reformatted. The Roberts Brothers printing of *Speaking Likenesses* (1874), for example, includes the same illustrations as the British printing, but chooses a different illustration, "Edith and her kettle" to use as the frontispiece instead of the slightly frightening image ("Maggie meets the fairies in the woods") featured in Macmillan's version. During Rossetti's lifetime, Macmillan's collections of her poems reprinted Dante Rossetti's illustrations for *Goblin Market and Other Poems* (1862) and *The Prince's Progress and Other Poems* (1866), invariably retaining the 1862 frontispiece as the frontispiece for each successive volume. But as early as 1882, Roberts Brothers began to use a portrait of Christina Rossetti by Dante Rossetti as the volume frontispiece, effectively refocusing attention away from the interaction of Christina's text and Dante Rossetti's image to emphasize Christina Rossetti's presence in the book.

Section B: Appearances in Books

In author bibliographies, it is standard practice to limit sections other than separate works to first publications. While there is practical value in implementing a method of limitation that is both clearly defined and consistent with previous practice, the focus on first publications also obscures reception history: we know which items were published in venues other than single author books, but we do not know how many times those items were subsequently reprinted. I have adopted the "first publication" rule to the extent that first publications of Rossetti's work (in this section, as well as in the periodicals section) have always been included, but I have also used my judgment in including subsequent publications that are of particular significance in highlighting some aspect of Rossetti's career and reception history. In other words, I have omitted nothing that could prove to be of value or interest to scholars simply because it was a "nonfirst."

A glance at Christina Rossetti's early appearances in books reveals the wide range of Victorian

12. Roberts Brothers advertisement, *New York Times* (10 July 1866): 5.

genres included within this section, as well as Christina Rossetti's focused and persistent efforts to establish herself as a published author. In 1850, Rossetti—whose only previous publications consisted of two poems in the *Athenaeum* in 1848—placed two "enigmas" and two "charades" in *Marshall's Ladies Daily Remembrancer*, a pocket book that contained an almanac, various useful information (including weights, measures, and "Cabriolet fares") and ruled pages for memoranda along with literary contributions. Four years later, she published poems in three illustrated gift anthologies, edited by Mary Howitt and each geared to a different audience: *Pictorial Calendar of the Seasons*, an illustrated almanac; *Midsummer Flowers for the Young*, a collection of fiction and poetry for children; and *The Dusseldorf Artist's Album*. The Howitt publications form quite a contrast to the biographical sketches Rossetti contributed to the *Imperial Dictionary of Universal Biography* in the late 1850s and early 1860s. The *Imperial Dictionary* entries demonstrate the value of paying close attention to publications that might initially seem to have little to add to our understanding of Rossetti's primary body of work. Rossetti would eventually write over 100 entries for the utilitarian *Dictionary*, mostly on figures from Italian history (including poets Tasso and Petrarch), but including a brief but significant paragraph on Priscilla Lydia Sellon, the controversial founder of one of the first Anglican sisterhoods. Rossetti's carefully worded endorsement of Sellon was her only published commentary on the monastic movement.

The bulk of Rossetti's appearances in books took place within poetry anthologies, though it must be understood that the word "anthology" covers a lot of ground. Rossetti's work appeared not only in lavish gift books such as the Howitt volumes and *A Welcome* (printed at Emily Faithfull's Victoria Press in commemoration of the marriage of the Prince of Wales), but in secular and devotional calendars, textbooks, and various themed collections, especially collections of religious poetry and prose. Following Macmillan's publication of *Goblin Market and Other Poems* in 1862 (but before Roberts Brothers published the first American collection of her poems in 1866), Rossetti's "Goblin Market" made its American debut in an American gift book, *Household Friends For Every Season* (1864), and six more poems were included in Richard Stoddard's *The Late English Poets* (1865). But British editors were also showing interest: the Rev. R. H. Baynes asked to include "From House to Home" in *English Lyrics: A Collection Of English Poetry Of The Present Day* (1865). Rossetti considered such opportunities carefully, weighing the financial and critical impact they might have on her career. She informed Macmillan that she would only accept Baynes's invitation if it would not "prejudice our 2nd edition" of *Goblin Market and Other Poems*, and reported to Gabriel on the quality of Baynes's other contributors: "Jean Ingelow is in his list of contributors; and Dean Alford, not that I rate him very high poetically" (*Letters* 1: 206, 211). For the rest of the century, Rossetti's poetic talent would be recognized in similar collections of contemporary poetry, such as *Works Of The British Poets* (1876), *Representative Poems Of Living Poets* (1886), and *Fifty Years Of English Song* (1887), culminating in her appearances in two of the century's landmark poetry surveys, Alfred H. Miles's *The Poets and The Poetry of the Century* (1892), and Francis Palgrave's second series of the *Golden Treasury* (1897), published three years after her death. Rossetti's work also turned up in handbooks and student textbooks ranging from the illustrated *Student's Treasury Of English Song* (1873), in which the page margins are filled with brief quotations, intended to be memorized so as to "furnish the student with pleasant food for the fancy and suggestive matter for reflection" (vi), to more pedestrian volumes such as *Progressive Exercises in Latin Elegiac Verse* (1871), *Philips' Series Of Reading Books* (1874) for British public elementary schools and *A Second School Poetry Book* (1887), which introduced young readers to "Goblin Market."

As one of the century's most prominent women writers, Rossetti appeared in two major (and ideologically opposed) collections of British women's poetry: Eric Robertson's *English Poetesses*

(1883), prefaced by Robertson's enumeration of the reasons why "no woman has equaled man as a poet" (xv), as well as Elizabeth ("Mrs. William") Sharp's *Women's Voices* (1887), in which Sharp countered that it was "as possible to form an anthology of "pure poetry" from the writings of women as from those of men" (ix). Rossetti's work frequently appeared in popular quotation books drawn from the work of women writers, such as Rose Porter's compilations *From Queen's Gardens* (1889, later reprinted as *Love's Thread of Gold*) and *Women's Thoughts for Women* (1891, reprinted 1899). Women artists and illustrators also found inspiration in Rossetti's "pure poetry," beginning with Alice Donlevy's *Practical Hints On the Art of Illumination* (1867), a textbook in which Rossetti's poem "Consider" figures, decorated with illuminated capitals and displayed within specially designed ornamental borders, as an example for students to study, copy or paint. Other women illustrators of Rossetti's poems in collections include Lady Caroline Blanche Elizabeth Lindsay, co-founder of the Grosvenor Gallery (*About Robins*, 1889), and Marie Low and Maud West (*Through Woodland And Meadow*, 1891).

One of the largest subgroups of books within which Rossetti's writing figured were religious collections, though these too took many forms. The popularity of hymns in the Victorian period led to the creation of collections of religious poetry that, while not intended for singing, were marketed to readers who would be favorably impressed by words like "hymn" and "song" in the books' titles. Among the earliest such books listed here are several hymnal-like compilations, such as the Rev. Orby Shipley's various "Lyra" collections: *Lyra Eucharistica*, subtitled *Hymns And Verses On The Holy Communion* (1863, second edition 1864); *Lyra Messianica* (1864, second edition 1865); and *Lyra Mystica* (1865). Many similar titles were compiled by other authors, with titles like *Christ in Song* (1870), *Heaven in Song* (1874), *Songs of Rest* (1878, second series), *Victorian Hymns* (1887), and Francis Palgrave's *Treasury Of Sacred Song* (1891). Rossetti's Church of England affiliation is evident in her appearance in the section of devotional "hymns" within *A Manual For Holy Communion* (1869, reprinted 1878), compiled by the industrious Rev. Baynes, who by that time had included Rossetti's poetry in two anthologies. Rossetti's popularity as a religious poet, along with the manifest difficulty of discovering "who were, and who were not, Catholics" (vi) among contemporary writers, also accounts for her otherwise inexplicable inclusion in the *Household Library Of Catholic Poets* (1881). Other themed religious collections in which Rossetti appeared include both the New Testament (1883) and Old Testament (1890) volumes of W. Garrett Horder's *The Poets' Bible*; Horder also dropped poems by Rossetti into at least two prose works: *Intimations of Immortality* (1883) and *The Supreme Argument for Christianity* (1899).

In 1874—the year in which Rossetti's devotional calendar *Annus Domini* was published—her work was excerpted in another devotional calendar, titled *Day after Day*. Rossetti's poetry and prose would soon become a favorite source of excerpts for devotional calendars, birthday books, and various other excerpt collections. Frederick Langbridge included nine poems by Rossetti in an unusual collection, *The Tablets of the Heart* (1883), created to provide its readers with extracts suitable for copying upon blank greeting cards. Among the Rossetti contributions is a short, previously unknown poem in the vein of "No, Thank You, John" (which Langbridge also included). The poem, "Stop Thief!," is not particularly memorable, but interesting nonetheless, if only by its contrast to the devotional writing that was Rossetti's primary focus at the time:

> My heart is yours. What can you want with *two*
> *Hearts*? oh you traitor, you!
> What can you keep a second heart to do?

Although "Stop Thief!" was reprinted in at least one other compilation (*Love-Knots and Bridal Bands*, also 1883), it was never published in Rossetti's collected volumes—though it may well have been inscribed, or printed upon, any number of Victorian greeting cards!

The most prolific anthologizers of Rossetti were three American women: Mary Tileston, Rose Porter, and Julia Louisa Matilda Woodruff, better known by her pseudonym, W. M. L. Jay. Mary Tileston was the compiler of *Daily Strength for Daily Needs* (1884), an extremely popular devotional calendar offering daily selections from the Bible paired with literary and devotional text. While Tileston included only three excerpts from Rossetti's devotional prose in *Daily Strength for Daily Needs*, Rossetti was the most frequently quoted writer in her later (also very popular), calendar-style compilation, *Prayers Ancient and Modern* (1897), which includes no less than fifty seven separate excerpts from *Annus Domini* and *The Face of the Deep*. But Tileston's borrowings are modest in comparison to those of Rose Porter and W. M. L. Jay. Jay included quotations from Rossetti in several devotional collections, including *He Giveth Songs* (1880, reprinted as *At the Evening Time* in 1892); *The Farrar Year Book* (1895), a devotional calendar ostensibly based on the writings of Frederic Farrar, Archdeacon and Canon of Westminster, but including 29 excerpts from *The Face of the Deep*; a similar compilation, *Good Cheer for a Year* (1896), supposedly drawn from the work of Phillips Brooks, but containing healthy portions of the work of other writers, including 25 Rossetti excerpts; and *Reflected Lights from The Face of the Deep* (1899), a collection composed entirely of quotations from Rossetti (and therefore listed in Section A). Porter's samplings from Rossetti include not only the previously mentioned collections *From Queens Gardens* and *Women's Thoughts for Women*, but at least seven additional quotation books: *In The Shadow Of His Hand* (1882), *Foregleams Of Immortality* (1884), *The Story Of Mary The Mother* (1888), *A Gift Of Love* (1891), *A Gift Of Peace* (1894), *A Charm Of Birds* (1897) and *The Pilgrim's Staff* (1897).

Section C: Appearances in Periodicals

In order to create some degree of uniformity in books of excerpts, alteration of the quoted texts is to be expected—titles are omitted or changed, the text of the excerpts is often modified, and the excerpts, removed from their original context, take on new meanings. The same is true, to varying degrees, for all anthologies: certainly the social activism of Rossetti's "A Royal Princess" takes on greater significance when one realizes that it first appeared in (and was probably composed for) *Poems: An Offering to Lancashire* (1863), a collection printed gratis at the Victoria Press, on donated paper, so that proceeds from its sale could be used to support the workers affected by the "cotton famine." Periodicals are even more likely than anthologies to present opportunities for textual meanings to be obscured, intensified, shifted, or changed entirely through context. At the same time, Rossetti's placement of particular items in particular journals was often strategic, in any number of ways: aesthetically, politically, and theologically. As Diane D'Amico has observed, "Identifying the periodicals in which Rossetti published is central to an understanding of her private views" on contemporary issues (20).[13]

Although over 130 periodical appearances within Rossetti's lifetime are listed in this bibliography, no doubt more remain to be discovered. Aside from a few early items, Rossetti's periodical pieces invariably appear under her own name, "Christina G. Rossetti," but Rossetti was not averse to publishing her work unsigned or under a pseudonym: she offered at least one piece to *Cornhill Magazine* with the proviso that it could not appear under her name (*Letters* 1: 308), and

---

13. See "Christina Rossetti and *The English Woman's Journal*," *Journal of Pre-Raphaelite Studies*, n.s. 3 (Spring 1994): 20-24.

in 1873, William Michael Rossetti recorded in his diary that Christina was considering publishing some of her "old poems, that were considered hardly good enough to be printed in her 2 vols" and offering them to "some magazine (Argosy or other) under a pseudonym" (WMRD 23 January). William discouraged this idea; we do not know if Christina followed his advice. It is also quite likely that Christina Rossetti published under her own name in scarce or little-known periodicals, especially religious periodicals, that thus far have remained beyond the scope of bibliographical indexes, microfilms, and commercial digitization projects.

Rossetti worked hard to establish a presence in the periodical press. After her initial appearances in the *Athenaeum*, she contributed, as "Ellen Alleyn," to that ill-fated pre-Raphaelite manifesto the *Germ* in 1850, and, writing in Italian as "Calta," to *The Bouquet, culled from Marylebone Gardens* in 1852. She placed two short stories in major venues: "The Lost Titian" appeared in William Stillman's the *Crayon* in 1856, and "Nick"—which she had first attempted to place in 1853 (*Letters* 1:78)—appeared in the *National Magazine* in 1857, though another story, the now lost "Case 2, Folio Q," was rejected by *Cornhill* and *Blackwood's* (*Letters* 1: 130, 138). She struggled to find similar success with poems, approaching *Blackwood's* unsuccessfully in 1854 (*Letters* 1: 98), but eventually publishing "The Round Tower at Jhansi: June 8, 1857" and "Maude Clare" in *Once a Week* in 1859. Her fortunes improved dramatically in 1861, when the publication of "Up-Hill" in *Macmillan's Magazine* initiated what would become Rossetti's most important publishing arrangement. Macmillan become Rossetti's primary British publisher and *Macmillan's Magazine* became the main outlet for her poetry in periodicals. Between 1861 and 1869, Rossetti published 22 poems in the *Magazine*, followed by one last contribution, "A Wintry Sonnet," in 1883. Other periodicals to which Rossetti contributed with some frequency include the *Athenaeum* (to which she sent eight poems and two letters) and *Argosy* (seven contributions).

In *Christina Rossetti and Illustration*, Lorraine Kooistra identifies Rossetti's preference for illustrated periodicals as a conscious strategy through which Rossetti sought to enhance the beauty and interpretive possibilities of her work (44-54). Her appearances in the *Germ* and in the art journal the *Crayon*, while not illustrated, aligned Rossetti with the Pre-Raphaelite artistic project of connecting literary and visual art. Rossetti's first illustrated poem was "Maude Clare," which appeared in *Once a Week* accompanied by a surprisingly unimpressive drawing by John Millais. More interesting interpretations of Rossetti's texts include Frederick Sandys's illustration for "Amor Mundi" in the *Shilling Magazine* (1865) and Charles Ricketts's illustration for "An Echo from Willowwood" in the *Magazine of Art*. Of course, not all illustrations that appeared with Rossetti's writings were created for the purpose. In at least one instance, the opposite was true: Rossetti's brief reminiscence of her brother Dante's residence in Cheyne Walk in *Literary Opinion* (1892) was prompted by Margaret Thomas's illustration (*Letters* 4: 276-278). And when "A Christmas Carol" (better known by its first line, "In the bleak mid-winter") was published in *Scribner's Monthly* for January 1872, it appeared with an illustration that was probably created for another work. Between the title and the text of the poem is an illustration of the nativity by John Leighton, engraved by Dalziel, featuring a center vignette of Joseph, Mary, the Christ child, and three shepherds, as well as two satellite vignettes framed within Biblical texts and Christian symbols (stars, crosses, a lamb). John Leighton had been one of the illustrators of Henry Bramley and John Stainer's *Christmas Carols New and Old* (1871), a popular and influential collection of traditional carols. Since Leighton's design for Rossetti's poem has several elements in common with his work for Bramley and Stainer's volume (such as the incorporation of scrolls bearing Biblical texts), his illustration enhanced the poem by visually situating Rossetti's contribution within the larger carol tradition celebrated in Bramley and Stainer's work. However, while Leighton's depiction of the surroundings of the infant Christ are in keeping with Rossetti's depiction of "a mangerful of hay," other elements of the illustration suggest that it was not designed especially for this poem. The shepherds and wise men in Leighton's vignette appear only in passing within the poem, and while both Leighton's image and Rossetti's poem place special emphasis upon Mary, Leighton presents a passive, reverent, and slightly distant Mary who grasps Christ's swaddling clothes but does not touch his body. By contrast, Rossetti's Mary is active and physically intimate, sustaining her child with a "breastful of milk" and worshiping him with a mother's kiss.

Rossetti's publications in religious periodicals show her working in a variety of genres, from politically laden fiction to devotional prose and poetry. Pointing specifically to Rossetti's critique of the practice of pew rents in "Some Pros and Cons about Pews" (1867), published in the Rev. Baynes's the *Churchman's Shilling Magazine*, Mary Arseneau argues that Rossetti's contributions to such "forgotten religious periodicals" allowed her to present political statements "publicly and with a sense of urgency and commitment" (*Recovering Christina Rossetti*, 36). Other fiction in the *Churchman's Shilling Magazine* and in the SPCK monthly the *Dawn of Day*, while less overtly political, still offered a strong critique of Victorian materialism and (with her sister Maria's example in mind) advocated both compassion and practical assistance for the poor. Only one example of Rossetti's devotional prose is to be found among her periodical contributions: in 1879, "A Harmony on First Corinthians XIII" was published in *New and Old*, the parish magazine of St. Cyprian's, Marylebone. *New and Old* was edited by St. Cyprian's perpetual curate, the Rev. Charles Gutch, who later became one of Rossetti's spiritual advisors. *New and Old* also published three of Rossetti's poems ("A Helpmeet for Him," 1888; "Son, Remember," 1889; and "Mary Magdalene and the Other Mary," 1890). The poems "Ash Wednesday," "Good Lord, to-day," and "Lent" appeared together in the *Dawn of Day* (1890), while Rossetti's last known periodical publication—probably unauthorized—was of the poem "If Thou Sayest, Behold We Knew it Not" in the September, 1894 *Heathen Woman's Friend* (Boston). Although Rossetti tended to choose religious periodicals associated with the Church of England, an excerpt from "Dost Thou Not Care?" appeared in the Quaker *British Friend* (1875), where it was placed beneath a paragraph warning readers not to "procrastinate in the hope of being saved" by a death-bed conversion. Read in this context, Rossetti's excerpt, retitled "To-morrow," drives the point home by depicting Christ's rejection of the speaker's seemingly modest plea for future "rest from toil" and escape from sorrow.

Despite Rossetti's placement of "A Helpmeet for Him" in the decidedly anti-feminist environment of *New and Old*,[14] she also published in periodicals that supported aspects of the Victorian women's movement, particularly women's right to greater opportunities for education and employment, such as the *English Woman's Journal*, founded by Bessie Parkes and Barbara Bodichon, and the *Victoria Magazine*, printed by Emily Faithfull. As Diane D'Amico has argued, Rossetti's appearance in the *English Woman's Journal* indicated her willingness to be associated with a politically-motivated journal that aimed "to employ, educate and organize middle-class women" ("Christina Rossetti and The English Woman's Journal," 22). Something like that willingness was evident even earlier, in Rossetti's contributions to *The Bouquet, culled from Marylebone Gardens*. The *Bouquet*'s "Address" to its supporters, while quick to point out that the journal would not advocate women "trenching on the prerogatives of men," nevertheless acknowledged that "women are asserting a right to greater consideration than they formerly held; and are maintaining it by the position which many, who are a glory to their sex, have achieved in literature and

---

14. See D'Amico, "Christina Rossetti's 'Helpmeet'," *Victorian Newsletter* (Spring 1994): 25-29.

science" (vi).[15] In 1876, Rossetti contributed the poem "Johnny" to *Friendly Leaves*, a periodical issued on behalf of the newly founded Girls Friendly Society. The Society, the first organization for girls and women within the Church of England, created the journal to extend its mission of providing spiritual and moral support to young rural women who left home to work as servants or in urban factories.

While Rossetti authorized these publications, her later appearances in the *Woman's Journal* (Boston)—six in 1874, two in 1881, and one misattribution in 1890—probably occurred without her permission. The front page of each number of the *Woman's Journal* reiterated its devotion "to the interests of Woman, to her educational, industrial, legal and political Equality, and especially to her right of Suffrage." Rossetti, who objected to suffrage on religious grounds, and who refused to publish in periodicals that endorsed positions she could not support, is not likely to have willingly contributed to a pro-suffrage venue. The appearance of other notable British women writers who did not support suffrage, such as George Eliot, further suggests that the editors did not seek permission to publish poems by British women. The *Journal* tended to group poetry into a single column, sometimes headed with the phrase "For the Woman's Journal"—presumably intended to refer only to the poem at the top of the column, but sometimes giving the impression that all poems in the column (including some of the poems by Rossetti) were written expressly for the *Journal* (see 4 July 1874, 31 December 1881). In any event, the juxtaposition of Rossetti's work with poems such as the anonymous welcome to a meeting of "The Woman Suffrage Club of Needham" (4 July 1874) served visually and contextually to induct Rossetti into the pro-suffrage ranks, regardless of her position on the issue.

Newly identified periodical publications listed in this bibliography include an 1868 letter to the editor of the *Athenaeum*, "Books in the Running Brooks" in the *Englishman's Magazine of Literature, Religion, Science, and Art* (1865), and a number of American printings of Rossetti's work, many of which, like *The Woman's Journal*, were probably unauthorized, but are nevertheless important in our understanding of Rossetti's reception in the United States. Among the new discoveries, Rossetti's previously unidentified contribution of "'Thy Brother's Blood Crieth'" to the *Graphic* is arguably Rossetti's most striking published political statement. A total of three publications of Rossetti's poem, first in the *Graphic*, and subsequently in two American periodicals, *Every Saturday* and *Harper's Weekly*, took place before it was included in Rossetti's 1875 collection, *Goblin Market, The Prince's Progress, and Other Poems*, where it appears, along with "To-Day for Me," under the explanatory title "The German-French Campaign, 1870-1871." No such explanation would have been needed in 1870: the Franco-Prussian war dominated reporting in the periodical press, and the *Graphic* was a leading provider of commentary and illustrations from the front (one of the *Graphic*'s artists was arrested under suspicion of being a Prussian spy).[16] American readers looked to *Every Saturday* for reproductions of the *Graphic*'s war pictures, and imported copies of *The Graphic* itself sold out quickly.[17] By publishing her poem in *The Graphic*, Rossetti boldly opted to express her response to "the awful reality of horror of this horrible war" (*Letters* 1: 361) within the pages of what was arguably the most highly visible international outlet for news, commentary, and poetry concerning the war. It is unclear whether she was aware of the American publications, but the appearance of her poem in large-circulation periodicals in the United States as well as in Britain guaranteed that her anti-war poem would be one of the most widely

15. "Address to the Supporters of The Bouquet," *The Bouquet, Culled from Marylebone Gardens*. June 1851-January 1852. London: Printed at the "Bouquet" Press, 1852.
16. *Cassell's History of the War Between France and Germany*, Vol. 1 (London: Cassell and Company Limited, 1894): 116.
17. "Our American Letter," *Athenaeum*, No. 2240 (1 October 1870): 430.

distributed poems she ever published. In Rossetti's 1875 (and subsequent) collections, she prefaced "The German-French Campaign" poems with a note disavowing their political import—"These two pieces, written during the suspense of a great nation's agony, aim at expressing human sympathy, not political bias." But none who read "'Thy Brother's Blood Crieth'" in the pages of the *Graphic* or its American counterparts would have had any doubt as to Rossetti's outrage on behalf of France, or to her even more powerful, Biblically-based rejection of warfare in general.

Section D: Hymnals and Musical Settings

Although Rossetti's musical settings offer fascinating insights into her contemporary (and continuing) reception, scholars who wish to study them must rely upon Brian N. S. Gooch and David S. Thatcher's *Musical Settings of Early- and Mid-Victorian Literature: A Catalogue* (1979), a valuable resource, but one which is now dated and incomplete. This bibliography augments Gooch and Thatcher's work both by including additional musical settings, and by recognizing that Rossetti's presence in music also extended into the realm of hymnals, the focus of the first part of the music section. Hymnals present some difficulties for the bibliographer: although all hymnals were used in singing and are relevant to the larger history of Rossetti and music, not all hymnals were published with music. To further complicate the matter, the rather large class of Victorian poetry anthologies of "sacred song" played upon the popularity of hymnals per se, but may or may not have actually functioned as hymnals. For the Victorians, then, whether a given text was to be understood either as hymn text or devotional poem depended almost entirely upon the context within which it was published, and even here, savvy publishers managed to have it both ways: a book with the word "Hymns" in the title might well contain a prefatory note explaining that the contents were not intended to be sung! Rossetti herself was well aware of the slipperiness of the "hymnal" designation, asking W. Garrett Horder if his definition of hymnal would "include collections of sacred verse not intended to be sung in Church?" (*Letters* 4: 92). Yet Rossetti's own practice of titling devotional poems with scriptural quotations, in much the same way that hymn texts were presented, further blurred the already flimsy boundary between the two genres. For present purposes, the hymnal section (DH) is reserved for the smaller subset of collections that functioned primarily, and unquestionably, as hymn texts, whether or not they included music. Collections of religious poetry that were not primarily intended for use in hymn singing are located in the anthology section (B), but are also separately listed before the hymnal section, so that those who are interested in studying the relationships between hymnals and "sacred song" anthologies can easily do so. As in sections B and C, I have also usually included any book that was likely to have played a part in establishing Rossetti's publication history within hymnals, regardless of whether the Rossetti poem(s) are printed in them for the first time.

Though small in number, Rossetti's appearances in hymnals reinforced her high standing among religious poets, and enlarged the avenues through which her work was known and distributed. Rossetti was included in several collections with Church of England ties, such as *The People's Hymnal* (1868), anonymously edited by the Rev. Richard Littledale; the *Savoy Hymnary* (1880), for use in the Queen's Savoy Chapel; and *The Children's Hymn Book* (1881), edited by "Mrs. Carey" (Frances Elizabeth Georgina) Brock, with oversight from Bishop William Walsham How and other prominent clergy. The publication of "Patience of Hope" in *The Children's Hymn Book* marked the first publication of that poem; it also marked Rossetti's place alongside famed Victorian hymnists such as Frances Ridley Havergal and C. F. Alexander, whose "All things bright and beautiful," and "There is a green hill far away" were already acknowledged as classics of hymn writing for children. Still, Rossetti's work did not appear in a major Church of England-oriented collection until "A Christmas Carol" ("In the bleak mid-winter") appeared in Percy Dearmer's *The English Hymnal* (1906). Although "A Christmas Carol" was a popular choice for reprinting in anthologies and periodicals, and had already been set to music at least once, the poem's appearance in *The English Hymnal* was pivotal in the poem's emergence in the twentieth century as one of the most frequently set pieces in Rossetti's canon. The few other post-1900 hymnals listed in this section trace Rossetti's gradual emergence within other Church of England hymnals, concluding with her (belated) appearance in *Hymns Ancient & Modern Revised* in 1950.

Rossetti's appearances in hymnals reveal the varied audiences and theological perspectives to which her work appealed—or was made to appeal. After its publication in *The Children's Hymn Book*, Rossetti's "Patience of Hope" reappeared in *Christian Chorals for the Chapel & Fireside* (1880), edited by Melanchton Woolsey Stryker, a Presbyterian minister, hymnist, and the president of Hamilton College in New York. Since the poem had still not been published in Rossetti's collected volumes, *The Children's Hymn Book* was Stryker's most likely source for the text. But while *The Children's Hymn Book* set out to provide hymns that conveyed "sentiments" and "expressions" that were within the "possible experience, and, as far as may be, [. . .] comprehension" of children (iii), Stryker's collection offered "A limited number of hymns, set to thoughtful music" to an elite, adult audience who "tired of compromise with the paltry and the common-place" ("Foreword"). In 1884, W. Garrett Horder, who had included Rossetti's work in *The Poets' Bible*, published "Weary in Well Doing" in *Congregational Hymns* (though in his 1889 survey of hymnody, *The Hymn Lover*, he introduced it as an example of a poem not well suited for singing). Although Horder had sought Rossetti's permission to include her work in other collections, he did not do so for *Congregational Hymns*. Rossetti responded graciously to his appropriation of her work, and apparently valued his friendship, despite theological differences: Horder is one of the "friends" identified in Rossetti's annotations to the Texas copy of *Time Flies*. But while Horder made few alterations to the text of Rossetti's poem (eliminating Rossetti's patterned line indentations and making minor changes in punctuation), he did follow the customary practice of removing Rossetti's title, supplying in its place a relevant epigraph: "Let us not be weary in well-doing" (Galatians 6.9). Horder's epigraph demonstrates the transformative power of even the smallest changes likely to occur when a poem is printed within a hymnal. Rossetti's title clearly echoes Paul, who uses the phrase "weary in well-doing" both in Galatians (6.9) and in Second Thessalonians (3.13). But Rossetti's echo is allusive, not prescriptive, leaving readers free to understand the title as an endorsement of the general implications of Paul's phrase (do what God asks, don't lose heart, and especially in Thessalonians, get a job), but also inviting them to move beyond the specific Biblical context of the title to explore the emotional cost of obedience: "My soul is wrung with doubts that lurk and vex it so." Unlike Rossetti's title, Horder's epigraph restricts the reader's frame of reference, tying the poem to a specific quotation, which is further truncated by the omission of the encouraging words that temper Paul's warning (the full verse reads "Let us not be weary in well-doing, for in due season we shall reap, if we faint not"). Horder's highlighting of Paul's admonition against weariness undercuts Rossetti's representation of weariness as a natural human response to God's demands.

Horder's alteration of Rossetti's text pales by comparison to the poem's later appearance in A. B. Earle's *Sought-Out Songs For Christian Workers* (Boston, 1888). Earle, a Baptist evangelist, was active in the revival movement, and as he explains in the preface to *Sought-Out Songs*, the purpose of his collection is evangelical: it includes only hymns that "have been used by the Holy Spirit in leading souls to Christ." Earle's recontextualization of Rossetti's poem includes not only a new title ("Submission") and the customary Biblical citations (in this instance, Psalm 51: 17 and

Romans 8.1), but the addition of two new stanzas, credited to C.B.J. Root, who also composed the hymn tune. C.B.J. Root's poetic talent was somewhat limited, and Root's theology, while appropriate for the audience of the hymnal, was not in keeping either with Rossetti's intentions in the poem, or with Church of England doctrine. Root's verses blunt the poem's raw expression of frustration and longing for rest by moving the speaker—that is, the singing congregation—to a clearly stated consecration of the self to God, followed by a calm acknowledgment of peace and reconciliation:

> I yield my will, My Lord to Thee,
> And consecrate my all to Thee;
> And Thou doth witness to the deed,
> That I am ever Thine to be entirely Thine.
>
> Oh! Blessed bond of perfect peace,
> For Thou dost keep me thro' Thy grace;
> And in Thy love, alone I trust,
> Until I see Thee, face to face, forever more.

In the terms of nineteenth century American evangelicalism, particularly the interdenominational holiness movement, Roots' stanzas show the speaker of the hymn progressing from struggle to "consecration" (yielding the will and consecrating the self to God), and ultimately to sanctification, a state in which the soul is freed from sin. Root's language clearly derives from contemporary discourse on consecration and sanctification, including the idea that God will "witness" the sanctification of the believer (Stanley 77).[18] An endorsement of sanctification makes sense within a collection edited by Earle, who experienced, preached on, and wrote about sanctification in works such as *The Rest of Faith* (1871), but one can hardly imagine a more complete departure from the poem as Rossetti wrote it.

Musical settings of Rossetti's work outside of hymnals rarely offer such drastic changes, although it must be remembered that the addition of music, in and of itself, can dramatically affect a poem's meaning. Rossetti understood that her work would be altered when set, but she nevertheless welcomed any opportunity to have her work circulated in this manner: "The more of my things get set to music the better pleased I am" (*Letters* 1: 211). Contemporaries such as Edmund Gosse recognized that Rossetti's verse was especially well suited for music, placing her "next to Lord Tennyson in this branch of the art, in the spontaneous and complete quality of her lieder, and in their propriety for the purpose of being sung."[19] During Rossetti's lifetime, the most frequently set of her poems was "Song" ("When I am dead, my dearest"), with forty known settings. In 1890, Rossetti feigned astonishment when a composer wrote to ask permission to set the song again: "fancy not knowing whether 'When'– has ever been set ! ! ! (Authorial conceit)" (*Letters* 4: 176). "A Birthday" was the second most popular, set to music at least thirteen times. Theo Marzials composed one of the most popular settings of "A Birthday." Titled "My Love is

---

18. Susie Stanley, *Holy Boldness* (Knoxville: University of Tennessee Press, 2002). On Earle, see Timothy Smith, *Revivalism and Social Reform* (Baltimore: Johns Hopkins UP, 1957, 1980): 74, 75, 139-40. Earle was influenced by Phoebe Palmer, who promoted the idea of sanctification through her writings and through the "Tuesday Meetings" that she and her husband held (and which Earle attended). On Palmer, Susie Stanley explains that while "Wesley believed that growth both preceded and followed the experience of sanctification, Palmer eliminated the growth period prior to sanctification and wrote and preached that a Christian could be sanctified immediately upon consecrating her life to Christ and believing in Christ's promise . . . both she and Wesley contended that the experience of sanctification itself is received merely by faith and given instantaneously" (*Holy Boldness*, 70).

19. Edmund Gosse, "Christina Rossetti," *Century Illustrated Monthly Magazine* 46 (June 1893): 216.

Come," Marzials's setting was frequently reprinted in a variety of formats, including a newspaper supplement. In 1898, "A Birthday" was among the first published settings by Henry Thacker Burleigh, one of the most important African-American composers of the early twentieth century.

Among other composers who set Christina Rossetti's work were several friends and acquaintances of the family, including Malcolm Lawson, Francis Hueffer (William Rossetti's brother-in-law), Mary Carmichael, Emanuel Aguilar, and Marzials. The Rossetti family often attended first performances of Rossetti's settings at the composers' homes. Rossetti's poems also appealed to some of the most prominent and prolific composers of the day, including Frederic Cowen, George Alexander MacFarren, and Arthur Somervell. Nearly 40 musical settings by women were published before 1900, including the first known (but no longer extant) setting of Rossetti's poetry by Alice Mary Smith. Mary Carmichael, whom Marzials introduced to the Rossettis, became the first of several composers to produce collections of songs chosen from *Sing-Song*. Carmichael became a "particular friend" of Lucy Rossetti (*WMRD*, 29 April 1881), and William Michael Rossetti tried to assist her in publishing her settings of Christina's poems.

I have provided entries for all known settings prior to 1900, many of which are not previously documented. Unfortunately, much popular sheet music of the Victorian era has literally disappeared, as is indicated in several instances in which copies of settings that once existed, identified through reviews or other means, cannot be traced. Even extant settings can be difficult to locate, since musical settings of literary works are often retitled; those that are located may still be difficult or impossible to examine without travel to collections, given the fragile condition of surviving documents. For these reasons, the information I have been able to provide varies considerably depending on the information source(s) available to me. While later settings are easier to find and to examine, to include anything like a full listing of these later settings (by such figures as Samuel Coleridge-Taylor, Edward Elgar, John Ireland, Gustav Holst, C. Hubert H. Parry, Martin Shaw, and Ralph Vaughan Williams) is impossible within the limits of this volume. A very few later settings are included of poems that are important in Rossetti's canon (such as "Goblin Market"), and of poems that have been especially appealing to composers (such as "A Christmas Carol" and *Sing-Song*).

Most Rossetti settings took the form of songs for solo voice and piano, though MacFarren's 1869 setting of "Songs in a Cornfield" as a cantata was popular enough to remain in print through the 1890s. Rossetti's "Goblin Market" was also set as a cantata and published in 1880 by Emanuel Aguilar, brother of author Grace Aguilar. *Goblin Market, Cantata* marks one of the rare instances in which Rossetti worked with the composer to create a version of her text that would be suitable for music, an instance made more significant by the nature of the changes in the published cantata. Several of these changes contradict aspects of the poem that have been influential in contemporary readings of it. For example, it has often been noted that Rossetti's initial depiction of sisters Lizzie and Laura deliberately blurs the distinctions between them; both are tempted by the goblins, and Laura's interaction with them hardly seems less culpable than Lizzie's decision to run away from danger, leaving her sister behind. The cantata text allows for no such ambiguity, presenting Lizzie as a model of resistance who consistently and firmly rejects the goblins: instead of running away from them to save herself, she urges her sister to depart with her. And although the poem ends with a depiction of Laura telling her children the story of her temptation and of her sister's heroism, this important scene is omitted from the conclusion of the cantata, which makes no reference to Laura's social recuperation as wife, mother and aunt. Laura never reappears after her recovery, and the moral of her story—"there is no friend like a sister"—is sung by the chorus. In the cantata, Laura never regains her voice or her place within the community, a far cry from the poem's politically and socially challenging depiction of a fallen woman's complete reintegration into society. Because Rossetti promised Aguilar that she would not allow anyone else to set the poem, there were no further settings of "Goblin Market" during her lifetime, but two later settings, by Vittorio Ricci (1901) and Ruth Gipps (1954), follow Aguilar's lead, making no reference to Laura's future as a wife and mother.

Section E: Translations, Printed Ephemera, Rossettiana

The production of printed ephemera and other artifacts related to Rossetti's life and work began in Rossetti's lifetime and continues through the present day, a testament to the growth and strength of her literary reputation. The materials presented in this bibliography are not intended to form a comprehensive list of Rossetti's representation in media other than printed books; rather, they are to give readers a better sense than what currently exists of Rossetti's presence in these varied media.

Visual art is largely excluded from this section, as portraits of Christina by Dante Gabriel Rossetti are included in Virginia Surtees's *The Paintings and Drawings of Dante Gabriel Rossetti (1828-1882): A Catalogue Raisonné*, while Victorian (and later) paintings based upon Rossetti's poetry are discussed in Lorraine Jantzen Kooistra's *Christina Rossetti and Illustration* (254-262). Photographs of Rossetti (with her mother and siblings) were taken by Lewis Carroll in 1863; professional photographs were also taken in 1863 and by Elliott and Fry in 1877.[20] Translations are also limited to the small number made by or of Rossetti's work through 1900. Of the items included here, perhaps the most important is Rossetti's collaboration with her cousin Teodorico Pietrocola Rossetti, an evangelist who established the Christian Brethren in Italy. Current scholarly interest in the role played by Rossetti's religious commitment in her writing life has yet to extend to her relationship with Teodorico, with whom Rossetti worked upon an Italian translation of the Bible, and who himself translated Rossetti's "Goblin Market" (as well as Lewis Carroll's *Alice in Wonderland*) into Italian.

Rossetti's printed ephemera and Rossettiana runs a considerable gamut, from Victorian and early twentieth century chromolithography, to late twentieth century collectibles. Three especially important items are included in Section A: Rossetti's first printed poem, "To My Mother on the Anniversary of Her Birth," printed as a broadside by her grandfather Polidori in 1842; Alice Donlevy's designs for "Consider," issued in the form of separately-printed chromolithographed plates (1867); and a broadside of "Roses and Roses," printed to raise money for a charitable cause. Although additional surviving examples of Rossetti-inspired ephemera in the nineteenth century are scarce, examples such as Anne G. Morse's *Christmas Offerings*, a design incorporating text from "A Christmas Carol" that took fourth place in Louis Prang's competition for Christmas card designs, points to the popularity of Rossetti's poetry, and to some of the more unusual ways in which it was presented to Victorian audiences (one wonders if the terra-cotta sculpture based on Morse's design incorporated a line or two of Rossetti's verse). And while the history of Victorian "outlines for illuminating" remains fairly obscure,[21] the impulse to draw upon Rossetti's work to create opportunities for amateur artists persists: poems from *Sing-Song* appeared in Susan Gaber's *Favorite Poems for Children* coloring book (1980), and an excerpt from "Goblin Market" forms

20. Portraits and photographs of Christina Rossetti are also discussed by William Michael Rossetti in *The Poetical Works of Christina Rossetti* (London: Macmillan, 1904, revised 1906); the locations of several of these works are listed in the *Dictionary of British Portraiture*, volume 3 (New York: Oxford University Press, 1981). Some of Carroll's photographs of the Rossettis are reproduced in Gernsheim, *Lewis Carroll: Photographer* (New York: Chanticleer, 1949); Edward Wakeling lists all of the Rossetti photographs, along with their current locations, in the Register included in *Lewis Carroll Photographer: The Princeton University Library Albums* (Princeton: Princeton University Press, 2002). Two early studio photographs (circa 1855 and 1863) are reproduced in Jan Marsh's biography.

21. See Ives, "Teaching Women's Art in America: Alice Donlevy's Designs for Christina Rossetti's Consider," *Textual Cultures* 4.1 (Spring 2009): 26-54.

the basis of a cross stitch design by Patricia Andrle (1990). Other items produced purely for the collector's market, such as the various enamel boxes produced by Halcyon Days, mirror the use of Rossetti's work in fine press and collectible books that emerged in the early twentieth century.

A note on the use of electronic sources:

While I have directly examined books and periodicals described here whenever possible, I have not always been able to do so. However, electronic full-text databases and digital archives have made it possible to locate, search, and view images of materials that would otherwise remain either inaccessible or entirely unknown. This bibliography may be one of the first to take full advantage of electronic resources that offer page images and searchable text for nineteenth century documents, including the *American Periodicals Online* database, and digital archives, especially the two Making of America collections (at Michigan, moa.umdl.umich.edu and at Cornell, http://cdl.library.cornel.edu/moa/), and digitized full text available from various sources through the Internet Archive (www. archive. org) and Google Books (www.google.com/books). Especially in sections B, C and D, I have found it not only useful but necessary to make use of digital facsimiles, either to confirm the existence of or gather information about items known to exist but not readily available, or to locate publications of Rossetti's work that have not previously been identified. The potential benefits of such materials are obvious: there are many entries in this bibliography that would not be present had I not chosen to include findings from digital archives and other electronic resources. At the same time, the quality of digital materials varies considerably, and the drawbacks of using any facsimile, electronic or print, cannot be taken lightly. Important details are lost (and some new details may be created) in any process of reproduction, and the materials from which reproductions are made are not always wisely chosen, appropriately identified, or processed with appropriate care.[22] For these reasons, whenever it has been possible to examine a copy of a book first identified via electronic means, I have done so, though it must be noted that the availability of microfilm, full text databases, and digital archives has in effect increased the difficulty of obtaining original materials through any means other than travel to collections, as libraries have become unwilling to lend materials for which a digital facsimile is available. Rather than exclude materials that I could not personally examine, I have, in every instance in which an entry is based wholly or in part upon reproductions of any kind (photocopies, microfilm, or digital text), made note of the fact, and identified the locations of the source copies.

Bibliographical Format and Taxonomy

General Considerations

The methodology, taxonomy, and organizational principles of this bibliography follow the standard practices in the field, as articulated by scholars such as Fredson Bowers and G. Thomas Tanselle.[23] As previously noted, each section of this bibliography operates upon slightly different principles of selection and presentation. The fullest descriptions are reserved for separate works

22. Exceptions to the usual caveats about both digital materials and the losses entailed in reproductive processes can be found, especially in the work of scholars active in the (still relatively new) field of digital humanities. Of particular value for Rossetti scholars is Jerome McGann's groundbreaking *Rossetti Archive* (www.rossetti.org). The Rossetti Archive focuses upon the work of Dante Rossetti, which is why it does not play a larger role in this bibliography.

23. Fredson Bowers's *Principles of Bibliographical Description* (1949) remains the standard guide; as well as the significant body of work in the area by G. Thomas Tanselle, including essays such as "The Bibliographical Concepts of Issue and State" (*PBSA* 69:1 (1975): 17-66), "A Sample Bibliographical Description with Commentary (*Studies in Bibliography* 40 (1997): 1-30), and the collection *Selected Studies in Bibliography* (Charlottesville: University Press of Virginia, 1979).

published during Rossetti's lifetime and by her brother William in the early twentieth century; less detailed entries are provided for the remaining sections of the book. Some common elements among them include the following:

All measurements are in millimeters. When appropriate, measurements are presented in the format of height x width.

Quasi-facsimile is a form of transcription that attempts to represent the details of an original document's fonts, lineation, and punctuation. Any text that is enclosed in single quotation marks is in quasi-facsimile (with the exception of certain titles, as explained below). Title page transcriptions and printer's imprints in quasi-facsimile do not include closing punctuation other than that which appeared in the original document. Text in double quotation marks retains only the wording and internal punctuation of the original document.

Locations are provided for the materials described in each entry. Locations of copies examined are indicated by National Union Catalog symbols; if a library does not have a National Union Catalogue symbol, the library's name is given instead. Some alternate designations for books in private collections are identified in the list of abbreviations. When I have not been able to examine relevant materials that are known to exist, the location of the materials is designated as "Not seen," and the source(s) of information about the item (such as listings in library catalogs) are identified. Presentation copies are listed at the end of each entry. I have not identified recipients other than providing their names, as most are friends and family of the Rossettis (and thus easily identifiable from other sources), or impossible to identify with any certainty (such as Charles P. O'Connor in entry A11.ic).

Format for Section A: Separate Works

TAXONOMY: The purpose of bibliographical taxonomy is to display and clarify the printing history of a book. Printing and publishing history are interrelated, but they are also distinct; my organization of Section A thus aims to present a clear a picture of the printing history of Rossetti's books without neglecting important aspects of publishing history. The main organizational scheme of this section is to present Rossetti's books title by title, in chronological order of their printing history. The exceptions I have made—specifically, presenting subeditions in separate entries—serve to clarify the complexities of Rossetti's publishing history.

The primary organization of each entry is by *edition*, defined in the usual sense of all books printed from a single setting of type. Books printed from standing type, as well as books printed from any plates that were derived from that same typesetting, form a single edition. An edition includes at least one, and often multiple, print runs (here termed "*printings*"), depending on demand, and in the nineteenth century it was not uncommon for the plates of an edition to be reused to generate additional printings years, or decades, after the initial typesetting. Later printings that differ from the original printing either by significant changes in presentation or by the addition of new material are termed *subeditions*.

The sheets produced in any given print run can be packaged in multiple forms through such means as variation in paper size or type, or alterations in the title page to allow for multinational distribution. These distinctions, which affect the book as a whole and are made for the purposes of marketing and distributing the book to different audiences, are identified as *issues*. Changes made to some copies of a printing for other purposes (usually to correct errors) result in variant *states* of the printing.

SIGLA: Each item listed in Section A is identified by a sigla, which is composed of the section letter, followed by a title number in arabic; an edition or subedition number, also in arabic; and a lower case letter designating where the item falls in the sequence of printings within the edition. Multiple issues are designated by lower case roman numerals following the printing letter. Thus the designation "A1.1a" represents the first printing of the first edition of the first title represented in section A.

EDITIONS AND SUBEDITIONS: First and subsequent editions of the same title are listed in sequence under a single edition number. An exception is made for separate American and British editions of the same title, which are numbered separately (A15 and A16; A20 and A21; A28 and A29) so as to facilitate the tracking of individual editions within the larger chain of British or American collected editions.

Subeditions are usually assigned separate edition numbers. Specifically, Roberts Brothers and Macmillan subeditions (A12, A17, A22, A30, A32) are presented as separate entries, and rendered in full detail, with relationships to previous editions and subeditions indicated. However, subeditions resulting from simultaneous printing from duplicate plates in Britain and the United States are included within a single title number. This arrangement highlights the chronology of publication without obscuring printing history.

PRINTINGS AFTER THE FIRST: It can be difficult to determine the number of impressions of nineteenth century books—the majority of which were printed from plates, on machine-made, wove paper—with any degree of certainty. Fortunately, collected editions of Rossetti's poems published by Macmillan present relatively few difficulties, given the information available in the Macmillan archive regarding print runs of Rossetti titles (although the Editions Books often do not distinguish between the date of printing and publication).

For collected editions published in the United States by Roberts Brothers, however, the situation is less clear, since no relevant publisher's records remain. There is usually little or no decisive evidence of the number of printings of later Roberts Brothers titles; moreover, extant copies of some Roberts Brothers subeditions from the late 1880s and 1890s are often scarce, leaving open the possibility of intervening printings that have yet to be identified. For example, the listing for A12 includes descriptions of copies dated 1880 and 1896. There may or may not have been one or more additional printings in the sixteen years between 1880 and 1896, so 1896 is designated "later printing" instead of "seventh printing." In other instances, multiple later printings in chronological sequence are treated as numbered printings (as in A30), but readers should treat such designations as matters of convenience rather than of bibliographical fact.

TITLE PAGE TRANSCRIPTIONS: Throughout the bibliography letterpress title pages are transcribed in quasi-facsimile. Fonts other than italic (primarily black letter) are designated by underlining and specified in a note preceding the transcription; ink colors other than black are also mentioned in a note and designated by underlining or other means. Visual content such as publisher's devices or illustrations are briefly described, with measurements provided in millimeters (height x length).

PAGINATION: Blank pages in a book's pagination are either inferred (represented by underlining) or unnumbered pages (presented in brackets). The pagination of unnumbered pages in the middle of a sequence is inferred; the end of a sequence is also inferred. Brackets are used to indicate unnumbered pages at beginning or mid-sequence that cannot be inferred.

Thus the sequence 'I-xi xii 1' indicates that an unnumbered page followed 'xi' and its number is inferred to be xii, while the sequence '[2] I-xi' indicates that two unnumbered, uninferred pages preceded 'I.'

PLATES: The location and description of plates includes measurements in millimeters (height x width). Measurements of images do not include appended captions unless indicated in the description. All captions are transcribed and should be assumed to be engraved unless they are identified as letterpress.

Plate marks and tissue guards are indicated if present (if any plates in a book have tissues, then all plates are indicated with or without).

Illustrations that were printed along with the text are described within or at the end of the "Contents" section.

COLLATION: Collation formulas are usually prefaced with a statement of a book's format, format being the way in which the pages were imposed (or, arranged for printing) and folded. But format statements do not mean the same thing for pre- and post-industrial printing. As Philip Gaskell explains, for hand-press books, the format statement conveys "the size and folding of the gatherings" as well as "the sheet size and the imposition used in printing it" (328).[24] However, for machine-press books, which were "commonly printed in large work-and-turn impositions on double or quad paper," format "refers only to the paper size and folding as they appear in the book" (Gaskell, 328). As a result, it can be difficult to determine format (in the sense of folios, quartos, or octavos) for Victorian machine-made books. Therefore, when possible, I have provided statements of format (e.g., 2°, 4°, 8°), but I have usually followed Bowers's recommendation to replace the format statement with the measurement of a typical leaf (Bowers, 429-430). Thus in most entries, format is not determined; instead, a leaf measurement is given in parentheses, followed by collation statement indicating how the book is gathered. Most of the books included here used alphabetical or numerical signing. When an unsigned gathering can be inferred, the inferred signature is represented by underlining. Since Victorian printers almost always omitted the letters J, V and W, readers should assume that those letters were not used in alphabetical signatures for the books in this section unless the entry specifies that they were present. Unsigned leaves in inferred gatherings are not specified in the statement of signing (that is, for a book signed A⁶ B-F⁶, the statement of signing will read "$1 signed" rather than "$1 signed (-A1)". The entire collation statement appears in brackets if the book is unsigned or if it is not gathered as signed, in which case a separate statement of the obsolete signing will follow, along with the number of leaves.

CONTENTS: This section attempts to account for the various divisions within a book, including not only the main text, but preliminary pages, prefaces or introductions, illustrations (other than plates), and appendixes, indexes, and advertisements that were printed along with the sheets of the book. While I do not list individual poems in this section, I do indicate chapter and division sections, usually in quasi-facsimile (presented in single quotation marks). Most of Rossetti's books do not have many divisions so there is no practical need to omit them; more important is that her use of sectional divisions (for example, her designation of "devotional" sections in collections of poetry) is of some interest to scholars. While visual content, such as type ornaments and illustrations, is indicated in contents when it is feasible or useful to do so (in *Called to Be Saints*, for example, the extensive patterning of the book's textual and visual content makes it helpful to indicate not only type ornaments but some font changes within contents), more complex visual elements are presented in a separate list. If publisher's advertisements were printed with the sheets of the book, the contents section will briefly describe them; otherwise they will be discussed in the binding section. Headings, numbers of titles advertised per page, and the first and last titles per page are indicated, and titles by Rossetti are mentioned. Book titles listed in advertisements are

24. Gaskell, *A New Introduction to Bibliography* (New York: Oxford University Press, 1972); see also Terry Belanger, "Descriptive Bibliography," in *Book Collecting: A Modern Guide*, ed. Jean Peters (New York: R.R. Bowker, 1977): 106-107.

presented in italics, regardless of how they appeared on the page, unless the titles appear within a quoted passage (as in the Contents section of A16.1a and A18.1).

POEMS: All poems included in a book are listed in the order of their occurrence. The titles of poems are not presented in quasi-facsimile, though in some instances, aspects of the original typography are retained (but line breaks within titles are not retained). I have generally not retained subtitles or epigraphs printed with poem titles unless they are necessary to identify the poem. However, for poems that are printed in numbered sections or parts, the number of sections or parts, and subtitles if present, are included in parentheses after the title, for example: "Title" (sections x-x)."

In titles printed with closing punctuation marks, closing periods are omitted, but other possibly substantive closing punctuation, such as exclamation points and question marks, is retained.

All titles are enclosed in double quotation marks. However, Rossetti's titles are sometimes direct quotations from the Bible, and such titles frequently appear in quotation marks within her works. Rather than using two sets of double marks around such titles, any titles that were printed in quotation marks, whether double or (as rarely happened) single, are regularized to single quotation marks within the usual double quotation marks.

Additional information is included to assist in the identification of poems that do not have unique titles, that have undergone title changes, were at some point published without a title, or for which the title status is unclear.

1. Poems without unique titles: several poems have the same title, such as "Song." In instances where Rossetti has used the same title for more than one poem, the first words of the poem's first line are given in parenthesis after the title.

2. Untitled poems: I do not distinguish between titled and untitled poems, for which all or part of the first line is given as the title.

3. Poems published both with and without titles: when Rossetti provides a title for a previously untitled poem, as frequently happens in the collection *Verses* (1893), the new title is followed by the first line in parentheses. When a titled poem is reprinted with no title (as happened when the poem "Roses and Roses," published first as a broadside, was reprinted in *Time Flies* and later collections), the first line is given as title, and the former title is provided in square brackets.

4. Retitled poems: when Rossetti retitles a poem (as happened with "Under the Rose"), the new title is followed by the former title in square brackets: "'The Iniquity of the Fathers Upon the Children'" ["Under the Rose"].

5. Unclear titles: sometimes, especially in Rossetti's devotional collections, it is unclear whether text that prefaces a poem is intended to serve as a title, and the same prefatory text may be presented in more (or less) "title-like" ways from one collection to the next. For example, in *Time Flies*, the poem for February 15 (first line: "My love whose heart is tender said to me"), includes this prefatory text: "'Doeth well, ... doeth better.'—(I Cor. vii.38.)." Rossetti generally does not provide full citations for Biblical quotations used as titles, and thus the format of this quotation suggests that it is to be understood as an epigraph rather than a title. However, when the same poem was reprinted in *Verses* the prefatory quotation is clearly presented as a title, with simplified internal punctuation and no citation: "'Doeth well . . . . doeth better.'" However, Rossetti's entries for Saint's days in *Time Flies* include both the calendar date and the name of the Saint in small capitals before the text of the entry: 'August 7. | FEAST OF THE NAME OF JESUS.' In the context of *Time Flies*, such poems might be considered untitled, since the Saint's day designation is a function of the calendar format; but the Saint's day titles are retained in *Verses*. The changes made

in *Verses* could be the result of authorial revision, but they may also reflect differing compositorial practices or house styling. In listing the poems for *Time Flies*, I have presented the Saint's day headings as titles, followed by the first line in parentheses. When these poems are reprinted with titles in *Verses*, the title is followed by the first line in parentheses.

TYPOGRAPHY AND PAPER: The character of a typical type page is indicated through measurements in millimeters of total page height (in parentheses), the text height, and the text width. These measurements are followed by the page number on which the measurements were taken and the number of lines on that page. When the number of lines per page varies (as often happens with poetry collections), a page with the largest number of lines is used for the purpose of type measurement. Whenever possible, measurements are taken on a page that includes both a headline and direction line. Exceptions (such as subsections with smaller fonts) are noted, as is the presence of rule frames, type ornaments, and significant typographical patterns.

The pattern of the book's paper, wove (lacking distinct chain lines) or laid (with chain lines), is also indicated in this part of the entry along with the presence or absence of watermarks. Most of Rossetti's books were printed on machine made white paper without watermarks or chain lines. When chain lines are present, the distance between them in millimeters is provided; unusual papers, or characteristics that distinguish between printings, are indicated. Watermarks are briefly described.

RUNNING TITLES: A running title (abbreviated 'RT') is a phrase descriptive of the page's contents (a shortened form of a book's title, a chapter title, or a poem title) that appears in a line of type placed above the text proper. Running titles are transcribed in quasi-facsimile, within single quotation marks, and divided into two subsections: rectos (right hand pages) and versos (left hand pages).

BINDING: Binding cloth and other materials, cloth and paper patterns, and cloth and paper colors are identified and described as needed; the binding itself, endpapers, and the treatment of the book's edges are all indicated. Whenever possible, color names follow the nomenclature recommended in *The ISCC-NBS Method of Designating Colors and a Dictionary of Color Names*. Centroid chart references are provided as a guide only, as there is rarely an exact match between a particular book cloth and color chart samples, and individual copies may vary widely due to storage conditions and other variables. Measurements of binding design elements, such as rules and ornaments, and measurements of boards, are generally not given unless they play a part in distinguishing binding variants. Locations of copies that display significant binding variants are indicated.

PUBLICATION: The size of the print run is provided, if known, along with the date of publication, price, existence of deposit copies, and the dates and locations of publication announcements and reviews. A brief narrative account of the book's composition and production also appears here.

PRINTING: Imprints included in the book are transcribed in quasi-facsimile.

Formats for Section B-E

These sections include less detailed, and (in D and E especially), more varied entry formats given the nature of the materials described. While I present a brief explanation of the main organization of each section here, full details about the organization and scope of these sections is presented in a note at the beginning of each section. Misattributions are presented at the end of each section. All correspondence published for the first time in books and periodicals is reprinted in Antony Harrison's *The Letters of Christina Rossetti* unless otherwise indicated.

Section B: Appearances in Books

Books in this section are arranged in chronological order by year, and in alphabetical order within each year.

Each entry includes a title page transcription in quasi-facsimile; first line or titles and inclusive page numbers of Rossetti material, an indication of whether and how Rossetti's name appears with the text (e.g., unsigned or signed, "C. G. Rossetti"); notes; and the location(s) of copies examined. Additional information about the section format appears at the beginning of the section.

Section C: Appearances in Periodicals

Items in this section are arranged in chronological order; within a given month, monthly periodicals are listed before periodicals issued more frequently.

Each entry includes a genre symbol if needed; the title of the item; the title of the periodical or newspaper and place of publication; volume and/or issue numbers; inclusive page numbers of the Rossetti material; indication of whether and how Rossetti's name appears with the text (e.g., unsigned or signed, "C. G. Rossetti"); notes; and location(s) of copies examined or other sources of information.

Section D: Hymnals and Poems Set to Music

Books in the hymnal section are listed in chronological order by year; musical settings are organized alphabetically by poem title within each year.

DH (hymnals): Each entry includes a title page transcription in quasi-facsimile, first line or titles and inclusive page numbers of Rossetti material, an indication of whether and how Rossetti's name appears with the text (e.g., unsigned or signed, "C. G. Rossetti"); tune designation (if any); notes; and the location(s) of copies examined. For entries that include music, the name of the composer, the tune name or other identification (if any), and the major key signature and instrumentation (if any) are indicated.

DM (musical settings): For each entry, the title of the Rossetti poem, the name of the composer, and the publication date are given in the entry heading. All entries also include the title of the setting, publication information (including plate or publisher's numbers), and locations of extant copies (or citations of sources that reference settings that cannot be located). All entries are for separately published sheet music unless otherwise indicated.

For sheet music, a brief description or a transcription of the front cover or other title page equivalent is provided when possible.

Section E: Translations, Printed Ephemera, Rossettiana

This section is numbered consecutively but divided into the following subsections: translations; printed ephemera; and other Rossettiana, including memorials, plaques, and commercially produced items incorporating text by Rossetti.

Indexes of Poems and Prose

Poems are indexed under the latest title given to them by Christina Rossetti. Alternate titles of first lines of poems retitled by Christina Rossetti, as well as of poems given titles by William Michael Rossetti, are included, with a "see" reference to Rossetti's title. Former titles appear in brackets; first line references appear in parentheses. The prose index includes fiction, nonfiction, and correspondence. Both complete works and excerpts from them are indexed. Rossetti rarely retitled prose works; the few instances in which a significant title change occurs are clarified through cross-references.

ABBREVIATIONS

1. LIBRARIES and PRIVATE COLLECTIONS

For most United States, Canadian and British libraries, this bibliography uses the library symbols provided in the National Union Catalog. The following additional symbols are also used:

Baylor	Baylor University
BL	British Library
DAM	Delaware Art Museum
Fitz	Fitzwilliam Museum, Cambridge
Fredeman	Collection of William E. Fredeman. Current location unknown.
Ives	Collection of Maura Ives
Macmillan	File copy kept at the Macmillan Archives, Basingstoke
MSL	Collection of Mark Samuels Lasner
UMs	University of Mississippi

2. OTHER ABBREVIATIONS

Account book	CGR's account book 1874-1894. Angeli-Dennis Collection, University of British Columbia, Box 10 Folder 1.
CGR	Christina Rossetti
Crump	*The Complete Poems of Christina Rossetti*. Ed. R. W. Crump. 3 vols. Baton Rouge: Louisiana State University Press, 1979-90.
Diary	*The Diary of W. M. Rossetti 1870-1873*. Ed. Odette Bornand. Oxford: Clarendon, 1977.
DGR	Dante Gabriel Rossetti
DRLetters	*The Correspondence of Dante Gabriel Rossetti*. 3 vols. to date. Ed. William E. Fredeman. Cambridge: D. S. Brewer, 2002-.
Family Letters	*The Family Letters of Christina Georgina Rossetti*. Ed. William Michael Rossetti. London: Brown, Langham, 1908
FLR	Frances Mary Lavinia Rossetti
GTT	Tanselle, G. Thomas. "The Bibliographical Description of Patterns." *Selected Studies in Bibliography*. Charlottesville: U Press of Virginia, 1979. 171-202.
Kooistra	Kooistra, Lorraine J. *Christina Rossetti and Illustration*. Athens: Ohio UP, 2002.
Kent and Stanwood	*Selected Prose of Christina Rossetti*. Ed. David A. Kent and P. G. Stanwood. New York: St. Martin's, 1998.
LAM	*Letters of Alexander Macmillan*. Ed. George Macmillan. Glasgow: privately printed, 1908.
Letters	*The Letters of Christina Rossetti*. 4 vols. Ed. Antony Harrison. Charlottesville: University Press of Virginia, 1997-2004.
Macmillan Archives	Records kept at Macmillan Archives, Basingstoke.

MFR	Maria Francesca Rossetti
PW	*The Poetical Works of Christina Rossetti*. Ed. William Michael Rossetti. London: Macmillan, 1904.
RP	*Rossetti Papers 1862 to 1870*. Comp. William Michael Rossetti. New York: Charles Scribner's Sons, 1903.
SPCK	Society for Promoting Christian Knowledge.
SWMR	*Selected Letters of William Michael Rossetti*. Ed. Roger W. Peattie. University Park: Penn State U P, 1990.
Troxell	Janet Camp Troxell Collection of Rossetti Manuscripts, Department of Rare Books and Special Collections, Princeton University Library.
WMR	William Michael Rossetti
WMRD	Unpublished diary of W. M. Rossetti. Angeli-Dennis Collection, University of British Columbia.

A: BOOKS AND SEPARATE WORKS

SEPARATE PUBLICATIONS, 1842-1899

A1   TO MY MOTHER ON THE ANNIVERSARY OF HER BIRTH (1842)

A2   VERSES (1847)

A3   GOBLIN MARKET AND OTHER POEMS (1862)

A4   POEMS (Roberts Brothers, 1866)

A5   THE PRINCE'S PROGRESS AND OTHER POEMS (1866)

A6   CONSIDER (1867)

A7   COMMONPLACE AND OTHER SHORT STORIES (1870)

A8   SING-SONG (1872)

A9   ANNUS DOMINI (1874)

A10   SPEAKING LIKENESSES (1874)

A11   GOBLIN MARKET, THE PRINCE'S PROGRESS, AND OTHER POEMS (1875)

A12   POEMS (Roberts Brothers First Subedition, 1876)

A13   SEEK AND FIND (1879)

A14   CALLED TO BE SAINTS (1881)

A15   A PAGEANT AND OTHER POEMS (Macmillan, 1881)

A16   A PAGEANT AND OTHER POEMS (Roberts Brothers, 1881)

A17   POEMS (Roberts Brothers Second Subedition, 1882)

A18   LETTER AND SPIRIT (1883)

A19   ROSES AND ROSES (1884)

A20   TIME FLIES (SPCK, 1885)

A21   TIME FLIES (Roberts Brothers, 1886)

A22   POEMS, NEW AND ENLARGED (Macmillan Subedition, 1890)

A23   THE FACE OF THE DEEP (1892)

A24   VERSES (1893)

A25   GOBLIN MARKET (1893)

A26   NEW POEMS (1896)

A27   THE ROSSETTI BIRTHDAY BOOK (1896)

A28   MAUDE (Stone, 1897)

A29   MAUDE (Bowden, 1897)

A30   POEMS (Little, Brown Subedition, 1898)

A31   MONNA INNOMINATA (1899)

A32   POETICAL WORKS (Little, Brown Subedition, 1899)

SELECTED LATER WORKS

A33   REFLECTED LIGHTS FROM THE FACE OF THE DEEP (1899, 1900)
A34   POETICAL WORKS (1904)
A35   POEMS OF CHRISTINA ROSSETTI (GOLDEN TREASURY SERIES) (1904)
A36   THE FAMILY LETTERS OF CHRISTINA GEORGINA ROSSETTI (1908)
A37   THE COMPLETE POEMS OF CHRISTINA GEORGINA ROSSETTI (1979-1990)
A38   THE LETTERS OF CHRISTINA ROSSETTI (1999-2004)

A1   **TO MY MOTHER ON THE ANNIVERSARY OF HER BIRTH (1842)**

A1.1   *First Edition, Only Printing (1842)*

TO MY MOTHER | ON THE ANNIVERSARY OF HER BIRTH. | April 27. 1842. | To-day's your natal day; | Sweet flow'rs I bring; | Mother, accept, I pray, | My offering. | And may you happy live, | And long us bless; | Receiving, as you give, | Great happiness. | CHRISTINA GEORGINA ROSSETTI.

Note: Broadside, printed on recto only. 154 x 95 mm. Privately printed by CGR's maternal grandfather, Gaetano Polidori. Included in *Verses* (A2) and in WMR's *New Poems* (A26). WMR's note in *New Poems* claims that these are "the first verses that Christina ever composed" (394). According to WMR, the family was "a little surprised" by Christina's "coming out" as a poet, which might explain why Polidori "printed the lines at once on a card" (394).

Locations: BL; Fredeman.

A2   VERSES (1847)

A2.1   *First Edition, Only Printing (1847)*

VERSES | BY CHRISTINA G. ROSSETTI | *DEDICATED TO HER MOTHER.* | *Perchè temer degg' io?* *Son le mie voci* | *Inesperte, lo so: ma il primo omaggio* | *D'accettarne la* MADRE | *Perciò non sdegnerà;* *ch' anzi assai meglio* | *Quanto a lei grata io sono* | *L' umil dirà semplicità del dono.* | Metastasio. | PRIVATELY PRINTED | AT G. POLIDORI'S, NO. 15, PARK VILLAGE EAST, | REGENT'S PARK, LONDON. 1847.

Pagination: [4] 1-66.

Collation: 8° in 4s: π^2 1-6^4 7^4 ($\pm7_4$) 8^4 (8$_4$ + 9). \$1 signed. 35 leaves, 173 x 107 mm. A single leaf, signed "9," is glued to the last leaf of gathering 8. See *Note one* and *Note two*.

Contents: [1]: title page; [2]: blank; [3]: preface 'A FEW WORDS TO THE READER.'; [4] blank; 1-66 text.

Poems: "The Dead City," "The Water Spirit's Song," "The Song of the Star," "Summer" ("Hark to the song of greeting"), "To My Mother, With A Nosegay," ["To My Mother"], "The Ruined Cross," "Eva," "Love Ephemeral," "Burial Anthem," "Sappho," "Tasso and Leonora," "On The Death of a Cat, A Friend Of Mine, Aged Ten Years And A Half," "Mother and Child," "Fair Margaret," "Earth and Heaven," "The Rose," "Love Attacked," "Love Defended," "Divine and Human Pleading," "Gone For Ever," "To My Friend Elizabeth," "Amore E Dovere," "Amore E Dispetto," "Love And Hope," "Serenade," "The Rose," "Present And Future," "Will These Hands Ne'er Be Clean?," "Sir Eustace Grey," "The Time Of Waiting," "Charity," "The Dead Bride," "Life Out Of Death," "The Solitary Rose," "Lady Isabella" ("Lady Isabella"), "Sonnet. Lady Isabella" ("Heart warm as summer, fresh as spring"), "The Dream," "The Dying Man To His Betrothed," "The Martyr," "The End Of Time," "'Vanity Of Vanities,'" "Resurrection Eve," "Zara."

Typography and paper: (127) 119 x 65 (p. 13); various lines per page (up to 35). Wove paper, unwatermarked.

No running titles.

Binding: According to WMR, there was no "original binding" other than a paper wrapper (letter to Mackenzie Bell, 21 March 1895, Troxell CO 189, folder 11); he also retained several copies in sheets. Several copies in unprinted grayish green (Centroid 150) wrappers are extant (TxU, Baylor, CaBVaU, NjP). Three copies exist in embossed dark greenish blue cloth (TxCM, TxU, NjP, PBm), with an additional copy reported at the Guildhall Library (not seen). Edges: cut flush or untrimmed.

Publication: Privately printed by Gaetano Polidori, Rossetti's maternal grandfather, in 1847 sometime before July 24 (Marsh 75). A number of errors on pages 55-56 caused Polidori to reprint the page, thus the cancellation and replacement of leaf 7$_4$ in most copies. However, some copies retain both the corrected and uncorrected leaves (see *Note one*), and various additional hand corrections occur on various other pages in other extant copies, as detailed in *Note two*. In 1882 a copy was advertised in a bookseller's catalogue for 5 guineas (*Family Letters* 108).

The University of Illinois at Urbana-Champaign reports a copy with extensive annotations by WMR in addition to hand corrections (see *Note two*). The annotations include dates for poems that WMR reprinted in *New Poems* (A26); this, along with notations that correlate with page numbers in *New Poems*, indicates that this copy may have served as printer's copy for the latter volume. I would like to thank Alvan Bregman for providing information about this copy.

Printing: No printer's imprint.

Note one: A set of unbound, unsewn gatherings (missing 7), with unfolded 4-leaf gatherings measuring 34.1 x 20.7 cm, and including the original single leaf 7₄ (pp.55-56) with corrections by WMR, is at CaBVaU.

In addition, four extant copies have been bound with both the corrected and uncorrected leaf 7₄ (NjP, BL (Ashley); not seen: CtY (Tinker), Huntington). Two other libraries report copies with the uncorrected leaf only (MWelC, DLC). The DLC copy is inscribed to William Bryant, who probably received the book from CGR in response to one of his repeated requests for financial assistance (see Lasner, "Christina Rossetti's 'Common Looking Booklet': A New Letter about her *Verses* of 1847," C156).

The reprinted leaf includes the following seven corrections in the poem "The Dream." Hand corrections are usually present in copies that retain the uncorrected leaf.

On page 55:

1. In line nine from the bottom, the uncorrected phrase "now thou" is corrected to "now that thou". Hand corrected by WMR in CaBVaU unbound copy; also corrected in BL (Ashley), CtY (Tinker), DLC, MWelC.

2. In line six from the bottom, the uncorrected phrase "see in the clouds" is corrected to "see the clouds". Hand corrected by WMR in CaBVaU unbound copy. Also corrected in BL (Ashley), CtY (Tinker), MWelC. Uncorrected in DLC.

3. In line four from bottom, the uncorrected phrase "its row" is corrected to "it now". Hand corrected by WMR in CaBVaU unbound copy; also corrected in BL (Ashley), CtY (Tinker), DLC, MWelC.

On page 56:

4. In line seven, double quotation marks are inserted before "It". Hand corrected by WMR in CaBVaU unbound copy. Also corrected in BL (Ashley), CtY (Tinker), MWelC. Uncorrected in DLC.

5. In line seven, punctuation after "it" is corrected from a period to a semicolon. Hand corrected by WMR in CaBVaU unbound copy. Also corrected in BL (Ashley), CtY (Tinker), MWelC. Uncorrected in DLC.

6. In line eight, double quotation marks are inserted after "me". Hand corrected by WMR in CaBVaU unbound copy. Also corrected in BL (Ashley), CtY (Tinker), MWelC. Uncorrected in DLC.

7. Beneath line 22, the date "1847." is inserted. Hand corrected by WMR in CaBVaU unbound copy. Also corrected in BL (Ashley), CtY (Tinker), MwelC. Uncorrected in DLC.

Note two: The following MS corrections have been noted in copies examined. Information from copies not examined was provided via a survey completed by the respective libraries. See also William Baker's report of a privately owned copy with corrections similar to those recorded here ("Christina Rossetti: An Unpublished Letter and an Unrecorded Copy of *Verses*," C162).

In eight copies (TxCM, TxU [3], MSL, NjP, PBm, UkCU), including five presentation copies, "Thou" (p. 52 line 3 of "The Solitary Rose") is hand corrected in black ink or pencil (MSL, TxU) to "That." Additional copies with this correction were reported by AzTeS, Guildhall Library, IU, and the John Rylands University library.

In five copies (TxU [2], MSL, NjP, UkCU), including three presentation copies, "no" (p. 63 line 6) is crossed out in pencil (TxU, MSL) or ink (NjP, UkCU). Additional copies with this correction were reported by AzTeS, IU, the John Rylands University library and the University of Richmond.

In four copies (NjP, Fitz, TxU, UkCu), including one presentation copy (TxU), the word "twelve" is stricken and replaced with "eleven" (p. 3, line 5) in pencil (TxU) or ink; in the TxU and Fitz copies, "December" (TxU) or "5th Dec"(Fitz) is inserted in line 2 before "1830"; in Fitz, "April" was inserted in line 3 before "1842." The Fitz copy was owned by DGR. An additional copy with this correction was reported by IU.

In three copies (TxU [2], UkCU) there is a pencil or ink caret between the b and ò in "sembò" (p. 38 line 12) and an "r" in margin. An additional copy with this correction was reported by the University of Richmond. This correction is not noted in Crump.

In one copy (UkCU), the word "fears" has been corrected to "tears" (p. 53, line 6 from bottom of page). An additional copy with this correction was reported by IU.

Note three: A copy with DGR's hand illustrations is extant (TxU); a copy with CGR's hand illustrations, mentioned by WMR in the notes to *New Poems* (395 & passim), was extant in 1959; its current location is unknown (Kooistra 28, 277).

Note four: The bookseller Frank W. Burgess informed WMR of a "facsimile piracy" of this book (WMRD, April 5, 1898, A. 1. 1. 8), and WMR referred to an unauthorized "reissue" in the preface to *Poetical Works* (1904). No copies of the facsimile have been located.

Locations: Baylor; BL (2); CaBVaU (2); DeU; Fitz; Fredeman; MSL (presentation copy); NjP (4, including presentation copy); PBm; TxU (4, including presentation copy); TxCM (presentation copy); TxU, UkCU.

Additional copies not seen: AzTeS; CtY (2); CU; DLC; GEU; Guildhall; Huntington; InU; MH-Houghton; MwelC; John Rylands University Library, Manchester University; NN; University of Richmond.

Presentation copies: Fredeman: "To my very dear daughter Mary I give this one of the few remaining copies of her Aunt's early Verses. W. M. Rossetti 22 June /95"; MSL: inscribed to Charles Hare "with C. G. R's compliments" with CGR's AMS of "Looking forward" dated 1849; NjP: copy 4, inscribed to Mrs. Edwards from G. Polidori, dated 1848; TxU: copy 1, inscribed "Mrs Nichol from C. G. R."; copy 2: inscribed 'Miss Bessie R. Parkes with C. G. R's regards"; copy 3: multiple Rossetti family inscriptions, including CGR to her mother (dated 1854) and to WMR ("Fratri Soror C. G. R Sept. 25. 1890"; TxCM: inscribed to WMR from CGR, no date.

A2.2   *Second Edition, Only Printing (1906)*

Same as 1847 edition, except:

See *Note one*. All trefoil ornaments measure 4 x 4:
[trefoil, stem pointing left] VERSES BY CHRISTINA G. ROSSETTI. | [trefoil, stem pointing left] REPRINTED FROM G. POLIDORI'S EDITION OF 1847. EDITED by J. D. SYMON. | [circular printer's device, 76 x 76 mm: in foreground, seated woman holding book with 'ERAGNY | PRESS' on cover; above woman, banner reading (left of woman) 'E• ET• L• (above woman) PISSARRO (right of woman) LONDON •'] | THIS REPRINT IS MADE BY ARRANGE- | MENT WITH MESSRS. MACMILLAN & | CO., LTD., AND SOLD AT THE ERAGNY | PRESS, THE BROOK, HAMMERSMITH, | LONDON, W.

Pagination: i-ii iii-v vi 1-3 4-75 76.

Collation: 8° in 4s: a1 b⁴ (B2 + χ1.2) c-i⁴ j⁴ k²; $1 signed; signing includes both "i" and "j." 41 leaves, 210 x 124.

Contents (see *Note two*): i: title; ii: blank; iii: 'PREFACE.'; vi: blank; 1: within red rule frame, text of 1847 title; 2-76: text and on 76, printer's imprint.

Typography and paper: (133) 129 x 83 (p. 18); various lines per page (up to 31); ornamental capitals in first line of preface and first lines of all poems. Laid paper, vertical chainlines 25 mm apart. Watermarked 'ARCHES' (13 x 100); countermarked with Eragny Press monogram, 50 x 42; see *Note three*. Vellum copies not seen.

No running titles.

Binding: Paper covered boards, spine light bluish gray (Centroid 190), boards with brownish-white paper printed with green and yellow floral design. On front, in gilt '[two intertwined leaves, 4 x 12] VERSES. | CHRISTINA | G. ROSSETTI.' Endpapers: same as sheets, and conjugate with a four-leaf gathering of blank pages that precede and follow the sheets. Edges: top edge rough trimmed, fore and tail edges untrimmed.

Publication: November 1906. Printing began in July 1906, but was not completed until November, due to negotiations with WMR and Macmillan regarding copyright (Genz 104; *SWMR* , 651-53; WMRD, August 3, 1906, September 19, 1906) and problems with the binding and endpapers (Genz 215). Printing costs for 175 paper and 10 vellum copies were approximately £69.03.11 (Genz 63).

The "Preface" states that "this reprint follows exactly the edition of 1847 printed by G. Polidori" (iv). The Eragny text follows the corrected version of 7_4 in A2.1. Of the hand corrections noted in various copies of A2.1, only one, the correction of "fears" to "tears" in "Lady Isabella" (p. 61) appears here.

Announced in the *Athenaeum* (3 November 1906: 551; "List of New Books," 24 November 1906: 655); Genz lists notices in London *Evening News*, November 1906; *Illustrated London News*, 1 December 1906.

Price: 1 guinea; vellum copies, 5 guineas (Genz 215).

Printing (all trefoil ornaments measure 4 x 4 mm): p. 76, '[trefoil, stem pointing left] THIS REPRINT OF CHRISTINA G. | ROSSETTI'S EARLIEST VERSES FOL- | LOWS THE TEXT OF G. POLIDORI'S | EDITION OF 1847, & HAS BEEN EDITED | AND SEEN THROUGH THE PRESS BY | J. D. SYMON. [trefoil, stem pointing left] THE DECORATIONS | HAVE BEEN DESIGNED BY LUCIEN | PISSARRO AND ENGRAVED ON THE | WOOD BY ESTHER & LUCIEN PISSAR- | RO, BY WHOM THE BOOK, FINISHED IN OCTOBER 1906, HAS BEEN PRIN- |TED AT THEIR ERAGNY PRESS. | [trefoil, stem pointing left] This edition is strictly limited to 175 paper | and 10 vellum copies.'

Note one: Title page device is Genz's "Pressmark III" (Genz 55, 56).

Note two: An errata slip is glued to 76, with contents as follows: 'Page 21, line 12: for <<band;>> read <<bands;>> | Page 40, line 8: for <<his>>, read <<His>>'.

Note three: Paper manufactured for Eragny Press in France by Perrigot-Masure; see Genz, 52.

Location: TxCM.

A3   **GOBLIN MARKET AND OTHER POEMS (1862)**

A3.1   ***First Edition, Only Printing (1862)***

Some text in <u>black letter</u>:
GOBLIN MARKET | AND | OTHER POEMS. | BY | CHRISTINA ROSSETTI. | WITH TWO DESIGNS BY D. G. ROSSETTI. | <u>Cambridge</u> | MACMILLAN AND CO. | AND 23, HENRIETTA STREET, COVENT GARDEN. | <u>London</u> | 1862.

Pagination: <u>i-v</u> vi-vii <u>viii</u> <u>1</u> 2-129 <u>130-133</u> 134-192.

Plates: Two (conjugate) leaves of plates with woodcut engravings are inserted before the title. The leaves are separated by a tissue guard.
1) Leaf 1 (verso): frontispiece vignette, 110.7 x 92, height measured with caption; image of woman (Laura) kneeling at left, clipping a lock of hair, and facing goblin animals, with another woman (Lizzie) in upper left, walking away; caption '"Buy from us with a golden curl"' engraved below vignette, and initials 'MMF & Co' in lower left corner; 'DGR' in lower right.
2) Leaf 2 (recto): engraved title (131 x 96.5), with intersecting horizontal and vertical lines forming compartments containing text and vignette, as follows: 'GOBLIN MARKET | and other poems | by Christina Rossetti | [vignette, Lizzie and Laura asleep with circular design of goblins in upper left] | '"Golden head by golden head"' | London and Cambridge | Macmillan and Co. 1862'; Initials 'WJL' in lower right corner, 'DGR' in lower left. See *Note one* below.

Collation: Three states have been noted (see *Note two*). In all states: size of leaf 170 x 107, \$2 signed, 100 leaves.
First state (uncorrected):
1. [A]⁴ B-N⁸; p. 26, line 17: "Shaking with anguish, fear, and pain."
Second state (corrected in the press):
2. [A]⁴ B-N⁸; p. 26, line 17: 'Shaking with aguish fear, and pain."
Third state (corrected by cancellation):
3. [A]⁴ B-C⁸ (±C4,5) D-N⁸;. p. 26, line 17: "Shaking with aguish fear, and pain."

Contents: <u>i</u>: title page; <u>ii</u>: printer's imprint; <u>iii</u>: dedication 'TO | MY MOTHER, | IN ALL REVERENCE AND LOVE, | I INSCRIBE THIS BOOK.'; <u>iv</u>: blank; <u>v-vii</u>: 'CONTENTS.'; <u>viii</u>: blank; 1-129: text; <u>130</u>: blank; <u>131</u>: section title 'DEVOTIONAL PIECES.'; <u>132</u>: blank;. <u>133</u>-192: text and on 192, printer's imprint.

Poems: "Goblin Market," "In The Round Tower At Jhansi, June 8, 1857," "Dream Land," "At Home," "A Triad," "Love From The North," "Winter Rain," "Cousin Kate," "Noble Sisters," "Spring," "The Lambs Of Grasmere, 1860," "A Birthday," "Remember," "After Death," "An End," "My Dream," "Song" ("Oh roses for the flush of youth"), "The Hour And The Ghost," "A Summer Wish," "An Apple Gathering," "Song" ("Two doves upon the selfsame branch"), "Maude Clare," "Echo," "My Secret," "Another Spring," "A Peal Of Bells," "Fata Morgana," "'No Thank You, John'," "May" ("I cannot tell you how it was"), "A Pause Of Thought," "Twilight Calm," "Wife To Husband," "Three Seasons," "Mirage," "Shut Out," "Sound Sleep," "Song" ("She sat and sang alway"), "Song" ("When I am dead, my dearest"), "Dead Before Death," "Bitter For Sweet," "Sister Maude," "Rest," "The First Spring Day," "The Convent Threshold," "Up-Hill," "'The Love Of Christ Which Passeth Knowledge'," "'A Bruised Reed Shall He Not Break'," "A Better Resurrection," "Advent" ("This Advent moon shines cold and clear"), "The Three Enemies" in three parts, "The Flesh," "The World," "The Devil," "The One Certainty," "Christian And Jew," "Sweet Death," "Symbols," "'Consider The Lilies Of The Field'" ("Flowers preach to us if we will hear"), "The World," "A Testimony," "Sleep At Sea," "From House To Home," "Old And New Year Ditties" (sections 1-3), "Amen."

Typography and paper: (135)122 x 55 (p. 3); various lines per page (up to 20). Wove paper, unwatermarked.

Running titles:

Rectos: <u>i-v</u>: no RT; vii: 'CONTENTS.'; <u>1</u>: no RT; 3-29: 'GOBLIN MARKET.'; 31-37: no RT; 39: 'LOVE FROM THE NORTH.'; 41: no RT; 43: 'WINTER RAIN.'; 45: 'COUSIN KATE.'; 47: no RT; 49: 'NOBLE SISTERS.'; 51: no RT; 53: 'SPRING.'; 55: 'THE LAMBS OF GRASMERE, 1860.'; 57: 'A BIRTHDAY.'; 61: 'AN END.'; 63: 'MY DREAM.'; 65: no RT; 67-69: 'THE HOUR AND THE GHOST.'; 71-75: no RT; 77-79: 'MAUDE CLARE.'; 81: 'ECHO.'; 83: 'MY SECRET.'; 85-89: no RT; 91: '"NO THANK YOU, JOHN."'; 93: no RT; 95: 'A PAUSE OF THOUGHT.'; 97-99: 'TWILIGHT CALM.'; 101: 'WIFE TO HUSBAND.'; 103: 'THREE SEASONS.'; 105-109: no RT; 111: 'SONG.'; 113: no RT; 115: 'SISTER MAUDE.'; 117-119: no RT; 121-127: 'THE CONVENT THRESHOLD.'; 129: 'UP-HILL.'; 131-139: no RT; 141: 'ADVENT.'; 145: 'THE THREE ENEMIES.'; 149-151: 'CHRISTIAN AND JEW.'; 153-159: no RT; 161-163: 'A TESTIMONY.'; 165: no RT; 167-169: 'SLEEP AT SEA.'; 171: no RT; 173-185: 'FROM HOUSE TO HOME.'; 187-189: 'OLD AND NEW YEAR DITTIES.'; 191: no RT.

Versos: <u>ii-iv</u>: no RT; vi: 'CONTENTS.'; <u>viii</u>: no RT; 2-30: 'GOBLIN MARKET.'; 32: 'IN THE ROUND TOWER AT JHANSI.'; 34: 'DREAM LAND.'; 36: 'AT HOME.'; 38: no RT; 40: 'LOVE FROM THE NORTH.'; 42: 'WINTER RAIN.'; 44: no RT; 46: 'COUSIN KATE.'; 48-50: 'NOBLE SISTERS.'; 52: 'SPRING.'; 54-62: no RT; 64: 'MY DREAM.'; 66: no RT; 68-70: 'THE HOUR AND THE GHOST.'; 72: 'A SUMMER WISH.'; 74: 'AN APPLE GATHERING.'; 76: no RT; 78: 'MAUDE CLARE.'; 80-82: no RT; 84: 'MY SECRET.'; 86: 'ANOTHER SPRING.'; 88: 'A PEAL OF BELLS.'; 90: no RT; 92: '"NO THANK YOU, JOHN."'; 94-96: no RT; 98: 'TWILIGHT CALM.'; 100-104: no RT; 106: 'SHUT OUT.'; 108: 'SOUND SLEEP.'; 110-116: no RT; 118: 'THE FIRST SPRING DAY.'; 120-126: 'THE CONVENT THRESHOLD.'; 128-132: no RT; 134: '"THE LOVE OF CHRIST WHICH PASSETH KNOWLEDGE."'; 136: '"A BRUISED REED SHALL HE NOT BREAK."'; 138: 'A BETTER RESURRECTION.'; 140-142: 'ADVENT.'; 144-146: 'THE THREE ENEMIES.'; 150-152: 'CHRISTIAN AND JEW.'; 154: 'SWEET DEATH.'; 156: 'SYMBOLS.'; 158: '"CONSIDER THE LILIES OF THE FIELD."'; 160: no RT; 162-164: 'A TESTIMONY.'; 166-170: 'SLEEP AT SEA.'; 172-184: 'FROM HOUSE TO HOME.'; 186: no RT; 188-190: 'OLD AND NEW YEAR DITTIES.'; 192: 'AMEN.'

Binding: Two forms have been noted, priority undetermined:

Binding A: Vertical rib cloth, dark blue (Centroid 183). Front: in gilt, four horizontal lines, intersecting with two vertical lines extending across spine; six groups of three hollow circles (rings) in corners. Back: blind-stamped, same design as front. Spine: in gilt, '[rule, with two small rings above] | GOBLIN | MARKET | & other | Poems. | [rule] | CHRISTINA | ROSSETTI. | [rule, with three rings beneath, arranged in inverted pyramid] | [bottom rule]'. Endpapers: coated paper, pale greenish-yellow (Centroid 104) or grayish reddish brown (Centroid 46). Edges: top rough trimmed, fore-edge and tail trimmed. Locations: BL; TxU (4); MSL (2) NjP (2); CaBVaU (3); PBm (3); OkU; MH-Houghton; UkCU.

Binding B: Horizontal rib cloth, dark blue (Centroid 183), same design as *Binding A*. Endpapers grayish reddish-brown (Centroid 46). All copies examined have undated advertisements (see *Note three*). Locations: PBm; TxCM; TxU; MH-Houghton.

Trial bindings: One copy in grayish red horizontal rib cloth, stamped as above, with inscription "Jane Morris June 1862" is at the Fitzwilliam Museum; another copy in smooth red cloth, stamping as above, was owned by William Fredeman. Both copies have undated advertisements.

Publication: March 1862. 750 copies printed (Editions Book, Macmillan Archives). On 28 October 1861, Alexander Macmillan wrote to DGR that he would "run the risk of a small edition" and that he intended "to bring it out as a small Christmas book" (*LAM* 95). Notices of the book "in press" appeared in the London *Times* on 30 November and 7 December 1861. On 11 December CGR wrote to Macmillan about her preferences for binding cloth: "The *dark* colours, especially the *puce*, *red*, and *violet*, which I return, appear to me among the best" (*Letters* 1: 153). CGR also required that several errors be corrected while the book was in press (see *Note two*). On 25 March CGR wrote to Macmillan that "I have seen my little book at last" (*Letters* 1: 159).

Announced in the *Athenaeum* (29 March 1862: 418; 5 April 1862: 475), London *Times* (5 April 1862: 13).

Price: 5s.

Reviewed in the *London Review* (12 April 1862: 353-354); *Spectator* (12 April 1862: 414-415; *Press* (19 April 1862: 378); *Critic* (19 April 1862: 392-393); *Athenaeum* (26 April 1862: 557-58); *English Woman's Journal* (May 1862: 206-207); *Saturday Review* (24 May 1862: 595).

Printing: 192: 'LONDON: | BRADBURY AND EVANS, PRINTERS, WHITEFRIARS.'; ii: 'BRADBURY AND EVANS, PRINTERS, WHITEFRIARS.'

Note one: The vignette on the engraved title was incorrectly cut. The chin of the woman on the right is blurred, and the line between the chin and the ear is faint. Problems with the block contributed to the delay in publication. On 26 February 1862 CGR wrote to Macmillan "If you, or Messrs Bradbury and Evans, still have the block last sent in for Goblin Market . . . my brother requests that you will kindly send it to the above address, as it still requires alteration" (*Letters* 1: 158).

Note two: On December 9 CGR wrote to Alexander Macmillan "I received *Goblin Market* on Saturday; and found with dismay on reading through three errors, one of which I am sure was corrected in the proof [. . .] I shall be much vexed if the book appears as it stands" (*Letters* 1: 133). In March, after the book's publication, Rossetti informed Macmillan that Bradbury and Evans had supplied her with "2 copies of the wood cuts and cancels [. . .] to complete two imperfect copies in our possession" (*Letters* 1: 161).

Rossetti does not identify the three corrections in her December letter to Macmillan. However, a presentation copy of what appears to be a set of duplicate author's proofs at the Harry Ransom Humanities Research Center at the University of Texas (TxU) contains three penciled corrections: in "Goblin Market," "anguish" is changed to "aguish" on 26; in "Wife to Husband," "fault" is changed to "faults" on 100; in 'From House to Home," "space change," is corrected to "space, change" on 181. Presumably gathering C (containing p. 26) was already in press when CGR wrote to Macmillan, thus necessitating a stop-press correction and the cancellation and replacement of C4.5 in some copies (another set of bound proofs, uncorrected, is at Baylor). The state 1 copy (TxU) contains the uncorrected sheet without cancellation. In state 3 (BL, Fitz, MH-Houghton (2), OkU, NjP (2), TxU (2), UkCU), C4.5 are sometimes slightly yellowish and smoother than other leaves; also, micrometer readings of state 3 copies show C4.5 to be thinner than other leaves in C by at least .01 mm. The state 2 copies (CaBVaU (4), TxU (2), TxCM) contain the correction on p. 26 but without cancellation or changes in micrometer readings for C4.5. See Ives, "A Stop Press Correction in Christina Rossetti's *Goblin Market*, *PBSA* 94.1 (2000), 35-48.

Note three: In some copies a 16 page gathering of advertisements follows the text. Two forms have been noted:
1) Undated, presumably earlier form; titles on first page are *The Lady of Garaye*; *The Golden Treasury* with note "Eighth Thousand"; *The Children's Garland*.
2) Dated (at lower left: '2,000 | 1:7:62"; titles on first page are *The Golden Treasury* with note "Eleventh Thousand"; *The Children's Garland* with note "Third Thousand"; *The Pilgrim's Progress* by John Bunyan.

Note four: A copy with CGR's watercolor illustrations, mentioned by WMR in the notes to *Poetical Works* (460 & passim), was owned by Mrs. Imogene Dennis; its current location is unknown (Kooistra 28, 40, 277). In one of the copies at PBm (binding B), the text has been illustrated; a handwritten note on the title page, "And with Etchings by E. Cotton" apparently identifies the artist.

Locations: BL; CaBVaU (3); Fitz; Fredeman; MH-Houghton (2); MSL (2); OkU; PBm (4); NjP (2); TxCM; TxU (5); UkCU.

Presentation copies: MSL: inscribed "Mrs Heimann from her old friend C. G. R. 3rd April 1862."

A3.2   *Second Edition, Only Printing (1865)*

Same as 1862 edition except:

Some text in <u>black letter</u>:
GOBLIN MARKET | AND | OTHER POEMS. | BY | CHRISTINA ROSSETTI. | WITH TWO DESIGNS BY D. G. ROSSETTI. | SECOND EDITION. | MACMILLAN AND CO. | <u>London</u> <u>and</u> <u>Cambridge</u> | 1865. | *The Right of Translation and Reproduction is reserved.*

Collation: A⁴ B-N⁸.

Running titles: 91-92: '"NO, THANK YOU, JOHN."'

Binding: Calico, deep purplish blue (Centroid 197). Design same as A3.1 except that towards the outer edge of the boards, the horizontal and vertical lines do not extend beyond their intersection. Endpapers: coated paper, moderate reddish brown (Centroid 43) or dark grayish green (Centroid 151).

Publication: March 1865. 1000 copies printed (Edition Book, Macmillan Archives). The second edition is a line by line resetting of 1862, with a number of text revisions as well as errors, such as "alvalanche" (p. 176). CGR first mentions the second edition in a letter to Alexander Macmillan in June 1864 (*Letters* I: 197), and completed reading proof in mid-January 1865 (*Letters* I: 218).
   Announced in the *Athenaeum* (21 January 1865: 99; 28 January 1865: 109; 4 February 1865: 147).
   Price: 5s.
   Reviewed in the *Examiner* (6 October 1866: 629-630).

Printing: 192: 'LONDON: | BRADBURY AND EVANS, PRINTERS, WHITEFRIARS.'; ii: 'BRADBURY AND EVANS, PRINTERS, WHITEFRIARS.'

Note one: Several changes were made to the engraved title page: the damage to the vignette is repaired (see A3.1, *Note one*); the words '*SECOND EDITION*' are added in the space above the vignette; the date is changed to 1865. See Gail Lynn Goldberg, "Dante Gabriel Rossetti's 'Revising Hand': His Illustrations for Christina Rossetti's Poems" and the accompanying "Editorial Note" by W. E. Fredeman, *Victorian Poetry* 20 (1982): 145-159.

Locations: BL; CaBVaU; MH-Houghton; NjP; PBm; TxCM; TxU.

A4 POEMS (Roberts Brothers, 1866)

A4.1a *First Edition, First Printing (1866)*

See also A12 (Roberts Brothers First Subedition, 1876), A17 (Roberts Brothers Second Subedition, 1882), A30 (Little, Brown Subedition, 1898) and A32 (Little, Brown Subedition, 1899).

POEMS | BY | CHRISTINA G. ROSSETTI. | [device, shield with pointed bottom, 32 x 26 mm; within, upon foliage background, an anchor with dolphin curled around it] | BOSTON: | ROBERTS BROTHERS. | 1866.

Pagination: [2] i-vii viii-x [1] 4-77 78-81 82-116 [1] 120-239 240-243 244-256.
The frontispiece is preceded by one blank leaf [2]; the first text page, [1], has a numeral '1' at the bottom left, beneath the text, but this page is identified as '3' in the book's table of contents, and the verso is paginated '4.' The second pair of plates is inserted between 116 and an unnumbered leaf [1], designated as '119' in the contents and with pagination '120' on verso.

Plates: Two conjugate pairs, both with tissue guards:
1) First pair, between [2] and i, reproduces the frontispiece (verso of first plate, 112 x 92, height measured with caption) and engraved title (recto of second plate, 132 x 95) from 1865 *Goblin Market*. The designs are same as A3.2 except the title has no "Second edition" and in place of Macmillan publishing information reads 'BOSTON, ROBERTS BROS.'
2) Second pair, between pp. 116 and [1] (H1, H2), reproduces the frontispiece (verso of first plate, 152 x 97, height measured with caption) and engraved title (recto of second plate, 144 x 90) from *Prince's Progress* (A5), a proof of which was supplied to Roberts Brothers before publication in the UK. The designs are the same except the title replaces Macmillan publishing information with 'BOSTON, ROBERTS BROS.' and the words 'W. J. LINTON SC.' do not appear beneath the design frame.

Collation: (175 x 110): pi² 2pi⁴ A⁸ B-O⁸ P⁶. Signatures include J. $1 signed, 132 leaves.

Contents: [1-2]: blank; i: title; ii: 'AUTHOR'S EDITION.' and printer's imprint; iii: text headed 'THE AUTHOR TO HER AMERICAN | READERS.' dated 'London, May, 1866' and signed 'CHRISTINA G. ROSSETTI.'; iv: blank; v: dedication 'TO | MY MOTHER, | IN ALL REVERENCE AND LOVE, | *I INSCRIBE THIS BOOK*.'; vi: blank; vii: 'CONTENTS.'; [1]-116 text of *Goblin Market and Other Poems* including 79: sectional half-title 'DEVOTIONAL PIECES' and 80: blank; [1]-256: text of *The Prince's Progress* including 240: blank and 241: sectional half-title 'DEVOTIONAL PIECES.'; 242: blank; 256: printer's imprint.

Poems: "Goblin Market," "In The Round Tower At Jhansi, June 8, 1857," "Dream-Land," "At Home," "A Triad," "Love From The North," "Winter Rain," "Cousin Kate," "Noble Sisters," "Spring," "The Lambs of Grasmere, 1860," "A Birthday," "Remember," "After Death," "An End," "My Dream," "Song" ("O roses for the flush of youth"), "The Hour And The Ghost," "A Summer Wish," "An Apple Gathering," "Song" ("Two doves upon the selfsame branch"), "Maude Clare," "Echo," "My Secret," "Another Spring," "A Peal Of Bells," "Fata Morgana," "'No, Thank You, John'," "May" ("I cannot tell you how it was"), "A Pause of Thought," "Twilight Calm," "Wife To Husband," "Three Seasons," "Mirage," "Shut Out," "Sound Sleep," "Song" ("She sat and sang alway"), "Song" ("When I am dead, my dearest"), "Dead Before Death," "Bitter For Sweet," "Sister Maude," "Rest," "The First Spring Day," "The Convent Threshold," "Up-Hill," "'The Love Of Christ Which Passeth Knowledge'," "'A Bruised Reed Shall He Not Break'," "A Better Resurrection," "Advent" ("This Advent moon shines cold and clear"), "The Three Enemies" in three parts, "The Flesh," "The World," "The Devil," "The One Certainty," "Christian And Jew," "Sweet Death," "Symbols," "'Consider The Lilies of The Field'" ("Flowers preach to us if we will hear"), "The World," "A Testimony," "Sleep At Sea," "From House To Home," "Old And New Year Ditties" (sections 1-3), "Amen," "The Prince's Progress," "Maiden-Song," "Jessie Cameron," "Spring Quiet," "The Poor Ghost," "A Portrait" (sections I-II), "Dream-Love,"

"Twice," "Songs In A Cornfield," "A Year's Windfalls," "The Queen Of Hearts," "One Day," "A Bird's-Eye View," "Light Love," "A Dream," "A Ring Posy," "Beauty Is Vain," "Lady Maggie," "What Would I Give?," "The Bourne," "Summer" ("Winter is cold-hearted"), "Autumn" ("I dwell alone"), "The Ghost's Petition," "Memory" (sections I-II), "A Royal Princess," "Shall I Forget?," "Vanity Of Vanities" ("Ah woe is me for pleasure that is vain"), "L. E. L," "Life And Death," "Bird Or Beast?," "Eve," "Grown And Flown," "A Farm Walk," "Somewhere Or Other," "A Chill," "Child's Talk In April," "Gone Forever," "Under The Rose," "Despised And Rejected," "Long Barren," "If Only," "Dost Thou Not Care?," "Weary In Well-Doing," "Martyrs' Song," "After This The Judgment," "Good Friday" ("Am I a stone and not a sheep"), "The Lowest Place."

Typography and paper: (140) 130.7 x 69.5 (p. 35); various lines per page (up to 30). Laid paper, vertical chainlines 25 mm apart. Unwatermarked.

Running titles: In italic. In some copies, the question mark is missing on recto page 207.

Rectos: [1]: no RT; i-vii: no RT; ix: 'CONTENTS.'; [1]: no RT; 5-21: 'GOBLIN MARKET.'; 23: 'IN THE ROUND TOWER AT JHANSI.'; 25: 'AT HOME.'; 27: 'LOVE FROM THE NORTH.'; 29: 'WINTER RAIN.'; 31: 'COUSIN KATE.'; 33: 'NOBLE SISTERS.'; 35: 'SPRING.'; 37: 'A BIRTHDAY.'; 39: 'AFTER DEATH.'; 41: 'MY DREAM.'; 43-45: 'THE HOUR AND THE GHOST.'; 47: 'AN APPLE GATHERING.'; 49: 'MAUDE CLARE.'; 51: 'ECHO.'; 53: 'ANOTHER SPRING.'; 55: 'FATA MORGANA.'; 57: 'MAY.'; 59: 'TWILIGHT CALM.'; 61: 'WIFE TO HUSBAND.'; 63: 'MIRAGE.'; 65: 'SOUND SLEEP.'; 67: 'SONG.'; 69: 'SISTER MAUDE.'; 71-75: 'THE CONVENT THRESHOLD.'; 77: 'UP-HILL.'; 79-81: no RT; 83: 'A BETTER RESURRECTION.'; 85: 'ADVENT.'; 87: 'THE THREE ENEMIES.'; 89: 'THE ONE CERTAINTY.'; 91: 'CHRISTIAN AND JEW.'; 93: 'SWEET DEATH.'; 95: 'CONSIDER THE LILIES OF THE FIELD.'; 97-99: 'A TESTIMONY.'; 101: 'SLEEP AT SEA.'; 103-111: 'FROM HOUSE TO HOME.'; 113: 'OLD AND NEW YEAR DITTIES.'; 115: 'AMEN.'; [1]: no RT; 121-139: 'THE PRINCE'S PROGRESS.'; 141-147: 'MAIDEN-SONG.'; 149-151: 'JESSIE CAMERON.'; 153: 'SPRING QUIET.'; 155: 'THE POOR GHOST.'; 157-159: 'DREAM-LOVE.'; 161: 'TWICE.'; 163-165: 'SONGS IN A CORNFIELD.'; 167-169: 'A YEAR'S WINDFALLS.'; 171: 'ONE DAY.'; 173-175: 'A BIRD'S-EYE VIEW.'; 177: 'LIGHT LOVE.'; 179: 'A DREAM.'; 181: 'BEAUTY IS VAIN.'; 183: 'LADY MAGGIE.'; 185: 'SUMMER.'; 187: 'AUTUMN.'; 189-191: 'THE GHOST'S PETITION.'; 193: 'MEMORY.'; 195-201: 'A ROYAL PRINCESS.'; 203: 'VANITY OF VANITIES.'; 205: 'L. E. L.'; 207: 'BIRD OR BEAST?'; 209: 'EVE.'; 211: 'GROWN AND FLOWN.'; 213: 'A FARM WALK.'; 215: 'SOMEWHERE OR OTHER.'; 217: 'CHILD'S TALK IN APRIL.'; 219: 'GONE FOREVER.'; 221-239: 'UNDER THE ROSE.'; 241-243: no RT; 245: 'LONG BARREN.'; 247: 'DOST THOU NOT CARE?'; 249-251: 'MARTYRS' SONG.'; 253: 'AFTER THIS THE JUDGMENT.'; 255: 'GOOD FRIDAY.'

Versos: [2], ii-vi: no RT; viii-x: 'CONTENTS.'; 4-22: 'GOBLIN MARKET.'; 24: 'DREAM-LAND.'; 26: 'A TRIAD.'; 28: 'LOVE FROM THE NORTH.'; 30: 'COUSIN KATE.'; 32: 'NOBLE SISTERS.'; 34: 'SPRING.'; 36: 'THE LAMBS OF GRASMERE.'; 38: 'REMEMBER.'; 40: 'AN END.'; 42: 'MY DREAM.'; 44: 'THE HOUR AND THE GHOST.'; 46: 'A SUMMER WISH.'; 48: 'SONG.'; 50: 'MAUDE CLARE.'; 52: 'MY SECRET.'; 54: 'A PEAL OF BELLS.'; 56: '"NO, THANK YOU, JOHN."'; 58: 'A PAUSE OF THOUGHT.'; 60: 'TWILIGHT CALM.'; 62: 'WIFE TO HUSBAND.'; 64: 'SHUT OUT.'; 66: 'SONG.'; 68: 'BITTER FOR SWEET.'; 70: 'THE FIRST SPRING DAY.'; 72-76: 'THE CONVENT THRESHOLD.'; 78-80: no RT; 82: 'A BRUISED REED SHALL HE NOT BREAK.'; 84-86: 'ADVENT.'; 88: 'THE THREE ENEMIES.'; 90-92: 'CHRISTIAN AND JEW.'; 94: 'SYMBOLS.'; 96: 'THE WORLD.'; 98: 'A TESTIMONY.'; 100-102: 'SLEEP AT SEA.'; 104-110: 'FROM HOUSE TO HOME.'; 112: 'FROM HOUSE TO HOME' [no period]; 114: 'OLD AND NEW YEAR DITTIES.'; 116: 'AMEN.'; 120-138: 'THE PRINCE'S PROGRESS.'; 140-146: 'MAIDEN-SONG.'; 148: 'JESSIE-CAMERON.'; 150-152: 'JESSIE CAMERON.'; 154: 'THE POOR GHOST.'; 156: 'A PORTRAIT.'; 158: 'DREAM-LOVE.'; 160: 'TWICE.'; 162-164: 'SONGS IN A CORNFIELD.'; 166-168: 'A YEAR'S WINDFALLS.'; 170: 'THE QUEEN OF HEARTS.'; 172-174: 'A BIRD'S-EYE VIEW.'; 176-178: 'LIGHT LOVE.'; 180: 'A RING

POSY.'; 182: 'LADY MAGGIE.'; 184: 'WHAT WOULD I GIVE?'; 186: 'SUMMER.'; 188: 'AUTUMN.'; 190-192: 'THE GHOST'S PETITION.'; 194: 'MEMORY.'; 196-200: 'A ROYAL PRINCESS.'; 202: 'SHALL I FORGET?'; 204: 'L. E. L.'; 206 'LIFE AND DEATH.'; 208-210: 'EVE.'; 212-214: 'A FARM WALK.'; 216: 'A CHILL.'; 218: 'CHILD'S TALK IN APRIL.'; 220-238: 'UNDER THE ROSE.'; 240-242: no RT; 244: 'DESPISED AND REJECTED.'; 246: 'IF ONLY.'; 248: 'WEARY IN WELL-DOING.'; 250: 'MARTYRS' SONG.'; 252-254: 'AFTER THIS THE JUDGMENT.'; 256: 'THE LOWEST PLACE.'

Binding: Sand-textured cloth, dark grayish reddish brown (Centroid 47) or reddish black (Centroid 24). Front: blind-stamped thick-thin rule border; in center, gilt signature, 'Christina G. Rossetti.' Back: same blind-stamped border as front; no text. Spine: in gilt, '[rule] | [three rings clustered in center, forming an inverted pyramid] | CHRISTINA | ROSSETTI'S | POEMS | [black letter] Boston | ROBERTS BROTHERS | [three rings clustered in center, forming a pyramid] | [rule]'. Endpapers: moderate reddish brown (Centroid 43) or grayish reddish brown (Centroid 46) coated paper, with one wove paper binder's leaf between endpapers and sheets, front and back. Edges: top edge gilt, fore-edge and tail trimmed, plain.

Publication: In January 1866, Rossetti asked Macmillan to provide Thomas Niles with a copy of the second edition of *Goblin Market and Other Poems* and a copy of the then "forthcoming" *Prince's Progress* (Letters I: 267). Two errors in the poem "Songs in a Cornfield" (164, lines 6-7) that were to have been hand-corrected by Macmillan before publication of *The Prince's Progress* remain uncorrected in the first printing of the American edition (there is a period after "coil" in line 6, and a comma after "thickest" in line 7).

Announced in the *New York Times* (25 June 1866: 5) as "Nearly Ready" and again (10 July 1866: 5) as ready "On Wednesday, July 11." Another *Times* advertisement (25 July 1866: 5) declared the "FIRST EDITION ALL SOLD."

Price: $1.75.

Reviewed in the *New York Times* (6 July 1866: 2); the *Nation* (19 July 1866: 47-48); *Saturday Evening Post* (28 July 1866: 2); *Hours at Home* (August 1866: 387); *Galaxy* 2.2 (15 September 1866: 192-196).

Printing: ii: 'UNIVERSITY PRESS: WELCH, BIGELOW, & CO., | CAMBRIDGE.'; 255: 'Cambridge: Electrotyped and Printed by Welch, Bigelow, & Co.'

Locations: BL; NjP; TxU; TxCM.

A4.1b   *First Edition, Second Printing (1866)*

Same as first printing except:

Contents: ii: 'AUTHOR'S EDITION. | SECOND THOUSAND. | UNIVERSITY PRESS: WELCH, BIGELOW, & CO., | CAMBRIDGE.'; 164: "Songs in a Cornfield" is corrected with no period after "coil" (line 6) and a colon after "thickest" (line 7).

Binding: Deep yellowish green (Centroid 132) or moderate reddish brown (Centroid 43).

Publication: Printed from corrected plates of the first edition. The *New York Times* announced on July 25 1866 that the "new edition . . . will be ready in a few days" (p.5). Advertised as "second edition" of *Poems* in the *American Literary Gazette* (1 Aug 1866: 164).

Note one: The correction to "Songs in a Cornfield" seems to have been made before CGR sent an errata list to Thomas Niles on August 20, 1866 (*Letters* 1: 280). The errata list is not extant. In one copy (PBm), the numeral 'I' does not appear on the first text page, and the double closing quotation marks following the word "children" in the subtitle of "Under the Rose" (p. 220) have been damaged so that only a single quotation mark is visible. These characteristics, which reappear in later printings, may indicate that two sets of plates were in use.

Locations: PBm; TxCM.

A4.1c   *First Edition, Third Printing (1866)*

Same as A4.1a except:

Pagination: The page between x and 3 is now unnumbered.

Contents: ii: 'AUTHOR'S EDITION. | THIRD THOUSAND. | UNIVERSITY PRESS: WELCH, BIGELOW, & CO., | CAMBRIDGE.'; 164: "Songs in a Cornfield" is corrected with no period after "coil" (line 6) and a colon after "thickest" (line 7).

Binding: Moderate reddish brown (Centroid 43).

Publication: The "third thousand" was advertised in the *American Literary Gazette* on September 1, 1866. By February, 1867, WMR recorded that CGR had received £38.10 from Roberts Brothers (her 10% royalty), and that "3000 copies have been printed, & all disposed of save 400 (or else 600)" (WMRD, 14 February 1867); by August 1867, WMR reported that Roberts Brothers "say they have issued no more of her book lately" (WMRD, 12 August 1867).

Note one: Damage to plates is apparent in the headline of page 89. As in A4.1b (PBm copy), there is no numeral 'I' on the first text page, and only a single closing quotation mark visible in the subtitle of "Under the Rose" (220).

Location: Ives.

A4.1d   *First Edition, Fourth Printing (1872)*

Same as A4.1a except:

POEMS | BY | CHRISTINA G. ROSSETTI. | [circular printer's device, 22 x 24.3: winged child holding scepter, seated on globe, reading book; foliage on either side of globe & scroll at bottom with motto, 'QUI LEGIT REGIT.'] | BOSTON: | ROBERTS BROTHERS. | 1872.

Pagination: The first page is i (no prefatory blank leaf); last pages are 257-258.

Collation: (173.3 x 114): [1-11¹²]. Obsolete signing for 8s is retained from 1866. 132 leaves.

Contents: no [1-2]; ii reads 'AUTHOR'S EDITION.', no printer's imprint; 256: no printer's imprint; 257: advertisements for Roberts Brothers children's books: 4 titles, *Sing-Song, Posies for Children, Max and Maurice, Puck's Nightly Pranks. Sing-Song* is prominently featured at the top of the page, by inclusion of a "specimen picture" from the book and accompanying verse "Eight o'clock." Description of *Sing-Song* as follows: 'SING-SONG. A Book of Original New Nursery Rhymes, by Miss Rossetti, | contains one hundred and twenty songs, and an illustration to each song by Arthur Hughes. One elegant square 8vo, bound in cloth, black and gilt lettered, Price, $2.00.' 258: advertisement for William Morris's works, including "A New Edition of *The Defence of Guinevere*," "in preparation."

Paper: laid, unwatermarked, horizontal chainlines 29 mm apart.

Running titles: No running titles on 257-258.

Binding: Sand-patterned cloth, dark green (Centroid 146) or moderate reddish brown (Centroid 43). Front, back: same as 1866. Spine: '[thick rule] | [thin rule with center triangular ornament, pointing down] | CHRISTINA | ROSSETTI'S | POEMS | [ornament, with heart shape in center & foliage] | [thin rule] | [thick rule] | *ROBERTS BROS.* | [thick rule]'. Endpapers grayish reddish brown (Centroid 46) coated paper, with one binder's leaf between endpapers and sheets, front and back. In two copies (NjP and TxCM) the binder's leaves are laid with horizontal chainlines 29 mm apart, but micrometer readings of the NjP copy show them to be considerably thinner (.116, .115 mm) than the sheets, which range from .145 to .170 mm. In another copy (PBm) the binder's leaves are wove.

Publication: No information on the publication of this book has been discovered. According to Kilgour, the title page device of "a cherub seated on the globe reading a book" was introduced in 1871, when it appeared in Joaquin Miller's *Songs of the Sierras* (105).

Printing: No printer's imprint.

Note one: Type damage on p. 220 indicates the book was printed from the same plates as A4.1c, but with some corrections to the text as follows:

p. 88, line 23: comma after "dust" (exclamation point in 1866 printings).

p. 93, line 18: colon after "truth" (no punctuation in 1866 printings).

p. 101, line 18: semicolon after "ears" (no punctuation in 1866 printings).

p. 210, line 19: "evil grin" ("awful grin" in 1866 printings).

Locations: PBm; NjP; TxCM.

A5   THE PRINCE'S PROGRESS AND OTHER POEMS (1866)

A5.1   *First Edition, Only Printing (1866)*

Letterpress title page: THE | PRINCE'S PROGRESS | AND | OTHER POEMS. | BY | CHRISTINA ROSSETTI. | WITH TWO DESIGNS BY D. G. ROSSETTI. | London: | MACMILLAN AND CO. | 1866. | *The Right of Translation and Reproduction is reserved.*

Pagination: i-vii viii 1 2-192 193-194 195-216.

Plates: Two (conjugate) leaves of plates are inserted before the title. The leaves are separated by a tissue guard.
1) Leaf 1 (verso): frontispiece vignette of the Prince's arrival, 150 x 97, height measured with caption 'You should have wept her yesterday'; initials 'DGR' in bottom right corner of vignette, and below, 'W. J. LINTON Sc.'
2) Leaf 2 (recto): engraved title, with intersecting horizontal and vertical lines forming compartments containing text and vignette, as follows: 'THE PRINCE'S PROGRESS | AND OTHER POEMS | BY CHRISTINA ROSSETTI| | [vignette of woman seated in front of window] | *The long hours go and come and go* | MACMILLAN & CO. 1866'. Beneath compartment, '*W. J. LINTON SC.*'

Collation: (174 x 109): A⁴ B-O⁸ P⁴. $1, 2 signed (-P2). 112 leaves.

Contents: i: half-title 'THE | PRINCE'S PROGRESS, | *AND OTHER POEMS.*'; ii: blank; iii: title page; iv: printer's imprint; v: dedication 'TO | MY MOTHER, | IN ALL REVERENCE AND LOVE, | I INSCRIBE THIS BOOK.'; vi: blank; vii: 'CONTENTS.'; 1-192: text; 193: section half-title 'DEVOTIONAL PIECES.'; 194: blank; 195-216 text and on 216, printer's imprint.

Poems (see Note one): "The Prince's Progress," "Maiden-Song," "Jessie Cameron," "Spring Quiet," "The Poor Ghost," "A Portrait" (sections I-II), "Dream-Love," "Twice," "Songs in a Cornfield," "A Year's Windfalls," "The Queen of Hearts," "One Day," "A Bird's-Eye View," "Light Love," "A Dream," "A Ring Posy," "Beauty is Vain," "Lady Maggie," "What Would I Give?" "The Bourne," "Summer" ("Winter is cold-hearted"), "Autumn" ("I dwell alone"), "The Ghost's Petition," "Memory" (sections I-II), "A Royal Princess," "Shall I Forget?," "Vanity of Vanities" ("Ah woe is me for pleasure that is vain"), "L. E. L.," "Life and Death," "Bird or Beast?," "Eve," "Grown and Flown," "A Farm Walk," "Somewhere or Other," "A Chill," "Child's Talk in April," "Gone For Ever," "Under the Rose," "Despised and Rejected," "Long Barren," "If Only," "Dost Thou Not Care?," "Weary in Well-Doing," "Martyrs' Song," "After This The Judgment," "Good Friday" ("Am I a stone, and not a sheep"), "The Lowest Place."

Typography and paper: (131) 119 x 50 (p. 177); various lines per page (up to 20). Wove paper, unwatermarked.

Running titles:

Rectos: i-vii, 1: no RT; 3-29: 'THE PRINCE'S PROGRESS.'; 31: no RT; 33-43: 'MAIDEN-SONG.'; 45: no RT; 47-51: 'JESSIE CAMERON.'; 53: 'SPRING QUIET.'; 55: 'THE POOR GHOST.'; 57-59: no RT; 61: 'DREAM-LOVE.'; 65-67: 'TWICE.'; 69-73: 'SONGS IN A CORNFIELD.'; 75: no RT: 77-81: 'A YEAR'S WINDFALLS.'; 83: 'THE QUEEN OF HEARTS.'; 85: 'ONE DAY.'; 87-91: 'A BIRD'S-EYE VIEW.'; 93: 'LIGHT LOVE.'; 97: no RT; 99: 'A RING POSY.'; 101: 'BEAUTY IS VAIN.'; 103-105: 'LADY MAGGIE.'; 107: no RT; 109: 'SUMMER.'; 111-113: 'AUTUMN.'; 115-119: 'THE GHOST'S PETITION.'; 121: 'MEMORY.'; 123: no RT; 125-133: 'A ROYAL PRINCESS.'; 135: no RT; 137: 'L. E. L.'; 139-143: no RT; 145-147: 'EVE.'; 149: 'GROWN AND FLOWN.'; 151-153: 'A FARM-WALK.'; 155-157: no RT; 159: 'CHILD'S TALK IN APRIL.'; 161-163: no RT; 165-191: 'UNDER THE ROSE.'; 193-195: no RT; 197: 'DESPISED AND REJECTED.'; 199-201: no RT; 203: 'DOST THOU NOT

CARE?'; 205: 'WEARY IN WELL-DOING.'; 207-209: 'MARTYRS' SONG.'; 211-213: 'AFTER THIS THE JUDGMENT.'; 215: 'GOOD FRIDAY.'

Versos: ii-vi: no RT; viii: 'CONTENTS.'; 2-30: 'THE PRINCE'S PROGRESS.'; 32-44: 'MAIDEN-SONG.'; 46-50: 'JESSIE CAMERON.'; 52-54: no RT; 56: 'THE POOR GHOST.'; 58: 'A PORTRAIT.'; 60-62: 'DREAM-LOVE.'; 64: no RT; 66: 'TWICE.'; 70-74: 'SONGS IN A CORNFIELD.'; 76-80: 'A YEAR'S WINDFALLS.'; 82-86: no RT; 88-90: 'A BIRD'S-EYE VIEW.'; 92: no RT; 94-96: 'LIGHT LOVE.'; 98-102: no RT; 104: 'LADY MAGGIE.'; 106-110: no RT; 112: 'AUTUMN.'; 114: no RT; 116-118: 'THE GHOST'S PETITION.'; 120: no RT; 122: 'MEMORY.'; 124-132: 'A ROYAL PRINCESS.'; 134-136: no RT; 138: 'L. E. L.'; 140: 'LIFE AND DEATH.'; 142: 'BIRD OR BEAST?'; 144-146: 'EVE.'; 148-150: no RT; 152-154: 'A FARM-WALK.'; 156: no RT; 158-160: 'CHILD'S TALK IN APRIL.'; 162: 'GONE FOR EVER.'; 164-192: 'UNDER THE ROSE.'; 196-198: 'DESPISED AND REJECTED.'; 200: 'LONG BARREN.'; 202-206: no RT; 208: 'MARTYRS' SONG.'; 212: 'AFTER THIS THE JUDGMENT.'; 214-216: no RT.

Binding: Calico cloth, dark green (Centroid 146). Front and back: In gilt, two horizontal lines intersecting with one vertical line, which branches into a spiral at head and tail. Four clusters of three circular rings are arranged with one cluster at each inner corner of the three-sided square formed by the intersecting horizontal and vertical lines. Two additional short horizontal lines, each terminating in a spiral, emerge from the spine, ending before, and not intersecting with, the vertical line. Spine: in gilt, '[rule] | CHRISTINA | ROSSETTI | [rule | [ornament, six rings, in two groups of three] | THE | PRINCE'S | PROGRESS | and | other | poems. | [ornament, six rings, in two groups of three] | [rule] | 1866. | [rule]'. Endpapers: coated paper, between moderate and grayish reddish brown (Centroid 43, 46) or dark blue (Centroid 183). Edges: top, fore-edge rough trimmed, tail trimmed.

Trial binding: Boston Public Library reports a presentation copy, probably an author's proof, from CGR to Philip Bourke Marston, bound in white muslin, with gilt stamping as above, but with gilt rings filled in. DGR had suggested white as a binding color to Macmillan *(DRLetters* III: 2860, and this is probably the same binding to which DGR refers in a December 1865 letter to Macmillan, requesting that the cover lines "be made half their present thickness (from the outside in each instance) and the gold balls turned into rings—the colour I chose is a green one which I have by me" *(Rossetti-Macmillan Letters*, 54). The title page of this copy is dated 1865.

Publication: June 1866. 750 copies printed from type (Edition Book, Macmillan Archives). In March 1865, CGR asked DGR to finalize the order of the poems, and to transmit the MS to Macmillan *(Letters* 1: 228), which he did on 4 April *(DRLetters* iii: 276). Although printed in July 1865, the book was not published until June 1866 because of DGR's slow completion of the woodcuts for the frontispiece and engraved title. By 1871, only 25 copies were in stock (WMRD, 1 December 1871).

Announced in the *Athenaeum* (18 March 1865: 387), as well as the *Guardian* and the *Morning Star* *(Letters* 1: 236, 237).

Price 6s.

Reviewed in the *Athenaeum* (23 June 1866: 824-25); *London Review* (23 June 1866: 708-709); *Illustrated London News* (23 June 1866: 610); *Saturday Review* (23 June 1866: 761-762); *Reader* (30 June 1866: 613); *Westminster Review* (July 1866: 275-277), *Eclectic Review* (August 1866: 124-130); *Spectator* (1 September 1866: 974-75); *Examiner* (6 October 1866: 631); *Contemporary Review* (December 1866: 502-504).

Printing: iv: 'LONDON: | R. CLAY, SON, AND TAYLOR, PRINTERS, | BREAD STREET HILL.'; 216: 'LONDON: R. CLAY, SON, AND TAYLOR, PRINTERS.'

Note one: Both CGR and DGR read proof, and requested that Macmillan make corrections to the text. DGR specifically mentioned the errors on page 71 *(DRLetters* III: 352-353). The author's proof at Boston

Public Library has text corrections marked on pages 37, 55, 71 and 89, presumably in CGR's hand. CGR stipulated for "an *Errata* and . . . two *Cancels*" in December 1865 (*Letters* 1, 263), but accepted Macmillan's offer to make hand corrections to the text (*Letters* 1, 265). On receiving the published volume in June 1866, CGR found "the worst misprint of all left uncorrected" (274). Apparently Macmillan failed to correct all copies of the book before they were released for sale. Packer, noting the existence of both corrected and uncorrected versions of page 71, infers that the "worst misprint" refers to the punctuation errors on that page (see "Christina Rossetti's 'Songs in a Cornfield'," 99).

The following uncorrected and corrected states have been identified:

Page 37, line 9 (leaf D3 recto, in poem "Maiden-Song"):

a) uncorrected: an accent mark appears over the letter "e" in "turned" [marked in Boston proof copy].

b) corrected: the accent mark over "e" in "turned" has been erased. Baylor; TxCM; TxU (3 copies), LNT, DAM, MSL, MoSW.

Page 55, line 1 (leaf E4 recto, in poem "The Poor Ghost"):

a) uncorrected: there are no quotation marks before the word "And"[marked in Boston proof copy].

b) corrected: double quotation marks are inked in before the word "And"; locations: Baylor; TxCM; TxU (3 copies); LNT, DAM, MSL, MoSW.

Page 71, lines 9 and 10 (leaf F4 recto, in poem "Songs in a Cornfield"):

a) uncorrected state: on p. 71, there is a period after "coil" (line 9), and a comma after "thickest" (line 10). [marked in Boston proof copy] Locations: TxU (2), CaBVaU (1), LNT, MSL.

b) corrected state: on p. 71, the period after "coil" is erased, and the comma after "thickest" is changed to a colon by erasing the tail and drawing the colon in black ink. locations: Baylor; TxCM; TxU (1), CaBVaU (3), DAM, MoSW.

c) variant corrected state: on p. 71, the period after "coil" is erased (line 9); the comma after "thickest" (line 10) is intact, but a semicolon has been added in light pen. locations: CaBVaU(1).

Page 89, line 4 (leaf G5 recto, in poem "A Bird's-Eye View"):

a) uncorrected: there are no quotation marks after the word "too."[marked in Boston proof copy].

b) corrected: double quotation marks appear after the word "too." Locations: Baylor, TxCM, TxU (3), LNT, DAM, MSL, MoSW.

Locations: Baylor; BL (2); CaBVaU (5); DAM; LNT; MH-Houghton; MoSW; NjP; TxCM; TxU (4); UkCU. Not seen: Boston Public Library.

Presentation copies: TxU (2) "To Fanny from her affectionate R. June 1866" (presumably to Fanny Cornforth); "George P. Boyce from his affectionate friend D. G. Rossetti 1866."

A6   **CONSIDER (1867)**

A6.1   *First Edition, Only Printing (1867)*

Printed in gold ink; text block is within triple rule frame (outermost rule, 184 x 121; second rule, 175 x 112; innermost rule, 172 x 110); text appears in white on gold background:
CONSIDER | BY | [in black letter with ornamented capitals] Christina G. Rossetti | [within scroll, to left of medallion, with ornamented capital and remaining letters in outlines] Illuminated [within medallion centered upon horizontal scroll] DESIGNED by ALICE DONLEVY.

Set of five broadsides, printed on recto only, 190 x 250.

Pagination: Each plate is printed and numbered on one side only: 4 75-78. See *Publication*.

Contents: 4: title, with designation 'PLATE 1' at top, above rule border; 75: 'PLATE 2' at top; stanza beginning "Consider / The lilies of the field, whose bloom is brief;" 76: 'PLATE 3' at top; stanza beginning "Consider / The sparrows of the air, of small account:"; 77: 'PLATE 4' at top; stanza beginning "Consider / The lilies, that neither spin nor toil,"; 78: 'Plate 5' at top; "Consider / The birds, that have no barns nor harvest=ricks:". Each stanza of the poem (pp. 75-78) is placed within a decorative border.

Poems: "Consider."

Publication: March 1867. This set of plates, containing the text of Rossetti's poem along with decorative borders, initial letters, and other ornamentation designed by Alice Donlevy, was intended for completion by students of illumination. Donlevy's designs—constituting the first published illustration of Rossetti's work by a female artist—were offered both in this form, and on pages 74-78 of her book, *Practical Hints on the Art of Illumination* (New York: A. D. F. Randolph, 1867; see section B). The plates and the book were printed from the same formes and retain the book's pagination (except for the loss, whether from loose type or poor inking, of the "7" in 74). See Ives, "Teaching Women's Art in America: Alice Donlevy's Designs for Christina Rossetti's Consider" (*Textual Cultures* 4.1, Spring 2009: 26-54).

   Announced, along with *Practical Hints on the Art of Illumination,* in *American Literary Gazette* (1 March 1867), p. 276, as "Five Outlines for Illuminating, in paper case."
   Priced at $2.00.
   Reviewed with *Practical Hints* in the *New York Times* (26 February 1867: 2), and *Catholic World* (April 1867: 144).

Location: BL.

A7   **COMMONPLACE AND OTHER SHORT STORIES (1870)**

A7.1a.i   ***First Edition, First Printing, British Issue***

COMMONPLACE, | AND | OTHER SHORT STORIES. | BY | CHRISTINA G. ROSSETTI, | AUTHOR OF 'GOBLIN MARKET,' AND | 'THE PRINCE'S PROGRESS.' | 'From sea to sea.' | LONDON: | F. S. ELLIS, 33 KING STREET, COVENT GARDEN. | 1870.

Pagination: i-v vi vii-viii 1-3 4-142 143-145 146-163 164-167 168-179 180-183 184-211 212-215 216-238 239-241 242-253 254-257 258-267 268-271 272-329 330-336.

Collation: (191 x 128): A⁴ B-Y⁸. $1 signed. 172 leaves.

Contents: i: half-title 'COMMONPLACE, | AND | OTHER SHORT STORIES.'; ii: blank; iii: title; iv: printer's imprint; v: 'PREFATORY NOTE.'; vii: 'CONTENTS.'; viii: blank; 1: half-title 'COMMONPLACE.'; 2: blank; 3: 'COMMONPLACE. | CHAPTER 1.'; 9: 'CHAPTER II.'; 19: 'CHAPTER III.'; 26: 'CHAPTER IV.'; 33: 'CHAPTER V.'; 39: 'CHAPTER VI.'; 46: 'CHAPTER VII.'; 54: 'CHAPTER VIII.'; 65: 'CHAPTER IX.'; 75: 'CHAPTER X.'; 86: 'CHAPTER XI.'; 94: 'CHAPTER XII.'; 101: CHAPTER XIII.'; 110: 'CHAPTER XIV.'; 120: 'CHAPTER XV.'; 127: 'CHAPTER XVI.'; 134: 'CHAPTER XVII.'; 139: 'CHAPTER XVIII.'; 143: half-title 'THE LOST TITIAN.'; 144: blank; 145: 'THE LOST TITIAN.'; 164: blank; 165: half-title 'NICK.'; 166: blank; 167: 'NICK.'; 180: blank; 181: half-title 'HERO. | *A METAMORPHOSIS*.'; 182: blank; 183: 'HERO.'; 212: blank; 213: half-title 'VANNA'S TWINS.'; 214: blank; 215: 'VANNA'S TWINS.'; 239: half-title 'A SAFE INVESTMENT.'; 240: blank; 241: 'A SAFE INVESTMENT.'; 254: blank; 255: half-title 'PROS AND CONS.'; 256: blank; 257: 'PROS AND CONS.'; 268: blank; 269: half-title 'THE WAVES OF THIS | TROUBLESOME WORLD. | *A TALE OF HASTINGS FIFTEEN | YEARS AGO*.'; 270: blank; 271: 'THE WAVES OF THIS | TROUBLESOME WORLD. | Part I.'; 299: 'PART II.'; 330: printer's imprint; 331: 'F. S. ELLIS'S PUBLICATIONS.'; advertisement for 'POEMS. | By DANTE GABRIEL ROSSETTI.'; 332: advertisement for parts I, II and III of William Morris, *The Earthly Paradise* and announcement that "in October will be published the Fourth and concluding portion"; 333: advertisement for Morris, *The Life and Death of Jason*; 334: advertisement, three titles: *The Story of Grettir the Strong*, *The Story of the Volsungs and Niblungs* (both by Morris and E. Magnusson), and Swinburne, *Songs Before Sunrise*; 335: advertisement, *The Voyage and Travaile of Sir John Maundevile, Kt.* by J. O. Halliwell; 336: blank.

Poems: "Love hath a name of Death," "'Giani My Friend and I both Strove to Excel'," "Peter Grump," "Forss."

Typography and paper: (136.3) 124.3 x 76.3 (p. 81); 24 lines per page. Wove paper, unwatermarked.

Running titles:

Rectos: i-vii, 1-3: no RT; 5-7: 'COMMONPLACE.'; 9: no RT; 11-17: 'COMMONPLACE.'; 19: no RT; 21-31: 'COMMONPLACE.'; 33: no RT; 35-37: 'COMMONPLACE.'; 39: no RT; 41-63: 'COMMONPLACE.'; 65: no RT; 67-73: 'COMMONPLACE.'; 75: no RT; 77-99: 'COMMONPLACE.'; 101: no RT; 103-125: 'COMMONPLACE.'; 127: no RT; 129-137: 'COMMONPLACE.'; 139: no RT; 141: 'COMMONPLACE.'; 143-145: no RT; 147-163: 'THE LOST TITIAN.'; 165-167: no RT; 169-179: 'NICK.'; 181-183: no RT; 185-211: 'HERO.'; 213-215: no RT; 217-237: 'VANNA'S TWINS.'; 239-241: no RT; 243-253: 'A SAFE INVESTMENT.'; 255-257: no RT; 259-267: 'PROS AND CONS.'; 269-271: no RT; 273-329: 'TROUBLESOME WORLD.'; 331: no RT; 333-335: 'F. S. Ellis's Publications.'

Versos: ii-iv: no RT; vi: 'PREFATORY NOTE.'; viii-2: no RT; 4-24: 'COMMONPLACE.'; 26: no RT; 28-44: 'COMMONPLACE.'; 46: no RT; 48-52: 'COMMONPLACE.'; 54: no RT; 56-84: 'COMMONPLACE.'; 86: no RT; 88-92: 'COMMONPLACE.'; 94: no RT; 96-108: 'COMMONPLACE.'; 110: no RT; 112-118: 'COMMONPLACE.'; 120: no RT; 122-132: 'COMMONPLACE.'; 134: no RT; 136-142:

'COMMONPLACE.'; 144: no RT; 146-162: 'THE LOST TITIAN.'; 164-166: no RT; 168-178: 'NICK.';
180-182: no RT; 184-210: 'HERO.'; 212-214: no RT; 216-238: 'VANNA'S TWINS.'; 240: no RT; 242-
252: 'A SAFE INVESTMENT.'; 254-256: no RT; 258-266: 'PROS AND CONS.'; 268-270: no RT; 272-
328: 'THE WAVES OF THIS'; 330: no RT; 332-334: 'F. S. Ellis's Publications.'; 336: no RT.

Binding: Calico cloth, very dark green (Centroid 147). Front and back: blind-stamped with two single
rule frames, 14 mm apart; outer 190 x 121; inner, 158 x 92. Spine: in gilt, '[thin rule] | [thick rule, 2mm] |
COMMONPLACE | AND | OTHER STORIES | C. G. ROSSETTI | ELLIS | [thick rule, 2mm] | [thin
rule]'. Endpapers: brownish-white wove paper, slightly thinner than sheets (.125, .113). Edges: head and
tail rough trimmed, fore-edge untrimmed.

Publication: May 1870. CGR proposed to send the MS to Ellis in March 1870 (*Letters* 1: 344), on the
terms of 25% for the first 500 copies (*Letters* 1: 347). According to WMR's diary, CGR received the final
proof on 29 April (*Diary* 4), and on 30 April, Ellis sent CGR "£46.17.6 as the quarter due to her upon
the published price of the first issue (500 copies)" (*Diary* 5). However, only 250 copies were printed by 7
May (Marsh, 385; *Letters* 1: 352-353).
    Announced in the *Athenaeum*, No. 2220 (14 May 1870: 634) as "Now ready," and advertised in *Pall
Mall Gazette* May 24 and May 28.
    Price: 7s.6d.
    Reviewed in the *Athenaeum* (4 June 1870: 734-35); *Pall Mall Gazette* (7 June 1870: 12); the *Sunday
Times* (12 June 1870: 7); *Victoria Magazine* 25 (June 1870: 191); *Academy* (9 July 1870: 252); *Spectator*
(29 October 1870: 1292-1293); *Examiner* (3 September 1870: 566), *London Quarterly Review* (April
1871: 258-259); *Graphic* (11 June 1870: 35). CGR refers to additional reviews in *Churchman's Shilling
Magazine*, and the *Guardian* (*Letters* 1: 358).
    BL depository copy: "BRITISH MUSEUM 3 JU 70."

Printing: iv: 'LONDON: | Strangeways and Walden, Printers, Castle St. Leicester Sq.'; 330:
'LONDON:| Strangeways and Walden, Printers, | Castle St. Leicester Sq.'

Note one: Princeton holds the MS which served as printer's copy for the stories 'Commonplace' and
'Vanna's Twins' (Troxell, Collection of Rossetti MS, Box 1, Folder 29; compositors' markings on text).

Locations: Baylor; BL (2); CaBVaU (3); NjP (2); UMs.

Presentation copies: CaBVaU: Copy 1 (Colbeck entry 12) inscribed from CGR to Janet S. Clayton;
Copy 2 (Colbeck entry 13) inscribed from WMR to Marie Spartali; NjP: inscribed 'Ellen Heaton with
Christina's love."

A7.1a.ii   *First Edition, First Printing, First American Issue (1870)*

Same as British issue except:

Cancellans title page:
COMMONPLACE, | A Tale of To-Day; | AND OTHER STORIES. | BY | CHRISTINA G. ROSSETTI, |
AUTHOR OF 'GOBLIN MARKET,' AND | 'THE PRINCE'S PROGRESS.' | 'From sea to sea.' | BOSTON:
| ROBERTS BROTHERS. | 1870.

Collation: (187 x 121): A⁴ (±A2) B-Y⁸. 172 leaves.

Contents: iv: blank; 330: blank.

Binding: Sand-patterned cloth, very dark green (Centroid 147) or dark red (Centroid 16). Front and
back: blind-stamped triple rule frame, outer rule thick, two inner rules thin. Spine: in gilt, '[ornamental

band composed of two thin rules, a Greek key design, and two additional thin rules] | COMMONPLACE [swash Ms, N, P, L, A] | AND [swash A, N] | OTHER STORIES | [ornamented rule with inverted pyramid in center] | ROSSETTI. [swash R, Ts] | BOSTON [swash B, S, T, N] | ROBERTS BROS. [swash R, B, R, T, S, B, R, S] | [ornamental band, same as head]'. Endpapers: reddish brown coated paper, with one wove paper binder's leaf between endpapers and sheets, front and back. Edges trimmed.

Publication: November 1870. As early as June 1867, WMR recorded that "Roberts Bros propose to publish the few prose tales &c written by Christina" (WMRD); CGR sent the MS to Thomas Niles in September 1867, but the book was not accepted; in April 1869, and again in November 1869, she wrote to ask for the MS to be returned (*Letters* 1: 319, 331-332). The Roberts Brothers issue consists of British sheets with a cancel title page.

Announced among books recently published in *American Literary Gazette* (15 November 1870: 43). Price $1.50.

Reviewed in the *Ladies' Repository* (January 1871: 72-73).

Printing: no printer's imprint.

Locations: Ives; TxCM.

A7.1a.iii   *First Edition, First Printing, Second American Issue (1871)*

Same as first American issue except:

Cancellans title page:
COMMONPLACE, | AND | OTHER SHORT STORIES. | BY | CHRISTINA G. ROSSETTI, | AUTHOR OF 'GOBLIN MARKET,' AND | 'THE PRINCE'S PROGRESS.' | 'From sea to sea.' | Second Edition. | BOSTON | ROBERTS BROTHERS. | 1871.

Contents: 330: printer's imprint.

Binding: Two forms have been noted, priority undetermined:
Binding A: Morocco-patterned cloth, very dark green (Centroid 147). Location: ELZ.
Binding B: Sand-patterned cloth, moderate reddish brown (Centroid 43). Location: TxCM.
In both forms: Endpapers: coated paper, grayish reddish brown (Centroid 46).

Printing: 330: 'LONDON: | STRANGEWAYS AND WALDEN, PRINTERS, | Castle St. Leicester Sq.'

Locations: ELZ; TxCM.

A8   SING-SONG (1872)

A8.1a.i   **First Edition, First British Printing, First Issue (Routledge Subedition) (1872)**

SING-SONG. | A NURSERY RHYME BOOK. | By CHRISTINA G. ROSSETTI. | [illustration, seated girl sewing, facing left, 48 x 43] | WITH ONE HUNDRED AND TWENTY ILLUSTRATIONS | By ARTHUR HUGHES. | *ENGRAVED BY THE BROTHERS DALZIEL*. | LONDON: | GEORGE ROUTLEDGE AND SONS, | THE BROADWAY, LUDGATE. | 1872.

Pagination: i-vii viii-x xi-xii 1-130 131-132.

Plates: None, but see contents for illustrations.

Collation: (181 x 135): π⁶ 1-2⁸ 5-6⁴ 4-²5⁴ 9-16⁴ ²9². $1 signed except π; $1,2 in 1, 2, 4, and ²5. Despite the disruption in sequence of signatures there is no disruption in the pagination. 72 leaves.

Contents: A separate list of illustrations follows. i: blank; ii: frontispiece (with tissue guard), 155 x 106.3, beneath a tree, a woman knitting, with a child sitting in her lap; signed at bottom left 'DALZIEL' and at bottom right 'AH'; iii: title; iv: device, circular, with text "DALZIEL BROTHERS ENGRAVERS & PRINTERS"; v: dedication 'RHYMES | DEDICATED | WITHOUT PERMISSION | TO | THE BABY | WHO | SUGGESTED THEM.'; vi: blank; vii: 'CONTENTS.'; xi: half-title 'SING-SONG.'; xii: blank; 1-130: poems and illustrations; 131: advertisements: five titles, *National Nursery Rhymes* through *The Children's Poetry Book*; 132: five titles: *Sage Stuffing for Green Goslings* through *The Golden Harp*.

Illustrations: Illustrations appear on the title page and on the first page of each poem (thus on pages 1-29, 32-44, 46, 48-49, 51, 53-54, 56-62, 64-116, 118-130). The illustrations on 17, 46 (simplified version) and 102 are repeated on the binding; the illustration on the title page is repeated on page 41.

Poems: (Untitled, identified by first line): "Angels at the foot," "Love me, – I love you," "My baby has a father and a mother," "Our little baby fell asleep," "'Kookoorookoo! kookoorookoo!'," "Baby cry –," "Eight o'clock," "Bread and milk for breakfast," "There's snow on the fields," "Dead in the cold, a song-singing thrush," "I dug and dug amongst the snow," "A city plum is not a plum," "Your brother has a falcon," "Hear what the mournful linnets say," "A baby's cradle with no baby in it," "Hop-o'-my-thumb and little Jack Horner," "Hope is like a harebell trembling from its birth," "O wind, why do you never rest," "Crying, my little one, footsore and weary?," "Growing in the vale," "A linnet in a gilded cage," "Wrens and robins in the hedge," "My baby has a mottled fist," "Why did baby die," "If all were rain and never sun," "O wind, where have you been," "On the grassy banks," "Rushes in a watery place," "Minnie and Mattie," "Heartsease in my garden bed," "If I were a Queen," "What are heavy? sea-sand and sorrow," "There is but one May in the year," "The summer nights are short," "The days are clear," "Twist me a crown of wind-flowers," "Brown and furry," "A toadstool comes up in a night," "A pocket handkerchief to hem," "If a pig wore a wig," "Seldom 'can't,'" "1 and 1 are 2," "How many seconds in a minute?," "What will you give me for my pound?," "January cold desolate," "What is pink? a rose is pink," "Mother shake the cherry-tree," "A pin has a head, but has no hair," "Hopping frog, hop here and be seen," "Where innocent bright-eyed daisies are," "The city mouse lives in a house," "What does the donkey bray about?," "Three plum buns," "A motherless soft lambkin," "Dancing on the hill-tops," "When fishes set umbrellas up," "The peacock has a score of eyes," "Pussy has a whiskered face," "The dog lies in his kennel," "If hope grew on a bush," "I planted a hand," "Under the ivy bush," "There is one that has a head without an eye," "If a mouse could fly," "Sing me a song," "The lily has an air," "Margaret has a milking-pail," "In the meadow–what in the meadow?," "A frisky lamb," "Mix a pancake," "The wind has such a rainy sound," "Three little children," "Fly away, fly away over the sea," "Minnie bakes oaten cakes," "A white hen sitting," "Currants on a bush," "I have but one rose in the world," "Rosy maiden Winifred," "When the cows come home the milk is coming," "Roses blushing red and white," "'Ding a ding,'" "A ring upon her finger," "Ferry me across the water," "When a mounting skylark sings," "Who has seen the wind?," "The horses of the sea," "O sailor, come ashore," "A diamond or a coal?," "An emerald is as green as grass," "Boats sail on the rivers," "The lily has a smooth stalk," "Hurt no living thing," "I caught a little ladybird," "All the bells were ringing," "Wee wee husband," "I have a little husband," "The dear old woman in the lane," "Swift and sure the swallow," "'I dreamt I caught a little owl'," "What does the bee do?," "I have a Poll parrot," "A house of cards," "The rose with such a bonny blush," "The rose that blushes rosy red," "Oh, fair to see," "Clever little Willie wee," "A peach for brothers, one for each," "A rose has thorns as well as honey," "Is the moon tired? she looks so pale," "If stars dropped out of heaven," "'Goodbye in fear, goodbye in sorrow'," "If the sun could tell us half," "If the moon came from heaven," "O Lady Moon, your horns point toward the east," "What do the stars do," "Motherless baby and babyless mother," "Crimson curtains round my mother's bed," "Baby lies so fast asleep," "I know a baby, such a baby," "Lullaby, oh, lullaby!," "Lie a-bed."

Typography and paper: (137) 121.7 x 57 (p. 30); various lines per page, up to 18. Wove paper, unwatermarked. In some copies, the numeral '3' in signature '13' is shifting down.

Running titles: In italic.

Rectos: i-vii: no RT; ix: 'CONTENTS.'; xi, 1-29: no RT; 31: 'SING-SONG.'; 33-43: no RT; 45-47: 'SING-SONG.'; 49-53: no RT; 55: 'SING-SONG.'; 57-61: no RT; 63: 'SING-SONG.'; 65-115: no RT; 117: 'SING-SONG.'; 119-131: no RT.

Versos: ii-vi: no RT; viii-x: 'CONTENTS.'; xii, 2-28: no RT; 30: 'SING-SONG.'; 32-48: no RT; 50-52: 'SING-SONG.'; 54-132: no RT.

Binding: Two patterns of cloth and a range of blue and green colors have been noted among the early bindings (A and B); while the priority of cloth patterns and colors is undetermined, calico is presumed earlier. Environmental or other factors may account for some of the differences among blue and among green copies. Binding C is presumed later. Copies in paper binding were also advertised in the early 1880s (see *Publication*).

Binding A: Calico, very dark bluish green (Centroid 166: TxU); dark yellowish green (Centroid 137: NjP both copies; CaBVaU, Colbeck entry 14); vivid purplish blue (Centroid 194: NjP, presentation copy from DGR). Front: in gilt: across top, ornamental band composed of circles with bells; centered beneath this, a small star (7.3 x 8); below star, text 'Sing-Song [with bouquet of lilies behind first "S"] | A NURSERY-RHYME | BOOK'; below text, a row of ornaments including (at left) a circle (15 mm), in center: a wreath of harebells with a bird (37.3 wide) and at right, a moon (16 mm); at bottom left, a boy at a sundial, with two rules (thin at top, thick at bottom) in the background extending to the right edge. To the right of the sundial, between the rules, text: 'BY | CHRISTINA • G • | ROSSETTI •' with a bird above "TINA" and daisies springing up from the bottom rule beneath "HRIS." Several of the front cover ornaments are drawn from illustrations in the text (the bells on 102; the harebell wreath on 17; the sundial on 46). Back: blind-stamped, four horizontal rules. Spine: '[ornament, two birds, 34.3 high] | Sing- | Song | [ornament, mother and baby, 58 mm high] | [two rules] | BY [swash Y] | Christina G [swash C, G] | Rossetti [swash R] | [two rules] | [thick rule].' Endpapers: coated paper, dark grayish reddish brown (Centroid 47). Edges: all edges gilt.

Binding B: Same design as *Binding A* except pebble-patterned cloth, medium green. Location: BL.

Binding C: See *Note two*. Pebble-patterned cloth, reddish brown. Design same except front: in black ink except 'Sing-Song'; and spine: again in black ink except for title, with different ornamentation: '[ornament, lily, 23 mm high] | [in gilt] SING- | [in gilt] SONG | [ornament, leaves and flowers, 58 mm high] | [two rules] | BY [swash Y] | CHRISTINA G | ROSSETTI [two rules] | [thick rule]'; Endpapers: coated papers, very light reddish brown. Edges: all edges gilt. The copy examined bears an 1878 inscription. Location: CaBVaU.

Publication: November 1871. The initial print run was 1000 copies, with a total of 1100 sold by March 1872 (WMRD, 27 March 1872). In January 1870, CGR offered the MS to Macmillan, but was not pleased with Macmillan's generally "meager" terms (*RP* 489), which included exclusive control of illustrations (Kooistra 92-93). The book was next offered to F. S. Ellis, but ultimately rejected on grounds of cost. CGR accepted an offer from Dalziel in April 1871 (*Letters* 1: 369), provided that she be consulted about the illustrator. The book was published by Routledge for Dalziel.

CGR's illness made it necessary for WMR to assist in negotiations with Dalziel and Roberts Brothers; WMR and CGR were both active in approving Hughes as the book's illustrator and determining details such as type size (*Letters* 1: 317). WMR and CGR read proofs from August through September 1871. See Kooistra for detailed treatment of CGR's collaboration with Hughes.

Sales had begun to lag by October 1873, at which point CGR authorized Routledge to reduce the price of the book (*Letters* 1: 437). As late as June, 1875, however, CGR reported to Dalziel that the book was still selling at the original price (*Letters* 2: 46). Routledge may have chosen an alternate way to increase profits by using a less expensive binding: the firm's 1875 catalog advertised the book "In chaste binding, Five Shillings." But by September 1875, CGR attributed her difficulty in finding a copy to purchase to "the *bound* copies being exhausted," asking for Dalziel's help in arranging for more copies to be bound (*Letters* 2: 58). By 1882, both a reduction in price and a change in binding were evident in Routledge's catalogue, which offered copies in a paper cover for 1 shilling, and in cloth gilt for 2s 6d (the same prices had been listed for a "new edition" of the book in the *English Catalogue* for 1878). When the Dalziel firm declared bankruptcy in 1893, Rossetti bought from them "the residue of my edition and the material thereto appertaining," including "328 Quire stock copies and covers" along with electroplates and woodblocks; at that time, only 50 copies remained with Routledge (*Letters* 4: 341-342).

Announced in the *Athenaeum* (29 July 1871: 146; 9 December 1871: 741) and the *Orchestra* (4 August 1871: 280).

Price: 5s.

BL depository copy: "BRITISH MUSEUM 26 FE 75"

Reviewed in the *Examiner* (9 December 1871: 1223); *Sunday Times*, (16 December 1871); *Saturday Review* (23 December 1871: 824); *Athenaeum* (6 January 1872: 11); *Academy* (15 January 1872: 23-24).

Printing: 132: 'GEORGE ROUTLEDGE AND SONS, the Broadway, Ludgate.'

Note one: CGR's manuscript of *Sing-Song*, including CGR's pencil illustrations, is at the British Library.

Note two: The Binding C copy (CaBVaU) is also gathered and bound differently from other 1872 copies, with a resulting change in the preliminaries, as follows: $\pi 2$ $^2\pi^4$ 1-2^8 5-6^4 4-^{2}5^4 9-16^4 ^{2}9^2; pagination: [2] i-vii viii-x 1-130 131-132. Whereas other 1872 copies are bound so that the unpaginated half-title falls after the last page of contents (x), this copy moves the half-title leaf to the beginning of the preliminaries, thus changing the contents as follows: : [1] half-title 'SING-SONG.' [2] b; no xi-xii. These changes suggest that this copy is a later binding of 1872 sheets.

Note three: The MSL copy varies from other early copies in both content (it lacks the final leaf of advertisements), and in its binding, which presents most of the characteristics of Binding A but varies in color (very dark green, Centroid 147) and more significantly, in the placement of the hyphen in the title on the spine, which in this copy appears on the second line ('-SONG') rather than the first ('SING-'). Most probably this is a pre-publication copy in a trial binding.

Locations: CaBVaU (2 copies); NjP (3 copies); TxU; BL (one copy rebound); MSL.

Presentation copies: NjP: inscribed "To A C Swinburne from his affectionate D G R"; MSL: inscribed by CGR "To my very dear brother William Michael Rossetti" (see *Note three*).

A8.1a.ii   *First Edition, First British Printing, Later Issue (Routledge Subedition)*

Same as A8.1ai, Binding C, except:

Title Page: no date.

Pagination: i-<u>vii</u> viii-x 1-130.

Collation: Note smaller leaf size and single leaf following gathering 16: (175.3 x 127): π2 ²π⁴ 1-2⁸ 5-6⁴ 4-²5⁴ 9-16⁴ (16 + ²9); 71 leaves.

Contents: No advertisements.

Binding: Pebble-patterned cloth, very dark greenish blue (Centroid 175). Front, back plain. Spine: in gilt, '[double rule] | SING | SONG. | [double rule]. Endpapers: white wove paper. Edges: trimmed, with red speckles.

Note one: The undated title and plain binding, along with the absence of advertisements, indicate that this is among the later, less expensive issues of the original impression.

Location: NjP.

A8.1b.i   *First Edition, First American Printing (Roberts Brothers Subedition) (1872)*

Same as British issue except:

Some text in <u>black letter</u>:
SING-SONG. | A NURSERY RHYME BOOK. | By CHRISTINA G. ROSSETTI. | [illustration, seated girl sewing, facing left, 48 x 43, signed 'AH' and 'DALZIEL'] | <u>With One Hundred and Twenty Illustrations</u> | By ARTHUR HUGHES. | ENGRAVED BY THE BROTHERS DALZIEL. | BOSTON: | ROBERTS BROTHERS.| 1872.

No tissue guard visible in copy examined.

Pagination: [2] i-<u>vii</u> viii-x 1-130 <u>131-132</u>.

Collation: (191 x 128): π⁶ 1-8⁸ 9²; page number '1' also serves as signature '1'; $1, 2 (-7¹) signed.

Contents: [1-2]: blank; no half-title, instead: vii-x: 'CONTENTS.'; 1-130: poems and illustrations; no advertisements, instead: <u>131-132</u>: blank.

Running titles: In italic.
Rectos: [1], i-<u>vii</u>: no RT; ix: 'CONTENTS.'; 1-29: no RT; 31: 'SING-SONG.'; 33-43: no RT; 45-47: 'SING-SONG.'; 49-53: no RT; 55: 'SING-SONG.'; 57-61: no RT; 63: 'SING-SONG.'; 65-115: no RT; 117: 'SING-SONG.'; 119-129, <u>131</u>: no RT.
Versos: [2], ii-<u>vi</u>: no RT; <u>viii-x</u>: 'CONTENTS.'; 2-28: no RT; 30: 'SING-SONG.'; 32-48: no RT; 50-52: 'SING-SONG.'; 54-130, <u>132</u>: no RT.

Typography and paper: Micrometer readings indicate that this paper is slightly thinner than that of the British issue (micrometer readings .129 to .146 mm; British issues range from .163 to .177).

Binding: Pebble-pattern cloth, burnt orange. Front: at the top and bottom, a black ink rectangle containing a thin black and gilt frame, and black horizontal ornament. In the center, between two horizontal gilt bands, a black ink square frame contains text: 'Sing-song | by Christina G. Rossetti.' At the bottom right corner of center compartment, in gilt, a bell design and a girl sewing. Back: plain. Spine: in black ink: vertical text, within three oval lozenges: '[within first lozenge] SING- [within second lozenge] SONG [within third lozenge] CHRISTINA ROSSETTI.' Medium reddish brown coated end papers, with one wove paper binder's leaf between endpapers and sheets, front and back. Edges trimmed, plain.

Publication: Printed from a set of duplicate plates supplied by Dalziel, who wrote on September 1, 1870 that the two books were intended for simultaneous publication "in November if not before" (*Letters* 1: 381). On October 17, the *New York Times* reported that the book was to be published "this month" (p. 2); it was listed as a "New Publication" in a Roberts Brothers advertisement on December 7 (*New York Times*, 3). According to Kilgour, the book "passed practically unnoticed." (100).

    Priced at $2.00.

    Reviewed in *Harper's New Monthly Magazine* (January 1872: 299); the *Nation* (2 May 1872: 295); *Scribner's Monthly* (March 1872: 629).

Printing: iv: 'CAMBRIDGE: | PRESS OF JOHN WILSON AND SON.'

Location: TxCM.

A8.1b.ii   *First Edition, First American Printing, Second Issue (Roberts Brothers Subedition) (1875)*

Not seen; no copies have been located. A Roberts Brothers advertisement for the book in the Ives copy of *Speaking Likenesses* (see A10.1b) features specimen pages from *Sing-Song*, including a reproduction of the title page (but with the date changed to 1875). Given that sales of the book were not particularly strong, it is likely that the 1875 issue consisted of a new title page bound with existing sheets (see A8.1b.iii).

A8.1b.iii   *First Edition, First American Printing, Third Issue (Roberts Brothers Subedition) (1894)*

Sheets of the first American printing with cancel title page.

Title Page: Same as 1872 but with date changed to '1894.'

Contents: Note no half-title, no advertisements. [1]-i: blank; ii: frontispiece (no tissue guard); iii: title; iv: blank; v: dedication; vi: blank; vii: 'CONTENTS.'; 1-130: poems and illustrations; 131-132: blank.

Binding: Fine diagonal rib patterned cloth, dark orange yellow (Centroid 72). Same binding design as Roberts Brothers 1872 but printed in moderate reddish brown ink (Centroid 43), no gilt.

Publication: Possibly prompted by Macmillan's 1893 edition (A8.2a, below), but without the added poems, as this issue consists of the 1872 sheets with a new title page glued to the stub of the original title.

Printing: no printer's imprint.

Location: NSbSU.

A8.2   *Second Edition, Only Printing (1893)*

Some text in black letter:
SING-SONG | A NURSERY RHYME BOOK | BY | CHRISTINA G. ROSSETTI | [illustration, seated girl sewing, facing left, 47.7 x 43, signed 'AH' and 'DALZIEL'] | WITH ONE HUNDRED AND TWENTY ILLUSTRATIONS | By ARTHUR HUGHES | ENGRAVED BY THE BROTHERS DALZIEL | London | MACMILLAN AND CO. | AND NEW YORK | 1893 | *All rights reserved*

Pagination: [2] i-ix x-xiv 1-135 136.

Collation: (184 x 133): A⁸ B-I⁸ K⁴; $1 signed; 76 leaves.

Contents: [1]-[2]: blank; i: half-title 'SING-SONG'; ii: Macmillan device, "MM& Co," 9 x 33; iii: blank; iv: frontispiece; v: title; vi: '*New and Enlarged Edition*'; vii: dedication (without period); viii: blank; ix: 'CONTENTS'; 1-135: poems and illustrations; 136: printer's imprint.

Illustrations: Illustrations appear on the title page and on the first page of poems originally printed in 1872; new additions are not illustrated (thus illustrations occur on pages 1-26, 28-30, 33-35, 37-46, 48, 50-51, 53, 55-56, 58-64, 66-72, 74-87, 89-90, 92-121, 123-135).

Poems: Five poems are added: "Brownie, brownie, let down your milk," "Stroke a flint, and there is nothing to admire," "I am a King," "Playing at bob cherry," "Blind from my birth." Rossetti also added a new opening stanza to the poem "A peach for brothers, each for each," so that the first line (and thus the title) changes to "The peach tree on the southern wall."

Typography and paper: (128) 124 x 54.7 (p. 31); 18 lines per page. Wove paper, unwatermarked.

Running titles: In italic.
Rectos: [1], i-ix: no RT; xi-xiii: 'CONTENTS' with swash Ts; 1-135: no RT.
Versos: [2], ii-viii: no RT; x-xiv: 'SING-SONG'; 2-136: no RT.

Binding: Silk, moiré pattern, moderate olive green (Centroid 125). Front, back plain. Spine: 'SING | SONG | CHRISTINA | ROSSETTI | MACMILLAN & C.º [the 'o' is superscript, with a small dot or line beneath]'. Endpapers: white wove paper, no watermarks, thinner than sheets. Edges: all edges gilt.

Publication: December 1893. 2000 copies were printed from type in November 1893 (Editions Book, Macmillan Archives). Having purchased from Dalziel not only the remaining copies, but also the plates and original woodblocks, Rossetti approached Macmillan in September 1893 with the idea of producing a "new and enlarged" edition (Letters 4: 341). Macmillan, who was already committed to a new illustrated edition of *Goblin Market*, purchased the copyright, electroplates, and woodblocks from Rossetti for £20 and offered Rossetti half-profits on sales (*Letters* 4: 342, 346; Terms Books, Macmillan Archives). Macmillan reset the text, retaining Hughes's illustrations. Rossetti read and returned proof for the new volume on October 19 (Letters 4: 351); it was published on December 9.
　　Listed among "Publications To-Day," London *Times* (9 December 1893: 11). Announced in the *Academy* (25 November 1893: 462), *Publishers' Weekly* (6 January 1894: 7) and the *Literary World* (Boston) (27 January 1894: 31).
　　Priced at 4s. 6d. and $1.50 in the United States.
　　BL depository copy: 'BRITISH MUSEUM 4 LA 94'.
　　Reviewed in the London *Times* (December 1893: 13).

Printing: 136: '*Printed by* R. & R. CLARK, *Edinburgh.*'

Locations: BL; CaBVaU (rebound); NjP (2, including presentation copy); TxCM.

Presentation copy: NjP: inscribed by WMR 'W M Rossetti from Christina 1893'.

A8.3a　　*Third Edition, First Printing: Macmillan 1907*

A line for line resetting of the 1893 second edition.

SING-SONG | A NURSERY RHYME BOOK | BY | CHRISTINA G. ROSSETTI | [illustration, seated girl sewing, facing left, 48 x 44, signed 'AH' and 'DALZIEL'] | WITH ONE HUNDRED AND

TWENTY ILLUSTRATIONS BY | ARTHUR HUGHES | ENGRAVED BY THE BROTHERS DALZIEL | MACMILLAN AND CO., LIMITED | ST. MARTIN'S STREET, LONDON | 1907

Pagination, Collation: same as 1893.

Contents: same as 1893 except: ii: [Macmillan device, "MM & Co." 9 x 33] | MACMILLAN AND CO., Limited | LONDON • BOMBAY • CALCUTTA | MELBOURNE | THE MACMILLAN COMPANY | NEW YORK • BOSTON • CHICACO | ATLANTA • SAN FRANCISCO | THE MACMILLAN CO. OF CANADA, Ltd. | TORONTO'; vi: '*Originally published elsewhere.* | *First published by Macmillan and Co., 1893.* | *"Illustrated Pocket Classics for the Young," 1907.*'

Typography and paper: (140) 134 x 51 (p. 34); 18 lines per page. Wove paper, unwatermarked.

Running titles: same as 1893 except *Rectos*: no swash 'T' in 'CONTENTS'.

Binding A: Calico cloth, deep blue (Centroid 179). Front: blindstamped rule at edges, and shield in center with initials 'M M'; above shield, in gilt: 'SING • SONG'; back plain. Spine, in gilt: 'SING | SONG | [two rows of five dots: •• • ••] | CHRISTINA | ROSSETTI [| [ornamental linear and floral band, separated from text by a rule at top and bottom] MACMILLAN'. Endpapers: plain, wove, thinner than sheets.

  Dust Jacket: yellowish tan paper, printed in blue ink. Front: same text and shield design as binding. Front flap: list of twelve series titles, ten illustrated, by various authors (*Cranford* through *John Inglesant: A Romance*), and two titles, "Without Illustrations." Back: List of "Illustrated Pocket Classics for the Young," described as "A Series of Dainty Volumes, with Beautiful Illustrations," and listing two bindings, "Cloth elegant" and "Limp leather"; ten titles listed: seven by various authors (*Tom Brown's School Days* through *Sing-Song*) followed by three books by J. Fenimore Cooper. Back flap: Heading "Dainty Gift Books"; seven titles, "The Works of Jane Austen" (five titles) and "The Works of Maria Edgeworth" (six titles). Spine: Same as binding; copy examined shows damage at tail, but beneath publisher's name the price '2/' appears.

Binding B: Leather, not seen (described on dust jacket of Binding A).

Publication: The Macmillan Editions Book shows 3000 copies printed from type and electroplates in October 1907. Additional printings of 2000 each took place in August 1915 and October 1920. The plates were destroyed in 1937.

  Announced in the "Autumn Announcements" supplement to *Macmillan's Magazine*, "Autumn Announcements" (October 1907), *Bookseller* (13 December 1907, p. 1080), *Publishers' Weekly* (11 January 1908, 50).

  Price 2s. cloth, 3s. "limp leather"; in US: .80 cloth, $1.25 leather.

Printing: same as 1893.

Location: MSat (rebound); Ives (Binding A, no dust jacket); TxCM (Binding A, with dust jacket).

A9   **ANNUS DOMINI (1874)**

A9.1a   First Edition, British Printing (Parker Subedition) (1874)

Within single rule frame, with cross pattée ornaments at corners, 97 x 63.3; some text in ornamental
<u>black letter</u>:
<u>Annus Domini:</u> | A PRAYER FOR EACH DAY OF THE | YEAR, FOUNDED ON A TEXT | OF HOLY
SCRIPTURE. | BY | CHRISTINA G. ROSSETTI. | Job ix. 15. | "I would make supplication to my Judge."
| <u>Oxford and London:</u> | JAMES PARKER AND CO. | 1874.

Pagination: <u>i-vii</u> viii-xii 1-366 <u>367-368</u>. Page numbers are within rule frame. The numerals 1-366 serve as
reference numbers for prayers (one per page) as well as page numbers.

Collation: (119 x 92) : <u>A</u>⁶ B-Z⁸ Aa⁸. $1 signed. 190 leaves.

Contents: <u>i</u>: title; <u>ii</u>: printer's device; <u>iii</u>: text beginning "I have had great pleasure" signed "H. W. Burrows";
<u>iv</u>: blank; <u>v</u>: text beginning "I have planned my little Book" and signed "C. G. R."; <u>vi</u>: blank; <u>vii-viii</u>:
'CALENDAR.'; ix-xii: poem, first line 'ALAS my Lord'; 1-366: prayers; <u>367</u>: advertisement, *Oxford
Editions of Devotional Works*; <u>368</u> advertisement, *The Practical Christian's Library*.

Poems: Untitled, first line: "Alas my lord" (see *Note one*).

Typography and paper: (98.3, signature to top of frame) 81.3 x 56 (p. 225). All text pages, except
advertisements, are printed within the same 97 x 63.3 rule frame with cross pattée ornaments. Each page
also includes a scripture quotation in italic. To accommodate the frame, lines per page, as well as leading
between lines, varies up to 25 lines (p. 236). Wove paper, unwatermarked.

No running titles.

Binding: Three forms noted; Binding A presumed earliest. All bindings have white wove endpapers and
trimmed edges.

Binding A: Calico cloth, dark grayish red (Centroid 20: BL), or blackish purple (CaBVaU), or very dark
purplish red (Centroid 260: MSL). Front: in black ink, a grid pattern formed of four sets of two vertical
double rules (two sets at either side) and four sets of two horizontal double rules (two sets at top, two at
bottom). Back: blind-stamped, same design as front. Spine: in black and gilt, '[double rule] | [text in gilt
and within gilt compartment] Annus |Domini | [short rule] | *ROSSETTI* | [two sets of double rules],' with
the double rules extending from the front; and the "A" in "Annus" with a chevron-shaped serif.

Binding B: Calico cloth, bluish black (Centroid 193); same as Binding A, but with front and back design
blind-stamped. Location: NjP.

Binding C: Calico cloth, dark grayish red (Centroid 20); design same as Binding A, but both front and back
stamped in black; text on spine "Annus | Domini"; spine rules do not extend from front. Location: NjP.

Publication: Announced as "just published" in the *Athenaeum* (4 April 1874: 447).
     Price: 3s 6d.
     BL depository copy: 'BRITISH MUSEUM 7 MY 74'.
     Reviewed in the *London Quarterly Review* (July 1874: 494); *Academy* (25 July 1874: 95).

Printing: ii: device, 19 x 18, with crown in center, three discs behind, upon ornamental background, and
text 'PRINTED BY PARKER OXFORD'.

Note one: A copy with CGR's annotations is at NjP (Princeton (Ex) 5866.786 c1, Binding C). The annotations include the addition of three lines to the poem titled "Alas my lord" (see notations for p. x in
the transcription that follows). The poem was reprinted in 1904 by WMR with the title "Wrestling." The
annotations are as follows:

On front free endpaper: in pencil: 'See p. x'.

p. x: In ink, written in margin with arrow pointing to indicate insertion between stanzas 2 ('Elias prayed') and 3 ('All Nineveh'):

> Gulped by the fish,
> As by the pit, lost Jonah made his moan;
> And thou forgivest, waiting to atone.

p. 47: In pencil, in margin beside line 2 from bottom ('our care on Thee, for thou carest for us.'): the 't' in 'thou' is crossed out and a capital 'T' is in margin.

p. 259: In pencil, in margin beside line 4 of prayer ('Father in Heaven. Suffer no sin to serve'), 'serve' crossed out, & 'sever' in margin.

p. 362: In pencil, in line 3 of text ("Father in his throne, by virtue of Thy"), slash mark over comma.

p. 362: In pencil, a slash mark after last word in last line, "Amen.'

Locations: BL, CaBVaU, MSL, NjP (2 copies).

Presentation copies: MSL: inscribed "Katherine Aspinell with Christina's love."

A9.1b   *First Edition, American Printing (Roberts Brothers Subedition) (1875)*

Same as British printing except:

Within single rule frame, with cross pattée ornaments at corners, 96.9 x 63; some text in ornamental black letter:
Annus Domini: | A PRAYER FOR EACH DAY OF THE | YEAR, FOUNDED ON A TEXT | OF HOLY SCRIPTURE. | BY | CHRISTINA G. ROSSETTI. | | [rule, 17] Job ix. 15. | "I would make supplication to my Judge." | [rule, 17.3] Printed by Jas. Parker and Co. | Oxford and London, | FOR MESSRS. ROBERTS BROTHERS, | BOSTON. | 1875.

Contents: ii: blank.

Typography and paper: Roberts Brothers copies are printed on thinner paper than British copies.

Binding: Sand patterned cloth, dark grayish red (Centroid 20) or moderate reddish brown (Centroid 43). Front: in black ink, ornamental band at top and bottom, and in center, in gilt, '[cross pattée, 3.3 x 3.3. | Annus [with chevron serif in A] | Domini | [cross pattée, 3.3 x 3.3] | Rossetti | [cross pattée 3.3 x 3.3].' Back: blind-stamped, pattern same as front. Spine: black ornamental band at top and bottom, same as front, and gilt text in center, same as front. Edges: stained, strong red (Centroid 12). Endpapers: coated paper, grayish brown (Centroid 61). One wove paper binders leaf, front and back.

Publication: Printed from corrected plates of British first printing. Noted among "New Publications" in *New York Times* (16 December 1874: 2), and reviewed in *Appleton's Journal* (9 January 1875: 53).

Printing: no printer's imprint.

Note one: Of the corrections noted in the annotated copy of the British printing at Princeton, only the change from "serve" to "sever" has been made.

Locations: Ives; NcD; PBm. Not seen: presentation copy from CGR to Amelia Heimann at Beinecke (Tinker 1789).

A10 SPEAKING LIKENESSES (1874)

A10.1a *First Edition, First Printing (1874)*

Some text in <u>black letter</u>; last line brackets in original:
SPEAKING LIKENESSES | BY | CHRISTINA ROSSETTI | WITH PICTURES THEREOF | BY | ARTHUR HUGHES | [vignette, chair & girl, 52 x 63.6] | <u>London</u> | MACMILLAN AND CO. | 1874 | [*The right of Translation and Reproduction is reserved*]

Pagination: i-<u>vii</u> viii <u>1</u> 2-11 <u>12</u> 13-19 <u>20</u> 21-29 <u>30</u> 31-61 <u>62</u> 63-79 <u>80</u> 81-89 <u>90</u> 91-96.

Plates: No plates, but see contents for illustrations.

Collation: (183 x 122): <u>A</u>⁴ B-G⁸. $1,2 signed (-<u>A</u>1,2; C2); also 'G' in 'G2' is missing in all copies examined. 52 leaves.

Contents: <u>i</u>: blank; <u>ii</u>: frontispiece, girl and children (129 x 90); <u>iii</u>: title; <u>iv</u>: printer's imprint; <u>v</u>: dedication [with <u>black letter</u>] 'TO MY | <u>Dearest Mother,</u> | IN GRATEFUL REMEMBRANCE OF THE | STORIES | WITH WHICH SHE USED TO ENTERTAIN HER | CHILDREN.'; <u>vi</u>: blank; <u>vii</u>: 'LIST OF ILLUSTRATIONS.'; <u>1</u>: text headed 'SPEAKING | LIKENESSES.'; 3: text and illustration, girl in bed, same as cover; 11: full page illustration (124 x 86), Medusa-like figure and six children; <u>12</u>: blank; 19: full page illustration (127 x 87), girl at door; <u>20</u>: blank; 22: text and illustration (52 x 63) same as title page; 24: text and illustration (72 x 90), girl at tea table; 29: full page illustration (125 x, 85.7), girl and nightmare children; <u>30</u>: blank; 56: text and illustration (64.3 x 77), girl with dog, bird, cat; 61: full page illustration (125 x 86.3), girl seated, with animals; <u>62</u>: blank; 79: full page illustration (129 x 90.3), same as frontispiece, girl & children; <u>80</u>: blank; 85: text and illustration, girl and mouth boy (62.3 x 88); 89: full page illustration (131.7 x 91), girl looking back at gypsies; <u>90</u>: blank; 95: text and illustration (58.7 x 72.3), girl & woman, girl has basket, animals; 96: text and printer's imprint.

Typography and paper: (146.7) 132 x 89.3 (p. 33); 19 lines per page. Thick wove paper, unwatermarked.

Running titles:
Rectos: i-<u>vii</u>, <u>1</u>: no RT; 3-11: 'LIKENESSES.'; 13: 'SPEAKING LIKENESSES.'; 15-19: 'LIKENESSES.'; 21: 'SPEAKING LIKENESSES.'; 23-29: 'LIKENESSES.'; 31: 'SPEAKING LIKENESSES.'; 33-61: 'LIKENESSES.'; 63: 'SPEAKING LIKENESSES.'; 65-79: 'LIKENESSES.'; 81: 'SPEAKING LIKENESSES.'; 83-89: 'LIKENESSES.'; 91: 'SPEAKING LIKENESSES.'; 93-95: 'LIKENESSES.'
Versos: ii-iv: no RT; viii: 'LIST OF ILLUSTRATIONS.'; 2-10: 'SPEAKING.'; 12: no RT; 14-18: 'SPEAKING.'; 20: no RT; 22-28: 'SPEAKING.'; 30: no RT; 32-60: 'SPEAKING.'; 62: no RT; 64-78: 'SPEAKING.'; 80: no RT; 82-88: 'SPEAKING.'; 90: no RT; 92-94: 'SPEAKING.'; 96: 'SPEAKING LIKENESSES.'

Binding: Two forms noted, Binding A presumed earlier:
Binding A: Calico, vivid purplish blue (Centroid 194) or deep blue (Centroid 179). Front: In gilt, single rule border and illustration (occupying the upper third and extending down the left side), same as page 3 of text, of girl being put to bed by mother, including cat at top right and a rooster at bottom left; at lower right, text: 'Speaking | Likenesses'. Back: blind-stamped single-rule border.
 Two forms of the *Binding A* spine have been noted, A presumed earlier:
Binding A, Spine A: Note small caps; also wrong initial, "C", in author's name: '[2 rules] | Speaking | Likenesses | CHRISTINA C. | ROSSETTI | [circular Macmillan device, 10 mm] | [rule] | Macmillan | [rule]'; Locations: with dust jacket: MSL; NjP; without dust jacket: BL; CaBVaU; DAM; Macmillan Archive; NjP; TxU.
Binding A, Spine B: Note removal of wrong initial and addition of chevron-bar 'A' in 'Macmillan'; coincides with stapled binding: '[double rule] | Speaking | Likenesses | CHRISTINA | ROSSETTI |

[circular Macmillan device, 10 mm] | [rule] | MACMILLAN | [rule]'; Locations: CaBVaU, call number A PR5237.S7 1874.

Endpapers: coated paper, dark grayish reddish brown (Centroid 47; CaBVaU (2); NjP) or dark grayish brown (Centroid 62, NjP). Edges: all edges gilt.

Dust jacket: very light greenish blue paper (Centroid 171); Front: in black ink, and with double hairline rule frame (168 x 109 outer; 109 x 103, inner): '[above frame] *Crown 8vo. 4s. 6d.* [within frame] SPEAKING LIKENESSES | BY | CHRISTINA ROSSETTI | WITH PICTURES THEREOF | BY | ARTHUR HUGHES | [illustration of chair and girl as on title page, 52 x 64] | [black letter] London | MACMILLAN AND CO. | 1874'. Back: plain. Spine: thick-thin rule at top, thin-thick rule at bottom, text vertical, reading bottom to top 'ROSSETTI'S SPEAKING LIKENESSES.'

Binding B: Same cloth as A, but front and back are plain except for a blind-stamped single rule border. Spine, text in gilt: [at head] [blind-stamped double rule] | 'Speaking | Likenesses | Christina | Rossetti | [at tail] [blind-stamped single rule] | MACMILLAN | [blind-stamped single rule].' Endpapers: white wove paper. Edges: trimmed. According to Carter, the book was remaindered, probably with this plain binding rather than the more ornate original cloth (*Binding Variants*, 149). Carter does not mention the dust jacket, which is also lacking on the copy examined for this bibliography. Location: TxCM.

Publication: 3000 copies were printed from type and electrotype in October 1874 (Editions Book, Macmillan Archives), with more than 1000 copies sold by late January 1875 (*Letters* 2: 38). Rossetti had offered the "little prose story" to Macmillan on 3 February 1874 (*Letters* 2: 6), and requested Arthur Hughes as illustrator, but seems not to have worked closely with him (Kooistra 128-129). Upon receiving a copy of the book she expressed displeasure with the wording of the title page and list of illustrations, neither of which she had seen in proof. Although she wrote to Macmillan to request that the title page be cancelled, no changes to the text of the title or the list of illustrations have been discovered (*Letters* 2: 30-31).

Early mention in the *Illustrated Review* (May 1874: 310); announced in the *Athenaeum* (3 October 1874: 437; published "This day," 31 October 1874: 567).

Price: 4s. 6d.

Reviewed in the *Examiner* (November 1874: 1304-1305); *Academy* (5 December 1874: 606); *Athenaeum* (27 December 1874: 878).

Printing: <u>iv</u>: 'LONDON | R. CLAY, SONS, AND TAYLOR, PRINTERS, | BREAD STREET HILL.'; 96: 'LONDON: R. CLAY, SONS, AND TAYLOR, PRINTERS.'

Locations: BL; CaBVaU (2); DAM; Macmillan; MSL; NjP (2); TxCM; TxU.

A10.1b   *First Edition, Second Printing (Roberts Brothers Subedition) (1874)*

Reprinted from the British plates with minor changes; see *Note one*.

See *Note one*:
SPEAKING LIKENESSES. | BY | CHRISTINA ROSSETTI. | WITH PICTURES THEREOF BY ARTHUR HUGHES. | [vignette: chair & girl, 52 x 61] | BOSTON: | ROBERTS BROTHERS. | 1875.

Pagination: The last gathering includes 4 unpaginated leaves of advertisements, thus i-<u>vii</u> viii <u>1</u> 2-11 <u>12</u> 13-19 <u>20</u> 21-29 <u>30</u> 31-61 <u>62</u> 63-79 <u>80</u> 81-89 <u>90</u> 91-96 [8].

Collation: (191 x 127): [1-7⁸]. Obsolete signatures of British issue remain. 56 leaves.

Contents: Same as British printing except for the following (see *Note two*):
ii: frontispiece illustration is now taken from page 61 of the text, depicting Edith in the woods with her kettle and various animals); iv: blank; 3: illustration same as cover of British issue (but not used on the

American cover); 79: illustration same as British issue (but not used as the frontispiece in the American issue); advertisements: [1]: full page illustration (155 x 106), with caption "Frontispiece of Sing-Song."; [2]: title page of *Sing-Song*; [3]: "Specimen page" of *Sing-Song* with illustration and poem "Love me, – I love you"; [4]: heading "Messrs. Roberts Bros. Illustrated Books" with Susan Coolidge's *What Katy Did at School* announced as "just ready"; [5]: two titles, Coolidge's *What Katy Did* and *The New Year's Bargain*; [6]: one title, *Bed-Time Stories* by Louise Chandler Moulton; [7]: eight Louisa M. Alcott titles; [8]: seven titles.

Typography and paper: on slightly thinner paper than the British issue.

Running titles: same; no RT on pages with advertisements.

Binding: Dotted line cloth, dark green (Centroid 146: Ives) or sand-patterned cloth, vivid purplish blue (Centroid 194: TxCM). Front: Divided into three black ink compartments with thick-thin rule borders. The top and bottom compartments are rectangular; each contains an asymmetrical, horizontal ornamental rule. The center compartment is square and is separated from the top and bottom compartments by an ornamented band featuring a row of circles. The center compartment is also subdivided into an L-shaped section on the left and a square at the lower right. Within the L-shaped compartment: at left, a black ink ornament with stylized foliage in three groups of three leaves; across the top of the L-shaped compartment, in gilt, an ornamental medallion with cloth show-through (except for the letter L) forming the text 'SPEAKING LIKENESSES' and beneath medallion, gilt text 'BY CHRISTINA ROSSETTI'. Within inner square compartment: title page vignette of girl with chair. Back: plain. Spine: gilt flower at head and tail; three oval, vertically-oriented black ink compartments; gilt fill within compartments with cloth show-through forming text as follows: upper compartment: 'SPEAKING'; middle compartment: 'CHRISTINA | ROSSETTI'; bottom compartment: 'LIKENESSES'. Endpapers: coated paper, dark grayish green (Centroid 151). Edges: trimmed.

Publication: December 1874. Rossetti approached Roberts Brothers at least twice before offering the book to Macmillan. In January 1873 she informed Niles that the book "is now about twice the length it was when you looked at it" (*Letters* 1: 418), and indicated that if she did not hear from Roberts Brothers "in the course of the week" she would instead "try my first publisher Mr. Macmillan in whose hands "Wonderland" . . . has had so appropriately wonderful a success." Perhaps the strategic reference to Lewis Carroll caught Roberts Brothers' attention, as some negotiation must have ensued, given the year-long delay between Rossetti's ultimatum and her letter to Macmillan in February 1874. Roberts Brothers reprinted the book from Macmillan's plates in late 1874.

Announced as "ready this day" with price as $1.50 in the *New York Times* (1 December 1874: 7); reviewed in the *Christian Union* (16 December 1874: 24); *Appleton's Journal* (9 January 1875: 53); *Unitarian Review* (March 1875: 327).

Printing: no printer's imprint.

Note one: Although the book was published, announced and reviewed in late 1874, no copies with an 1874 title page have been found. There probably were no copies published with an 1874 title page, given that it was common practice for books published late in the year to bear the subsequent year's date.

Note two: Although the text of the Roberts Brothers issue is printed from the British plates, the title page is reset, as is the heading on page 1. The frontispiece is changed: whereas the British issue uses the illustration from page 79 of Maggie and the children in the woods, the Roberts Brothers issue reproduces the illustration of Maggie and her kettle from page 61, altering the frontispiece designation in the "List of Illustrations" accordingly. Roberts Brothers also places captions beneath each full page illustration, and fills out the last gathering with a section of advertisements for children's books in which Rossetti's *Sing-Song* is prominently featured.

Location: Ives, TxCM.

A11   GOBLIN MARKET, THE PRINCE'S PROGRESS AND OTHER POEMS (1875)

A11.1a   *First Edition, First Printing*

Some text in <u>black letter</u>:
GOBLIN MARKET | THE PRINCE'S PROGRESS | AND | OTHER POEMS | BY | CHRISTINA G. ROSSETTI | *WITH FOUR DESIGNS BY D. G. ROSSETTI* | NEW EDITION | <u>London</u> | MACMILLAN AND CO. | 1875 | *The Right of Translation and Reproduction is reserved.*

Pagination: <u>i</u>-<u>vii</u> viii-xi <u>xii</u> <u>1</u> 2-218 <u>219-220</u> 221-287 <u>288</u>.

Plates: Four plates, printed on same paper as sheets but glued in to the book (see *Note one*).
1) Facing title, image and caption (111 x 92.7, height measured with caption) from frontispiece of *Goblin Market* 1866/1865. With tissue guard.
2) Facing 7, vignette and caption (62 x 92.7, height measured with caption) from engraved title of *Goblin Market* 1865.
3) Facing 21, vignette and caption (77 x 84.7, height measured with caption) from engraved title of *Prince's Progress* 1866.
4) Facing 41, image and caption (150 x 98, height measured with caption) from frontispiece of *Prince's Progress* 1866.

Collation: (173 x 116.7): π² <u>A</u>⁴ B-T⁸. \$1 signed (-π, <u>A</u>). 150 leaves.

Contents: <u>1</u>: half-title 'GOBLIN MARKET | THE PRINCE'S PROGRESS | AND | OTHER POEMS'; <u>ii</u>: circular publisher's device with two Ms in center and four compartments, diameter 20; <u>iii</u>: title; <u>iv</u>: blank; <u>v</u>: dedication 'TO | MY MOTHER, | IN ALL REVERENCE AND LOVE, | I INSCRIBE THIS BOOK.'; <u>vi</u>: blank; <u>vii</u>: 'CONTENTS.'; <u>xii</u>: blank; <u>1</u>-218: text; <u>219</u>: section half-title 'DEVOTIONAL PIECES.'; <u>220</u>: blank; <u>221</u>-287: text and on 287: printer's imprint; <u>288</u>: blank.

Poems: (poems appearing for the first time are marked with an asterisk; see Note two):
"Goblin Market," "The Prince's Progress," "Maiden-Song," "Dream Land," "At Home," "The Poor Ghost," "Grown And Flown," "A Farm Walk," "A Portrait" (sections I-II), *"By The Sea," "Gone For Ever," "Love From The North," "Maggie A Lady," *"From Sunset To Star Rise," "Spring Quiet," "Winter Rain," "Vanity Of Vanities" ("Ah woe is me for pleasure that is vain"), *"Days Of Vanity," "The Ghost's Petition," *"Once For All. (Margaret.)," *"Enrica, 1865," "A Chill," "Somewhere Or Other," "Noble Sisters," "Jessie Cameron," "Spring," "Summer" ("Winter is cold-hearted"), "Autumn" ("I dwell alone"), "Winter: My Secret" ["My Secret"], *"Autumn Violets," *"A Dirge" ("Why were you born when the snow was falling?"), "A Bird's-Eye View," "Fata Morgana," "Memory" (sections I-II), *"'They Desire A Better Country'" (sections I-III), "Child's Talk In April," *"A Green Cornfield," "The Lambs Of Grasmere, 1860," "A Birthday," *"A Bride Song," *"Confluents," "Remember," "After Death," *"The Lowest Room," "Dream-Love," "An End," *"Dead Hope," "Twice," "My Dream," "Songs In A Cornfield," "On The Wing," "L. E. L.," "Song" ("Oh roses for the flush of youth"), "The Hour And The Ghost," "Shall I Forget?," "Life And Death," "A Summer Wish," "A Year's Windfalls," "An Apple Gathering," "Song" ("Two doves upon the selfsame branch"), "Maude Clare," "Echo," "Another Spring," "Bird Or Beast?," "Eve," *"A Daughter Of Eve," "A Peal Of Bells," "The Bourne," *"Song" ("Oh what comes over the sea"), *"Venus's Looking-Glass," *"Love Lies Bleeding," *"Bird Raptures," "The Queen Of Hearts," "'No, Thank You, John'," "Beauty Is Vain," "May" ("I cannot tell you how it was"), "A Pause Of Thought," "Twilight Calm," "Wife To Husband," "Three Seasons," "Mirage," "A Royal Princess," *"My Friend," "Shut Out," "Sound Sleep," "Song" ("She sat and sang alway"), "Song" ("When I am dead, my dearest"), "Dead Before Death," *"Twilight Night" (sections I-II), "Bitter For Sweet," "What Would I Give?," "The First Spring Day," *"A Bird Song," *"A Smile And A Sigh," "One Day," "Rest," "The Convent Threshold," *"Amor Mundi," "Up-Hill," "'The Iniquity Of

The Fathers Upon The Children'" ["Under The Rose"], "In The Round Tower At Jhansi, June 8, 1857," *"The German-French Campaign. 1870-1871" in two parts, "I. 'Thy Brother's Blood Crieth'" and "II. 'To-Day For Me'," *"A Christmas Carol" ("In the bleak mid-winter"), "'The Love Of Christ Which Passeth Knowledge'," "'A Bruised Reed Shall He Not Break'," "Long Barren," "Despised And Rejected," "A Better Resurrection," "If Only," "Advent" ("This Advent moon shines cold and clear"), "The Three Enemies" in three parts, "The Flesh," "The World," "The Devil," *"Consider," "Dost Thou Not Care?," "Weary In Well-Doing," "One Certainty," *"By The Waters Of Babylon. B. C. 570," "Christian And Jew," "Good Friday" ("Am I a stone, and not a sheep"), "Sweet Death," "Symbols," "'Consider The Lilies Of The Field'" ("Flowers preach to us if we will hear"), "The World," "A Testimony," *"Paradise" ("Once in a dream I saw the flowers"), "Sleep At Sea," *"Mother Country," *"'I Will Lift Up Mine Eyes Unto The Hills'" ("I am pale with sick desire"), *"'The Master Is Come, And Calleth For Thee'," *"Who Shall Deliver Me?" *"'When My Heart Is Vexed, I Will Complain'"("O Lord, how canst Thou say Thou lovest me"), *"After Communion," "Martyrs' Song," "After This The Judgment," *"Saints And Angels," *"A Rose Plant In Jericho," "From House To Home," "Old And New Year Ditties" (sections 1-3), "Amen," "The Lowest Place."

Title changes: The following poems are retitled in this edition: "Winter: My Secret" (was "My Secret"); "One Certainty" (was "The One Certainty"); "On the Wing" (was "A Dream"); "Maggie a Lady" (was "Lady Maggie"), "The Iniquity of The Fathers Upon The Children" (was "Under the Rose").

Typography and paper: (135) 125 x 76 (p. 209); 30 lines per page. Wove paper, unwatermarked.

Running titles:

Rectos: i-vii: no RT; ix, xi: 'CONTENTS.'; 1: no rt; 3-19: 'GOBLIN MARKET.'; 21-39: 'THE PRINCE'S PROGRESS.'; 41-49: 'MAIDEN-SONG.'; 51: 'AT HOME.'; 53: 'THE POOR GHOST.'; 55, 57: 'A FARM WALK.'; 59: 'BY THE SEA.'; 61: 'LOVE FROM THE NORTH.'; 63: 'MAGGIE A LADY.'; 65: 'SPRING QUIET.'; 67: 'VANITY OF VANITIES.'; 69-71: 'THE GHOST'S PETITION.'; 73: 'ENRICA.'; 75: 'NOBLE SISTERS.'; 77-81: 'JESSIE CAMERON.'; 83: 'SUMMER.'; 85: 'AUTUMN.'; 87: 'WINTER: MY SECRET.'; 89-91: 'A BIRD'S-EYE VIEW.'; 93: 'FATA MORGANA–MEMORY.'; 95: '"THEY DESIRE A BETTER COUNTRY."'; 97: 'CHILD'S TALK IN APRIL.'; 99: 'A GREEN CORNFIELD.'; 101: 'A BIRTHDAY.'; 103: 'CONFLUENTS.'; 105: 'REMEMBER.'; 107-117: 'THE LOWEST ROOM.'; 119: 'DREAM-LOVE.'; 121: 'AN END.'; 123: 'TWICE.'; 125: 'MY DREAM.'; 127-129: 'SONGS IN A CORNFIELD.'; 131: 'ON THE WING.'; 133: 'L. E. L.'; 135: 'THE HOUR AND THE GHOST.'; 137: 'SHALL I FORGET?'; 139: 'A SUMMER WISH.'; 141: 'A YEAR'S WINDFALLS.'; 143: 'AN APPLE GATHERING.'; 145: 'SONG–MAUDE CLARE.'; 147: 'ECHO.'; 149: 'BIRD OR BEAST?'; 151: 'EVE.'; 153: 'A DAUGHTER OF EVE.'; 155: 'THE BOURNE–SONG.'; 157: 'BIRD RAPTURES.'; 159: '"NO, THANK YOU, JOHN."'; 161: 'MAY.'; 163: 'TWILIGHT CALM.'; 165: 'WIFE TO HUSBAND.'; 167: 'THREE SEASONS–MIRAGE.'; 169-173: 'A ROYAL PRINCESS.'; 175: 'MY FRIEND.'; 177: 'SOUND SLEEP.'; 179: 'SONG.'; 181: 'TWILIGHT NIGHT.'; 183: 'THE FIRST SPRING DAY.'; 185: 'ONE DAY.'; 187-191: 'THE CONVENT THRESHOLD.'; 193: 'AMOR MUNDI.'; 195: '"THE INIQUITY OF THE FATHERS.'; 197-231: 'UPON THE CHILDREN."'; 215: '"THY BROTHER'S BLOOD CRIETH."'; 217: '"TO-DAY FOR ME."'; 219: no RT; 221: 'A CHRISTMAS CAROL.'; 223: 'WHICH PASSETH KNOWLEDGE."'; 225: 'LONG BARREN.'; 227: 'DESPISED AND REJECTED.'; 229: 'IF ONLY.'; 231: 'ADVENT.'; 233: 'THE THREE ENEMIES.'; 235: 'DOST THOU NOT CARE?'; 237: 'ONE CERTAINTY.'; 239: 'BY THE WATERS OF BABYLON.'; 241-243: 'CHRISTIAN AND JEW.'; 245: 'SWEET DEATH.'; 247: '"CONSIDER THE LILIES."'; 249-251: 'A TESTIMONY.'; 253: 'PARADISE.'; 255: 'SLEEP AT SEA.'; 257-259: 'MOTHER COUNTRY.'; 261: 'UNTO THE HILLS."'; 263: 'WHO SHALL DELIVER ME?'; 265: 'I WILL COMPLAIN."'; 267: 'MARTYRS' SONG.'; 269: 'AFTER THIS THE JUDGMENT.'; 271: 'SAINTS AND ANGELS.'; 273: 'A ROSE PLANT IN JERICHO.'; 275-283: 'FROM HOUSE TO HOME.'; 285: 'OLD AND NEW YEAR DITTIES.'; 287: 'THE LOWEST PLACE.'

Versos: ii-vi: no RT; viii-x: 'CONTENTS.'; xii: no RT; 2-20: 'GOBLIN MARKET.'; 22-40: 'THE PRINCE'S PROGRESS.'; 42-48: 'MAIDEN-SONG.'; 50: 'DREAM LAND.'; 52: 'THE POOR GHOST.'; 54: 'GROWN AND FLOWN.'; 56: 'A FARM WALK.'; 58: 'A PORTRAIT.'; 60: 'GONE FOR EVER.'; 62: 'MAGGIE A LADY.'; 64: 'FROM SUNSET TO STAR RISE.'; 66: 'WINTER RAIN.'; 68: 'DAYS OF VANITY.'; 70: 'THE GHOST'S PETITION.'; 72: 'ONCE FOR ALL.'; 74: 'A CHILL.'; 76: 'NOBLE SISTERS.'; 78-80: 'JESSIE CAMERON.'; 82: 'SPRING.'; 84-86: 'AUTUMN.'; 88: 'AUTUMN VIOLETS.'; 90-92: 'A BIRD'S-EYE VIEW.'; 94: 'MEMORY.'; 96: '"THEY DESIRE A BETTER COUNTRY."'; 98: 'CHILD'S TALK IN APRIL.'; 100: 'THE LAMBS OF GRASMERE.'; 102: 'A BRIDE SONG.'; 104: 'CONFLUENTS.'; 106: 'AFTER DEATH.'; 108-118: 'THE LOWEST ROOM.'; 120: 'DREAM-LOVE.'; 122: 'DEAD HOPE.'; 124: 'TWICE.'; 126: 'MY DREAM.'; 128-130: 'SONGS IN A CORNFIELD.'; 132: 'L. E. L.'; 134-136: 'THE HOUR AND THE GHOST.'; 138: 'LIFE AND DEATH.'; 140-142: 'A YEAR'S WINDFALLS.'; 144: 'AN APPLE GATHERING.'; 146: 'MAUDE CLARE.'; 148: 'ANOTHER SPRING.'; 150-152: 'EVE.'; 154: 'A PEAL OF BELLS.'; 156: 'LOVE LIES BLEEDING.'; 158: 'THE QUEEN OF HEARTS.'; 160: 'BEAUTY IS VAIN.'; 162: 'A PAUSE OF THOUGHT.'; 164: 'TWILIGHT CALM.'; 166: 'WIFE TO HUSBAND.'; 168-174: 'A ROYAL PRINCESS.'; 176: 'SHUT OUT.'; 178: 'SONG.'; 180: 'DEAD BEFORE DEATH.'; 182: 'WHAT WOULD I GIVE?'; 184: 'A SMILE AND A SIGH.'; 186: 'REST – THE CONVENT THRESHOLD.'; 188-190: 'THE CONVENT THRESHOLD.'; 192: 'AMOR MUNDI.'; 194: 'UP-HILL.'; 196-212: '"THE INIQUITY OF THE FATHERS'; 214: 'IN THE ROUND TOWER AT JHANSI.'; 216: '"THY BROTHER'S BLOOD CRIETH."'; 218: '"TO-DAY FOR ME."'; 220: no RT; 222: '"THE LOVE OF CHRIST'; 224: '"A BRUISED REED."'; 226: 'DESPISED AND REJECTED.'; 228: 'A BETTER RESURRECTION.'; 230: 'ADVENT.'; 232: 'THE THREE ENEMIES.'; 234: 'CONSIDER.'; 236: 'WEARY IN WELL-DOING.'; 238-240: 'BY THE WATERS OF BABYLON.'; 242: 'CHRISTIAN AND JEW.'; 244: 'GOOD FRIDAY.'; 246: 'SYMBOLS.'; 248: 'THE WORLD – A TESTIMONY.'; 250: 'A TESTIMONY.'; 252: 'PARADISE.'; 254-256: 'SLEEP AT SEA.'; 258: 'MOTHER COUNTRY.'; 260: '"I WILL LIFT UP MINE EYES'; 262: '"THE MASTER IS COME."'; 264: '"WHEN MY HEART IS VEXED,'; 266: 'AFTER COMMUNION.'; 268: 'MARTYRS' SONG.'; 270: 'AFTER THIS THE JUDGMENT.'; 272: 'SAINTS AND ANGELS.'; 274-282: 'FROM HOUSE TO HOME.'; 284: 'OLD AND NEW YEAR DITTIES.'; 286: 'AMEN.'; 288 no RT.

Binding (see *Note three*): Fine diagonal rib cloth, grayish brown (Centroid 61). Front: in gilt, same design as *Goblin Market* 1865. Back: blind-stamped, same as front. Spine: gilt; top and bottom rules extend from front cover: '[rule below two small rings (one at left, one at right)] | POEMS | CHRISTINA | ROSSETTI | [rule, with three rings beneath, in inverted pyramid] | MACMILLAN & Cᵒ | [rule]' with a period beneath the 'o' in 'Co'. Endpapers: coated paper, dark grayish green (Centroid 151) or very dark greenish blue (Centroid 175). Edges: top rough trimmed, fore-edge and tail trimmed.

Publication: 1000 copies printed in October 1875 (Editions Book, Macmillan Archives). Printed from type and from stereotype plates, identified by stereotype symbol "S" on B1. Reset and rearranged contents of Rossetti's first two volumes, *Goblin Market* and *The Prince's Progress*, with additions and deletions as noted in contents section.

Rossetti expressed interest in the prospect of a "fattish volume" of collected poems in January 1875, apparently in response to a suggestion by Alexander Macmillan (*Letters* 2: 38), and stipulated that she would determine the arrangement of the poems and correct proofs (*Letters* 2: 42). Although she supplied the manuscript on February 16 (*Letters* 2: 43), the process of proofreading and finalizing the text began in March (at which time she requested that a set of proof sheets be sent to Roberts Brothers) and continued through September (*Letters* 2: 44, 53, 59). Writing to Macmillan in September, Rossetti asked for additional time to complete her work, having noticed "a few poems (e. g. "Sister Maude") I do not want to reprint at all" and admitting her anxiety to "do all thoroughly now I am about it" (*Letters* 2: 59). Her thoroughness seems to have prompted her to ask for "revises of various proofs" (*Letters* 2: 61). As usual, Rossetti's involvement extended beyond proofreading and revisions to the text to include the illustrations and binding (see notes).

Early mention in the *Academy* (27 February 1875: 214) and *Athenaeum* (21 August 1875: 247); announced in the *Athenaeum* ("In a few days," 30 October 1875: 565; published "This day," 20 November 1875: 663).

Price 6s.

BL depository copies: 'BRITISH MUSEUM 14 JAN 22' (stereotype copy); 'BRITISH MUSEUM 21 JA 76' (letterpress copy).

Reviewed in the *Examiner* (18 December 1875: 1418-1419) and *Academy* (22 January 1876: 73-74). CGR mentions additional reviews in the *Glasgow News* (*Letters* 2: 68), *Pictorial World* (*Letters* 2: 69), and the *Hour* (*Letters* 2: 71, 84).

Printing: 287: '*Printed by* R. & R. CLARK, *Edinburgh*.'

Note one: Rossetti asked Macmillan to retain the frontispiece and title page vignettes from Macmillan's previous editions of *Goblin Market* and *The Prince's Progress*, "each to be inserted opposite the incident it represents" (*Letters* 2: 54).

Note two: The thirty-seven poems added to this collection are listed in Crump (1: 191-230). Rossetti also removed five poems that had previously appeared in *Goblin Market* ("A Triad," "Cousin Kate," "Sister Maude") or *The Prince's Progress* ("Light Love," "A Ring Posy").

Note three: Rossetti requested that Macmillan use the "old blocks, one or both," from previous DGR bindings, "with a widened back to suit increased bulk" and asked that "magenta, dense blue [. . .] & vermillion" be excluded from the list of possible binding colors (*Letters* 2: 54).

Locations: Letterpress copies: BL, CaBVaU (Colbeck entry 16), NjP. Stereotype copies: BL, PBm, TxCM.

Presentation copies: BL: "Eliza Harriet Polidori with her niece Christina's warm and grateful love. Xmas 1875."

A11.1b   *First Edition, Second Printing (1879)*

Same as 1875 except:

Some text in <u>black letter</u>:
GOBLIN MARKET | THE PRINCE'S PROGRESS | AND | OTHER POEMS | BY | CHRISTINA G. ROSSETTI | *WITH FOUR DESIGNS BY D. G. ROSSETTI* | NEW EDITION | <u>London</u> | MACMILLAN & CO. | 1879 | *The Right of Translation and Reproduction is reserved*.

Contents: v: Damage to comma after 'LOVE' (broken tail).

Running titles:
Rectos: 63: no period after 'LADY'; 109: faint period after 'ROOM'; 149: no question mark after 'BEAST'.
Versos: 74: period faint.

Binding: Cloth color seems slightly lighter than 1875; front seems to have been reblocked, as the small rings are closer together; spine: '[rule below two small rings (one at left, one at right)] | POEMS | CHRISTINA G. | ROSSETTI | [rule, with three rings beneath in inverted pyramid] | Macmillan & Co. | [rule].' Note that bar on the 'A' in 'Macmillan' is chevron shaped, pointing down.

Publication: 1000 copies printed from plates in July 1879 (Editions Book, Macmillan Archives). BL depository copy: 'BRITISH MUSEUM 15 OCT 71'.

Location: BL.

A11.1c   *First Edition, Third Printing (1884)*

Same as 1879 printing except:

Title Page: Date changed to 1884.

Contents: <u>ii</u>: new publisher's device, interlinked "M M & Co" above ornamental rule, 19 x 33.

Running titles: Damage on almost every page.

Binding: Endpapers: coated paper, blackish blue (Centroid 188). Two leaf advertisement gathering follows sheets; on recto of leaf 2, Rossetti's books *A Pageant* and *Speaking Likenesses* are included.

Publication: 1000 copies printed in August 1884 (Editions Book, Macmillan Archives).

Location: PBm.

Presentation copies: PBm: "Charles P. O'Connor Esq. from Christina G. Rossetti October 1885."

A11.1d   *First Edition, Fourth Printing (1888)*

Same as 1884 printing except:

Some text in <u>black letter</u>:
GOBLIN MARKET I THE PRINCE'S PROGRESS I AND I OTHER POEMS I BY I CHRISTINA G. ROSSETTI I *WITH FOUR DESIGNS BY D. G. ROSSETTI* I NEW EDITION I <u>London</u> I MACMILLAN & CO. I AND NEW YORK I 1888 I *The Right of Translation and Reproduction is reserved*

Note that there is no period after "reserved" in the last line.

Plates: Paper is browner than that of the sheets and noticeably flecked with wood pulp. On plate 1, a 1.5 cm scratch in the block between the woman's chin and her hand, slightly noticeable in 1875, is more visible now.

Contents: <u>ii</u>: change in printer's device; <u>iv</u>: 'This Edition first printed 1875. I *Reprinted 1879, 1884, 1888.*'; <u>v</u>: period instead of comma after 'MOTHER' (the comma's tail may have broken off).

Running titles:
Rectos: 185: no period after 'DAY'.

Binding: Although the design for the binding is unchanged, there are several changes to the spine: the rings on the spine are larger (nearly 3 mm as opposed to 2 mm in 1884); the rule after Rossetti is thinner (1 mm as opposed to 2 mm in 1884); the ampersand now resembles an E.

   Two leaf advertisement gathering follows sheets; on recto of leaf 1, Rossetti's books *A Pageant* and *Speaking Likenesses* are included.

Location: PBm.

A12   POEMS (Roberts Brothers First Subedition, 1876)

See also A4 (Robert Brothers parent edition), A17 (Roberts Brothers Second Subedition, 1882), A30 (Little, Brown Subedition, 1898) and A32 (Little, Brown Subedition, 1899).

A12.1a   First Edition, First Printing (First Subedition)(1876)

See *Note one*:
POEMS. | BY | CHRISTINA G. ROSSETTI. | [vignette, 62 x 69, with script '"Golden head by golden head"'] | BOSTON: | ROBERTS BROTHERS. | 1876.

Pagination: i-vii viii-xi xii 1-3 4-77 78-81 82-118 119 120-284 285-287 288-300.

Plates: Three plates, with tissue guards; designs same as A4, as follows.
1) Facing title, frontispiece from the 1865 Macmillan *Goblin Market* as reproduced in Roberts Brothers 1866 (A4). Note that the engraved title page that was conjugate with the frontispiece in 1866 and 1872 no longer appears.
2) Between 118 and 119, conjugate pair, reproducing the frontispiece (verso of first plate) and engraved title (recto of second plate) from the 1866 Macmillan *Prince's Progress* as reproduced in Roberts Brothers 1866, 1872 (A4).

Collation: (174 x 114): 1¹² 2-13¹². $2, 6 signed (signatures on leaf 6 are followed by an asterisk, for example, 2*). 156 leaves.

Contents: i: title; ii: '[circular printer's device, 21 x 24: winged child holding scepter, seated on globe, reading book; foliage at either side of globe & scroll at bottom with motto 'QUI LEGIT REGIT.'] | AUTHOR'S EDITION, REVISED AND ENLARGED. | 1876. | *Cambridge*: | *Press of John Wilson & Son*.'; iii: dedication 'TO | MY MOTHER, | IN ALL REVERENCE AND LOVE, | *I INSCRIBE THIS BOOK*.'; iv: blank; v: 'THE AUTHOR TO HER AMERICAN | READERS.' and at bottom, 'London.' (no date); vi: blank; vii: 'CONTENTS.'; xxi: blank; 1: half-title 'POEMS.'; 2: blank; 3-300: text including section half-titles 'DEVOTIONAL PIECES.' on 79 and 285.

Poems: Same as A4 (1872) except for the following substitutions and additions; see *Note two*:
"From Sunset to Star Rise" (replaces "A Triad. Sonnet"); "A Dirge" and "Confluents"(replaces "Cousin Kate"); "'The Master is Come, and Calleth for Thee'" (replaces "Sister Maude"); "Mother Country" (added on p. 116); "The German-French Campaign. 1870-1871" in two parts, "I. 'Thy Brother's Blood Crieth'" and "II. 'To-Day for Me'" (replaces "Light Love"); "Consider" (replaces "A Ring Posy"). An additional twenty-nine poems are inserted after "Under the Rose" (pp. 239-284): "Song" ("Oh what comes over the sea"), "By The Sea," "Days of Vanity," "Enrica, 1865," "Once for all. (Margaret)," "Autumn Violets," "'They Desire a Better Country'," "A Green Cornfield," "A Bride Song," "The Lowest Room," "Dead Hope," "A Daughter of Eve," "Venus' Looking-Glass," "Love Lies Bleeding," "Bird Raptures," "My Friend," "Twilight Night," "A Bird Song," "A Smile and a Sigh, "Amor Mundi," "A Christmas Carol" ("In the bleak mid-winter"), "By The Waters of Babylon B. C 570," "Paradise," "'I Will Lift Up Mine Eyes Unto The Hills'" ("I am pale with sick desire"), "Saints and Angels," "'When My Heart Is Vexed, I Will Complain'," "After Communion," "A Rose Plant in Jericho," "Who Shall Deliver Me?"

Title changes: The following title changes, adopted in Macmillan 1875 (A11), also appear here: "Winter: My Secret" (was "My Secret"); "One Certainty" (was "The One Certainty"); "On the Wing" (was "A Dream"); "Maggie a Lady" (was "Lady Maggie").

Typography and paper: (128.3) 121 x 76.3 (p. 272); various lines per page (up to 30). Laid paper, horizontal chainlines 29 mm apart. Unwatermarked.

Running titles: In italic (See *Note two*).

Rectos: i-vii: no RT; ix-xi: 'CONTENTS.'; [1]-3: no RT; 5-21: 'GOBLIN MARKET.'; 23: 'IN THE ROUND TOWER AT JHANSI.'; 25: 'AT HOME.'; 27: 'LOVE FROM THE NORTH.'; 29: 'WINTER RAIN.'; 31: 'CONFLUENTS.'; 33: 'NOBLE SISTERS.'; 35: 'SPRING.'; 37: 'A BIRTHDAY.'; 39: 'AFTER DEATH.'; 41: 'MY DREAM.'; 43-45: 'THE HOUR AND THE GHOST.'; 47: 'AN APPLE GATHERING.'; 49: 'MAUDE CLARE.'; 51: 'ECHO.'; 53: 'ANOTHER SPRING.'; 55: 'FATA MORGANA.'; 57: 'MAY.'; 59: 'TWILIGHT CALM.'; 61: 'WIFE TO HUSBAND.'; 63: 'MIRAGE.'; 65: 'SOUND SLEEP.'; 67: 'SONG.'; 69: 'THE MASTER CALLETH.'; 71-75: 'THE CONVENT THRESHOLD.'; 77: 'UP-HILL.'; 79-81: no RT; 83: 'A BETTER RESURRECTION.'; 85: 'ADVENT.'; 87: 'THE THREE ENEMIES.'; 89: 'THE ONE CERTAINTY.'; 91: 'CHRISTIAN AND JEW.'; 93: 'SWEET DEATH.'; 95: 'CONSIDER THE LILIES OF THE FIELD.'; 97-99: 'A TESTIMONY.'; 101: 'SLEEP AT SEA.'; 103-111: 'FROM HOUSE TO HOME.'; 113: 'OLD AND NEW YEAR DITTIES.'; 115: 'AMEN.'; 117: 'MOTHER COUNTRY.'; 119: no RT; 121-139: 'THE PRINCE'S PROGRESS.'; 141-147: 'MAIDEN-SONG.'; 149-151: 'JESSIE CAMERON.'; 153: 'SPRING QUIET.'; 155: 'THE POOR GHOST.'; 157-159: 'DREAM-LOVE.'; 161: 'TWICE.'; 163-165: 'SONGS IN A CORNFIELD.'; 167-169: 'A YEAR'S WINDFALLS.'; 171: 'ONE DAY.'; 173-175: 'A BIRD'S-EYE VIEW.'; 177: '"TO-DAY FOR ME."'; 179: 'ON THE WING.'; 181: 'BEAUTY IS VAIN.'; 183: 'LADY MAGGIE.'; 185: 'SUMMER.'; 187: 'AUTUMN.'; 189-191: 'THE GHOST'S PETITION.'; 193: 'MEMORY.'; 195-201: 'A ROYAL PRINCESS.'; 203: 'VANITY OF VANITIES.'; 205: 'L. E. L.'; 207: 'BIRD OR BEAST?'; 209: 'EVE.'; 211: 'GROWN AND FLOWN.'; 213: 'A FARM WALK.'; 215: 'SOMEWHERE OR OTHER.'; 217: 'CHILD'S TALK IN APRIL.'; 219: 'GONE FOREVER.'; 221-237: 'UNDER THE ROSE.'; 239: 'SONG.'; 241: 'DAYS OF VANITY.'; 243: 'AUTUMN VIOLETS.'; 245: 'A BETTER COUNTRY DESIRED.'; 247: 'A BRIDE SONG.'; 249-259: 'THE LOWEST ROOM.'; 261: 'A DAUGHTER OF EVE.'; 263: 'BIRD RAPTURE.'; 265: 'TWILIGHT NIGHT.'; 267: 'AMOR MUNDI.'; 269: 'A CHRISTMAS CAROL.'; 271-273: 'BY THE WATERS OF BABYLON.'; 275: 'PARADISE.'; 277: 'UPLIFTING OF EYES.'; 279: 'SAINTS AND ANGELS.'; 281: 'AFTER COMMUNION.'; 283: 'WHO SHALL DELIVER ME?'; 285-287: no RT; 289: 'LONG BARREN.'; 291: 'DOST THOU NOT CARE?'; 293-295: 'MARTYRS' SONG.'; 297: 'AFTER THIS THE JUDGMENT.'; 299: 'GOOD FRIDAY.'

Versos: ii-vi: no RT; viii-x: 'CONTENTS.'; xi-2: no RT; 4-22: 'GOBLIN MARKET.'; 24: 'DREAM-LAND.'; 26: 'FROM SUNSET TO STAR RISE.'; 28: 'LOVE FROM THE NORTH.'; 30: 'A DIRGE.'; 32: 'NOBLE SISTERS.'; 34: 'SPRING.'; 36: 'THE LAMBS OF GRASMERE.'; 38: 'REMEMBER.'; 40: 'AN END.'; 42: 'MY DREAM.'; 44: 'THE HOUR AND THE GHOST.'; 46: 'A SUMMER WISH.'; 48: 'SONG.'; 50: 'MAUDE CLARE.'; 52: 'WINTER: MY SECRET.'; 54: 'A PEAL OF BELLS.'; 56: '"NO, THANK YOU, JOHN."'; 58: 'A PAUSE OF THOUGHT.'; 60: 'TWILIGHT CALM.'; 62: 'WIFE TO HUSBAND.'; 64: 'SHUT OUT.'; 66: 'SONG.'; 68: 'BITTER FOR SWEET.'; 70: 'THE FIRST SPRING DAY.'; 72-76: 'THE CONVENT THRESHOLD.'; 78-80: no RT; 82: 'A BRUISED REED SHALL HE NOT BREAK.'; 84-86: 'ADVENT.'; 88: 'THE THREE ENEMIES.'; 90-92: 'CHRISTIAN AND JEW.'; 94: 'SYMBOLS.'; 96: 'THE WORLD.'; 98: 'A TESTIMONY.'; 100-102: 'SLEEP AT SEA.'; 104-110: 'FROM HOUSE TO HOME.'; 112: 'FROM HOUSE TO HOME'; 114: 'OLD AND NEW YEAR DITTIES.'; 116-118: 'MOTHER COUNTRY.'; 120-138: 'THE PRINCE'S PROGRESS.'; 140-146: 'MAIDEN-SONG.'; 148: 'JESSIE-CAMERON.'; 150-152: 'JESSIE CAMERON.'; 154: 'THE POOR GHOST.'; 156: 'A PORTRAIT.'; 158: 'DREAM-LOVE.'; 160: 'TWICE.'; 162-164: 'SONGS IN A CORNFIELD.'; 166-168: 'A YEAR'S WINDFALLS.'; 170: 'THE QUEEN OF HEARTS.'; 172-174: 'A BIRD'S-EYE VIEW.'; 176: 'GERMAN-FRENCH CAMPAIGN.'; 178: '"TO-DAY FOR ME."'; 180: 'CONSIDER.'; 182: 'MAGGIE A LADY.'; 184: 'WHAT WOULD I GIVE?'; 186: 'SUMMER.'; 188: 'AUTUMN.'; 190-192: 'THE GHOST'S PETITION.'; 194: 'MEMORY.'; 196-200: 'A ROYAL PRINCESS.'; 202: 'SHALL I FORGET?'; 204: 'L. E. L.'; 206: 'LIFE AND DEATH.'; 208-210: 'EVE.'; 212-214: 'A FARM WALK.'; 216: 'A CHILL.'; 218: 'CHILD'S TALK IN APRIL.'; 220-238: 'UNDER THE ROSE.'; 240: 'DAYS OF VANITY.'; 242: 'ENRICA, 1865.'; 244: 'A BETTER COUNTRY DESIRED.'; 246: 'A GREEN CORNFIELD.'; 248: 'A BRIDE SONG.'; 250-260: 'THE LOWEST ROOM.'; 262: 'VENUS' LOOKING-GLASS.'; 264: 'MY

FRIEND.'; 266: 'A BIRD SONG.'; 268: 'AMOR MUNDI.'; 270: 'A CHRISTMAS CAROL.'; 272: 'BY THE WATERS OF BABYLON.'; 274: 'PARADISE.'; 276: 'UPLIFTING OF EYES.'; 278: 'SAINTS AND ANGELS.'; 280: 'THE VEXED HEART.'; 282: 'A ROSE PLANT IN JERICHO.'; 284: 'WHO SHALL DELIVER ME?'; 286: no RT; 288: 'DESPISED AND REJECTED.'; 290: 'IF ONLY.'; 292: 'WEARY IN WELL-DOING.'; 294: 'MARTYRS' SONG.'; 296-298: 'AFTER THIS THE JUDGMENT.'; 300: 'THE LOWEST PLACE.'

Binding: Dot-and-line-patterned cloth (GTT 110), moderate reddish brown (Centroid 43) or dark green (Centroid 146). Front: blind-stamped thick and thin rule borders, with center gilt signature 'Christina G. Rossetti.' Back: same, without signature. Spine: '[ornamented band: between two thin horizontal rules, a row of ovals alternating with vertical lines of three dots] | CHRISTINA | ROSSETTI'S | POEMS | [publisher's device, "RB"] | [ornamented band same as at head]'. Endpapers: coated papers, moderate brown (Centroid 58) or dark grayish reddish brown (Centroid 47), with one wove paper binder's leaf between endpapers and sheets, front and back. Edges: top edge gilt, fore-edge and tail trimmed.

Publication: No later than May 1876. Printed from corrected and revised plates of 1872 combined with newly-set pages.

A copy of 1872 with corrections by Rossetti was owned by John Quinn and included in the auction catalog of his library. The book included "numerous" changes to accidentals in Rossetti's hand, as well as text changes on three pages (23, 34 and 52), a "new stanza of five lines" inserted in "The Prince's Progress" (136) and "three new lines" inserted in "Under the Rose" (229) (Quinn 798-799). The catalog states that the revisions were "for the new edition of 1876," and the book apparently included an ALS to Rossetti's publishers (Roberts Brothers?) referring to their "new edition." Neither the book nor the letter listed in the Quinn catalogue has been located. Crump notes that the revisions mentioned in the Quinn catalogue correspond to revisions present in the Macmillan edition of 1875 (*Complete Poems* I: 7).

CGR's correspondence with Macmillan indicates that by March 1875, Roberts Brothers had requested permission to publish a revised version of Rossetti's *Poems*, and that by August, Macmillan had sent Roberts Brothers proof sheets of the 1875 collected edition at Rossetti's request (*Letters* 2: 44, 53).

Announced among Roberts Brothers' New Publications in the *New York Times*, (4 May 1876: 5) as "A new revised edition, with more than fifty additional pages of new poems. 16 mo. Price, $1.50."

Reviewed in the *New York Times* (3 June 1876: 5); *Godey's Lady's Book and Magazine* (July 1876: 93).

Printing: <u>ii</u>: '[circular device, 21 x 24: winged child holding scepter, seated on globe, reading book, foliage at either side of globe & scroll at bottom with motto 'QUI LEGIT REGIT.'] | AUTHOR'S EDITION, REVISED AND ENLARGED. | 1876. | *Cambridge: Press of John Wilson & Son.*'

Note one: The title page vignette consists of the illustration and caption that had appeared on the engraved title in the previous Macmillan and Roberts Brothers editions.

Note two: Roberts Brothers' desire to reuse existing plates accounts for the marked difference in arrangement of poems in this volume as compared to Macmillan 1875, as Roberts Brothers either substitutes new poems in place of old ones (as in the replacement of "Cousin Kate" with "A Dirge" and "Confluents" on 30-31), inserts new poems into blank spaces (as in the addition of "Song" on 239) or inserts entirely new pages (240-284). The reuse of 1872 plates also results in several running titles remaining unchanged from previous impressions, despite changes in poem titles; see, for example, 'THE ONE CERTAINTY.' (89) and 'LADY MAGGIE.' (183). The incorrect running title 'JESSIE-CAMERON.' (148) is also retained. Previously noted type damage to running titles is still visible, as on 236 (damage to final 'E' in 'ROSE.'), but some type damage within the text is corrected, for example, the double closing quotation marks on the subtitle on 220.

Locations: Ives; TxCM.

A12.1b   *First Edition, Second Printing (First Subedition) (1880)*

Same as 1876 printing except:

Title Page: Date changed to 1880.

Contents: <u>ii</u>: last two lines read 'UNIVERSITY PRESS: | JOHN WILSON & SON, CAMBRIDGE.'

Typography and paper: Laid paper pattern same as 1876, but slightly thinner.

Binding: Two forms noted, priority undetermined:

Binding A: Dotted-line-patterned cloth (GTT 108), dark green (Centroid 146). Front: near top edge, gilt signature 'Christina G. Rossetti.' and in center, blind-stamped diagonal lines forming an X shape. Back: blind-stamped Roberts Brothers device, shield with initials "R B" on either side of an anchor. Spine: [ornamented band, within top and bottom horizontal rules, two branches crossed at center with blossoms at ends] | CHRISTINA | ROSSETTI'S | POEMS | [ornament, foliage] | [floral ornament, pointing up] | [within rectangular compartment, text in italic] 'Roberts Bros.' Endpapers: pattern of light grayish olive (Centroid 109) foliage on white paper. Top edge stained moderate greenish yellow (Centroid 102); other edges trimmed, plain. Location: DAM.

Binding B: Fine diagonal rib pattern cloth, light olive brown (Centroid 94) or very dark green (Centroid 147). Front: in gilt, near top, signature 'Christina G. Rossetti.' with two small circular ornaments, one above signature (towards the left) and another below signature (towards the right). Back: plain. Spine: in gilt, 'CHRISTINA | ROSSETTI'S | POEMS | [horizontal rule] | [small circular ornament, similar to front]'. Endpapers: same as binding A or coated paper, dark grayish blue (Centroid 187). Edges: top edge gilt, fore-edge and tail plain, trimmed. Locations: Ives.

Locations: DAM; Ives (2).

A12.1c.i   *First Edition, Later Printing, Tall Issue (First Subedition) (1896)*

Same as 1880 except:

Title Page: Date changed to 1896.

Pagination: Same except preliminaries, <u>i-vi</u> vii-ix <u>x</u> <u>3</u>.

Plates: Four plates, all with tissue guards; some designs same as A4, as follows:
1) Facing title, portrait of CGR by DGR. This is the same portrait that appears in A16, but enlarged (113.5 h x 76 w), with single rule border, and without caption.
2) Facing <u>3</u>, frontispiece from the 1865 Macmillan *Goblin Market* as reproduced in Roberts Brothers 1866, 1872 (A4).
3) Facing 119, vignette and caption (76 x 85, height measured with caption) from the engraved title page of 1866 Macmillan *Prince's Progress* as reproduced in Roberts Brothers 1866, 1872 (A4).
4) Facing 139, frontispiece and caption (150 x 97.3, height measured with caption) from the 1866 Macmillan *Prince's Progress* as reproduced in Roberts Brothers 1866, 1872 (A4).

Collation: (175 x 120): [1² 2-20⁸]. Retains obsolete signing for 12s as in 1786/1880.

Contents: same except preliminaries: <u>iv</u>: "THE AUTHOR TO HER AMERICAN | READERS'; <u>v</u>: 'CONTENTS'; <u>x</u>: blank; <u>3</u>: text (no half-title before text).

Typography and paper: Wove paper, unwatermarked.

Running titles: same except preliminaries, as follows:

Rectos: <u>i</u>-<u>v</u>: no RT; vi-ix: 'CONTENTS.'

Versos: <u>ii</u>-<u>iv</u>: no RT; vi-vii: 'CONTENTS.'; x: no RT.

Binding: Two forms noted, priority undetermined:

Binding A: Fine diagonal rib cloth, color between dark yellowish brown (Centroid 78) and dark grayish yellowish brown (Centroid 81). Front and back: plain. Spine: in silver ink, 'CHRISTINA | ROSSETTI'S | POEMS | ["RB" device]'. Endpapers: white wove paper. One laid paper binder's leaf precedes and follows sheets. Edges trimmed. Boards: 181 x 119 mm. Location: Ives.

Binding B: Similar to 1880 form B. Fine diagonal rib cloth, dark bluish green. Front: in addition to the gilt signature and two circular ornaments, black ink horizontal rule at head and tale, and to the side and beneath gilt, three black ink stamped squares with floral ornamentation. Back: plain. Spine obscured by repair tape. Location: IDeKN.

Note one: The removal of the half-title page results in the irregular pagination in the preliminaries between <u>x</u> and <u>3</u>.

Locations: Ives; IDeKN (incomplete copy).

A12.1c.ii   *First Edition, Later Printing, Short Issue (First Subedition) (1896)*

Same as other 1896 copies, but with shorter leaves and boards and title change on spine.

Collation: leaf size 170 x 115.

Binding: Linen textured cloth, moderate olive (Centroid 107). Front and back: plain. Spine: in silver ink, 'THE | Goblin | Market | AND OTHER | •Poems• | ["RB" device].' Edges trimmed, plain. Endpapers: white laid paper. One laid paper binder's leaf precedes and follows sheets. Boards: 175 x 113 mm.

Location: Ives.

A13 SEEK AND FIND (1879)

A13.1a *First Edition, First Printing (1879)*

See *Note one*:

SEEK AND FIND | A DOUBLE SERIES OF SHORT STUDIES | OF THE | BENEDICITE. | BY | CHRISTINA G. ROSSETTI. | "Treasure hid in a field." – St. Matthew xiii. 44. | [rule, 8.3] | PUBLISHED UNDER THE DIRECTION OF THE TRACT COMMITTEE. | [rule, 8] | LONDON: | SOCIETY FOR PROMOTING CHRISTIAN KNOWLEDGE. | NORTHUMBERLAND AVENUE, CHARING CROSS; | 4, ROYAL EXCHANGE; AND 48, PICCADILLY. | New York: Pott, Young, & Co.

Pagination: 1-5 6-10 11-13 14-165 166-169 170-327 328.

Collation: (171 x 118): B⁸ C-X⁸ Y⁴. $1, 2 signed. 164 leaves.

Contents: 1: title; 2: blank; 3: 'PREFATORY NOTE.' signed 'C.G.R.'; 4: blank; 5: 'THE BENEDICITE.'; 11: section half-title 'THE FIRST SERIES:| CREATION.'; 12: blank; 13: 'ALL WORKS.'; 16: 'ANGELS.'; 20: 'HEAVENS.'; 23: 'WATERS ABOVE THE | FIRMAMENT.'; 25: 'POWERS.'; 29: 'SUN AND MOON.'; 35: 'STARS.'; 39: 'SHOWERS AND DEW.'; 43: 'WINDS.'; 49: 'FIRE AND HEAT.'; 55: 'WINTER AND SUMMER.'; 57: 'DEWS AND FROSTS.'; 60: 'FROST AND COLD.'; 64: 'ICE AND SNOW.'; 68: 'NIGHTS AND DAYS.'; 73: 'LIGHT AND DARKNESS.'; 80: 'LIGHTNINGS AND CLOUDS.'; 86: 'EARTH.'; 90: 'MOUNTAINS AND HILLS.'; 96: 'GREEN THINGS.'; 103: 'WELLS.'; 106: 'SEAS AND FLOODS.'; 110: 'WHALES AND ALL THAT MOVE | IN THE WATERS.'; 116: 'FOWLS OF THE AIR.'; 121: 'BEASTS AND CATTLE.'; 127: 'CHILDREN OF MEN.'; 135: 'ISRAEL.'; 140: 'PRIESTS.'; 144: 'SERVANTS OF THE LORD.'; 150: 'SPIRITS AND SOULS OF THE | RIGHTEOUS.'; 155: 'HOLY AND HUMBLE MEN OF | HEART.'; 162: 'ANANIAS, AZARIAS, AND | MISAEL.'; 166: blank; 167: section half-title 'THE SECOND SERIES. | REDEMPTION.'; 168: blank; 169: 'ALL WORKS.'; 171: 'ANGELS.'; 174: 'HEAVENS.'; 179: 'WATERS ABOVE THE | FIRMAMENT.'; 182: 'POWERS.'; 187: 'SUN AND MOON.'; 192: 'STARS.'; 197: 'SHOWERS AND DEW.'; 200: 'WINDS.'; 204: 'FIRE AND HEAT.'; 210: 'WINTER AND SUMMER.'; 214: 'DEWS AND FROSTS.'; 217: 'FROST AND COLD.'; 221: 'ICE AND SNOW.'; 225: 'NIGHTS AND DAYS.'; 235: 'LIGHT AND DARKNESS.'; 240: 'LIGHTNINGS AND CLOUDS.'; 245: 'EARTH.'; 252: 'MOUNTAINS AND HILLS.'; 259: 'GREEN THINGS.'; 267: 'WELLS.'; 271: 'SEAS AND FLOODS.'; 276: 'WHALES AND ALL THAT MOVE | IN THE WATERS.'; 280: 'FOWLS OF THE AIR.'; 285: 'BEASTS AND CATTLE.'; 292: 'CHILDREN OF MEN.'; 299: 'ISRAEL.'; 305: 'PRIESTS.'; 310: 'SERVANTS OF THE LORD.'; 316: 'SPIRITS AND SOULS OF THE | RIGHTEOUS.'; 321: 'HOLY AND HUMBLE MEN OF | HEART.'; 325: 'ANANIAS, AZARIAS, AND | MISAEL.'; 327: text and printer's imprint; 328: blank.

Typography and paper: (133)122.3 x 76.3 (p. 33); 26 lines per page. Pages 5-10 printed in three columns separated by vertical rules. Wove paper, unwatermarked.

Running titles:

Rectos: 1-13: no RT; 15: 'ALL WORKS.'; 17-19: 'ANGELS.'; 21: 'HEAVENS.'; 23: 'WATERS ABOVE THE FIRMAMENT.'; 25-27: 'POWERS.'; 29-33: 'SUN AND MOON.'; 35-37: 'STARS.'; 39-41: 'SHOWERS AND DEW.'; 43-47: 'WINDS.'; 49-53: 'FIRE AND HEAT.'; 55: 'WINTER AND SUMMER.'; 57-59: 'DEWS AND FROSTS.'; 61-63: 'FROST AND COLD.'; 65-67: 'ICE AND SNOW.'; 69-71: 'NIGHTS AND DAYS.'; 73-79: 'LIGHT AND DARKNESS.'; 81-85: 'LIGHTNINGS AND CLOUDS.'; 87-89: 'EARTH.'; 91-95: 'MOUNTAINS AND HILLS.'; 97-101: 'GREEN THINGS.'; 103-105: 'WELLS.'; 107-109: 'SEAS AND FLOODS.'; 111-115: 'ALL THAT MOVE IN THE WATERS.'; 117-119: 'FOWLS OF THE AIR.'; 121-125: 'BEASTS AND CATTLE.'; 127-133: 'CHILDREN OF MEN.'; 135-139: 'ISRAEL.'; 141-143: 'PRIESTS.'; 145-149: 'SERVANTS OF THE LORD.'; 151-153: 'SPIRITS AND SOULS OF THE RIGHTEOUS.'; 155-161: 'HOLY AND HUMBLE MEN OF HEART.'; 163-165: 'ANANIAS, AZARIAS,

AND MISAEL.'; 167-169: no RT; 171-173: 'ANGELS.'; 175-177: 'HEAVENS.'; 179-181: 'WATERS ABOVE THE FIRMAMENT.'; 183-185: 'POWERS.'; 187-191: 'SUN AND MOON.'; 193-195: 'STARS.'; 197-199: 'SHOWERS AND DEW.'; 201-203: 'WINDS.'; 205-209: 'FIRE AND HEAT.'; 211-213: 'WINTER AND SUMMER.'; 215: 'DEWS AND FROSTS.'; 217-219: 'FROST AND COLD.'; 221-223: 'ICE AND SNOW.'; 225-233: 'NIGHTS AND DAYS.'; 235-239: 'LIGHT AND DARKNESS.'; 241-243: 'LIGHTNINGS AND CLOUDS.'; 245-251: 'EARTH.'; 253-257: 'MOUNTAINS AND HILLS.'; 259-265: 'GREEN THINGS.'; 267-269: 'WELLS.'; 271-275: 'SEAS AND FLOODS.'; 277-279: 'ALL THAT MOVE IN THE WATERS.'; 281-283: 'FOWLS OF THE AIR.'; 285-291: 'BEASTS AND CATTLE.'; 293-297: 'CHILDREN OF MEN.'; 299-303: 'ISRAEL.'; 305-309: 'PRIESTS.'; 311-315: 'SERVANTS OF THE LORD.'; 317-319: 'SPIRITS AND SOULS OF THE RIGHTEOUS.'; 321-323: 'HOLY AND HUMBLE MEN OF HEART.'; 325-327: 'ANANIAS, AZARIAS, AND MISAEL.'

Versos: 2-12: no RT; 14-164: 'SEEK AND FIND.'; 166-168: no RT; 170-326: 'SEEK AND FIND.'; 328: no RT.

Binding: Calico cloth, light grayish blue (CaBVaU, copies with 22-9-79 and 1-10-84 advertisements) or dark grayish blue (Centroid 187, PBm) or very dark bluish green (Centroid 166, all other copies). Front: Black stamped design at top and bottom, text in gilt. Design at top, near the edge, includes a horizontal black rule which intersects with a semicircular design (an outer single curved rule, an inner thin-thick-thin curved rule, and within the curved rules, a geometric design with a diamond pattern and flower petals) in the upper right corner. The same design, reversed (horizontal rule intersects with circular design at lower left corner) appears near the bottom edge. Below the top rule, text in gilt: 'SEEK AND FIND | *CHRISTINA ROSSETTI.*' Back: One black stamped rule extending from front, across spine, to back cover. Spine: in black (first rule only) and gilt, with small caps: '[rule] | SEEK | AND | FIND | [gilt rule] | CHRISTINA | ROSSETTI | ["SPCK" device]'; all copies have chevron bar in 'A' in 'AND' on front and spine. Endpapers: coated paper, several colors noted, priority undetermined: brownish gray (Centroid 64; PBm, NjP); grayish brown (Centroid 66; Ives, TxU); reddish brown, dark brown (CaBVaU); blackish brown (BL). Edges trimmed.

With one exception (BL), all copies contain two to four pages of advertisements following the text, as follows:

1) Two leaf advertisements, dated 22-9-79 (CaBVaU; NjP; Ives; BL, Ashley copy; TxU, TxLT):
   1: 'PUBLICATIONS | OF THE | [black letter] Society for Promoting Christian Knowledge.'; information about ornamental bindings; seven titles, *Australia's Heroes* through *Fifth Continent (The)*; 2: eleven titles, *For Faith and Fatherland* through *King's Warrant (The)*; 3: ten titles, *Kitty Bligh's Birthday* through *Owen Hartley; Or, Ups and Downs*; 4: nine titles, *Percy Trevor's Training* through *Wilford Family (The): or, Hero Worship in the Schoolroom* and at bottom, list of depositories.

2) Two leaf advertisements, dated 3-5-80 (PBm):
   1: eight titles, *Steps to Faith* through *Some Witnesses for the Faith*; 2: ten titles, *Theism and Christianity* through *Scripture Doctrine of Creation*; 3: ten titles, *Thoughts on the First Principles of the Positive* through *When was the Pentateuch Written?*; 4: eight titles, *The Credibility of Mysteries* through *The Origin of the World According to Revelation and Science*.

3) Two leaf advertisements, dated 1-10-84 (see Colbeck, entry 17, p. 690):
   1: 'Society for Promoting Christian Knowledge. | [rule] | [black letter] Publications on | THE CHRISTIAN EVIDENCE. | [short rule]'; ten titles, *Christianity Judged by its Fruits* through *Theism and Christianity*; 2: twelve titles, *Being of God, Six Addresses on the* through *Scripture Doctrine of Creation*; 3: twelve titles, *The Witness of the Heart to Christ* through *The Credibility of Mysteries*; 4: eleven titles, *The Gospels of the New Testament* through *What is Natural Theology*.

4) Four leaf advertisements (AL):
   1: 'PUBLICATIONS | OF THE | Society for Promoting Christian Knowledge.'; five titles, *Star Atlas* through *Sinai And Jerusalem*; 2: ten titles, *Bible Places* through *A Chapter of English Church History*; 3: eleven titles, *Africa, seen through its Explorers* through *Man and his Handiwork*; 4: three headings: 'DIOCESAN HISTORIES.' (16 titles) 'HEROES OF LITERATURE' (1 title) 'HEROES OF SCIENCE.'

(5 titles); 5: two headings: 'COMMENTARY ON THE BIBLE.' (7 vols) 'THE ROMANCE OF SCIENCE.' (9 titles); 6: heading 'CHRISTIAN EVIDENCE | PUBLICATIONS. | BOOKS.' (13 titles); 7: sixteen titles, *The Analogy of Religion* through *Paley's Horae Paulinae*; 8: sixteen titles, *Religion and Morality* through *What is Natural Theology?*

Publication: October 1879. In March 1879, the SPCK's General Literature Committee rejected CGR's MS (Kent and Stanwood, 221). By 21 July, however, CGR reported to WMR that she had sold the copyright for "a little book" to SPCK for £40 (*Letters* 2: 204). By July 25, she had finished reading "all the proofs and even the revises" (*Letters* 2: 206), but the book was not published until October (*Letters* 2: 213). CGR sold the MS to Charles Fairfax Murray in August 1879 for £10 (*Letters* 2: 209-211). A MS, retaining Rossetti's original title, "Treasure-Trove," is held by the Fitzwilliam Museum, Cambridge (Kent and Stanwood 220), and from their description seems to be the Murray MS. This MS "differs from the printed text in many respects, including verbal changes" (Kent and Stanwood 220).

Early mention in the *Athenaeum* (30 August 1879: 274) and later advertised in SPCK's "new publications" (4 October 1879: 422). Reviewed in the *Examiner* (6 December 1879: 1581); *Saturday Review* (6 December 1879: 704).

Price: 2s. 6d.

BL depository copy: 'BRITISH MUSEUM 27 NOV 57'.

Printing: 327: 'CLARENDON PRESS, OXFORD. | FOR THE SOCIETY FOR PROMOTING CHRISTIAN KNOWLEDGE.'

Note one: As noted in Colbeck, in all copies examined, the last line of the title page ("New York: Pott, Young, & Co." is in darker type (Colbeck 690).

Note two: In some copies, the binding is stapled, not sewn (CaBVaU, both copies; Ives; NjP; TxU).

Locations: AL; BL (2); CaBVaU (2); Ives; PBm (2); NjP; TxU; TxLT (rebound).

Presentation copies: NjP: inscribed "Mrs Heimann with her old friend's love."

A13.1b   *First Edition, Second Printing (1906)*

Not seen; title page transcription from image provided by Boston University.

SEEK AND FIND | A DOUBLE SERIES OF SHORT STUDIES | OF THE | BENEDICITE. | BY THE LATE | CHRISTINA G. ROSSETTI. | "Treasure hid in a field." – St. Matthew xiii. 44. | [short rule] | PUBLISHED UNDER THE DIRECTION OF THE TRACT COMMITTEE. | [short rule] | LONDON: | SOCIETY FOR PROMOTING CHRISTIAN KNOWLEDGE. | NORTHUMBERLAND AVENUE, W.C.; | BRIGHTON: 129, North Street. | New York: E. S. GORHAM. | 1906.

Location: School of Theology Library at MBU.

A14 CALLED TO BE SAINTS (1881)

A14.1a *First Edition, First Printing (1881)*

Within rule frame, 144 x 94; see *Typography*:
CALLED TO BE SAINTS: | THE | <u>Minor Festivals</u> | DEVOTIONALLY STUDIED, | BY | CHRISTINA G. ROSSETTI, | AUTHOR OF "SEEK AND FIND." | [wavy rule, 16.3] | "<u>Ye</u> <u>are</u> <u>God's</u> <u>husbandry</u>, <u>ye</u> <u>are</u> <u>God's</u> <u>building</u>." | i Cor. iii. 9. | "<u>That</u> <u>our</u> <u>sons</u> <u>may</u> <u>grow</u> <u>up</u> <u>as</u> <u>the</u> <u>young</u> <u>plants</u>: | <u>and</u> <u>that</u> <u>our</u> <u>daughters</u> <u>may</u> <u>be</u> <u>as</u> <u>the</u> <u>polished</u> <u>corners</u> | <u>of</u> <u>the</u> <u>temple</u>."–Ps. cxliv. 12. | [rule, 16] | PUBLISHED UNDER THE DIRECTION OF THE TRACT COMMITTEE. | [rule, 15.7] | LONDON: | SOCIETY FOR PROMOTING CHRISTIAN KNOWLEDGE: | NORTHUMBERLAND AVENUE, CHARING CROSS; | 43 QUEEN VICTORIA STREET; 48 PICCADILLY; | AND 135 NORTH STREET, BRIGHTON. | [rule, 11.3] | New York: E. & J. B. Young & Co.

Pagination: i-<u>vii</u> viii-xi <u>xii</u>-<u>xiii</u> xiv-xix <u>xx</u> <u>1</u> 2-22 <u>23</u> 24-44 <u>45</u> 46-61 <u>62</u> 63-91 <u>92</u> 93-100 <u>111</u> 112-129 <u>130</u> 131-150 <u>151</u> 152-171 <u>172</u> 173-193 <u>194</u> 195-215 <u>216</u> 217-242 <u>243</u> 244-267 <u>268</u> 269-296 <u>297</u> 298-337 <u>338</u> 339-358 <u>359</u> 360-377 <u>378</u> 379-403 <u>404</u> 405-450 <u>451</u> 452-472 <u>473</u> 474-495 <u>496</u> 497-519 <u>520</u>.

Collation: (172 x 117.3): $\underline{a}^8$ b^2 B-Z^8 Aa-Kk^8 Ll^4. \$1,2 signed (-B2). 280 leaves.

Contents: Type ornaments appear frequently, but are only mentioned here on pages that contain no text. A separate list of botanical drawings follows. All pages are within rule frame (see *Typography*). Black letter <u>underlined</u>.
<u>i</u>: title; <u>ii</u>: ornament, cross, 32 x 32; <u>iii</u>: dedication, 'IN HOPE OF OUR RE-UNION, | TO | THE DEAR AND GRACIOUS MEMORY | OF | <u>My Sister</u>.'; <u>iv</u>: floral ornament, 28 x 25; <u>v</u>: text beginning "Hooker, in Book 5 of his *Ecclesiastical Polity*, speaking"; <u>vi</u>: floral ornament, 21 x 22; <u>viii</u>: 'CONTENTS'; <u>xii</u>: ornament, cross with lilies, 22 x 22; <u>xiii</u>: 'THE KEY TO MY BOOK.'; xviii: poem; <u>xx</u>: ornament, daffodil, 35 x 20; <u>1</u>: '<u>St. Andrew</u>, | APOSTLE.'; 3: 'BIOGRAPHICAL ADDITIONS.'; 6: '*A Prayer for Large-heartedness*.'; 7: 'A Memorial of St. Andrew.'; 17: 'The First Foundation. | <u>Jasper</u>.'; 20: 'The Daisy.'; <u>23</u>: '<u>St. Thomas</u>, | APOSTLE.'; 25: 'BIOGRAPHICAL ADDITIONS.'; 28: '*A prayer for Confidence of Love*.' and 'A Memorial of St. Thomas.'; 39: 'The Second Foundation. | <u>Sapphire</u>.'; 42: 'Ivy.'; <u>45</u>: '<u>St. Stephen</u>, | DEACON.'; 47: 'BIOGRAPHICAL ADDITIONS.'; 51: '*A Prayer for Victory*.'; 52: 'A Memorial of St. Stephen.'; 59: 'Holly.'; <u>62</u>: '<u>St. John</u>, | APOSTLE AND EVANGELIST.'; 70: 'BIOGRAPHICAL ADDITIONS.'; 76: '*A Prayer for Union with Christ*.'; 77: 'A Memorial of St. John the Evangelist.'; 85: 'The Fourth Living Creature. | <u>An Eagle</u>.'; 87: 'The Third Foundation. | <u>A Chalcedony</u>.'; 88: 'Mistletoe.'; 90: poem; <u>92</u>: '<u>Holy Innocents</u>.'; 96: '*A Prayer for Cleansing*.'; 97: 'A Memorial for the Feast of the Holy Innocents.'; 107: 'Groundsel and Chickweed.'; 109: poem; <u>111</u>: '<u>St. Paul</u>, | APOSTLE.'; 113: 'BIOGRAPHICAL ADDITIONS.'; 118: '*A Prayer for Grace*.'; 119: 'A Memorial of St. Paul.'; 127: 'Gorse.'; <u>130</u>: 'THE | <u>Presentation of Christ</u> | IN THE TEMPLE, | AND | <u>Purification of St. Mary</u> | THE VIRGIN.'; 132: '*GLORIES OF THE PRESENTATION*.'; 134: '<u>The Sacred Text</u>.'; 136: 'BIOGRAPHICAL ADDITIONS.'; 138: '*A Prayer for Acceptance in Christ*.' and 'A Memorial of the Presentation and Purification.'; 148: 'The Snowdrop.'; 149: poem; 151: '<u>St. Matthias</u>, | APOSTLE.'; 152: 'BIOGRAPHICAL ADDITIONS.'; 158: '*A Prayer for Holy Fear*.' and 'A Memorial of St. Matthias.'; 167: 'The Fourth Foundation. | <u>An Emerald</u>.'; 169: 'Hepaticas.'; <u>172</u>: '<u>The Annunciation of the</u> | <u>Blessed Virgin Mary</u>.'; 173: '*GLORIES OF THE ANNUNCIATION*.'; 176: '<u>The Sacred Text</u>.'; 182: '*A Prayer for Self-Devotion*.'; 183: 'A Memorial of the Annunciation.'; 191: 'Violets.'; 193: poem; <u>194</u>: '<u>St. Mark</u>, | EVANGELIST.'; 195: 'BIOGRAPHICAL ADDITIONS.'; 200: '*A Prayer for Steadfastness*.'; 201: 'A Memorial of St. Mark.'; 209: 'The First Living Creature. | <u>A Lion</u>.'; 213: 'Wood Sorrel.'; 214: poem; <u>216</u>: '<u>St. Philip</u> | AND | <u>St. James the Less</u>, | APOSTLES.'; 219: 'BIOGRAPHICAL ADDITIONS.'; 225: '*A Prayer for Sympathy of Love*.'; 226: 'A Memorial of St. Philip and St. James.'; 237: 'The Fifth and Sixth Foundations. | <u>Sardonyx and Sardius</u>.'; 239: 'Cowslips and Veronica.'; 242: poem 'Great

or small below,'; 243: 'St. Barnabas, | APOSTLE.'; 250: 'BIOGRAPHICAL ADDITIONS.'; 255: '*A Prayer for Goodwill of Love.*'; 256: 'A Memorial of St. Barnabas.'; 265: 'Honeysuckle.'; 267: poem; 268: 'St. John, | BAPTIST.'; 277: 'BIOGRAPHICAL ADDITIONS.'; 284: '*A Prayer for Conformity to God's Will.*'; 285: 'A Memorial of St. John Baptist.'; 293: 'St. John's Wort: | Dedicated to the Baptist.'; 295: poem; 297: 'St. Peter, | APOSTLE.'; 318: 'BIOGRAPHICAL ADDITIONS.'; 321: '*A Prayer for Repentance unto Love.*'; 323: 'A Memorial of St. Peter.'; 331: 'The Seventh Foundation. | Chrysolyte.'; 333: 'The Yellow Flag.'; 335: poem; 338: 'St. James, | (STYLED THE GREAT), | APOSTLE.'; 342: 'BIOGRAPHICAL ADDITIONS.'; 344: "*A Prayer for Final Perseverance.*'; 345: 'A Memorial of St. James.'; 353: 'The Eighth Foundation. | Beryl.'; 357: 'The Flowering Rush.'; 359: 'St. Bartholomew, | APOSTLE.'; 361: 'BIOGRAPHICAL ADDITIONS.'; 363: '*A Prayer for Progress.*'; 364: 'A Memorial of St. Bartholomew.'; 373: 'The Ninth Foundation. | A Topaz.'; 376: 'Harebells.'; 378: 'St. Matthew, | APOSTLE AND EVANGELIST.'; 379: 'BIOGRAPHICAL ADDITIONS.'; 384: '*A Prayer for Use of Talents.*'; 385: 'A Memorial of St. Matthew.'; 395: 'The Third Living Creature. | An Angel.'; 400: 'The Tenth Foundation. | A Chrysoprase.'; 402: 'The Scarlet Pimpernel.'; 404: 'St. Michael | AND | All Angels.'; 431: '"Things too wonderful for me." *Job* xlii.3.'; 436: 'A Prayer for Angelic Fellowship.'; 437: 'A Memorial for the Feast of St. Michael and | All Angels.'; 446: 'Ferns.'; 450: poem; 451: 'St. Luke, | EVANGELIST.'; 452: 'BIOGRAPHICAL ADDITIONS.'; 455: '*A Prayer for Final Acceptance.*'; 456: 'A Memorial of St. Luke.'; 465: 'The Second Living Creature. | An Ox.'; 470: 'Marigolds.'; 473: 'St. Simon and St. Jude, | APOSTLES.'; 474: 'BIOGRAPHICAL ADDITIONS.'; 478: '*A Prayer of Trembling.*'; 479: 'A Memorial of St. Simon and St. Jude.'; 489: 'The Eleventh and Twelfth Foundations. | A Jacinth and an Amethyst.'; 492: 'Blackberries and Blackthorn.'; 494: poem; 496: 'All Saints.'; 504: '*A Prayer of Desire.*' and 'A Memorial for the Feast of All Saints.'; 515: 'The Arbutus and Grass.'; 518: poem; 520: printer's imprint.

Illustrations: Botanical drawings attributed to Emily Stackhouse, Anne Pratt, or unidentified; see *Publication*:
iv: snowdrop?, 28 x 25; vi: primrose?, 21 x 30; xx: daffodil, 35 x 20; 21: daisy, 31 x 45; 43: ivy, 74 x 65; 60: holly leaf, 44 x 40; 89: mistletoe, 60 x 39; 108: chickweed, 66 x 40; 128: gorse, 75 x 40; 148: snowdrop, 75 x 38; 170: hepaticas, 65 x 72, signed "T? or S? S"; 172: violets, 75 x 53; 214: wood sorrel, 61 x 42, signed "ES"; 240: cowslip and veronica, 68 x 51, signed "ES"; 268: honeysuckle, 94 x 59; 294: St. John's wort, 80 x 56; 334: yellow flag (iris), 79 x 50; 358: flowering rush, 76 x 43; 377: harebell, 76 x 36; 402: scarlet pimpernel, 66 x 47, signed "ES"; 447: maidenhair fern, 96 x 57; 471: marigold, 54 x 65; 493: blackberry, 69 x 55; 516: arbutus, 43 x 69, signed "ES."

Poems (Untitled, identified by first lines): "This near-at-hand land breeds pain by measure," "Jerusalem is built of gold," "They scarcely waked before they slept," "O Firstfruits of our grain," "Herself a rose, who bore the Rose," "Once like a broken bow Mark sprang aside," "Great or small below," "St. Barnabas, with John his sister's son," "Sooner or later: yet at last," "I followed Thee, my God, I followed Thee," "Service and strength, God's Angels and Archangels," "Leaf from leaf Christ knows," "Light is our sorrow for it ends to-morrow."

Typography and paper: (142, signature to top of frame) 122 x 80 (p. 131); 31 lines per page. All text (including running titles and page numbers) within rule frame with ornamental corners, height and width slightly variable, 144-145 x 94-95. The "memorial" sections are printed in columns separated by a 122.7 vertical rule (see p. 163). The highly decorative and patterned typography includes ornamental capitals and various religious or botanical ornaments throughout. Wove paper, unwatermarked.

Running titles: In black letter.
Rectos: i-vii: no RT; ix-xi: 'Contents.'; xiii: no RT; xv-xix: 'The Key to my Book.'; 1: no RT; 3-21: 'St. Andrew, Apostle.'; 23: no RT; 25-43: 'St. Thomas, Apostle.'; 45: no RT; 47-61: 'St. Stephen, Deacon.'; 63-91: 'St. John, Apostle and Evangelist.'; 93-109: 'Holy Innocents.'; 111: no RT; 113-129: 'St. Paul,

Apostle.'; 131-149: 'The Presentation and Purification.'; 151: no RT; 153-171: 'St. Matthias, Apostle.'; 173-193: 'The Annunciation.'; 195-215: 'St. Mark, Evangelist.'; 217-241: 'St. Philip and St. James the Less, Apostles.'; 243: no RT; 245-267: 'St. Barnabas, Apostle.'; 269-295: 'St. John, Baptist.'; 297: no RT; 299-337: 'St. Peter, Apostle.'; 339-357: 'St. James the Great, Apostle.'; 359: no RT; 361-377: 'St. Bartholomew, Apostle.'; 379-403: 'St. Matthew, Apostle and Evangelist.'; 405-449: 'St. Michael and All Angels.'; 451: no RT; 453-471: 'St. Luke, Evangelist.'; 473: no RT; 475-495: 'St. Simon and St. Jude, Apostles.'; 497-519: 'All Saints.'

Versos: ii-vi: no RT; viii-x: 'Contents.'; xii: no RT; xiv-xviii: 'The Key to my Book.'; xix: no RT; 2-60: 'Called to be Saints.'; 62: no RT; 64-90: 'Called to be Saints.'; 92: no RT; 94-128: 'Called to be Saints.'; 130: no RT; 132-170: 'Called to be Saints.'; 172: no RT; 174-192: 'Called to be Saints.'; 194: no RT; 196-214: 'Called to be Saints.'; 216: no RT; 218-266: 'Called to be Saints.'; 268: no RT; 270-336: 'Called to be Saints.'; 338: no RT; 340-376: 'Called to be Saints.'; 378: no RT; 380-402: 'Called to be Saints.'; 404: no RT; 406-494: 'Called to be Saints.'; 496: no RT; 498-518: 'Called to be Saints.'; 520: no RT.

Binding (see *Note one*): Calico cloth, very dark greenish blue (Centroid 175). Front: in black, three sets of seven horizontal lines; each set of lines begins at the left or right edge of the board and extends to meet a set of four concentric black ink rings, with a gilt ornament stamped within the innermost ring. The first set of lines and rings begins at upper left edge of the board and includes a gilt cross within the innermost ring. The second set starts at the right edge of the board and includes a gilt crown within the inner ring. The third set, with lines beginning at the lower left side of the board, includes a gilt chi χ within the inner ring. Back: two sets of black stamped horizontal lines, continued from front and spine. Spine: in gilt, except for horizontal lines, and with chevron-shaped bars in all appearances of the letter A: '[seven horizontal lines, continued from front] | CALLED | TO BE | SAINTS | CHRISTINA G. | ROSSETTI | [seven horizontal lines, continued from front] | [device, "S • P • C • K •" within banner]'. Endpapers: coated paper, black (Centroid 267). Edges stained strong red (Centroid 12).

Three forms of advertisements have been noted, dated 1-2-81 or 22-7-81, as follows:
1) Two leaf advertisement contents, dated 1-2-81 (PBm):
   [1]: nine titles, *Alone with God; or, Helps to Thought and Prayers* through *Church History in England*; [2]: ten titles, *Church History, Sketches of* through *Narrative of a Modern Pilgrimage through Palestine on Horseback, and with Tents*; [3]: thirteen titles, *On the Nature and Office of God the Holy Ghost* to *Scenes in the East*; [4]: ten titles, *Seek and Find* through *Ventures of Faith; or, Deeds of Christian Heroes*.
2) Two leaf advertisement contents, dated 1-2-81 (TxCM):
   1: '[black letter] Society for Promoting Christian Knowledge. | [orn rule] | Publications on | [no black letter] THE CHRISTIAN EVIDENCES.' eight titles, *Steps to Faith* through *Some Witnesses for the Faith*; date in lower left corner; 2: ten titles, *Theism and Christianity* through *Scripture Doctrine of Creation*; 3: ten titles, *Thoughts on the First Principles of the Positive* through *When was the Pentateuch Written?*; 4: eight titles, *The Credibility of Mysteries* through *The Origin of the World*.
3) Two leaf advertisement contents, dated 22-7-81 (BL; CaBVaU, both copies):
   1: '[black letter] Society for Promoting Christian Knowledge. | [orn rule] | Publications on | [no black letter] THE CHRISTIAN EVIDENCES.' eight titles, *Steps to Faith* through *When was the Pentateuch Written?*, date in lower left corner; 2: ten titles, *Theism and Christianity* to *Scripture Doctrine of Creation*; 3: ten titles, *The Witness of the Heart to Christ* through *The Theory of Prayer; with Special Reference*; 4: eight titles, *The Credibility of Mysteries* through *The Origin of the World*.

Publication: October 1881. Rossetti offered the book, titled "Young Plants & Polished Corners," to Macmillan in November 1876 *(Letters* 2: 109), who quickly rejected it, citing "commercial considerations" (Kooistra 143). Rossetti approached the Society for Promoting Christian Knowledge in January 1880, which eventually approved publication in October (Kooistra 145). Rossetti sold the copyright to SPCK for £30 (Account book). Rossetti reported that the book was "in press" in December 1880 (*Letters* 2: 256), but not published until October 1881 (*Letters* 2: 304). The overall complexity of the book's typography may account for the delay, but in any event, the slow production was not, as Kooistra speculates, because of the cost of commissioning an illustrator for the botanical ornaments (Kooistra 153), since nearly all of the ornaments had been used in previously published SPCK titles, notably several botanical works by Charles Alexander Johns, especially *Flowers of the Field*. Some of the botanical illustrations of Rossetti's text can be attributed to Johns's illustrator, Emily Stackhouse (who used the initials "ES"), while a smaller number can be attributed to Anne Pratt (violets, 172; honeysuckle, 266) or have not yet been identified (hepaticas, 170; marigold, 471). CGR offered the MS "of the original (not the compiled), portion" of the book to Charles Fairfax Murray in June (*Letters* 2: 278), but there is no record of the sale in Rossetti's account book. The MS is not extant.

Early mention in the *Athenaeum* (26 February 1881: 300); in SPCK's "New and Recent Publications," the *Academy* (8 October 1881: 1).

American distribution by E & J. B. Young announced in the *New York Times* (4 April 1881: 2); publication announced in the *Publishers' Weekly* (15 October 1881: 488; see *Note two*). American copies priced at $1.50; British copies priced at 5s.

BL depository copy: 'BRITISH MUSEUM 11 OC 81'; stamp legible but not inked.

Reviewed in the *Academy* (5 November 1881: 341); the *Literary Churchman* (11 November 1881: 479).

Printing: 520: 'CLARENDON PRESS, OXFORD. I FOR THE SOCIETY FOR PROMOTING CHRISTIAN KNOWLEDGE.'

Note one: Several copies have stapled bindings.

Note two: Although copies were distributed simultaneously in the United States and Britain, separate issues have not been identified.

Locations: BL; CaBVaU (2 copies); PBm; TxCM.

A14.1b   *First Edition, Later Printing (1883?)*

Same as 1881 printing except:

Title Page: Undated, text unchanged except for the three lines listing SPCK depository information, as follows: 'NORTHUMBERLAND AVENUE, CHARING CROSS, W. C.; I 43, QUEEN VICTORIA STREET, E. C.; I BRIGHTON: 135, NORTH STREET.'

Advertisements: Three forms have been noted, priority undetermined:
1) Two leaf advertising section, undated but including Rossetti's *Time Flies* (1885) (NjP):
   1: heading 'PUBLICATIONS I OF THE I Society for Promoting Christian Knowledge. I [swelled rule] I BOOKS BY THE AUTHOR OF I "*The Chronicles of the SCHÖNBERG-COTTA FAMILY.*"' six titles, *By Thy Cross and Passion* through *An Old Story of Bethlehem*; 2: seven titles, *Three Martyrs of the Nineteenth Century* through *Thought and Characters*; 3: headed "Miscellaneous Publications" ten titles, *Aids to Prayer* through *Peace with God* and including *Called to be Saints*; 4: nine titles, *Perfecting Holiness* through Rossetti's *Time Flies* and including *Seek and Find*.
2) Eight leaf advertising section, undated but including Rossetti's *Time Flies* (1885) (CUY):
   1: heading 'PUBLICATIONS I OF THE I Society for Promoting Christian Knowledge.' eight titles, *Aids to Prayer* through *Christus Comprobator*; includes ad for *Called to be Saints*; 2: nine titles, *Church History in England* through *History of the English Church*; 3: eight titles, *Land of Israel, The* through *Plain Words for Christ*; 4: eight titles, *Readings on the First Lessons* through *Spiritual*

Counsels; 5: seven titles, *Thoughts for Men and Women* through *Turning-Points of General Church History*; 6: two headings "Non-Christian Religious Systems" and "The Heathen World and St. Paul"; 7: two headings "Conversion of the West" and "Ancient History From The Monuments"; 8: heading "The Fathers For English Readers."

3) Two leaf advertising section, dated 1.11.88:
1: heading 'PUBLICATIONS | OF THE | Society for Promoting Christian Knowledge.' and nine titles, *Abbotsnid* through *Baron's Head (The)*; 2: eleven titles, *Behind the Clouds* through *Fortunes of Hassan (The)*; 3: eleven titles, *Great Captain (The)* through *Our Valley*; 4: nine titles, *Percy Trevor's Training* through *Will's Voyages*.

Printing: 520: 'Oxford | PRINTED BY HORACE HART, PRINTER TO THE UNIVERSITY.'

Note one: Although undated, this (presumed second) impression could have been printed no earlier than 1883, when Horace Hart began his tenure at Oxford; note also the advertisements, which indicate that individual copies examined were bound in 1885 or later.

Locations: CoDI, CUY, NjP.

A14.1c   *First Edition, Later Printing (1895)*

Printed from same plates as 1881/1883, with reset title.
Same as 1883 printing except:

CALLED TO BE SAINTS: | THE | Minor Festivals | DEVOTIONALLY STUDIED, | BY THE LATE | CHRISTINA G. ROSSETTI, | AUTHOR OF "SEEK AND FIND." | [wavy rule, 16.3] | "Ye are God's husbandry, ye are God's building." | i Cor. iii. 9. | "That our sons may grow up as the young plants: | and that our daughters may be as the polished corners | of the temple." – Ps. cxliv. 12. | [rule, 15] | PUBLISHED UNDER THE DIRECTION OF THE TRACT COMMITTEE. | [rule, 15] | LONDON: | SOCIETY FOR PROMOTING CHRISTIAN KNOWLEDGE. | NORTHUMBERLAND AVENUE, W.C.; | 43, QUEEN VICTORIA STREET, E. C.; | BRIGHTON: 129, NORTH STREET. | [rule 11.3] | New York: E. & J. B. YOUNG & CO. | 1895.

Typography and paper: Laid paper, vertical chainlines 27 mm apart. Watermarked with a crown and text "Abbey Mills | Greenfield".

Running titles: same except 347: comma missing after 'Great'.

Binding: Buckram, blackish blue (Centroid 188). Front: in gilt, with chevron-bar A in first line: 'CALLED TO BE SAINTS | *CHRISTINA ROSSETTI*'. Back: plain. Spine, with chevron-bar A: 'CALLED | TO BE | SAINTS | [rule] | CHRISTINA | ROSSETTI | ["SPCK" device].' Endpapers: laid paper, vertical chainlines 24 mm apart. Edges: top edge gilt, fore-edge and tail untrimmed. Binding is sewn, not stapled.

Publication: Listed in the *English Catalogue* with December publication date. Price 5s. Reviewed in the *Expository Times* (January 1896: 211-216).

Locations: Ives; PBm.

A14.1d   *First Edition, Later Printing (1902)*. *Not seen*.

Location: Copy located at University of St. Andrews Library, call number r BV194.C6R7.

A14.1e   *First Edition, Later Printing (1912).*

Not seen; information drawn from an electronic version of University of British Columbia copy.

Title Page: same as 1895 except for presentation of publisher's information: 'SOCIETY FOR PROMOTING CHRISTIAN KNOWLEDGE. | LONDON: NORTHUMBERLAND AVENUE, W. C.; | 43, QUEEN VICTORIA STREET, E.C. | BRIGHTON: 129, NORTH STREET. | 1912.'

Location: CaBVaU (via Internet Archive).

A15   **A PAGEANT AND OTHER POEMS (Macmillan, 1881)**

A15.1   ***First British Edition, Only Printing (1881)***

Some text in <u>black letter</u>:
A PAGEANT | AND | OTHER POEMS | BY | CHRISTINA G. ROSSETTI | <u>London</u> | MACMILLAN AND CO. | 1881 | *The right of translation and reproduction is reserved.*

Pagination: [2] <u>i-vii</u> viii-ix <u>x</u> <u>1-3</u> 4-198 <u>199-200</u>.

Collation: (174 x 120): π² <u>A</u>⁴ B-N⁸ O⁴. $1 signed. 106 leaves.

Contents: [1]-[2]: blank; <u>i</u>: half-title 'A PAGEANT | AND | OTHER POEMS'; <u>ii</u>: circular publisher's device with two Ms in center and four compartments, 19.7 x 19.7; <u>iii</u>: title; <u>iv</u>: printer's imprint; <u>v</u>: poem, first line: 'Sonnets are full of love, and this my tome'; <u>vi</u>: blank; <u>vii</u>: 'CONTENTS.'; <u>x</u>: blank; <u>1</u>: 'THE KEY-NOTE.'; <u>2</u>: blank; 3-198: text and on 198: printer's imprint; <u>199-200</u>: blank.

Poems: "Sonnets are full of love, and this my tome," "The Key-Note," "The Months: A Pageant," "Pastime," "'Italia, Io Ti Saluto!'," "Mirrors of Life and Death," "A Ballad of Boding," "Yet A Little While" ("I dreamed and did not seek: today I seek"), "He and She," "Monna Innominata." (sonnets 1-14), "'Luscious and Sorrowful'," "De Profundus," "Tempus Fugit," "Golden Glories," "Johnny," "'Hollow-Sounding and Mysterious'," "Maiden May," "Till To-Morrow," "Death-Watches," "Touching 'Never'," "Brandons Both," "A Life's Parallels," "At Last," "Golden Silences," "In The Willow Shade," "Fluttered Wings," "A Fisher-Wife," "What's In A Name?," "Mariana," "Memento Mori," "'One Foot On Sea, And One On Shore'," "Buds and Babies," "Boy Johnny," "Freaks of Fashion," "An October Garden," "'Summer is Ended'," "Passing and Glassing," "'I Will Arise'," "A Prodigal Son," "Sœur Louise De La Miséricorde," "An 'Immurata' Sister," "'If Thou Sayest, Behold, We Knew It Not'" (sections 1-3), "The Thread of Life" (sections 1-3), "An Old-World Thicket," "'All Thy Works Praise Thee, O Lord'," "Later Life: A Double Sonnet Of Sonnets" (sonnets 1-28), "'For Thine Own Sake, O My God'," "Until The Day Break," "'Of Him That Was Ready To Perish'," "'Behold the Man!'," "The Descent From The Cross," "'It Is Finished'," "An Easter Carol," "'Behold A Shaking'" (sections 1-2), "All Saints" ("They are flocking from the East"), "'Take Care of Him'," "A Martyr" ("Inner not outer, without gnash of teeth"), "Why?," "'Love Is Strong As Death'" ("I have not sought Thee, I have not found Thee").

Typography and paper: (132.3) 122 x 73 (p. 193); 26 lines per page. Wove paper, unwatermarked.

Running titles: In italic.

Rectos: [1], <u>i-vii</u>: no RT; ix: 'CONTENTS.'; <u>1-3</u>: no RT; 5-21: 'PAGEANT.'; 23: 'PASTIME.'; 25-31: 'MIRRORS OF LIFE AND DEATH.'; 33-41: 'A BALLAD OF BODING.'; 43: 'HE AND SHE.'; 45-57: 'MONNA INNOMINATA'; 59: '"LUSCIOUS AND SORROWFUL."'; 61: 'TEMPUS FUGIT.'; 63-65: 'JOHNNY.'; 67: '"HOLLOW-SOUNDING & MYSTERIOUS."'; 69-73: 'MAIDEN MAY.'; 75: 'DEATH-WATCHES.'; 77-81: 'BRANDONS BOTH.'; 83: 'AT LAST.'; 85-87: 'IN THE WILLOW SHADE.'; 89: 'FLUTTERED WINGS.'; 91: 'WHAT'S IN A NAME?'; 93: 'MARIANA.'; 95: '"ONE FOOT ON SEA,'; 97: 'BUDS AND BABIES.'; 99-101: 'FREAKS OF FASHION.'; 103: 'AN OCTOBER GARDEN.'; 105: 'PASSING AND GLASSING.'; 107: '"I WILL ARISE."'; 109: 'A PRODIGAL SON.'; 111: 'SŒUR LOUISE DE LA MISÉRICORDE.'; 113: 'AN "IMMURATA" SISTER.'; 115: '"IF THOU SAYEST . . ."'; 117-119: 'THE THREAD OF LIFE.'; 121-129: 'AN OLD-WORLD THICKET.'; 131-143: 'O LORD.'" 145-171: 'LATER LIFE.'; 173: 'UNTIL THE DAY BREAK.'; 175: '"READY TO PERISH."'; 177: '"BEHOLD THE MAN."'; 179-181: '"IT IS FINISHED."'; 183: 'AN EASTER CAROL.'; 185: '"BEHOLD A SHAKING."'; 187: 'ALL SAINTS.'; 189: '"TAKE CARE OF HIM."'; 191-195: 'A MARTYR.'; 197: 'WHY?'; 199: no RT.

Versos: [2], ii-vi: no RT; viii: 'CONTENTS.'; x: no RT; 2: no RT; 4-20: 'THE MONTHS:'; 22: 'THE MONTHS: A PAGEANT.'; 24: 'ITALIA, IO TI SALUTO!'; 26-30: 'MIRRORS OF LIFE AND DEATH.'; 32-40: 'A BALLAD OF BODING.'; 42: 'YET A LITTLE WHILE.'; 44-58: 'MONNA INNOMINATA.'; 60: 'DE PROFUNDIS.'; 62: 'GOLDEN GLORIES.'; 64-66: 'JOHNNY.'; 68: '"HOLLOW-SOUNDING & MYSTERIOUS."'; 70-72: 'MAIDEN MAY.'; 74: 'TILL TO-MORROW.'; 76: 'TOUCHING "NEVER."'; 78-80: 'BRANDONS BOTH.'; 82: 'A LIFE'S PARALLELS.'; 84: 'GOLDEN SILENCES.'; 86-88: 'IN THE WILLOW SHADE.'; 90: 'A FISHER-WIFE.'; 92: 'WHAT'S IN A NAME?'; 94: 'MEMENTO MORI.'; 96: 'AND ONE ON SHORE."'; 98: 'BOY JOHNNY.'; 100-102: 'FREAKS OF FASHION.'; 104: '"SUMMER IS ENDED."'; 106: 'PASSING AND GLASSING.'; 108: '"I WILL ARISE."'; 110: 'SŒUR LOUISE DE LA MISÉRICORDE.'; 112: 'AN "IMMURATA" SISTER.'; 114-116: '"IF THOU SAYEST . . ."'; 118: 'THE THREAD OF LIFE.'; 120-128: 'AN OLD-WORLD THICKET.'; 130-142: '"ALL THY WORKS PRAISE THEE,'; 144-166: 'LATER LIFE.'; 168: 'LATER LIFE'[no period]; 170: 'LATER LIFE.'; 172: '"FOR THINE OWN SAKE, O MY GOD."'; 174: 'UNTIL THE DAY BREAK.'; 176: '"READY TO PERISH."'; 178: 'THE DESCENT FROM THE CROSS.'; 180: '"IT IS FINISHED."'; 182: 'AN EASTER CAROL.'; 184: '"BEHOLD A SHAKING."'; 186-188: 'ALL SAINTS.'; 190: '"TAKE CARE OF HIM."'; 192-196: 'A MARTYR.'; 198: '"LOVE IS STRONG AS DEATH."'; 200: no RT.

Binding: Calico cloth, blackish blue (Centroid 188) or dark to very dark greenish blue (Centroid 174-175). Front: in gilt, geometrical design of intersecting rules, with rings placed in groups of three at intersections; the rules extend across the spine. Back: blind-stamped same design as front.

Spine: several forms noted, priority uncertain but may correlate with dated inscriptions, as follows; all spines printed in gilt:

Spine A: (1882): '[2 rings] | [rule] | A | PAGEANT | AND | OTHER POEMS | CHRISTINA G. | ROSSETTI | [rule] | [group of 3 rings, arranged in inverted pyramid] | MACMILLAN & C.ᵒ | [rule]'; the o in 'Co' in last line is lower case, with a period beneath. Also, the bar in letter 'A' in 'Macmillan' is chevron-shaped (pointing down), not straight; bottom rule is thinner (1.3 mm) than Form B. Locations: BL (Ashley), UkCU (library deposit stamp January 1882), TxCM (2, including presentation copy).

Spine B: (1882?): same as form A except bottom rule is 1.9 (nearly 2 mm) thick. Locations: CaBVaU (inscribed and dated 1882), PBm.

Spine C: '[2 rings] | [rule] | A | PAGEANT | AND | OTHER POEMS | CHRISTINA G. | ROSSETTI | [rule] | [group of 3 rings, arranged in inverted pyramid] | MACMILLAN & Cᵒ | [rule]'; straight bars in letter A in Macmillan; the o in 'Co' in last line is lower case, with short rule beneath. Bottom rule about 1.9 mm thick. Locations: NjP (inscribed and dated 1885), MSL (presentation copy, dated 1882).

Spine D: same as Spine C, but the o in 'Co" is small capital, not lower case, with a period rather than a short rule beneath; bottom rule 1.9 mm thick. Location: PBm.

Spine E: '[2 rings] | [rule] | A | PAGEANT | AND | OTHER POEMS | CHRISTINA | ROSSETTI | [rule] | [group of three rings, arranged in inverted pyramid] | MACMILLAN & Cᵒ'; in this form, the 'G' is omitted from Rossetti's name; there are straight bars in the letter A in Macmillan; the o in 'Co' is lower case, with short rule beneath; bottom rule 1.3 mm thick. Location: TxCM.

Spine F: (1890?): '[rule, with ring at either end] | A | PAGEANT | AND | OTHER POEMS | CHRISTINA | ROSSETTI | [thin rule between two rings, ○—○ at ends, .7 mm thick, with group of three small rings arranged in inverted pyramid beneath rule] | MACMILLAN & C.ᵒ | [rule, 1.7 mm]'; note absence of initial 'G' in author's name; rule after 'ROSSETTI' thinner than other spines (.7 mm); rings are slightly larger than other copies; in last line, straight bar 'A' in 'Macmillan'; instead of regular ampersand '&' the ampersand is shaped like a cursive letter 'E'; period after superscript 'o' in 'Co'; boards are also taller than other copies examined, 182 mm vs. 180 mm height. Location: NjP; CaBVaU (inscribed and dated 1890); Baylor.

Endpapers: white wove paper. Edges: top rough trimmed, others untrimmed.

Publication: 1500 copies printed on July 26, 1881 (Editions Book, Macmillan Archives). In April, CGR offered her new volume of poems to Macmillan "on the old terms" (*Letters* 2: 269); as CGR informed DGR, Macmillan accepted the book "without even asking to see it" (*Letters* 2: 272). Apparently Macmillan suggested that the book be stereotyped, but the notation in the Editions Book in the Macmillan Archive indicates that it was printed from type. No further printings are noted. The contract for the publication is at the Macmillan Archive, British Library. Rossetti began receiving proofs in June (*Letters* 2: 276).

Announced in the *Athenaeum* (23 July 1881: 124); London *Times* (28 July 1881: 12).

Price: 6s.

Reviewed in the *Tablet* (*Letters* 2: 297), *St. James's Gazette* (9 August 1881: 13-14), *Academy* (27 August 1881: 152); *Athenaeum* (10 September 1881: 327-328); *British Quarterly Review* (October 1881: 480-481); *London Quarterly Review* (October 1881: 250-253); *Westminster Review* (October 1881: 561-562), *Pall Mall Gazette* (probably September; see *Letters* 2: 303).

Printing: iv, 198: 'Printed by R & R Clark, Edinburgh.'

Locations: Baylor, BL, CaBVaU (3), NjP (3), PBm (2), UkCU, TxCM (3).

Presentation copies: TxCM: undated inscription "F. M. L. R." and poem by William Bell Scott written in CGR's hand; note by WMR presenting the book to Robert and Martha Garnett, dated June 1896. MSL: inscribed to C. L. Dodgson (Lewis Carroll) from CGR, with note "received Nov. 8/82" in Dodgson's hand.

A16   A PAGEANT AND OTHER POEMS (Roberts Brothers, 1881)

See also A17 (Roberts Brothers Second Subedition, 1882), A30 (Little, Brown Subedition, 1898) and A32 (Little, Brown Subedition, 1899).

A16.1a   First American Edition, First Printing (1881)

Same as A15 except:

A PAGEANT | *AND OTHER POEMS* | BY | CHRISTINA G. ROSSETTI | [circular printer's device, 22.3 x 24.3: winged child holding scepter, seated on globe, reading book; foliage on either side of globe & scroll at bottom with motto 'QUI LEGIT REGIT'] | BOSTON | ROBERTS BROTHERS | 1881

Pagination: i-vii viii-ix x [2] 13 14-208. Note the shift from Roman to Arabic numerals in preliminaries.

Collation: (176 x 117): [12°: 1-8¹² 9⁸]. Signed for 8s, 2 (p. 17) to 13 (p. 193); all $1. 104 leaves. See *Note one.*

Contents: i: half-title; ii: advertisement for '*Miss Rossetti's first volume of Poems, containing* | "*The Goblin Market,*" "*The Prince's Progress,*" *&c., in* | *one volume. 16mo. Price $1.50.* | *ROBERTS BROTHERS,* | *Publishers,* | *BOSTON.*'; iii: title; iv: 'AUTHOR'S EDITION.' and printer's imprint; v: poem, first line 'Sonnets are full of love, and this my tome'; vi: blank; vii: 'CONTENTS.'; x: blank; [1]: 'THE KEY-NOTE.'; [2]: blank; 13-208: poems and on 208: printer's imprint.

Poems: same as A15 (Macmillan 1881).

Typography and paper: (136.3) 124.3 x 66.7 (p. 49); various lines per page (up to 26). Laid paper, horizontal chainlines 30 mm apart. Unwatermarked.

Running titles: In italic. All copies have battered type in the headline on page 69.

Rectos: i-vii: no RT; xi: 'CONTENTS.'; [1]: no RT; 13: no RT; 15-31: 'A PAGEANT.'; 33: 'PASTIME.'; 35-41: 'MIRRORS OF LIFE AND DEATH.'; 43-51: 'A BALLAD OF BODING.'; 53: 'HE AND SHE.'; 55-67: 'MONNA INNOMINATA.'; 69: '"LUSCIOUS AND SORROWFUL."'; 71: 'TEMPUS FUGIT.'; 73-75: 'JOHNNY.'; 77: '"HOLLOW-SOUNDING & MYSTERIOUS."'; 79-83: 'MAIDEN MAY.'; 85: 'DEATH-WATCHES.'; 87-91: 'BRANDONS BOTH.'; 93: 'AT LAST.'; 95-97: 'IN THE WILLOW SHADE.'; 99: 'FLUTTERED WINGS.'; 101: 'WHAT'S IN A NAME?'; 103: 'MARIANA.'; 105: '"ONE FOOT ON SEA,'; 107: 'BUDS AND BABIES.'; 109-111: 'FREAKS OF FASHION.'; 113: 'AN OCTOBER GARDEN.'; 115: 'PASSING AND GLASSING.'; 117: '"I WILL ARISE."'; 119: 'A PRODIGAL SON.'; 121: 'SŒUR LOUISE DE LA MISÉRICORDE.'; 123: 'AN "IMMURATA" SISTER.'; 125: '"IF THOU SAYEST . . ."'; 127-129: 'THE THREAD OF LIFE.'; 131-139: 'AN OLD-WORLD THICKET.'; 141-153: 'O LORD."'; 155-181: 'LATER LIFE.'; 183: 'UNTIL THE DAY BREAK.'; 185: '"READY TO PERISH."'; 187: '"BEHOLD THE MAN!"'; 189-191: '"IT IS FINISHED."'; 193: 'AN EASTER CAROL.'; 195: '"BEHOLD A SHAKING."'; 197: 'ALL SAINTS.'; 199: '"TAKE CARE OF HIM."'; 201-205: 'A MARTYR.'; 207: 'WHY?'

Versos: ii-vi: no RT; viii: 'CONTENTS.'; x-[2]: no RT; 14-30: 'THE MONTHS:'; 32: 'THE MONTHS: A PAGEANT.'; 34: '"ITALIA, IO TI SALUTO!"'; 36-40: 'MIRRORS OF LIFE AND DEATH.'; 42-50: 'A BALLAD OF BODING.'; 52: 'YET A LITTLE WHILE.'; 54-68: 'MONNA INNOMINATA.'; 70: 'DE PROFUNDIS.'; 72: 'GOLDEN GLORIES.'; 74-76: 'JOHNNY.'; 78: '"HOLLOW-SOUNDING & MYSTERIOUS."'; 80-82: 'MAIDEN MAY.'; 84: 'TILL TO-MORROW.'; 86: 'TOUCHING "NEVER."'; 88-90: 'BRANDONS BOTH.'; 92: 'A LIFE'S PARALLELS.'; 94: 'GOLDEN SILENCES.'; 96-98: 'IN THE WILLOW SHADE.'; 100: 'A FISHER-WIFE.'; 102: 'WHAT'S IN A NAME?'; 104: 'MEMENTO MORI.'; 106: 'AND ONE ON SHORE."'; 108: 'BOY JOHNNY.'; 110-112: 'FREAKS OF FASHION.';

114: '"SUMMER IS ENDED."'; 116: 'PASSING AND GLASSING.'; 118: '"I WILL ARISE."'; 120: 'SŒUR LOUISE DE LA MISÉRICORDE.'; 122: 'AN "IMMURATA" SISTER.'; 124-126: '"IF THOU SAYEST . . ."'; 128: 'THE THREAD OF LIFE.'; 130-138: 'AN OLD-WORLD THICKET.'; 140-152: '"ALL THY WORKS PRAISE THEE,'; 154-180: 'LATER LIFE.'; 182: '"FOR THINE OWN SAKE, O MY GOD."'; 184: 'UNTIL THE DAY BREAK.'; 186: '"READY TO PERISH."'; 188: 'THE DESCENT FROM THE CROSS.'; 190: '"IT IS FINISHED."'; 192: 'AN EASTER CAROL.'; 194: '"BEHOLD A SHAKING."'; 196-198: 'ALL SAINTS.'; 200: '"TAKE CARE OF HIM."'; 202-206: 'A MARTYR.'; 208: '"LOVE IS STRONG AS DEATH."'.'

Binding: Two forms of binding have been noted, A probably earlier.

Binding A: Fine diagonal rib pattern cloth, medium brown (Centroid 58) or deep brown (Centroid 56) or dark orange yellow (Centroid 72) or dark purplish gray, faded (Centroid 234) or very dark green (Centroid 147). Front: gilt, '[circular ornament] | THE • PAGEANT • | AND OTHER POEMS | [circular ornament] | [signature] Christina G. Rossetti.' The bars on the letters A in "Pageant" and H in "The" and "Other" are chevron-shaped. Back: plain. Spine: in gilt, 'THE | PAGEANT | AND | OTHER POEMS | [rule] | [circular ornament, same as front] | CHRISTINA • G • ROSSETTI'. Edges trimmed, plain (NjP) or top edge stained medium grayish yellow (Centroid 102) or strong greenish yellow (Centroid 99). Endpapers: brownish-white paper printed with floral design (foreground) and vertical lines (background) in dark grayish green (Centroid 151) or grayish olive green (Centroid 127), with one laid paper binder's leaf between endpapers and sheets, front and back (binder's leaves are same paper as sheets). Locations: DAM, Ives, NjP, PBm (2), TxCM.

Binding B: Linen textured cloth, deep red (Centroid 13). Front and back plain. Spine (in silver): 'A | PAGEANT | AND OTHER | • POEMS • | ["RB" device, 16 x 14]'. Edges trimmed, plain. Endpapers: brownish-white laid paper same as sheets, with one laid paper binder's leaf inserted between front free endpaper and text. Leaf height of binding B copy is shorter than that of binding A copies. Location: Ives.

Publication: October 1881. A line for line resetting of the Macmillan volume. In the course of negotiations with Macmillan, CGR asked about plans for American publication, and wrote to Roberts Brothers with Macmillan's approval (*Letters* 2: 271). CGR wrote to Thomas Niles of Roberts Brothers, offering to forego her royalties on the new book to resolve a "clash of interests among us all" since otherwise Roberts Brothers would have to pay CGR as well as Macmillan (*Letters* 2: 275), but in February 1882 CGR received £ 12.4.6 from Roberts Brothers, representing combined royalties from *A Pageant* and *Poem*s; at that point less than 500 copies of *A Pageant* had sold (*Letters* 3: 9).

In August 1881, CGR received a letter from "Boston" informing her that sheets from Macmillan had not yet arrived (*Letters* 2:292). The book was announced as "ready this week" on October 15 (*Publishers' Weekly*: 500).

Advertised in the *New York Times* (19 October 1881: 5).

Price: $1.25.

Reviewed in the *Critic* (24 September 1881: 257); *Literary World* (Boston) (22 October, 1881: 372; 5 November 1881: 395-396); *New York Tribune* (14 November 1881: 6); *Appleton's Journal* (December 1881), *Atlantic Monthly* (January 1882: 121); *Dial* (February 1882: 239-24); *International Review* (February 1882: 213-225).

Printing: <u>iv</u>: 'UNIVERSITY PRESS: | JOHN WILSON AND SON, CAMBRIDGE.'; 208: 'University Press: John Wilson and Son, Cambridge.'

Locations: DAM, Ives (2), NjP, PBm (2), TxCM (presentation copy).

Presentation copies: TxCM: inscription in WMR's hand "W. M. Rossetti from Christina's books 1894."

A17   POEMS (Roberts Brothers Second Subedition, 1882)

See also A4 (Roberts Brothers parent edition, 1866, 1872), A12 (Roberts Brothers first subedition, 1876, 1880) and A16 (Roberts Brothers, *A Pageant*, 1881).

A17.1a   ***Second Subedition, First Printing (1882)*** Combined plates of A12 and A16.

Within red rule frame, see *Typography*:
POEMS. | BY | CHRISTINA G. ROSSETTI. | [vignette, 62 x 69, with caption '"Golden head by golden head"'] | BOSTON: | ROBERTS BROTHERS. | 1882.

Pagination: i-v vi-x 1-3 4-77 78-81 82-118 119 120-284 285-287 288-300 [7] 14-208.

Plates: Two plates, both with tissue guards:
1) Facing title, portrait (109 x 75) of CGR by DGR, whose signature appears in the upper right corner. Letterpress caption: "FROM AN ORIGINAL DRAWING BY DANTE G. ROSSETTI, IN THE POSSESSION OF THE PUBLISHERS.'
2) Facing 3, frontispiece and caption (111 x 92, height measured with caption) from the 1865 Macmillan *Goblin Market* as reproduced in Roberts Brothers 1866 (A4).

Collation: (184 x 122): [1-32⁸]. Obsolete signings retained, as follows: first sections (pp. i-[2]) signed for gathering in 12s ($1, 5) beginning on p. 15 (signed '2') through p. 279 (signed '13'), second section (pp. [3]-208) signed for gathering in 8s ($1) beginning on p. 17 (signed '2') through 193 (signed '13'), but missing signature 3. 256 leaves. See *Note one*.

Contents: i: title; ii: [circular printer's device, 21.7 x 23.3, with winged child holding scepter, seated on globe, reading book; foliage at either side & at bottom scroll with motto 'QUI LEGIT REGIT.'] | 'AUTHOR'S EDITION, REVISED AND ENLARGED. | 1876.' and printer's imprint; iii: dedication, 'TO | MY MOTHER, | IN ALL REVERENCE AND LOVE, | *I INSCRIBE THIS BOOK*.'; iv: 'THE AUTHOR TO HER AMERICAN | READERS.' signed 'CHRISTINA G. ROSSETTI. | London.' (no date); v: 'CONTENTS.'; 1: section half-title 'POEMS.'; 2: blank; 3-77: poems; 78: blank; 79: section half-title 'DEVOTIONAL PIECES.'; 80: blank; 81-284: poems; 285: section half-title 'DEVOTIONAL PIECES'; 286: blank; 287-300: poems; [1]: section half-title 'A PAGEANT | AND | OTHER POEMS.'; [2]: blank; [3]: untitled poem 'Sonnets are full of love, and this my tome'; [4]: blank; [5]: 'THE KEY-NOTE.'; [6]: blank; [7]-208: poems, and on 208 printer's imprint.

Poems: Same poems as in Roberts Brothers 1880 (A12) and 1881 (A16):
"Goblin Market," "In The Round Tower At Jhansi, June 8, 1857," "Dream-Land," "At Home," "From Sunset To Star Rise," "Love From The North," "Winter Rain," "A Dirge" ("Why were you born when the snow was falling?"), "Confluents," "Noble Sisters," "Spring," "The Lambs Of Grasmere, 1860," "A Birthday," "Remember," "After Death," "An End," "My Dream," "Song" ("O roses for the flush of youth"), "The Hour And The Ghost," "A Summer Wish," "An Apple Gathering," "Song" ("Two doves upon the selfsame branch"), "Maude Clare," "Echo," "Winter: My Secret" ["My Secret"], "Another Spring," "A Peal Of Bells," "Fata Morgana," "'No, Thank You, John'," "May" ("I cannot tell you how it was"), "A Pause Of Thought," "Twilight Calm," "Wife To Husband," "Three Seasons," "Mirage," "Shut Out," "Sound Sleep," "Song" ("She sat and sang alway"), "Song" ("When I am dead, my dearest"), "Dead Before Death," "Bitter For Sweet," "'The Master Is Come, And Calleth For Thee,'" "Rest," "The First Spring Day," "The Convent Threshold," "Up-Hill," "'The Love Of Christ Which Passeth Knowledge','" "'A Bruised Reed Shall He Not Break'," "A Better Resurrection," "Advent" ("This Advent moon shines cold and clear"), "The Three Enemies" in three parts, "The Flesh," "The World," "The Devil," "One Certainty," "Christian And Jew," "Sweet Death," "Symbols," "'Consider The Lilies Of The Field'" ("Flowers preach to us if we will hear"), "The World," "A Testimony," "Sleep At Sea,"

"From House To Home," "Old And New Year Ditties" (sections 1-3), "Amen," "Mother Country," "The Prince's Progress," "Maiden-Song," "Jessie Cameron," "Spring Quiet," "The Poor Ghost," "A Portrait" (sections I-II), "Dream-Love," "Twice," "Songs In A Cornfield," "A Year's Windfalls," "The Queen Of Hearts," "One Day," "A Bird's-Eye View," "The German-French Campaign. 1870-1871," in two parts, "I. 'Thy Brother's Blood Crieth,'" and "II. 'To-Day For Me,'" "On The Wing," "Consider," "Beauty Is Vain," "Maggie A Lady," "What Would I Give?," "The Bourne," "Summer" ("Winter is cold-hearted"), "Autumn" ("I dwell alone"), "The Ghost's Petition," "Memory" (sections I-II), "A Royal Princess," "Shall I Forget?," "Vanity Of Vanities" ("Ah, woe is me for pleasure that is vain")," "L. E. L.," "Life And Death," "Bird Or Beast?," "Eve," "Grown And Flown," "A Farm Walk," "Somewhere Or Other," "A Chill," "Child's Talk In April," "Gone Forever," "Under The Rose," "Song" ("Oh what comes over the sea"), "By The Sea," "Days Of Vanity," "Enrica, 1865," "Once For All. (Margaret.)," "Autumn Violets," "'They Desire A Better Country'" (sections I-III), "A Green Cornfield," "A Bride Song," "The Lowest Room," "Dead Hope," "A Daughter Of Eve," "Venus's Looking-Glass," "Love Lies Bleeding," "Bird Raptures," "My Friend," "Twilight Night," "A Bird Song," "A Smile And A Sigh," "Amor Mundi," "A Christmas Carol" ("In the bleak mid-winter"), "By The Waters Of Babylon. B. C. 570," "Paradise," "'I Will Lift Up Mine Eyes Unto The Hills,'" ("I am pale with sick desire"), "Saints And Angels," "'When My Heart Is Vexed, I Will Complain'" ("O Lord, how canst Thou say Thou lovest me"), "After Communion," "A Rose Plant In Jericho," "Who Shall Deliver Me?," "Despised And Rejected," "Long Barren," "If Only," "Dost Thou Not Care?," "Weary In Well-Doing," "Martyrs' Song," "After This The Judgment," "Good Friday" ("Am I a stone and not a sheep"), "The Lowest Place," "Sonnets are full of love, and this my tome," "The Key-Note," "The Months: A Pageant," "Pastime," "'Italia, Io Ti Saluto!'," "Mirrors Of Life And Death," "A Ballad Of Boding," "Yet A Little While" ("I dreamed and did not seek: to-day I seek"), "He And She," "Monna Innominata" (sonnets 1-14), "'Luscious And Sorrowful'," "De Profundis," "Tempus Fugit," "Golden Glories," "Johnny," "'Hollow-Sounding And Mysterious'," "Maiden May," "Till To-Morrow," "Death-Watches," "Touching 'Never'," "Brandons Both," "A Life's Parallels," "At Last," "Golden Silences," "In The Willow Shade," "Fluttered Wings," "A Fisher-Wife," "What's In A Name?," "Mariana," "Memento Mori," "'One Foot On Sea, And One On Shore'," "Buds And Babies," "Boy Johnny," "Freaks Of Fashion," "An October Garden," "'Summer Is Ended'," "Passing And Glassing," "'I Will Arise'," "A Prodigal Son," "Sœur Louise De La Miséricorde," "An 'Immurata' Sister," "'If Thou Sayest, Behold, We Knew It Not'" (sections 1-3), "The Thread Of Life" (sections 1-3), "An Old-World Thicket," "All Thy Works Praise Thee, O Lord," "Later Life: A Double Sonnet Of Sonnets" (sonnets 1-28), "'For Thine Own Sake, O My God'," "Until The Day Break," "'Of Him That Was Ready To Perish'," "'Behold The Man!'," "The Descent From The Cross," "'It Is Finished'," "An Easter Carol," "'Behold A Shaking'" (sections 1-2), "All Saints," "'Take Care Of Him'," "A Martyr" ("Inner not outer, without gnash of teeth"), "Why?," "'Love Is Strong As Death'" ("I have not sought Thee, I have not found Thee'").

Typography and paper: All sheets are printed with a red rule frame with ornamental, cross pattée corners, 184 x 102. First section (pp. 3-300): (129) 122 x 76 (p. 272); 30 lines per page. Second section (pp. 11-208): (136.3) 124.3 x 66.5 (p. 49); 25 lines per page; see *Note two*. Brownish-white wove paper.

Running titles: In italic.

Rectos: i-v: no RT; vii-ix: 'CONTENTS.'; 1-3: no RT; 5-21: 'GOBLIN MARKET.'; 23: 'IN THE ROUND TOWER AT JHANSI.'; 25: 'AT HOME.'; 27: 'LOVE FROM THE NORTH.'; 29: 'WINTER RAIN.'; 31: 'CONFLUENTS.'; 33: 'NOBLE SISTERS.'; 35: 'SPRING.'; 37: 'A BIRTHDAY.'; 39: 'AFTER DEATH.'; 41: 'MY DREAM.'; 43-45: 'THE HOUR AND THE GHOST.'; 47: 'AN APPLE GATHERING.'; 49: 'MAUDE CLARE.'; 51: 'ECHO.'; 53: 'ANOTHER SPRING.'; 55: 'FATA MORGANA.'; 57: 'MAY.'; 59: 'TWILIGHT CALM.'; 61: 'WIFE TO HUSBAND.'; 63: 'MIRAGE.'; 65: 'SOUND SLEEP.'; 67: 'SONG.'; 69: 'THE MASTER CALLETH.'; 71-75: 'THE CONVENT THRESHOLD.'; 77: 'UP-HILL.'; 79-81: no RT; 83: 'A BETTER RESURRECTION.'; 85: 'ADVENT.'; 87: 'THE THREE ENEMIES.'; 89: 'THE ONE

CERTAINTY.'; 91: 'CHRISTIAN AND JEW.'; 93: 'SWEET DEATH.'; 95: 'CONSIDER THE LILIES OF THE FIELD.'; 97-99: 'A TESTIMONY.'; 101: 'SLEEP AT SEA.'; 103-111: 'FROM HOUSE TO HOME.'; 113: 'OLD AND NEW YEAR DITTIES.'; 115: 'AMEN.'; 117: 'MOTHER COUNTRY.'; [1]: no RT; 121-139: 'THE PRINCE'S PROGRESS.'; 141-147: 'MAIDEN-SONG.'; 149-151: 'JESSIE CAMERON.'; 153: 'SPRING QUIET.'; 155: 'THE POOR GHOST.'; 157-159: 'DREAM-LOVE.'; 161: 'TWICE.'; 163-165: 'SONGS IN A CORNFIELD.'; 167-169: 'A YEAR'S WINDFALLS.'; 171: 'ONE DAY.'; 173-175: 'A BIRD'S-EYE VIEW.'; 177: '"TO-DAY FOR ME."'; 179: 'ON THE WING.'; 181: 'BEAUTY IS VAIN.'; 183: 'LADY MAGGIE.'; 185: 'SUMMER.'; 187: 'AUTUMN.'; 189-191: 'THE GHOST'S PETITION.'; 193: 'MEMORY.'; 195-201: 'A ROYAL PRINCESS.'; 203: 'VANITY OF VANITIES.'; 205: 'L. E. L.'; 207: 'BIRD OR BEAST?'; 209: 'EVE.'; 211: 'GROWN AND FLOWN.'; 213: 'A FARM WALK.'; 215: 'SOMEWHERE OR OTHER.'; 217: 'CHILD'S TALK IN APRIL.'; 219: 'GONE FOREVER.'; 221-237: 'UNDER THE ROSE.'; 239: 'SONG.'; 241: 'DAYS OF VANITY.'; 243: 'AUTUMN VIOLETS.'; 245: 'A BETTER COUNTRY DESIRED.'; 247: 'A BRIDE SONG.'; 249-259: 'THE LOWEST ROOM.'; 261: 'A DAUGHTER OF EVE.'; 263: 'BIRD RAPTURE.'; 265: 'TWILIGHT NIGHT.'; 267: 'AMOR MUNDI.'; 269: 'A CHRISTMAS CAROL.'; 271-273: 'BY THE WATERS OF BABYLON.'; 275: 'PARADISE.'; 277: 'UPLIFTING OF EYES.'; 279: 'SAINTS AND ANGELS.'; 281: 'AFTER COMMUNION.'; 283: 'WHO SHALL DELIVER ME?'; 285-287: no RT; 289: 'LONG BARREN.'; 291: 'DOST THOU NOT CARE?'; 293-295: 'MARTYRS' SONG.'; 297: 'AFTER THIS THE JUDGMENT.'; 299: 'GOOD FRIDAY.'; [1]-[7]: no RT; 15-31: 'A PAGEANT.'; 33: 'PASTIME.'; 35-41: 'MIRRORS OF LIFE AND DEATH.'; 43-51: 'A BALLAD OF BODING.'; 53: 'HE AND SHE.'; 55-67: 'MONNA INNOMINATA.'; 69: '"LUSCIOUS AND SORROWFUL."'; 71: 'TEMPUS FUGIT.'; 73-75: 'JOHNNY.'; 77: '"HOLLOW-SOUNDING & MYSTERIOUS."'; 79-83: 'MAIDEN MAY.'; 85: 'DEATH-WATCHES.'; 87-91: 'BRANDONS BOTH.'; 93: 'AT LAST.'; 95-97: 'IN THE WILLOW SHADE.'; 99: 'FLUTTERED WINGS.'; 101: 'WHAT'S IN A NAME?'; 103: 'MARIANA.'; 105: '"ONE FOOT ON SEA,'; 107: 'BUDS AND BABIES.'; 109-111: 'FREAKS OF FASHION.'; 113: 'AN OCTOBER GARDEN.'; 115: 'PASSING AND GLASSING.'; 117: '"I WILL ARISE."'; 119: 'A PRODIGAL SON.'; 121: 'SŒUR LOUISE DE LA MISÉRICORDE.'; 123: 'AN "IMMURATA" SISTER.'; 125: '"IF THOU SAYEST . . ."'; 127-129: 'THE THREAD OF LIFE.'; 131-139: 'AN OLD-WORLD THICKET.'; 141-153: 'O LORD."'; 155-181: 'LATER LIFE.'; 183: 'UNTIL THE DAY BREAK.'; 185: '"READY TO PERISH."'; 187: '"BEHOLD THE MAN!"'; 189-191: '"IT IS FINISHED."'; 193: 'AN EASTER CAROL.'; 195: '"BEHOLD A SHAKING."'; 197: 'ALL SAINTS.'; 199: '"TAKE CARE OF HIM."'; 201-205: 'A MARTYR.'; 207: 'WHY?'

Versos: Period faint on p. 114. ii-iv: no RT; vi-x: 'CONTENTS.'; 2: no RT; 4-22: 'GOBLIN MARKET.'; 24: 'DREAM-LAND.'; 26: 'FROM SUNSET TO STAR RISE.'; 28: 'LOVE FROM THE NORTH.'; 30: 'A DIRGE.'; 32: 'NOBLE SISTERS.'; 34: 'SPRING.'; 36: 'THE LAMBS OF GRASMERE.'; 38: 'REMEMBER.'; 40: 'AN END.'; 42: 'MY DREAM.'; 44: 'THE HOUR AND THE GHOST.'; 46: 'A SUMMER WISH.'; 48: 'SONG.'; 50: 'MAUDE CLARE.'; 52: 'WINTER: MY SECRET.'; 54: 'A PEAL OF BELLS.'; 56: '"NO, THANK YOU, JOHN."'; 58: 'A PAUSE OF THOUGHT.'; 60: 'TWILIGHT CALM.'; 62: 'WIFE TO HUSBAND.'; 64: 'SHUT OUT.'; 66: 'SONG.'; 68: 'BITTER FOR SWEET.'; 70: 'THE FIRST SPRING DAY.'; 72-76: 'THE CONVENT THRESHOLD.'; 78-80: no RT; 82: 'A BRUISED REED SHALL HE NOT BREAK.'; 84-86: 'ADVENT.'; 88: 'THE THREE ENEMIES.'; 90-92: 'CHRISTIAN AND JEW.'; 94: 'SYMBOLS.'; 96: 'THE WORLD.'; 98: 'A TESTIMONY.'; 100-102: 'SLEEP AT SEA.'; 104-110: 'FROM HOUSE TO HOME.'; 112: 'FROM HOUSE TO HOME' [no period]; 114: 'OLD AND NEW YEAR DITTIES.'; 116-118: 'MOTHER COUNTRY.'; 120-138: 'THE PRINCE'S PROGRESS.'; 140-146: 'MAIDEN-SONG.'; 148: 'JESSIE-CAMERON.'; 150-152: 'JESSIE CAMERON.'; 154: 'THE POOR GHOST.'; 156: 'A PORTRAIT.'; 158: 'DREAM-LOVE.'; 160: 'TWICE.'; 162-164: 'SONGS IN A CORNFIELD.'; 166-168: 'A YEAR'S WINDFALLS.'; 170: 'THE QUEEN OF HEARTS.'; 172-174: 'A BIRD'S-EYE VIEW.'; 176: 'GERMAN-FRENCH CAMPAIGN.'; 178: '"TO-DAY FOR ME."'; 180: 'CONSIDER.'; 182: 'MAGGIE A LADY.'; 184: 'WHAT WOULD I GIVE?'; 186: 'SUMMER.'; 188: 'AUTUMN.'; 190-192: 'THE GHOST'S PETITION.'; 194: 'MEMORY.';

196-200: 'A ROYAL PRINCESS.'; 202: 'SHALL I FORGET?'; 204: 'L. E. L.'; 206: 'LIFE AND DEATH.'; 208-210: 'EVE.'; 212-214: 'A FARM WALK.'; 216: 'A CHILL.'; 218: 'CHILD'S TALK IN APRIL.'; 220-238: 'UNDER THE ROSE.'; 240: 'DAYS OF VANITY.'; 242: 'ENRICA, 1865.'; 244: 'A BETTER COUNTRY DESIRED.'; 246: 'A GREEN CORNFIELD.'; 248: 'A BRIDE SONG.'; 250-260: 'THE LOWEST ROOM.'; 262: 'VENUS' LOOKING-GLASS.'; 264: 'MY FRIEND.'; 266: 'A BIRD SONG.'; 268: 'AMOR MUNDI.'; 270: 'A CHRISTMAS CAROL.'; 272: 'BY THE WATERS OF BABYLON.'; 274: 'PARADISE.'; 276: 'UPLIFTING OF EYES.'; 278: 'SAINTS AND ANGELS.'; 280: 'THE VEXED HEART.'; 282: 'A ROSE PLANT IN JERICHO.'; 284: 'WHO SHALL DELIVER ME?'; 286: no RT; 288: 'DESPISED AND REJECTED.'; 290: 'IF ONLY.'; 292: 'WEARY IN WELL-DOING.'; 294: 'MARTYRS' SONG.'; 296-298: 'AFTER THIS THE JUDGMENT.'; 300: 'THE LOWEST PLACE.'; [2]-[6]: no RT; 14-30: 'THE MONTHS'; 32: 'THE MONTHS: A PAGEANT.'; 34: '"ITALIA, IO TI SALUTO!"'; 36-40: 'MIRRORS OF LIFE AND DEATH.'; 42-50: 'A BALLAD OF BODING.'; 52: 'YET A LITTLE WHILE.'; 54-68: 'MONNA INNOMINATA.'; 70: 'DE PROFUNDIS.'; 72: 'GOLDEN GLORIES.'; 74-76: 'JOHNNY.'; 78: '"HOLLOW-SOUNDING & MYSTERIOUS."'; 80-82:'MAIDEN MAY.'; 84: 'TILL TO-MORROW.'; 86: 'TOUCHING "NEVER."'; 88-90: 'BRANDONS BOTH.'; 92: 'A LIFE'S PARALLELS.'; 94: 'GOLDEN SILENCES.'; 96-98: 'IN THE WILLOW SHADE.'; 100: 'A FISHER-WIFE.'; 102: 'WHAT'S IN A NAME?'; 104: 'MEMENTO MORI.'; 106: 'AND ONE ON SHORE."'; 108: 'BOY JOHNNY.'; 110-112: 'FREAKS OF FASHION.'; 114: '"SUMMER IS ENDED."'; 116: 'PASSING AND GLASSING.'; 118: '"I WILL ARISE."'; 120: 'SŒUR LOUISE DE LA MISÉRICORDE.'; 122: 'AN "IMMURATA" SISTER.'; 124-126: '"IF THOU SAYEST . . ."'; 128: 'THE THREAD OF LIFE.'; 130-138: 'AN OLD-WORLD THICKET.'; 140-152: '"ALL THY WORKS PRAISE THEE,'; 154-180: 'LATER LIFE.'; 182: '"FOR THINE OWN SAKE, O MY GOD."'; 184: 'UNTIL THE DAY BREAK.'; 186: '"READY TO PERISH."'; 188: 'THE DESCENT FROM THE CROSS.'; 190: '"IT IS FINISHED."'; 192: 'AN EASTER CAROL.'; 194: '"BEHOLD A SHAKING."'; 196-198: 'ALL SAINTS.'; 200: '"TAKE CARE OF HIM."'; 202-206: 'A MARTYR.'; 208: '"LOVE IS STRONG AS DEATH."'

Binding: Two forms noted, no priority. Both were advertised in Roberts Brothers' "Autumn Announcements" (*Publishers' Weekly*, 16 September 1882: 365), which included the "Household Edition" of "Christina G. Rossetti's Poetical Works."

Binding A: Fine diagonal rib cloth, medium brown or moderate green (Centroid 145). Front: in black ink, a set of three rules (one thick rule nearest the edge, and two thin) at top and bottom, and across center, a wide black ornamental band of passion flowers and foliage; also within the black band at upper left, a gilt medallion with cloth showing through to form text 'Christina Rossetti's Poems'. Back: plain. Spine: in black, top and bottom rules, ornamental band continued from front; with gilt stamped square at top with cloth show-through forming text 'Christina | Rossetti's | Poems' and gilt rectangle at bottom with cloth show-through forming text 'Roberts | Bros'. Endpapers light brown (Centroid 57) with white show-through creating foliage design with repeating diamond pattern. Edges: all edges gilt. Locations: BL, TxCM.

Binding B: See *Note two*. Moderate reddish-brown (Centroid 43) imitation calf quarter binding on spine, marbled paper-covered boards. Marbling colors and patterns vary: one copy examined (Ives), marbled in an antique spot pattern (GTT 1206), is predominantly very dark greenish blue (Centroid 175) with veins of strong reddish brown (Centroid 40) and moderate greenish yellow (Centroid 102), the other copy (PBm) marbled in a Dutch pattern (GTT 1204), is predominantly red, with blue, green and orange scallops. Front, back plain. Spine: gilt, scalloped head and tail band, with overall background of alternating small rings and diamonds divided by horizontal rules into six compartments, with a leather label pasted over the second uppermost compartment, and text printed on the label 'CHRISTINA | ROSSETTI'S | POEMS.' Endpapers: edges marbled, same as boards. One wove paper binder's leaf between endpapers and sheets, front and back. Locations: PBm, Ives.

Publication: No later than September 1882. Printed from combined plates of 1876 *Poems* and *A Pageant* with no text changes noted. A reference to Roberts Brothers' plans for the holiday market, including "new editions of the poetical works" of Rossetti and other "leading authors" appeared in the *New York Times*, (August 28, 1882: 3), and the "Household edition" of Rossetti's "Poetical Works" was included in a list of the "Household Editions of Popular Poets" in *Publishers' Weekly* (16 September: 365). The price of the cloth binding was $2.00; the whole set of "Popular Poets," including Christina and Dante Rossetti, Jean Ingelow, Joqauin Miller, Edwin Arnold and John Keats, bound in "imitation half calf" and packaged in a "neat box" was available for $10.00, and the individual volumes could also be purchased bound in tree calf for $5.00. No copies of Rossetti's volume in tree calf have been located.

BL depository copy: 'BRITISH MUSEUM 28 MY 83.'

Printing: <u>ii</u>: same as A12.1b. 208: same as A16: 'University Press: John Wilson and Son, Cambridge.'

Note one: The TxCM and BL copies are not signed on page 49 (second part), which in other copies is signed "4."

Note two: The "imitation calf" binding was introduced in 1881 and promoted by Roberts Brothers as a "device" to "popularize certain books hitherto printed in more expensive form" (*Our Continent*, 6 December 1882: 700). A November, 1881 Roberts Brothers advertisement for "Library Books" described the "new style" as having "a cloth back, full gilt, with illuminated titles, marble paper sides and linings, marble edge or gilt top edge with head band—a style possessing all the attractions of the more expensive full or half bound in leather book at a more nominal price" (*Literary World* (Boston), 18 November 1882: 408).

Locations: BL, Ives, PBm, TxCM.

A17.1b   Second Subedition, Later Printing (1888)

Printed from same plates as 1882; same except:

Title Page: Date changed to 1888.

Collation: In second series of signatures (that is, the *Pageant* section), the signature number '4' is printed on p. 49 ('4' is missing from some copies of 1882).

Typography and paper: no red rule frame.

Binding: Same design as 1882 Binding A (diagonal rib cloth with black and gilt), but color changed to grayish brown (Centroid 61); floral endpaper design differs from that of 1882, with color changed to grayish olive (Centroid 110) on light yellowish brown (Centroid 76) background; boards 188 mm height, slightly shorter than 1882.

Note one: Although one of Crump's references to the 1888 edition suggests that it may have appeared as a two volume set ("Poems (2 vols.; Roberts Brothers, 1888)," *Poems* 1: 231), I have not been able to locate any two volume presentation of the poems prior to Little, Brown (1898). Some library catalogues record this title as two volumes in one, which might explain Crump's notation.

Location: TxCM.

A17.1c   Second Subedition, First Expanded Printing (1888?)

Same as A17.1b, except:

Pagination: i-v vi-xi xii 1-3 4-77 78-81 82-118 119 120-284 285-287 288-300 [7] 14-231 232.

Plates: Two additional plates added:
3) Facing 119, vignette and caption (76 x 85, height measured with caption) from the engraved title page of 1866 Macmillan *Prince's Progress* as reproduced in Roberts Brothers 1866, 1872 (A4).
4) Facing 139, frontispiece and caption (150 x 97.3, height measured with caption) from the 1866 Macmillan *Prince's Progress* as reproduced in Roberts Brothers 1866, 1872 (A4).

Collation: leaf height 185; [π1 1⁶ (1₄ + χ1) 2-32⁸ 33⁴], with obsolete signatures as in A17.1b.

Contents, Poems: Additional poems on pp. 209-231, as follows:
"Birchington Churchyard," "One Sea-Side Grave," "Brother Bruin," "'A Helpmeet for Him'," "A Song of Flight," "A Wintry Sonnet," "Resurgam," "To-Day's Burden," "'There is a Budding Morrow in Midnight'," "Exultate Deo," "A Hope Carol," "Christmas Carols" in three parts, "1. Whoso hears a chiming," "2. A holy, heavenly chime," "3. Lo, newborn Jesus," "A Candlemas Dialogue," "Mary Madgalene and the Other Mary," "Patience of Hope."

Running titles (for xi-xii, 209-231):
Rectos: xi: CONTENTS.'; 209: 'BIRCHINGTON CHURCHYARD.'; 211-213: 'BROTHER BRUIN.'; 215: 'A SONG OF FLIGHT.'; 217: 'RESURGAM.'; 219: '"THERE IS A BUDDING MORROW."'; 221: 'A HOPE CAROL.'; 223-227: 'CHRISTMAS CAROLS.'; 229: 'A CANDLEMAS DIALOGUE.'; 231: 'PATIENCE OF HOPE.'

Versos: xii: no RT; 210: 'ONE SEA-SIDE GRAVE.'; 212: 'BROTHER BRUIN.'; 214: '"A HELPMEET FOR HIM."'; 216: 'A WINTRY SONNET.'; 218: 'TO-DAY'S BURDEN.'; 220: 'EXULTATE DEO.'; 222: 'A HOPE CAROL.'; 224-226: 'CHRISTMAS CAROLS.'; 228: 'A CANDLEMAS DIALOGUE.'; 230: 'MARY MAGDALENE.'; 232: no RT.

Binding: Same as 1882 binding A (diagonal rib cloth with black and gilt), but color changed to light olive brown (Centroid 94) or strong red (Centroid 12). Endpapers: coated paper, blackish blue (Centroid 188).

Note one: The additional poems following page 290 in this printing do not appear in British printings prior to Macmillan 1890. Crump reasons that the new poems first appeared in "[s]ome of the 1888 copies," and were subsequently added to Macmillan (*Poems* 2: 13), but Rossetti's offer to "collect" her "stray magazine pieces" for the Macmillan volume in June, 1890 indicates that she had not previously collected them for the purpose of adding to the Roberts Brothers volume (*Letters* 4: 204). Assuming this is true, the expanded American printing probably appeared no earlier than 1890, despite the 1888 title page date.

Locations: Ives, PBm.

A17.1d   *Second Subedition, Later Expanded Printing (1895)*

Same as expanded 1888 printing except:

Title Page: Date changed to 1895.

Pagination: No pp. 1-2.

Plates: Four plates, same as 1882 expanded printing, except first plate altered as follows:
1) Facing title, same portrait of CGR by DGR as previous printings, but enlarged (113.5 x 76), with single rule border, and without letterpress caption.

Collation: (183 x 122): [1-33⁸ 34⁴], with obsolete signatures as in previous printings.

Contents: No half-title between <u>xii</u> and <u>3</u>.

Binding: Same as 1882 binding A, but color changed to vivid purplish blue (Centroid 194) and as in 1888, shorter boards (188 mm). Endpapers: white wove paper.

Note one: This combination of plates, with the alteration to the portrait frontispiece, also appears in other later issues of Roberts Brothers editions; see A12.1c.i, 1896.

Locations: BL; Ives.

A17.1e   *Second Subedition, Later Expanded Printing (1897)*

Same as 1895 printing except:

Title Page: Date changed to 1897.

Collation: Obsolete signature missing from p.113 (should be '8').

Binding: Fine diagonal rib cloth, strong red (Centroid 12) or light olive brown (Centroid 94) or grayish olive green (Centroid 127). Front: '[in gilt, across top] Christina G. Rossetti's | Poems' and in grayish brown (Centroid 61) or deep reddish brown (Centroid 41) ink, within thick-thin top rule and thin-thick bottom rule, an ornamental band with repeating hexagon motif. Back: brown ink ornamental band, same as front. Spine: '[in gilt] Christina | G. | Rossetti's | Poems' above brown ink ornamental band continued from front; at tail [in gilt] 'Roberts Bros'. Endpapers: white wove. Edges: all edges gilt. One wove paper binder's leaf between endpapers and sheets, front and back.

Note one: This is the last of the Roberts Brothers subedition printings. In 1898, Roberts Brothers was sold to Little, Brown, which continued to reprint Rossetti's poetry from Roberts Brothers' plates. Thus the Little, Brown first subedition of *Poems* is in most respects identical to the 1897 Roberts Brothers printing (see A30).

Locations: Ives, PBm (2).

A18   **LETTER AND SPIRIT (1883)**

A18.1   ***First Edition, Only Printing (1883)***

Within rule frame, 145.3 x, 95.3; some text in <u>black letter</u>; see *Typography* and *Note one*:
<u>Letter</u> and <u>Spirit</u>. | NOTES | ON THE | COMMANDMENTS. | BY | CHRISTINA G. ROSSETTI, | AUTHOR OF "SEEK AND FIND," AND "CALLED TO BE SAINTS." | [wavy rule, 22.3] | "What is written in the law? how readest thou? | . . . . This do, and thou shalt live."–*St. Luke* x. 26, 28. | [ornamented rule, 13.3] | <u>Published</u> <u>under</u> <u>the</u> <u>Direction</u> <u>of</u> <u>the</u> <u>Tract</u> <u>Committee</u>. | [ornamented rule, 13.3] LONDON: | SOCIETY FOR PROMOTING CHRISTIAN KNOWLEDGE, | NORTHUMBERLAND AVENUE, CHARING CROSS, W.C.; | 43, QUEEN VICTORIA STREET, E.C.; | 26, ST. GEORGE'S PLACE, HYDE PARK CORNER, S.W. | BRIGHTON: 135, NORTH STREET. | NEW YORK: E. & J. B. YOUNG & CO.

Pagination: <u>1</u>-<u>5</u> 6-206 <u>207</u>-<u>208</u>.

Collation: (170 x 115): <u>B</u>⁸ C-O⁸. $1,2 signed. 104 leaves.

Contents (some text in <u>black letter</u>): <u>1</u>: title; <u>2</u>: circular ornament, 15 x 15; <u>3</u>: 'TO | <u>My Mother</u> | IN THANKFULNESS FOR HER | DEAR AND HONOURED | EXAMPLE.'; <u>4</u>: circular ornament, foliage, 18 x 18; <u>5</u>: text headed '<u>Letter and Spirit</u>. | [rule, 21 mm] | ST. MARK xii.28-30: ST. MATTHEW xxii. | 39, 40: EXODUS xx. 3-17.'; 200: 'A HARMONY ON PART OF I CORINTHIANS XIII.'; <u>207</u> advertisement '*By the same Author*. | <u>Called to be Saints</u>. | THE MINOR FESTIVALS DEVOTIONALLY | STUDIED. | With Illustrations. Crown 8vo. *Cloth boards*, | *red edges, 5s.*' and '<u>Seek and Find</u>. | A DOUBLE SERIES OF SHORT STUDIES | OF THE BENEDICITE. | Crown 8vo. *Cloth boards, 2s. 6d.*'; <u>208</u>: printer's imprint.

Typography and paper: (145) 115 x 75 (p. 163); 23 lines per page, wove paper. All printed pages (including running titles and page numbers) are within a rule frame with small square floral ornaments at corners and with a lily-shaped ornament extending from the corners; total frame measurement 144 x 93. Some pages (5-7, 200-206) printed in two columns separated by 113.7 vertical rule (see p. 6).

Running titles: In black letter.
Rectos: <u>1</u>-<u>5</u>: no RT; 7-205: 'Letter and Spirit.'; 207: no RT.
Versos: <u>2</u>-<u>4</u>: no RT; 6-206: 'Letter and Spirit.'; 208: no RT.

Binding: Calico cloth, in dark grayish olive (Centroid 111) or very dark greenish blue (Centroid 175). Front: In dark reddish orange ink (Centroid 38), an outer red double rule frame and an inner single rule compartment with a group of three triangles at each inner corner and a snowflake ornament at top and bottom. In center, text in gilt: 'LETTER AND SPIRIT | *CHRISTINA ROSSETTI*' with chevron bar 'A' in 'AND.' Back: in dark reddish orange ink, circular "SPCK" printer's device. Spine: (with the double and single rules at head and tail in dark reddish orange ink, rest in gilt) '[double rule] | [single rule] | LETTER | AND | SPIRIT | [rule] | CHRISTINA | ROSSETTI | ["SPCK" device] | [single rule] | [double rule]'; chevron bar in the 'A' in 'AND.' Endpapers: coated paper, blackish blue (Centroid 188). Edges trimmed. Binding stapled, not sewn.

Advertisements: A two-leaf advertising section dated '1-11-82' appears in all copies examined.
    <u>1</u>: *Publications on the Christian Evidences* 9 titles, *Natural Theology of Natural Beauty (The)* to *When was the Pentateuch Written?*; 2: ten titles, *Theism and Christianity* to *Scripture Doctrine of Creation*; 3: ten titles, *The Witness of the Heart to Christ* to *The Theory of Prayer*; 4: eight titles, *The Credibility of Mysteries* to *The Origin of the World* and list of depositories.

Publication: May 1883. CGR completed the manuscript and sent it to SPCK for review sometime before 11 October 1882 (WMRD). By February 1, the SPCK had accepted the book for publication (*Letters* 3: 95).

CGR was reading proofs before the end of the month (WMRD, entry for February 28), finishing the revision process in March. She was "surprised" to find the book "already published" in early May (*Letters* 3: 116). In June, CGR recorded that she sold the copyright for £26 (Account book). An autograph manuscript "with many verbal differences" from the printed text is held by the Humanities Research Center at the University of Texas at Austin (Kent and Stanwood, 266). Rossetti also made corrections in her copy of the published book (see *Note two*) but no corrected states of the book have been located.

Announced in the *Academy* (28 April 1883: 292; "just published," 12 May 1883: 1); in the *Athenaeum*'s list of new books (12 May 1883: 601).

Price 2s.

BL depository copy: 'BRITISH MUSEUM 11 MY 83'.

Reviewed in the *Academy* (June 1883), 395-396; mentioned in the *Literary World* (29 December 1883: 470), and the *Official Year-Book of the Church of England* (1884: 510).

Printing: 208: 'CLARENDON PRESS, OXFORD. | FOR THE SOCIETY FOR PROMOTING CHRISTIAN KNOWLEDGE.'

Note one: This book uses the same ornamental rule frame as *Called to Be Saints* (A14).

Note two: The DAM copy includes multiple inscriptions as well as corrections by CGR. The inscriptions are on the verso of the front free endpaper. The first, in ink, "To my dearest and best of Daughters, Christina Rossetti Xmas Day, 1883" reveals that the book was given to CGR by her mother. Beneath that inscription, in pencil, is the note "This copy to be sent to the SPCK having been corrected by CGR"; with everything but "corrected by CGR" crossed out in black crayon. The final inscription reads "W. M. Rossetti from Christina's books 1894."

The corrections to the book are as follows:

On page 15, three corrections:
1) In the last paragraph, seven lines from the bottom of the page, in the phrase "naturally range themselves" the word "naturally" is crossed out in pencil, and "presumably may" is written in the left margin.
2) In the same line of text, a caret is added following the phrase "though not" and the word "necessarily" is written in the margin.
3) In the last paragraph, six lines from the bottom of the page, the word "exactly" is crossed out, and a delete mark is written in the margin.

On page 21: A blue sheet of paper with text handwritten in ink is inserted between pages 20 and 21, presumably to replace lines 1-3 of page 21, which are crossed out in ink.

On page 77, two corrections:
1) In the last paragraph, sixth line from the bottom, the comma after the phrase "are even" is circled in pencil, with a caret drawn to show that it should be moved to follow "are" and "tr" is written in the margin.
2) In the last paragraph, second line from the bottom of the page, a caret is inserted between the words "may be" with "truly" written in the right margin.

On page 90: In the first paragraph, eight lines from the top of the page, the word "Hard" is crossed out in pencil and the words "A stone" are written in the left margin.

Locations: BL, CaBVaU, DAM (presentation copy, see *Note two*), MSL, NjP, PBm, SdU, TxCM, Ives.

A19   ROSES AND ROSES (1884)

A19.1   *First Edition, Only Printing (1884)*

Heading: Roses and Roses. | [wavy rule, 25] | BY CHRISTINA G. ROSSETTI. | [wavy rule, 26] | C
Copyright of the Author.
  Note chevron bar 'A' in first line.

Broadside, printed on recto only, 203 x 129.

Contents: Heading and text of poem "Roses and Roses."

Note: One of the BL copies includes a note in WMR's hand on the verso, dated 17 June 1904. WMR's note explains that "This . . . is the first form in wh. these verses were printed—for a Bazaar, held in June 1884, for the Boy's Home at Barnet, founded by an old acquaintance of ours, Colonel Gillum—Christina afterwards, 1893, introduced the poem into her volume 'Verses' (S. P. C. K.)"; however, the poem had also appeared in *Time Flies*. A signed holograph copy of the poem is extant in the W. Hugh Peal Collection at the University of Kentucky.

Location: BL (2).

A20   TIME FLIES (SPCK, 1885)

A20.1a   **First Edition, First Printing (1885)**

TIME FLIES: | A READING DIARY | BY | CHRISTINA G. ROSSETTI, | AUTHOR OF "LETTER AND SPIRIT," ETC. | "A day's march nearer home." | JAMES MONTGOMERY. | [rule, 14.3] | PUBLISHED UNDER THE DIRECTION OF THE TRACT COMMITTEE. | [rule, 14.3] | LONDON: | SOCIETY FOR PROMOTING CHRISTIAN KNOWLEDGE, | NORTHUMBERLAND AVENUE, CHARING CROSS, W. C.; | 43, QUEEN VICTORIA STREET, E. C.; | 26, ST. GEORGE'S PLACE, HYDE PARK CORNER, S.W. | BRIGHTON: 135, NORTH STREET. | 1885.

Pagination: [4] 1 2-280 1 2-4.

Collation: (167 x 114): A² B-S⁸ T⁶. $1, 2 signed. 144 leaves.

Contents: (Some text in black letter): [1]: title; [2]: blank; [3]: dedication 'TO | MY BELOVED EXAMPLE, FRIEND, | **MOTHER**. | *"Her children arise up, and call her blessed."*'; [4]: blank; 1: heading 'TIME FLIES: | A Reading Diary. | [rule, center diamond, 8.3]' and diary entry for January 1; 2-253: diary entries through December 31; 254: heading 'APPENDIX. | Readings for certain movable Holy Days.' and 'Advent Sunday.'; 255: 'Advent: Ember Wednesday.' and 'Advent: Ember Friday.'; 256: 'Advent: Ember Saturday.'; 257: 'Ash Wednesday.' and 'Lent: Ember Wednesday.'; 258: 'Lent: Ember Friday.'; 259: 'Lent: Ember Saturday.' and 'Palm Sunday.'; 260: 'Monday in Holy Week.'; 261: 'Tuesday in Holy Week.' and 'Wednesday in Holy Week.'; 262: 'Thursday in Holy Week.'; 263: 'Good Friday.' and 'Easter Even.'; 264: 'Easter Day.'; 265: 'Easter Monday.' and 'Easter Tuesday.'; 266: 'Rogation Monday.'; 267: 'Rogation Tuesday.'; 268: 'Vigil of the Ascension: Rogation | Wednesday.'; 270: 'Ascension Day.'; 271: 'Whitsun Eve.' and 'Whitsun Day.'; 272: 'Whitsun Monday.' and 'Whitsun Tuesday.'; 273: 'Whitsuntide: Ember Wednesday.'; 274: 'Whitsuntide: Ember Friday.'; 276: 'Whitsuntide: Ember Saturday.'; 277: 'Trinity Sunday.' and 'Trinitytide: Ember Wednesday.'; 278: 'Trinitytide: Ember Friday.'; 279: 'Trinitytide: Ember Saturday.'; 280: printer's imprint; 1: advertisement 'PUBLICATIONS | OF THE | Society for Promoting Christian Knowledge.', seven titles, *Australia's Heroes* to *Fifth Continent*; 2: eleven titles, *For Faith and Fatherland* to *King's Warrant (The)*; 3: ten titles, *Kitty Bligh's Birthday* to *Owen Hartley: or, Ups and Downs*; 4: nine titles, *Percy Trevor's Training* to *Wilford Family (The)*.

Poems: (Some untitled, identified by first line; titles that function also as headings are marked with an asterisk and followed by first line; see *Note one*):
"A heavy heart, if ever heart was heavy," *"Feast of the Epiphany" ("Lord Babe, if Thou art He"), "Who cares for earthly bread though white?," "Where love is, there comes sorrow," "Love understands the mystery, whereof," "Joy is but sorrow," "O blessed Paul elect to grace," "Oh Christ our All in each, our All in All!," "A life of hope deferred too often is," *"Feast of the Presentation of Christ in the Temple, Commonly Called, the Purification of St. Mary the Virgin" ("Purity born of a Maid"), "Up, my drowsing eyes!," "Who scatters tares shall reap no wheat," "1. 'I see that all things come to an end'," "2. 'But Thy commandment is exceeding broad,'" "'Doeth well, . . . doeth better.'–(I Cor. vii. 38.)" ("My love whose heart is tender said to me"), "Love is all happiness, love is all beauty," "Home by different ways. Yet all," "'One sorrow more?' I thought the tale complete', "A handy Mole who plied no shovel," "Laughing Life cries at the feast," "Where shall I find a white rose blowing?" ["Roses and Roses"], "After midnight, in the dark," "Earth has clear call of daily bells," "Thy lilies drink the dew," "What is it Jesus saith unto the soul?," "Watch yet a while," "It is good to be last not first," "Christ's heart was wrung for me, if mine is sore," "A burdened heart that bleeds and bears," "Lie still, my restive heart, lie still," "A Castle-Builder's World," "Heaven's chimes are slow, but sure to strike at last," "Weigh all my faults and follies righteously," "Rest remains, when all is done," "A cold wind stirs the blackthorn," "Oh! what is earth, that we should build," "Piteous my rhyme is," "Lord, I had chosen another lot," "Lord, what have I to offer?

sickening fear," "When sick of life and all the world," "'Eye hath not seen:'—yet man hath known and weighed," "Man's life is death. Yet Christ endured to live," "'One swallow does not make a summer'," "Love said nay, while Hope kept saying," "Lord, when my heart was whole I kept it back," "Young girls wear flowers," "If love is not worth loving, then life is not worth living," "That Song of Songs which is Solomon's," "'The half was not told me,' said Sheba's Queen," "They lie at rest, our blessed dead," "Parting after parting," "'As cold waters to a thirsty soul, so is good news from a far country'" ("'Golden haired, lily white"), "O Christ my God Who seest the unseen," "Heartsease I found, where Love-lies-bleeding," "Roses on a brier," "A rose, a lily and the Face of Christ," "The lowest place. Ah, Lord, how steep and high," "Friends, I commend to you the narrow way," "O ye, who are not dead and fit," "Lord, grant me grace to love Thee in my pain," "Saints are like roses when they flush rarest," "Lord God of Hosts most Holy and most High," "Love doth so grace and dignify," "Innocent eyes not ours," "Contemptuous of his home beyond," "Man's life is but a working day," "Have I not striven, my God, and watched and prayed?", "A Word for the Dumb," "The sinner's own fault? So it was," "Who would wish back the Saints upon our rough," "Through burden and heat of the day," "A Dialogue" ("'The fields are white to harvest, look and see"), "Of each sad word, which is more sorrowful," *"Feast of the Name of Jesus" ("Jesus, Lord God from all eternity"), "Lord Jesus, who would think that I am Thine?," "Yea, if Thou wilt, Thou canst put up Thy sword," "To meet, worth living for," "When all the overwork of life," *"Feast of St. Bartholomew, Apostle" ("He bore an agony whereof the name"), "One step more, and the race is ended," "If I should say 'My heart is in my home'," "Whereto shall we liken this Blessed Mary Virgin," "Treasure plies a feather," "In weariness and painfulness St. Paul," "Lord, what have I that I may offer Thee?," "Sorrow hath a double voice," "Our life is long—Not so wise Angels say," "Darkness and light are both alike to Thee," "1. No thing is great on this side of the grave," "2. While all creation sang its hymn anew," "Lying a-dying," "1. All heaven is blazing yet," "2. That which I chose, I choose," "1. Together once, but never more" and "2. Whatso it be, howso it be, Amen," "How can one man, how can all men," "Of all the downfalls in the world," "Who is this that cometh up not alone," *"Feast of All Saints" ("As grains of sand, as stars, as drops of dew"), "Our heaven must be within ourselves," "Scarce-tolerable life which all life long," "'Lift up your hearts'—'We lift them up'—Ah me!", "It seems an easy thing," "The goal in sight! Look up and sing," "We know not when, we know not where," "Everything that is born must die," "In that world we weary to attain," "'A Merry heart is a continual feast'," "Bury Hope out of sight," "Is any grieved or tired? Yea, by God's will," "Have dead men long to wait?," "Earth grown old yet still so green," "Shall not the Judge of all the earth do right?," "Christmas Eve" ("Christmas hath a darkness"), "Christmas Day" ("A baby is a harmless thing"), "'Beloved, let us love one another,' says St. John," "Love came down at Christmas," "Looking back along life's trodden way," *"Advent Sunday" ("Behold, the bridegroom cometh:—go ye out"), *"Ash Wednesday" ("My God, my God, have mercy on my sin"), *"Monday in Holy Week" ("Once I ached for thy dear sake"), *"Tuesday in Holy Week" ("By Thy long drawn anguish to atone"), *"Thursday in Holy Week" ("The great Vine left its glory to reign as Forest King"), *"Good Friday" ("Lord Jesus Christ grown faint upon the Cross"), *"Easter Even" ("The tempest over and gone, the calm begun"), *"Easter Day" ("Words cannot utter"), *"Easter Tuesday" ("Out in the rain a world is growing green"), *"Ascension Day" ("When Christ went up to Heaven the Apostles stayed"), *"Whitsun Day" ("At sound as of rushing wind and sight as of fire"), *"Whitsun Tuesday" ("Lord Jesus Christ our Wisdom and our Rest").

Typography and paper: (139.3) 128.3 x 84 (p. 51); 35 lines; wove paper.

Running titles:

Rectos: [1]-[3], <u>1</u>: no RT; 3-279: 'A READING DIARY.'; <u>1</u>: no RT; 3: 'PUBLICATIONS OF THE SOCIETY.'

Versos: [2]-[4]: no RT; 2-278: 'TIME FLIES:'; 280: 'TIME FLIES: A READING DIARY.'; 2-4: 'PUBLICATIONS OF THE SOCIETY.'

Binding: Several forms and colors of cloth and endpapers noted, priority undetermined.

Calico cloth, dark brown (CaBVaU) or olive green (BL) or dark olive brown (Centroid 96: TxCM), or calico with slight linen grain, very dark bluish green (Centroid 166; BL, DAM, MSL, NjP, TxU). Front: in gilt, 'TIME FLIES | *A READING DIARY* | *CHRISTINA ROSSETTI* | [ornament, butterfly above winged hourglass]. Back: plain. Spine: 'TIME | FLIES | [rule] | CHRISTINA | ROSSETTI| ["SPCK" device]'. Endpapers: coated paper, black or dark greenish blue or blackish green (Centroid 152). Edges stained strong red (Centroid 12), except CaBVaU top edge is plain. Binding stapled, not sewn.

Publication: May 1885. Rossetti mentioned the book in correspondence as early as February 5, 1885 (*Letters* 3: 247); by early April she expected that the book to be "coming out—soon, I hope" (*Letters* 3: 252). Although Rossetti's friend Frederick Shields, who had agreed to prepare a cover design for the book, fell ill and was unable to carry out the commission (*Letters* 3: 254), by April 22, Rossetti assured Shields that the book would not be delayed: the SPCK had produced an alternate design, "not at all unpleasing," with publication set for May 1 (*Letters* 3: 257). After the book was printed, Rossetti noted an error in her commentary for St. Mark's Day (p. 79). She wrote to SPCK secretary Edmund McClure to alert him to the error, which was corrected in later printings (*Letters* 3: 260; see *Note two* and A20.1b).

Early mention in the *Athenaeum* (28 March 1885: 409); advertised by SPCK in *Athenaeum* (2 May 1885: 558).

Price: 2s 6d.

BL depository copies: 'BRITISH MUSEUM 21 MY 85'; '14 JUL 34' (presentation copy).

Reviewed in the *Academy* (27 June 1885: 454); *British Quarterly Review* (July 1885: 245); *Saturday Review* (22 August 1885: 267); *Athenaeum* (31 October 1885: 569); *Merry England* (Dec. 1885: 133-134).

Printing: 280: '*Printed at the University Press, Oxford* | *By* HORACE HART, *Printer to the University*.'

Note one: When the content of an entry consists only of a poem, and when that entry includes a heading denoting a feast day, Saint's day, or other event in the Church calendar, it is unclear whether the heading functions also as a poem title. In such cases, the first line of the poem is also given. Also, Rossetti sometimes numbers sequential calendar entries, apparently to indicate subgroups of entries that pursue a related theme or idea. In four instances, a pair of numbered calendar entries consists only of poetry, thus raising the question of whether the numbered poems are to be considered as separate entities or as a single poem in two parts. The poems, listed below, are treated in the *Contents* as separate poems.
1) "1. 'I see that all things come to an end'" and "2. 'But thy commandment is exceeding broad'" (February 11 and 12, p. 31). Reprinted in *Verses* with section numbers "1" and "2" but with separate first line entries in the index);
2) "1. 'No thing is great on this side of the grave'" and "2. 'While all creation sang its hymn anew'" (October 4 and 5, p. 192-193). Reprinted as a single poem, without section numbers, in *Verses*.
3) "1. 'All heaven is blazing yet'" and "2. 'That which I chose, I choose'" (October 10 and 11, p. 196). Reprinted as a single poem, without section numbers, in *Verses*.
4) "1. 'Together once, but never more'" and "2. 'Whatso it be, howso it be, Amen'" (October 15 and 16, p. 199). Reprinted as a single poem, with section numbers, in *Verses*.

Note two: Copies with annotations and hand corrections by CGR are held at BL, DAM, and TxU, while a copy with WMR's annotations is owned by Mark Samuels Lasner. The TxU copy is the most extensively annotated, with references to family and friends and locations identified, along with a few corrections to the text; the DAM copy provides only text corrections, most (but not all) of which also appear in TxU. In the DAM and BL copies, CGR draws attention to the error in the entry for April 25 (p. 79) but does not provide alternate wording. In the TxU copy, the passage is crossed out, and the revised passage is provided on a piece of writing paper tipped in to the book. The uncorrected passage reads as follows:

p. 79: "Either with Moses at the Red Sea he bids the people go forward: or else with a Greater than

Moses at another stormy sea he tenderly revives hope, saying, 'O thou of little faith, wherefore didst thou doubt?'—Divine words recorded in no Gospel besides his own."

In the TxU copy, everything following "Greater than Moses" is crossed out; CGR's revised text does not differ from the revised version in A20.1b (see *Note one* in that entry).

The additional corrections in DAM and TxU are as follows. None of these corrections are made in subsequent printings of this book, but the corrections to poems appear in *Verses* (A24).

p. 17 (TxU): in pencil, in the inner margin across from line 7 of the first entry, "8" (presumably to correct the word "sixteen" in the text).

p. 109 (DAM only): In pencil, in line 3, the word "things" crossed out, and "growths" is written in the right margin. (In the poem "Heartsease I found").

p. 126 (TxU, DAM): in pencil (TxU), in line 1, the words "in the sky" are crossed out and the "hid on high" is written above. (In the poem "Lord God of Hosts").

p. 129 (TxU, DAM) in pencil (DAM) or purple pencil (TxU), in line 17, the word "not" is crossed out and a delete sign written in the right margin. (In the entry for July 6).

p. 145 (TxU, DAM) in purple pencil, in line 8, the word "grow" crossed out and "show /" is written in the right margin. (In the poem "Through burden and heat of the day").

p. 162 (TxU, DAM) in pencil (DAM) or purple pencil (TxU), in line 4, the word "stop" crossed out and "conclude" is written in the left margin. (In the entry for August 21).

p. 177 (DAM), in pencil, in line 8 from the bottom, the "a" in "Haraclius" is crossed out, and "e /" is written in the right margin. (In the entry for September 14).

Locations: BL (2, including one presentation copy); CaBVaU (2); DAM (presentation copy); MSL (presentation copy); NjP; TxCM; TxU.

Presentation copies: BL (shelf mark 12356 p39): Inscribed on free front endpaper "Dear Nurse Abrey with Christina G. Rossetti's love and grateful remembrance. May 13. 1886." DAM: The free front endpaper is inscribed "Frances Mary Lavinia Rossetti with the love of her daughter Christina May 6. 1885; below this inscription, CGR has attached a rectangular piece of paper to form a pocket which holds two dried trefoils. Beneath the pocket, in CGR's hand, is written "See April 2. Four & five leaved "Trefoil" from Cornwall given CGR by Miss Lisa Wilson"; on the rear free endpaper, in WMR's hand, is a note explaining CGR's inscriptions and in turn presenting the book to "Mrs Garnett" (presumably Olivia Garnett) in February 1895. MSL: inscribed by CGR, "William M. Rossetti from his affectionate sister Christina May 8. 1885" and in WMR's hand, "A few pencilings of mine here. W. M. R. 1905".

A20.1b   *First Edition, Corrected Printing (SPCK 1890)*

Same as 1885 except:

Note changes in last three lines:
TIME FLIES: | A READING DIARY | BY | CHRISTINA G. ROSSETTI, | AUTHOR OF "LETTER AND SPIRIT," ETC. | "A day's march nearer home." | James Montgomery. | [rule 14.3] | PUBLISHED UNDER THE DIRECTION OF THE TRACT COMMITTEE. | [rule, 14.3] | LONDON: | SOCIETY FOR PROMOTING CHRISTIAN KNOWLEDGE, | NORTHUMBERLAND AVENUE, CHARING CROSS, W. C.; | 43, QUEEN VICTORIA STREET, E. C.; 97, WESTBOURNE GROVE, W. | BRIGHTON: 135, north street. | 1890.

Contents: Same, including advertisements, but with revised text on 79 (see *Publication*), and on the last page of advertisements, the list of depositories now includes '43, Queen Victoria Street, E. C.; 97 Westbourne Grove, W.'

Publication: Other than the revision to page 79 (see *Note one*), the text of this printing seems not to have been reset. There is no reference to this printing in CGR's extant correspondence. Apparently the first printing had sold out, since in 1887 CGR commented that she did not have a copy of the book to send to her friend Caroline Gemmer (*Letters* 4: 33).

Printing: 280: 'OXFORD: HORACE HART, PRINTER TO THE UNIVERSITY'

Binding: Binding is sewn. Calico cloth, very dark greenish blue (Centroid 175: AZU) or glossy calico, dark olive brown (Centroid 96: CaBVaU). Endpapers: coated paper, black (Centroid 267). Edges: stained strong red (Centroid 12).

Note one: In bringing the error on page 79 to the attention of Edmund McClure, Rossetti noted that "if ever I can afford it I may perhaps indulge in a "cancel" at my own expense, SPCK permitting," adding that she had already "rewritten the passage and sent it to my Boston publishers as well as to the SPCK" in case there were to be a second edition (*Letters* 3: 260). Although CGR made numerous other corrections in copies of the first printing (see *Note one*, entry A20.1a), none of those revisions were printed in 1890 or later editions. The corrected passage in the entry for April 25 (p. 79) reads:
"Either with Moses at the Red Sea he bids the people go forward: or else with a Greater than Moses beside another sea he tenderly provokes to good works, saying, 'Go home to thy friends, and tell them how great things the Lord have done for thee, and hath had compassion on thee'–Divine words so fully recorded in no Gospel besides his own."

Locations: CaBVaU; AzU.

A20.1c   *First Edition, Corrected Printing (SPCK 1895)*

Same as 1890 printing except:

Title Page: Change in last three lines (depository information and date), as follows:
NORTHUMBERLAND AVENUE, CHARING CROSS, W. C. | 43, QUEEN VICTORIA STREET, E. C. | BRIGHTON: 135, NORTH STREET. | 1895.

Contents: Change in advertisements, as follows: <u>1</u>: three titles, *History of India* through *Sinai And Jerusalem*; <u>2</u>: four titles, *Bible Places* through *The Natural History of the Bible*; <u>3</u>: four titles, *A History of the Jewish Nation* through *Some Heroes of Travel*; <u>4</u>: four titles, *Christians Under the Crescent in Asia* through *Russia: Past and Present* and depository list.

Binding: Glossy calico, dark olive brown (Centroid 96).

Location: PBm.

A20.1d   *First Edition, Corrected Printing (SPCK 1897)*

Not seen; information drawn from an electronic version of University of Toronto copy.

TIME FLIES: | A READING DIARY | BY THE LATE | CHRISTINA G. ROSSETTI, | AUTHOR OF "LETTER AND SPIRIT," ETC. | "A day's march nearer home." | JAMES MONTGOMERY. | [rule] | PUBLISHED UNDER THE DIRECTION OF THE TRACT COMMITTEE. | [rule] | LONDON: | SOCIETY FOR PROMOTING CHRISTIAN KNOWLEDGE, | NORTHUMBERLAND AVENUE, W. C.; QUEEN VICTORIA STREET, E. C. | BRIGHTON: 129, NORTH STREET. | NEW YORK: E. & J. B. YOUNG & CO. | 1897.

Location: University of Toronto at Downsview (via Internet Archive).

A20.1e   *First Edition, Corrected Printing (SPCK 1902)*

Same as 1890 printing except:

TIME FLIES: | A READING DIARY | BY THE LATE | CHRISTINA G. ROSSETTI, | AUTHOR OF "LETTER AND SPIRIT," ETC. | "A day's march nearer home." | JAMES MONTGOMERY. | [rule, 20.7] | PUBLISHED UNDER THE DIRECTION OF THE TRACT COMMITTEE. | [rule, 20] | *SEVENTH THOUSAND* | LONDON: | SOCIETY FOR PROMOTING CHRISTIAN KNOWLEDGE, | NORTHUMBERLAND AVENUE, W. C.; QUEEN VICTORIA STREET, E. C. | BRIGHTON: 129, NORTH STREET. | NEW YORK: E. & J. B. YOUNG & CO. | 1902.

Collation: leaf size 186 x 127.

Contents: Change in advertisements: 1: four titles, *The Dawn of Civilization* through *Art Pictures from the Old Testament*; 2: six titles, *Bible Places* through *Star Atlas*; 3: seven titles, *The Art Teaching of the Primitive Church* through *Man and his Handiwork*; 4: five titles, *The Fifth Continent* through *Russia: Past and Present*.

Typography and paper: laid paper, chainlines 25 mm apart.

Binding: Buckram, dark purplish blue (Centroid 201) or blackish blue (Centroid 188). Stamping same except there is no ornament on the front. Endpapers: coated paper, blackish blue (Centroid 188). Edges: top edge gilt, fore-edge and tail rough trimmed.

Locations: Ives; TxLT.

A21   **TIME FLIES (Roberts Brothers, 1886)**

A21.1   ***First American Edition, Only Printing (1886)***

TIME FLIES: | A READING DIARY. | BY | CHRISTINA G. ROSSETTI. | "A day's march nearer home." | James Montgomery. | [ornament, 14 x 20.3, butterfly above winged hourglass] | BOSTON: | ROBERTS BROTHERS. | 1886.

Pagination: 1-7 8-307 308-309 310-340.

Collation: (145 x 101): 1⁸ 2-21⁸ 22². $1 signed. 170 leaves.

Contents: (Some text in black letter): 1: half-title 'TIME FLIES: A READING DIARY.'; 2: blank; 3: title; 4: printer's imprint; 5: dedication 'TO | MY BELOVED EXAMPLE, FRIEND, | MOTHER. | [rule 11.3 mm] | "*Her children arise up, and call her blessed.*"'; 6: blank; 7: text headed 'TIME FLIES: | [this line black letter] A Reading Diary. | [orn rule 9 mm]' and diary entry for 'January 1.'; 8-306: diary entries through 'December 31.'; 308: blank; 309: text headed 'APPENDIX. | [rule 11 mm] | Readings for certain movable Holy Days. | [rule 11.3 mm]' and 'Advent Sunday.'; 310: 'Advent: Ember Wednesday.'; 311: 'Advent: Ember Friday.'; 312: 'Advent: Ember Saturday.' and 'Ash Wednesday.'; 313: 'Lent: Ember Wednesday.'; 314: 'Lent: Ember Friday.'; 315: 'Lent: Ember Saturday.'; 316: 'Palm Sunday.'; 317: 'Monday in Holy Week.' and 'Tuesday in Holy Week.'; 318: 'Wednesday in Holy Week.'; 319: 'Thursday in Holy Week.'; 320: 'Good Friday.'; 321: 'Easter Even.' and 'Easter Day.'; 322: 'Easter Monday.' and 'Easter Tuesday.'; 323: 'Rogation Monday.'; 324: 'Rogation Tuesday.'; 326: 'Vigil of the Ascension: Rogation | Wednesday.'; 328: 'Ascension Day.'; 329: 'Whitsun Eve.'; 330: 'Whitsun Day.' and 'Whitsun Monday.'; 331: 'Whitsun Tuesday.'; 332: 'Whitsuntide: Ember Wednesday.'; 333: 'Whitsuntide: Ember Friday.'; 335: 'Whitsuntide: Ember Saturday.'; 336: 'Trinity Sunday.'; 337: 'Trinitytide: Ember Wednesday.'; 338: 'Trinitytide: Ember Friday.'; 339: 'Trinitytide: Ember Saturday.'; 340: printer's imprint.

Poems: Same as A20.

Typography and paper: (120) 109.3 x 68 (p. 177); 32 lines per page. Wove paper.

Running titles:
Rectos: 1-7: no RT; 9-307: 'A READING DIARY.'; 309: no RT; 311-339: 'A READING DIARY.'
Versos: 2-6: no RT; 8-284: 'TIME FLIES:'; 286: 'TIME FLIES' [no colon]; 288-306: 'TIME FLIES:'; 308: no RT; 310-338: 'TIME FLIES:'; 340: 'TIME FLIES: A READING DIARY.'

Binding: Two forms noted, priority undetermined. Although Binding A's similarity to the British publisher's binding might suggest priority, the *Literary World* (Boston) announcement (28 November 1885) noted that Rossetti's book would be bound "in a style uniform with *Daily Strength for Daily Needs*, a manual of devotion published last year" (449).

Binding A: Fine diagonal rib patterned cloth, dark orange yellow (Centroid 72). Front: in dark yellowish brown ink (Centroid 78), 'Time Flies | By | Christina Rossetti.'. Back plain. Spine: in gilt, 'Time | Flies | A | Reading Diary | [rule] | Christina Rossetti | [ornament, hourglass]'. Edges stained dark reddish orange (Centroid 38); endpapers printed in moderate yellow green (Centroid 120), floral vine design on diagonally striped background. One binder's leaf between endpapers and sheets, front and back. Location: NjP.

Binding B: Fine diagonal rib patterned cloth, very dark green (Centroid 147: PBm) or smooth calico, light olive gray (Centroid 112: Ives). Front: in dark reddish brown ink (Centroid 44), a three-sided rule frame open at the outer edge; within the frame, a background design of foliage and passion flowers, with a rectangular open compartment near the top edge, and another square compartment at the bottom right corner; in gilt, within top compartment, 'Time Flies [swash M, S] | By | Christina Rossetti'; in bottom compartment, also in gilt, ornament of butterfly above winged hourglass. Back: plain. Spine: in dark reddish brown ink, background design same as front; single rules extending across the head and tail; two additional rules forming a large open compartment in upper spine, with a small rectangular compartment in the middle of the spine and a circular compartment near the tail. In gilt, in the first compartment: 'TIME [swash M] | FLIES [swash S] | A | READING | DIARY | [gilt rule] | CHRISTINA | ROSSETTI'; within second compartment, in gilt, hourglass ornament; within third compartment, in gilt, "RB" device. Endpapers: printed in moderate orange yellow (Centroid 71: PBm) or dark orange yellow (Centroid 72: Ives), foliage and flowers on dotted background. Edges: all edges gilt. One binder's leaf between endpapers and sheets, front and back. Locations: Ives, PBm.

Publication: Published in late 1885 but with 1886 date. Rossetti knew of this edition, as indicated by her having sent a corrected version of the entry for April 25 to Roberts Brothers (too late, apparently, as the passage in question remains uncorrected on p. 100 of the American edition). Unfortunately, the American volume did not have strong sales; in February 1887, CGR learned from Thomas Niles that "Poor Time Flies has failed in their hands" (*Letters* 4: 11).

Announced in the *Literary World* (Boston) (28 November 1885: 449); listed among "New Publications" in *Publishers' Weekly* (26 December 1885: 963).

Price: $1.00.

Reviewed in the *Washington Post* (27 December 1885: 6); *Critic* (10 April 1886: 180); *Unitarian Review* (April 1886: 380); *Godey's Lady's Book* (May 1886: 536).

Printing: 4 (first line black letter): 'University Press: | JOHN WILSON AND SON, CAMBRIDGE.'; 340: 'University Press: John Wilson & Son, Cambridge.'

Locations: Ives; NjP; PBm; TxU (rebound).

A22   POEMS, NEW AND ENLARGED (Macmillan Subedition, 1890)

A22.1a   *First Edition, First Printing (October 1890)*

Some text in <u>black letter</u>:
POEMS | BY | CHRISTINA G. ROSSETTI | *NEW AND ENLARGED EDITION* | <u>London</u> | MACMILLAN AND CO. | AND NEW YORK | 1890

Pagination: <u>i</u>-<u>vii</u> viii-xiv <u>xv</u>-<u>xvi</u> <u>1</u> 2-218 <u>219</u>-<u>220</u> 221-287 <u>288</u>-<u>295</u> 296-450 <u>451</u>-<u>452</u>.

Plates: Same as A11 (*Goblin Market, The Princes Progress, and Other Poems*, 1875):
1) Facing title, frontispiece and caption (110.7 x 92.7, height measured with caption) from *Goblin Market* 1866/1865 as reproduced in A11; note the scratch between the woman's chin and hand, consistent with plate damage that was visible in A11, especially the 1888 printing (A11.1d). With tissue guard.
2) Facing 7, vignette and caption (62.3 x 69, height measured with caption) from engraved title of *Goblin Market* 1865, as reproduced in A11. No tissue guard.
3) Facing 21, vignette and caption (77.3 x 84.7, height measured with caption) from engraved title of *Prince's Progress* 1866. No tissue guard.
4) Facing 41, image and caption (150 x 98, height measured with caption) from frontispiece of *Prince's Progress* 1866. No tissue guard.

Collation: (175 x 120): <u>A</u>8 B-Z^8 2A-2F^8 2G^2. $1 signed. 234 leaves.

Contents: <u>i</u>: half-title 'POEMS'; <u>ii</u>: publisher's device, "MM & Co" with ornamented rule beneath, 9 x 32; <u>iii</u>: title; <u>iv</u>: blank; <u>v</u>: dedication 'TO | MY MOTHER, | IN ALL REVERENCE AND LOVE, | I INSCRIBE THIS BOOK.'; <u>vi</u>: blank; <u>vii</u>: 'CONTENTS.'; <u>xv</u>: section half-title 'THE FIRST SERIES.'; <u>xvi</u>: blank; 1-218: poems; <u>219</u>: section half-title 'DEVOTIONAL PIECES.'; <u>220</u>: blank; 221-287: poems and on 287 'END OF THE FIRST SERIES.'; <u>288</u>: blank; <u>289</u>: section half-title 'THE SECOND SERIES.'; <u>290</u>: blank; <u>291</u>: untitled poem 'Sonnets are full of love, and this my tome'; <u>292</u>: blank; <u>293</u>: poem 'THE KEY-NOTE.'; <u>294</u>: blank; <u>295</u>-450: poems and on 450, printer's imprint; <u>451</u>: advertisement for 'MESSRS. MACMILLAN AND CO.'S PUBLICATIONS.', seven titles, Rossetti's *A Pageant and Other Poems* through *Matthew Arnold's Poetical Works*; <u>452</u>: advertisement, 18 titles, *Charles Kingsley's Poems* through *Hymns for School Worship*.

Poems: "Goblin Market," "The Prince's Progress," "Maiden-Song," "Dream Land," "At Home," "'The Poor Ghost," "Grown and Flown," "A Farm Walk," "A Portrait" (sections I-II), "By The Sea," "Gone For Ever," "Love From The North," "Maggie a Lady," "From Sunset To Star Rise," "Spring Quiet," "Winter Rain," "Vanity of Vanities" ("Ah, woe is me for pleasure that is vain"), "Days Of Vanity," "The Ghost's Petition," "Once For All. (Margaret.)," "Enrica, 1865," "A Chill," "Somewhere Or Other," "Noble Sisters," "Jessie Cameron," "Spring," "Summer" ("Winter is cold-hearted"), "Autumn" ("I dwell alone"), "Winter: My Secret" ["My Secret"], "Autumn Violets," "A Dirge" ("Why were you born when the snow was falling?"), "A Bird's-Eye View," "Fata Morgana," "Memory," "'They Desire A Better Country'" (sections I-III), "Child's Talk In April," "A Green Cornfield," "The Lambs Of Grasmere, 1860," "A Birthday," "A Bride Song," "Confluents," "Remember," "After Death," "The Lowest Room," "Dream-Love," "An End," "Dead Hope," "Twice," "My Dream," "Songs In A Cornfield," "On The Wing," "L. E. L.," "Song" ("Oh roses for the flush of youth"), "The Hour And The Ghost," "Shall I Forget?," "Life And Death," "A Summer Wish," "A Year's Windfalls," "An Apple Gathering," "Song" ("Two doves upon the selfsame branch"), "Maude Clare," "Echo," "Another Spring," "Bird Or Beast?," "Eve," "A Daughter Of Eve," "A Peal Of Bells," "The Bourne," "Song" ("Oh what comes over the sea"), "Venus's Looking-Glass," "Love Lies Bleeding," "Bird Raptures," "The Queen Of Hearts," "'No, Thank You, John'," "Beauty Is Vain," "May" ("I cannot tell you how it was"), "A Pause Of Thought," "Twilight Calm," "Wife To Husband," "Three Seasons," "Mirage," "A Royal Princess," "My Friend,"

"Shut Out," "Sound Sleep," "Song" ("She sat and sang alway"), "Song" ("When I am dead, my dearest"), "Dead Before Death," "Twilight Night," "Bitter For Sweet," "What Would I Give?," "The First Spring Day," "A Bird Song," "A Smile And A Sigh," "One Day," "Rest," "The Convent Threshold," "Amor Mundi," "Up-Hill," "'The Iniquity Of The Fathers Upon The Children'" ["Under the Rose"], "In The Round Tower At Jhansi, June 8, 1857," "The German-French Campaign. 1870-1871" in two parts, "I. 'Thy Brother's Blood Crieth'," "2.'To-Day For Me'," "A Christmas Carol" ("In the bleak midwinter"), "'The Love Of Christ Which Passeth Knowledge'," "'A Bruised Reed Shall He Not Break'," "Long Barren," "Despised and Rejected," "A Better Resurrection," "If Only," "Advent" ("This Advent moon shines cold and clear"), "The Three Enemies" in three parts, "The Flesh," "The World," "The Devil," "Consider," "Dost Thou Not Care?," "Weary In Well-Doing," "One Certainty," "By The Waters Of Babylon. B.C. 570," "Christian And Jew," "Good Friday" ("Am I a stone, and not a sheep"), "Sweet Death," "Symbols," "'Consider The Lilies Of The Field'" ("Flowers preach to us if we will hear"), "The World," "A Testimony," "Paradise," "Sleep at Sea," "Mother Country," "'I Will Lift Up Mine Eyes Unto The Hills'" ("I am pale with sick desire"), "'The Master Is Come, And Calleth For Thee'," "Who Shall Deliver Me?," "'When My Heart Is Vexed, I Will Complain'" ("O Lord, how canst Thou say Thou lovest me"), "After Communion," "Martyrs' Song," "After This The Judgment," "Saints And Angels," "A Rose Plant In Jericho," "From House To Home," "Old And New Year Ditties" (sections 1-3), "Amen," "The Lowest Place," "Sonnets are full of love, and this my tome," "The Key-Note," "The Months: A Pageant," "Pastime," "'Italia, Io Ti Saluto!'," "Mirrors Of Life And Death," "Birchington Churchyard," "A Ballad Of Boding," "Yet A Little While" ("I dreamed and did not seek"), "He And She," "Monna Innominata" (sonnets 1-14), "'Luscious And Sorrowful'," "One Sea-Side Grave," "De Profundis," "Tempus Fugit," "Golden Glories," "Johnny," "Brother Bruin," "'Hollow-Sounding And Mysterious'," "'A Helpmeet For Him'," "Maiden May," "Till To-Morrow," "Death-Watches," "Touching 'Never'," "Brandons Both," "A Life's Parallels," "At Last," "Golden Silences," "In The Willow Shade," "Fluttered Wings," "A Fisher-Wife," "What's In a Name?," "Mariana," "Memento Mori," "'One Foot On Sea, And One On Shore'," "A Song Of Flight," "Buds And Babies," "A Wintry Sonnet," "Boy Johnny," "Freaks Of Fashion," "An October Garden," "Summer Is Ended," "Passing And Glassing," "'I Will Arise'," "Resurgam," "A Prodigal Son," "Sœur Louise De La Misericorde," "To-Day's Burden," "An 'Immurata' Sister," "'There Is A Budding Morrow In Midnight'," "'If Thou Sayest, Behold, We Knew It Not" (sections 1-3), "The Thread Of Life" (sections 1-3), "An Old-World Thicket," "Exultate Deo," "'All Thy Works Praise Thee, O Lord," "Later Life: A Double Sonnet Of Sonnets" (sonnets 1-28), "'For Thine Own Sake, O My God," "Until The Day Break," "A Hope Carol," "'Of Him That Was Ready To Perish'," "Christmas Carols" in three parts, "1. Whoso hears a chiming," "2. A holy, heavenly chime," "3. Lo, newborn Jesus," "A Candlemas Dialogue," "'Behold The Man!'," "The Descent From The Cross," "Mary Magdalene And The Other Mary," "'It Is Finished'," "An Easter Carol," "'Behold A Shaking'" (sections 1-2), "All Saints" ("They are flocking from the East"), "'Take Care Of Him'," "Patience Of Hope," "A Martyr" ("Inner not outer, without gnash of teeth")," "Why?," "'Love Is Strong As Death'" ("I have not sought Thee, I have not found Thee").

Typography and paper: (133.3) 124.7 x 72.3 (p. 17); various lines per page (up to 30).

Running titles: In italic.

Rectos: i-vii: no RT; ix-xiii: 'CONTENTS.'; xv: no RT; 1: no RT; 3-19: 'GOBLIN MARKET.'; 21-39: 'THE PRINCE'S PROGRESS.'; 41-49: 'MAIDEN-SONG.'; 51: 'AT HOME.'; 53: 'THE POOR GHOST.'; 55-57: 'A FARM WALK.'; 59: 'BY THE SEA.'; 61: 'LOVE FROM THE NORTH.'; 63: 'MAGGIE A LADY.'; 65: 'SPRING QUIET.'; 67: 'VANITY OF VANITIES.'; 69-71: 'THE GHOST'S PETITION.'; 73: 'ENRICA.'; 75: 'NOBLE SISTERS.'; 77-81: 'JESSIE CAMERON.'; 83: 'SUMMER.'; 85: 'AUTUMN.'; 87: 'WINTER: MY SECRET.'; 89-91: 'A BIRD'S-EYE VIEW.'; 93: 'FATA MORGANA – MEMORY.'; 95: '"THEY DESIRE A BETTER COUNTRY."'; 97: 'CHILD'S TALK IN APRIL.'; 99: 'A GREEN CORNFIELD.'; 101: 'A BIRTHDAY.'; 103: 'CONFLUENTS.'; 105: 'REMEMBER.'; 107-117: 'THE LOWEST ROOM.';

119: 'DREAM-LOVE.'; 121: 'AN END.'; 123: 'TWICE.'; 125: 'MY DREAM.'; 127-129: 'SONGS IN A CORNFIELD.'; 131: 'ON THE WING.'; 133: 'L. E. L.'; 135: 'THE HOUR AND THE GHOST.'; 137: 'SHALL I FORGET?'; 139: 'A SUMMER WISH.'; 141: 'A YEAR'S WINDFALLS.'; 143: 'AN APPLE GATHERING.'; 145: 'SONG–MAUDE CLARE.'; 147: 'ECHO.'; 149: 'BIRD OR BEAST?'; 151: 'EVE.'; 153: 'A DAUGHTER OF EVE.'; 155: 'THE BOURNE–SONG.'; 157: 'BIRD RAPTURES.'; 159: '"NO, THANK YOU, JOHN."'; 161: 'MAY.'; 163: 'TWILIGHT CALM.'; 165: 'WIFE TO HUSBAND.'; 167: 'THREE SEASONS–MIRAGE.'; 169-173: 'A ROYAL PRINCESS.'; 175: 'MY FRIEND.'; 177: 'SOUND SLEEP.'; 179: 'SONG.'; 181: 'TWILIGHT NIGHT.'; 183: 'THE FIRST SPRING DAY.'; 185: 'ONE DAY.'; 187-191: 'THE CONVENT THRESHOLD.'; 193: 'AMOR MUNDI.'; 195: '"THE INIQUITY OF THE FATHERS."'; 197-213: 'UPON THE CHILDREN."'; 215: '"THY BROTHER'S BLOOD CRIETH."'; 217: '"TO-DAY FOR ME."'; <u>219</u>: no RT; 221: 'A CHRISTMAS CAROL.'; 223: 'WHICH PASSETH KNOWLEDGE."'; 225: 'LONG BARREN.'; 227: 'DESPISED AND REJECTED.'; 229: 'IF ONLY.'; 231: 'ADVENT.'; 233: 'THE THREE ENEMIES.'; 235: 'DOST THOU NOT CARE?'; 237: 'ONE CERTAINTY.'; 239: 'BY THE WATERS OF BABYLON.'; 241-243: 'CHRISTIAN AND JEW.'; 245: 'SWEET DEATH.'; 247: '"CONSIDER THE LILIES."'; 249-251: 'A TESTIMONY.'; 253: 'PARADISE.'; 255: 'SLEEP AT SEA' [no period]; 257-259: 'MOTHER COUNTRY.'; 261: 'UNTO THE HILLS."'; 263: 'WHO SHALL DELIVER ME?'; 265: 'I WILL COMPLAIN."'; 267: 'MARTYRS' SONG.'; 269: 'AFTER THIS THE JUDGMENT.'; 271: 'SAINTS AND ANGELS.'; 273: 'A ROSE PLANT IN JERICHO.'; 275-283: 'FROM HOUSE TO HOME.'; 285: 'OLD AND NEW YEAR DITTIES.'; 287: 'THE LOWEST PLACE.'; <u>289-295</u>: no RT; 297-311: 'A PAGEANT.'; 313-317: 'MIRRORS OF LIFE AND DEATH.'; 319-325: 'A BALLAD OF BODING.'; 327: 'YET A LITTLE WHILE.'; 329-337: 'MONNA INNOMINATA.'; 339: 'ONE SEA-SIDE GRAVE.'; 341: 'GOLDEN GLORIES–JOHNNY.'; 343: 'JOHNNY.'; 345: 'BROTHER BRUIN.'; 347: '"HOLLOW-SOUNDING & MYSTERIOUS."'; 349-351: 'MAIDEN MAY.'; 353: 'DEATH-WATCHES.'; 355-357: 'BRANDONS BOTH.'; 359: 'AT LAST.'; 361: 'IN THE WILLOW SHADE.'; 363: 'FLUTTERED WINGS.'; 365: 'WHAT'S IN A NAME?'; 367: 'MARIANA–MEMENTO MORI.'; 369: 'A SONG OF FLIGHT.'; 371: 'BOY JOHNNY.'; 373: 'FREAKS OF FASHION.'; 375: 'AN OCTOBER GARDEN.'; 377: '"I WILL ARISE."'; 378: 'SŒUR LOUISE DE LA MISÉRICORDE.'; 381: 'AN "IMMURATA" SISTER.'; 383: '"IF THOU SAYEST . . ."'; 385: 'THE THREAD OF LIFE.'; 387-393: 'AN OLD WORLD THICKET.'; 395: '"THY WORKS PRAISE THEE, O LORD."'; 397-405: 'O LORD."'; 407-423: 'LATER LIFE.'; 425: '"FOR THINE OWN SAKE, O MY GOD."'; 427: 'A HOPE CAROL.'; 429-431: 'CHRISTMAS CAROLS.'; 433: 'A CANDLEMAS DIALOGUE.'; 435: 'THE DESCENT FROM THE CROSS.'; 437: '"IT IS FINISHED."'; 439: '"BEHOLD A SHAKING."'; 441: 'ALL SAINTS.'; 443: 'PATIENCE OF HOPE.'; 445-447: 'A MARTYR.'; 449: 'WHY?'; 451: no RT.

Versos: <u>ii-vi</u>: no RT; viii-xiv: 'CONTENTS.'; xvi: no RT; 2-20: 'GOBLIN MARKET.'; 22-40: 'THE PRINCE'S PROGRESS.'; 42-48: 'MAIDEN-SONG.'; 50: 'DREAM LAND.'; 52: 'THE POOR GHOST.'; 54: 'GROWN AND FLOWN.'; 56: 'A FARM WALK.'; 58: 'A PORTRAIT.'; 60: 'GONE FOR EVER.'; 62: 'MAGGIE A LADY.'; 64: 'FROM SUNSET TO STAR RISE.'; 66: 'WINTER RAIN.'; 68: 'DAYS OF VANITY.'; 70: 'THE GHOST'S PETITION.'; 72: 'ONCE FOR ALL.'; 74: 'A CHILL.'; 76: 'NOBLE SISTERS.'; 78-80: 'JESSIE CAMERON.'; 82: 'SPRING.'; 84-86: 'AUTUMN.'; 88: 'AUTUMN VIOLETS.'; 90-92: 'A BIRD'S-EYE VIEW.'; 94: 'MEMORY.'; 96: '"THEY DESIRE A BETTER COUNTRY."'; 98: 'CHILD'S TALK IN APRIL.'; 100: 'THE LAMBS OF GRASMERE.'; 102: 'A BRIDE SONG.'; 104: 'CONFLUENTS.'; 106: 'AFTER DEATH.'; 108-118: 'THE LOWEST ROOM.'; 120: 'DREAM-LOVE.'; 122: 'DEAD HOPE.'; 124: 'TWICE.'; 126: 'MY DREAM.'; 128-130: 'SONGS IN A CORNFIELD.'; 132: 'L. E. L.'; 134-136: 'THE HOUR AND THE GHOST.'; 138: 'LIFE AND DEATH.'; 140-142: 'A YEAR'S WINDFALLS.'; 144: 'AN APPLE GATHERING.'; 146: 'MAUDE CLARE.'; 148: 'ANOTHER SPRING.'; 150-152: 'EVE.'; 154: 'A PEAL OF BELLS.'; 156: 'LOVE LIES BLEEDING.'; 158: 'THE QUEEN OF HEARTS.'; 160: 'BEAUTY IS VAIN.'; 162: 'A PAUSE OF THOUGHT.'; 164: 'TWILIGHT CALM.'; 166: 'WIFE TO HUSBAND.'; 168-174: 'A ROYAL PRINCESS.'; 176: 'SHUT OUT.'; 178: 'SONG.'; 180: 'DEAD BEFORE DEATH.'; 182: 'WHAT WOULD I GIVE?'; 184: 'A SMILE AND A SIGH.'; 186:

'REST – THE CONVENT THRESHOLD.'; 188-190: 'THE CONVENT THRESHOLD.'; 192: 'AMOR MUNDI.'; 194: 'UP-HILL.'; 196-212: '"THE INIQUITY OF THE FATHERS"'; 214: 'IN THE ROUND TOWER AT JHANSI.'; 216: '"THY BROTHER'S BLOOD CRIETH."'; 218: '"TO-DAY FOR ME."'; 220: no RT; 222: '"THE LOVE OF CHRIST"; 224: '"A BRUISED REED."'; 226: 'DESPISED AND REJECTED.'; 228: 'A BETTER RESURRECTION.'; 230: 'ADVENT.'; 232: 'THE THREE ENEMIES.'; 234: 'CONSIDER.'; 236: 'WEARY IN WELL-DOING.'; 238-240: 'BY THE WATERS OF BABYLON.'; 242: 'CHRISTIAN AND JEW.'; 244: 'GOOD FRIDAY.'; 246: 'SYMBOLS.'; 248: 'THE WORLD – A TESTIMONY.'; 250: 'A TESTIMONY.'; 252: 'PARADISE.'; 254-256: 'SLEEP AT SEA.'; 258: 'MOTHER COUNTRY.'; 260: '"I WILL LIFT UP MINE EYES"; 262: '"THE MASTER IS COME."'; 264: '"WHEN MY HEART IS VEXED,'; 266: 'AFTER COMMUNION.'; 268: 'MARTYRS' SONG.'; 270: 'AFTER THIS THE JUDGMENT.'; 272: 'SAINTS AND ANGELS.'; 274-282: 'FROM HOUSE TO HOME.'; 284: 'OLD AND NEW YEAR DITTIES.'; 286: 'AMEN.'; 288-294: no RT; 296-310: 'THE MONTHS:'; 312: 'PASTIME.'; 314-316: 'MIRRORS OF LIFE AND DEATH.'; 318: 'BIRCHINGTON CHURCHYARD.'; 320-326: 'A BALLAD OF BODING.'; 328: 'HE AND SHE.'; 330-336: 'MONNA INNOMINATA.'; 338: '"LUSCIOUS AND SORROWFUL."'; 340: 'TEMPUS FUGIT.'; 342: 'JOHNNY.'; 344: 'BROTHER BRUIN.'; 346: '"HOLLOW-SOUNDING & MYSTERIOUS."'; 348: '"A HELPMEET FOR HIM."'; 350: 'MAIDEN MAY.'; 352: 'TILL TO-MORROW.'; 354-356: 'BRANDONS BOTH.'; 358: 'A LIFE'S PARALLELS.'; 360: 'GOLDEN SILENCES.'; 362: 'IN THE WILLOW SHADE.'; 364: 'A FISHER-WIFE.'; 366: 'WHAT'S IN A NAME?'; 368: '"ONE FOOT ON SEA, & ONE ON SHORE."'; 370: 'BUDS AND BABIES.'; 372-374: 'FREAKS OF FASHION.'; 376: 'PASSING AND GLASSING.'; 378: 'RESURGAM – A PRODIGAL SON.'; 380: 'TO-DAY'S BURDEN.'; 382: '"A BUDDING MORROW."'; 384: '"IF THOU SAYEST . . ."'; 386: 'THE THREAD OF LIFE.'; 388-392: 'AN OLD-WORLD THICKET.'; 394: 'EXULTATE DEO.'; 396-404: '"ALL THY WORKS PRAISE THEE,'; 406: '"THY WORKS PRAISE THEE, O LORD."'; 408-424: 'LATER LIFE.'; 426: 'UNTIL THE DAY BREAK.'; 428: '"OF HIM THAT WAS READY TO PERISH."'; 430-432: 'CHRISTMAS CAROLS.'; 434: '"BEHOLD THE MAN!"'; 436: '"IT IS FINISHED."'; 438: 'AN EASTER CAROL.'; 440: 'ALL SAINTS.'; 442: '"TAKE CARE OF HIM."'; 444-448: 'A MARTYR.'; 450: '"LOVE IS STRONG AS DEATH."'; 453: no RT.

Binding: Calico cloth, between dark grayish blue (Centroid 187) and blackish blue (Centroid 188). Binding same as A11.1d (1888 printing of *Goblin Market, The Prince's Progress and Other Poems*): Front: gilt, stamped with same design (intersecting lines and with rings grouped at corners) as 1865 *Goblin Market*. Back: blind-stamped, same design as cover. Spine: gilt, '[rule below two small rings (one at left, one at right)] | POEMS | CHRISTINA G. | ROSSETTI | [rule between two small rings, ○—○ with a group of three rings in inverted pyramid beneath rule] | MACMILLAN & C.° | [rule]'. Endpapers: white wove paper, unwatermarked. Edges: plain, top trimmed, fore-edge and tail rough trimmed.

Publication: November 1890. In June 1890, CGR began correspondence with Macmillan about the content and arrangement of the new volume, which was to combine *Goblin Market, The Prince's Progress and Other Poems*, and *A Pageant* along with "a few stray magazine pieces" (*Letters* 4: 204). This was the closest Macmillan could come to a complete edition, given that they did not hold the copyright to *Sing-Song* or to poems that had been published by the Society for Promoting Christian Knowledge. The "considerable rearrangement" (*Letters* 4: 205) that CGR initially planned for the combined volume was impossible, given that Macmillan would not allow changes to the plates of *Goblin Market and The Prince's Progress*. CGR's response was to "achieve a tolerable (?) arrangement [by] keeping the 2 sets of pieces so far distinct as to style them "First Series," "Second Series," respectively" (*Letters* 4: 206), and to make all additions to the *Pageant* section. CGR asked to revise proofs of the *Pageant* section, and by the end of June was expecting to "soon have the pleasure of returning the sheets" (*Letters* 4: 208), but she did not receive a copy of the published book until October (*Letters* 4: 215).

Macmillan's Editions book records a total of eleven impressions, each of 1000 copies, with two in 1890

(October and December), two in 1891 (in February and August), and continuing nearly every year into the new century (December 1892, July 1894, April 1895, February 1896, December 1897, May 1899, and March 1901). The October 1890 impression was printed from type and from plates (but no copies from type have been located); all remaining impressions were printed from plates exclusively. Impressions after the first have an impression statement on iv (verso of title); this page is blank in first impression copies. Copies printed from plates bear the usual black letter "S" in the direction line on page 1.

Announced in the *Athenaeum* (1 November 1890: 571) as ready "next week."

Price: 7 s. 6d.

Reviewed in the *Academy* (7 February 1891: 130-131); *Literary World* (Boston) (14 March 1891: 95-96).

Printing: 450: '*Printed by* R. & R. CLARK, E*dinburgh*.'

Note one: The Macmillan Archives copy has a hand correction in pencil on p. 261. At the end of line 7 (from the bottom of the page), the ending punctuation (apparently a semicolon with damage to the top) is crossed out, and ';/' is added in the margin.

Locations: KKS, Macmillan. Not seen (information provided by libraries): CSt, NjP, California State at Northridge.

A22.1b   *First edition, Second Printing (December 1890)*

Same as first printing except:

Contents: iv: '*First complete edition printed November* 1890. *Reprinted December* 1890.'

Running titles:

Rectos: 37: damage to 'THE'; 149: 'BIRD OR BEAST' [no question mark]; 163: period moved up; 185: no period; 195: damage to 'THE'.

Versos: 70: no period; 156: no period; 334: no period; 420: no period.

Binding: Color between dark grayish blue (Centroid 187) and blackish blue (Centroid 188). Two forms of spine noted, priority undetermined:

Spine A: Same as first printing: gilt, '[rule below two small rings (one at left, one at right)] | POEMS | CHRISTINA G. | ROSSETTI | [rule, with ring at either end and a group of three rings in inverted pyramid beneath] | MACMILLAN & C.° | [rule]'; Location: TxCM.

Spine B: Same as first printing except publisher's name: instead of a period after the C in 'Co" there is a short rule beneath the 'o.' Location: Ives.

Locations: Ives; TxCM.

A22.1c   *First Edition, Third Printing (February 1891)*

Not seen; see Publication, A22.1a and Contents, A22.1e.

A22.1d   *First edition, Fourth printing (August 1891)*

Not seen; see Publication, A22.1a and Contents, A22.1e.

A22.1e   *First edition, Fifth Printing (December 1892)*

Title Page: Date changed to 1892.

Contents: same except iv: '*First complete edition printed November* 1890 | *Reprinted December* 1890, *January* 1891, *August* 1891, 1892'; 451: advertisement for two Rossetti titles, *A Pageant and Other Poems* and *Speaking Likenesses* and for Macmillan's Standard Poets, with volumes by Tennyson, Lowell, Wordsworth, Shelley, Arnold, and Coleridge; 452: advertisement, 13 titles, *Charles Kingsley's Poems* to *The Works Of William Shakespeare.*

Running titles: same except:

Rectos: 255: no period.

Versos: 334: period faint.

Binding: Color changed to very dark greenish blue (Centroid 175); period after C in "Co" on spine.

Location: NjP.

A22.1f   *First Edition, Sixth Printing (July 1894)*

Title Page: Date changed to 1894.

Contents: same except iv: '*First complete edition printed November* 1890 | *Reprinted December* 1890, *January* 1891, *August* 1891, 1892, 1894'; 451: advertisement, heading "By Miss Rossetti" and three titles, *Goblin Market, Sing-Song* and *Speaking Likenesses*; heading "Complete Editions of the Poets" with six titles, *The Works of Alfred Lord Tennyson* through *The Poetical Works of William Wordsworth*; 452: advertisement heading "Some Volumes of the Golden Treasury Series" and nineteen titles, *The Golden Treasury of the Best Songs and Lyrical Poems in the English Language* through *The Sunday Book of Poetry for the Young.*

Running titles:

Rectos: 63: no period; 109: no period; 149: 'BIRD OR BEAST.'; 255: no period.

Versos: 2: no period; 102: no period; 334: no period.

Binding: Color closest to blackish blue (Centroid 188); same design, but on spine, 'MACMILLAN & C.ᵒ' at tail is reset and the rule is thinner than that of the 1890 binding.

Note one: Changes in damage to running titles visible in earlier printings (such as the appearance of a period in the RT on 149) suggests that this printing used a different set of plates.

Location: Ives.

A22.1g   *First Edition, Seventh Printing (April 1895)*

Not seen; see Publication, A22.1a and Contents, A22.1j.

Locations: University of Waterloo, call number PR5237.A1 1895; Bodleian, shelfmark Dunston B 1542.

A22.1h   *First Edition, Eighth Printing (February 1896)*

Not seen; information drawn from an electronic version of University of California copy.

Title Page: Date changed to 1896.

Contents: same as A22.1f except: iv: '*First complete edition printed November* 1890 | *Reprinted December* 1890, *January* 1891, *August* 1891, 1892, | 1894, 1895, 1896'; <u>451</u>: advertisement, heading "By the late Christina G. Rossetti" and five titles, *New Poems, The Poems of Christina Rossetti, Speaking Likenesses, Sing-Song*, and *The Rossetti Birthday Book*; second heading "Complete Editions of the Poets" with six titles, *The Complete Works of Alfred Lord Tennyson* through *The Poetical Works of William Wordsworth*; <u>452</u>: advertisement heading "Works By Matthew Arnold" (eleven titles) and "Edited By Matthew Arnold" (four titles).

Location: CU (via Internet Archive).

A22.1i   *First Edition, Ninth Printing (December 1897)*

Some text in <u>black letter</u>:
POEMS | BY | CHRISTINA G. ROSSETTI | *NEW AND ENLARGED EDITION* | <u>London</u> | MACMILLAN AND CO., Limited | NEW YORK: THE MACMILLAN COMPANY | 1897 | *All rights reserved*

Contents: same as A22.1h except: iv: '*First complete edition printed November* 1890 | *Reprinted December* 1890, *January* 1891, *August* 1891, 1892, | 1894, 1895, 1896, 1897'.

Running titles: frequent damage and signs of wear, including:
Rectos: 63: no period: 109: faint period; 149: "BIRD OR BEAST."; 255: no period.
Versos: 2: no period; 102: faint period; 334: no period.

Binding: Color: blackish blue (Centroid 188); Spine: gilt, '[rule below two small rings (one at left, one at right)] | POEMS | CHRISTINA G. | ROSSETTI | [rule between two small rings, ○—○ with a group of three rings in inverted pyramid beneath rule] | MACMILLAN & CO. | [rule]'.

Printing: '*Printed by* R & R Clark, Limited, *Edinburgh*.'

Location: University of Texas at Dallas.

A22.1j   *First Edition, Tenth Printing (May 1899)*

Same as earlier printings except:

Some text in <u>black letter</u>:
POEMS | BY | CHRISTINA G. ROSSETTI | *NEW AND ENLARGED EDITION* | <u>London</u> | MACMILLAN AND CO., Limited | NEW YORK: THE MACMILLAN COMPANY | 1899 | *All rights reserved*

Contents: same except iv: '*First complete edition printed November* 1890 | *Reprinted December* 1890, *January* 1891, *August* 1891, 1892, 1894, 1895, 1896, 1897, 1899'; 451: advertisement, heading "By the late Christina G. Rossetti" and five titles, *New Poems, The Poems of Christina Rossetti, Speaking Likenesses, Sing-Song* and *The Rossetti Birthday Book*; second heading "Complete Editions of the Poets" with six titles, *The Complete Works of Alfred Lord Tennyson* through *The Poetical Works of William Wordsworth*; 452: advertisement headed "Works by Alfred Lord Tennyson" and list of 32 titles.

Running titles: frequent damage and signs of wear, including:
Rectos: 63: no period; 109: no period; 149: "BIRD OR BEAST."; 255: no period.
Versos: 2: no period; 102: no period; 334: no period.

Binding: Same as A22.1h.

Printing: 'Printed by R & R Clark, Limited, *Edinburgh*.'

Location: Ives.

A22.1k   *First Edition, Eleventh Printing (March 1901)*

Not seen; see Publication, A22.1a.

Location: copy listed in University of Arkansas library catalog, PR5237 .A1 1901.

A23 THE FACE OF THE DEEP (1892)

A23.1a *First Edition, First Printing (1892)*

The Face of the Deep: | A DEVOTIONAL COMMENTARY | ON | THE APOCALYPSE. | BY | CHRISTINA G. ROSSETTI, | AUTHOR OF "SEEK AND FIND," "TIME FLIES," ETC. | "Thy judgments are a great deep."–Psalm xxxvi. 6. | PUBLISHED UNDER THE DIRECTION OF THE TRACT COMMITTEE. | LONDON: | SOCIETY FOR PROMOTING CHRISTIAN KNOWLEDGE, | NORTHUMBERLAND AVENUE, W. C.; 43, QUEEN VICTORIA STREET, E. C. | Brighton: 135, north street. | New York: E. & J. B. YOUNG & CO. | 1892.

Pagination: 1-9 10-46 47 48-84 85 86-145 146 147-164 165 166-192 193 194-220 221 222-240 241 242-256 257 258-273 274 275-285 286 287-308 309 310-329 330 331-350 351 352-370 371 372-379 380 381-394 395 396-411 412 413-427 428 429-457 458 459-476 477 478-520 521 522-552 1 2-8.

Collation: (216 x 138): A⁸ B-Z⁸ AA-MM⁸. $1 signed. 280 leaves.

Contents: (some text in black letter): An errata slip is tipped in between pages 6 and 7 (see *Note one*). 1: half-title 'THE FACE OF THE DEEP.'; 2: blank; 3: title; 4: printer's imprint; 5: dedication 'TO | My Mother, | FOR THE FIRST TIME | TO HER | BELOVED, REVERED, CHERISHED MEMORY.'; 6: blank; 7: 'PREFATORY NOTE.'; 8: blank; 9: text headed 'THE APOCALYPSE. | [rule, 16 mm] | CHAPTER I.'; 47: 'CHAPTER II.'; 85: 'CHAPTER III.'; 146: 'CHAPTER IV.'; 165: 'CHAPTER V.'; 193: 'CHAPTER VI.'; 221: 'CHAPTER VII.'; 241: 'CHAPTER VIII.'; 257: 'CHAPTER IX.'; 274: 'CHAPTER X.'; 286: 'CHAPTER XI.'; 309: 'CHAPTER XII.'; 330: 'CHAPTER XIII.'; 351: 'CHAPTER XIV.'; 371: 'CHAPTER XV.'; 380: 'CHAPTER XVI.'; 395: 'CHAPTER XVII.'; 412: 'CHAPTER XVIII.'; 428: 'CHAPTER XIX.'; 458: 'CHAPTER XX.'; 477: 'CHAPTER XXI.'; 521: 'CHAPTER XXII.'; 552: text and printer's imprint; 1: advertisement headed 'PUBLICATIONS | OF THE | Society for Promoting Christian Knowledge," fifteen titles in the series "The Fathers For English Readers," *Leo the Great* through *The Venerable Bede*; 2: heading 'THE ROMANCE OF SCIENCE.' with nine titles, 'NON-CHRISTIAN RELIGIOUS SYSTEMS.' with eight titles; 3: heading 'DIOCESAN HISTORIES.' with sixteen titles, 'CHIEF ANCIENT PHILOSOPHIES.' with three titles; 4: heading 'CHURCH HYMNS.' with three titles, 'COMMENTARY ON THE BIBLE.' with seven titles, 'ANCIENT HISTORY FROM THE MONUMENTS.' with five titles; 5: heading 'MISCELLANEOUS PUBLICATIONS.' with twelve titles, *Aids to Prayer* through *Church in the New Testament* and including Rossetti's *Called to Be Saints*; 6: twelve titles, *Devotional (A) Life Of Our Lord* through *Paley's Evidences* and including Rossetti's *Letter and Spirit*; 7: twelve titles, *Paley's Horæ Paulinæ* through *Servants Of Scripture (The)* and including Rossetti's *Seek and Find*; 8: ten titles, *Sinai And Jerusalem; or, Scenes from Bible Lands* through *Within The Veil* and including Rossetti's *Time Flies*.

Poems: (Untitled poems identified by first line):
"O, ye who love to-day," "Heaven is not far, though far the sky," "Lord, I am feeble and of mean account," "Astonished Heaven looked on when man was made," "My God, Thyself being Love Thy heart is love," "Long and dark the nights, dim and short the days," "While Christ lay dead the widowed world," "If thou be dead, forgive and thou shalt live," "Ah, Lord, we all have pierced Thee: wilt Thou be," "Thy lovely saints do bring Thee love," "O Lord Almighty, Who has formed us weak," "Earth cannot bar flame from ascending," "Lord, I am here, – But, child, I look for thee," "O Lord, on Whom we gaze and dare not gaze," "O Jesu, gone so far apart," "What will it be, O my soul, what will it be," "We are of those who tremble at Thy word," "Lord, Thou art fulness, I am emptiness," "All weareth, all wasteth," "Light colourless doth colour all things else," "The twig sprouteth," "'As dying, and behold we live!'," "Little Lamb, who lost thee?," "Love, to be love, must walk Thy way," "Lord, make me one with Thine own faithful ones," "O Shepherd with the bleeding Feet," "Lord, make me pure," "O Christ

the Life, look on me where I lie," "That Eden of earth's sunrise cannot vie," "My God, wilt Thou accept, and will not we," "Cast down but not destroyed, chastened not slain," "Be faithful unto death. Christ proffers thee," "Hidden from the darkness of our mortal sight," "Lord, make us all love all: that when we meet," "What is the beginning? Love. What the course? Love still," "O Lord, seek us, O Lord, find us," "Lord, carry me. – Nay, but I grant thee strength," "Beloved, yield thy time to God, for He," "O foolish Soul! to make thy count," "O Lord, I cannot plead my love of Thee," "As froth on the face of the deep," "Contempt and pangs and haunting fears," "Lord, grant us eyes to see and ears to hear," "All that we see rejoices in the sunshine," "Thy Name, O Christ, as ointment is poured forth," "Ah me, that I should be," "Trembling before Thee we fall down to adore Thee," "Bone to his bone, grain to his grain of dust," "Can I know it? – Nay," "Patience must dwell with Love, for Love and Sorrow," "Wisest of sparrows that sparrow which sitteth alone," "Oh knell of a passing time," "I, Lord, Thy foolish sinner low and small," "Once within, within for evermore," "O Lord, I am ashamed to seek Thy Face," "O Saviour, show compassion!," "As dying, – and behold, we live!," "I long for joy, O Lord, I long for gold," "From shame that is neither glory nor grace," "Life that was born to-day," "'As many as I love,' – Ah, Lord, Who lovest all," "St Peter once: 'Lord, dost Thou wash my feet?'," "Lord, we are rivers running to Thy sea," "Who sits with the King in His Throne? Not a slave but a Bride," "Lord, dost Thou look on me, and will not I," "O Jesu, better than Thy gifts," "O God Eternal, Who causest the vapours to ascend from the ends of the earth," "Tumult and turmoil, trouble and toil," "O God the Holy Ghost Who art Light unto Thine elect," "All things are fair, if we had eyes to see," "Love loveth Thee, and wisdom loveth Thee," "Ah Lord, Lord, if my heart were right with Thine," "Shadows to-day, while shadows show God's Will," "I saw a Saint. – How canst thou tell that he," "Lord, give me blessed fear," "Hope is the counterpoise of fear," "Thou Who wast Centre of a stable, with two saints and harmless cattle," "None other Lamb, none other Name," "Whoso hath anguish is not dead in sin," "The joy of Saints, like incense turned to fire," "My heart is yearning," "Because Thy Love hath sought me," "O Lord God, hear the silence of each soul," "From worshipping and serving the creature more than the Creator," "They throng from the east and the west," "The world, –what a world, ah me!," "Voices from above and from beneath," "Love still is Love, and doeth all things well," "Faith and Hope are wings to Love," "Experience bows a sweet contented face," "Such is Love, it comforts in extremity," "'Because He First Loved Us'," "Safe where I cannot lie yet," "How know I that it looms lovely that land I have never seen," "Sorrow of saints is sorrow of a day," "From any sword that would devour for ever," "It is not death, O Christ, to die for Thee," "Once slain for Him Who first was slain for them," "'Thou Shalt Hear a Voice Behind Thee'," "Dear Angels and dear disembodied Saints," "Lord, grant us calm, if calm can set forth Thee," "A Sorrowful Sigh of a Prisoner," "Jesus Who didst touch the leper," "Thy Cross cruciferous doth flower in all," "Good Lord, to-day," "The half moon shows a face of plaintive sweetness," "'Out of the Angel's hand,'" "As the dove which found no rest," "Love us unto the end, and prepare us," "Thy fainting spouse, yet still Thy spouse," "How great is little man!," "A moon impoverished amid stars curtailed," "Oh fallen star! a darkened light," "Who knows? God knows: and what He knows," "One woe is past. Come what come will," "Lord God Whom we fear, protect us," "O Christ our Light Whom even in darkness we," "Life that was born to-day," "O mine enemy," "Time seems not short," "Grant, O Lord," "Thou Who was straitened till Thy baptism was accomplished," "Lord, grant us eyes to see," "Alone Lord God, in Whom our trust and peace," "As flames that consume the mountains, as winds that coerce the sea," "Where never tempest heaveth," "Toll, bell, toll. For hope is flying," "Yet earth was very good in days of old," "Lord, grant us grace to mount by steps of grace," "Marvel of marvels, if I myself shall behold," "So brief a life, and then an endless life," "I think of the saints I have known, and lift up mine eyes," "Tempest and terror below: but Christ the Almighty above," "O Lord, when Thou didst call me, didst Thou know," "Behold in heaven a floating, dazzling cloud," "If not with hope of life," "O Lamb of God, slain from the foundation of the world, save us," "Day and night the Accuser makes no pause," "'Launch out into the deep,' Christ spake of old," "Lord, grant us grace to rest upon Thy word," "Love is alone the worthy law of love," "Slain in their high places: – fallen on rest," "In tempest and storm blackness of darkness for ever," "Slain for man, slain for me, O Lamb of God, look down," "Grant us, O Lord, that patience and that faith," "Hail, garden of confident hope!" "Lord, give me grace | To take the lowest place," "As the voice of many waters all saints sing as one," "Unspotted lambs to follow the one Lamb," "Can peach renew lost bloom," "Sweetness of rest when Thou sheddest rest," "Jerusalem of fire," "The Passion Flower hath sprung up tall," "Time lengthening, in the lengthening seemeth long," "Seven vials hold Thy wrath: but what can hold," "Tremble, thou earth, at the Presence of the Lord," "Lord, I believe, help Thou mine unbelief," "Solomon most glorious in array," "Fear, Faith, and Hope have sent their hearts above," "From love that cleaveth not to Thee," "Lord, give me love that I may love Thee much," "Our Mothers, lovely women pitiful," "Crimson as the rubies, crimson as the roses," "Foul is she and ill-favoured, set askew," "Content to come, content to go," "I peered within, and saw a world of sin," "'I sit a queen, and am no widow,'" "Standing Afar Off For the Fear of Her Torment," "The hills are tipped with sunshine, while I walk," "What is this above thy head," "From all kinds of music which worship an idol in thy stead," "Alleluia! or Alas! my heart is crying," "I lift mine eyes to see: earth vanisheth," "The least, if so I am," "When wickedness is broken as a tree," "Lord, to thine own grant watchful hearts and eyes," "As violets so be I recluse and sweet," "Worship God," "Grant us such grace that we may work Thy Will," "Passing away the bliss," "As one red rose in a garden where all other roses are white," "'He Treadeth the Winepress of the Fierceness and Wrath of Almighty God','" "King of Kings, and Lord of Lords," "Nerve us with patience, Lord, to toil or rest," "Before the beginning Thou has foreknown the end," "O Christ Who once wast condemned that we might never be condemned," "The end of all things is at hand. We all," "Lord, grant us wills to trust Thee with such aim," "Time passeth away with its pleasure and pain," "O Lord, fulfil Thy Will," "Yea, blessed and holy is he that hath part in the First Resurrection!," "Lift up thine eyes to seek the invisible," "On the dead for whom once Thou diedst, Lord Jesus, have mercy," "Clother of the lily, Feeder of the sparrow," "The sea laments with unappeasable," "I, laid beside thy gate, am Lazarus," "A lovely city in a lovely land," "Whiteness most white. Ah, to be clean again," "Together with my dead body shall they arise," "A Churchyard Song of Patient Hope," "New creatures; the Creator still the Same," "Tune me, O Lord, into one harmony," "Lord, whomsoever Thou shalt send to me," "Lord, by what inconceivable dim road," "The King's Daughter is all glorious within," "What are these lovely ones, yea, what are these?" "Lord, hast Thou so loved us: and will not we," "A chill blank world. Yet over the utmost sea," "Short is time, and only time is bleak," "Love builds a nest on earth and waits for rest," "Bring me to see, Lord, bring me yet to see," "Day that hath no tinge of night," "Lord Jesu, Thou art sweetness to my soul," "We know not a voice of that River," "It is the greatness of Thy Love, dear Lord, that we would celebrate," "Alas, alas! for the self-destroyed," "A Song for the Feast of all Saints" ("Love is the key of life and death"), "The night is far spent, the day is at hand," "Hark! the Alleluias of the great salvation," "The shout of a King is among them. One day may I be," "Me and my gift: kind Lord, behold," "Jesus alone: –if thus it were to me," "Can man rejoice who lives in hourly fear?," "For Each," "For All."

Typography and paper: (160) 150.7 x 89 (p. 321); 44 lines per page, wove paper. Bible verses printed in bold type; poetry in smaller font than other text.

Running titles: In italic.
Rectos: <u>1</u>-<u>9</u>: no RT; 11-45: 'THE FACE OF THE DEEP.'; 47: no RT; 49-83: 'THE FACE OF THE DEEP.' 85: no RT; 87-163: 'THE FACE OF THE DEEP.'; 165: no RT; 167-191: 'THE FACE OF THE DEEP.'; 193: no RT; 195-219: 'THE FACE OF THE DEEP.'; 221: no RT; 223-239: 'THE FACE OF THE DEEP.'; 241: no RT; 243-255: 'THE FACE OF THE DEEP.'; 257: no RT; 259-307: 'THE FACE OF THE DEEP.'; 309: no RT; 311-349: 'THE FACE OF THE DEEP.'; 351: no RT; 353-369: 'THE FACE OF THE DEEP.'; 371: no RT; 373-393: 'THE FACE OF THE DEEP.'; 395: no RT; 397-475: 'THE FACE OF THE DEEP.'; 477: no RT; 479-519: 'THE FACE OF THE DEEP.'; 521: no RT; 523-551: 'THE FACE OF THE DEEP.'; <u>1</u>: no RT; <u>3</u>: 'FOR PROMOTING CHRISTIAN KNOWLEDGE' [no period]; <u>5</u>-<u>7</u>: 'FOR PROMOTING CHRISTIAN KNOWLEDGE.'

Versos: 2-8: no RT; 10-144: 'THE FACE OF THE DEEP.'; 146: no RT; 148-272: 'THE FACE OF THE DEEP.'; 274: no RT; 276-284: 'THE FACE OF THE DEEP.'; 286: no RT; 288-328: 'THE FACE OF THE DEEP.'; 330: no RT; 332-378: 'THE FACE OF THE DEEP.'; 380: no RT; 382-410: 'THE FACE OF THE DEEP.'; 412: no RT; 414-426: 'THE FACE OF THE DEEP.'; 428: no RT; 430-456: 'THE FACE OF THE DEEP.'; 458: no RT; 460-552: 'THE FACE OF THE DEEP.'; 2-6: 'PUBLICATIONS OF THE SOCIETY'; 8: 'PUBLICATIONS OF THE S. P. C. K.'

Binding: Calico cloth, blackish blue (Centroid 188). Front: in gilt; across top near edge, group of four wavy rules; beneath rules, 'THE FACE | OF THE DEEP | *CHRISTINA ROSSETTI*'; across bottom, another set of four wavy rules, blind-stamped. Back: two sets of wavy rules, as on front, but both sets blind-stamped. Spine, in gilt: '[four wavy rules, extending from front] | THE | Face | OF THE | Deep | [single rule] | CHRISTINA G. | ROSSETTI | [device, "SPCK"] | [blind-stamped wavy rules, extending from front and back]'; note the 'A' in 'CHRISTINA' has a chevron-shaped bar. Boards have beveled edges. Endpapers: coated paper, black (Centroid 267). Edges trimmed.

Publication: April 1891. On October 19, 1891, Rossetti noted in her account book that she had been paid £100 for the copyright, the largest sum she ever received from the SPCK However, in February 1894, WMR noted in his diary that when CGR "was paid, some months ago, the stipulated price of her book, *The Face of the Deep*, she voluntarily returned the money" because the SPCK had published a book that supported vivisection, to which CGR was deeply opposed (*Family Letters*, 218). By February 1892, Rossetti informed Edmund McClure that she hoped for a "felicitous" binding, "as invests *Called to be Saints* and . . . *Time Flies*" in a dark color: "black, but if that might repel a cheerful purchaser I should at any rate vote for something dark and grave not to say sombre" (*Letters* 4: 264). The book was published on April 29. In May, Rossetti again wrote to McClure to express her approval of the binding's "border of waving lines" (*Letters* 4: 276). Unfortunately, Rossetti had also noted a number of errors, and by May 20, mentioned to WMR that she hoped a copy of the book she was ordering for Theodore Watts "will be one with a sadly-needed slip of "errata," for at the end of an investigation I sent a list to Mr. McClure and he wrote back that already the list was given in hand," noting also that "the list was so long I omitted trivial printer's errors" (*Letters* 4: 279). In July, writing to Frederick Shields, Rossetti enclosed a list of corrections of the book's "grave mistakes (some my own, some I think the printer's)," explaining that "Since those first issues a slip of errata has been prepared and printed, so that I trust the book as now on sale exhibits fewer glaring imperfections." (*Letters* 4: 289; see *Note one*). In addition to printing the errata slip (albeit, apparently, after some copies had already been sold), the SPCK also made corrections in the text of later printings.

The title "Song for the Feast of All Saints" (529) later appears in *Verses* (A24) as "Song for the Least of All Saints." Most likely this represents yet another error in *The Face of the Deep*, rather than an authorial revision, as "Least" seems to be more appropriate for the poem's content.

Announced in "Publications To-Day," London *Times*, (29 April 1892: 11); announced in the United States as available "next week" in the *International Bookseller* (21 May 1892), 164.

Price: 7s 6d; in the United States, $3.00.

BL depository copy: 'BRITISH MUSEUM 7 NOV 52'.

Reviewed in the *Rock* (*Letters* 4: 298); *Expository Times* (July 1892: 469); *Independent* (New York) (27 October 1892: 1524, also 12 January 1893: 54); *Literary World* (Boston) (19 November 1892: 411); *Saturday Review* (26 November 1892: 625).

Printing: 4: 'RICHARD CLAY & SONS, LIMITED, | LONDON & BUNGAY.'; 552: '*Richard Clay & Sons, Limited, London & Bungay.*'

Note one: The Princeton copy is inscribed "H. R. from C. G. R." ("H. R." being Henrietta Rintoul). This is apparently one of the early copies, as it contains no printed errata slip, but is instead corrected by hand in pencil and ink. Princeton also holds a handwritten errata slip (Troxell collection, #C0189, box 2, folder

27) that was removed from this copy. In the list of hand corrections below, those that are marked with a dagger (†) do not appear on either the handwritten or printed errata slips, nor in the corrected second edition of the book. There is only one correction that appears in the printed and handwritten lists (to page 509) but not in the hand corrected book. Finally, although the corrections to poems on pages 198, 402, and 410 do not appear in later editions of *The Face of the Deep*, they do appear in *Verses* (1893). For the printed errata slip, see *Note two*.

Hand corrections in Princeton copy are in pencil unless ink is specified.

Page 1: inscription

page 92, line 12, in ink: 'there' corrected to 'their'

† page 93, line 11, in ink: 'move' corrected to 'move,'

page 115, line 24: 'two' corrected to 'too'

page 126 , line 13: 'Father,' corrected to "Father:'

page 149, line 5 from bottom: 'we' corrected to 'He'

† page 198, line 8 from bottom: 'Hope' corrected to 'Hope,' (in the poem 'Experience bows a sweet')

page 292, line 16: 'Thy' deleted

† 304, line 12 from bottom: 'al ife' corrected to 'a life'

† 402 line 18: 'discloses' corrected to 'discloses,' (in the poem 'Crimson as the rubies')

† 402 line 25: 'God' corrected to 'God,' (in the poem 'Crimson as the rubies')

† 410 line 27: 'sit high or low' corrected to 'sit, high or low,' (in the poem 'Content to come, content to go')

456 line 14 from bottom, in ink: 'was forsaken' corrected to 'wast forsaken'

456 line 12 from bottom, in ink: 'was slain' corrected to 'wast slain'

Note two: The text of the printed errata slip is as follows. Note that the handwritten errata slip includes all of these corrections except for the spelling of patience (115).

Page	92,	line	12,	*for* there *read* their
”	115,	”	24,	” two *read* too
”	”	”	33,	” patence *read* patience
”	126,	”	13,	” 2nd comma, *substitute* colon (:)
”	149,	”	5 from bottom,	*for* we in Him *read* He in him
”	170,	”	26,	*for* crouched *read* couched
”	292,	”	16,	*omit* Thy
”	363,			*Instead of final sentence of paragraph* 1 *on* v. 14, *substitute* As *"the* Son of Man" I adore

my Lord as Head indeed of the race, but as so separate from sinners that Him alone it befits to be constituted Judge of human-kind. As *"a* Son of Man" I worship Him as the Representative Man in Whose perfect Will all sanctified human wills concur, Whose righteous Acts all holy souls approve.

Page 456, lines 12, 14 from bottom, *for* was *read* wast

Page 509, lines 13, 14, *for* "We have found the Messiah." *read* "We have found" the Messiah.

Locations: BL; CaBVaU; NjP (presentation copy; see *Note one*).

A23.2a   *Second (Corrected) Edition, First Printing (1893)*

Same as 1892 printing except:

THE FACE OF THE DEEP: | A DEVOTIONAL COMMENTARY | ON | THE APOCALYPSE. | BY | CHRISTINA G. ROSSETTI, | AUTHOR OF "SEEK AND FIND," "TIME FLIES," ETC. | "Thy judgments are a great deep." – Psalm xxxvi. 6. | *SECOND EDITION.* | PUBLISHED UNDER THE DIRECTION OF THE TRACT COMMITTEE. | LONDON: | SOCIETY FOR PROMOTING CHRISTIAN KNOWLEDGE, | NORTHUMBERLAND AVENUE, W. C.; 43, QUEEN VICTORIA STREET, E. C. | BRIGHTON: 135, NORTH STREET. | NEW YORK: E. & J. B. YOUNG & CO. | 1893.

Typography and paper: (158) 149 x 88.7 (p. 321); 44 lines.

Running titles: same as 1892 except:
Rectos: 61: faint or no period after 'DEEP'; 3: period inserted after 'KNOWLEDGE'.
Versos: 394: faint or no period after 'DEEP'.

Paper: Thicker paper than 1892 (micrometer readings from .091 to .117), which noticeably increases the bulk of the book.

Publication: In January 1893, Rossetti wrote "Some days ago I received 6 copies of my 2nd ed. "Face of the Deep," a *corrected* ed. much to my satisfaction" (*Letters* 4: 309). All corrections listed in the printed errata sheet for 1892 have been made in the text. The smaller typography measurements of 1893 indicate a line for line resetting of the first edition. The second edition is otherwise indistinguishable from the first except for the few corrections.

Locations: NjP (presentation copy); BL; Ives.

Presentation copies: NjP: inscribed in ink on front free endpaper: "Mrs Catterson in memory of much kindness received from her by Christina G. Rossetti. Christmas 1892."

A23.2b   *Second (Corrected) Edition, Second Printing (1895)*

Same as 1893 printing except:

THE FACE OF THE DEEP: | A DEVOTIONAL COMMENTARY | ON | THE APOCALYPSE. | BY THE LATE | CHRISTINA G. ROSSETTI, | AUTHOR OF "SEEK AND FIND," "TIME FLIES," ETC. | "Thy judgments are a great deep." – Psalm xxxvi. 6. | *THIRD EDITION.* | PUBLISHED UNDER THE DIRECTION OF THE TRACT COMMITTEE. | LONDON: | SOCIETY FOR PROMOTING CHRISTIAN KNOWLEDGE, | NORTHUMBERLAND AVENUE, W.C.; 43, QUEEN VICTORIA STREET, E.C. | NEW YORK: E. & J. B. YOUNG & CO. | 1895.

Contents: Changes in advertisements: 2: 'THE ROMANCE OF SCIENCE' ten titles, *Our Secret Friends and Foes* added after *Diseases Of Plants*; 3: 'DIOCESAN HISTORIES' 17 titles, *Sodor and Man* added after *Salisbury*; 8: eleven titles, *Verses* added after *Turning-Points*; text regarding Rossetti's *Verses* as follows: 'VERSES. | By the late CHRISTINA G. ROSSETTI. Sm. Post 8vo. Printed | in Red and Black on hand-made paper . . . . *Cloth boards* 3 6'. All advertisements for Rossetti's books are now designated "By the late Christina".

Running titles:
Rectos: 61: period restored after 'DEEP'.

Publication: BL depository copy: 'BRITISH MUSEUM 12 FEB 49'.

Printing: 4: no comma after 'Limited'; in some copies, a thin rule above the printer's imprint on 552 is broken (BL).

Locations: BL; NjP.

A23.2c   *Second (Corrected) Edition, Third Printing (1902)*

Same as 1895 except:

THE FACE OF THE DEEP: | A DEVOTIONAL COMMENTARY | ON | THE APOCALYPSE. | BY THE LATE | CHRISTINA G. ROSSETTI, | AUTHOR OF "SEEK AND FIND," "TIME FLIES," ETC. | "Thy judgments are a great deep."–Psalm xxxvi. 6. | *FOURTH EDITION.* | PUBLISHED UNDER THE DIRECTION OF THE TRACT COMMITTEE. | LONDON: | SOCIETY FOR PROMOTING CHRISTIAN KNOWLEDGE, | NORTHUMBERLAND AVENUE, W.C.; 43, QUEEN VICTORIA STREET, E.C. | BRIGHTON: 129, NORTH STREET. | NEW YORK: E. & J. B. YOUNG & CO. | 1902

Contents: additional changes on most pages of advertisements, as follows: <u>1</u>: 17 titles, *Boniface* through *The Venerable Bede*; 2: 'THE ROMANCE OF SCIENCE' 13 titles; 'NON-CHRISTIAN RELIGIOUS SYSTEMS" 10 titles; 3: 'DIOCESAN HISTORIES' 20 titles; 4: 'CHURCH HYMNS' three titles; 'COMMENTARY ON THE BIBLE' seven titles; 'ANCIENT HISTORY' four titles.

Running titles:
Versos: 352: no period and damage to "EP" in 'DEEP'; 4: 'PUBLICATIONS OF THE S.P.C.K.'

Binding: Calico cloth, dark blue (Centroid 183). Front: same, but gilt ornament across top edge is now a triangular design between two rules, with same blind-stamped near bottom edge. Back plain. Spine same except the ornamental band from front extends to top edge of spine (and is blind-stamped at the tail); text is same but in a new font with no chevron-shaped bar in 'CHRISTINA'.

Location: OrU.

A23.2d   *Second (Corrected) Edition, Fourth Printing (1907)*

Same as 1902 printing except:

The Face of the Deep: | A DEVOTIONAL COMMENTARY | ON | THE APOCALYPSE. | BY THE LATE | CHRISTINA G. ROSSETTI, | AUTHOR OF "SEEK AND FIND," "TIME FLIES," ETC. | "Thy judgments are a great deep."–Psalm xxxvi. 6. | *FIFTH EDITION.* | PUBLISHED UNDER THE DIRECTION OF THE TRACT COMMITTEE. | LONDON: | SOCIETY FOR PROMOTING CHRISTIAN KNOWLEDGE, | NORTHUMBERLAND AVENUE, W.C.; 43, QUEEN VICTORIA STREET, E.C. | BRIGHTON: 129, NORTH STREET. | NEW YORK: E. S. GORHAM. | 1907

Contents: some changes in advertisements: 2: 'THE ROMANCE OF SCIENCE' 14 titles; 'NON-CHRISTIAN RELIGIOUS SYSTEMS" 10 titles; 3: 'DIOCESAN HISTORIES' 21 titles; 4: 'COMMENTARY ON THE BIBLE' seven titles; 'ANCIENT HISTORY' nine titles; 7: 13 titles.

Running titles: additional damage (broken, bent, or flattened letters); also:
Versos: 4: 'PUBLICATIONS OF THE SOCIETY'.

Binding: Same as 1902 except back: blind-stamped ornamental bands at top and bottom.

Printing: 4: 'RICHARD CLAY & SONS, LIMITED, | BREAD STREET HILL, E. C., AND | BUNGAY, SUFFOLK.'

Location: TxHR.

A23.2e   ***Second (Corrected) Edition, Fifth Printing (1911)***

Same as 1907 printing except:

Title Page: Same as 1907 except for line 9: 'SIXTH EDITION' and date changed to 1911.

Contents: Same as 1907 except 2: 'THE ROMANCE OF SCIENCE' 15 titles; 8: 10 titles.

Running titles: additional damage; otherwise same as 1907.

Binding: Color changed to blackish blue (Centroid 188).

Locations: Baylor.

A24   VERSES (1893)

A24.1a   *First Edition, First Printing (1893)*

Within red ink rule frame, 162 x 120:
VERSES | BY | CHRISTINA G. ROSSETTI. | *Reprinted from "Called to be Saints," "Time Flies,"* | *"The Face of the Deep."* | [rule, 23.3] | PUBLISHED UNDER THE DIRECTION OF THE TRACT COMMITTEE. | [rule, 23] | LONDON: | SOCIETY FOR PROMOTING CHRISTIAN KNOWLEDGE, | NORTHUMERLAND AVENUE, W.C.; 43, QUEEN VICTORIA STREET, E. C. | BRIGHTON: 135, NORTH STREET. | NEW YORK: E. & J. B. YOUNG & CO. | 1893.

Pagination: 1-7 8-15 16-19 20-47 48-51 52-98 99-101 102-118 119-121 122-126 127-129 130-147 148-151 152-170 171-173 174-225 226-227 228-236 237-240.

Collation: (180 x 125): A⁸ B-P⁸. $1,2 signed. 120 leaves.

Contents: (some text in black letter): 1: title; 2: printer's imprint; 3: 'CONTENTS.'; 4: ornament; 5: section half-title '"*OUT OF THE DEEP HAVE* | *I CALLED UNTO THEE,* | *O LORD."*' with small ornaments above and below text; 6: ornament; 7: poems headed 'Verses.'; 16: ornament; 17: section half-title '*CHRIST OUR ALL IN ALL.*' with small ornaments above and below text; 18: ornament; 19: poems headed '*CHRIST OUR ALL IN ALL.*'; 48: ornament; 49: section half-title '*SOME FEASTS AND FASTS.*' with small ornaments above and below text; 50: ornament; 51: poems headed '*SOME FEASTS AND FASTS.*'; 99: section half-title '*GIFTS AND GRACES.*' with small ornaments above and below text; 100: ornament; 101: poems headed '*GIFTS AND GRACES.*'; 119: section half-title '*THE WORLD.* | *SELF-DESTRUCTION.*' with small ornaments above and below text; 120: ornament; 121: poems headed '*THE WORLD. SELF-DESTRUCTION.*'; 127: section half-title '*DIVERS WORLDS.* | *TIME AND ETERNITY.*' with small ornaments above and below text; 128: ornament; 129: poems headed '*DIVERS WORLDS. TIME AND* | *ETERNITY.*'; 148: blank; 149: section half-title '*NEW JERUSALEM AND ITS* | *CITIZENS.*' with small ornaments above and below text; 150: ornament; 151: poems headed '*NEW JERUSALEM AND ITS* | *CITIZENS.*'; 171: section half-title '*SONGS FOR STRANGERS AND* | *PILGRIMS.*' with small ornaments above and below text; 172: ornament; 173: poems headed '*SONGS FOR STRANGERS AND* | *PILGRIMS.*'; 226: ornament; 227: 'INDEX OF FIRST LINES.'; 237: section half-title 'PUBLICATIONS | OF THE | Society for Promoting Christian | Knowledge.'; 238: blank; 239: 'BOOKS BY THE SAME AUTHOR.' five titles: *Called to be Saints, Letter and Spirit, Seek and Find, The Face of the Deep, Time Flies*; 240: blank.

Poems: (Some untitled, identified by first line. For titled poems that were untitled in previous appearances, first lines are given in parentheses; for retitled poems, former titles are given in square brackets). See *Note one*.
 "Alone Lord God, in whom our trust and peace," "Seven vials hold Thy wrath: but what can hold," "'Where neither rust nor moth doth corrupt'" ("Nerve us with patience, Lord, to toil or rest"), "'As the sparks fly upwards'" ("Lord grant us wills to trust Thee with such aim"), "Lord, make us all love all: that when we meet," "O Lord, I am ashamed to seek Thy Face," "It is not death, O Christ, to die for Thee," "Lord, grant us eyes to see and ears to hear," "'Cried out with Tears'" ("Lord, I believe, help Thou mine unbelief"), "O Lord, on Whom we gaze and dare not gaze," "'I will come and heal him'" ("O Lord God, hear the silence of each soul"), "Ah Lord, Lord, if my heart were right with Thine," "'The gold of that land is good'" ("I long for joy, O Lord, I long for gold"), "Weigh all my faults and follies righteously," "Lord, grant me grace to love Thee in my pain," "Lord, make me one with Thine own faithful ones," "'Light of Light'" ("O Christ our Light, whom even in darkness we"), "'The ransomed of the Lord'" ("Thy lovely saints do bring Thee love"), "Lord, we are rivers running to Thy sea," "'An exceeding bitter cry'" ("Contempt and pangs and haunting fears"), "O Lord, when Thou didst call me, didst Thou know,"

"'Thou, God, seest me'" ("Ah me, that I should be"), "Lord Jesus, who would think that I am Thine?," "'The Name of Jesus'" ("Jesus, Lord God from all eternity"), "Lord God of Hosts, most Holy and most High," "Lord, what have I that I may offer Thee?," "If I should say 'My heart is in my home'," "Leaf from leaf Christ knows," "Lord, carry me. – Nay, but I grant thee strength," "Lord, I am here. – But child, I look for thee," "New creatures; the Creator still the Same," "'King of kings and Lord of lords'," "Thy Name, O Christ, as incense streaming forth," "'The Good Shepherd'" ("O Shepherd with the bleeding Feet"), "'Rejoice with Me'" ("Little Lamb, who lost thee?"), "Shall not the Judge of all the earth do right?," "Me and my gift: kind Lord, behold," "'He cannot deny Himself'" ("Love still is love, and doeth all things well"), "'Slain from the foundation of the world'" ("Slain for man, slain for me, O Lamb of God, look down"), "Lord Jesu, Thou art sweetness to my soul," "I, Lord, Thy foolish sinner low and small," "'Because He first loved us'," "Lord, has Thou so loved us, and will not we," "As the dove which found no rest," "'Thou art Fairer than the children of men'" ("A rose, a lily and the Face of Christ"), "'As the Apple Tree among the trees of the wood'" ("As one red rose in a garden where all other roses are white"), "None other Lamb, none other Name," "'Thy Friend and thy Father's Friend forget not'" ("Friends, I commend to you the narrow way"), "'Surely he hath borne our griefs'" ("Christ's heart was wrung for me, if mine is sore"), "'They toil not, neither do they spin'" ("Clother of the lily, Feeder of the sparrow"), "Darkness and light are both alike to Thee," "'And now why tarriest thou?'" ("Lord, grant us grace to mount by steps of grace"), "Have I not striven, my God, and watched and prayed?," "'God is our Hope and Strength'" ("Tempest and terror below; but Christ the Almighty above"), "Day and night the Accuser makes no pause," "O mine enemy," "Lord, dost Thou look on me, and will not I," "'Peace I leave with you'" ("Tumult and turmoil, trouble and toil"), "O Christ our All in each, our All in all!," "Because Thy Love hath sought me," "Thy fainting spouse, yet still Thy spouse," "'Like as the hart desireth the water brooks'" ("My heart is yearning"), "'That where I am, there ye may be also'" ("How know I that it looms lovely that land I have never seen"), "'Judge not according to the appearance'," "My God, wilt Thou accept," "A chill blank world. Yet over the utmost sea," "'The Chiefest among ten thousand'" ("O Jesu, better than Thy gifts"), "Advent Sunday," "Advent" ("Earth grown old, yet still so green"), "Sooner or later: yet at last," "Christmas Eve," "Christmas Day," "Christmastide" ("Love came down at Christmas"), "St. John, Apostle" ("Earth cannot bar flame from ascending"), "'Beloved, let us love one another', says St. John," "Holy Innocents" ("They scarcely waked before they slept"), "Unspotted lambs to follow the one Lamb," "Epiphany" ("Lord Babe, if thou art He"), "Epiphanytide" ("Trembling before Thee we fall down to adore Thee"), "Septuagesima" ("One step more, and the race is ended"), "Sexagesima" ("Yet Earth was very good in days of old"), "That Eden of earth's sunrise cannot vie," "Quinquagesima" ("Love is alone the worthy law of love"), "Piteous my rhyme is," "Ash Wednesday" ("My God, My God, have mercy on my sin"), "Good Lord, to-day," "Lent" ("It is good to be last not first"), "Embertide" ("I saw a Saint. – How canst thou tell that he"), "Mid-Lent" ("Is any grieved or tired? Yea, by God's Will"), "Passiontide" ("It is the greatness of Thy love, dear Lord, that we would celebrate"), "Palm Sunday" ["'He Treadeth the Winepress of the Fierceness and Wrath of Almighty God'"], "Monday in Holy Week," "Tuesday in Holy Week," "Wednesday in Holy Week" ("Man's life is death. Yet Christ endured to live"), "Maundy Thursday" ("The great vine left its glory to reign as Forest King"), "Good Friday Morning," "Good Friday" ("Lord Jesus Christ, grown faint upon the Cross"), "Good Friday Evening" ["Out of the Angel's Hand"], "A bundle of myrrh is my Well-beloved unto me'" ("Thy Cross cruciferous doth flower in all"), "Easter Even" ("The tempest over and gone, the calm begun"), "Our Church Palms are budding willow twigs" ("While Christ lay dead the widowed world"), "Easter Day," "Easter Monday" ("Out in the rain a world is growing green"), "Easter Tuesday" ("'Together with my dead body shall they arise'"), "Rogationtide" ("Who scatters tares shall reap no wheat"), "Ascension Eve" ("O Lord Almighty, Who hast formed us weak"), "Ascension Day," "Whitsun Eve" ("As many as I love. – Ah, Lord, who lovest all"), "Whitsun Day," "Whitsun Monday" ("We know not a voice of that River"), "Whitsun Tuesday," "Trinity Sunday" ("My God, Thyself being Love Thy heart is love"), "Conversion of St Paul" ("O blessed Paul elect to grace"), "In weariness and painfulness St. Paul," "Vigil of the Presentation" ("Long and dark the nights, dim and short the days"), "Feast of the Presentation" ("O firstfruits of our grain"), "The Purification of St. Mary the Virgin" ("Purity born of a Maid"), "Vigil of the Annunciation" ("All weareth, all wasteth"), "Feast of the Annunciation" ("Whereto shall we liken this Blessed Mary Virgin"), "Herself a rose, who bore the Rose," "St. Mark" ("Once like a broken bow Mark sprang aside"), "St. Barnabas" ("St. Barnabas, with John his sister's son"), "Vigil of St. Peter" ("O Jesu, gone so far apart"), "St. Peter" ("'Launch out into the deep,' Christ spake of old"), "St. Peter once: "Lord, dost Thou wash my feet?," "I followed Thee, my God, I followed Thee," "Vigil of St. Bartholomew" ("Lord, to thine own grant watchful hearts and eyes"), "St. Bartholomew" ("He bore an agony whereof the name"), "St. Michael and All Angels" ("Service and strength, God's Angels and Archangels"), "Vigil of All Saints" ("Up, my drowsing eyes"), "All Saints" ("As grains of sand, as stars, as drops of dew"), "All Saints: Martyrs" ("Once slain for Him who first was slain for them"), "'I gave a sweet smell'" ("Saints are like roses when they flush rarest"), "Hark! the Alleluias of the great salvation," "A Song for the Least of All Saints" ("Love is the key of life and death"), "Sunday Before Advent" ("The end of all things is at hand. We all"), "Love loveth Thee, and wisdom loveth Thee," "Lord, give me love that I may love Thee much," "'As a king, ... unto the King'" ("Love doth so grace and dignify"), "O ye who love to-day," "Life that was born to-day," "'Perfect Love casteth out Fear'" ("Lord, give me blessed fear"), "Hope is the counterpoise of fear," "'Subject to like Passions as we are'" ("Whoso hath anguish is not dead in sin"), "Experience bows a sweet contented face," "'Charity never faileth'" ("Such is Love, it comforts in extremity"), "'The Greatest of these is Charity'" ("A moon impoverished amid stars curtailed"), "All beneath the sun hasteth," "If thou be dead, forgive and thou shalt live," "'Let Patience have her perfect work'" ("Can man rejoice who lives in hourly fear?"), "Patience must dwell with Love, for Love and Sorrow," "'Let everything that hath breath praise the Lord'" ("All that we see rejoices in the sunshine"), "What is the beginning? Love. What the course? Love still," "Lord, make me pure," "Love, to be love, must walk Thy way," "Lord, I am feeble and of mean account," "Tune me, O Lord, into one harmony," "'They shall be as white as snow'" ("Whiteness most white. Ah, to be clean again"), "Thy lilies drink the dew," "'When I was in trouble I called upon the Lord'" ("A burdened heart that bleeds and bears"), "Grant us such grace that we may work Thy Will," "'Who hath despised the day of small things?'" ("As violets so be I recluse and sweet"), "'Do this, and he doeth it'" ("Content to come, content to go"), "'That no man take thy Crown'" ("Be faithful unto death. Christ proffers thee"), "'Ye are come unto Mount Sion'" ("Fear, faith and hope have sent their hearts above"), "'Sit down in the lowest room'" ("Lord give me grace"), "'Lord, it is good for us to be here'" ("Grant us, O Lord, that patience and that faith"), "Lord, grant us grace to rest upon Thy word," "'A vain Shadow'" ("The world, –what a world, ah me!"), "'Lord, save us, we perish'" ("O Lord, seek us, O Lord, find us"), "What is this above thy head," "Babylon the Great" ("Foul is she and ill-favoured, set askew"), "'Standing afar off for the fear of her torment'," "'O Lucifer, Son of the Morning!'" ("Oh fallen star! a darkened light"), "Alas, alas! for the self-destroyed," "As froth on the face of the deep," "'Where their worm dieth not, and the fire is not quenched'" ("In tempest and storm blackness of darkness forever"), "Toll, bell, toll. For hope is flying," "Earth has clear call of daily bells," "'Escape to the Mountain'" ("I peered within, and saw a world of sin"), "I lift mine eyes to see: earth vanisheth," "'Yet a little while'" ("Heaven is not far, tho' far the sky"), "'Behold, it was very good'" ("All things are fair, if we had eyes to see"), "'Whatsoever is right, that shall ye receive'" ("When all the overwork of life"), "This near-at-hand land breeds pain by measure," "'Was Thy Wrath against the Sea?'" ("The sea laments with unappeasable"), "'And there was no more Sea'" ("Voices from above and from beneath"), "Roses on a brier," "We are of those who tremble at Thy word," "'Awake, thou that sleepest'" ("The night is far spent, the day is at hand"), "We know not when, we know not where," "'I will lift up mine eyes unto the hills'" ("When sick of life and all the world"), "'Then whose shall those things be'" ("Oh what is earth, that we should build"), "'His Banner over me was Love'" ("In that world we weary to attain"), "Beloved, yield thy time to God," "Time seems not short," "The half moon shows a face of plaintive sweetness," "'As the Doves to their windows'" ("They throng from the east and the west"), "O knell of a passing time," "Time passeth away with its pleasure and pain," "'The Earth shall tremble at the Look of Him'" ("Tremble, thou earth, at the Presence of the Lord"), "Time lengthening, in the lengthening seemeth long," "'All Flesh is Grass'" ("So brief a life, and then an endless life"), "Heaven's chimes are slow, but sure to strike at last," "'There remaineth therefore a Rest to the People of God'" ("Rest remains when all is done"), "Parting after parting," "'They put their trust in Thee, and were not confounded'" ("Together once, but never more"), "Short is time, and only time is bleak," "For Each," "For All," "'The Holy City, New Jerusalem'" ("Jerusalem is built of gold"), "When wickedness is broken as a tree," "Jerusalem of fire," "'She shall be brought unto the King'" ("The King's Daughter is all glorious within"), "Who is this that cometh up not alone," "Who sits with the King in His throne? Not a slave but a bride," "Antipas" ("Hidden from the darkness of our mortal sight"), "'Beautiful for situation'" ("A lovely city in a lovely land"), "Lord, by what inconceivable dim road," "'As cold waters to a thirsty soul, so is good news from a far country'" ("'Golden haired, lily white"), "Cast down but not destroyed, chastened not slain," "Lift up thine eyes to seek the invisible," "'Love is strong as Death'" ("As flames that consume the mountains, as winds that coerce the sea"), "'Let them rejoice in their beds'" ("Crimson as the rubies, crimson as the roses"), "Slain in their high places: fallen on rest," "'What hath God wrought'" ("The shout of a King is among them. One day may I be"), "'Before the Throne, and before the Lamb'" ("As the voice of many waters all saints sing as one"), "'He shall go no more out'" ("Once within, within for evermore"), "Yea, blessed and holy is he that hath part in the First Resurrection!," "The joy of Saints, like incense turned to fire," "What are these lovely ones, yea, what are these?," "'The General Assembly and Church of the Firstborn'" ("Bring me to see, Lord, bring me yet to see"), "'Every one that is perfect shall be as his master'" ("How can one man, how can all men"), "As dying, and behold we live," "'So great a cloud of Witnesses'" ("I think of the saints I have known, and lift up mine eyes"), "Our Mothers, lovely women pitiful," "Safe where I cannot lie yet," "'Is it well with the child?'" ("Lying a-dying"), "Dear Angels and dear disembodied Saints," "'To every seed his own body'" ("Bone to his bone, grain to his grain of dust"), "'What good shall my life do me?'" ("Have dead men long to wait?"), "'Her Seed; It shall bruise thy head'" ("Astonished Heaven looked on when man was made"), "'Judge nothing before the time'" ("Love understands the mystery, whereof"), "How great is little man!," "Man's life is but a working day," "If not with hope of life," "'The day is at hand'" ("Watch yet a while"), "'Endure hardness'" ("A cold wind stirs the blackthorn"), "'Whither the Tribes go up, even the Tribes of the Lord'" ("Light is our sorrow for it ends tomorrow"), "Where never tempest heaveth," "Marvel of marvels, if I myself shall behold," "'What is that to thee? follow thou me'" ("Lie still, my restive heart, lie still"), "'Worship God,'" "'Afterward he repented, and went'" ("Lord, when my heart was whole I kept it back"), "'Are they not all Ministering Spirits?'" ("Lord, whomsoever Thou shalt send to me"), "Our life is long. Not so, wise Angels say," "Lord, what have I to offer? sickening fear," "Joy is but sorrow," "Can I know it? –Nay," "'When my heart is vexed I will complain'" ("'The fields are white to harvest, look and see"), "'Praying always'" ("After midnight, in the dark"), "'As thy days, so shall thy strength be'" ("Day that hath no tinge of night"), "A heavy heart, if ever heart was heavy," "If love is not worth loving, then life is not worth living," "What is it Jesus saith unto the soul?," "They lie at rest, our blessed dead," "'Ye that fear him, both small and great'" ("Great or small below"), "'Called to be Saints'" ("The lowest place. Ah, Lord, how steep and high"), "The sinner's own fault? So it was," "Who cares for earthly bread tho' white?," "Laughing Life cries at the feast," "'The end is not yet'" ("Home by different ways. Yet all"), "Who would wish back the Saints upon our rough," "'That which hath been is named already, and it is known that it is Man'" ("'Eye hath not seen': –yet man hath known and weighed"), "Of each sad word which is more sorrowful," "'I see that all things come to an end'" ("No more! while sun and planets fly"), "'But Thy Commandment is exceeding broad'" ("Once again to wake, nor wish to sleep"), "Sursum Corda" ("Lift up your hearts." "We lift them up." Ah me!"), "O Ye, who are not dead and fit," "Where shall I find a white rose blowing?" ["Roses and Roses"], "'Redeeming the Time'" ("A life of hope deferred too often is"), "'Now they desire a Better Country'" ("Love said nay, while Hope kept saying"), "A Castle-Builder's World," "'These all wait upon Thee'," ("Innocent eyes not ours"), "'Doeth well . . . doeth better'" ("My love whose heart is tender said to me"), "Our heaven must be within ourselves," "'Vanity of Vanities'" ("Of all the downfalls in the world"), "The hills are tipped with sunshine, while I walk," "Scarce tolerable life, which all life long," "All heaven is blazing yet," "'Balm in Gilead'" ("Heartsease I found, where Love-lies-bleeding"), "'In the day of his Espousals,'" ("That Song of Songs which is Solomon's"), "'She came from the uttermost part of the earth'" ("'The half was not told me', said Sheba's Queen"), "Alleluia! or Alas! my heart is crying," "The Passion Flower hath sprung up tall," "'God's Acre'" ("Hail, garden of confident hope"), "'The Flowers appear on the Earth'" ("Young girls wear flowers"), "'Thou knewest . . . thou oughtest therefore'" ("Behold in heaven a floating dazzling cloud"), "'Go in Peace'" ("Can peach renew lost bloom"), "'Half dead'" ("O Christ the Life, look on me where I lie"), "'One of the Soldiers with a Spear pierced His Side'" ("Ah, Lord, we all have pierced Thee: wilt Thou be"), "Where love is, there comes sorrow," "Bury Hope out of sight," "A Churchyard Song of Patient Hope," "One woe is past. Come what come will," "'Take no thought for the morrow'" ("Who knows? God knows: and what he knows"), "'Consider the Lilies of the field'" ("Solomon most glorious in array"), "'Son, remember'" ("I, laid beside thy gate, am Lazarus"), "'Heaviness may endure for a night, but Joy cometh in the morning'" ("No thing is great on this side of the grave"), "'The Will of the Lord be done'" ("O Lord, fulfil thy will"), "'Lay up for yourselves treasures in Heaven'" ("Treasure plies a feather"), "'Whom the Lord loveth he chasteneth'" ("'One sorrow more? I thought the tale complete'"), "'Then shall ye shout'" ("It seems an easy thing"), "Everything that is born must die," "Lord, grant us calm, if calm can set forth Thee," "Changing Chimes" ["'Thou Shalt Hear a Voice Behind Thee'"], "'Thy Servant will go and fight with this Philistine'" ("Sorrow of saints is sorrow of a day"), "Thro' burden and heat of the day," "'Then I commended Mirth'" ("A merry heart is a continual feast"), "Sorrow hath a double voice," "Shadows to-day, while shadows show God's Will," "'Truly the Light is sweet'" ("Light colourless doth color all things else"), "'Are ye not much better than they?'" ("The twig sprouteth"), "'Yea, the sparrow hath found her an house'" ("Wisest of sparrows that sparrow which sitteth alone"), "'I am small and of no reputation'" ("The least, if so I am"), "O Christ my God Who seest the unseen," "Yea, if Thou wilt, Thou canst put up Thy sword," "Sweetness of rest when Thou sheddest rest," "O foolish Soul! to make thy count," "Before the beginning Thou hast foreknown the end," "The goal in sight! Look up and sing," "Looking back along life's trodden way."

Typography and paper: (122.7) 111.3 x 71.3 (p. 67); variable lines per page (up to 32). Laid paper, horizontal chainlines 26 mm apart. Unwatermarked.

On all pages, including blanks, a red rule frame, with double rule across top and all horizontal rules extending to fore-edge; all text (including running titles, page numbers, and signatures) is within the frame. Frame measurement (slightly variable): p. 213, top rule to bottom rule, 129.3. The typography throughout is highly patterned, including black letter running titles and poem titles; italic section half-titles and section titles; and ornamental capitals for the first letter of each poem.

Running titles: In black letter.

Rectos: 1-7: no RT; 9-15: 'unto Thee, O Lord.'; 17-19: no RT; 21-47: 'Christ our All in all.'; 49-51: no RT; 53-97: 'Some Feasts and Fasts.'; 99-101: no RT; 103-117: 'Gifts and Graces.'; 119-121: no RT; 123-125: 'The World. Self-Destruction.'; 127-129: no RT; 131-147: 'Divers Worlds. Time and Eternity.'; 149-151: no RT; 153-169: 'New Jerusalem and its Citizens.'; 171-173: no RT; 175-225: 'Songs for Strangers and Pilgrims.'; 227: no RT; 229-235: 'Index of First Lines.'; 237-239: no RT.

Versos: 2-6: no RT; 8-14: '"Out of the Deep have I called'; 16-18: no RT; 20-46: 'Christ our All in all.'; 48-50: no RT; 52-98: 'Some Feasts and Fasts.'; 100: no RT; 102-118: 'Gifts and Graces.'; 120: no RT; 122-126: 'The World. Self-Destruction.'; 128: no RT; 130-146: 'Divers Worlds. Time and Eternity.'; 148-150: no RT; 152-170: 'New Jerusalem and its Citizens.'; 172: no RT; 174-224: 'Songs for Strangers and Pilgrims.'; 226: no RT; 228-236: 'Index of First Lines.'; 238-240: no RT.

Binding: Buckram, blackish blue (Centroid 188) or dark greenish blue, boards with slightly beveled edges. Front: in gilt, 'Verses | *CHRISTINA ROSSETTI*'. Back plain. Spine: in gilt, 'Verses | [rule] |

CHRISTINA | ROSSETTI | [device, "SPCK", 12.3 x 11]'. Endpapers: brownish white laid paper, not same as sheets; chainlines 24 mm apart. Edges: top edge gilt; fore-edge and tail untrimmed.

Publication: September 1893. In late 1892, after WMR "proposed . . that the poems contained in her various books published by the Society for Promoting Christian Knowledge should all be collected together" CGR approached Edmund McClure with the idea (*Letters* 4:301). CGR copied the poems by hand; as Crump notes, this manuscript was sold by Maggs Brothers in 1931 but has not been traced (*Poems* II: 14). Comparison of the published text with previous versions reveals numerous changes "in punctuation, spelling, paragraphing, and even some wording"; in addition, Rossetti "added titles to many of the previously untitled poems" (*Poems* II: 14). In March she was nearly finished with the manuscript; on June 16, she returned the final revises to the SPCK: "I hope it is already for "press" when a few marked corrections are made. I quite admire the pretty red lined pages" (*Letters* 4: 328). The book was published on September 27. In December, WMR alerted CGR to some errors in the text; CGR in turn wrote to McClure regarding the changes (*Letters* 4: 359; see A24.1b).

Sales of the book were strong. By the end of 1893, CGR reported that "Mrs Garnett called one day and told me there was no meeting the demand for Verses . . . I wish the new edition may now be out, but I have not heard," (Letters 4: 364).

Listed among "Publications To-Day," London *Times* (27 September 1893: 8); noticed in the *Times* "Books of the Week" (29 September 1893), and advertised among the SPCK's new books in the *Times* "Column of New Books and Editions" (20 October 1893: 10), with emphasis on book's distinctive appearance ("printed in red and black on hand-made paper").

Price: 3s. 6d.

BL depository copy: date illegible.

Reviewed in the *Saturday Review* (21 October 1893: 476); *Speaker* (25 November 1893: 558); *Athenaeum* (16 December 1893: 842-43); *Bookman* (December 1893: 78-79); *Academy* (24 February 1894: 162-164); *Sunday at Home* (5 May 1894: 425-428).

Printing: <u>2</u> (first line black letter): 'Oxford | HORACE HART, PRINTER TO THE UNIVERSITY'.

Note one: First lines are provided only for poems that had not previously appeared with a heading or title, including poems in A20 (*Time Flies*) for which the status of the heading or title is unclear, or for titles that appear on more than one poem in Rossetti's canon (such as *Easter Even*). One poem, titled "'Judge not according to the appearance'" in *Verses*, appeared in *Time Flies* as "Lord, grant us eyes to see"; in *Verses*, the "grant us" has been revised to "purge our."

Locations: BL; CaBVaU; KMK; NjP; TxU.

A24.1b   *First Edition, Second Printing ("Fourth Thousand") (1894)*

Within red rule frame:
VERSES | BY | CHRISTINA G. ROSSETTI. | *Reprinted from "Called to be Saints," "Time Flies,"* | *"The Face of the Deep."* | [rule, 23] | PUBLISHED UNDER THE DIRECTION OF THE TRACT COMMITTEE. | [rule, 23] | Fourth Thousand. | LONDON: SOCIETY FOR PROMOTING CHRISTIAN KNOLWEDGE, | NORTHUMBERLAND AVENUE, W.C.; 43, QUEEN VICTORIA STREET, E.C. | BRIGHTON: 135, NORTH STREET. | NEW YORK: E. & J. B. YOUNG & CO. | 1894.

Binding: Copy examined is same as 1893, but additional bindings were advertised in late 1894, including "limp roan, 5s.; Levantine, 6s.6d; limp German calf, 7s.; limp morocco, 7s. 6d." (*Academy*, 6 October 1894: 398). No 1894 copies in these bindings have been located.

Publication: Presumably the "new edition" CGR referred to in late 1893 (*Letters* 4: 364) and received by late January 1894: "I see the book is *4th thousand* which looks grand" (*Letters* 4: 367). In December 1893, Rossetti had informed Edmund McClure of three errors in the text, "I fear too late to be available for the reissue" (*Letters* 4: 359). The errors Rossetti lists are on p. 96 (missing period at the end of line 4), 207 (the poem "Half Dead" "should be in three line stanzas throughout") and p. 215 (missing semicolon at the end of the second line of "Then shall ye shout") (*Letters* 4: 359). The errors are corrected in this printing.

Location: Ives.

A24.1c   *First Edition, Third Printing ("Sixth Edition") (1894)*

Within red rule frame:
VERSES | BY | CHRISTINA G. ROSSETTI. | *Reprinted from "Called to be Saints," "Time Flies,"* | *"The Face of the Deep."* | [rule, 22.3] | PUBLISHED UNDER THE DIRECTION OF THE TRACT COMMITTEE. | [rule, 22.7] | Sixth Edition. | LONDON: | SOCIETY FOR PROMOTING CHRISTIAN KNOWLEDGE, | NORTHUMBERLAND AVENUE, W. C.; 43, QUEEN VICTORIA STREET, E. C. | BRIGHTON: 135, NORTH STREET. | NEW YORK: E. & J. B. YOUNG & CO. | 1894.

Publication: In March 1894, CGR thanked Edmund McClure for "the gratifying news of my 3rd edition"; the book was not yet printed, as he had apparently asked if she wished to make further textual changes, prompting a negative response ("No, I have no further emendations to proffer") (*Letters* 4: 376).

Location: Ives.

A24.1d   *First Edition, Fourth Printing ("Seventh Thousand") (1894)*

Same as 1893 except:

Within red rule frame:
VERSES | BY | CHRISTINA G. ROSSETTI. | *Reprinted from "Called to be Saints," "Time Flies,"* | *"The Face of the Deep."* | [rule, 22.7] | PUBLISHED UNDER THE DIRECTION OF THE TRACT COMMITTEE. | [rule, 22.3] | Seventh Thousand. | LONDON: | SOCIETY FOR PROMOTING CHRISTIAN KNOWLEDGE, | NORTHUMBERLAND AVENUE, W. C.; 43, QUEEN VICTORIA STREET, E. C. | BRIGHTON: 129, NORTH STREET. | NEW YORK: E. & J. B. YOUNG & CO. | 1894.

Location: NjP.

A24.1e   *First Edition, Fifth Printing ("Eighth Thousand") (1895)*

Not seen.

Locations: no holdings located; identified via bookseller's listing (Fortune Green Books).

A24.1f   *First Edition, Later Printing ("Tenth Thousand") (1895)*

Same as 1894 "Seventh Thousand" except:

Title Page: No period after 'COMMITTEE' in line seven, and change to "Tenth Thousand" in line nine.

Binding: Rebound.

Location: Ives.

A24.1g   *First Edition, Later Printing ("Twelfth Thousand") (1895)*

Same as 1893 except:

Within red rule frame:
VERSES | BY | CHRISTINA G. ROSSETTI. | *Reprinted from "Called to be Saints," "Time Flies,"* | *"The Face of the Deep."* | [rule, 22] | PUBLISHED UNDER THE DIRECTION OF THE TRACT COMMITTEE. | [rule, 22] | Twelfth Thousand. | LONDON: | SOCIETY FOR PROMOTING CHRISTIAN KNOWLEDGE, | NORTHUMBERLAND AVENUE, W. C.; 43, QUEEN VICTORIA STREET, E. C. | BRIGHTON: 129, NORTH STREET. | NEW YORK: E. & J. B. YOUNG & CO. | 1895.

Location: Ives, TxCM.

A24.2a   *Second Edition, First Printing (1896)*

Reset from the 1893 edition (see *Note one*) with few changes, as follows:

Within red rule frame:
VERSES | BY | CHRISTINA ROSSETTI | REPRINTED FROM | "CALLED TO BE SAINTS," "TIME FLIES," "THE FACE OF THE DEEP" | *Published under the Direction of the Tract Committee* | Fifteenth Thousand | Re-set and Electrotyped | LONDON | SOCIETY FOR PROMOTING CHRISTIAN KNOWLEDGE | NEW YORK: E. & J B. YOUNG & CO. | 1896
    Note that the period after 'J' in the last line is faint or missing in copies examined.

Contents: 148: ornament; 237: instead of section half-title: 'BOOKS BY THE SAME AUTHOR.' (same as 239 in first edition); 238-240: blank.

Typography and paper: same except total length: 125.

Publication: The *English Catalogue* lists another printing of the "15th thou" in March 1897.

Printing: additional printer's imprint on 236: 'OXFORD: HORACE HART, PRINTER TO THE UNIVERSITY'.

Note one: A line-for-line resetting, with a very close resemblance to the previous edition, not only in the text and typography but also in materials. The only notable exception is in the typography, which has been somewhat simplified by the replacement of the ornamental capitals with dropped capitals in the first lines of poems.

Locations: Ives, NjP.

A24.2b   *Second Edition, Later Printing (1898)*

Same as 1896 except:

VERSES | BY | CHRISTINA G. ROSSETTI | REPRINTED FROM | "CALLED TO BE SAINTS," "TIME FLIES," "THE FACE OF THE DEEP" | *Published under the Direction of the Tract Committee* | Twentieth Thousand | LONDON | SOCIETY FOR PROMOTING CHRISTIAN KNOWLEDGE | NORTHUMBERLAND AVENUE, W. C. | NEW YORK: E. & J. B. YOUNG & CO. | 1898

Contents: 237: the binding of *Time Flies* is now described as 'buckram boards, gilt top edges. 3s. 6d.' indicating that the book is now bound to match *Verses*, and the price has increased from 2s. 6d. to 3s. 6d.

Printing: no printer's imprint on 2 (but imprint 236 same as 1896 printing).

Location: NjP

A24.2c   *Second Edition, Later Printing (1904)*

Same as 1898 except:

VERSES | BY | CHRISTINA G. ROSSETTI | REPRINTED FROM | "CALLED TO BE SAINTS," "TIME FLIES," "THE FACE OF THE DEEP" | *Published under the Direction of the Tract Committee* | Twentieth Thousand | LONDON | SOCIETY FOR PROMOTING CHRISTIAN KNOWLEDGE | NORTHUMBERLAND AVENUE, W. C. | NEW YORK: E. S. GORHAM | 1904

Binding: Boards are slightly smaller (183 x 126).

Location: Ives.

A24.2d   *Second Edition, Last Printing (1912)*

Not seen.

Location: Copy listed in Cambridge University library catalog, Classmark: 9720.d.6974.

A24.3a   *Third Edition, First Printing (1925)*

A line-for-line resetting of the second edition.

VERSES | BY | CHRISTINA G. ROSSETTI | LONDON | SOCIETY FOR PROMOTING CHRISTIAN KNOWLEDGE | NEW YORK AND TORONTO: THE MACMILLAN CO. | *Printed in Great Britain*

Pagination: [19] 8-15 <u>16</u>-<u>19</u> 20-47 <u>48</u>-<u>51</u> 52-98 <u>99</u>-<u>101</u> 102-118 <u>119</u>-<u>121</u> 122-126 <u>127</u>-<u>129</u> 130-147 <u>148</u>-<u>151</u> 152-170 <u>171</u>-<u>173</u> 174-225 <u>226</u>-<u>227</u> 228-236 <u>237</u>-<u>240</u>.

Collation: (123 x 104): <u>A</u>^{8} B-P^8 Q^6. $1 signed, except Q2 signed 'R'. 126 leaves.

Contents: Changes primarily to preliminaries and advertisements: [1]: half-title 'VERSES'; [2]: blank; [3]: title; [4]: '*Printed to* 1912 – 21,000 *copies* | *New edition* 1925'; [5]: 'CONTENTS' and 'ILLUSTRATIONS.'; [6]: blank; [7]: 'Introduction' signed on [15] 'W. K. L. C. | *October*, 1925.'; 236: printer's imprint; <u>237</u>-<u>239</u>: blank; <u>240</u>: advertisement headed 'BY THE SAME AUTHOR' lists three titles: *Called to be Saints*, *Redeeming the Time*, and *Time Flies*.

Plates:
1) Facing title, frontispiece (93 x 76) reproduction of DGR's painting "The Girlhood of Mary Virgin," and letterpress caption 'W. F. *Mansell, Photo.* | "THE GIRLHOOD OF THE VIRGIN. | DANTE GABRIEL ROSSETTI. | *Frontispiece*.' No tissue guard.
2) Facing 19, portrait of CGR and her mother Frances Mary Lavinia Rossetti (68 x 76) and letterpress caption 'CHRISTINA ROSSETTI WITH HER MOTHER, MARY | LAVINIA ROSSETTI. | CRAYON DRAWING BY DANTE GABRIEL ROSSETTI. | face page 19.'

Typography and paper: (127) 113 x 72 (p. 213); variable lines up page, up to 32. Wove paper, unwatermarked. Unlike previous editions, no rule frames.

Running titles: In black letter. Same as previous edition from pp. 8 on; preliminaries as follows:
Rectos: [1]-[5]: no RT; [7]-[15]: 'Introduction.'; [17]-[19]: no RT.
Versos: [2]-[6]: no RT; [8]-[14]: 'Introduction.'; [16]-[18]: no RT.

Binding: Calico cloth, vivid purplish blue (Centroid 194); front, back plain; spine (in silver ink) '[rule] | Verses | [ornament, leaf] | Christina | Rossetti | S•P•C•K | [rule]'. Endpapers: white wove paper. Edges trimmed.

Printing: 236: '*Wyman & Sons Ltd., Printers, London, Reading and Fakenham*'.

Note one: Introduction by William Kemp Lowther Clarke, editorial secretary of the Society for Promoting Christian Knowledge.

Location: Sonoma State University.

A25   GOBLIN MARKET (1893)

A25.1a.i   *First Edition, First Printing, Small Paper Issue (1893)*

Title Page is engraved (no letterpress), 125 x 66 overall size. The design features three pomegranate trees; standing by the trunks of the trees are four 'goblin' animals with baskets of fruit, with more goblins represented among the tree branches. Beneath the trees, in the center of the design is a river; at the lower left, a seated woman, facing the goblins; at the right, another woman is facing the reader, and covering her face with her hands. The text is dispersed within the overall design, as follows:
[within tree branches] GOBLIN MARKET | [beneath trees] BY | CHRISTINA ROSSETTI | illustrated by | LAURENCE HOUSMAN | [at bottom, centered] 1893 | MACMILLAN & Co LONDON [in lower right corner] L HOUSMAN

Pagination: [6] 1-2 <u>3-4</u> 5-6 <u>7-10</u> 11-12 <u>13-16</u> 17-18 <u>19-20</u> 21-28 <u>29-30</u> 31-32 <u>33-34</u> 35-42 <u>43-46</u> 47-50 <u>51-54</u> 55-63 <u>64-66</u>.

Plates: No plates, but there is a tissue guard inserted before title.

Collation: (183 x 104): <u>A</u>⁶ B-F⁶. $1 signed. 36 leaves.

Contents: [1]-[2]: blank; [3]: half-title 'GOBLIN | MARKET | [ornament, goblin within fruit, 25 x 25]'; [4]: blank; [5]: title; [6]: blank; <u>1</u>-64: poem and illustrations headed 'GOBLIN MARKET' (except blank pages <u>4</u> , <u>7</u>, <u>10</u> , <u>13</u> ,<u>16</u> , <u>19</u>, <u>29</u>, <u>33</u> , <u>43</u>, <u>46</u> , <u>51</u>, <u>54</u>); <u>64</u>: printer's device; <u>65-66</u>: blank.
    Ornaments and illustrations on pp. [3], [5] (full page illustration: title page); <u>1</u>, <u>3</u> (full page illustration of goblins), 5, <u>8-9</u> (paired full page illustrations of goblins gathering fruit), 12, 14-15 (paired full page illustrations, on 14: Laura kneeling at the brook; on 15: goblins with baskets of fruit), 17, 18, <u>20</u> (full page illustration of Laura with goblins), 21-22, 24-28, <u>30</u> (full page illustration of goblins), 31-32, 34 (full page illustration of sisters, one standing, one seated); 35-39, 41-42 , <u>44-45</u> (paired full page illustrations, on 44: goblins calling and tossing fruit; on 45: goblins attacking Lizzie), 48-49, <u>52-53</u> (paired full page illustrations, on 52: Lizzie holding on to tree; on 53: goblins departing); <u>55-63</u>.

Poems: "Goblin Market."

Typography and paper: (134) 119.3 x 57 (p. 6); text height measured without catchword; various lines per page (up to 21; 22 with catchword). Laid paper, vertical chainlines, 26 mm apart. Unwatermarked.

Catchwords: <u>1</u>: 'Apples'; 2: 'Currants'; 5: '"Lie close,"'; 6: 'Whose'; 11: 'Laura'; 12: 'When'; 17: 'Of welcome,'; 18: '"You'; 21: 'Lizzie'; 22: 'While'; 23: 'Pellucid'; 24: 'Like'; 25: 'Fetched'; 26: 'Lizzie'; 27: 'Not'; 28: 'Each'; 31: 'Her'; 32: '"Come"'; 35: 'She'; 36: 'Tender'; 37: 'But'; 38: 'At twilight'; 39: 'Chuckling,'; 40: 'Bite'; 41: 'Held'; 42: 'Cheer'; 47: 'Tore'; 48: 'Like'; 49: 'Though'; 50: 'Some'; 55: 'She'; 56: 'Squeezed'; 57: 'She'; 58: 'Rent'; 59: 'Ah! fool,'; 60: 'But'; 61: 'Days,'; 62: 'Then'.

Running titles:

Rectos: [1]-[5], 1-3: no RT; 5: 'GOBLIN MARKET'; 7-9: no RT; 11: 'GOBLIN MARKET'; 13-15: no RT; 17: 'GOBLIN MARKET'; 19: no RT; 21-27: 'GOBLIN MARKET'; 29: no RT; 31: 'GOBLIN MARKET'; 33: no RT; 35-41: 'GOBLIN MARKET'; 43-45: no RT; 47-49: 'GOBLIN MARKET'; 51-53: no RT; 55-63: 'GOBLIN MARKET'; 65: no RT.

Versos: [2]-[6]: no RT; 2: 'GOBLIN MARKET'; 4: no RT; 6: 'GOBLIN MARKET'; 8-10: no RT; 12: 'GOBLIN MARKET'; 14-16: no RT; 18: 'GOBLIN MARKET'; 20: no RT; 22-28: 'GOBLIN MARKET'; 30: no RT; 32: 'GOBLIN MARKET'; 34: no RT; 36-42: 'GOBLIN MARKET'; 44-46: no RT; 48-50: 'GOBLIN MARKET'; 52-54: no RT; 56-62: 'GOBLIN MARKET'; 64-66: no RT.

Binding: Calico cloth, between moderate and grayish olive green (Centroid 125, 127). Front and back stamped in gilt with repeating leaf and vine design, with outline letters 'GOB- | -LIN | MAR- | -KET' in the upper left on the front, and in the upper right on back (back is reversed version of front). Note initials "LH" in lower left corner of back. The front and back designs are continued by six groups of three horizontal lines across spine. At top of spine, in gilt: 'GOB- | -LIN | MAR- | -KET' | [six groups of three horizontal lines] | [at tail: Macmillan device, two interlocked "M"s with "&" and "Co" above an ornamented rule]'; endpapers: same as sheets. Edges: all edges gilt.

Dust jacket: grayish yellowish white wrapper printed with cover design in very dark yellowish green ink (Centroid 138). Location: TxCM.

Publication: 2000 copies printed from type and electrotype plates in November 1893 (Editions Book, Macmillan Archives). In all copies examined, the characteristic black letter 'E' with which Macmillan designated printing from plates appears on page 1, to the left of the page number. Housman sent a specimen drawing and some "rough sketches" to Macmillan in March 1893 (Nowell-Smith, 238). CGR accepted Housman's illustrations, stipulating only that they not be masked (*Letters* 4: 318), but according to WMR, the finished drawings "did not correspond to Christina's notions, and [. . .] in sending me a copy of the book, she wrote on the wrapper the single word 'Alas'" (*Family Letters* 190). Rossetti was to be paid half profits, and Housman was paid £50.3.6 for his illustrations (Terms Book, Macmillan Archives).

Announced among "Publications To-Day" in the London *Times* (13 December 1893: 12) and in *Publishers' Weekly* (6 January 1894: 7).

Price: 5s.; in the United States; $1.50.

Reviewed in the London *Times* (23 December 1893: 13), *Academy* (23 December 1893: 573); *Bookman* (January 1894: 122); *Dial* (16 January 1894: 59).

Printing: 64: rectangular R&R Clark device, 29 x 24 mm.

Note one: In the TxLT copy, the lower right corner of the title page is embossed with a circular seal including the words "PRESENTATION COPY."

Locations: DAM (2); DeU; CaBVaU (Colbeck entry 21); Macmillan; TxU (3 copies); TxCM; TxLT.

A25.1a.ii   *First Edition, First Printing, Large Paper Issue (1893)*

Same as small paper except:

Pagination: [8] 1 2 3-4 5-6 7-10 11-12 13-16 17-18 19-20 21-28 29-30 31-32 33-34 35-42 43-46 47-50 51-54 55-63 64.

Collation: (261 x 170): π2 A² B-E⁸. 36 leaves.

Contents: same except for preliminaries and absence of final blank leaf, as follows: [1]-[2]: blank; [3]: '*ONE HUNDRED AND SIXTY COPIES | OF THIS LARGE PAPER EDITION WERE PRINTED | DECEMBER 1893*'; [4]: blank; [5]: half-title; [6]: blank; [7]: title; [8]: blank; 1-63 poem and illustrations headed 'GOBLIN MARKET'; 64: printer's device.

Running titles:

Rectos: [1]-[7], 1-3: no RT; 5: 'GOBLIN MARKET'; 7-9: no RT; 11: 'GOBLIN MARKET'; 13-15: no RT; 17: 'GOBLIN MARKET'; 19: no RT; 21-27: 'GOBLIN MARKET'; 29: no RT; 31: 'GOBLIN MARKET'; 33: no RT; 35-41: 'GOBLIN MARKET'; 43-45: no RT; 47-49: 'GOBLIN MARKET'; 51-53: no RT; 55-63: 'GOBLIN MARKET'.

Versos: [2]-[8]: no RT; <u>2</u>: 'GOBLIN MARKET'; <u>4</u>: no RT; 6: 'GOBLIN MARKET'; 8-10: no RT; 12: 'GOBLIN MARKET'; 14-16: no RT; 18: 'GOBLIN MARKET'; 20: no RT; 22-28: 'GOBLIN MARKET'; 30: no RT; 32: 'GOBLIN MARKET'; 34: no RT; 36-42: 'GOBLIN MARKET'; 44-46: no RT; 48-50: 'GOBLIN MARKET'; 52-54: no RT; 56-62: 'GOBLIN MARKET'; 64: no RT.

Typography and paper: Wove paper, unwatermarked; see *Publication*.

Binding: Linen cloth, moderate greenish yellow (Centroid 102). Front, back plain. Spine: label of marbled paper (light pink, brown, white, green, yellow) with black ink: '[double rules] | Gob- | *lin* | Mar- | *ket* | [double rule]'. Endpapers: white wove, not same as sheets. Edges: top edges rough trimmed, fore-edge and tail untrimmed.

Publication: The Editions Book records 170 copies from standing type printed in November, presumably after the small paper copies, which are listed first (Macmillan Archives); however, all copies examined have a black letter 'E' to the left of the signature 'B' on p. <u>1</u> which usually indicates printing from plates. In August, *Publishers' Weekly* had reported that the publisher planned to print only 100 copies, but also indicated that "Messrs. Macmillan propose to print as many large-paper copies of each book as are ordered in advance, but not more, and to state the number actually printed on the title-page of each volume" (26 August 1893: 261). In October, Macmillan advertised the large paper issue as "an Édition de Luxe, Super Royal 8vo, Hand-made paper." In November, CGR noted in a letter to Macmillan that "I see in your announcements the large paper *Goblin Market* marked as 'all sold'," noting that her copy had not arrived (*Letters* 4: 357).

Priced at 21 shillings; in the United States, $9.00.

BL depository copy: 'BRITISH MUSEUM 4 JA 94'.

Locations: BL; DeU; NjP.

A25.2   *Second Edition, First Printing (1909)*

Within compartment of interlocking stylized foliage, 93 x 61:
GOBLIN | MARKET | BY | CHRISTINA ROSSETTI | ILLUSTRATED BY | LAURENCE HOUSMAN | MACMILLAN AND CO. LIMITED | ST. MARTIN'S STREET, | LONDON | 1909

Pagination: <u>1</u>-<u>9</u> 10 <u>11</u>-<u>12</u> 13-14 <u>15</u>-<u>18</u> 19-20 <u>21</u>-<u>24</u> 25-28 <u>29</u>-<u>30</u> 31-44 <u>45</u>-<u>46</u> 47-50 <u>51</u>-<u>52</u> 53-64 <u>65</u>-<u>68</u> 69-76 <u>77</u>-<u>80</u> 81-92 <u>93</u>-<u>96</u>.

Collation: (183 x 104): <u>A</u>⁸ B-F⁸. $1 signed. 36 leaves.

Contents: <u>1</u>: halftitle 'GOBLIN MARKET | [ornament, goblin within fruit, 25 x 25]'; 2: Macmillan device, 'MACMILLAN AND CO., Limited | LONDON BOMBAY CALCUTTA | MELBOURNE | THE MACMILLAN COMPANY | NEW YORK • BOSTON • CHICAGO | ATLANTA • SAN FRANCISCO | THE MACMILLAN COMPANY OF CANADA, Ltd | TORONTO'; 3: blank; 4: frontispiece; 5: title; 6: 'First published, 1862. | first published with illustrations by | L. Housman, 1893.' 7: illustrated halftitle; 8: blank; 9-92: poem and illustrations headed 'GOBLIN MARKET' (except blank pages <u>11</u>, <u>15</u>, <u>18</u>, <u>21</u>, <u>24</u>, <u>29</u>, <u>45</u>, <u>51</u>, <u>65</u>, <u>68</u>, <u>77</u>, <u>80</u>); <u>94</u>: blank; <u>95</u>: imprint; <u>96</u>: blank.

Ornaments and illustrations (see *Note one*) on pp. <u>1</u>, <u>4</u>, <u>7</u>, <u>12</u>, 13, <u>16</u>-<u>17</u>, <u>22</u>-<u>23</u>, 25-27, <u>30</u>, 31, 33-34, 37-39, 41-43, <u>46</u>, 48, 50, <u>52</u>, 53-54, 55, 58-59, 62-63, <u>66</u>-<u>67</u>, 71-72, 75-76, <u>78</u>-<u>79</u>, 81, 84, 86-87, 89-90, <u>93</u>.

Poems: "Goblin Market."

Typography and paper: (85) 76 x 59 (p. 49); 15 lines per page. Wove paper, unwatermarked. See *Note one*.

Running titles:

Rectos: 1-11: no RT; 13: 'GOBLIN MARKET'; 15-17: no RT; 19: 'GOBLIN MARKET'; 21-23: no RT; 25-27: 'GOBLIN MARKET'; 29: no RT; 31-43: 'GOBLIN MARKET'; 45: no RT; 47-49: 'GOBLIN MARKET'; 51: no RT; 53-63: 'GOBLIN MARKET'; 65-67: no RT; 69-75: 'GOBLIN MARKET'; 77-79: no RT; 81-91: 'GOBLIN MARKET'; 93-95: no RT.

Versos: [2]-8: no RT; 10: 'GOBLIN MARKET'; 12: no RT; 14: 'GOBLIN MARKET'; 16-18: no RT; 20: 'GOBLIN MARKET'; 22-24: no RT; 26-28: 'GOBLIN MARKET'; 30: no RT; 32-44: 'GOBLIN MARKET'; 46: no RT; 48-50: 'GOBLIN MARKET'; 52: no RT; 54-64: 'GOBLIN MARKET'; 66-68: no RT; 70-76: 'GOBLIN MARKET'; 78-80: no RT; 82-92: 'GOBLIN MARKET'; 94-96: no RT.

Binding: Calf, dark purplish blue (Centroid 201) with yapp edges. Front: within blindstamped oval medallion of foliated branches, round gilt ornament of a goblin nestling within a pomegranate fruit (25 x 26). Back: plain. Spine: in gilt, reading vertically from tail to head, 'GOBLIN MARKET CHRISTINA ROSSETTI' Endpapers wove, same as sheets. Edges: t.e.g.

Publication: A number of publishers produced separate issues of Goblin Market after the poem went out of copyright in 1904 (see Kooistra, 206-207); this miniature edition was probably intended to compete with productions such as George Harrap's Sesame Booklet edition, also published in 1909 and illustrated by Willy Pogany.

Printing: 95: 'Glasgow: Printed at the University Press | by Robert MacLehose and Co. Ltd.'

Note one: Printed in brown ink. The illustrations are from the 1893 edition. The order of the illustrations varies slightly. While the vignettes and ornaments are not resized, the full page illustrations have been reduced to fit the 1909 edition's smaller size. The only other significant alteration occurs to the 1893 title page, which is truncated (to omit the bottom portion with Rossetti's name and publishing information) and appears as a full page illustration on 7.

Location: Ives.

A26 NEW POEMS (1896)

A26.1a *First Edition, First (Uncorrected) Printing (1896)*

Some text in <u>black letter</u>:
NEW POEMS | BY | CHRISTINA ROSSETTI | HITHERTO UNPUBLISHED | OR UNCOLLECTED | EDITED BY | WILLIAM MICHAEL ROSSETTI | I rated to the full amount | Must render mine account | <u>London</u> | MACMILLAN AND CO. | AND NEW YORK | 1896 | *All rights reserved*

Pagination: <u>i-vii</u> viii-xiv <u>xv</u> xvi-xxiv <u>xxv-xxvi</u> <u>1-3</u> 4-184 <u>185-187</u> 188-265 <u>266-269</u> 270-302 <u>303-305</u> 306-376 <u>377</u> 378-397 <u>398-400</u>.

Plates: 1) Facing title, frontispiece portrait of Christina Rossetti (81 x 79), in profile, facing left. See preface p. xiii: "The portrait of my sister given in the present volume is taken from a pencil drawing done by Dante Gabriel . . . ". With tissue guard.

Collation: (174.7 x 115): <u>a</u>⁸ b⁴ B⁸ (χ + B1) C-Z⁸ 2A-2C⁸. $1 signed. 213 leaves. An errata sheet is glued either to the last leaf of b (NjP, BL) or the first leaf in B (Baylor).

Contents: <u>i</u>: half-title 'NEW POEMS | BY | CHRISTINA ROSSETTI'; <u>ii</u>: publisher's device, "M M & Co," 9 x 30; <u>iii</u>: title; <u>iv</u>: blank; <u>v</u>: dedication 'TO | ALGERNON CHARLES SWINBURNE | A GENEROUS EULOGIST OF | CHRISTINA ROSSETTI | WHO HAILED HIS GENIUS AND PRIZED HIMSELF | THE GREATEST OF LIVING BRITISH POETS | MY OLD AND CONSTANT FRIEND | I DEDICATE THIS BOOK | W. M. R.'; <u>vi</u>: blank; <u>vii</u>: 'PREFACE'; <u>xv</u>: 'CONTENTS'; <u>xxv</u>: 'ERRATA'; <u>xxvi</u>: blank; <u>1</u>: section half-title 'GENERAL POEMS'; <u>2</u>: blank; <u>3</u>-184: poems; <u>185</u>: section half-title 'DEVOTIONAL POEMS'; <u>186</u>: blank; 187-265: poems; <u>266</u>: blank; <u>267</u>: section half-title 'ITALIAN POEMS'; <u>268</u>: blank; <u>269</u>-302: poems; <u>303</u>: section half-title 'JUVENILIA'; <u>304</u>: blank; 305-376: poems; <u>377</u>: 'NOTES | BY WILLIAM M. ROSSETTI'; 397: printer's imprint; <u>398</u>: blank; <u>399</u>: advertisement headed 'By the late CHRISTINA G. ROSSETTI' including *Poems*, *Speaking Likenesses*, *Goblin Market* and *Sing-Song* and 'COMPLETE EDITIONS OF THE POETS.' including volumes by Tennyson, Arnold, Lowell, Shelley, Coleridge, Wordsworth; <u>400</u>: advertisement for 'WORKS BY MATTHEW ARNOLD.' (17 items).

Poems: "The Whole Head is Sick and the Whole Heart Faint," "Repining," "Lady Montrevor," "Sonnets Written to Bouts-Rimés" (sonnets I-Xc), "On Keats," "Have Patience," "To Lalla Reading my Verses Topsy-Turvy," "Three Nuns" (sections I-III), "The End of the First Part," "Two Enigmas" (sections I-II), "Two Charades" (sections I-II), "Looking Forward," "Life Hidden," "Queen Rose," "How One Chose," "Seeking Rest," "Two Thoughts Of Death" (sections I-II), "Three Moments," "Is And Was," "Song" ("We buried her among the flowers"), "Annie," "A Dirge" ("She was as sweet as violets in the Spring"), "Song" ("It is not for her even brow"), "A Fair World Though A Fallen," "Books in The Running Brooks," "The Summer Is Ended," "After All," "From The Antique" ("The wind shall lull us yet"), "To What Purpose Is This Waste?," "Next Of Kin," "Portraits," "What?," "Near The Styx," "A Pause," "Holy Innocents" ("Sleep, little Baby, sleep"), "Seasons" ("In springtime when the leaves are young"), "Buried," "A Wish," "Two Parted," "For Rosaline's Album," "Autumn" ("Care flieth"), "Seasons" ("Crocuses and snowdrops wither"), "Ballad," "A Soul," "From The Antique" ("It's a weary life, it is, she said"), "Restive," "Long Looked For," "Listening," "The Last Look," "I Have A Message Unto Thee," "Cobwebs," "An After-Thought," "To The End," "May" ("Sweet life"), "By The Water," "A Chilly Night," "Let Patience Have Her Perfect Work" ("I saw a bird alone"), "In The Lane," "Acme," "A Bed Of Forget-Me-Nots," "Look On This Picture And On This," "Gone Before," "Light Love," "Winter," "A Triad," "In An Artist's Studio," "Introspective," "Day-Dreams," "A Nightmare," "For One Sake," "From Metastasio," "To-Day And To-Morrow," "Yet A Little While" ("These days are long before I die"), "Father And Lover," "What Good Shall My Life Do Me?" ("No hope in life: yet is there hope"), "Cousin Kate," "Sister Maude," "Promises Like Pie-Crust," "Better So," "Our Widowed Queen,"

"In Progress," "Seasons" ("Oh the cheerful Budding-time!"), "June," "Jess And Jill," "Helen Grey," "A Dumb Friend," "To-Morrow" ("Where my heart is"), "Margery," "Last Night," "If," "Sunshine," "Meeting" ("If we shall live, we live"), "Under Willows," "A Sketch," "If I Had Words," "En Route" (sections 1-3), "Husband And Wife," "What To Do?," "In A Certain Place," "Cannot Sweeten," "Of My Life," "What Comes?," "Love's Name" ("Love hath a name of death"), "By Way Of Remembrance," "An Echo From Willow-wood," "Golden Holly," "An Alphabet," "Cor Mio"" ("Still sometimes in my secret heart of hearts"), "Who Shall Say?," "Life," "Meeting" ("I said good-bye in hope"), "Lines," "Hadrian's Death-Song Translated," "Valentines To My Mother" (eleven poems, dated "1876" through "1886"), "My Mouse," "A Poor Old Dog" ["A Word for the Dumb"], "Parted," "To-Day's Burden," "Counterblast On Penny Trumpet," "Michael F. M. Rossetti" (sections 1-4), "The Way Of The World," "To My Fior-Di-Lisa," "Sleeping At Last," "I Do Set My Bow In The Cloud," "Death Is Swallowed Up In Victory," "A Christmas Carol" ("Thank God, thank God, we do believe"), "For Advent," "Two Pursuits," "The Watchers," "Behold, I Stand At The Door And Knock," "Advent" ("'Come,' Thou dost say to Angels"), "All Saints" ("They have brought gold and spices to my King"), "Eye Hath Not Seen" ("Our feet shall tread upon the stars"), "St. Elizabeth Of Hungary," "Moonshine," "I Look For The Lord," "The Heart Knoweth Its Own Bitterness" ("Weep yet awhile"), "Whitsun Eve" ("The white dove cooeth in her downy nest"), "There Remaineth Therefore A Rest For The People Of God" ("Come, blessed sleep") (sections I and II), "A Harvest," "The Eleventh Hour," "For Under A Crucifix," "Who Have A Form Of Godliness," "There Remaineth Therefore A Rest" ("In the grave will be no space"), "Ye Have Forgotten The Exhortation," "Unforgotten," "Zion Said," "Hymn After Gabriele Rossetti," "How Long?," "A Martyr," "Now They Desire," "A Christmas Carol" ("The shepherds had an Angel"), "Not Yours But You," "The Heart Knoweth Its Own Bitterness" ("When all the overwork of life"), "A Burden," "Only Believe," "A Shadow Of Dorothea" ("Golden haired, lily-white), "For Henrietta Polydore," "Ash Wednesday" ("Jesus, do I love thee?"), "A Christmas Carol" ("Before the paling of the stars"), "Easter Even," "The Offering Of The New Law," "By The Waters Of Babylon," "Within The Veil," "Out Of The Deep," "For A Mercy Received," "Conference Between Christ, The Saints, And The Soul" ["I Will Lift Up Mine Eyes Unto The Hills"], "Come Unto Me," "In Patience," "None With Him," "Birds Of Paradise," "I Know You Not," "Thou Art The Same And Thy Years Shall Not Fail" ["Patience of Hope"], "A Christmas Carol" ("Whoso hears a chiming"), "Cardinal Newman," "Yea I Have A Goodly Heritage," "A Death Of A First-Born," "Faint Yet Pursuing" (sections I and II), "Heaven Overarches," "Versi," "L' Incognita," "Nigella," "Chiesa E Signore," "Il Rosseggiar Dell' Oriente" (stanzas 1-21), "L'Uommibatto," "Cor Mio"("Cor mio, cor mio"), "Adriano," "Ninna-Nanna" (1-33), "Sognando," "To My Mother On the Anniversary of her Birth," "Hymn," "Love And Hope," "On Albina," "Forget Me Not," "Charity," "Earth And Heaven," "Love Ephemeral," "Burial Anthem," "Summer" ("Hark to the song of greeting"), "Serenade," "The End Of Time," "Amore E Dovere," "Mother And Child," "On The Death Of A Cat," "Love Attacked," "Love Defended," "The Martyr," "The Dying Man To His Betrothed," "Lisetta All' Amante," "The Dead Bride," "Will These Hands Ne'er Be Clean?," "Present And Future," "The Time Of Waiting," "Tasso And Leonora," "The Solitary Rose," "The Song Of The Star," "Resurrection Eve," "The Dead City," "The Rose," "I Have Fought A Good Fight," "Wishes," "The Dream," "Eleanor," "Isidora," "Zara," "The Novice," "Immalee," "Lady Isabella" ["Sonnet. Lady Isabella"], "Night And Death," "The Lotus-Eaters," "Sonnet," "Song" ("The stream moaneth as it floweth"), "The World's Harmonies," "The Last Answer."

Contents of errata sheet:

Page		line			
Page	33,	line	7 from bottom, *after* out *add* (,).
"	45,	"	4	"	" grieve *add* (:).
"	48,	"	7, *after* playfellow *add* (,).
"	74,	"	13, *before* 1853 *add* February [and the poem ought to be transferred to p. 66].
"	81,	"	4 from bottom, *after* me *add* (,).

” 163, ” 8, *after* kins *dele* (,).

” ” ” ” ” nations *dele* (,).

” 168, ” 4, ” due *add* (,).

” 171, ” last, *before* 1876 *add* 16 March [and the poem ought to be transferred to p. 178].

” 216, ” 9, end of poem, *add* 1853.

” 227, ” 4 from bottom, *after* attend *add* (.).

” 269, ” 9 ” *for* sai *read* sei.

” 288, ” 7, *before* 1876 *add* 16 March.

” 296, ” 5 from bottom, *for* ohime *read* ohimè.

” 380, ” 10 ” ” two *read* four.

” 381, ” 11, etc., from bottom, I am not sure *to* Odds and Ends, *dele.*

” 383, ” last but one, *for* I take it to be several years prior to 1870, *read* it cannot have been later than 1865.

” 384, ” 8 from bottom, *for* Shilling *read* Cornhill.

” 387, ” 16 ” *after* vivid, *add* The scientific name of this creature is *Aphrodita Aculeata:* hence the allusion to "Venus."

” ” ” 6 ” *after* day, *add* After the present volume was in print, I learned that these verses are printed in *Time Flies* (Society for Promoting Christian Knowledge).

” 395, ” 25, *after* hour-glass, *add* The MS. does not give any line rhyming to "lagni": this appears to be an oversight.

Typography and paper: (137) 127 x 57.3 (p. 33), variable lines per page (up to 30). Wove paper, unwatermarked.

Rectangular type ornaments head the text on pp. vii, xv, 3 and 377. Smaller font for Notes (pp. 377-398).

Running titles: In italic.

Rectos: i-vii: no RT; ix-xiii: 'PREFACE'; xv: no RT; xvii-xxiii: 'CONTENTS'; xxv: no RT; 1-3: no RT; 5-13: 'REPINING'; 15-21: 'BOUTS-RIMÉS SONNETS'; 23: 'HAVE PATIENCE'; 25: 'TO LALLA'; 27-35: 'THREE NUNS'; 37: 'TWO ENIGMAS'; 39: 'TWO CHARADES'; 41: 'LIFE HIDDEN'; 43: 'HOW ONE CHOSE'; 45: 'SEEKING REST'; 47-49: 'THREE MOMENTS'; 51: 'SONG'; 53: 'ANNIE'; 55: 'SONG'; 57: 'BOOKS IN THE RUNNING BROOKS'; 59: 'AFTER ALL'; 61-65: 'TO WHAT PURPOSE IS THIS WASTE?'; 67: 'PORTRAITS'; 69: 'NEAR THE STYX'; 71: 'SEASONS'; 73: 'TWO PARTED'; 75: 'BALLAD'; 77: 'A SOUL'; 79: 'RESTIVE'; 81: 'LONG LOOKED FOR'; 83: 'THE LAST LOOK'; 85-87: 'I HAVE A MESSAGE UNTO THEE'; 89: 'AN AFTER-THOUGHT'; 91-93: 'TO THE END'; 95: 'BY THE WATER'; 97: 'A CHILLY NIGHT'; 99: 'HAVE HER PERFECT WORK'; 101: 'ACME'; 103: 'LOOK ON THIS PICTURE'; 105-107: 'AND ON THIS'; 109-111: 'LIGHT LOVE'; 113: 'A TRIAD'; 115: 'INTROSPECTIVE'; 117: 'DAY-DREAMS'; 119: 'FOR ONE SAKE'; 121: 'TO-DAY AND TO-MORROW'; 123: 'YET A LITTLE WHILE'; 125: 'WHAT GOOD SHALL MY LIFE DO ME?'; 127: 'COUSIN KATE'; 129: 'SISTER MAUDE'; 131: 'BETTER SO'; 133: 'OUR WIDOWED QUEEN'; 135: 'SEASONS'; 137: 'JESS AND JILL'; 139: 'A DUMB FRIEND'; 141-143: 'MARGERY'; 145: 'IF'; 147: 'SUNSHINE'; 149: 'UNDER WILLOWS'; 151: 'IF I HAD WORDS'; 153: 'EN ROUTE'; 155: 'HUSBAND AND WIFE'; 157: 'IN A CERTAIN PLACE'; 159: 'CANNOT SWEETEN'; 161: 'LOVE'S NAME'; 163: 'BY WAY OF REMEMBRANCE'; 165-167: 'AN ALPHABET'; 169: 'LIFE'; 171: 'HADRIAN'S DEATH-SONG'; 173-177: 'VALENTINES TO MY MOTHER'; 179: 'PARTED'; 181: 'MICHAEL F. M. ROSSETTI'; 183: 'TO MY FIOR-DI-LISA'; 185-187: no RT; 189: 'DEATH IS SWALLOWED UP IN VICTORY'; 191: 'IN VICTORY'; 193: 'FOR ADVENT'; 195: 'TWO PURSUITS';

197: 'THE WATCHERS'; 199: 'ADVENT'; 201-203: 'EYE HATH NOT SEEN'; 205: 'MOONSHINE'; 207: 'I LOOK FOR THE LORD'; 209: 'ITS OWN BITTERNESS'; 211: 'THERE REMAINETH A REST'; 213: 'A HARVEST'; 215: 'THE ELEVENTH HOUR'; 217: 'THERE REMAINETH A REST'; 219: 'THE EXHORTATION'; 221: 'UNFORGOTTEN'; 223-225: 'HYMN AFTER GABRIELE ROSSETTI'; 227: 'A MARTYR'; 229: 'NOW THEY DESIRE'; 231: 'A CHRISTMAS CAROL'; 233: 'HEART'S BITTERNESS'; 235-237: 'A BURDEN'; 239: 'ONLY BELIEVE'; 241: 'A SHADOW OF DOROTHEA'; 243: 'ASH WEDNESDAY'; 245: 'EASTER EVEN'; 247: 'THE OFFERING OF THE NEW LAW'; 249: 'BY THE WATERS OF BABYLON'; 251: 'FOR A MERCY RECEIVED'; 253: 'CHRIST, THE SAINTS, AND THE SOUL'; 255: 'IN PATIENCE'; 257: 'BIRDS OF PARADISE'; 259: 'I KNOW YOU NOT'; 261: 'CARDINAL NEWMAN'; 263: 'A DEATH OF A FIRST-BORN'; 265: 'HEAVEN OVERARCHES'; 267-269: no RT; 271: 'CHIESA E SIGNORE'; 273-285: 'IL ROSSEGGIAR DELL' ORIENTE'; 287: 'COR MIO'; 289-301: 'NINNA-NANNA'; 303-305: no RT; 307: 'CHARITY'; 309: 'LOVE EPHEMERAL'; 311-313: 'SUMMER'; 315: 'THE END OF TIME'; 317: 'AMORE E DOVERE'; 319: 'ON THE DEATH OF A CAT'; 321: 'LOVE ATTACKED'; 323: 'THE MARTYR'; 325-327: 'THE DYING MAN TO HIS BETROTHED'; 329: 'THE DEAD BRIDE'; 331: 'WILL THESE HANDS NE'ER BE CLEAN?'; 333: 'PRESENT AND FUTURE'; 335: 'THE TIME OF WAITING'; 337: 'THE SOLITARY ROSE'; 339: 'THE SONG OF THE STAR'; 341: 'RESURRECTION EVE'; 343-351: 'THE DEAD CITY'; 353: 'THE ROSE'; 355: 'WISHES'; 357: 'THE DREAM'; 359-361: 'ISIDORA'; 363: 'ZARA'; 365: 'THE NOVICE'; 367-369: 'NIGHT AND DEATH'; 371: 'SONNET FROM THE PSALMS'; 373: 'THE WORLD'S HARMONIES'; 375: 'THE LAST ANSWER'; 377: no RT; 379-397: 'NOTES'; 399: no RT.

Versos: ii-vi: no RT; viii-xiv: 'PREFACE'; xvi-xxiv: 'CONTENTS'; xxvi: no RT; 2: no RT; 4-12: 'REPINING'; 14: 'LADY MONTREVOR'; 16-20: 'BOUTS-RIMÉS SONNETS'; 22: 'ON KEATS'; 24: 'HAVE PATIENCE'; 26: 'TO LALLA'; 28-34: 'THREE NUNS'; 36: 'THE END OF THE FIRST PART'; 38: 'TWO CHARADES'; 40: 'LOOKING FORWARD'; 42: 'QUEEN ROSE'; 44: 'HOW ONE CHOSE'; 46: 'TWO THOUGHTS OF DEATH'; 48: 'THREE MOMENTS'; 50: 'IS AND WAS'; 52: 'ANNIE'; 54: 'A DIRGE'; 56-58: 'BOOKS IN THE RUNNING BROOKS'; 60: 'FROM THE ANTIQUE'; 62-64: 'TO WHAT PURPOSE IS THIS WASTE?'; 66: 'NEXT OF KIN'; 68: 'WHAT?'; 70: 'HOLY INNOCENTS'; 72: 'A WISH'; 74: 'AUTUMN'; 76: 'BALLAD'; 78: 'FROM THE ANTIQUE'; 80: 'RESTIVE'; 82: 'LISTENING'; 84-86: 'I HAVE A MESSAGE UNTO THEE'; 88: 'COBWEBS'; 90: 'AN AFTER-THOUGHT'; 92: 'TO THE END'; 94: 'MAY'; 96: 'A CHILLY NIGHT'; 98: 'LET PATIENCE'; 100: 'IN THE LANE'; 102: 'A BED OF FORGET-ME-NOTS'; 104-106: 'LOOK ON THIS PICTURE'; 108: 'GONE BEFORE'; 110: 'LIGHT LOVE'; 112: 'WINTER'; 114: 'IN AN ARTIST'S STUDIO'; 116: 'DAY-DREAMS'; 118: 'A NIGHTMARE'; 120: 'TO-DAY AND TO-MORROW'; 122: 'YET A LITTLE WHILE'; 124: 'FATHER AND LOVER'; 126: 'WHAT GOOD SHALL MY LIFE DO ME?'; 128: 'COUSIN KATE'; 130: 'PROMISES LIKE PIE-CRUST'; 132: 'BETTER SO'; 134: 'IN PROGRESS'; 136: 'JUNE'; 138: 'HELEN GREY'; 140: 'TO-MORROW'; 142: 'MARGERY'; 144: 'LAST NIGHT'; 146: 'IF'; 148: 'MEETING'; 150: 'A SKETCH'; 152: 'EN ROUTE'; 154: 'HUSBAND AND WIFE'; 156: 'IN A CERTAIN PLACE'; 158: 'CANNOT SWEETEN'; 160: 'OF MY LIFE'; 162: 'BY WAY OF REMEMBRANCE'; 164: 'AN ECHO FROM WILLOW-WOOD'; 166: 'AN ALPHABET'; 168: 'WHO SHALL SAY?'; 170: 'MEETING'; 172-176: 'VALENTINES TO MY MOTHER'; 178: 'MY MOUSE'; 180: 'TO-DAY'S BURDEN'; 182: 'MICHAEL F. M. ROSSETTI'; 184: 'SLEEPING AT LAST'; 186: no RT; 188: 'I DO SET MY BOW IN THE CLOUD'; 190: 'DEATH IS SWALLOWED UP'; 192: 'A CHRISTMAS CAROL'; 194: 'FOR ADVENT'; 196: 'THE WATCHERS'; 198: 'I STAND AT THE DOOR AND KNOCK'; 200: 'ALL SAINTS'; 202: 'EYE HATH NOT SEEN'; 204-206: 'MOONSHINE'; 208: 'THE HEART KNOWETH'; 210: 'WHITSUN EVE'; 212: 'A HARVEST'; 214: 'THE ELEVENTH HOUR'; 216: 'WHO HAVE A FORM OF GODLINESS'; 218: 'YE HAVE FORGOTTEN'; 220: 'EXHORTATION FORGOTTEN'; 222: 'ZION SAID'; 224: 'HYMN AFTER GABRIELE ROSSETTI'; 226: 'HOW LONG?'; 228: 'NOW THEY DESIRE'; 230: 'A CHRISTMAS CAROL'; 232: 'NOT YOURS BUT YOU'; 234: 'HEART'S BITTERNESS'; 236-238: 'A BURDEN'; 240: 'A SHADOW OF DOROTHEA'; 242: 'ASH WEDNESDAY'; 244: 'A

CHRISTMAS CAROL'; 246: 'EASTER EVEN'; 248: 'BY THE WATERS OF BABYLON'; 250: 'OUT OF THE DEEP'; 252: 'FOR A MERCY RECEIVED'; 254: 'CHRIST, THE SAINTS, AND THE SOUL'; 256: 'NONE WITH HIM'; 258: 'I KNOW YOU NOT'; 260: 'THOU ART THE SAME'; 262: 'YEA I HAVE A GOODLY HERITAGE'; 264: 'FAINT YET PURSUING'; 266-268: no RT; 270: 'NIGELLA'; 272-286: 'IL ROSSEGGIAR DELL' ORIENTE'; 288-300: 'NINNA-NANNA'; 302: 'SOGNANDO'; 304: no RT; 306: 'ON ALBINA'; 308: 'EARTH AND HEAVEN'; 310: 'BURIAL ANTHEM'; 312: 'SUMMER'; 314: 'SERENADE'; 316: 'THE END OF TIME'; 318: 'MOTHER AND CHILD'; 320: 'LOVE ATTACKED'; 322: 'LOVE DEFENDED'; 324: 'THE MARTYR'; 326: 'THE DYING MAN TO HIS BETROTHED'; 328: 'LISETTA ALL' AMANTE'; 330: 'THE DEAD BRIDE'; 332: 'WILL THESE HANDS NE'ER BE CLEAN?'; 334-336: 'THE TIME OF WAITING'; 338-340: 'THE SONG OF THE STAR'; 342-352: 'THE DEAD CITY'; 354: 'I HAVE FOUGHT A GOOD FIGHT'; 356: 'THE DREAM'; 358: 'ELEANOR'; 360: 'ISIDORA'; 362: 'ZARA'; 364: 'THE NOVICE'; 366: 'LADY ISABELLA'; 368: 'NIGHT AND DEATH'; 370: 'THE LOTUS-EATERS'; 372: 'SONG'; 374: 'THE WORLD'S HARMONIES'; 376: 'THE LAST ANSWER'; 378-396: 'NOTES'; 398-400: no RT.

Binding: Calico cloth, very dark greenish blue (Centroid 175). Front: same design as 1865 *Goblin Market*, in gilt: three vertical lines intersected by three-sided square, with groups of three rings in the corners. Back: blind-stamped, same as front. Spine: in gilt: '[rule below two small rings (one at left, one at right)] | NEW | POEMS | CHRISTINA | ROSSETTI | [rule with a ring at either end, and a group of three rings in inverted pyramid centered beneath] | MACMILLAN & Cᵒ [dot under the "o"] | [rule]'; in most copies, the rings at either end of the second rule are only partially printed. Endpapers: white wove, thicker than sheets; top edges rough trimmed, fore-edge and tail untrimmed.

Publication: 2000 printed in January 1896, from type and electrotype (Editions Book, Macmillan Archives). An additional 2000 were printed in June from corrected plates, with a final 1000 printed in August 1900.

On May 20, 1895, WMR proposed "a supplementary volume" of CGR's poems; two days later, WMR recorded that Macmillan had accepted (WMRD). WMR's contract with Macmillan, dated June 5, 1895, stipulate half profits and a royalty of 15% on the American edition (Terms book). By early August, WMR had assembled the poems and sent them to be typed; and on October 3, he delivered the complete manuscript to Macmillan, noting that "the Printers in England will print, & send me proofs, & the proofs, as revised by me, will be forwarded to the United States, where Amer[ican] Printers will print other sheets" (WMRD, 3 October 1895). WMR returned the last set of proofs on November 10; these may be the same set, stamped 7 November 1895, with WMR's signature and corrections that is currently held at the Bancroft Library at the University of California at Berkeley. On January 13, WMR received "an advance-copy" of the book, which was to be published on January 17 (WMRD, 13 January 1895).

As noted in the entry for A2, a copy of CGR's *Verses* (1847) now held at the University of Illinois at Urbana-Champaign probably served as printer's copy for the early poems included in *New Poems*.

Announced in the *Dial* (16 September 1895: 150; 16 February 1896: 121); in the London *Times* (17 January 1896: 12; in "Publications To-Day," 18 January: 8).

Price: 7s. 6d; in United States, $1.75.

BL depository copy: 'BRITISH MUSEUM 5 MH 96'.

Reviewed in the *Times* (7 February 1896: 13); *Athenaeum* (15 February 1896: 207-209); *Spectator* (29 February 1896: 309-310); *Bookman* (March 1896: 55-56); *Dial* (1 April 1896: 205-206); *Atlantic Monthly* (April 1896: 570-571); *London Quarterly Review* (April 1896): 180-181); *Blackwood's Edinburgh Magazine* (June 1896: 922-924); *Academy* (25 July 1896: 59-60); *Speaker* (22 August 1896: 204-205).

Printing: 397: '*Printed by* R & R CLARK, LIMITED, *Edinburgh*.'

Locations: BL (rebound); Ives; NjP; TxCM; Baylor.

A26.1b   *First Edition, Second (Corrected) Printing (1896)*

Same as first printing except:

Some text in <u>black letter</u>:
NEW POEMS | BY | CHRISTINA ROSSETTI | HITHERTO UNPUBLISHED | OR UNCOLLECTED | EDITED BY | WILLIAM MICHAEL ROSSETTI | I rated to the full amount | Must render mine account | <u>London</u> | MACMILLAN AND CO., Ltd. | NEW YORK: MACMILLAN & CO. | 1896 | *All rights reserved*

Pagination: Same except no pp. <u>xxv</u>-<u>xxvi</u>.

Collation: <u>a</u>^{8} b^4 B^8 C-Z^8 2A-2C^8. \$1 signed. 212 leaves.

Contents: same except iv: '*First Edition* 1895 | *Reprinted* 1896' (see *Note one*); poem "For Rosaline's Album" moved from 74 to 67; poem "Hadrian's Death-Song Translated" moved from 171 to 177; on 399 and 400, at the bottom of page, the presentation of the publisher's name changes to 'MACMILLAN AND CO., Ltd'.

Running titles: Same except:
Rectos: 69: 'WHAT?'; 71: 'HOLY INNOCENTS'; 171: 'VALENTINES TO MY MOTHER'; 177: 'HADRIAN'S DEATH-SONG'.
Versos: 70: 'A PAUSE'; 72: 'BURIED'.

Publication: Printed in June 1896 from corrected plates. On June 6, WMR noted in his diary that he had "returned to the printers R & R Clark some pages wh. they had sent me out of C, as a 2nd edition is about to appear" (WMRD).

Note one: The notation "First Edition 1895" (iv) seems to reflect the printing rather than the publication dates. Although an 1895 proof is held at the Bancroft Library (see A261a, *Publication*), no published copies with an 1895 date on the title page have been located.

Locations: CUV (rebound), DeU, CaBVaU (Colbeck entry 25), TxCM.

A26.1c   *First Edition, Third Printing (1900)*

Not seen; information drawn from an electronic version of University of California copy.

Some text in black letter:
NEW POEMS | BY | CHRISTINA ROSSETTI | HITHERTO UNPUBLISHED | OR UNCOLLECTED | EDITED BY | WILLIAM MICHAEL ROSSETTI | I rated to the full amount | Must render mine account | <u>London</u> | MACMILLAN AND CO., Limited | NEW YORK: THE MACMILLAN COMPANY | 1900 | *All rights reserved*

Contents: Edition statement reads "*First Edition* 1895 | *Reprinted* 1896, 1900."
Two poems removed: "Conference between Christ, the Saints, and the Soul," and "A Christmas Carol" ("Whoso hears a chiming"); "Jess and Jill" retitled "A Ring-Posy."

Publication: 1000 copies printed (Editions Book, Macmillan Archives). As early as August 1896, WMR noted in his diary that he had sent a list of corrections that would be needed for a new edition, consisting mostly of "omissions of a few poems wh. prove to have been already published in her vols" (28 August 1896), and in September, he "Began setting C. to rights for the next reissue (when it comes) – cutting out 2 pieces &c" (10 September 1896). This accounts for the removal of "Conference between Christ, the Saints, and the Soul" (published in 1875 under the title "I Will Lift Up Mine Eyes Unto The Hills"), and "A Christmas Carol," along with the retitling of "Jess and Jill," and various corrections to the volume's

Preface and Notes. However, "Thou Art the Same and Thy Years Shall Not Fail," previously published under the title "Patience of Hope," remains in the volume.

Locations: University of California, Santa Cruz (via Google Books).

A26.2a.i   *Second Edition, First Printing, Large Paper Issue (1896)*

Some text in <u>black letter</u>:
NEW POEMS | BY | CHRISTINA ROSSETTI | HITHERTO UNPUBLISHED OR | UNCOLLECTED | EDITED BY | WILLIAM MICHAEL ROSSETTI | I rated to the full amount | Must render mine account | <u>New York</u> | MACMILLAN AND CO. | AND LONDON | 1896 | *All rights reserved*

Pagination: <u>i</u>-<u>vii</u> viii-xxiv <u>1</u>-<u>3</u> 4-184 <u>185</u>-<u>187</u> 188-265 <u>266</u>-<u>269</u> 270-302 <u>303</u>-<u>305</u> 306-397 <u>398</u>-<u>400</u>.

Plates: Frontispiece profile of Christina Rossetti, same as first edition.

Collation: (205 x 131): [1-25⁸ 26-28⁴]; 212 leaves.

Contents: <u>i</u>: half-title 'NEW POEMS | BY | CHRISTINA ROSSETTI'; <u>ii</u>: Macmillan device, "M M & Co," 8 x 34.3; <u>iii</u>: title; <u>iv</u>: 'Copyright, 1896, | By MACMILLAN AND CO. | [rule, 11] | *One hundred copies of this large paper edition printed on hand-made | paper, January, 1896, of which this is No.* [nine dot ellipsis]' and printer's imprint; <u>v</u>: dedication 'TO | ALGERNON CHARLES SWINBURNE | GENEROUS EULOGIST OF | CHRISTINA ROSSETTI | WHO HAILED HIS GENIUS AND PRIZED HIMSELF | THE GREATEST OF LIVING BRITISH POETS | MY OLD AND CONSTANT FRIEND | I DEDICATE THIS BOOK | W. M. R.'; <u>vi</u>: blank; <u>vii</u>: 'PREFACE'; <u>xv</u>: 'CONTENTS'; <u>1</u>: section half-title 'GENERAL POEMS'; <u>2</u>: blank; <u>3</u>-184: poems; <u>185</u>: section half-title 'DEVOTIONAL POEMS'; <u>186</u>: blank; <u>187</u>-265: poems; <u>266</u>: blank; <u>267</u>: section half-title 'ITALIAN POEMS'; <u>268</u>: blank; <u>269</u>-302: poems; <u>303</u>: section half-title 'JUVENILIA'; <u>304</u>: blank; <u>305</u>-376: poems; <u>377</u>: 'NOTES | BY WILLIAM M. ROSSETTI'; <u>398</u>-<u>400</u>: blank.

Running titles: Same as British edition, uncorrected printing, except:
Rectos: no errata sheet (that is, no xxv); period on 41 ('LIFE HIDDEN.'); 209: 'KNOWETH ITS OWN BITTERNESS'.
Versos: no errata sheet (that is, no xxvi); 208: 'THE HEART'.

Typography and paper: Laid paper, vertical chainlines 26 mm apart. Two watermarks: text 'John Dickinson & Co'; also fleur de lys and crown above script "J D Co."

Binding: Buckram, light brown (Centroid 57). Front and back plain. Spine: on grayish white paper label, in grayish reddish orange ink: 'NEW POEMS | BY | CHRISTINA ROSSETTI | EDITED BY | WILLIAM MICHAEL ROSSETTI'. Endpapers: same as sheets. Edges: top rough trimmed, fore-edge and tail untrimmed.

Publication: WMR noted in his diary that the American edition was to be printed from corrected sheets of the British edition. However, only two items listed on the errata sheet of the British edition are corrected in this edition: on 33, line 7 from bottom, comma after 'out'; and on 227, 4 from bottom, period after 'attend'.
 Advertised (with small paper issue) among Macmillan's "New Books" in *New York Times* (8 February 1896: 5).
 Price $3.50.

Printing: <u>iv</u> (first line black letter): 'Norwood Press | J. S. Cushing & Co.–Berwick & Smith | Norwood Mass. U. S. A.'

Locations: NjP, TxU (2).

A26.2a.ii   **Second Edition, First Printing, Small Paper Issue (1896)**

Same as large paper issue except:

Collation: (175 x 119): A-B⁸ C-2C⁸ 4C⁴, $5 signed.

Contents: iv: no edition statement; 399: advertisement, "Works By William Watson," three titles; 400: advertisement, two titles, *The Humours of the Court* and *The Selections From the Poems of Aubrey de Vere*

Typography and paper: Wove paper, unwatermarked.

Binding: Calico cloth, very dark yellowish green (Centroid 138). Front, back: blind-stamped single rule border. Spine: in gilt '[rule] | NEW POEMS | BY | CHRISTINA | ROSSETTI | EDITED BY | WILLIAM MICHAEL | ROSSETTI | MACMILLAN & Cᵃ | [rule]'. Endpapers: wove paper. Edges: top edge gilt, fore-edge, tail rough trimmed.

Publication: Announced in the *Dial*, "List of New Books" (16 February 1896: 121).
    Price: $1.75.
    Reviewed in *New York Observer* (27 February 1896: 280); *New York Times* (1 March 1896: 31); *Bookman* (March 1896: 55); *Literary World* (Boston) (March 1896: 85); *Independent* (New York) (26 March 1896: 18); *Dial* (1 April 1896: 205-206); *Critic* (brief mention) (27 June 1896: 463).

Location: Ives.

A27 THE ROSSETTI BIRTHDAY BOOK (1896)

A27.1a **First Edition, First Printing (1896)**

Within single rule frame, 102 x 68; some text in <u>black letter</u>:
THE ROSSETTI | BIRTHDAY BOOK | EDITED BY | OLIVIA ROSSETTI | <u>London</u> | MACMILLAN AND CO., Ltd. | NEW YORK: MACMILLAN & CO. | 1896

Pagination: [4] 1-278 <u>279-280</u>.

Collation: A² B-S⁸ T⁴. $1 signed. 142 leaves.

Contents: [1]: half-title 'THE | ROSSETTI BIRTHDAY BOOK'; [2]: '*All rights reserved*'; [3]: title; [4]: poem 'Tempus Fugit'; 1: section half-title 'JANUARY.'; 2-23: poems and calendar pages; 24: ornament, 8 x 29, floral (tulips?); 25: section half-title 'FEBRUARY.'; 26-45: poems and calendar pages; 46: ornament 11 x 28, lily of the valley; 47: section half-title 'MARCH.'; 48-69: poems and calendar pages; 70: ornament, 14 x 30, honeysuckle; 71: section half-title 'APRIL.'; 72-91: poems and calendar pages; 92: ornament, 10 x 31, morning glory; 93: section half-title 'MAY.'; 94-115: poems and calendar pages; 116: ornament, 10 x 28, floral; 117: section half-title 'JUNE.'; 118-137: poems and calendar pages; 138: ornament, same as on 70; 139: section half-title 'JULY.'; 140-161: poems and calendar pages; 162: ornament, 10 x 28, flowers on branch; 163: section half-title 'AUGUST.'; 164-185: poems and calendar pages; 186: ornament, 11 x 27, marigolds; 187: section half-title 'SEPTEMBER'; 188-207: poems and calendar pages; 208: ornament, 10 x 26, sunflower; 209: section half-title 'OCTOBER.'; 232: ornament, 9 x 25, acorns; 233: section half-title 'NOVEMBER'[no period]; 234-253: poems and calendar pages; 254: ornament,10 x 33, floral; 255: section half-title 'DECEMBER.'; 256-277: poems and calendar pages; 278: printer's imprint; 279: advertisement for books by CGR, five titles, *New Poems*, *The Poems of Christina Rossetti*, *Speaking Likenesses*, *Goblin Market*, *Sing-Song*; 280: advertisement for 'COMPLETE EDITIONS OF THE POETS,' six titles, Tennyson through Wordsworth.

Birth and death dates of Rossetti family members are also included in the text, as follows: 16: '(MICHAEL F. M. ROSSETTI, died 24*th January* 1883)'; 36: '(MARIA FRANCESCA ROSSETTI, born 17*th Feb.* 1827)'; 44: '(GABRIELE ROSSETTI, born 28*th February* 1783)'; 76: '(FRANCES L. M. ROSSETTI, died 8*th April* 1886)' and '(D. G. ROSSETTI, died 9*th April* 1882)'; 78: '(LUCY MADOX ROSSETTI, died 12*th April* 1894)'; 88: '(GABRIELE ROSSETTI, died 26*th April* 1854)' and April 27 '(FRANCES L. M. ROSSETTI, born 27*th April* 1800)'; 100: '(D. G. ROSSETTI, born 12*th May* 1828)'; 152: '(LUCY MADOX ROSSETTI, born 19*th July* 1843)'; 248: '(MARIA FRANCESCA ROSSETTI, died 24*th Nov.* 1876)'; 258: '(CHRISTINA G. ROSSETTI, born 5*th December* 1830)'; 274: '(CHRISTINA G. ROSSETTI, died 29*th December* 1894)' .

Poems: "Tempus Fugit" and excerpts from the following; poems excerpted multiple times are marked with asterisks (see *Note one*):
"Old and New Year Ditties," "A Year's Windfalls," "Spring Quiet," "Mirrors of Life and Death," "Goblin Market," "Long Barren," "Up-Hill," "Somewhere or Other," "A Birthday," "Dead in the cold, a song-singing thrush" ["cold" altered to "snow"], "What do the stars do," "Is the moon tired? she looks so pale," "O Lady Moon, your horns point towards the east," "O wind, why do you never rest," "Growing in the vale," "Who has seen the wind?," "On the grassy banks," "O wind, where have you been," "Wrens and robins in the hedge," "A frisky lamb," "O, fair to see," "If all were rain and never sun," "There is but one May in the year," "Hope is like a harebell," "The lily has an air," "When the cows come home the milk is coming," "Roses blushing red and white," "When a mounting skylark," "Hurt no living thing," "What are heavy?," "The lily has a smooth stalk," "Rushes in a watery place," "The wind has such a rainy sound," "Fly away, fly away over the sea," "If hope grew on a bush," "My baby has a mottled fist," "The dog lies in his kennel," "The horses of the sea," "Swift and sure the swallow," "I know a baby, such a baby," "An emerald is as green as grass," "Bread and milk for

breakfast," "A diamond or a coal?," "There's snow on the fields," "A linnet in a gilded cage," "A rose has thorns as well as honey," "Good-bye in fear, good-bye in sorrow," "'The Love of Christ Which Passeth Knowledge'," "A Wintry Sonnet," "'There is a budding Morrow in Midnight'," "A Testimony," "Mother Country," "The Master is Come and Calleth for Thee," "Saints and Angels," "The Key-Note," "Monna Innominata," "Michael M. F. Rossetti," "'Hollow-Sounding and Mysterious'," "A Helpmeet for Him," "Maiden May," "Death-Watches," "Amen," "A Better Resurrection," "A Candlemas Dialogue," "To The End," "The Months: A Pageant," "Brandons Both," "A Life's Parallels," "The First Spring Day," "In the Willow Shade," "An "Immurata" Sister," "One Foot on Sea, and One on Shore," "Passing and Glassing," "I Will Arise," "What's in a Name?," "All Thy Works Praise Thee, O Lord," "Later Life," "Love hath a name of death," "For Thine Own Sake, O My God," "'Take Care of Him'," "En Route," "Another Spring," "Advent" ("This Advent moon shines cold and clear"), "Consider the Lilies of the Field" ("Flowers preach to us if we will hear"), "I Will Lift up Mine Eyes Unto The Hills" ("I am pale with sick desire"), "A Fisher-Wife," "A Song of Flight," "Freaks of Fashion," "A Farm Walk," "By the Sea," "Three Seasons," "The Thread of Life," "If thou Sayest, Behold, We Knew it Not," "Mariana," "Spring," "One Day," "Sleeping at Last," "Birchington Churchyard," "A Chill," "Rest," "At Last," "An Easter Carol," "Buds and Babies," "Paradise," "Valentine 1876," "A Martyr" ("Inner not outer, without gnash of teeth"), "L. E. L.," "May" ("I cannot tell you how it was"), "Dream-Love," "Sweet Death," "A Bird Song," "Golden Glories," "An Old World Thicket," "Exultate Deo," "Patience of Hope," "A Summer Wish" ["Wish" altered to "Walk"], "A Peal of Bells," "Confluents," "Twilight calm," "Sound Sleep," "Echo," "A Smile and a Sigh," "Consider," "Symbols," "Beauty is Vain," "Sleep at Sea," "When my Heart is Vexed I will Complain" ("O Lord, how canst Thou say Thou lovest me?"), "From House to Home," "Bird Raptures," "Summer" ("Winter is cold-hearted"), "Martyrs' Song," "Songs in a Cornfield," "Life and Death," "The Prince's Progress," "Enrica, 1865," "Thy Brother's Blood Crieth," ["The German-French Campaign"], "Amor Mundi," "Until the Day Break," "To-Day and To-morrow," "The Lowest Place," "A Green Cornfield," "Looking Forward," "Annie," "A Wish," "Seasons"("Crocuses and snowdrops wither"), "From Metastasio," "What Good shall My Life Do Me?" ("No hope in life: yet is there hope"), "Golden Silences," "Seasons" ("Oh the cheerful Budding-time!"), "Sunshine," "One Sea-Side Grave," "Autumn Violets," "The Convent Threshold," "Autumn" ("I dwell alone"), "A Poor Old Dog," "Resurgam," "St. Elizabeth of Hungary," "Yet a Little While" ("These days are long before I die"), "A Bed of Forget-me-nots," "I Have a Message Unto Thee," "From the Antique" ("The wind shall lull us yet"), "An October Garden," "Summer is Ended," "After this the Judgment," "Touching 'Never'," "Song" ("It is not for her even brow"), "Song" ("O what comes over the sea"), "Johnny," "Golden Holly," "Bitter for Sweet," "Heaven Overarches," "If Only," "Winter," "Seasons" ("In Springtime when the leaves are young"), "Winter: My Secret" ["My Secret"], "Love Defended," "The Iniquity of the Fathers Upon the Children"["Under The Rose"], "For Advent," "A Christmas Carol" ("In the bleak mid-winter"), "Christmas Carols (2)" ("A holy, heavenly chime"), "Song" ("O roses for the flush of youth").

Typography and paper: (106) 92 x 48 (p. 62); various lines per page (up to 26). Wove paper, unwatermarked.

All text, exclusive of pagination and calendar date, within rule frame, 102 x 69. Calendar pages are also divided into three sections by two horizontal rules. Each rule extends to the left and right of letterpress for the date (e.g., "January 1"). Calendar dates are in black letter; poem titles in italic; names of months printed on section half-titles are in an unidentified ornamented san serif font.

No running titles.

Binding: Linen-textured cloth, moderate reddish brown (Centroid 43). Front: in blackish green ink (Centroid 152), repeating diagonal design of carnations with bud and single leaf. Back: same ink color and design, with a center medallion containing the interlaced initials "C G R" in outline font. Spine: in gilt, 'The | Rossetti | Birthday | Book | [in blackish green ink, ornament of carnation with two blossoms] | [in gilt] Macmillan and Co.'. Endpapers: same floral design as front, printed in moderate red (Centroid 15). Edges: stained moderate reddish brown (Centroid 43).

Publication: June 23, 1896. 2000 copies printed in May 1896 from type and plates (Edition Book, Macmillan Archives).

On May 16, 1895, Macmillan sent WMR a manuscript for a CGR birthday book. Although WMR was not averse to the idea — "I have no antipathy to such a volume" — he was unimpressed with Macmillan's manuscript, noting in his diary that it was "in a most disagreeable handwri[ting]; seems to me to be "less well done t[ha]n. it might be" (WMRD). He responded to Macmillan on May 20 that "the selection does not appear to me to be made on quite the right principle" (Peattie, 76-77). WMR's negative response deterred Macmillan from publishing the original manuscript, which is no longer extant (WMRD, May 23 1895). However, WMR subsequently asked his daughter Olivia to compile a new manuscript, and Macmillan accepted the proposed volume in June (WMRD 5 June). Olivia finished the compilation on November 2; five days later, WMR sent the manuscript to Macmillan, with first proofs arriving on November 25 (WMRD). Macmillan promptly sent the manuscript to R. & R. Clark, instructing them to set the book "uniform with the Tennyson Birthday Book" (Letter Books, 60).

Announced in *Book Reviews* (September 1895: 133); London *Times* (24 April 1896: 10 and "Publications Today," 24 June 1896: 16); *Publishers' Weekly* (25 July 1896: 152).

Price: 2s. 6d.; in United States, 75 cents.

Reviewed in *New York Times* (20 July 1896: 3); the *Academy* (25 July 1896: 59-60); *Bookseller* (7 August 1896: 740); *Literary World* (21 August 1896: 145).

Printing: 278: '*Printed by* R. & R. Clark, Limited, *Edinburgh.*'

Note one: Many of the poems were excerpted multiple times, with "The Months: A Pageant" providing 30 separate excerpts.

Location: Ives.

A27.1b   *First Edition, Second Printing (1897)*

Same as 1896 printing except:

Within single rule frame, 102 x 68; some text in black letter:
THE | CHRISTINA ROSSETTI | BIRTHDAY BOOK | EDITED BY | OLIVIA ROSSETTI | London | MACMILLAN AND CO., Limited | NEW YORK: THE MACMILLAN COMPANY | 1897

Contents (see *Note one*): [1]: half-title 'THE | CHRISTINA ROSSETTI | BIRTHDAY BOOK'; on [4], printed below rule frame '*First edition* 1896; *Reprinted* 1897'.

Binding: Ives copy is rebound; see note.

Publication: 2000 copies printed from plates in January, 1897 (Editions Book, Macmillan Archives).

Note one: Pages 279-280 are missing from the Ives copy; they may have been removed when the book was rebound. Only one library copy is extant, at the Bancroft Library at the University of California at Berkeley. The binding of this copy, as described in the catalog record and personal correspondence, is similar to that of the 1896 edition, with the addition of a dust jacket upon which the carnation design of the cloth binding is repeated.

Location: Ives.

A28 MAUDE (Stone, 1897)

A28.1a.i   ***First American Edition, First Printing, First Issue (1897)***

Within plate mark, 105 x 65; tree ornament is printed in green ink:
MAUDE: *Prose & Verse* | *by* Christina Rossetti; 1850 | [in green ink: ornament, tree, 88 x 38.7; remaining text printed in black, on either side of ornament, as follows:]
    CHICAGO [ornament] HERBERT S. |
   MDCCCXC [ornament] STONE & COM |
       VII [ornament] PANY

Pagination: [8] 1-122 <u>123</u>-<u>124</u> [4]. Note that a sixteen page advertising section is inserted after <u>124</u> (that is, in the middle of gathering 17, before the last two unpaginated leaves). The advertising section is paginated <u>1</u>-<u>2</u> 3-15 <u>16</u>.

Collation: (174 x 113): [1-16⁴ 17⁴]. Gathering 17 with insertion consisting of an unsigned 8 leaf gathering of advertisements. 68 leaves.

Contents: [1-4]: blank; [5]: half-title 'MAUDE: *Prose & Verse*'; [6]: blank; [7]: title; [8]: 'COPYRIGHT, 1897, BY | HERBERT S. STONE & CO.'; 1: 'Prefatory Note'; 7: text headed 'Maude | Part I | I'; 19: text headed 'II'; 33: text headed 'III'; 41: text headed 'Part II | I'; 52: text headed 'II'; 63: text headed 'III'; 80: text headed 'Part III | I'; 89: text headed 'II'; 106: text headed 'III'; <u>123</u>: printer's imprint; <u>124</u>: blank: [1]-[4]: blank.

Poems: "Yes, I too could face," "Would that I were a turnip," "I fancy the good fairies," "Some ladies dress in muslin," "She sat and sang alway," ["Song"], "Sweet, sweet sound of distant waters," "Vanity of vanities, the Preacher saith" ["One Certainty"], "I listen to the holy antheming," "Thank God, thank God, we do believe," "Three Nuns," (sections I-III), "I watched a rosebud very long" ["Symbols"], "Sleep, let me sleep," "Fade, tender lily," "What is it Jesus saith unto the soul?"

Typography and paper: (95) 86 x 55 (p. 21); 19 lines per page. Poems in smaller font: (93) 83.3 x 55 (p. 121), 20 lines per page. Laid paper, vertical chainlines 27 mm apart. Unwatermarked.

Running titles:

Rectos: [1]-[7]: no RT; 1: no RT; 3-5: 'PREFATORY NOTE'; 7: no RT; 9-121: 'MAUDE'; <u>123</u>: no RT; [1]-[3]: no RT.

Versos: [2]-[8]: no RT; 2-6: 'PREFATORY NOTE'; 8-122: 'MAUDE'; <u>124</u>, [2]-[4]: no RT.

Binding: Paper covered boards, dark red (Centroid 16). Front and back: in center, yellow stamped design of a coat of arms within foliage, the shield ornamented with three open books, and an eagle shaped crest. Spine: brownish-yellow paper label, 52 x 20, printed in black ink: '[rule] | MAUDE | PROSE | [long dash] & | VERSE | [long dash] BY | CHRIST | [long dash] INA | ROSSET | [long dash] TI | 1 . 8 . 5 . 0 . | [rule]'. Endpapers same as sheets. Edges: top rough trimmed, fore-edge and tail untrimmed.
    An eight-leaf advertising section, dated March 1897, is inserted in the last gathering. The paper of the advertisements is different from that of the sheets (laid paper, chainlines 30 mm apart and with watermark "H. S. Stone & Company | Chicago" and "The Chap Book"):
    <u>1</u>: "CATALOGUE OF BOOKS | IN BELLES LETTRES" and date "MDCCCXCVII" <u>2</u>: Announcement of works "in preparation" including authors Harold Frederic, Henry Seton Merriman, George Ade, Henry M. Blossom <u>3</u>: in upper right date "March, mdcccxcvii"; one title, *Artie*; 4: two titles, *The Fourth Napoleon, Checkers*; 5: one title, *Chap-Book Essays*; 6: two titles, *A Volume of Reprints from the Chap-Book* and *The Land of the Castanet*; 7: three titles, *Episcopo and Company, Eve's Glossary* and *Curious Punishments of Bygone Days*; 8: two titles, *Flames* and *What Maisie Knew*; 9: two

titles, *The Fearsome Island* and *Prose Fancies*; 10: one title, *Miss Ayr of Virginia*; 11: one title, *The Carissima*; 12: two titles, *The Impudent Comedian and Others* and *The Jessamy Bride*; 13: one title, *A Child of the Jago*; 14: one title, *In Buncombe County*; 15: two titles, *Without Sin* and *The Fatal Gift of Beauty*; 16: in orange ink, same shield and crest as on binding, but with scroll and motto "FAIRE ET TAIRE."

Publication: No later than July 1897. After lending the manuscript to Mackenzie Bell in September 1896, WMR was approached by a representative of the publisher James Bowden, who apparently learned of the manuscript from Bell (WMRD, SWMR, 599-600; for details of WMR's negotiations with Bowden, see A29). Although no mention of Stone occurs in WMR's diaries, presumably Bowden and/or Rossetti approached Stone to arrange publication in the United States. The American edition includes Rossetti's preface. CGR's manuscript is held in the Huntington Library, San Marino, California.

Notices of the impending publication began to appear in May 1897; in that same month, Stone registered the title with the Copyright Office. Publication notices began to appear in July (though *Publishers' Weekly* marked the listing with an asterisk to indicate that the book had not been received). The appearance of several (mostly negative) reviews in June and July confirms that the book was published in the summer. The Stone edition includes the "Three Nuns" sequence, omitted from the British edition because Macmillan claimed copyright.

Announced in the *Dial*, "Literary Notes" (1 May 1897: 290), and in the list of "New Books" (1 July 1897: 27); and in *Publishers' Weekly* (3 July 1897: 9; 17 July 1897: 115).

Price: $1.00.

Reviewed in the *Outlook* (26 June 1897: 506); *Literary World* (Boston) (24 July 1897: 244); *Dial* (brief mention, 16 October 1897: 224).

Printing: <u>123</u>: 'PRINTED FOR HERBERT S. STONE | AND CO. BY R. R. DONNELLY AND | SONS CO. AT THE LAKESIDE PRESS | MDCCCXCVII'.

Locations: CoFS, NjP, Ives.

A28.1a.ii   First Edition, First Printing, "Court Series" Issue (1900)

Not seen. Sidney Kramer (*A History of Stone & Kimball*) notes that *Maude* appeared in Stone's "Court Series" in 1900, clothbound , and probably manufactured from remainder sheets (126).

Location: no copies or library holdings located.

A28.1a.iii   First Edition, First Printing, Duffield Issue (1906)

Same as A28.1.a.i except:

MAUDE: Prose & Verse | [device, 25 x 18, tree with text 'FIDE ET LITERIS' and Duffield initials, "D & Co"] | NEW YORK | DUFFIELD & COMPANY | 1906

Collation: (168 x 107): [1-8⁸].

Pagination: [1]-[6] 1-222.

Contents: [1]-[2]: blank; [3]: halftitle 'MAUDE: Prose & Verse'; [4]: blank; [6]: 'COPYRIGHT, 1897, BY | HERBERT S. STONE & CO. | *This edition published August 1906, by* | *Duffield & Company*' and imprint; 1-122: same as 1906.

Typography and paper: Laid paper, vertical chainlines 20 mm apart. Unwatermarked.

Publication: Printed from the Stone plates. Duffied & Company purchased the Stone list in 1906, and "remaindered many thousands of copies of books originally printed for Stone & Kimball and Herbert S. Stone Company" (Kramer, 127).

Printing: [6]: 'The Trow Press, N. Y.'

Location: FMU.

A29   MAUDE (Bowden, 1897)

A29.1   *Second Edition, Only Printing (1897)*

Some text in <u>red ink</u>:
<u>MAUDE</u> | A STORY FOR GIRLS | BY | CHRISTINA ROSSETTI | WITH AN INTRODUCTION BY | WILLIAM MICHAEL ROSSETTI | [ornament, leaf pointing down, 6.3 x 6] | LONDON | <u>JAMES BOWDEN</u> | 10 HENRIETTA STREET | COVENT GARDEN, W. C. | 1897

Pagination: i-<u>vi</u> vii-xi <u>xii</u> <u>1-2</u> 3-30 <u>31-32</u> 33-57 <u>58-60</u> 61-80 1 (=81) <u>82-84</u>.

Plates: 1) Facing title, portrait of CGR with caption 'Christina G. Rossetti | from a sketch by Dante G. Rossetti | towards 1848.'; 105 x 54 (height measured with caption); plate mark 116 x 70. With tissue guard.

Collation: (175 x 104): <u>A</u>⁸ B-F⁸. $1 signed. 48 leaves.

Contents: <u>i</u>: half-title 'MAUDE'; <u>ii</u>: '*This Edition is limited to 500 copies.*'; <u>iii</u>: title; <u>iv</u>: blank; <u>v</u>: copyright acknowledgement beginning "Thanks are due to Messrs"; <u>vi</u>: blank; vii: '*PREFATORY NOTE*'; xii: blank; <u>1</u>: section half-title 'PART FIRST' and ornament; <u>2</u>: blank; 3: 'MAUDE | I'; 13: 'II'; 25: 'III'; <u>31</u>: section half-title 'PART SECOND' and ornament; <u>32</u>: blank; 33: 'I'; 40: 'II'; 49: 'III'; <u>58</u>: blank; <u>59</u>: section half-title 'PART THIRD' and ornament; <u>60</u>: blank; 61: 'I'; 68: 'II'; 71: 'III'; <u>82</u>: printer's device, 33 x 25, and printer's imprint; 83: advertisement 'BY THE LATE | CHRISTINA G. ROSSETTI' with three titles: *The Poems of Christina Rossetti*, *New Poems*, *The Rossetti Birthday Book*; <u>84</u>: blank.

Poems: (see *Note one*). "Yes, I too could face death and never shrink," "Would that I were a turnip white," "I fancy the good fairies dressed in white," "Some ladies dress in muslin full and white," "Fade, tender lily," "What is it Jesus saith unto the soul?"

Typography and paper: (104) 95 x 51 (p. 53); 24 lines per page. Prefatory note in italic, and poetry in smaller font. Laid paper, vertical chainlines 27 mm apart. Unwatermarked.

Running titles: Prefatory note in italic.

Rectos: <u>i-v</u>: no RT; vii: no RT; ix-xi: '*PREFATORY NOTE*'; <u>1</u>-3: no RT; 5-11: 'MAUDE'; 13: no RT; 17-23: 'MAUDE'; 25: no RT; 27-29: 'MAUDE'; 31-33: no RT; 35-47: 'MAUDE'; 49: no RT; 51-57: 'MAUDE'; 59-61: no RT; 63-69: 'MAUDE'; 71: no RT; 73-81: 'MAUDE'; 83: no RT.

Versos: <u>ii-vi</u>: no RT; viii-x: '*PREFATORY NOTE*'; <u>xii</u>, <u>2</u>: no RT; 4-30: 'MAUDE'; <u>32</u>: no RT; 34-38: 'MAUDE'; 40: no RT; 42-56: 'MAUDE'; <u>58-60</u>: no RT; 62-66: 'MAUDE'; <u>68</u>: no RT; 70-80: 'MAUDE'; <u>82-84</u>: no RT.

Binding: Buckram, dark bluish green (Centroid 165). Front: in gilt, signature stamped in lower right corner, 'Christina G. Rossetti'. Back: plain. Spine, in gilt: 'Mᴀᴜᴅᴇ | CHRISTINA | ROSSETTI | WITH INTRODUC- | -TION BY | W. M. | ROSSETTI | Jᴀᴍᴇs Bᴏᴡᴅᴇɴ'. Endpapers: laid paper, chainlines 25 mm apart. Edges: top rough trimmed, fore-edge and tail untrimmed.

Publication: September 1897. In October 1896, WMR met with Coulson Kernahan, James Bowden's literary advisor, to discuss possible publication of *Maude*. WMR later assured Macmillan that Bowden "got to know something of this early performance not through me in any way"; presumably either Kerhanan or Bowden discovered *Maude* through Mackenzie Bell, to whom WMR had loaned the MS (SWMR 599). Although, as he told Macmillan, he himself "would not have volunteered in offering the tale to a Publisher" (SWMR 599), WMR agreed to allow publication by Bowden and to write the prefatory note that appears in both editions of the book. On December 3 he received £30 for the copyright (WMRD).

Difficulties regarding the prior publication of the poems in *Maude* ultimately resulted in the omission of eight poems from the British edition, which in turn resulted in some alterations to the text as well as the preface (see *Note one*). WMR informed Macmillan on December 9 that "11 of the poems have been already published by you [. . .] some of the compositions are in the New Poems" and asked Macmillan to give Bowden consent to publish (SWMR 599); on December 12, he wrote to Bowden to inform him that Macmillan refused to allow publication of the poems (WMRD). WMR left further negotiations up to Bowden, and upon learning in May 1897 that Macmillan at that point was still withholding permission, he "offered, if he prefers to relinquish the project, to repay him his £30" (WMRD). The *Bookman*'s notice of the volume indicated that it had been planned for simultaneous publication with Stone on May 17, but WMR received his copy of the book on 3 September (WMRD). CGR's manuscript of Maude is held at the Huntington Library in California.

Early mention in the *Bookman* (May 1897: 26) and the *Saturday Review* (31 July 1897: 123); announced in the *Athenaeum* (28 August 1897: 303); the London *Times* (10 September 1897: 10).

Price: 3s. 6d.

Printing: <u>82</u>: 'PRINTED BY W. H. WHITE AND CO. LTD., | RIVERSIDE PRESS, EDINBURGH.' and above text, device featuring trees & foliage, with text within two scrolls: 'THE RIVER-SIDE PRESS' and 'EDINBURGH' and within a compartment formed by the roots of the tree, 'W H W & CO'.

Note one: Eight poems are omitted from the British edition: "She sat and sang alway," "Sweet, sweet sound of distant waters," "Vanity of vanities, the Preacher saith," "I listen to the holy antheming," "Thank God, thank God, we do believe," "Three Nuns," (sections I-III), "I watched a rosebud very long," "Sleep, let me sleep."

Locations: CaBVaU (2 copies); GEU; KU; NjP; BL.

A30   **POEMS (Little, Brown Subedition, 1898)**

See also A4 (Roberts Brothers parent edition, 1866, 1872), A12 (Roberts Brothers first subedition, 1876, 1880), A16 (Roberts Brothers, *A Pageant*, 1881) and A17 (Roberts Brothers Second Subedition, 1882).

A30.1a   *First Edition, First Printing (Little, Brown Subedition) (1898).*
          Printed from same plates as A17.1e (Roberts Brothers second subedition,
          later expanded printing (1897).

POEMS. | BY | CHRISTINA G. ROSSETTI. | [vignette, 62 x 69, with caption "Golden head by golden head"] | BOSTON: | LITTLE, BROWN, AND COMPANY. | 1898.

Pagination: i-v vi-xi xii 3 4-77 78-81 82-118 119 120-284 285-287 288-300 [7] 14-231 232.

Plates: Four plates:
1) Facing title, same portrait of CGR by DGR that appears in A17.1e (113.5 x 76), with single rule border, and without caption. With tissue guard.
2) Facing 3, frontispiece and caption (112 x 92, height measured with caption) from *Goblin Market* 1862/1865 as reproduced in Roberts Brothers 1866 (A4), with same caption. No tissue guard.
3) Facing 119, vignette and caption (76 x 85, height measured with caption) from the engraved title page of *Prince's Progress 1866* as reproduced in Roberts Brothers 1866, 1872 (A4). No tissue guard.
4) Facing 139, frontispiece and caption (150 x 97.3, height measured with caption) from *Prince's Progress 1866* as reproduced in Roberts Brothers 1866, 1872 (A4). No tissue guard.

Collation: (183 x 122): [1-33⁸ 34⁸]. Obsolete signings in 12s and 8s, missing signatures '3' and '8' as in A17.1cii.

Contents: Same as Roberts Brothers 1897 (A17.1e).

Poems: Same as Roberts Brothers 1897 (A17.1e):
"Goblin Market," "In The Round Tower At Jhansi, June 8, 1857," "Dream-Land," "At Home," "From Sunset To Star Rise," "Love From The North," "Winter Rain," "A Dirge" ("Why were you born when the snow was falling?"), "Confluents," "Noble Sisters," "Spring," "The Lambs Of Grasmere, 1860," "A Birthday," "Remember. Sonnet," "After Death. Sonnet," "An End," "My Dream," "Song" ("O roses for the flush of youth"), "The Hour And The Ghost," "A Summer Wish," "An Apple Gathering," "Song" ("Two doves upon the selfsame branch"), "Maude Clare," "Echo," "Winter: My Secret" ["My Secret"], "Another Spring," "A Peal Of Bells," "Fata Morgana," "'No, Thank You, John'," "May" ("I cannot tell you how it was"), "A Pause Of Thought," "Twilight Calm," "Wife To Husband," "Three Seasons," "Mirage," "Shut Out," "Sound Sleep," "Song" ("She sat and sang alway"), "Song" ("When I am dead, my dearest"), "Dead Before Death. Sonnet," "Bitter For Sweet," "'The Master Is Come, And Calleth For Thee'," "Rest. Sonnet," "The First Spring Day," "The Convent Threshold," "Up-Hill," "'The Love Of Christ Which Passeth Knowledge'," "'A Bruised Reed Shall He Not Break'," "A Better Resurrection," "Advent" ("This Advent moon shines cold and clear"), "The Three Enemies" in three parts, "The Flesh," "The World," "The Devil," "One Certainty. Sonnet," "Christian And Jew. A Dialogue," "Sweet Death," "Symbols," "'Consider The Lilies Of The Field'" ("Flowers preach to us if we will hear"), "The World. Sonnet," "A Testimony," "Sleep At Sea," "From House To Home," "Old And New Year Ditties" (sections 1-3), "Amen," "Mother Country," "The Prince's Progress," "Maiden-Song," "Jessie Cameron," "Spring Quiet," "The Poor Ghost," "A Portrait" (sections I-II), "Dream-Love," "Twice," "Songs In A Cornfield," "A Year's Windfalls," "The Queen Of Hearts," "One Day," "A Bird's-Eye View," "The German-French Campaign. 1870-1871," in two parts, "I. 'Thy Brother's Blood Crieth'," and "II. ''To-Day For Me'," "On The Wing Sonnet," "Consider," "Beauty Is Vain," "Maggie A Lady," "What Would I Give?," "The Bourne," "Summer"("Winter is cold-hearted"), "Autumn" ("I dwell alone"), "The Ghost's Petition,"

"Memory" (sections I-II), "A Royal Princess," "Shall I Forget?," "Vanity Of Vanities. Sonnet," "L. E. L. ," "Life And Death," "Bird Or Beast?," "Eve," "Grown And Flown," "A Farm Walk," "Somewhere Or Other," "A Chill," "Child's Talk In April," "Gone Forever," "Under The Rose," "Song" ("Oh what comes over the sea"), "By The Sea," "Days Of Vanity," "Enrica, 1865," "Once For All. (Margaret.)," "Autumn Violets," "'They Desire A Better Country" (sections I-III), "A Green Cornfield," "A Bride Song," "The Lowest Room," "Dead Hope," "A Daughter Of Eve," "Venus's Looking-Glass," "Love Lies Bleeding," "Bird Raptures," "My Friend," "Twilight Night," "A Bird Song," "A Smile And A Sigh," "Amor Mundi," "A Christmas Carol" ("In the bleak mid-winter"), "By The Waters Of Babylon. B. C. 570," "Paradise," "'I Will Lift Up Mine Eyes Unto The Hills'," "Saints And Angels," "'When My Heart Is Vexed, I Will Complain'" ("O Lord, how canst Thou say Thou lovest me?"), "After Communion," "A Rose Plant In Jericho," "Who Shall Deliver Me?," "Despised And Rejected," "Long Barren," "If Only," "Dost Thou Not Care?," "Weary In Well-Doing," "Martyrs' Song," "After This The Judgment," "Good Friday" ("Am I a stone and not a sheep?"), "The Lowest Place," "Sonnets are full of love, and this my tome," "The Key-Note," "The Months: A Pageant," "Pastime," "'Italia, Io Ti Saluto!'," "Mirrors Of Life And Death," "A Ballad Of Boding," "Yet A Little While" ("I dreamed and did not seek"), "He And She," "Monna Innominata." (sonnets 1-14), "'Luscious And Sorrowful'," "De Profundis," "Tempus Fugit," "Golden Glories," "Johnny," "'Hollow-Sounding And Mysterious'," "Maiden May," "Till To-Morrow," "Death-Watches," "Touching 'Never'," "Brandons Both," "A Life's Parallels," "At Last," "Golden Silences," "In The Willow Shade," "Fluttered Wings," "A Fisher-Wife," "What's In A Name?," "Mariana," "Memento Mori," "'One Foot On Sea, And One On Shore'," "Buds And Babies," "Boy Johnny," "Freaks Of Fashion," "An October Garden," "'Summer Is Ended'," "Passing And Glassing," "'I Will Arise'," "A Prodigal Son," "Sœur Louise De La Miséricorde. (1674.)," "An 'Immurata' Sister," "'If Thou Sayest, Behold, We Knew It Not" (sections 1-3), "The Thread Of Life" (sections 1-3), "An Old-World Thicket," "All Thy Works Praise Thee, O Lord," "Later Life: A Double Sonnet Of Sonnets" (sonnets 1-28), "'For Thine Own Sake, O My God'," "Until The Day Break," "'Of Him That Was Ready To Perish'," "'Behold The Man!'," "The Descent From The Cross," "'It Is Finished'," "An Easter Carol," "'Behold A Shaking'" (sections 1-2), "All Saints," "'Take Care Of Him'," "A Martyr," "Why?," "'Love Is Strong As Death'" ("I have not sought Thee, I have not found Thee"), "Birchington Churchyard," "One Sea-Side Grave," "Brother Bruin," "'A Helpmeet for Him'," "A Song of Flight," "A Wintry Sonnet," "Resurgam," "To-Day's Burden," "'There is a Budding Morrow in Midnight'," "Exultate Deo," "A Hope Carol," "Christmas Carols" (sections 1-3), "A Candlemas Dialogue," "Mary Madgalene and the Other Mary," "Patience of Hope."

Typography and paper: Same as A17.1e, but paper is slightly thinner (micrometer readings range from .082 to .099), with a glossier finish.

Running titles: Same as A17.1e.

Rectos: i-v: no RT; vii-xi: 'CONTENTS.'; 3: no RT; 5-21: 'GOBLIN MARKET.'; 23: 'IN THE ROUND TOWER AT JHANSI.'; 25: 'AT HOME.'; 27: 'LOVE FROM THE NORTH.'; 29: 'WINTER RAIN.'; 31: 'CONFLUENTS.'; 33: 'NOBLE SISTERS.'; 35: 'SPRING.'; 37: 'A BIRTHDAY.'; 39: 'AFTER DEATH.'; 41: 'MY DREAM.'; 43-45: 'THE HOUR AND THE GHOST.'; 47: 'AN APPLE GATHERING.'; 49: 'MAUDE CLARE.'; 51: 'ECHO.'; 53: 'ANOTHER SPRING.'; 55: 'FATA MORGANA.'; 57: 'MAY.'; 59: 'TWILIGHT CALM.'; 61: 'WIFE TO HUSBAND.'; 63: 'MIRAGE.'; 65: 'SOUND SLEEP.'; 67: 'SONG.'; 69: 'THE MASTER CALLETH.'; 71-75: 'THE CONVENT THRESHOLD.'; 77: 'UP-HILL.'; 79-81: no RT; 83: 'A BETTER RESURRECTION.'; 85: 'ADVENT.'; 87: 'THE THREE ENEMIES.'; 89: 'THE ONE CERTAINTY.'; 91: 'CHRISTIAN AND JEW.'; 93: 'SWEET DEATH.'; 95: 'CONSIDER THE LILIES OF THE FIELD.'; 97-99: 'A TESTIMONY.'; 101: 'SLEEP AT SEA.'; 103-111: 'FROM HOUSE TO HOME.'; 113: 'OLD AND NEW YEAR DITTIES.'; 115: 'AMEN.'; 117: 'MOTHER COUNTRY.'; [1]: no RT; 121-139: 'THE PRINCE'S PROGRESS.'; 141-147: 'MAIDEN-SONG.'; 149-151: 'JESSIE CAMERON.'; 153: 'SPRING QUIET.'; 155: 'THE POOR GHOST.'; 157-159: 'DREAM-LOVE.'; 161: 'TWICE.'; 163-

165: 'SONGS IN A CORNFIELD.'; 167-169: 'A YEAR'S WINDFALLS.'; 171: 'ONE DAY.'; 173-175: 'A BIRD'S-EYE VIEW.'; 177: '"TO-DAY FOR ME."'; 179: 'ON THE WING.'; 181: 'BEAUTY IS VAIN.'; 183: 'LADY MAGGIE.'; 185: 'SUMMER.'; 187: 'AUTUMN.'; 189-191: 'THE GHOST'S PETITION.'; 193: 'MEMORY.'; 195-201: 'A ROYAL PRINCESS.'; 203: 'VANITY OF VANITIES.'; 205: 'L. E. L.'; 207: 'BIRD OR BEAST?'; 209: 'EVE.'; 211: 'GROWN AND FLOWN.'; 213: 'A FARM WALK.'; 215: 'SOMEWHERE OR OTHER.'; 217: 'CHILD'S TALK IN APRIL.'; 219: 'GONE FOREVER.'; 221-237: 'UNDER THE ROSE.'; 239: 'SONG.'; 241: 'DAYS OF VANITY.'; 243: 'AUTUMN VIOLETS.'; 245: 'A BETTER COUNTRY DESIRED.'; 247: 'A BRIDE SONG.'; 249-259: 'THE LOWEST ROOM.'; 261: 'A DAUGHTER OF EVE.'; 263: 'BIRD RAPTURE.'; 265: 'TWILIGHT NIGHT.'; 267: 'AMOR MUNDI.'; 269: 'A CHRISTMAS CAROL.'; 271-273: 'BY THE WATERS OF BABYLON.'; 275: 'PARADISE.'; 277: 'UPLIFTING OF EYES.'; 279: 'SAINTS AND ANGELS.'; 281: 'AFTER COMMUNION.'; 283: 'WHO SHALL DELIVER ME?'; 285-287: no RT; 289: 'LONG BARREN.'; 291: 'DOST THOU NOT CARE?'; 293-295: 'MARTYRS' SONG.'; 297: 'AFTER THIS THE JUDGMENT.'; 299: 'GOOD FRIDAY.'; [1]-[7]: no RT; 15-31: 'A PAGEANT.'; 33: 'PASTIME.'; 35-41: 'MIRRORS OF LIFE AND DEATH.'; 43-51: 'A BALLAD OF BODING.'; 53: 'HE AND SHE.'; 55-67: 'MONNA INNOMINATA.'; 69: '"LUSCIOUS AND SORROWFUL."'; 71: 'TEMPUS FUGIT.'; 73-75: 'JOHNNY.'; 77: '"HOLLOW-SOUNDING & MYSTERIOUS."'; 79-83: 'MAIDEN MAY.'; 85: 'DEATH-WATCHES.'; 87-91: 'BRANDONS BOTH.'; 93: 'AT LAST.'; 95-97: 'IN THE WILLOW SHADE.'; 99: 'FLUTTERED WINGS.'; 101: 'WHAT'S IN A NAME?'; 103: 'MARIANA.'; 105: '"ONE FOOT ON SEA,'; 107: 'BUDS AND BABIES.'; 109-111: 'FREAKS OF FASHION.'; 113: 'AN OCTOBER GARDEN.'; 115: 'PASSING AND GLASSING.'; 117: '"I WILL ARISE."'; 119: 'A PRODIGAL SON.'; 121: 'SŒUR LOUISE DE LA MISÉRICORDE.'; 123: 'AN "IMMURATA" SISTER.'; 125: '"IF THOU SAYEST . . ."'; 127-129: 'THE THREAD OF LIFE.'; 131-139: 'AN OLD-WORLD THICKET.'; 141-153: 'O LORD."'; 155-181: 'LATER LIFE.'; 183: 'UNTIL THE DAY BREAK.'; 185: '"READY TO PERISH."'; 187: '"BEHOLD THE MAN!"'; 189-191: '"IT IS FINISHED."'; 193: 'AN EASTER CAROL.'; 195: '"BEHOLD A SHAKING."'; 197: 'ALL SAINTS.'; 199: '"TAKE CARE OF HIM."'; 201-205: 'A MARTYR.'; 207: 'WHY?'; 209: 'BIRCHINGTON CHURCHYARD.'; 211-213: 'BROTHER BRUIN.'; 215: 'A SONG OF FLIGHT.'; 217: 'RESURGAM.'; 219: '"THERE IS A BUDDING MORROW."'; 221: 'A HOPE CAROL.'; 223-227: 'CHRISTMAS CAROLS.'; 229: 'A CANDLEMAS DIALOGUE.'; 231: 'PATIENCE OF HOPE.'

Versos: Period faint on page 114, faint and dropped below line on page 164. ii-iv: no RT; vi-x: 'CONTENTS.'; xii: no RT; 4-22: 'GOBLIN MARKET.'; 24: 'DREAM-LAND.'; 26: 'FROM SUNSET TO STAR RISE.'; 28: 'LOVE FROM THE NORTH.'; 30: 'A DIRGE.'; 32: 'NOBLE SISTERS.'; 34: 'SPRING.'; 36: 'THE LAMBS OF GRASMERE.'; 38: 'REMEMBER.'; 40: 'AN END.'; 42: 'MY DREAM.'; 44: 'THE HOUR AND THE GHOST.'; 46: 'A SUMMER WISH.'; 48: 'SONG.'; 50: 'MAUDE CLARE.'; 52: 'WINTER: MY SECRET.'; 54: 'A PEAL OF BELLS.'; 56: '"NO, THANK YOU, JOHN."'; 58: 'A PAUSE OF THOUGHT.'; 60: 'TWILIGHT CALM.'; 62: 'WIFE TO HUSBAND.'; 64: 'SHUT OUT.'; 66: 'SONG.'; 68: 'BITTER FOR SWEET.'; 70: 'THE FIRST SPRING DAY.'; 72-76: 'THE CONVENT THRESHOLD.'; 78-80: no RT; 82: 'A BRUISED REED SHALL HE NOT BREAK.'; 84-86: 'ADVENT.'; 88: 'THE THREE ENEMIES.'; 90-92: 'CHRISTIAN AND JEW.'; 94: 'SYMBOLS.'; 96: 'THE WORLD.'; 98: 'A TESTIMONY.'; 100-102: 'SLEEP AT SEA.'; 104-110: 'FROM HOUSE TO HOME.'; 112: 'FROM HOUSE TO HOME' [no period]; 114: 'OLD AND NEW YEAR DITTIES.'; 116-118: 'MOTHER COUNTRY.'; 120-138: 'THE PRINCE'S PROGRESS.'; 140-146: 'MAIDEN-SONG.'; 148: 'JESSIE-CAMERON.'; 150-152: 'JESSIE CAMERON.'; 154: 'THE POOR GHOST.'; 156: 'A PORTRAIT.'; 158: 'DREAM-LOVE.'; 160: 'TWICE.'; 162-164: 'SONGS IN A CORNFIELD.'; 166-168: 'A YEAR'S WINDFALLS.'; 170: 'THE QUEEN OF HEARTS.'; 172-174: 'A BIRD'S-EYE VIEW.'; 176: 'GERMAN-FRENCH CAMPAIGN.'; 178: '"TO-DAY FOR ME."'; 180: 'CONSIDER.'; 182: 'MAGGIE A LADY.'; 184: 'WHAT WOULD I GIVE?'; 186: 'SUMMER.'; 188: 'AUTUMN.'; 190-192: 'THE GHOST'S PETITION.'; 194: 'MEMORY.'; 196-200: 'A ROYAL PRINCESS.'; 202: 'SHALL I FORGET?'; 204: 'L. E. L.'; 206: 'LIFE AND DEATH.'; 208-210: 'EVE.'; 212-214: 'A FARM WALK.'; 216: 'A CHILL.';

218: 'CHILD'S TALK IN APRIL.'; 220-238: 'UNDER THE ROSE.'; 240: 'DAYS OF VANITY.'; 242: 'ENRICA, 1865.'; 244: 'A BETTER COUNTRY DESIRED.'; 246: 'A GREEN CORNFIELD.'; 248: 'A BRIDE SONG.'; 250-260: 'THE LOWEST ROOM.'; 262: 'VENUS' LOOKING-GLASS.'; 264: 'MY FRIEND.'; 266: 'A BIRD SONG.'; 268: 'AMOR MUNDI.'; 270: 'A CHRISTMAS CAROL.'; 272: 'BY THE WATERS OF BABYLON.'; 274: 'PARADISE.'; 276: 'UPLIFTING OF EYES.'; 278: 'SAINTS AND ANGELS.'; 280: 'THE VEXED HEART.'; 282: 'A ROSE PLANT IN JERICHO.'; 284: 'WHO SHALL DELIVER ME?'; 286: no RT; 288: 'DESPISED AND REJECTED.'; 290: 'IF ONLY.'; 292: 'WEARY IN WELL-DOING.'; 294: 'MARTYRS' SONG.'; 296-298: 'AFTER THIS THE JUDGMENT.'; 300: 'THE LOWEST PLACE.'; [2]-[6]: no RT; 14-30: 'THE MONTHS:'; 32: 'THE MONTHS: A PAGEANT.'; 34: '"ITALIA, IO TI SALUTO!"'; 36-40: 'MIRRORS OF LIFE AND DEATH.'; 42-50: 'A BALLAD OF BODING.'; 52: 'YET A LITTLE WHILE.'; 54-68: 'MONNA INNOMINATA.'; 70: 'DE PROFUNDIS.'; 72: 'GOLDEN GLORIES.'; 74-76: 'JOHNNY.'; 78: '"HOLLOW-SOUNDING & MYSTERIOUS."'; 80-82: 'MAIDEN MAY.'; 84: 'TILL TO-MORROW.'; 86: 'TOUCHING "NEVER."'; 88-90: 'BRANDONS BOTH.'; 92: 'A LIFE'S PARALLELS.'; 94: 'GOLDEN SILENCES.'; 96-98: 'IN THE WILLOW SHADE.'; 100: 'A FISHER-WIFE.'; 102: 'WHAT'S IN A NAME?'; 104: 'MEMENTO MORI.'; 106: 'AND ONE ON SHORE."'; 108: 'BOY JOHNNY.'; 110-112: 'FREAKS OF FASHION.'; 114: '"SUMMER IS ENDED."'; 116: 'PASSING AND GLASSING.'; 118: '"I WILL ARISE."'; 120: 'SŒUR LOUISE DE LA MISÉRICORDE.'; 122: 'AN "IMMURATA" SISTER.'; 124-126: '"IF THOU SAYEST . . ."'; 128: 'THE THREAD OF LIFE.'; 130-138: 'AN OLD-WORLD THICKET.'; 140-152: '"ALL THY WORKS PRAISE THEE,'; 154-180: 'LATER LIFE.'; 182: '"FOR THINE OWN SAKE, O MY GOD."'; 184: 'UNTIL THE DAY BREAK.'; 186: '"READY TO PERISH."'; 188: 'THE DESCENT FROM THE CROSS.'; 190: '"IT IS FINISHED."'; 192: 'AN EASTER CAROL.'; 194: '"BEHOLD A SHAKING."'; 196-198: 'ALL SAINTS.'; 200: '"TAKE CARE OF HIM."'; 202-206: 'A MARTYR.'; 208: '"LOVE IS STRONG AS DEATH."'; 210: 'ONE SEA-SIDE GRAVE.'; 212: 'BROTHER BRUIN.'; 214: '"A HELPMEET FOR HIM."'; 216: 'A WINTRY SONNET.'; 218: 'TO-DAY'S BURDEN.'; 220: 'EXULTATE DEO.'; 222: 'A HOPE CAROL.'; 224-226: 'CHRISTMAS CAROLS.'; 228: 'A CANDLEMAS DIALOGUE.'; 230: 'MARY MAGDALENE.'

Binding: Fine diagonal rib cloth, between grayish yellowish brown (Centroid 80) and dark grayish yellowish brown (Centroid 81). Front: '[in gilt, across top] CHRISTINA G. ROSSETTI'S | POEMS' and in dark grayish reddish brown ink (Centroid 47), within thick-thin top rule and thin-thick bottom rule, an ornamental band with repeating hexagon motif. Back: brown ink ornamental band, same as front. Spine: '[in gilt] CHRISTINA | G. | ROSSETTI'S | POEMS' above brown ink ornamental band continued from front; at tail [in gilt] 'LITTLE, BROWN & CO'. Endpapers: white wove. Edges: all edges gilt. One wove paper binder's leaf between endpapers and sheets, front and back.

Publication: Having purchased Roberts Brothers list in June, 1898, Little, Brown immediately began to reprint Rossetti's poems from plates of the Roberts Brothers expanded 1888 subedition, endeavoring to preserve similarity to the Roberts Brothers books by retaining the same binding design and making only those changes to the text that were necessary to indicate the change of publisher.

Printing: ii: 'AUTHOR'S EDITION, REVISED AND ENLARGED. | 1876. | UNIVERSITY PRESS: JOHN WILSON & SON, CAMBRIDGE.'

Location: Spalding University.

A30.1b   *First Edition, Second Printing (Little, Brown Subedition) (1899)*

Same as A30.1a, except:

Title Page: Date changed to 1899.

Binding: Calico cloth, vivid red (Centroid 11), with ornamental band in dark grayish red (Centroid 20).

Location: PBm.

A30.1c   *First Edition, Third Printing (Little, Brown Subedition) (1906)*
Not seen; information drawn from an electronic version of Stanford copy.

Title Page: Date changed to 1906.

Location: CSt (via Google Books).

A30.1d   *First Edition, Fourth Printing (Little, Brown Subedition) (1911)*
Same as previous printings, except:

Title Page: Date changed to 1911.

Running titles:
Versos: no period on pages 16, 56, 164.

Location: TxCM (rebound).

A30.1e   *First Edition, Fifth Printing (Little, Brown Subedition) (1915)*
Not seen.

Location: Copy listed in Princeton University library catalog, call number 3913.1 1915.

A30.1f   *First Edition, Sixth Printing (Little, Brown Subedition) (1918)*
Same as previous printings, except:

Title Page: Date changed to 1918.

Binding: Two forms noted:
Binding A: Same as 1898. Location: ICarbS.
Binding B: Same design as 1898, but deep Red (Centroid 13) linen-textured cloth, with ornamental band lightly stamped in dark grayish reddish brown ink (Centroid 47), trimmed edges. No binder's leaves. Location: Ives.

Printing: ii (some text in black letter): 'AUTHOR'S EDITION, REVISED AND ENLARGED | 1876. | Printers | S. J. Parkhill & Co., Boston, U. S. A.'

Note one: Plates 3 and 4 face pages 118 and 138 respectively, causing the illustration on plate 3 to face the wrong poem ("Mother Country" instead of "The Prince's Progress").

Location: ICarbS; Ives.

A31   MONNA INNOMINATA (1899)

A31.1a.i   *First Edition, First Printing, Van Gelder Issue (1899)*

First and last lines in red ink; see *Note one*.

MONNA INNOMINATA | SONNETS AND SONGS | BY CHRISTINA G. ROSSETTI | [Mosher device, two dolphins and book, 25 x 26] | Portland, Maine | *THOMAS B. MOSHER* | Mdcccxcix

Pagination: [2] i-iv v vi-viii 1-2 3-16 17-18 19-46 47-48 49-76 77-78 79-93 94-102. The first and last leaves are pasted to the wrapper and are not counted in the pagination or leaf count.

Collation: (181 x 93): [1-7⁸ 8²]. 56 leaves.

Contents: [1]-[2]: blank; i: '[first line with thin-thick underline] Old World Series. | [ornament 8 x 37] | MONNA INNOMINATA | SONNETS & SONGS | [triangular ornament 12 x 33]'; ii: blank; iii: title; iv: '*This First Edition on* | Van Gelder *paper con-* | *sists of 925 copies.*'; v: '[ornament, 12 x 16] | CONTENTS'; vii: section half-title '[ornament 8 x 37] | MONNA INNOMINATA | A SONNET OF SONNETS | [triangular ornament 11 x 33]'; viii: blank; 1: introduction beginning "Beatrice"; 2: blank; 3-16: poems; 17: section half-title '[ornament 8 x 38] | LATER LIFE | A DOUBLE SONNET OF SONNETS | [triangular ornament 10 x 34]'; 18: blank; 19-46: poems; 47: section half-title '[ornament 8 x 37] | SONGS | [triangular ornament 11 x 33]'; 48: blank; 49-76: poems; 77: section half-title '[ornament 8 x 38] | SONNETS | [triangular ornament 10 x 35]'; 78: blank; 79-94: poems; 95: printer's imprint; 96-102: blank.

Poems: "Monna Innominata" (sonnets I-XIV), "Later Life" (sonnets I-XXVIII), "Dream Land," "An End," "A Pause of Thought," "Song" ("Oh roses for the flush of youth"), "A Testimony," "Sweet Death," "Somewhere Or Other," "Dead Hope," "Shall I Forget?," "Life And Death," "The Bourne," "Song" ("When I am dead, my dearest"), "Amor Mundi," "Up-Hill," "L. E. L.," "The Three Enemies" in three parts, "I. The Flesh," "II. The World," "III. The Devil," "Passing Away, Saith the World," "Despised and Rejected," "A Rose Plant in Jericho," "Birchington Churchyard," "A Triad," "A Portrait" (sections I-II), "Autumn Violets," "'They Desire a Better Country'" (sections I-III), "Remember," "After Death," "Venus's Looking-Glass," "Love Lies Bleeding," "Dead Before Death," "Rest," "One Certainty," "The World."

Typography and paper: (120) 112 x 51 (p.55); 27 lines per page. Laid paper, vertical chainlines 25 mm apart. Watermarked "Van Gelder Zonen".

Running titles:
Rectos: No running titles.
Versos: No running titles except vi: 'CONTENTS'.

Binding: Japan vellum paper wrapper, yellowish white (Centroid 92), with yapp edges; see *Note three*. Front: in deep brown ink (Centroid 56): 'MONNA | INNOMINATA' above vine design attributed to Frederic Goudy (Bishop, *Thomas Bird Mosher*, 215). Back: plain. Spine: in same brown ink as front, 'MON | NA | IN | NOM | IN | ATA | 1899'. No endpapers. Edges: top rough trimmed, fore-edge and bottom untrimmed. A blue silk ribbon bookmark is sewn into the spine. Mosher's advertisements for the series also specify "white parchment wrappers, gold seals, and . . . slide cases," not present in copies examined. The wrappers, described by Bishop as "tissue paper . . . fastened with a gold seal" (58), are unlikely to have survived once removed from the book.

Publication: November 1899. Mosher may or may not have informed WMR of his plans to publish this book. The two were in contact in May 1898, when WMR responded to Mosher's invitation to write a preface for his edition of the *Germ* (SWMR, 614); WMR's diary also records a visit from Mosher in 1901 (WMRD). No reference to *Monna Innominata* occurs in either WMR's letter or his diary entry. Listed in the "Autumn List of Books" published by Mosher in the September, 1899 issue of the *Bibelot*. The Old

World Series is described as being printed "on a size of Van Gelder paper made for this edition only," with "Original head-bands and tail-pieces," and a "special cover design" for each book.

Announced in the *Literary World* (Boston) (25 November 1899: 418).

Price: $1.00.

Printing: 95: 'PRINTED BY | SMITH & SALE | PORTLAND | MAINE'.

Note one: The Mosher device on the title page is identified in Bishop (p. 72, number 2).

Note two: In the TxCM copy, an additional two-leaf conjugate pair has been inserted into the front of the book. The first leaf of the pair is pasted down; the second leaf has been rough excised (probably after the book was bound), with the stub glued to the first leaf of the first gathering. According to Bishop, the Mosher books were "folded, sewn, and bound by hand," and "the text block and the binding covers were kept separate until copies were needed to fill orders" (44), which would account for some variation.

Note three: As Bishop explains, "Japan vellum is . . . a paper hand-made in Japan from the fibers of a shrub distantly related to the Mulberry tree" (65).

Locations: Ives; TxCM.

A31.1a.ii   *First Edition, First Printing, Japan Vellum Issue (1899)*

Same as Van Gelder issue, except:

Pagination: Same except no page 101-102.

Contents: Same except <u>iv</u>: "OF THIS BOOK 100 | COPIES ARE PRINTED | ON JAPAN VELLUM. | THIS IS NO. . . . .'; 96-100: blank.

Typography and paper: Thick wove (vellum-patterned) paper.

Publication: Japan vellum copies were priced at $2.50.

Location: TxCM (Number 94).

A31.2   *Second Edition, Only Printing (1908)*

A line-by-line resetting of the first edition, same except:

Title Page: Same as first edition except device is 25 x 25 and date changed in last line to 'Mdccccviij'.

Pagination: [6] <u>i-iv</u> v <u>vi-vi</u> <u>1-4</u> 5-18 <u>19-20</u> 21-48 <u>49-50</u> 51-78 <u>79-80</u> 81-95 <u>96-104</u>. The first and last leaves are pasted to the wrapper and are not counted in the pagination or leaf count.

Collation: (181 x 95): [1⁴ 2-8⁸]. 58 leaves. The status of the first gathering of blank leaves is ambiguous; see *Note one*.

Contents: same except: [1]-[6]: blank; <u>iv</u>: 'This Second Edition on | Van Gelder paper con- | sists of 925 copies.'; <u>1</u>: section half-title '[ornament 8 x 37] | MONNA INNOMINATA | A SONNET OF SONNETS | [triangular ornament 11 x 33]'; <u>2</u>: blank; <u>3</u>: introduction beginning "Beatrice"; <u>4</u>: blank; 5-18: poems; <u>19</u>: section half-title '[ornament 9 x 39] | LATER LIFE | A DOUBLE SONNET OF SONNETS | [triangular ornament 10 x 33]'; <u>20</u>: blank; 21-48: poems; <u>49</u>: section half-title '[ornament 8 x 39] | SONGS | [triangular ornament 12 x 32]'; <u>50</u>: blank; 51-78: poems; <u>79</u>: section half-title '[ornament 9 x 39] | SONNETS | [triangular ornament 10 x 33]'; <u>80</u>: blank; 81-96: poems; <u>97</u>: printer's imprint; <u>98-104</u>: blank.

Typography and paper: (128) 110 x 52 (p.52); 27 lines per page. Laid paper, vertical chainlines 25 mm apart. Watermarked "Van Gelder Zonen | Holland".

Binding: Yellowish-white parchment spine (Centroid 92) and mottled pale blue (Centroid 185) paper covered boards. Front and back: plain. Spine: on paper label, '[thick-thin rule] | MON | NA | IN | NOM | IN | ATA | [thin-thick rule]'. No endpapers. Top and bottom edge rough trimmed, fore-edge untrimmed. Alternate bindings have not been seen (see *Note two*).

Printing: 97: 'PRINTED BY | GEORGE D. LORING | PORTLAND | MAINE'.

Note one: It is unclear whether the first gathering should be included within the collation formula, as there is no proof that this gathering actually went through the press. Since the final gathering concludes with four blank leaves, it is possible that the initial gathering was added in the binding process so that the book opens and closes with an equal number of blanks.

Note two: According to Bishop, the "Old World Series" was usually bound in "flexible Japan vellum covers with yapp fore-edges" but was also available "bound in 'old style' blue paper boards with white paper spine and spine label" and in "full smooth flexible leather with gilt top page edges" (58). I have not located any copies in the vellum or leather bindings.

Location: CU.

A32   **POETICAL WORKS (Little, Brown Subedition, 1899)**

See also A4 (Roberts Brothers parent edition, 1866, 1872), A12 (Roberts Brothers first subedition, 1876, 1880), A16 (Roberts Brothers, *A Pageant*, 1881), A17 (Roberts Brothers Second Subedition, 1882) and A30 (Little, Brown Subedition, 1898).

A32.1a   *First Edition, First Printing (1899)* Printed in two volumes from plates of A30.

Volume I:

THE | POETICAL WORKS | OF | CHRISTINA G. ROSSETTI | IN TWO VOLUMES | Vol. I. | BOSTON | LITTLE, BROWN, AND COMPANY | 1899

Pagination: [2] i-v vi-ix x 3 4-77 78-81 82-118 119 120-284 285-287 288-300 301-302.

Plates: 1) Facing title, portrait of CGR by DGR (114 x 78) same image as A17 (1882/1888), enlarged as in A30, but with no border and no caption.

Collation: (176 x 110): [1-19⁸ 20⁴]. Obsolete signing for 12s present. 155 leaves.

Contents: [1]: half-title 'THE POETICAL WORKS | OF | CHRISTINA G. ROSSETTI'; [2]: blank; i: title; ii: blank; iii: dedication 'TO | MY MOTHER, | IN ALL REVERENCE AND LOVE, | *I INSCRIBE THIS BOOK*.'; iv: blank; v: '*CONTENTS*.'; x: blank; 3-77: poems; 78: blank; 79: section half-title 'DEVOTIONAL PIECES'; 80: blank; 81-284: poems; 285: section half-title 'DEVOTIONAL PIECES.'; 286: blank; 287-300: poems.

Poems: Same contents as 1898 Little, Brown (A30), divided as follows:
"Goblin Market," "In The Round Tower At Jhansi, June 8, 1857," "Dream-Land," "At Home," "From Sunset To Star Rise," "Love From The North," "Winter Rain," "A Dirge" ("Why were you born when the snow was falling?"), "Confluents," "Noble Sisters," "Spring," "The Lambs Of Grasmere, 1860," "A Birthday," "Remember. Sonnet," "After Death. Sonnet," "An End," "My Dream," "Song" ("O roses for the flush of youth"), "The Hour And The Ghost," "A Summer Wish," "An Apple Gathering," "Song" ("Two doves upon the selfsame branch"), "Maude Clare," "Echo," "Winter: My Secret" ["My Secret"], "Another Spring," "A Peal Of Bells," "Fata Morgana," "'No, Thank You, John'," "May" ("I cannot tell you how it was"), "A Pause Of Thought," "Twilight Calm," "Wife To Husband," "Three Seasons," "Mirage," "Shut Out," "Sound Sleep," "Song" ("She sat and sang alway"), "Song" ("When I am dead, my dearest"), "Dead Before Death. Sonnet," "Bitter For Sweet," "'The Master Is Come, And Calleth For Thee'," "Rest. Sonnet," "The First Spring Day," "The Convent Threshold," "Up-Hill," "'The Love Of Christ Which Passeth Knowledge'," "'A Bruised Reed Shall He Not Break'," "A Better Resurrection," "Advent" ("This Advent moon shines cold and clear"), "The Three Enemies" in three parts, "The Flesh," "The World," "The Devil," "One Certainty. Sonnet," "Christian And Jew. A Dialogue," "Sweet Death," "Symbols," "'Consider The Lilies Of The Field'" ("Flowers preach to us if we will hear"), "The World. Sonnet," "A Testimony," "Sleep At Sea," "From House To Home," "Old And New Year Ditties" (sections 1-3), "Amen," "Mother Country," "The Prince's Progress," "Maiden-Song," "Jessie Cameron," "Spring Quiet," "The Poor Ghost," "A Portrait" (sections I-II), "Dream-Love," "Twice," "Songs In A Cornfield," "A Year's Windfalls," "The Queen Of Hearts," "One Day," "A Bird's-Eye View," "The German-French Campaign. 1870-1871," in two parts, "I. 'Thy Brother's Blood Crieth'," and "II. 'To-Day For Me'," "On The Wing. Sonnet," "Consider," "Beauty Is Vain," "Maggie A Lady," "What Would I Give?," "The Bourne," "Summer" ("Winter is cold-hearted"), "Autumn" ("I dwell alone"), "The Ghost's Petition," "Memory" (sections I-II), "A Royal Princess," "Shall I Forget?," "Vanity Of Vanities. Sonnet," "L. E. L.," "Life And Death," "Bird Or Beast?," "Eve," "Grown And Flown," "A Farm Walk," "Somewhere Or Other," "A Chill," "Child's Talk In April," "Gone Forever," "Under The Rose," "Song" ("Oh what comes over the sea"), "By The Sea," "Days Of Vanity," "Enrica, 1865," "Once For All. (Margaret.),"

"Autumn Violets," "'They Desire A Better Country" (sections I-III), "A Green Cornfield," "A Bride Song," "The Lowest Room," "Dead Hope," "A Daughter Of Eve," "Venus's Looking-Glass," "Love Lies Bleeding," "Bird Raptures," "My Friend," "Twilight Night," "A Bird Song," "A Smile And A Sigh," "Amor Mundi," "A Christmas Carol" ("In the bleak mid-winter"), "By The Waters Of Babylon. B. C. 570," "Paradise," "'I Will Lift Up Mine Eyes Unto The Hills'," "Saints And Angels," "'When My Heart Is Vexed, I Will Complain'," "After Communion," "A Rose Plant In Jericho," "Who Shall Deliver Me?," "Despised And Rejected," "Long Barren," "If Only," "Dost Thou Not Care?," "Weary In Well-Doing," "Martyrs' Song," "After This The Judgment," "Good Friday" ("Am I a stone and not a sheep?"), "The Lowest Place."

Typography and paper: (129) 122 x 76 (p. 272); 30 lines per page. Laid paper, horizontal chainlines 29 mm apart. Unwatermarked.

Running titles

Rectos: [1], i-v: no RT; vii-ix: 'CONTENTS.'; 3: no RT; 5-21: 'GOBLIN MARKET.'; 23: 'IN THE ROUND TOWER AT JHANSI.'; 25: 'AT HOME.'; 27: 'LOVE FROM THE NORTH.'; 29: 'WINTER RAIN.'; 31: 'CONFLUENTS.'; 33: 'NOBLE SISTERS.'; 35: 'SPRING.'; 37: 'A BIRTHDAY.'; 39: 'AFTER DEATH.'; 41: 'MY DREAM.'; 43-45: 'THE HOUR AND THE GHOST.'; 47: 'AN APPLE GATHERING.'; 49: 'MAUDE CLARE.'; 51: 'ECHO.'; 53: 'ANOTHER SPRING.'; 55: 'FATA MORGANA.'; 57: 'MAY.'; 59: 'TWILIGHT CALM.'; 61: 'WIFE TO HUSBAND.'; 63: 'MIRAGE.'; 65: 'SOUND SLEEP.'; 67: 'SONG.'; 69: 'THE MASTER CALLETH.'; 71-75: 'THE CONVENT THRESHOLD.'; 77: 'UP-HILL.'; 79-81: no RT; 83: 'A BETTER RESURRECTION.'; 85: 'ADVENT.'; 87: 'THE THREE ENEMIES.'; 89: 'THE ONE CERTAINTY.'; 91: 'CHRISTIAN AND JEW.'; 93: 'SWEET DEATH.'; 95: 'CONSIDER THE LILIES OF THE FIELD.'; 97-99: 'A TESTIMONY.'; 101: 'SLEEP AT SEA.'; 103-111: 'FROM HOUSE TO HOME.'; 113: 'OLD AND NEW YEAR DITTIES.'; 115: 'AMEN.'; 117: 'MOTHER COUNTRY.'; 119: no RT; 121-139: 'THE PRINCE'S PROGRESS.'; 141-147: 'MAIDEN-SONG.'; 149-151: 'JESSIE CAMERON.'; 153: 'SPRING QUIET.'; 155: 'THE POOR GHOST.'; 157-159: 'DREAM-LOVE.'; 161: 'TWICE.'; 163-165: 'SONGS IN A CORNFIELD.'; 167-169: 'A YEAR'S WINDFALLS.'; 171: 'ONE DAY.'; 173-175: 'A BIRD'S-EYE VIEW.'; 177: '"TO-DAY FOR ME."'; 179: 'ON THE WING.'; 181: 'BEAUTY IS VAIN.'; 183: 'LADY MAGGIE.'; 185: 'SUMMER.'; 187: 'AUTUMN.'; 189-191: 'THE GHOST'S PETITION.'; 193: 'MEMORY.'; 195-201: 'A ROYAL PRINCESS.'; 203: 'VANITY OF VANITIES.'; 205: 'L. E. L.'; 207: 'BIRD OR BEAST?'; 209: 'EVE.'; 211: 'GROWN AND FLOWN.'; 213: 'A FARM WALK.'; 215: 'SOMEWHERE OR OTHER.'; 217: 'CHILD'S TALK IN APRIL.'; 219: 'GONE FOREVER.'; 221-237: 'UNDER THE ROSE.'; 239: 'SONG.'; 241: 'DAYS OF VANITY.'; 243: 'AUTUMN VIOLETS.'; 245: 'A BETTER COUNTRY DESIRED.'; 247: 'A BRIDE SONG.'; 249-259: 'THE LOWEST ROOM.'; 261: 'A DAUGHTER OF EVE.'; 263: 'BIRD RAPTURE.'; 265: 'TWILIGHT NIGHT.'; 267: 'AMOR MUNDI.'; 269: 'A CHRISTMAS CAROL.'; 271-273: 'BY THE WATERS OF BABYLON.'; 275: 'PARADISE.'; 277: 'UPLIFTING OF EYES.'; 279: 'SAINTS AND ANGELS.'; 281: 'AFTER COMMUNION.'; 283: 'WHO SHALL DELIVER ME?'; 285-287: no RT; 289: 'LONG BARREN.'; 291: 'DOST THOU NOT CARE?'; 293-295: 'MARTYRS' SONG.'; 297: 'AFTER THIS THE JUDGMENT.'; 299: 'GOOD FRIDAY.'; 301: no RT.

Versos: [2], ii-iv: no RT; vi-viii: 'CONTENTS.'; x: no RT; 4-22: 'GOBLIN MARKET.'; 24: 'DREAM-LAND.'; 26: 'FROM SUNSET TO STAR RISE.'; 28: 'LOVE FROM THE NORTH.'; 30: 'A DIRGE.'; 32: 'NOBLE SISTERS.'; 34: 'SPRING.'; 36: 'THE LAMBS OF GRASMERE.'; 38: 'REMEMBER.'; 40: 'AN END.'; 42: 'MY DREAM.'; 44: 'THE HOUR AND THE GHOST.'; 46: 'A SUMMER WISH.'; 48: 'SONG.'; 50: 'MAUDE CLARE.'; 52: 'WINTER: MY SECRET.'; 54: 'A PEAL OF BELLS.'; 56: '"NO, THANK YOU, JOHN."'; 58: 'A PAUSE OF THOUGHT.'; 60: 'TWILIGHT CALM.'; 62: 'WIFE TO HUSBAND.'; 64: 'SHUT OUT.'; 66: 'SONG.'; 68: 'BITTER FOR SWEET.'; 70: 'THE FIRST SPRING DAY.'; 72-76: 'THE CONVENT THRESHOLD.'; 78-80: no RT; 82: 'A BRUISED REED SHALL HE NOT BREAK.'; 84-86: 'ADVENT.'; 88: 'THE THREE ENEMIES.'; 90-92: 'CHRISTIAN AND JEW.'; 94: 'SYMBOLS.';

96: 'THE WORLD.'; 98: 'A TESTIMONY.'; 100-102: 'SLEEP AT SEA.'; 104-110: 'FROM HOUSE TO HOME.'; 112: 'FROM HOUSE TO HOME' [no period]; 114: 'OLD AND NEW YEAR DITTIES.'; 116-118: 'MOTHER COUNTRY.'; 120-138: 'THE PRINCE'S PROGRESS.'; 140-146: 'MAIDEN-SONG.'; 148: 'JESSIE-CAMERON.'; 150-152: 'JESSIE CAMERON.'; 154: 'THE POOR GHOST.'; 156: 'A PORTRAIT.'; 158: 'DREAM-LOVE.'; 160: 'TWICE.'; 162-164: 'SONGS IN A CORNFIELD.'; 166-168: 'A YEAR'S WINDFALLS.'; 170: 'THE QUEEN OF HEARTS.'; 172-174: 'A BIRD'S-EYE VIEW.'; 176: 'GERMAN-FRENCH CAMPAIGN.'; 178: '"TO-DAY FOR ME."'; 180: 'CONSIDER.'; 182: 'MAGGIE A LADY.'; 184: 'WHAT WOULD I GIVE?'; 186: 'SUMMER.'; 188: 'AUTUMN.'; 190-192: 'THE GHOST'S PETITION.'; 194: 'MEMORY.'; 196-200: 'A ROYAL PRINCESS.'; 202: 'SHALL I FORGET?'; 204: 'L. E. L.'; 206: 'LIFE AND DEATH.'; 208-210: 'EVE.'; 212-214: 'A FARM WALK.'; 216: 'A CHILL.'; 218: 'CHILD'S TALK IN APRIL.'; 220-238: 'UNDER THE ROSE.'; 240: 'DAYS OF VANITY.'; 242: 'ENRICA, 1865.'; 244: 'A BETTER COUNTRY DESIRED.'; 246: 'A GREEN CORNFIELD.'; 248: 'A BRIDE SONG.'; 250-260: 'THE LOWEST ROOM.'; 262: 'VENUS' LOOKING-GLASS.'; 264: 'MY FRIEND.'; 266: 'A BIRD SONG.'; 268: 'AMOR MUNDI.'; 270: 'A CHRISTMAS CAROL.'; 272: 'BY THE WATERS OF BABYLON.'; 274: 'PARADISE.'; 276: 'UPLIFTING OF EYES.'; 278: 'SAINTS AND ANGELS.'; 280: 'THE VEXED HEART.'; 282: 'A ROSE PLANT IN JERICHO.'; 284: 'WHO SHALL DELIVER ME?'; 286: no RT; 288: 'DESPISED AND REJECTED.'; 290: 'IF ONLY.'; 292: 'WEARY IN WELL-DOING.'; 294: 'MARTYRS' SONG.'; 296-298: 'AFTER THIS THE JUDGMENT.'; 300: 'THE LOWEST PLACE.'; <u>302</u>: no RT.

Binding: Calico, moderate reddish brown (Centroid 43). Front: in gilt, diamond-shaped medallion with lyre and foliage. Back: Plain. Spine: 'THE POEMS | OF | CHRISTINA | G. | ROSSETTI | GOBLIN | MARKET | AND | OTHER POEMS | LITTLE, BROWN | & CO.' Endpapers: wove paper. Edges: top edge gilt, fore-edge and tail rough trimmed.

Publication: Advertised, along with volumes by Dante Rossetti and John Keats, under the heading Handy Volume Poets in the *Literary News* (November 1899: 352) and priced at $1.50.

Printing: no printer's imprint.

Locations: Ives; TxU (disbound).

Volume II:

THE | POETICAL WORKS | OF | CHRISTINA G. ROSSETTI | IN TWO VOLUMES | Vol. II. | BOSTON | LITTLE, BROWN, AND COMPANY | 1899

Pagination: <u>1</u>-<u>13</u> 14-231 <u>232</u>. Obsolete (1881) pagination remains in preliminaries, thus <u>6</u>-<u>8</u> are printed with page numbers viii-x.

Collation: 177 x 110: <u>1</u>⁸ 2⁸ <u>3</u>⁸ 4-7⁸ <u>8</u>⁸ 9-13⁸ <u>14</u>⁸ <u>15</u>⁴. $1 signed. 116 leaves.

Contents: <u>1</u>: halftitle 'THE POETICAL WORKS | OF | CHRISTINA G. ROSSETTI'; <u>2</u>: blank; <u>3</u>: title; <u>4</u>: blank; <u>5</u>: 'CONTENTS.'; <u>9</u>: poem "SONNETS are full of love . . ."; <u>10</u>: blank; <u>11</u>: poem 'THE KEY-NOTE.'; <u>12</u>: blank; <u>13</u>-231: poems; <u>232</u>: blank.

Poems: Same as A30 (Little, Brown, 1898, selections from "A Pageant" and from expanded 1888 subedition):
"'Sonnets are full of love, and this my tome'," "The Key-Note," "The Months: A Pageant," "Pastime," "'Italia, Io Ti Saluto!'," "Mirrors Of Life And Death," "A Ballad Of Boding," "Yet A Little While" ("I dreamed and did not seek"), "He And She," "Monna Innominata" (sonnets 1-14), "'Luscious And Sorrowful'," "De Profundis," "Tempus Fugit," "Golden Glories," "Johnny," "'Hollow-Sounding And Mysterious'," "Maiden May," "Till To-Morrow," "Death-Watches," "Touching 'Never'," "Brandons

Both," "A Life's Parallels," "At Last," "Golden Silences," "In The Willow Shade," "Fluttered Wings," "A Fisher-Wife," "What's In A Name?," "Mariana," "Memento Mori," "'One Foot On Sea, And One On Shore'," "Buds And Babies," "Boy Johnny," "Freaks Of Fashion," "An October Garden," "'Summer Is Ended'," "Passing And Glassing," "'I Will Arise'," "A Prodigal Son," "Sœur Louise De La Miséricorde. (1674.)," "An 'Immurata' Sister," "'If Thou Sayest, Behold, We Knew It Not'." (sections 1-3), "The Thread Of Life" (sections 1-3), "An Old-World Thicket," "All Thy Works Praise Thee, O Lord," "Later Life: A Double Sonnet Of Sonnets" (sonnets 1-28), "'For Thine Own Sake, O My God'," "Until The Day Break," "'Of Him That Was Ready To Perish'," "'Behold The Man!'," "The Descent From The Cross," "'It Is Finished'," "An Easter Carol," "'Behold A Shaking'" (sections 1-2), "All Saints," "'Take Care Of Him'," "A Martyr," "Why?," "'Love Is Strong As Death'" ("I have not sought Thee, I have not found Thee"), "Birchington Churchyard," "One Sea-Side Grave," "Brother Bruin," "'A Helpmeet for Him'," "A Song of Flight," "A Wintry Sonnet," "Resurgam," "To-Day's Burden," "'There is a Budding Morrow in Midnight'," "Exultate Deo," "A Hope Carol," "Christmas Carols" (sections 1-3), "A Candlemas Dialogue," "Mary Madgalene and the Other Mary," "Patience of Hope."

Running titles:

Rectos: <u>1-5</u>: no RT; 7 'CONTENTS.'; <u>9-13</u>: no RT; 15-31: 'A PAGEANT.'; 33: 'PASTIME.'; 35-41: 'MIRRORS OF LIFE AND DEATH.'; 43-51: 'A BALLAD OF BODING.'; 53: 'HE AND SHE.'; 55-67: 'MONNA INNOMINATA.'; 69: '"LUSCIOUS AND SORROWFUL."'; 71: 'TEMPUS FUGIT.'; 73-75: 'JOHNNY.'; 77: '"HOLLOW-SOUNDING & MYSTERIOUS."'; 79-83: 'MAIDEN MAY.'; 85: 'DEATH-WATCHES.'; 87-91: 'BRANDONS BOTH.'; 93: 'AT LAST.'; 95-97: 'IN THE WILLOW SHADE.'; 99: 'FLUTTERED WINGS.'; 101: 'WHAT'S IN A NAME?'; 103: 'MARIANA.'; 105: '"ONE FOOT ON SEA,'; 107: 'BUDS AND BABIES.'; 109-111: 'FREAKS OF FASHION.'; 113: 'AN OCTOBER GARDEN.'; 115: 'PASSING AND GLASSING.'; 117: '"I WILL ARISE."'; 119: 'A PRODIGAL SON.'; 121: 'SŒUR LOUISE DE LA MISÉRICORDE.'; 123: 'AN "IMMURATA" SISTER.'; 125: '"IF THOU SAYEST . . ."'; 127-129: 'THE THREAD OF LIFE.'; 131-139: 'AN OLD-WORLD THICKET.'; 141-153: 'O LORD."'; 155-181: 'LATER LIFE.'; 183: 'UNTIL THE DAY BREAK.'; 185: '"READY TO PERISH."'; 187: '"BEHOLD THE MAN!"'; 189-191: '"IT IS FINISHED."'; 193: 'AN EASTER CAROL.'; 195: '"BEHOLD A SHAKING."'; 197: 'ALL SAINTS.'; 199: '"TAKE CARE OF HIM."'; 201-205: 'A MARTYR.'; 207: 'WHY?'; 209: 'BIRCHINGTON CHURCHYARD.'; 211-213: 'BROTHER BRUIN.'; 215: 'A SONG OF FLIGHT.'; 217: 'RESURGAM.'; 219: '"THERE IS A BUDDING MORROW."'; 221: 'A HOPE CAROL.'; 223-227: 'CHRISTMAS CAROLS.'; 229: 'A CANDLEMAS DIALOGUE.'; 231: 'PATIENCE OF HOPE.'

Versos: 2-4: no RT; 6-8: 'CONTENTS.'; 10-12: no RT; 14-30: 'THE MONTHS:'; 32: 'THE MONTHS: A PAGEANT.'; 34: '"ITALIA, IO TI SALUTO!"'; 36-40: 'MIRRORS OF LIFE AND DEATH.'; 42-50: 'A BALLAD OF BODING.'; 52: 'YET A LITTLE WHILE.'; 54-68: 'MONNA INNOMINATA.'; 70: 'DE PROFUNDIS.'; 72: 'GOLDEN GLORIES.'; 74-76: 'JOHNNY.'; 78: '"HOLLOW-SOUNDING & MYSTERIOUS."'; 80-82: 'MAIDEN MAY.'; 84: 'TILL TO-MORROW.'; 86: 'TOUCHING "NEVER."'; 88-90: 'BRANDONS BOTH.'; 92: 'A LIFE'S PARALLELS.'; 94: 'GOLDEN SILENCES.'; 96-98: 'IN THE WILLOW SHADE.'; 100: 'A FISHER-WIFE.'; 102: 'WHAT'S IN A NAME?'; 104: 'MEMENTO MORI.'; 106: 'AND ONE ON SHORE."'; 108: 'BOY JOHNNY.'; 110-112: 'FREAKS OF FASHION.'; 114: '"SUMMER IS ENDED."'; 116: 'PASSING AND GLASSING.'; 118: '"I WILL ARISE."'; 120: 'SŒUR LOUISE DE LA MISÉRICORDE.'; 122: 'AN "IMMURATA" SISTER.'; 124-126: '"IF THOU SAYEST . . ."'; 128: 'THE THREAD OF LIFE.'; 130-138: 'AN OLD-WORLD THICKET.'; 140-152: '"ALL THY WORKS PRAISE THEE,'; 154-180: 'LATER LIFE.'; 182: '"FOR THINE OWN SAKE, O MY GOD."'; 184: 'UNTIL THE DAY BREAK.'; 186: '"READY TO PERISH."'; 188: 'THE DESCENT FROM THE CROSS.'; 190: '"IT IS FINISHED."'; 192: 'AN EASTER CAROL.'; 194: '"BEHOLD A SHAKING."'; 196-198: 'ALL SAINTS.'; 200: '"TAKE CARE OF HIM."'; 202-206: 'A MARTYR.'; 208: '"LOVE IS STRONG AS DEATH."'; 210: 'ONE SEA-SIDE GRAVE.'; 212: 'BROTHER BRUIN.';

214: '"A HELPMEET FOR HIM."'; 216: 'A WINTRY SONNET.'; 218: 'TO-DAY'S BURDEN.'; 220: 'EXULTATE DEO.'; 222: 'A HOPE CAROL.'; 224-226: 'CHRISTMAS CAROLS.'; 228: 'A CANDLEMAS DIALOGUE.'; 230: 'MARY MAGDALENE.'; <u>232</u>: no RT.

Typography and paper: (136) 124.3 x 66 (p. 49); variable lines per page (up to 25). Laid paper, vertical chainlines 30 mm apart. Unwatermarked.

Binding: Same as Volume I except spine: 'THE POEMS | OF | CHRISTINA | G. | ROSSETTI | THE | PAGEANT | AND | OTHER POEMS | LITTLE, BROWN | & CO.' Endpapers: wove. Edges: top edge gilt, fore-edge and tail rough trimmed. Binder's leaf follows the text.

Note: Half-title, and possibly front binder's leaf, missing in copy examined.

Printing: no printer's imprint.

Location: Ives.

A32.1b   *First Edition, Second Printing (1900)*

Volume I:

Same as 1899 except:

Title Page: Date changed to 1900.

Collation: 176 x 110: [1-19⁸ 20⁴]. Obsolete signing for 12s present. 156 leaves.

Paper: laid, horizontal chainlines 20 m. apart.

Binding: Endpapers: laid, thicker than sheets, with vertical chainlines 29 mm apart.

Location: Ives.

Volume II:

Same as 1899 except:

Title Page: Date changed to 1900.

Typography and paper: Laid paper, vertical chainlines 20 mm apart. Unwatermarked.

Binding: Endpapers: laid, thicker than sheets, with vertical chainlines 29 mm apart. One binder's leaf precedes and follows the text.

Location: Ives.

A32.1c   *First Edition, Third Printing (1902)*

Volume I: not seen.

Location: Copy located at Southwestern University (TX), call number 821.8 R735p.

Volume II:

Same as 1900 except:

Title Page: Date changed to 1902.

Collation: (177 x 109): <u>1</u>⁸ 2⁸ <u>3</u>⁸ 4-7⁸ <u>8</u>⁸ 9-13⁸ <u>14</u>⁸ <u>15</u>⁴.

Typography and paper: Laid paper, vertical chainlines 20 mm apart. Unwatermarked.

Binding: Endpapers laid, vertical chainlines 20 mm apart, but thicker than sheets.

Printing: iv (first line in black letter): 'Printers | S. J. PARKHILL & CO., BOSTON, U. S. A.'

Location: Ives.

A32.1d   *First Edition, Fourth Printing (1904)*

Volume I: not seen.

Volume II: not seen.

Location: Copies (both volumes) listed in Monmouth University library catalog, call number PR 5240 F4 Vol.1, Vol. 2.

A32.1e   *First Edition, Fifth Printing (1905)*

Volume I: not seen.

Location: Copy listed in Abilene Christian University Library catalog, 828.001 R829A2 V.1.

Volume II: same as 1902 except:

Title Page: Date changed to 1905.

Binding: Fine diagonal rib cloth; endpapers: same as sheets; otherwise same as 1902.

Printing: no printer's imprint.

Location: TxAbC.

A32.1f   *First Edition, Sixth Printing (1909)*

Volume I: same as 1899 except:

Title Page: Date changed to 1909.

Collation: [1-19⁸ 20⁴].

Pagination: same except: 300 <u>301</u>-<u>302</u>.

Plates: Portrait further enlarged, 115 x 78.

Contents: <u>ii</u>: printer's imprint; <u>301-302</u>: blank.

Typography and paper: vertical chainlines, 21 mm apart.

Binding: Same as 1900 except: Fine diagonal rib cloth, very dark red (Centroid 17). One blank laid paper binder's leaf precedes and follows the sheets.

Printing: ii (first line in black letter): 'Printers | S. J. PARKHILL & CO., BOSTON, U. S. A.'

Location: Ives.

Volume II:

Same as 1905 except:

Title Page: Date changed to 1909.

Printing: iv (first line in black letter): 'Printers | S. J. Parkhill & Co., Boston, U. S. A.'

Binding: Same as 1905 except fine diagonal rib cloth, very dark red (Centroid 17).

Location: Ives.

A32.1g   *First Edition, Seventh Printing (1917)*

Volume I: not seen.

Volume II: not seen.

Location: Copies (both volumes) listed in Texas Lutheran College library catalog, call number PR5237 .A1 1917.

SELECTED LATER WORKS

A33   **REFLECTED LIGHTS FROM THE FACE OF THE DEEP (1899, 1900)**

A33.1a   *First Edition, American Printing (1899)*

REFLECTED LIGHTS | FROM | "THE FACE OF THE DEEP" | BY | CHRISTINA ROSSETTI | SELECTED AND ARRANGED | BY | W. M. L. JAY | [ornament, Maltese cross, 3.7 x. 3.7] | NEW YORK | E. P. DUTTON & COMPANY | 31 West Twenty-third Street | 1899

Collation: $\underline{1}^8$ 2-3^8 $\underline{4}^8$ 5-7^8 $\underline{8}^8$ 9-12^8 $\underline{13}^8$ 14-16^8 $\underline{17}^2$, \$5 signed (-1, 4, 8, 13, 17). 130 leaves.

Pagination: i-ii iii-v vi vii viii 1 2 3-12 22 23-31 32 33-43 44 45-53 54 55 56 57-63 64 65-69 70 71-79 80 81-93 94 95 96 97-107 108 109 110 111-129 130 131-137 138 139 140 141-155 156 157-163 164 165 166 167-175 176 177-183 184 185-191 192 193 194 195-205 206 207-215 216 217-233 234 235-251 252.

Plates: In some instances I have been able to identify the artists and works represented in the illustrations; none are identified in the book.

1) Facing i, frontispiece, reproduction of DGR's "The Annunciation" (126.5 x 72), with letterpress caption '"Clothe us as Thy lilies." – *Page* 151. | *Frontispiece*'.
2) Facing 12, reproduction of "Christ the Consoler," signed B. Plockhorst (102 x 71), with letterpress caption '"O Lord, I cannot plead my love of Thee." – *Page 12.*'
3) Facing 16, reproduction of painting of the ascension of Christ, signature illegible (127 x 69) with letterpress caption '"When a cloud received Him out of sight." – *Page 16.*'
4) Facing 34, illustration of woman with uplifted arms, unsigned (127 x 69) with letterpress caption '"Hope, . . . with arms flung forth and backward floating hair." | – *Page 34.*'
5) Facing 48, reproduction of painting of Magi, unsigned (118 x 72), with vertical letterpress caption '"Did those three alone see the star?" – *Page 145.*'
6) Facing 62, reproduction of woman's portrait, unsigned (108 x 76), with letterpress caption '"Thus pondering, I glanced downward on the grass." – *Page 148.*'
7) Facing 74, reproduction of painting of standing woman, unsigned (108 x 77) with letterpress caption '"One sorrow more." – *Page 160.*'
8) Facing 88, reproduction of Alexandre Bida's "The Widow's Mite," unsigned (107 x 75), with vertical letterpress caption '"The widow who cast two mites into the treasury by so doing became rich." – *Page 160.*'
9) Facing 102, reproduction of painting, illegible signature (95 x 73), with letterpress caption "Sweet Spring must fail, and fail the choir of Spring, | But wisdom shall burn on when the lesser lights are gone." | – *Page 144.*'
10) Facing 116, reproduction Alexandre Bida's "The Prayer In Secret" (man preparing to pray), signed "Bida" (109 x 76), with letterpress caption '"If I pray not at the hour of prayer, the hour passes." – Page 117.'
11) Facing 130, reproduction of a painting of seascape, unsigned (119 x 75) with vertical letterpress caption '"*And there was no more sea.*' And wherefore not the sea?" – Page 153.'
12) Facing 142, reproduction of Elihu Vedder's "Girl With Poppies," unsigned (126 x 78), with letterpress caption '"The poppy saith, . . . | 'Yet juice of subtle virtue lies | Within my cup of curious dyes.'" – Page 143.'
13) Facing 156, reproduction of Heinrich Hofmann's "Christ and the Rich Young Man" (95 x 74),

vertical letterpress caption '"The 'rich young man' turned away sorrowful." – Page 157.'

14) Facing 168, reproduction of portrait of young woman (99 x 75), with letterpress caption '"Whiteness most white: ah, to be clean again!" – *Page* 168.'

15) Facing 186, reproduction of painting, burial of Christ, signed H Hofmann (106 x 77) with letterpress caption '"If Christ hath died, His brethren well may die." – *Page* 186.'

16) Facing 200, oval reproduction of "The Holy Innocents" by William Charles Thomas Dobson (77 x 75) with letterpress caption '"Unspotted lambs to follow the one Lamb." – *Page* 201."

17) Facing 210, reproduction of landscape (115 x 77) with vertical letterpress caption '"Though the things which are seen are temporal, yet —." – *Page* 210.'

18) Facing 224, reproduction of painting of woman holding flowering branch in left hand, right hand reaching upward (120 x 74), letterpress caption '"Lift up thine eyes to seek the invisible." – *Page* 224.'

Contents: i: title; ii: copyright statement and printer's imprint; iii: 'PREFACE'; vi: blank; vii: 'LIST OF ILLUSTRATIONS'; viii: blank; 1: text headed 'THE LIGHT OF LOVE'; 2: blank; 3-20: text; 21: text headed 'THE LIGHT OF FAITH'; 22: blank; 23-30: text; 31: text headed 'THE LIGHT OF HOPE'; 32: blank; 33-42: text; 43: text headed 'THE LIGHT OF PATIENCE'; 44: blank; 45-53: text; 54: blank; 55: text headed 'THE LIGHT OF HUMILITY'; 56: blank; 57-62: text; 63: text headed 'THE LIGHT OF OBEDIENCE'; 64: blank; 64-68: text; 69: text headed 'THE LIGHT OF WISDOM'; 70: blank; 71-78: text; 79: text headed 'THE LIGHT OF ENCOURAGE- | MENT'; 80: blank; 81-93: text; 94: blank; 95: text headed 'LIGHT FOR LABOR'; 96: blank; 97-107: text; 108: blank; 109: text headed 'LIGHT ON THE DAILY PATH'; 110: blank; 111-128: text; 129: text headed 'LIGHT THROUGH SHADOWS'; 130: blank; 131-137: text; 138: text headed 'LIGHT FROM NATURE'; 140: blank; 141-154: text; 155: text headed 'THE LIGHT OF SACRIFICE'; 156: blank; 157-163: text; 164: blank; 165: text headed 'THE LIGHT OF PENITENCE'; 166: blank; 167-174: text; 175: text headed 'LIGHT FROM THE CROSS'; 176: blank; 177-182: text; 183: text headed 'LIGHT FOR THE VALLEY OF THE | SHADOW OF DEATH'; 184: blank; 185-191: text; 192: blank; 193: text headed 'LIGHT FROM PARADISE'; 194: blank; 195-204: text; 205: text headed 'LIGHT FROM TIME'; 206: blank; 207-214: text; 215: text headed 'LIGHT HERE AND THERE'; 234: blank; 235-251: text; 252 blank.

Poems: Untitled excerpts from the following poems (first lines are provided for poems previously published in titled and untitled forms; one excerpt is unidentified; see *Note one*):
"If love is not worth loving, then life is not worth living," "What is the beginning? Love. What the course? Love still," "A Song for the Least of All Saints," "Quinquagesima" ("Love is alone the worthy law of love"); "Love, to be love, must walk Thy way"; "Lord, dost Thou look on me, and will not I," "The Ransomed of the Lord" ("Thy lovely saints do bring Thee love"), "'A Bruised Reed Shall He Not Break'," "Where love is, there comes sorrow," "Lord, save us, we perish" ("O Lord, seek us, O Lord, find us"), "O ye who are not dead and fit," "Because He first loved us," "Because thy love hath sought me," "Everything that is born must die," "Me and my gift: kind Lord, behold," "Lord God of Hosts, most Holy and most High," "Lord, give me love that I may love Thee much," "Our heaven must be within ourselves," "Alone Lord God, In Whom our trust and peace" (2 excerpts), "Like as the hart desireth the water brooks," "Every one that is perfect shall be as his master," "The Greatest of these is Charity" ("A moon impoverished amid stars curtailed"), "Judge nothing before the time," "From House to Home" (3 excerpts), "Take no thought for the morrow," "I lift mine eyes to see: earth vanisheth," "Life that was born to-day," "Peace I leave with you" ("Tumult and turmoil, trouble and toil"), "Shall not the judge of all the earth do right?," "Escape to the Mountain" ("I peered within, and saw a world of sin"), "After this the Judgment" (2 excerpts), "Tune me, O Lord, into one harmony," "Whatso it be, howso it be, Amen" ("They put their trust in Thee, and were not confounded"), "Experience bows a sweet contented face," "As froth on the face of the deep," "Light of Light" (2 excerpts), "All heaven is blazing yet," "God's Acre" ("Hail, garden of confident hope!"), "New creatures; the Creator still the Same," "Bury Hope out of sight," "Hope is the counterpoise of fear," "Redeeming the time" ("A life of hope deferred too often

is"), "Lord, grant us grace to rest upon thy word," "Have Patience," "The Will of the Lord Be Done" ("O Lord, fulfill Thy Will"), "Lord, it is good for us to be here" ("Grant us, O Lord, that patience and that faith"), "Patience must dwell with Love, for Love and Sorrow," "Where neither rust nor moth doth corrupt"("Nerve us with patience, Lord, to toil or rest"), "Then shall ye shout" ("It seems an easy thing"), "Sweetness of rest when Thou sheddest rest," "The Lowest Place," "Who hath despised the day of small things?" ("As violets so be I recluse and sweet"), "The Offering of the New Law," "Do this, and he doeth it" ("Content to come, content to go"), "Lord, I am feeble and of mean account," "I am small and of no reputation" ("The least, if so I am"), "The Lowest Room" (2 excerpts), "Lord, make me pure," "Ye are come unto Mount Sion," "Whitsun Tuesday," "Love loveth thee, and wisdom loveth thee" (2 excerpts), "Grant us such grace that we may work thy will" (2 excerpts), "Ah Lord, Lord, if my heart were right with Thine," "A merry heart is a continual feast" ("Then I commended mirth"), "What good shall my life do me?" ("Have dead men long to wait?"), "Love is Strong as Death" ("As flames that consume the mountains"), "When my heart is vexed I will complain" ("The fields are white to harvest, look and ·see"), "Lord, what have I that I may offer thee?," "'Can I know it?' 'Nay,'" "All flesh is grass" ("So brief a life, and then an endless life"), "What is it Jesus saith unto the soul?" (2 excerpts), "Ye have forgotten the exhortation," "Who Have a Form of Godliness," "Lord, carry me. – Nay, but I grant thee strength," "Yea I have a Goodly Heritage," "Through burden and heat of the day," "Amen," "Ascension Eve," "Vigil of All Saints" ("Up, my drowsing eyes!"), "Day and Night the Accuser makes no pause," "The sinner's own fault. So it was," "Are they not all Ministering Spirits?" ("Lord, whomsoever Thou shalt send to me")(3 excerpts), "Then whose shall those things be?" ("Oh, what is earth, that we should build"), "Looking back along life's trodden way," "Shadows to-day, while shadows show God's will" (2 excerpts), "What is that to thee? Follow thou me"("Lie still, my restive heart, lie still"), "Sorrow hath a double voice," "Surely he hath borne our griefs"("Christ's Heart was wrung for me, if mine is sore"),"Thy servant will go and fight with this Philistine" ("Sorrow of saints is sorrow of a day"), "Joy is but sorrow," "Consider the Lilies of the Field"("Flowers preach to us if we will hear") (2 excerpts), "Judge not according to the appearance," "And there was no more Sea" ("Voices from above and from beneath"), "Let everything that hath breath praise the Lord" ("All that we see rejoices in the sunshine"), "Lord, grant us calm, if calm can set forth Thee,""Are ye not much better than they?" ("The twig sprouteth"), "Thou knewest . . . thou oughtest therefore"("Behold in heaven a floating, dazzling cloud"), "The hills are tipped with sunshine, while I walk," "Consider the Lilies of the Field" ("Solomon most glorious in array"), "Truly the Light is Sweet" ("Light colourless doth color all things else"), "Sexagesima"("Yet earth was very good in days of old"), "A Churchyard Song of Patient Hope," "My God, wilt Thou accept, and will not we," "Whom the Lord loveth he chasteneth" ("One sorrow more? I thought the tale complete"), "Beloved, yield thy time to God, for he" (2 excerpts), "Vigil of Saint Peter"("O Jesu, gone so far apart"), "Go in Peace" ("Can peach renew lost bloom"), "They shall be as white as snow" ("Whiteness most white. Ah, to be clean again"), "Subject to like Passions as we are"("Whoso hath anguish is not dead in sin"), "Good Lord, to-day," "Before the beginning Thou hast foreknown the end," "None other Lamb, none other Name"),"Ash Wednesday" ("My God, my God, have mercy on my sin"), "Epiphanytide" ("Trembling before Thee we fall down to adore Thee"), "A bundle of Myrrh is my Well-Beloved unto Me" ("Thy Cross cruciferous doth flower in all"), "The Love of Christ which Passeth Knowledge," "Long Barren," "Easter Monday" (2 excerpts), "It is not death, O Christ, to die for Thee," "Yet a little while" ("Heaven is not far, though far the sky"), "Vigil of the Annunciation" ("All weareth, all wasteth"), "The goal in sight! Look up and sing," "Three Nuns" (2 excerpts), "Lord, make me one with Thine own faithful ones," "Advent" ("This Advent moon shines cold and clear"), "'To every Seed his own Body'" ("Bone to his bone, grain to his grain of dust"), "Safe where I cannot lie yet," "If I should say, 'My heart is in my home'," "Who would wish back the saints upon our rough," "Antipas" ("Hidden from the darkness of our mortal sight"), "Unspotted lambs to follow the one Lamb," "Christian and Jew," "Our Mothers, lovely women pitiful," "I Have a Message Unto Thee," "Time seems not short," "As thy days, so shall thy strength be" ("Day that hath no tinge of night"), "Our life is long. – Not so wise angels say,"

167

"Heaven's chimes are slow, but sure to strike at last," "Time passeth away with its pleasure and pain," "Short is time, and only time is bleak," "Time lengthening, in the lengthening seemeth long," "Trinity Sunday"("My God, Thyself being Love Thy heart is love"), "What will it be, O my soul, what will it be" ("What Will it Be"), "We know not when, we know not where," "Beautiful for situation" ("A lovely city in a lovely land"),"The gold of that land is good" ("I long for joy, O Lord, I long for gold"), "The end is not yet"("Home by different ways. Yet all"), "Lift up thine eyes to seek the invisible," "Before the Throne, and before the Lamb" ("As the voice of many waters all saints sing as one"), "What are these lovely ones, yea, what are these?," "He shall go no more out" ("Once within, within for evermore"), "All Things" ("Jesus alone: if thus it were to me"), "Lord, grant us eyes to see and ears to hear," "Lord, make us all love all, that when we meet" (2 excerpts), "Cast down but not destroyed, chastened not slain," "Whitsun Monday" ("We know not a voice of that River"), "'That which hath been is named already, and it is known that it is Man'" ("'Eye hath not seen': Yet man hath known and weighed"), "Old and New Year Ditties," "'He cannot deny Himself'" ("Love still is love, and doeth all things well"), "Thy name, O Christ, as incense streaming forth," "Beloved, yield thy time to God, for He," "Who Shall Deliver Me?," "Lord, we are rivers running to Thy sea," "Lent" ("It is good to be last, not first"), "The half moon shows a face of plaintive sweetness," "Whatsoever is right, that shall ye receive" ("When all the overwork of life").

Typography and paper: (117) 108 x 63 (p. 145); 26 lines per page. Wove paper, unwatermarked.

Running titles: In black letter.

Rectos: i-vii, 1-3: no RT; 5-19: 'The Light of Love'; 21-23: no RT; 25-29: 'The Light of Faith'; 31-33: no RT; 35-41: 'The Light of Hope'; 43-45: no RT; 47-53: 'The Light of Patience'; 55-57; no RT; 59-61: 'The Light of Humility'; 63-65: no RT; 67: 'The Light of Obedience'; 69-71: no RT; 73-77: 'The Light of Wisdom'; 79-81: no RT; 83-93: 'The Light of Encouragement'; 95-97: no RT; 99-107: 'Light for Labor'; 109-11: no RT; 113-127: 'Light on the Daily Path'; 129-131: no RT; 133-137: 'Light through Shadows'; 139-141: no RT; 143-153: 'Light from Nature'; 155-157: no RT; 159-163: 'The Light of Sacrifice'; 165-167: no RT; 169-173: 'The Light of Penitence'; 175-177: no RT; 179-181: 'Light from the Cross'; 183-185: no RT; 187-191: 'Light for the Valley of Death'; 193-195: no RT; 197-203: 'Light from Paradise'; 205-207: no RT; 209-213: 'Light from Time'; 215-217: no RT; 219-231: 'Light from Eternity'; 233-235: no RT; 237-251: 'Light Here and There'.

Versos: ii: no RT; iv: 'Preface'; vi-vii, 2: no RT; 4-20: 'Reflected Lights'; 22: no RT; 24-30: 'Reflected Lights'; 32: no RT; 34-42: 'Reflected Lights'; 44: no RT; 46-52: 'Reflected Lights'; 54-56: no RT; 58-62: 'Reflected Lights'; 64: no RT; 66-68: 'Reflected Lights'; 70: no RT; 72-78: 'Reflected Lights'; 80: no RT; 82-92: 'Reflected Lights'; 94-96: no RT; 98-106: 'Reflected Lights'; 108-110: no RT; 112-128: 'Reflected Lights'; 130: no RT; 132-136: 'Reflected Lights'; 138-140: no RT; 142-154: 'Reflected Lights'; 156: no RT; 158-162: 'Reflected Lights'; 164-166: no RT; 168-174: 'Reflected Lights'; 176: no RT; 178-182: 'Reflected Lights'; 184: no RT; 186-190: 'Reflected Lights'; 192-194: no RT; 196-204: 'Reflected Lights'; 206: no RT; 208-214: 'Reflected Lights'; 216: no RT; 218-232: Reflected Lights'; 234: no RT; 236-250: 'Reflected Lights'; 252: no RT.

Binding: Fine diagonal rib cloth, yellowish gray (Centroid 93). Front: at top, within gilt-outlined rectangular compartment, five gilt rays on greenish-gray (Centroid 154) background, above black (Centroid 267) horizon. Beneath compartment, in gilt: '•REFLECTED • LIGHTS• | •FROM• | "THE FACE OF THE DEEP" | •CHRISTINA ROSSETTI•'. Back plain. Spine (in gilt): 'REFLECTED | LIGHTS | [rule] | CHRISTINA | ROSSETTI | E. P. DUTTON & Cº.' White wove endpapers, smoother than sheets. Edges: top edge gilt, fore-edge and tail rough trimmed. A pale yellow ribbon marker is bound into the spine.

Publication: September 1899. Compiled by Julia Louisa Matilda Woodruff, primarily from *The Face of the Deep*. Woodruff, writing under the pseudonym W. M. L. Jay, compiled several volumes in which Rossetti is included.

Listed in *New York Times* "Books Received" (30 September 1899: BR649).
Price: $1.25.

Reviewed in the *Literary News* (November 1899: 344); the *Watchman (Boston)* (30 November, 1899: 17); *New York Observer* (7 December 1899: 752).

Printing: ii (last line in black letter): 'Copyright, 1899 | BY | E. P. DUTTON & CO. | The Knickerbocker Press, New York."

Note one: The following excerpt does not appear in any Rossetti work, or in any book other than this one: "Though knowledge fail, and sight be dim, / And way and end not understood, / Though life be masked with doubt's gray film, / Obedience is good" (68).

Location: FMU.

A33.1b.i   *First Edition, Second Printing (SPCK Subedition), Illustrated issue (1900)*

Same as American printing except:

REFLECTED LIGHTS | FROM | "THE FACE OF THE DEEP" | BY | CHRISTINA ROSSETTI | SELECTED AND ARRANGED | BY | W.M. L. JAY | [ornament, maltese cross, 3 x 3] | LONDON | SOCIETY FOR PROMOTING CHRISTIAN KNOWLEDGE | NORTHUMBERLAND AVENUE, W. C. | 1900

Pagination: Same except 252-256.

Collation: π^4 1^8 2-16^8; $1 signed.

Contents: ii: '[PUBLISHED UNDER THE DIRECTION OF THE TRACT COMMITTEE]'; 253: advertisement 'WORKS BY THE LATE | CHRISTINA G. ROSSETTI.' six titles, *Called to be Saints, Letter and Spirit, Seek and Find, The Face of the Deep, Time Flies, Verses*; 254-256: blank.

Typography and paper: Sheets and plates on thicker paper than that of the Dutton printing.

Running titles:
Rectos: 253-255 no RT.
Versos: ii-viii no RT; 254-256 no RT.

Binding: Spine: 'REFLECTED | LIGHTS | [rule] | CHRISTINA | ROSSETTI | S. P. C. K.'

Publication: Reprinted from Dutton's plates. There is no indication that WMR was involved, or knew much about, the publication. He ordered a copy and received it on December 29 1900, noting in his diary that the volume "seems likely to extend & deepen her [CGR's] fame in religious circles" (WMRD).
　　Announced in the London *Times* "Publications To-Day" (12 October 1900: 4).
　　Price: 2s. 6d.

Printing: 251: '*Richard Clay & Sons, Limited, London & Bungay.*'

Location: University of Memphis.

A33.1b.ii   *First Edition, Second Printing (SPCK Subedition), Unillustrated Issue*

Same as first British printing except:

Collation: π^2 (χ + π1) 1-16^8 (the title page is pasted to the first leaf of π). $1 signed. 131 leaves. No plates.

Pagination: No vii, <u>viii</u>.

Contents: No vii, <u>viii</u>.

Publication: Presumably a later binding of the first British sheets, without the illustrations (and thus without the list of illustrations on pp. vii-viii).

Location: Ives.

A33.1c   *First Edition, Third Printing (SPCK Subedition) (1900)*

Not seen; information drawn from an electronic version of Harvard copy.

REFLECTED LIGHTS | FROM | "THE FACE OF THE DEEP" | BY | CHRISTINA ROSSETTI | SELECTED AND ARRANGED | BY | W. M.L. JAY | [ornament, Maltese cross] | LONDON | SOCIETY FOR PROMOTING CHRISTIAN KNOWLEDGE | NORTHUMBERLAND AVENUE, W.C. | 1900 | [*First Reprint.*]

Note one: None of the copies located (at Harvard, Nazereth College and University of Western Ontario) has illustrations.

Location: MH (via Google Books).

A34 POETICAL WORKS (1904)

A34.1a *First Edition, First Printing*

Some text in <u>black letter</u>:
THE POETICAL WORKS | OF | CHRISTINA GEORGINA | ROSSETTI | WITH MEMOIR AND NOTES & c | BY | WILLIAM MICHAEL ROSSETTI | <u>London</u> | MACMILLAN AND CO., LIMITED | NEW YORK: THE MACMILLAN COMPANY | 1904 | *All rights reserved*

Pagination: [1]-[2] <u>i</u>-<u>iv</u> v-xi <u>xii</u> xiii-xxxvii <u>xxxviii</u> xxxix-lxxi <u>lxxii</u> lxxiii <u>lxxiv</u> <u>1</u> 2-507 <u>508</u>.

Plates: 1) Facing title, frontispiece portrait (81 x 79; with tissue guard) of CGR by DGR.

Collation: [190 x 123]: a⁶ b-e⁸ B-Z⁸ 2A-2I⁸ 2K⁶ $1 signed, 292 leaves.

Contents: [1]-[2]: blank; <u>i</u>: half-title 'THE POETICAL WORKS | OF | CHRISTINA GEORGINA ROSSETTI'; <u>ii</u>: publisher's device, "M M & Co" 32 x 10; <u>iii</u>: title; <u>iv</u>: blank; <u>v</u>: 'PREFACE'; <u>xii</u>: blank; xiii: 'CONTENTS'; <u>xxxviii</u>: blank; xxxix: 'APPENDIX'; xlv: 'MEMOIR'; <u>lxxii</u>: blank; lxxiii: 'DEDICATORY SONNET'; <u>lxxiv</u>: blank; <u>1</u>-458: poems headed 'THE LONGER POEMS'; 82: heading 'JUVENILIA'; 114: heading 'DEVOTIONAL POEMS'; 286: heading 'GENERAL POEMS'; 417: heading 'POEMS FOR CHILDREN | AND MINOR VERSES'; 446: heading 'ITALIAN POEMS'; 459: 'NOTES BY W. M. ROSSETTI'; 495: 'INDEX TO FIRST LINES'; 508: imprint.

Poems: WMR includes all poems published in CGR's previous collections and in *New Poems* (A26), except for the following:
"Amore E Dispetto," "Divine and Human Pleading," "Eva," "Fair Margaret," "For Under a Crucifix," "From all kinds of music which worship an idol in thy stead," "From any sword that would devour for ever," "From love that cleaveth not to Thee," "From shame that is neither glory nor grace," "From worshipping and serving the creature more than the Creator," "Grant, O Lord," "I listen to the holy antheming," "Jesus Who didst touch the leper," "Life," "Life Out of Death," "Lord God Whom we fear, protect us," "Lord, grant us eyes to see," "Lord, I had chosen another lot," "Love us unto the end, and prepare us," "Near the Styx," "O Christ Who once wast condemned that we might never be condemned," "O God Eternal, Who causest the vapours to ascend from the ends of the earth," "O God the Holy Ghost Who art Light unto Thine elect," "O Lamb of God, slain from the foundation of the world, save us," "O Saviour, show compassion!," "On the dead for whom once Thou diedst, Lord Jesus, have mercy," "The Ruined Cross," "Sappho," "Lady Isabella" ("Lady Isabella"), "Thou Who wast Centre of a stable, with two saints and harmless cattle," "Thou Who was straitened till Thy baptism was accomplished," "To-Morrow ("Where my heart is"), "The Water Spirit's Song."
  WMR includes the following poems that had not been published in CGR's previous collections:
"A Bouts-Rimés Sonnet," "Charon," "The Chinaman," "'Come cheer up, my lads, 'tis to glory we steer'" (titled by WMR "Couplet"), "Downcast," "Heart's Chill Between" and "Death's Chill Between" (both previously published in Mackenzie Bell's biography), "Mary Magdalene," "The P. R. B." (1-2), "A Sick Child's Meditation," "To Mary Rossetti," "To William Bell Scott," "Young Death."
  In addition, some poems are reprinted in new forms, including:
  The poem "To meet, worth living for," previously published in *Time Flies* (A20, A21) appears as the concluding stanza in "Meeting" ("If we shall live, we live").
  The poem "A peach for brothers, one for each" appears incorporated into CGR's revised version, "The peach tree on the southern wall."
  The poem "Three Stages" (in three parts; 1, "A Pause of Thought"; 2, "The End Of The First Part"; 3, "Restive") represents a new combination of previously published poems.

Typography and paper: (161) 150 x 101 (p. 209); up to 44 lines per page, except "Notes" section, up to 50 lines per page. Poems and notes printed in two columns. Wove paper, unwatermarked.

Running titles: In italic. Single quotation marks in original on recto pages 253, 255, 349 and verso pages 248, 400. Period in original on recto page 265 and verso page 264.

Rectos: [1], i-v: no RT; vii-xi: 'PREFACE'; xiii: no RT; xv-xxxvii: 'CONTENTS'; xxxix: no RT; xli-xliii: 'APPENDIX'; xlv: no RT; xlvii-lxxi: 'MEMOIR'; lxxiii-1: no RT; 3-7: 'GOBLIN MARKET'; 9-11: 'REPINING'; 13-15: 'THREE NUNS'; 17-19: 'THE LOWEST ROOM'; 21-25: 'FROM HOUSE TO HOME'; 27-33: 'THE PRINCE'S PROGRESS'; 35-37: 'A ROYAL PRINCESS'; 39: 'MAIDEN-SONG'; 41-47: 'THE INIQUITY OF THE FATHERS UPON THE CHILDREN'; 49-53: 'THE MONTHS: A PAGEANT'; 55-57: 'A BALLAD OF BODING'; 59-63: 'MONNA INNOMINATA'; 65-67: 'AN OLD-WORLD THICKET'; 69-71: 'ALL THY WORKS PRAISE THEE, O LORD'; 73-81: 'LATER LIFE'; 83: 'FORGET ME NOT'; 85: 'LINES TO MY GRANDFATHER'; 87: 'THE END OF TIME'; 89: 'ON THE DEATH OF A CAT'; 91: 'THE MARTYR'; 93: 'THE DEAD BRIDE'; 95: 'THE TIME OF WAITING'; 97: 'THE SONG OF THE STAR'; 99-101: 'THE DEAD CITY'; 103: 'I HAVE FOUGHT A GOOD FIGHT'; 105: 'ELEANOR'; 107: 'ZARA'; 109: 'NIGHT AND DEATH'; 111: 'THE LOTUS-EATERS'; 113: 'THE LAST ANSWER'; 115: 'DEATH IS SWALLOWED UP IN VICTORY'; 117: 'FOR ADVENT'; 119: 'A TESTIMONY'; 121-143: 'SONGS FOR STRANGERS AND PILGRIMS'; 145: 'THE WATCHERS'; 147: 'BEHOLD, I STAND AT THE DOOR AND KNOCK'; 149: 'EYE HATH NOT SEEN'; 151: 'I LOOK FOR THE LORD'; 153: 'A HARVEST'; 155: 'SLEEP AT SEA'; 157-179: 'SOME FEASTS AND FASTS'; 181: 'YE HAVE FORGOTTEN THE EXHORTATION'; 183: 'HYMN AFTER GABRIELE ROSSETTI'; 185: 'HOW LONG?'; 187: 'A CHRISTMAS CAROL'; 189: 'AFTER THIS THE JUDGMENT'; 191: 'A BETTER RESURRECTION'; 193-201: 'DIVERS WORLDS. TIME AND ETERNITY'; 203: 'CHRISTIAN AND JEW'; 205: 'ONLY BELIEVE'; 207-213: 'NEW JERUSALEM AND ITS CITIZENS'; 215: 'THE LOVE OF CHRIST WHICH PASSETH KNOWLEDGE'; 217: 'A CHRISTMAS CAROL'; 219-231: 'CHRIST OUR ALL IN ALL'; 233: 'BY THE WATERS OF BABYLON'; 235: 'FOR A MERCY RECEIVED'; 237: 'COME UNTO ME'; 239: 'BY THE WATERS OF BABYLON'; 241: 'DESPISED AND REJECTED'; 243: 'I KNOW YOU NOT'; 245: 'MOTHER COUNTRY'; 247: 'WRESTLING'; 249: 'SAINTS AND ANGELS'; 251: 'A PRODIGAL SON'; 253: 'OF HIM THAT WAS READY TO PERISH'; 255: 'BEHOLD A SHAKING'; 257-259: 'A MARTYR'; 261: 'WE KNEW IT NOT'; 263: 'A SICK CHILD'S MEDITATION'; 265: 'OUT OF THE DEEP HAVE I CALLED UNTO THEE, O LORD.'; 267-269: 'OUT OF THE DEEP HAVE I CALLED UNTO THEE, O LORD' [no period]; 271-277: 'GIFTS AND GRACES'; 279: 'CHRISTMAS CAROLS'; 281: 'MARY MAGDALENE AND THE OTHER MARY'; 283: 'THE WORLD. SELF-DESTRUCTION'; 285: 'ALL THINGS'; 287: 'VANITY OF VANITIES'; 289: 'THREE STAGES'; 291: 'HAVE PATIENCE'; 293: 'LOOKING FORWARD'; 295: 'HOW ONE CHOSE'; 297: 'TWILIGHT CALM'; 299: 'THREE MOMENTS'; 301: 'A DIRGE' 303: 'BOOKS IN THE RUNNING BROOKS'; 305: 'TO WHAT PURPOSE IS THIS WASTE?'; 307: 'FOR ROSALINE'S ALBUM'; 309: 'TWO PARTED'; 311: 'THE BOURNE;' 313: 'DEAD BEFORE DEATH'; 315: 'MY DREAM'; 317: 'COBWEBS'; 319: 'TO THE END'; 321: 'A CHILLY NIGHT'; 323: 'LOOK ON THIS PICTURE AND ON THIS'; 325: 'GONE BEFORE'; 327: 'LIGHT LOVE'; 329: 'LOVE FROM THE NORTH'; 331: 'A PEAL OF BELLS'; 333: ' FOR ONE SAKE'; 335: 'AN APPLE GATHERING' 337: 'AUTUMN'; 339: 'TO-DAY AND TO-MORROW'; 341: 'THE CONVENT THRESHOLD'; 343: 'BY THE SEA'; 345: 'SPRING'; 347: 'COUSIN KATE'; 349: 'NO, THANK YOU, JOHN'; 351: 'BETTER SO'; 353: 'THE QUEEN OF HEARTS'; 355: 'A YEAR'S WINDFALLS'; 357: 'A BIRD'S-EYE VIEW'; 359: 'THE POOR GHOST'; 361: 'LAST NIGHT'; 363: 'WHAT WOULD I GIVE!'; 365: 'HOPING AGAINST HOPE'; 367: 'A FARM WALK' 369: 'SONGS IN A CORNFIELD'; 371: 'JESSIE CAMERON'; 373: 'EVE'; 375: 'MAGGIE A LADY'; 377: 'ENRICA, 1865'; 379: 'A DIRGE'; 381: 'CANNOT SWEETEN'; 383: 'THEY DESIRE A BETTER COUNTRY'; 385: 'AN ECHO FROM WILLOW-WOOD'; 387: 'VENUS'S LOOKING-GLASS'; 389: 'A GREEN CORNFIELD'; 391: 'VALENTINES TO MY MOTHER'; 393: 'MIRRORS OF LIFE AND DEATH'; 395: 'FREAKS OF FASHION'; 397: 'THE KEY-NOTE'; 399: 'JOHNNY'; 401: 'MAIDEN MAY'; 403: 'BRANDONS BOTH'; 405: 'AT LAST'; 407: 'FLUTTERED WINGS'; 409: 'A SONG OF FLIGHT'; 411: 'PASTIME'; 413: 'ONE SEA-SIDE GRAVE'; 415: 'BROTHER

BRUIN'; 417-419: 'SONNETS WRITTEN TO BOUTS-RIMÉS'; 421: 'TO LALLA'; 423: 'CHARON'; 425: 'LOVE'S NAME'; 427-441: 'SING-SONG'; 443: 'AN ALPHABET'; 445: 'PLEADING'; 447-451: 'IL ROSSEGGIAR DELL' ORIENTE'; 453-457: 'NINNA-NANNA'; 459: no RT; 461-493: 'NOTES'; 495: no RT; 497-507: INDEX TO FIRST LINES.

Versos: [2] ii -iv: no RT; vi-x: 'POETICAL WORKS OF CHRISTINA ROSSETTI'; xii: no RT xiv-xxxvi: 'POETICAL WORKS OF CHRISTINA ROSSETTI'; xxxviii: no RT; xl- lxx: 'POETICAL WORKS OF CHRISTINA ROSSETTI'; lxxii - lxxiv: no RT; 2-8: 'GOBLIN MARKET'; 10: 'REPINING'; 12-14: 'THREE NUNS'; 16-18: 'THE LOWEST ROOM'; 20-24: 'FROM HOUSE TO HOME'; 26-34: 'THE PRINCE'S PROGRESS'; 36: 'A ROYAL PRINCESS'; 38-40: 'MAIDEN-SONG'; 42-46: 'THE INIQUITY OF THE FATHERS UPON THE CHILDREN'; 48-54: 'THE MONTHS: A PAGEANT'; 56: 'A BALLAD OF BODING'; 58-62: 'MONNA INNOMINATA'; 64-66: 'AN OLD-WORLD THICKET'; 68-72: 'ALL THY WORKS PRAISE THEE, O LORD'; 74-80: 'LATER LIFE'; 82: 'THE CHINAMAN'; 84: 'BURIAL ANTHEM'; 86: 'SUMMER'; 88: 'MOTHER AND CHILD'; 90: 'LOVE DEFENDED'; 92: 'THE DYING MAN TO HIS BETROTHED'; 94: 'WILL THESE HANDS NE'ER BE CLEAN?'; 96: 'TASSO AND LEONORA'; 98: 'RESURRECTION EVE'; 100-102: 'THE DEAD CITY'; 104: 'THE DREAM'; 106: 'ISIDORA'; 108: 'IMMALEE'; 110: 'DEATH'S CHILL BETWEEN'; 112: 'THE WORLD'S HARMONIES'; 114: 'DEATH IS SWALLOWED UP IN VICTORY'; 116: 'SWEET DEATH'; 118: 'TWO PURSUITS'; 120-144: 'SONGS FOR STRANGERS AND PILGRIMS'; 146: 'THE THREE ENEMIES'; 148: 'EYE HATH NOT SEEN'; 150: 'MOONSHINE'; 152: 'WHITSUN EVE'; 154: 'SLEEP AT SEA'; 156-178: 'SOME FEASTS AND FASTS'; 180: 'PARADISE'; 182: 'UNFORGOTTEN'; 184: 'I WILL LIFT UP MINE EYES UNTO THE HILLS'; 186: 'NOW THEY DESIRE'; 188: 'AFTER THIS THE JUDGMENT'; 190: 'OLD AND NEW YEAR DITTIES'; 192: 'THE HEART KNOWETH ITS OWN BITTERNESS'; 194 - 200: 'DIVERS WORLDS. TIME AND ETERNITY'; 202: 'ADVENT'; 204: 'A BURDEN'; 206 - 214: 'NEW JERUSALEM AND ITS CITIZENS'; 216: 'A SHADOW OF DOROTHEA'; 218 -230: 'CHRIST OUR ALL IN ALL'; 232: 'EASTER EVEN'; 234: 'OUT OF THE DEEP'; 236: 'MARTYRS' SONG'; 238: 'NONE WITH HIM'; 240: 'BY THE WATERS OF BABYLON'; 242: 'DOST THOU NOT CARE?'; 244: 'YOUNG DEATH'; 246: 'A CHRISTMAS CAROL'; 248: 'WHEN MY HEART IS VEXED I WILL COMPLAIN'; 250: 'PATIENCE OF HOPE'; 252: 'UNTIL THE DAY BREAK'; 254: 'IT IS FINISHED'; 256: 'ALL SAINTS'; 258: 'A MARTYR'; 260: 'WHY?'; 262: 'THE THREAD OF LIFE'; 264: 'OUT OF THE DEEP HAVE I CALLED UNTO THEE, OH LORD.'; 266- 268: 'OUT OF THE DEEP HAVE I CALLED UNTO THEE, OH LORD' [no period]; 270 - 276: 'GIFTS AND GRACES'; 278: 'CHRISTMAS CAROLS'; 280: 'YEA I HAVE A GOODLY HERITAGE'; 282: 'FAINT YET PURSUING'; 284: 'THE WORLD. SELF-DESTRUCTION'; 286: 'A PORTRAIT'; 288: 'THREE STAGES'; 290: 'SONG'; 292: 'AFTER DEATH'; 294: 'REMEMBER'; 296: 'SEEKING REST'; 298: 'TWO THOUGHTS OF DEATH'; 300: 'SONG'; 302: 'A FAIR WORLD THOUGH A FALLEN'; 304: 'FROM THE ANTIQUE'; 306: 'TO WHAT PURPOSE IS THIS WASTE?'; 308: 'THREE SEASONS'; 310: 'BALLAD'; 312: 'FROM THE ANTIQUE'; 314: 'THE FIRST SPRING DAY'; 316: 'I HAVE A MESSAGE UNTO THEE'; 318: 'AN AFTER-THOUGHT'; 320: 'SHUT OUT'; 322: 'IN THE LANE'; 324: 'LOOK ON THIS PICTURE AND ON THIS'; 326: 'THE HOUR AND THE GHOST'; 328: 'DOWNCAST'; 330: 'ONE DAY'; 332: 'DAY-DREAMS'; 334: 'MEMORY'; 336: 'MY FRIEND'; 338: 'AUTUMN'; 340: 'THE CONVENT THRESHOLD'; 342: 'YET A LITTLE WHILE'; 344: 'L.E.L.'; 346: 'WHAT GOOD SHALL MY LIFE DO ME?'; 348: 'NOBLE SISTERS'; 350: 'PROMISES LIKE PIE-CRUST'; 352: 'ON THE WING'; 354: 'A RING POSY'; 356: 'A YEAR'S WINDFALLS'; 358: 'LIFE AND DEATH'; 360: 'MARGERY'; 362: 'CHILL'; 364: 'THE GHOST'S PETITION'; 366: 'TWICE'; 368: 'A SKETCH'; 370: 'SONGS IN A CORNFIELD'; 372: 'JESSIE CAMERON'; 374: 'AMOR MUNDI'; 376: 'MAGGIE A LADY'; 378: 'ITALIA, IO TI SALUTO'; 380: 'A SMILE AND A SIGH'; 382: 'FROM METASTASIO'; 384: 'BY WAY OF REMEMBRANCE'; 386: 'THE GERMAN-FRENCH CAMPAIGN'; 388: 'A BIRD SONG'; 390: 'CONFLUENTS'; 392: 'VALENTINES TO MY MOTHER'; 394: 'MIRRORS OF LIFE AND DEATH'; 396: 'FREAKS OF FASHION'; 398: 'TEMPUS FUGIT'; 400: "'HOLLOW-

SOUNDING AND MYSTERIOUS'"; 402: 'DEATH-WATCHES'; 404: 'BRANDONS BOTH'; 406: 'IN THE WILLOW SHADE'; 408: 'MARIANA'; 410: 'PASSING AND GLASSING'; 412: 'MICHAEL F. M. ROSSETTI'; 414: 'A FROG'S FATE'; 416: 'EXULTATE DEO'; 418- 420: 'SONNETS WRITTEN TO BOUTS-RIMÉS'; 422: 'TWO CHARADES'; 424: 'CHILD'S TALK IN APRIL'; 426 - 442: 'SING-SONG'; 444: 'COUNTERBLAST ON PENNY TRUMPET'; 446: 'L'INCOGNITA'; 448 -452: 'IL ROSSEGGIAR DELL' ORIENTE'; 454-456: 'NINNA-NANNA'; 458: 'SOGNANDO'; 460- 506: 'POETICAL WORKS OF CHRISTINA ROSSETTI'; 508: no RT.

Binding: Fine diaper patterned cloth, dark green (Centroid 146). Front and back plain; spine, in gilt 'CHRISTINA | ROSSETTI'S | POEMS | MACMILLAN & Co'; endpapers wove paper, unwatermarked; head and fore-edge rough trimmed, tail trimmed.

Publication: Macmillan's Editions Book lists 3000 copies printed in January 1904 from type and electrotyped, with an additional 3000 in June 1904 from plates. Another printing of 3000 copies "with alterations" took place in January 1906, followed by printings of 2000 in July 1908, April 1911,and July 1914, and a final printing of 1000 in August 1920.

First proposed by WMR to Macmillan in 1895, and revisited in1897, at which point WMR, fearing that he might not live to complete the project, began work on it despite Macmillan's reluctance to commit to the project (*SWMR* 601, 618). In 1899, WMR informed Macmillan that the manuscript was complete, but Macmillan, noting strong sales of CGR's existing works, maintained that the time for a collected edition had not come (*SMWR*, 618-619). In March 1903, reminded by WMR that *Goblin Market* would be out of copyright in 1904, Macmillan agreed to publish, but proved reluctant to negotiate with the Society for Promoting Christian Knowledge, which held copyright for the poems reprinted in *Verses* (1893). Declaring that there was no "great call" for the collected edition without the SPCK poems, which were "among the best things that Christina ever did," WMR agreed to pay £50 towards the SPCK's £100 fee from his royalties (*SWMR* 638). Negotiations among WMR, Macmillan and the SPCK ran from April through July; WMR finished reading the first proof for the volume in August, and finished the last revise on November 15; he received the published book on January 19, 1904 (WMRD).

Printing: 508, '*Printed by* R & R. CLARK, LIMITED, *Edinburgh*.'

Note one: On the first leaf of each gathering of the TxCM copy the letter 'R' appears in the direction line beneath the first column of text, to the right of the signature.

Location: TxCM.

Presentation copies: TxCM: inscribed 'Olivia R. Garnett."

A34.1b   *First edition, Corrected Printing (June 1904)*

Same as first printing except:

Contents: iv: '*First Edition January* 1904 | *Reprinted June* 1904'.

Running titles: No periods in running titles on 264-265.

Publication: In August 1904, WMR presented Macmillan with a list of emendations for the 1904 volume, and received Macmillan's assurance that changes would be made at the next opportunity (WMRD). However, substantive changes were not made until the 1906 printing.

Location: TxU.

A34.1c   *First Edition, Corrected Printing (1906)*

Same as 1904 except:

Title Page: Date changed to 1906.

Contents: iv: 'First Edition January 1904 | *Reprinted June* 1904, 1906'; 415: poem "Brother Bruin" omitted, appears instead on 416; 446: 'Couplet' ("Faith and Hope") added.

Publication: WMR received a copy of the corrected printing in May 1906, noting in his diary that the book included "various revisions made by me a longish while ago, principally to my own editorial matter there" (WMRD). The revisions include corrected dates of several poems, reordering (and moving) poems on page 415-416; the addition of "Couplet" on 445; and several additions and alterations to WMR's notes.

Locations: MoSW; TxU.

A35   POEMS OF CHRISTINA ROSSETTI (GOLDEN TREASURY SERIES) (1904)

A35.1a   First Edition, First Printing

Not seen; information drawn from electronic version of Harvard copy.

Some text in <u>black letter</u>:
POEMS | OF | CHRISTINA ROSSETTI | CHOSEN AND EDITED BY | WILLIAM M. ROSSETTI |
<u>London</u> | MACMILLAN AND CO., Limited | NEW YORK: THE MACMILLAN COMPANY | 1904

Plates: Frontispiece portrait, right-facing profile by DGR of CGR, with caption "Christina Rossetti | from a drawing made by Dante Gabriel Rossetti in 1865. | Emery Walker Ph. Sc."

Poems: (see *Note one*): "Goblin Market," "Monna Innominata" (sonnets 1-14), "Sweet Death," "One Certainty," "A Testimony," "Advent" ("'Come,' Thou dost say to Angels"), "Eye Hath Not Seen," "A Bruised Reed Shall He Not Break," "Moonshine," "The Heart Knoweth Its Own Bitterness" ("Weep yet awhile"), "Whitsun Eve" ("The white dove cooeth in her downy nest"), "There Remaineth Therefore a Rest for the People of God" ("Come, blessed sleep")(sections I and II), "A Harvest," "Sleep at Sea," "Who Have a Form of Godliness," "There Remaineth Therefore a Rest" ("In the grave will be no space"), "Paradise," "Ye Have Forgotten the Exhortation," "The World," "Zion Said," "I Will Lift Up Mine Eyes Unto the Hills" ("I am pale with sick desire"), "How Long?," "Amen," "Now They Desire," "A Christmas Carol" ("The Shepherds had an Angel"), "Not Yours But You," "After This The Judgment," "Old and New Year Ditties" (sections 1-3), "A Better Resurrection," "The Heart Knoweth its Own Bitterness" ("When all the over-work of life"), "From House to Home," "Advent" ("This Advent moon shines cold and clear"), "The Love of Christ which Passeth Knowledge," "A Christmas Carol" ("Before the paling of the stars"), "Easter Even" ("There is nothing more that they can do"), "The Offering of the New Law," "By the Waters of Babylon," "Good Friday" ("Am I a stone, and not a sheep"), "For a Mercy Received," "Martyrs' Song," "The Lowest Place," "Come unto Me," "Who Shall Deliver Me?," "In Patience," "Weary in Well-Doing," "Birds of Paradise," "Dost Thou Not Care?," "If Only," "Long Barren," "Mother Country," "After Communion," "They Desire a Better Country" (sections I-III), "A Christmas Carol" ("In the bleak mid-winter"), "The Master is Come, and Calleth for Thee," "'When My Heart is Vexed I Will Complain'" ("O Lord, how canst Thou say Thou lovest me"), "Saints and Angels," "A Rose Plant in Jericho," "A Ballad of Boding," "An Old-World Thicket," "For Thine Own Sake, O My God," "'Of Him That Was Ready to Perish'," "The Descent From the Cross," "'Take Care of Him'," "A Martyr"("Inner not outer, without gnash of teeth"), "The Thread of Life" (sections 1-3), "Christmas Carol" ("Lo! newborn Jesus"), "A Hope Carol," "Yea I Have a Goodly Heritage," "Faint yet Pursuing"(sections 1-2), "Heaven Overarches," "Dream Land," "Rest," "Sleeping at Last," "The Prince's Progress," "My Dream," "A Chilly Night," "The Hour and the Ghost," "Love from the North," "In the Round Tower at Jhansi," "An Apple Gathering," "Maude Clare," "The Convent Threshold," "Sister Maude," "Noble Sisters," "A Royal Princess," "Maiden-Song," "A Bird's-Eye View," "The Poor Ghost," "A Farm Walk," "Songs in a Cornfield," "Jessie Cameron," "Eve," "Amor Mundi," "Husband and Wife," "Minnie and Mattie," "Brandons Both," "A Fisher-Wife," "One Foot on Sea, and One on Shore," "Three Stages" (sections 1-3), "Looking Forward," "Shut Out," "Acme," "Introspective," "Another Spring," "Memory" (sections I-II), "L. E. L.," "Mirage," "What would I give!," "Twice," "If I Had Words," "En Route," "An 'Immurata' Sister," "Of My Life," "By Way of Remembrance," "Love Lies Bleeding," "Confluents," "Valentines to my Mother" (sections 1-2), "One Sea-Side Grave," "Song" ("When I am dead, my dearest"), "The Summer is Ended," "Remember," "A Pause," "Up-Hill," "At Home," "To-day and To-morrow" (sections 1-2), "Yet a Little While" ("These days are long before I die"), "Life and Death," "Twilight Calm," "To What Purpose is This Waste?," "Child's Talk in April," "A Green Cornfield," "Freaks of Fashion," "Song" ("Oh roses for the flush of youth"), "Three Seasons," "Seasons" ("In Springtime when the leaves are young"), "Seasons" ("Crocuses and snowdrops wither"),

"The First Spring Day," "May" ("I cannot tell you how it was"), "May" ("'Sweet life'"), "Winter: My Secret," "Autumn," "Winter Rain," "Spring," "June," "A Year's Windfalls," "Autumn Violets," "Harebell, Rose, Lily" ("Hope is like a harebell trembling from its birth"), "An October Garden," "A Wintry Sonnet," "An End," "Withering," "A Wish," "A Soul," "Dream-Love," "From the Antique" ("It's a weary life, it is, she said"), "Echo," "Cobwebs," "Let Patience Have her Perfect Work," "A Triad," "In an Artist's Studio," "A Birthday," "Wife to Husband," "In Progress," "On the Wing," "A Dumb Friend," "Meeting"("If we shall live, we live"), "Grown and Flown," "From Sunset to Star Rise," "The German-French Campaign" (in two parts, "I. 'Thy Brother's Blood Crieth'" and "II. 'To-day for Me'"), "Venus's Looking-Glass," "I dug and dug" ("I dug and dug amongst the snow"), "Sea-Sand and Sorrow" ("What are heavy? sea-sand and sorrow"), "Wind-flowers" ("Twist me a crown of wind-flowers"), "Alice" ("Dancing on the hill-tops"), "Sisters" ("Sing me a song"), "Wind" ("The wind has such a rainy sound"), "Winifred" ("Rosy maiden Winifred"), "Emblem Flowers" ("Roses blushing red and white"), "Coral" ("O Sailor, come ashore"), "A Moon-Track" ("Is the moon tired? She looks so pale"), "Goodbye" ("'Goodbye in fear, goodbye in sorrow"), "Baby Asleep" ("Baby lies so fast asleep"), "Death-Watches," "Fluttered Wings," "Resurgam," "Later Life: a Double Sonnet of Sonnets" (sonnets 1-28), "The Months: A Pageant."

Printing: 332: '*Printed by* R. & R. CLARK, LIMITED, *Edinburgh.*'

Publication: In August 1904, WMR suggested that Macmillan publish a "small volume" of CGR's "best poems of whatever class" (*SWMR* 640). The Terms Book in the Macmillan Archives records a proposal to WMR for a book of CGR's poems to be published in the Golden Treasury series, with WMR receiving half profits.

By September 7, Macmillan had approved WMR's selections for the volume. However, upon learning that the arrangement Macmillan had made with the Society for Promoting Christian Knowledge to reprint poems in the 1904 *Poetical Works* would not hold for the Golden Treasury volume, WMR was forced to remove "several fine things" (WMRD, 5 September 1904). By 27 September, he had mailed the volume's Preface to Macmillan. He finished reading proofs for the volume on November 4 (WMRD).

The Macmillan Archives editions book lists 2000 copies printed from type and electroplate in November 1904. A second printing of 2000 copies from plates December, with additional printings of 3000 in October 1905 and November 1907, and of 2000 in July 1910, January 1913, March 1918, January 1923, September 1927, and May 1931.

Advertised in the *Academy* (3 December 1904: 549); *Publishers' Weekly,* "Weekly Record of New Publications" (4 February 1905: 537-538).

Price: Cloth bindings ("Pott 8vo" and "cloth elegant"), 2s. 6d.; limp leather, 3s. 6d. In United States: cloth $1.00, limp leather $1.50.

Reviewed in the *Academy* (24 December 1904: 641); *Journal of Education* (July 1905: 462).

Note one: WMR gives titles to several *Sing-Song* verses (for example, "Dancing on the hill-tops" becomes "Alice" and "O sailor, come ashore" becomes "Coral").

Location: MH (via Google Books).

A35.1b   *First Edition, Second Printing*

Same as first edition, first printing except:

Pagination (see Collation): [1-2] i-iv v-xix xx xxi-xxvi 1 2-325 326 327-332.

Plate: Plate mark 128 x 87.

Collation: (158 x 109): π² a⁴ b⁴ B-X⁸ Y⁶; $1 signed.

Contents (some text in <u>black letter</u>): [1]-[2] blank; i: half-title '<u>Golden Treasury Series</u> | POEMS OF CHRISTINA ROSSETTI'; ii: blank; iii: title; iv: '*First Edition, December* 1904 | *Reprinted December 1904*'; v: 'PREFACE'; xv: 'EXTRACTS FROM REVIEWS'; xx: blank; xxi 'CONTENTS'; 1-325: poems; 326: blank; 327: 'INDEX OF FIRST LINES'; 332: printer's imprint.

Typography and paper: (124) 115 x 61 (p. 17); various lines per page (up to 35). Preliminary text more closely set (41 lines per page). Wove paper, unwatermarked.

Running titles:

Rectos: [1], <u>i-iii</u>, v: no RT; vii-xiii: 'PREFACE'; xv: no RT; xvii-xix: 'EXTRACTS FROM REVIEWS'; xxi: no RT; xxiii-xxv: 'CONTENTS'; <u>1</u>: no RT; 3-17:'GOBLIN MARKET'; 19-25: 'MONNA INNOMINATA'; 27: 'SWEET DEATH'; 29: 'A TESTIMONY'; 31-33: 'EYE HATH NOT SEEN'; 35 'MOONSHINE'; 37: 'HEART'S BITTERNESS'; 39: 'REST FOR THE PEOPLE OF GOD'; 41-43: 'SLEEP AT SEA'; 45: 'THERE REMAINETH A REST'; 47-49: 'FORGOTTEN EXHORTATION'; 51: 'I WILL LIFT UP MINE EYES'; 53: 'AMEN'; 55: 'A CHRISTMAS CAROL'; 57: 'NOT YOURS BUT YOU'; 59: 'AFTER THIS THE JUDGMENT'; 61: 'OLD AND NEW YEAR DITTIES'; 63: 'HEART'S BITTERNESS'; 65-73: 'FROM HOUSE TO HOME'; 75: 'ADVENT'; 77: 'A CHRISTMAS CAROL'; 79: 'THE OFFERING OF THE NEW LAW'; 81: 'BY THE WATERS OF BABYLON'; 83: 'FOR A MERCY RECIEVED'; 85: 'MARTYRS' SONG'; 87: 'WHO SHALL DELIVER ME?'; 89: 'BIRDS OF PARADISE'; 91: 'DOST THOU NOT CARE?'; 93: 'MOTHER COUNTRY'; 95: 'AFTER COMMUNION'; 97: 'A CHRISTMAS CAROL'; 99: 'THE MASTER IS COME'; 101: 'SAINTS AND ANGELS'; 103: 'A ROSE PLANT IN JERICHO'; 105-109: 'A BALLAD OF BODING'; 111-115: 'AN OLD-WORLD THICKET'; 117: 'FOR THINE OWN SAKE, O MY GOD'; 119: 'TAKE CARE OF HIM'; 121-123: 'A MARTYR'; 125: 'THE THREAD OF LIFE'; 127: 'CHRISTMAS CAROL'; 129: 'FAINT YET PURSUING'; 131: 'DREAM LAND'; 133-149: 'THE PRINCE'S PROGRESS'; 151: 'MY DREAM'; 153: 'A CHILLY NIGHT'; 155: 'THE HOUR AND THE GHOST'; 157: 'LOVE FROM THE NORTH'; 159: 'IN THE ROUND TOWER AT JHANSI'; 161: 'MAUDE CLARE'; 163-167: 'THE CONVENT THRESHOLD'; 169: 'NOBLE SISTERS'; 171-175: 'A ROYAL PRINCESS'; 177-183: 'MAIDEN-SONG'; 185: 'A BIRD'S-EYE VIEW'; 187: 'THE POOR GHOST'; 189: 'A FARM WALK'; 191-193: 'SONGS IN A CORNFIELD'; 195-197: 'JESSIE CAMERON'; 199: 'EVE'; 201: 'AMOR MUNDI'; 203: 'HUSBAND AND WIFE'; 205-207: 'BRANDONS BOTH'; 209: 'FISHER-WIFE'; 211-213: 'THREE STAGES'; 215: 'SHUT OUT'; 217: 'ANOTHER SPRING'; 219: 'MEMORY'; 221: 'MIRAGE'; 223: 'TWICE'; 225: 'EN ROUTE'; 227: 'OF MY LIFE'; 229: 'BY WAY OF REMEMBRANCE'; 231: 'CONFLUENTS'; 233: 'SONG'; 235: 'UP-HILL'; 237: 'TO-DAY'; 239: 'YET A LITTLE WHILE'; 241: 'TWILIGHT CALM'; 243-245: 'TO WHAT PURPOSE IS THIS WASTE?'; 247: 'CHILD'S TALK IN APRIL'; 249: 'A GREEN CORNFIELD'; 251: 'FREAKS OF FASHION'; 253: 'THREE SEASONS'; 255: 'SEASONS'; 257: 'MAY'; 259: 'AUTUMN'; 261: 'WINTER RAIN'; 263: 'SPRING'; 265-267: 'A YEAR'S WINDFALLS'; 269: 'AN OCTOBER GARDEN'; 271: 'WITHERING'; 273: 'DREAM-LOVE'; 275: 'FROM THE ANTIQUE'; 277: 'LET PATIENCE HAVE HER PERFECT WORK'; 279: 'IN AN ARTIST'S STUDIO'; 281: 'WIFE TO HUSBAND'; 283: 'A DUMB FRIEND'; 285: 'GROWN AND FLOWN'; 287: 'THE GERMAN-FRENCH CAMPAIGN'; 289: 'I DUG AND DUG'; 291: 'SISTERS'; 293: 'CORAL'; 295: 'FLUTTERED WINGS'; 297: no RT; 299-309: 'LATER LIFE'; 311: no RT; 313-325: 'THE MONTHS: A PAGEANT'; 327: no RT; 329-331: 'INDEX OF FIRST LINES'

Versos: [2], <u>ii-iv</u>: no RT; vi-xiv: 'PREFACE'; xvi-xviii: 'EXTRACTS FROM REVIEWS'; xx: no RT; xxii-xxvi: 'CONTENTS'; 2-16: 'GOBLIN MARKET'; 18-26: 'MONNA INNOMINATA'; 28-30: 'A TESTIMONY'; 32: 'EYE HATH NOT SEEN'; 34: 'A BRUISED REED'; 36: 'MOONSHINE'; 38: 'WHITSUN EVE'; 40: 'A HARVEST'; 42: 'SLEEP AT SEA'; 44: 'A FORM OF GODLINESS'; 46: 'PARADISE'; 48: 'FORGOTTEN EXHORTATION'; 50: 'ZION SAID'; 52: 'HOW LONG?'; 54: 'NOW THEY DESIRE'; 56: 'A CHRISTMAS CAROL'; 58: 'AFTER THIS THE JUDGMENT'; 60: 'OLD AND NEW YEAR DITTIES'; 62: 'A BETTER RESURRECTION'; 64: 'HEART'S BITTERNESS'; 66-72: 'FROM HOUSE TO HOME'; 74: 'ADVENT'; 76: 'THE LOVE OF CHRIST'; 78: 'EASTER EVEN'; 80: 'THE

OFFERING OF THE NEW LAW'; 82: 'GOOD FRIDAY'; 84: 'MARTYRS' SONG'; 86: 'THE LOWEST PLACE'; 88: 'IN PATIENCE'; 90: 'BIRDS OF PARADISE'; 92: 'LONG BARREN'; 94: 'MOTHER COUNTRY'; 96: 'THEY DESIRE A BETTER COUNTRY'; 98: 'A CHRISTMAS CAROL'; 100: 'WHEN MY HEART IS VEXED'; 102: 'SAINTS AND ANGELS'; 104-110: 'A BALLAD OF BODING'; 112-116: 'AN OLD-WORLD THICKET'; 118: 'READY TO PERISH'; 120: 'TAKE CARE OF HIM'; 122-124: 'A MARTYR'; 126: 'THE THREAD OF LIFE'; 128: 'A HOPE CAROL'; 130: 'HEAVEN OVERARCHES'; 132: 'REST'; 134-150: 'THE PRINCE'S PROGRESS'; 152: 'MY DREAM'; 154: 'A CHILLY NIGHT'; 156: 'THE HOUR AND THE GHOST'; 158: 'LOVE FROM THE NORTH'; 160: 'AN APPLE GATHERING'; 162: 'MAUDE CLARE'; 164-166: 'THE CONVENT THRESHOLD'; 168: 'SISTER MAUDE'; 170: 'NOBLE SISTERS'; 172-174: 'A ROYAL PRINCESS'; 176-182: 'MAIDEN-SONG'; 184-186: 'A BIRD'S-EYE VIEW'; 188-190: 'A FARM WALK'; 192-194: 'SONGS IN A CORNFIELD'; 196-198: 'JESSIE CAMERON'; 200: 'EVE'; 202: 'HUSBAND AND WIFE'; 204: 'MINNIE AND MATTIE'; 206-208: 'BRANDONS BOTH'; 210: 'ONE FOOT ON SEA'; 212: 'THREE STAGES'; 214: 'LOOKING FORWARD'; 216: 'INTROSPECTIVE'; 218: 'MEMORY'; 220: 'L. E. L.'; 222: 'TWICE'; 224: 'IF I HAD WORDS'; 226: 'AN IMMURATA SISTER'; 228: 'BY WAY OF REMEMBRANCE'; 230: 'CONFLUENTS'; 232: 'VALENTINES TO MY MOTHER'; 234: 'REMEMBER'; 236: 'AT HOME'; 238: 'YET A LITTLE WHILE'; 240: 'LIFE AND DEATH'; 242: 'TWILIGHT CALM'; 244-246: 'TO WHAT PURPOSE IS THIS WASTE?'; 248: 'CHILD'S TALK IN APRIL'; 250-252: 'FREAKS OF FASHION'; 254: 'SEASONS'; 256: 'MAY'; 258: 'WINTER: MY SECRET'; 260: 'AUTUMN'; 262: 'WINTER RAIN'; 264: 'JUNE'; 266: 'A YEAR'S WINDFALLS'; 268: 'AUTUMN VIOLETS'; 270: 'AN END'; 272: 'A SOUL'; 274: 'DREAM-LOVE'; 276: 'ECHO'; 278: 'LET PATIENCE HAVE HER WORK'; 280: 'A BIRTHDAY'; 282: 'ON THE WING'; 284: 'MEETING'; 286-288: 'THE GERMAN-FRENCH CAMPAIGN'; 290: 'WIND-FLOWERS'; 292: 'WINIFRED'; 294: 'BABY ASLEEP'; 296: 'RESURGAM'; 298-310: 'LATER LIFE'; 312-324: 'THE MONTHS: A PAGEANT'; 326: no RT; 328-332: 'INDEX OF FIRST LINES'.

Binding: Calico cloth, dark blue (Centroid 183). Front: blindstamped thin-thick rule across top, two rules across the bottom; in center, gilt medallion with "GTS" in center. Back: blindstamped rules at top and bottom, same as front. Spine: in gilt, '[thin-thick rule] | POEMS | OF | CHRISTINA | ROSSETTI | [rule] MACMILLAN & Co [with dot beneath superscript 'o'] | [rule]'. Endpapers: white wove paper, thicker than sheets. Edges: top rough trimmed; foreedge untrimmed; tail trimmed.

A two leaf advertisement for the Golden Treasury series, dated '10.12.14' follows the sheets. The advertisement states that volumes in the series are "Uniformly printed in Pott 8vo, with Vignette Titles by Sir Noel Paton, T. Woolner, W. Holman Hunt, Sir J. E. Millais, Arthur Hughes, etc. Engraved on steel. Bound in extra cloth" and priced at 2s. 6d. The advertisement includes 'Select Poems of Christina Rossetti' and indicates that this is one of the titles also available in "Presentation Editions" of "Cloth elegant, full gilt backs and gilt tops" at 2s. 6d., and "Limp leather, full gilt backs and gilt edges" at 3s. 6d.

Location: UPB; Ives.

A36 THE FAMILY LETTERS OF CHRISTINA GEORGINA ROSSETTI (1908)

A36.1a.i *First edition, British issue*

The Family Letters | of | Christina Georgina Rossetti | With some Supplementary Letters | and Appendices | Edited by | William Michael Rossetti | She stands there patient, nerved with inner might, | Indomitable in her feebleness, | Her face and will athirst against the light. | LONDON | BROWN, LANGHAM & Co., Ltd. | 78 NEW BOND STREET | MCMVIII

Pagination: i-vi vii-xiii xiv xv-xxii xxiii-xxiv 1-233 234 235-242 243-244.

Plates:

1) Frontispiece, portrait of CGR with engraved caption, 125 x 94, plate mark 157 x 111; caption text 'Christina Georgina Rossetti. | From a tinted crayon drawing by Dante Rossetti 1877.' With tissue guard.

2) Facing 1, photograph of building with black line border, 159 x 99; letterpress caption 'CHRISTINA GEORGINA ROSSETTI'S BIRTH-HOUSE. | 10 Hallam Street, Portland Place; formerly 38 Charlotte Street. | *Photograph taken in* 1908. | [*To face p.* 1.' No tissue guard.

3) Facing 21, cartoon, 140.3 x 93, woman sketching a man, including caption '"WE NE'ER| SHALL LOOK | UPON HIS | LIKE AGAIN." | Oh Ah!" | S J'; letterpress caption 'SKETCH BY DANTE GABRIEL ROSSETTI. | *See p.* 22. | [*To face p.* 21.' No tissue guard.

4) Facing 22, facsimile of manuscript, 148.3 x 95; letterpress caption 'FACSIMILE FROM ROSSETTI'S LETTER. | *See p.* 22. | [*To face p.* 22.' No tissue guard.

5) Facing 29, photograph of Rossetti family with black line border, 128 x 92; letterpress caption 'DANTE, CHRISTINA, FRANCES AND WILLIAM ROSSETTI. | *From a Photograph taken by Rev. C. L. Dodgson* (*Lewis Carroll*) *in Dante Rossetti's Garden*, c. 1894. | [*To face p.* 29.' No tissue guard.

6) Facing 45, three line drawings of animals (womat, squirrels, fox) mounted on gray background with a black line border and headed by letterpress 'CHRISTINA ROSSETTI', 172 x 87; letterpress caption 'FROM PENCIL DRAWINGS BY CHRISTINA ROSSETTI. | *Animals in the Zöological Gardens, London*, c. 1862. | [*To face p.* 45.' No tissue guard.

7) Facing 84, portrait with black line border, 120 x 98.7, letterpress caption 'FRANCES M. L. ROSSETTI. | *From an Oil Portrait by Dante Rossetti*, c. 1865. | [*To face p.* 84.' No tissue guard.

8) Facing 142, photograph with black line border, 94 x 29; letterpress caption 'CHARLES BAGOT CAYLEY. | *From a Photograph*, c 1866. | *To face p.* 142.' No tissue guard.

9) Facing 144, photograph, 171.3 x 94.3; letterpress caption 'THE GRAVE-CROSS OF DANTE ROSSETTI. | *Designed by Ford Madox Brown*, 1883. | [*To face p.* 144.' No tissue guard.

10) Facing 206, facsimile of manuscript poem titled 'The End of the Year', 131 x 98; letterpress caption 'FACSIMILE OF A POEM BY CHRISTINA ROSSETTI. | [*To face p.* 206.' No tissue guard.

11) Facing 222, photograph of a building with black line border, 179 x 98; letterpress caption 'THE HOUSE IN WHICH CHRISTINA ROSSETTI DIED. | 30 Torrington Square. | *Photograph taken in* 1908. | [*To face p.* 222.' No tissue guard.

Collation: [213 x 135]: a^4 b^8 1-14^8 15^{10}. $1 signed, except 15 signed also '*15' on 2. 134 leaves.

Contents: i: half-title 'The Family Letters | of | Christina Georgina Rossetti'; ii: blank; iii: title; iv: printer's imprint; v: dedication 'THESE LETTERS | BY | CHRISTINA ROSSETTI | ARE INSCRIBED BY HER BROTHER TO THE | MEMORY OF OUR MOTHER | TO WHOM HER OWN BOOKS WERE | CONSTANTLY DEDICATED'; vi: blank; vii: 'PREFACE'; xiv: blank; xv: 'CONTENTS'; xxiii: 'LIST OF ILLUSTRATIONS'; xxiv: blank; 1: text headed 'THE FAMILY LETTERS | OF | CHRISTINA GEORGINA ROSSETTI'; 207: 'APPENDIX'; 234: blank; 235: 'INDEX'; 243: printer's imprint; 244: blank.

Poems: "So I Began My Walk of Life: No Stop."

Typography and paper: (178) 169 x 98 (p. 138, direction line p.17), 38 lines per page. *Notes* section is (181) 171 x 98, 42 lines per page (p. 209). Vertical chainlines, 25 mm apart. Unwatermarked.

Running titles:

Rectos: <u>i</u>-vii: no RT; ix-xiii: 'PREFACE'; xv: no RT; xvii-xxi: 'CONTENTS'; xxiii-1: no RT; 3: '1848–TO WILLIAM ROSSETTI'; 5-11: '1849–TO WILLIAM ROSSETTI'; 13-15: '1850–TO WILLIAM ROSSETTI'; 17-19: '1851–TO WILLIAM ROSSETTI'; 21: '1852–FROM DANTE ROSSETTI'; 23: '1853–TO WILLIAM ROSSETTI'; 25: '1858–TO WILLIAM ROSSETTI'; 27: '1862–TO DANTE ROSSETTI'; 29: 1866–TO WILLIAM ROSSETTI'; 31: '1870–TO DANTE ROSSETTI'; 33: 1871–TO DANTE ROSSETTI'; 35-37: '1872–TO WILLIAM ROSSETTI'; 39: '1873–TO LUCY BROWN'; 41: '1873–TO WILLIAM ROSSETTI'; 43-47: '1874–TO DANTE ROSSETTI'; 49: '1875–TO WILLIAM ROSSETTI'; 51-55: '1875–TO DANTE ROSSETTI'; 57: '1876–TO WILLIAM ROSSETTI'; 59: '1876–TO DANTE ROSSETTI'; 61-63: '1876–TO WILLIAM ROSSETTI'; 65: '1877–FROM CAYLEY'; 67-69: '1877–TO WILLIAM ROSSETTI'; 71: '1877–TO SHIELDS'; 73-77: '1878–TO DANTE ROSSETTI'; 79: '1879–TO WILLIAM ROSSETTI'; 81-83: '1878–TO DANTE ROSSETTI'; 85-89: '1880–TO DANTE ROSSETTI'; 90-99: '1881–TO DANTE ROSSETTI'; 101: '1881–FROM CAYLEY'; 103: '1881–TO LUCY ROSSETTI'; 105: '1882–FROM DANTE ROSSETTI'; 107-115: '1882–TO WILLIAM ROSSETTI'; 117: '1882–ROM LADY MOUNT-TEMPLE'; 119: '1882–TO WILLIAM ROSSETTI'; 121: '1882–TO LUCY ROSSETTI'; 123: '1883–TO CAYLEY'; 125: '1883–FROM SWINBURNE'; 127-135: '1883–TO WILLIAM ROSSETTI'; 137: '1883–TO LUCY ROSSETTI'; 139: '1883–FROM PROFESSOR CAYLEY'; 141: '1883–FROM SHIELDS'; 143-145: '1884–TO WILLIAM ROSSETTI'; 147: '1884–FROM SWINBURNE'; 149-153: '1886–TO LUCY ROSSETTI'; 155-157: '1886–TO WILLIAM ROSSETTI'; 159-161: '1887–TO WILLIAM ROSSETTI'; 163: '1887–TO LUCY ROSSETTI'; 165: '1888–TO LUCY ROSSETTI'; 167: '1888–TO WILLIAM ROSSETTI'; 169: '1888–TO LUCY ROSSETTI'; 171: '1889–TO ARTHUR ROSSETTI'; 173: '1889–TO LUCY ROSSETTI'; 175: '1890–TO WILLIAM ROSSETTI'; 177-179: '1891–TO WILLIAM ROSSETTI'; 181: '1891–TO LUCY ROSSETTI'; 183: '1892–TO LUCY ROSSETTI'; 185-189: '1892–TO WILLIAM ROSSETTI'; 191-201: '1893–TO WILLIAM ROSSETTI'; 203-205: '1894–TO WILLIAM ROSSETTI'; 207-221: 'APPENDIX–WILLIAM ROSSETTI'; 223-231: 'APPENDIX–FRANCES ROSSETTI'; 233: 'APPENDIX–CHRISTINA ROSSETTI'; 235: no RT; 237-241: 'INDEX'; 243: no RT.

Versos: ii-vi: no RT; viii-xii: 'PREFACE'; xiv: no RT; xvi-xxii: 'CONTENTS'; xxiv: no RT; 2-232: 'CHRISTINA ROSSETTI'S LETTERS'; 234: no RT; 236-242: 'INDEX'; 242-244: no RT.

Binding: Buckram, deep bluish green (Centroid 165). Front (in gilt): 'FAMILY LETTER | OF | CHRISTINA | ROSSETTI | W. M. ROSSETTI'; back plain. Spine (in gilt): 'FAMILY | LETTERS | OF | CHRISTINA | ROSSETTI | W. M. ROSSETTI | BROWN | LANGHAM | & Cº Lᵗᵈ'. Endpapers same as sheets. Edges: top edge gilt, fore-edge and tail rough trimmed.

Publication: Lacon Watson proposed a two volume collection of CGR's letters to WMR, who had begun work on the project by January 1907 (*SWMR*, 657-658). Later in the year, Watson asked WMR to shorten the collection, which resulted in his "cutting out 200 items, more or less" (*SWMR* 658).
    Advertised in the London *Times* (14 December 1908: 9).
    Price: 15s.
    Reviewed in the *Times Literary Supplement* (12 November 1908: 403).

Printing: printer's imprint on <u>iv</u>, <u>243</u>: 'RICHARD CLAY & SONS, LIMITED, | BREAD STREET HILL, E. C., AND | BUNGAY, SUFFOLK.'

Locations: TxCM (rebound); TxU.

A36.1a.ii   *First Edition, American Issue (1908)*

Same as British except:

The Family Letters | of | Christina Georgina Rossetti | With some Supplementary Letters | and Appendices | Edited by | William Michael Rossetti | She stands there patient, nerved with inner might, | Indomitable in her feebleness, | Her face and will athirst against the light. | NEW YORK | CHARLES SCRIBNER'S SONS | 1908

Binding: Linen, deep bluish green (Centroid 16). Endpapers same as sheets. Edges: top edge gilt, fore-edge and tail rough trimmed.

Publication: Priced at $3.50 as an "imported" book in *Scribners Magazine Advertiser* (December 1908: 63) and in the *American Catalogue* for 1908, but some mentions of the book give the price as $4.50 (*New York Times, Book Buyer*). Presumably composed, at least initially, of sheets from the British edition; I have not been able to confirm any additional printings in the United States.

Announced in *Book Buyer* (September 1908: 132) and *New York Times* (October 23 1908: BR597).

Reviewed in *New York Times* (December 5, 1908: 747); *Dial* (January 1, 1909: 24); *Bookman* (February 1909: 619); *North American Review* (April 1909: 618-621).

Locations: TxHR; Washington State University.

A37 **THE COMPLETE POEMS OF CHRISTINA ROSSETTI (1979-1990)**

A37.1 *First Edition*

The Complete | *Poems of* | CHRISTINA | ROSSETTI | A VARIORUM EDITION | VOLUME I | Edited, with Textual Notes | and Introductions, by | R. W. CRUMP | LOUISIANA STATE UNIVERSITY PRESS | BATON ROUGE & LONDON

Three volumes. First volume published 1979 (all dates from copyright notice on verso of title). Title Page unchanged in subsequent volumes except for line 6: 'VOLUME II' (published 1986); 'VOLUME III' (published 1990).

Contents: Volume III includes the following poems not published in CGR's lifetime or in WMR's collections: "Heaven"; "Corydon's Lament and Resolution"; "Rosalind"; "Pitia a Damone"; "The Faithless Sheperdess"; "Ariadne to Theseus"; "A Hymn for Christmas Day"; "Love and Death"; "Despair"; "Easter Morning"; "A Tirsi"; "The Last Words of St. Telemachus"; "Lord Thomas and Fair Margaret"; "Charade"; "Hope in Grief"; "Song" ("I saw her, she was lovely"); "Praise of Love"; "Young men were fickle found/Since summer trees were leafy"; "A Counsel"; "Lines/Given With a Penwiper"; "One of the Dead"; "O Death Where is thy Sting"; "Undine"; "Floral Teaching"; "Death"; "A Hopeless Case/Nydia"; "Ellen Middleton"; "Grown Cold"; "Zara" ("The pale sad face of her I wronged"); "Listen, and I Will Tell You Of A Face"; "Strange Voices Sing Among the Planets Which"; "Sleep, Sleep, Happy One"; "What Sappho would have said had her leap cured instead of killing her"; "Sonnet" ("Some say that love and joy are one, and so"); "The Last Complaint"; "Have You Forgotten?"; "A Year Afterwards"; "Once"; "A Dream"; "Song" ("I have loved you for long long years Ellen"); "Let Them Rejoice in their Beds"; "All Night I Dream You Love Me Well"; "Epitaph"; "Guesses"; "Zara" ("I dreamed that loving me he would love on"); "An Answer"; "A Yawn"; "'Then They That Feared The Lord Spake Often One to Another'"; "The Massacre of Prugia." "'I Have Done With Hope'"; "Along The High Road The Way Is Too Long"; "From Early Dawn Until The Flush Of Noon"; "O Glorious Sea That In Each Climbing Wave"; "Oh Thou Who Tell'st Me That All Hope Is Over"; "Surely There Is An Aching Voice Within"; "The Spring Is Come Again Not As At First"; "Who Shall My Wandering Thoughts Steady & Fix"; "You Who Look On Passed Ages As A Glass"; "The Succession of Kings"; "A True Story"; "Mr. And Mrs. Scott, And I"; "Gone to His Rest"; "I Said 'All's Over'– & I Made My"; "A Roundel Seems To Fit A Round Of Days"; "4th May Morning"; "Quanto A Lei Grata Io Sono"; "On The Note You Do Not Send Me"; "Hail, Noble Face of Noble Friend"; "Hymn" ("O the bitter shame and sorrow").

Location: Ives.

A38   **THE LETTERS OF CHRISTINA ROSSETTI (1999-2004)**

A38.1   *First Edition*

Within decorative compartment:
THE | LETTERS OF | CHRISTINA | ROSSETTI | VOLUME 1 • 1843-1873 | [ornament, leaf] | EDITED BY | Antony H. Harrison | THE UNIVERSITY PRESS OF VIRGINIA | CHARLOTTESVILLE & LONDON

Four volumes. Title Page unchanged in subsequent volumes except for line 5: 'VOLUME 2 • 1874-1881' (published 1999); 'VOLUME 3 • 1882-1886' (published 2000); 'VOLUME 4 • 1887-1894' (published 2004).

Location: Ives.

ILLUSTRATIONS

Dante Gabriel Rossetti, colored chalks on paper, circa 1866. Fitzwilliam Museum, Cambridge.

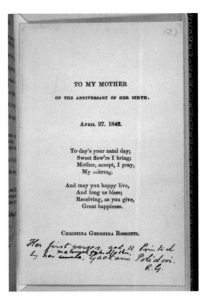

A1, *To My Mother on the Anniversary of her Birth* (1842).

A2.1, *Verses* (1847).

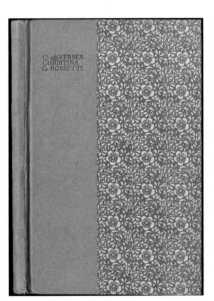

A2.2, *Verses* (1906).

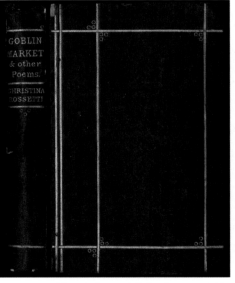

A3.1, *Goblin Market and Other Poems* (1862). Horizontal binding (above left); engraved title page (above right); letterpress title page (below left); frontispiece (below right).

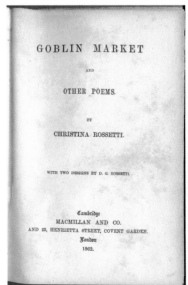

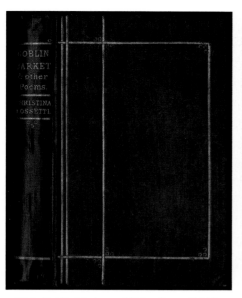

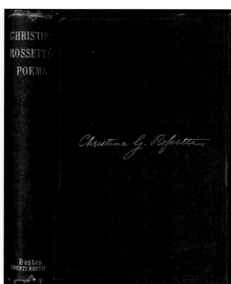

A3.2, *Goblin Market and Other Poems* (1865).

A4.1a, *Poems* (1866). First printing.

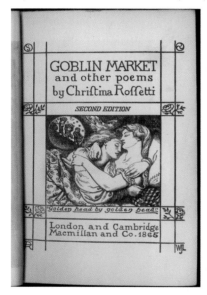

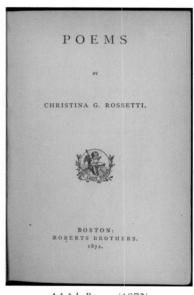

A4.1b, *Poems* (1866). Second printing.

A4.1d, *Poems* (1872).

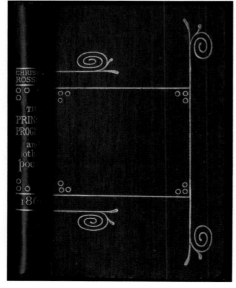

A5.1, *The Prince's Progress
and Other Poems* (1866).

A6.1, *Consider* (1867).

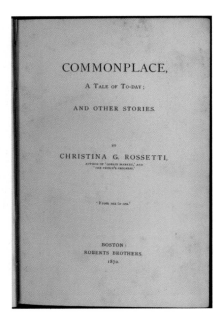

A7.1a.ii, *Commonplace, A Tale of To-Day; And Other Stories* (1870).

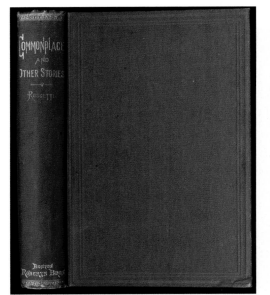

A7.1a.i, *Commonplace, And Other Short Stories* (1870).

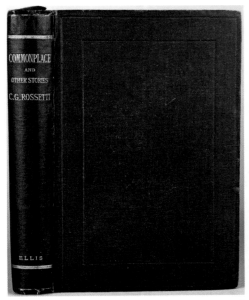

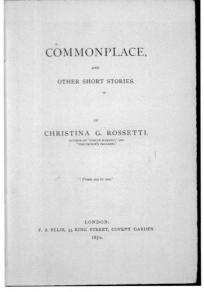

A7.1a.iii, *Commonplace, And Other Short Stories* (1871).

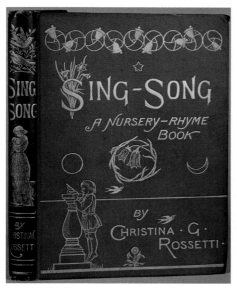
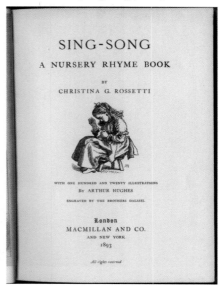

A8.1a.i, *Sing-Song* (1872). Binding A.

A8.2, *Sing-Song* (1893).

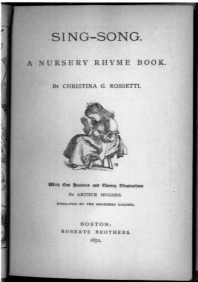

A8.1b.i, *Sing-Song* (Roberts Brothers, 1872).

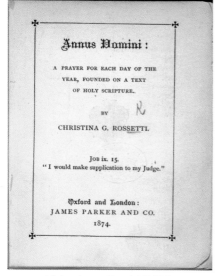

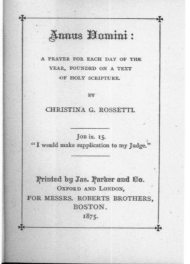

A9.1a, *Annus Domini* (1874).

A9.1b, *Annus Domini* (1875).

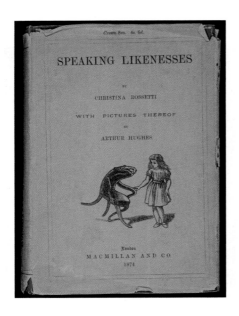
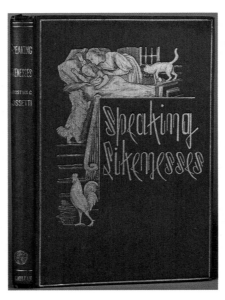
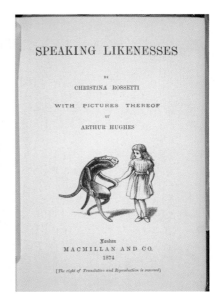

A10.1a, *Speaking Likenesses* (1874).

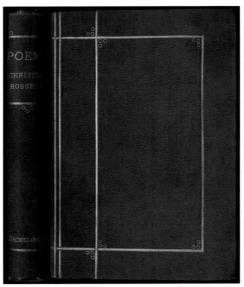
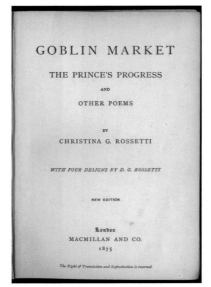

A11.1a, *Goblin Market, The Prince's Progress, and Other Poems* (1875).

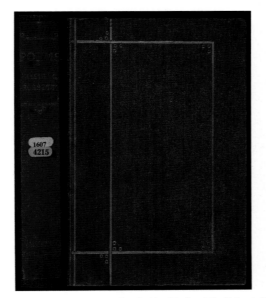
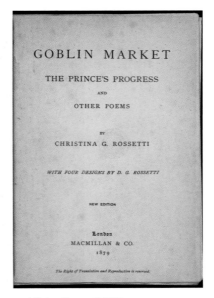

A11.1b, *Goblin Market, The Prince's Progress, and Other Poems* (1879).

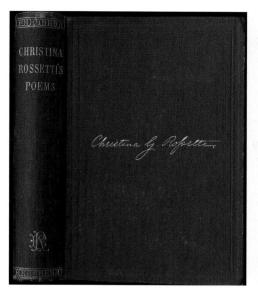

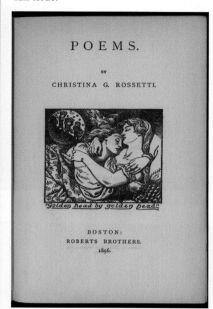

A12.1c.i *Poems*
(Roberts Brothers, 1896).
Tall Issue.

A12.1a, *Poems* (Roberts Brothers, 1876).

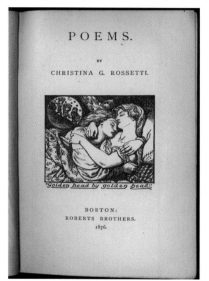

A12.1c.ii *Poems*
(Roberts Brothers, 1896).
Short Issue.

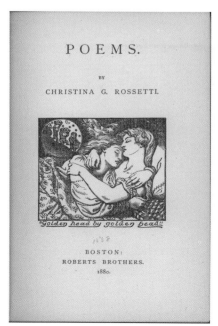

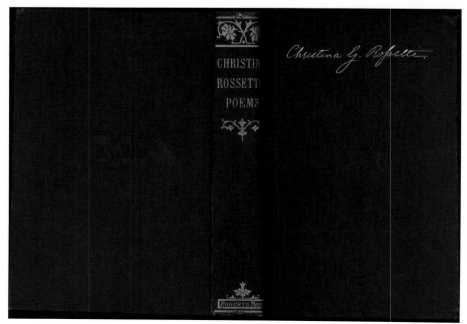

A12.1b, *Poems* (Roberts Brothers, 1880).

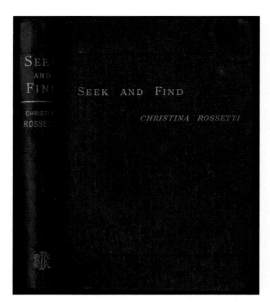
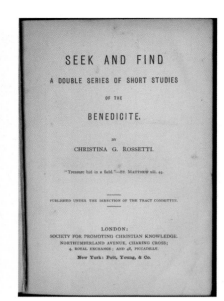

A13.1a, *Seek and Find* (1879).

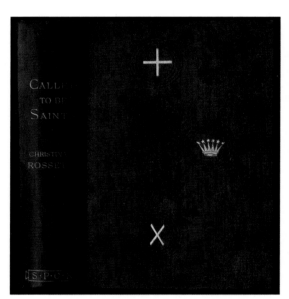
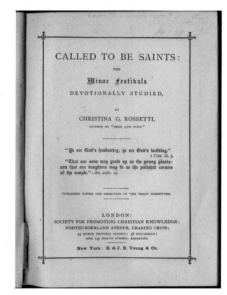

A14.1a, *Called To Be Saints* (1881).

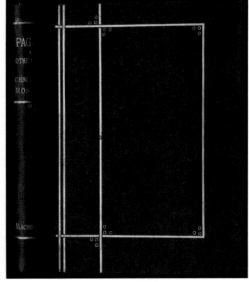
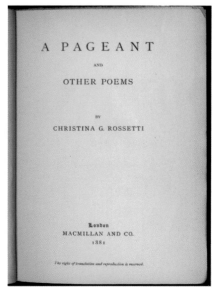

A15.1, *A Pageant and Other Poems* (Macmillan, 1881). Spine A.

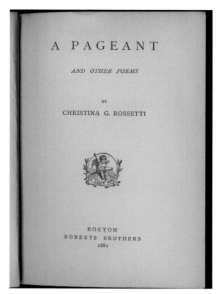 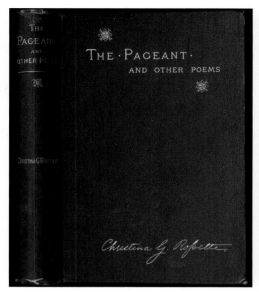 

A16.1a, *A Pageant and Other Poems* (Roberts Brothers, 1881). L-R: title page; binding A; binding B.

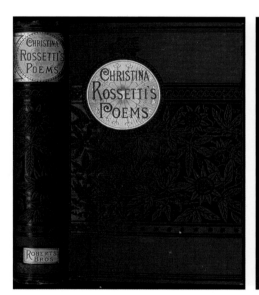 

A17.1a, *Poems* (Roberts Brothers, 1882). Left: binding A; right: binding B; below: title page.

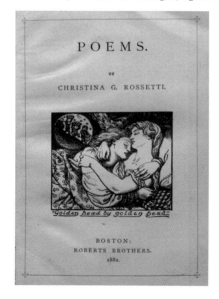 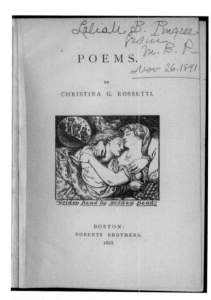

A17.1b, *Poems* (Roberts Brothers, 1888).

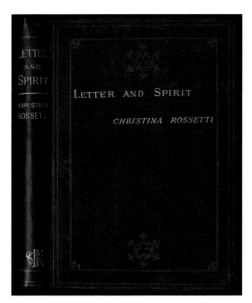
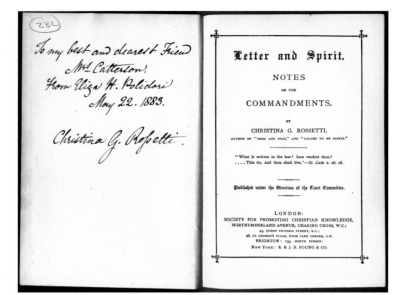

A18.1a, *Letter and Spirit* (1883).

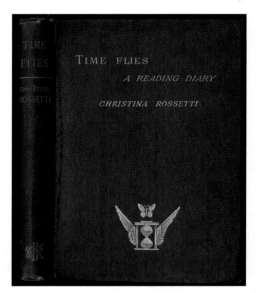
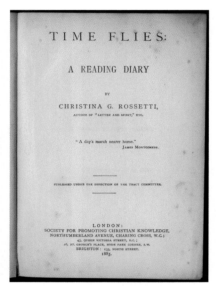

A20.1a, *Time Flies* (1885).

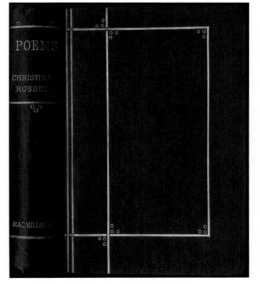
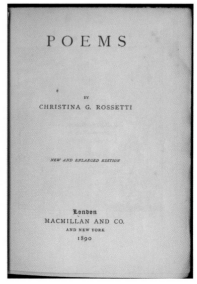

A22.1b, *Poems* (1890).

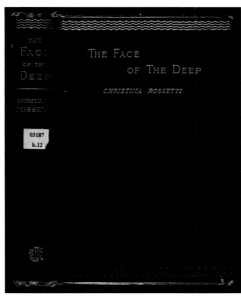
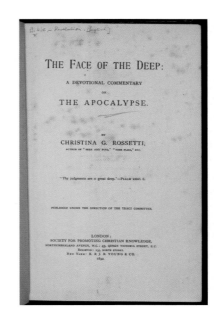

A23.1a, *The Face of the Deep* (1892).

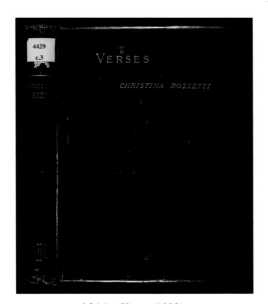

A24.1a, *Verses* (1893).

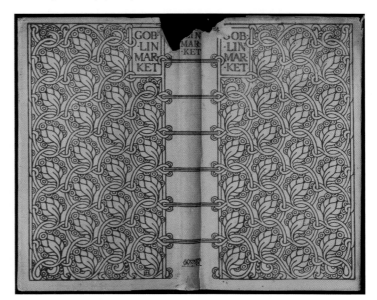

A25.1a, *Goblin Market* (1893).

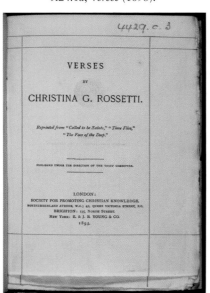

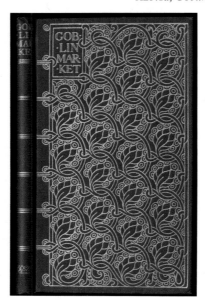

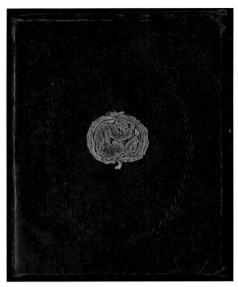
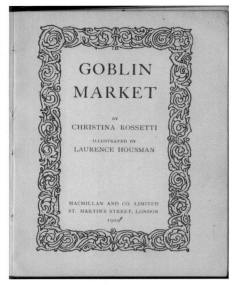
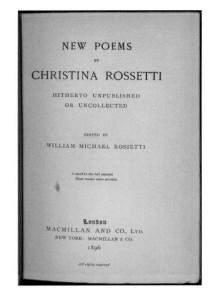

A25.2, *Goblin Market* (1909). A26.1b, *New Poems* (1896).

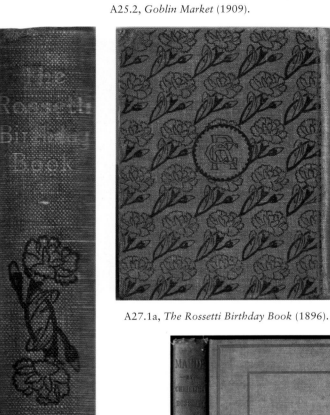
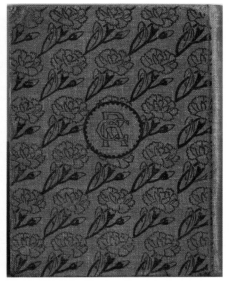
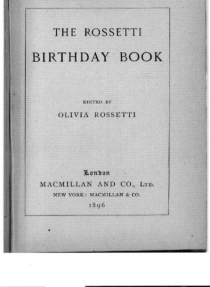

A27.1a, *The Rossetti Birthday Book* (1896).

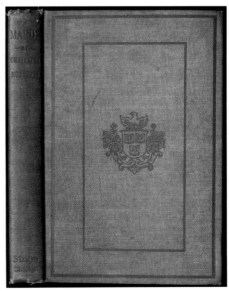

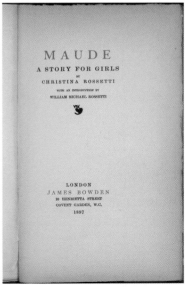

A28.1a.i, *Maude* (1897). A29.2, *Maude* (1897).

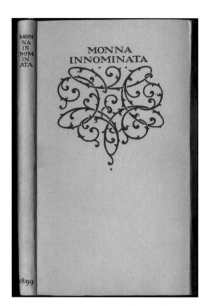
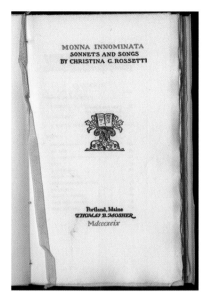

A31.1a.i, *Monna Innominata* (1899).

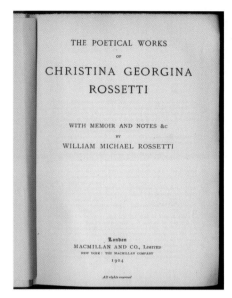

A34.1a, *The Poetical Works of Christina Georgina Rossetti* (1904).

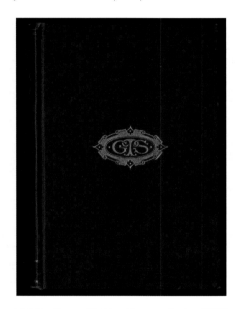

A35.1b, *Poems* (Golden Treasury Series, 1904).

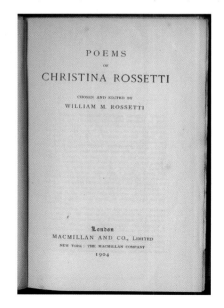

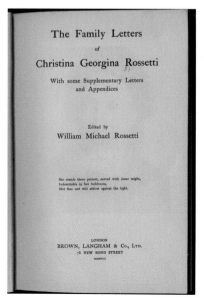

A36.1a.i, *The Family Letters of Christina Georgina Rossetti* (1908).

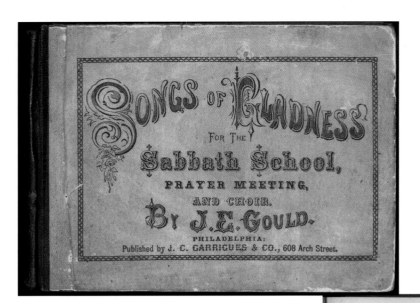

DH3, *Songs of Gladness for the Sabbath School* (1869).

DM29, *One May* (1875).

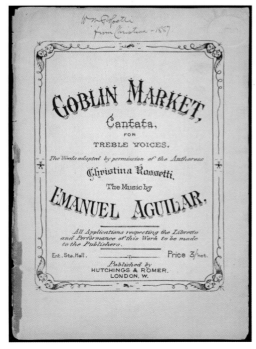

DM39, *Goblin Market, Cantata* (1880).

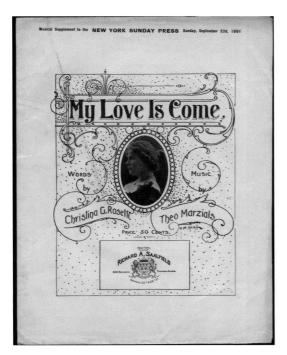

DM41, *My Love is Come* (1881).

E9, Christmas Offerings. Louis Prang
Prize Christmas Card (1880).

DM127-DM128, *Two Hymns* (1895).

Image credits

A1, *To My Mother on the Anniversary of her Birth* (1842). British Library, C.39.e.64.(2.).

A2.1, *Verses* (1847). Cushing Memorial Library and Archives, Texas A&M University, PR5237 .A1 1847.

A2.2, *Verses* (1906). Cushing Memorial Library and Archives, Texas A&M University, PR5237 .A1 1906.

A3.1, *Goblin Market and Other Poems* (1862). Horizontal binding: Cushing Memorial Library and Archives, Texas A&M University, PR5237 .G64 1862. Engraved title page, letterpress title page, frontispiece: Mark Samuels Lasner Collection, on loan to the University of Delaware Library.

A3.2, *Goblin Market and Other Poems* (1865). Cushing Memorial Library and Archives, Texas A&M University, PR5237.G64 1865.

A4.1a, *Poems* (1866). First printing. Cushing Memorial Library and Archives, Texas A&M University, PR5237 .A1 1866.

A4.1b, *Poems* (1866). Second printing. Cushing Memorial Library and Archives, Texas A&M University, PR5237 .A1 1866.

A4.1d, *Poems* (1872). Cushing Memorial Library and Archives, Texas A&M University, PR5237 .A1 1872.

A5.1, *The Prince's Progress and Other Poems* (1866). Cushing Memorial Library and Archives, Texas A&M University, PR5237 .P7 1866.

A6.1, *Consider* (1867). British Library, 11687.e.16.

A7.1a.i, *Commonplace, And Other Short Stories* (1870). Rare Books Division, Department of Rare Books and Special Collections, Princeton University Library, (Ex) 3913.1.326.

A7.1a.ii, *Commonplace, a Tale of To-Day; And Other Stories* (1870). Cushing Memorial Library and Archives, Texas A&M University, PR5237.C65 1870.

A7.1a.iii, *Commonplace, And Other Short Stories* (1871). Cushing Memorial Library and Archives, Texas A&M University, PR5237. C65 1871.

A8.1a.i, *Sing-Song* (1872). Binding A: Rare Books Division, Department of Rare Books and Special Collections, Princeton University Library, (Ex) 3913.1.395 c5.

A8.1b.i, *Sing-Song* (Roberts Brothers, 1872). Cushing Memorial Library and Archives, Texas A&M University, PR5237.S5 1872.

A8.2, *Sing-Song* (1893). Cushing Memorial Library and Archives, Texas A&M University, PR5237.S5 1893.

A9.1a, *Annus Domini* (1874). British Library, 3457.a. 59.

A9.1b, *Annus Domini* (1875). Bryn Mawr College Library, Special Collections, RBR.PR5237.dA55.1875b.

A10.1a, *Speaking Likenesses* (1874). Rare Books Division, Department of Rare Books and Special Collections, Princeton University Library, (Ex) 3919.1.386.

A11.1a, *Goblin Market, The Prince's Progress, and Other Poems* (1875). Cushing Memorial Library and Archives, Texas A&M University, PR5237.G65 1875.

A11.1b, *Goblin Market, The Prince's Progress, and Other Poems* (1879). British Library, 1607/4215.

A12.1a, *Poems* (Roberts Brothers, 1876). Cushing Memorial Library and Archives, Texas A&M University, PR5237 .A1 1876.

A12.1b, *Poems* (Roberts Brothers, 1880). Helen Farr Sloan Library & Archives, Delaware Art Museum, Bancroft, PR 5237 A1 1880.

A12.1c.i *Poems* (Tall Issue, Roberts Brothers, 1896). Ives collection.

A12.1c.ii *Poems* (Short Issue, Roberts Brothers, 1896). Ives collection.

A13.1a, *Seek and Find* (1879). Ives Collection.

A14.1a, *Called To Be Saints* (1881). Cushing Memorial Library and Archives, Texas A&M University, PR5237 .C34 1881.

A15.1, *A Pageant and Other Poems* (Macmillan, 1881). Spine A: Cushing Memorial Library and Archives, Texas A&M University, PR5237 .P3 1881.

A16.1a, *A Pageant and Other Poems* (Roberts Brothers, 1881). Title page, binding A: Cushing Memorial Library and Archives, Texas A&M University, PR5237.P3 1881b. Binding B: Ives Collection.

A17.1a, *Poems* (Roberts Brothers, 1882). Binding A: Cushing Memorial Library and Archives, Texas A&M University, PR5237 .A1 1882. Binding B; title page: Bryn Mawr College Library, Special Collections, RBR.PR5237 .A1 1882.

A17.1b, *Poems* (Roberts Brothers, 1888). Cushing Memorial Library and Archives, Texas A&M University, PR5237 .A1 1888.

A18.1, *Letter and Spirit* (1883). Binding: Cushing Memorial Library and Archives, Texas A&M University, BV4655.R67 1883. Title page: Mark Samuels Lasner Collection, on loan to the University of Delaware Library.

A20.1a, *Time Flies* (1885). Binding, title page: Cushing Memorial Library and Archives, Texas A&M University, PR5237 .T55 1885.

A20.1a, *Time Flies* (1885). Cushing Memorial Library and Archives, Texas A&M University, PR5237.T55 1885.

A22.1b, *Poems* (1890). Binding, title page: Cushing Memorial Library and Archives, Texas A&M University, PR5237 .A1 1890.

A23.1a, *The Face of the Deep* (1892). Binding, title page: British Library, 03187.k.12.

A24.1a, *Verses* (1893). Binding, title page: British Library, 4429.c.3.

A25.1a, *Goblin Market* (1893). Binding, title page, wrapper: Cushing Memorial Library and Archives, Texas A&M University, PR5237 .G6 1893.

A25.2, *Goblin Market* (1909). Binding, title page. Ives Collection.

A26.1b, *New Poems* (1896). Cushing Memorial Library and Archives, Texas A&M University, PR5237 .A1 1896.

A27.1a, *The Rossetti Birthday Book* (1896). Binding, title page. Ives Collection.

A28.1a.i, *Maude* (1897). Cushing Memorial Library and Archives, Texas A&M University, PR5237 .M38 1897.

A29.2 *Maude* (Second Edition, Only Printing, Bowden, 1897): Cushing Memorial Library and Archives, Texas A&M University, (not yet catalogued).

A31.1a.i, *Monna Innominata* (1899). Binding, title page: Cushing Memorial Library and Archives, Texas A&M University, PR5237 .M66 1899.

A34.1a, *The Poetical Works of Christina Georgina Rossetti* (1904). Cushing Memorial Library and Archives, Texas A&M University, PR5237 .A1 1904.

A35.1b, *Poems* (Golden Treasury Series, 1904). Frontispiece, title page, spine. Ives Collection.

A36.1a.i, *The Family Letters of Christina Georgina Rossetti* (1908). Cushing Memorial Library and Archives, Texas A&M University, PR5238 .A3 1973.

DH3, *Songs of Gladness for the Sabbath School* (1869). Binding, title page. Ives Collection.

DM29, *One May* (1875). Music Special Collections, Harold B. Lee Library, Brigham Young University, MSC Thurston Miscellaneous 4:27.

DM39, *Goblin Market, Cantata* (1880). Rare Books Division, Department of Rare Books and Special Collections, Princeton University Library, (Ex) 2006-3196N.

DM41, *My Love is Come* (1881). Ives Collection.

DM127-DM128, *Two Hymns* (1895). Ives Collection.

E9, *Christmas Offerings*. Louis Prang Prize Christmas Card (1880). Front and back. Ives Collection.

B: APPEARANCES IN BOOKS

This section includes all first appearances of Rossetti's work in books or pamphlets, including material published posthumously, and selected nonfirsts that bear particular significance. Books in series and annuals are included here rather than in Section C (Periodicals). Books are arranged in chronological order and arranged alphabetically within each year.

Each entry includes a title page transcription in quasi-facsimile; first line or title, and inclusive page numbers of Rossetti material; an indication of whether and how Rossetti's name appears with the text (e.g., unsigned or signed, "C. G. Rossetti"); notes (as needed); and the location(s) of copies examined.

Entries for contributions that appeared without a title (or with a title different from what appears in Rossetti's collected publications, or that present other difficulties) include the title or first line as printed in the listed item, followed by the title or first line as printed in collections authorized by Rossetti, with Rossetti's first lines or titles in parentheses. The term "signed" indicates that Rossetti's name appeared with the text either as a heading or a byline; if Rossetti's name appears elsewhere, its location is noted.

Information about publication in multiple issues (such as simultaneous British and American publication) and reprintings is provided if known. All entries are poems unless one of the following sigla appears in the heading after the entry letter and number: 'NF' (nonfiction prose), 'F' (fiction), or 'L' (letter). CGR's correspondence is reprinted in Harrison's edition of Rossetti's *Letters* unless otherwise indicated.

The term "First appearance" is difficult to define for works that appear in multiple versions, such as "From House to Home," which was first reprinted in an extremely abbreviated form, then later reprinted in its full form. In such cases, each version is treated as a separate first appearance (that is, as a first appearance of that version of the poem).

~

B1   **MARSHALL'S LADIES' DAILY REMEMBRANCER (1850)**

Within compartment of engraved title page:
MARSHALLS'S | LADIES' | DAILY | Remembrancer. | FOR | 1850. | [short hairline rule, slightly swelled, 15 mm] LONDON: | R & A. SUTTABY | AND J. TOULMIN.

"Name any gentleman you spy"("Two Enigmas"), 135; signed 'BY C.'; "My first is no proof of my second" ("Two Charades"), 140; signed 'BY C.'.

Note: There is no period after "R" in "R. & A. Suttaby" on the title page of the copy examined. This copy (at NjP) is a presentation copy from CGR to FMR ("Frances M. L. Rossetti from Christina Containing two of C's riddles"), subsequently inscribed "W M Rossetti from Christina's books 1894" and with WMR's note that the annotations within the book are those of CGR and FMR.
Location: NjP.

B2   PICTORIAL CALENDAR OF THE SEASONS (1854)

PICTORIAL CALENDAR | OF THE | SEASONS | EXHIBITING THE | PLEASURES, PURSUITS, AND CHARACTERISTICS OF COUNTRY | LIFE FOR EVERY MONTH IN THE YEAR | AND EMBODYING THE WHOLE OF | AIKIN'S CALENDAR OF NATURE. | EDITED BY | MARY HOWITT. | EMBELLISHED WITH UPWARDS OF | ONE HUNDRED ENGRAVINGS ON WOOD. | LONDON: | HENRY G. BOHN, YORK STREET, COVENT GARDEN. | 1854.

"O Rose, thou flower of flowers, thou fragrant wonder" ("The Rose"), 305. Signed "CHRISTINA G. ROSETTI." (misspelled).

Note: BL depository copy: '4 JA 54'.
Location: BL.

B3   MIDSUMMER FLOWERS FOR THE YOUNG (1854)

MIDSUMMER | FLOWERS. | FOR THE YOUNG. | BY | MARY HOWITT. | ILLUSTRATED. | [ornamented rule] | PHILADELPHIA: | LINDSAY & BLAKISTON. | 1854.

"The Trees' Counselling," 202-203, unsigned.

Location: MH.

B4   THE DUSSELDORF ARTIST'S ALBUM (1854)

Within single rule frame with ornamental corners, some text in <u>black letter</u>:
<u>The</u> | Dusseldorf Artist's Album. | Edited & Translated | By | Mrs. Mary Howitt, | With | <u>Original Contributions by Various English Poëts.</u> | [ornament] | Dusseldorf. | Arnz & Comp. | 1854.

"A Summer Evening," Part II ("Twilight Calm"), 7-8; signed "Christina Rossetti."

Note: "Translated by Mrs. Howitt" appears at the end of Rossetti's poem, which is in English. There is also a lithographed English title page which gives Trubner & Co. as the publishers.
Location: NjP.

B5 NF   THE IMPERIAL DICTIONARY OF UNIVERSAL BIOGRAPHY (1857-)

THE | IMPERIAL DICTIONARY | OF | UNIVERSAL BIOGRAPHY: | A SERIES OF | ORIGINAL MEMOIRS OF DISTINGUISHED MEN, | OF ALL AGES AND ALL NATIONS. | BY | WRITERS OF EMINENCE IN THE VARIOUS BRANCHES OF LITERATURE, | SCIENCE, AND ART. | CONDUCTED BY | [the next three lines are in two columns, separated by a vertical rule, represented as ‖] PROFESSOR JOHN EADIE, D.D., LL.D. ‖ EDWIN LANKESTER, M.D., F.R.S. | JOHN FRANCIS WALLER, LL.D., M.R.I.A. ‖ PROFESSOR FRANCIS BOWEN, M.A., UNITED STATES, | PROFESSOR W. J. M. RANKINE, LL.D. ‖ Late Editor of "North American Review." [end text in columns] | JOHN FRANCIS WALLER, LL.D., M.R.I.A., EDITOR. | VOL. I. | WILLIAM MACKENZIE: | LONDON, GLASGOW, EDINBURGH, | 22 PATERNOSTER ROW. 45 & 47 HOWARD STREET. 39 SOUTH BRIDGE. | [the next three lines in columns, with vertical rule between, represented by ‖] ABERDEEN, 61 ST. NICHOLAS STREET. ‖ LIVERPOOL, 54 SEEL STREET. | BIRMINGHAM, 56 ALBION STREET. ‖ LEEDS, 5 SOUTH PARADE. | BRISTOL, 7 STOKES CROFT. ‖ NEWCASTLE, 27 CARLIOL STREET. [end text in columns] | BOSTON, U.S., 12 TREMONT STREET. | [next line outside of rule frames, brackets in original] [THE PUBLISHER RESERVES THE RIGHT OF TRANSLATION.]

In division X, Volume II, Part 4:
"GIRAUD, GIOVANNI," 639, column 1; "GOLDONI, Carlo," 665, columns 1-2 – 666, column 1;

"GOVONA, Rosa," 689, column 2; "GRAVINA, Domenico da," 710, column 2; "GRAVINA, Giovanni Vincenzo," 710, column 2; "GUALDO-PRIORATO, Galeazzo," 745, column 2; "GUARINI, Giovanni Battista," 746, column 1; "GUERRAZZI, Francesco Domenico," 749, column 1. All signed 'C. G. R."

In division XII, Volume II, Part 6:
"INGHIRAMI, Francesco," 977, column 2 – 978, column 1. Signed 'C. G. R."

In division XII, Volume III, Part 1:
"JACOPONE da Todi," 6, column 1. Signed "C. G. R."

In division XIII, Volume III, Part 2:
"LIUTPRANDO or LUITPRAND, sometimes called Liuzio," 211, column 1; "MAVROCORDATO-SCARLOTOS, Alessandro," 338, column 1. Signed "C. G. R."

In division XIV, Volume III, Part 3:
"MONTI, Vincenzo," 395, column 1; "MOROSINI, Francesco," 405, column 1; "MURATORI, Ludovico Antonio," 419, columns 1-2; "NICCOLINI, Giovanni Battista," 449, column 2 – 450, column 1; "PACIO, Giulio," 491, column 2 – 492, column 1; "PALLAVICINO, Sforza," 499, column 1; "PANVINIO, Onofrio," 501, column 2; "PARINI, Giuseppe," 503, column 2 – 504 column 1; "PASSIONEI, Domenico, Carlo," 513, column 2; "PELLICO, Silvio," 525 columns 1-2; "PETRARCA, Francesco," 542 column 2 – 544 column 1. All signed "C. G. R."

In division XV, Volume III, Part 4:
"PICCOLOMINI, Ottavio," 559, column 1; "PINDEMONTE, Ippolito," 562, column 1; "POZZO, Modesta," 598, column 2; "QUADRIO, Francesco Saverio," 619, column 1; "QUIRINI or QUERINI, Angelo Maria," 622, column 2; "RAMUSIO or RANNUSIO, Giambattista," 633, column 2; "RINUCINNI, Ottavio," 663, column 2; "ROGER I., King of Sicily," 677, column 2 – 678 column 1; "ROSELLINI, Ippolito," 686, column 2; "SADOLETO, Jacopo," 710, columns 1-2; "SANNAZARO, Jacopo," 722 column 1. All signed "C. G. R."

In division XVI, Volume III, Part 5:
"SESTINI, Domenico, Numismatist," 761, column 1;"SFORZA: a house famous in medieval history," 763, column 1; "TASSO, Bernardo, poet," 824, column 2; "TIRABOSCHI, Girolamo," 844, column 2; "UGHELLI, Ferdinando," 856, column 1; "VALERIANO, Giovanni Pierio," 860, column 2; "VALLA or DALLA VALLE, Lorenzo," 860, column 2. All signed "C. G. R."

Note: The printing and publishing history of the *Imperial Dictionary* is complicated by the various formats in which it originally appeared. Beginning in 1857, the *Dictionary* was first published in 48 parts and in sixteen undated, cloth bound divisions, containing three volumes of material divided into numbered parts. Publication in these forms occurred over several years. The set of divisions examined at the University of Texas bear various dated inscriptions ranging from 1859 through 1862; the set at Texas A&M includes several advertisements tipped in between the front endpapers, the latest of which is dated 1862. The last of the divisions includes engraved title pages for volumes II and III to facilitate rebinding into three volumes upon conclusion of the series. Given the uncertain publication dates of individual divisions, all of the Rossetti entries located in bound divisions are presented in this entry.

Location: Publication in parts: not seen, information from BL copy description in C19 database; Publication in divisions: TxCM, TxU.

B6   NIGHTINGALE VALLEY (1860)

NIGHTINGALE VALLEY. | A COLLECTION, | INCLUDING A GREAT NUMBER | OF THE CHOICEST LYRICS | AND | SHORT POEMS | IN | THE ENGLISH LANGUAGE. | EDITED BY GIRALDUS. | *Sul lito un bosco era di querce ombrose, | Dove ognor par che Filomena piagna; | Ch' in mezzo avea un pratel con una fonte, | E quinci e quindi un solitario monte.* | Ariosto, *Orl. Fur.* x 113. | [rule] | LONDON: |

BELL AND DALDY, 186, FLEET STREET. | 1860.

"An End," 194-195; signed "Christina Rossetti."

Note: Edited by William Allingham. Reprinted in 1862.
Location: KMK.

B7　　　　**POEMS OF RELIGIOUS SORROW (1863)**

POEMS OF RELIGIOUS SORROW | COMFORT COUNSEL AND | ASPIRATION | 'Tis life whereof our nerves are scant | Oh life not death for which we pant | More life and fuller that I want | I am come that they might have life and that they | might have it more abundantly | NEW YORK | SHELDON AND COMPANY PUBLISHERS | 335 BROADWAY CORNER OF WORTH STREET | 1863

"A City That Hath Foundations" (excerpt from "From House to Home"), 52-53. Unsigned but attributed to "Christina Rossetti" in the table of contents.

Note: Edited by Francis James Child. Reprinted, by various publishers, in 1866, 1886, and 1889. The excerpt was subsequently reprinted in the third series of *Hymns of the Ages*, compiled by C. S. W. [Caroline Snowden Whitmarsh] and A. E. G. [Anne E. Guild] (Boston: Ticknor and Fields, 1865: 70-71).
Location: TxU.

B8　　　　**LYRA EUCHARISTICA (1863)**

Some text in black letter:
Lyra Eucharistica | HYMNS AND VERSES ON | THE HOLY COMMUNION, | ANCIENT AND MODERN; | *WITH OTHER POEMS.* | EDITED BY | The Rev. Orby Shipley, M. A. | [ornament, foliage] | London: | LONGMAN, GREEN, LONGMAN, ROBERTS, | AND GREEN. | 1863.

"The Offering of the New Law, the One Oblation Once Offered," 48-49; "Conference between Christ, the Saints, and the Soul," 167-168; both unsigned (but attributed to "Christina G. Rossetti" in the table of contents).

Note: Additional Rossetti poems were included in the second edition, 1864 (B11).
Location: NjP.

B9　　　　**A WELCOME (1863)**

A Welcome | ORIGINAL CONTRIBUTIONS IN | POETRY AND PROSE. | [Victoria Press device, "VP" above shield, within shield 'Non nobis solum.'] | LONDON: EMILY FAITHFULL, | *Printer and Publisher to Her Majesty,* | PRINCES STREET, HANOVER SQUARE, AND | 83A, FARRINGDON STREET. | 1863.

"Dream Love," 63-66. Signed "Christina G. Rossetti."

Locations: NjP (three copies), ViW.

B10　　　　**POEMS: AN OFFERING TO LANCASHIRE (1863)**

Some text in black letter:
POEMS: | An Offering to Lanchashire. | PRINTED AND PUBLISHED FOR THE ART EXHIBITION FOR THE | RELIEF OF DISTRESS IN THE COTTON DISTRICTS. | [Victoria Press device, "VP" above shield, within shield 'Non nobis solum.'] | LONDON: | EMILY FAITHFULL, | *Printer and Publisher in*

Ordinary to Her Majesty, | VICTORIA PRESS, 83a, FARRINGDON STREET, E. C. | 1863.

"A Royal Princess," 2-10.

Locations: NjP (2 copies); U of Western Ontario.

B11   **LYRA EUCHARISTICA, SECOND EDITION (1864)**

Some text in <u>black letter</u>:
<u>Lyra Eucharistica</u>: | HYMNS AND VERSES ON | THE HOLY COMMUNION, | ANCIENT AND MODERN; | *WITH OTHER POEMS.* | EDITED BY | THE REV. ORBY SHIPLEY, M. A. | Second Edition. | [ornament] | <u>London:</u> | LONGMAN, GREEN, LONGMAN, ROBERTS, | AND GREEN. | 1864.

"Come Unto Me," 5; "The Offering of the New Law," 61-62; "Conference between Christ, the Saints, and the Soul," 206-208; "Jesus, Do I love Thee?" 355-356. Unsigned but attributed to "Christina G. Rossetti" (first poem) or "C. G. Rossetti" (remaining poems) in the table of contents.

Note: "The Offering of the New Law" is printed here with revisions. Reprinted in 1869 by Longmans, Green, & Co.
Locations: 1864: University of California, Berkeley (via Internet Archive). 1869: CtMW.

B12   **HOUSEHOLD FRIENDS FOR EVERY SEASON (1864)**

In *red* and black, with ornate capitals and shadowed black letter in first line:
*H*OUSEHOLD *F*RIENDS | FOR EVERY SEASON | "The pleasant books, that silently among | Our household treasures take familiar places, | And are to us as if a living tongue | Spake from the printed leaves or pictured faces!" | *Longfellow* | [orn, 33 x 25, combined "TF" on shield suspended from scroll] | BOSTON | *TICKNOR AND FIELDS* | 1864

"Goblin Market," 74-91; signed "Christina Rossetti."

Note: Edited by James Thomas Shields.
Location: MsSM.

B13   **LYRA MESSIANICA (1864)**

Within double rule frame; some text in <u>black letter</u>:
<u>Lyra Messianica:</u> | HYMNS AND VERSES ON | THE LIFE OF CHRIST, | ANCIENT AND MODERN; | *WITH OTHER POEMS.* | EDITED BY | THE REV. ORBY SHIPLEY, M. A. | [ornament, foliage] | <u>London:</u> | LONGMAN, GREEN, LONGMAN, ROBERTS, | AND GREEN. | 1864.

"I know you not," 28-29; "Before the paling of the Stars" ("A Christmas Carol"), 63-64; "Good Friday" ("Am I a stone and not a sheep"), 236-237; "Easter Even" (first line "There is nothing more that they can do"), 251-252; "The Love of Christ which passeth Knowledge," 269. Individual poems not signed, but attributed to "Christina G. Rossetti" or "C. G. Rossetti" (second poem only) in the table of contents.

Note: A second edition was printed in 1865 with additional Rossetti poems; see B16.
Location: InND.

B14   **ENGLISH LYRICS (1865)**

Some text in <u>black letter</u>:
<u>English Lyrics</u> | A | COLLECTION OF ENGLISH POETRY | OF THE PRESENT DAY. | ARRANGED BY

THE | REV. ROBERT H. BAYNES, M. A. | *Editor of the "Lyra Anglicana"* | LONDON | HOULSTON AND WRIGHT | 65, PATERNOSTER ROW | MCCCCLXV.

"From House to Home," 109-117. Signed "Christina Rossetti."

Note: BL depository copy: '20 AP 65.'
Location: BL.

B15   THE LATE ENGLISH POETS (1865)

THE | LATE ENGLISH POETS | EDITED BY | RICHARD HENRY STODDARD. | [rule] | WITH SIX ILLUSTRATIONS. | [rule] | New York: | GEORGE ROUTLEDGE AND SONS, | 9 LAFAYETTE PLACE.

"Love from the North," 447-448; "At Home," 448-449; "Maude Clare," 449-451; "Up-Hill," 451; "A Peal of Bells," 452-453; "Noble Sisters," 453-455. Section of poems attributed to "Christina Rossetti."

Note: The spine title is *Golden Leaves from the Late English Poets*; on ii, *The Late English Poets* is listed as no. IV in *The Golden Leaves Series*. Various United States publishers are listed in library catalogs, including Hurst, Bunce & Huntington, and G. F. Huntington (1867).
Location: NjP.

B16   LYRA MESSIANICA, SECOND EDITION (1865)

Within double rule frame; some text in <u>black letter</u>:
<u>Lyra Messianica:</u> | HYMNS AND VERSES ON | THE LIFE OF CHRIST, | ANCIENT AND MODERN; | *WITH OTHER POEMS.* | EDITED BY | THE REV. ORBY SHIPLEY, M. A. | *SECOND EDITION,* | Revised and Enlarged. | [ornament, foliage] | <u>London:</u> | LONGMANS, GREEN, AND CO. | 1865.

"I know you not," 28-29; "The Advent Moon" ("Advent"), 65-67; "Before the paling of the stars" ("A Christmas Carol"), 81; "Good Friday"("Am I a stone and not a sheep"), 266-267; "Easter Even" ("There is nothing more that they can do"), 279-280; "The Love of Christ" ("The Love of Christ which passeth Knowledge"), 300; "Paradise: in a Dream" ("Paradise"), 365-366; "Within the Veil," 393; "Paradise: In a Symbol" ("Birds of Paradise"), 417-418. Individual poems not signed, but attributed to "C. G. Rossetti" in the table of contents.

Note: Reprinted by Longmans, Green and Co. in 1869.
Location: NcD; 1869 edition: OO.

B17   LYRA MYSTICA (1865)

Some text in <u>black letter</u>:
<u>Lyra Mystica</u> | HYMNS AND VERSES ON | SACRED SUBJECTS, | ANCIENT AND MODERN. | EDITED BY | THE REV. ORBY SHIPLEY, M. A. | [ornament, foliage] <u>London:</u> | LONGMAN, GREEN, LONGMAN, ROBERTS, | AND GREEN. | 1865.

"After this the Judgment," 33-36; "The Three Enemies: a Colloquy," 199-200; "Martyr's Song," 427-429. Individual poems not signed, but attributed to "Christina G. Rossetti" ("After this the Judgment") or "C. G. Rossetti" ("The Three Enemies" and "Martyrs' Song") in the table of contents.

Note: Reprinted by Longmans, Green and Co. in 1869.
Location: 1865: NjP; 1869: CtMW.

B18   POEMS OF THE INNER LIFE (1866)

POEMS | OF | THE INNER LIFE. | SELECTED | CHIEFLY FROM MODERN AUTHORS. | LONDON: | SAMPSON LOW, SON, AND MARSTON, | MILTON HOUSE, LUDGATE HILL. | [short rule] | 1866.

"A Summer Wish," 43-44; "Symbols," 51-52; "Advent" ("This Advent moon shines cold and clear"), 64-66; "Up-Hill," 208-209; "Sweet Death," 237-238. Signed "Christina Rossetti" except "C. Rossetti" on 52.

Note: Preface signed "R. C. J." (Robert Crompton Jones). New edition in 1872 omits "Advent."
Locations: 1866: CU-SB; NjP; 1872: NjP.

B19   A ROUND OF DAYS (1866)

Red ink as noted:
A | [this line in red] ROUND OF DAYS | DESCRIBED IN | ORIGINAL POEMS | BY SOME OF | OUR MOST CELEBRATED POETS, | AND IN | [this line in red] PICTURES | BY | EMINENT ARTISTS | ENGRAVED BY THE BROTHERS DALZIEL. | LONDON: | [this line in red] GEORGE ROUTLEDGE AND SONS, | BROADWAY, LUDGATE HILL. | MDCCCLXVI.

"An English Drawing-Room. 1865" ("Enrica, 1865"), 6; "By the Sea," 68. Signed "Christina G. Rossetti."

Note: Illustrated. Also published in the United States by Roberts Brothers. A second British edition, reset and retitled *Picture Posies*, was published in 1874 with same CGR poems (Location: BL). BL depository copy: '8 JA 66'.
Locations: BL; NjP.

B20   ELIM; OR HYMNS OF HOLY REFRESHMENT (1866)

Some text in <u>black letter</u>; red ink as noted:
[letter E and decorative background in red] <u>Elim:</u> | OR | HYMNS OF HOLY REFRESHMENT. | EDITED BY THE | [this line in red] REV. F. D. HUNTINGTON, D.D. | "And they came to Elim, where were twelve wells of water, and threescore and ten palm-trees: and they encamped there by the waters." | [illustration, camels at well] | [this line in red] BOSTON: | E. P. DUTTON AND COMPANY. | NEW YORK: HURD AND HOUGHTON. | 1866.

"The Love of Christ Which Passeth Knowledge," 34-35; "The Oblation" ("The Offering of the New Law"), 130-131. Not signed, but attributed to "Christina G. Rossetti" in contents.

Note: Nonfirst; first United States printing of these poems, which were frequently reprinted in collections of religious poetry and in hymnals. Frederick Huntington became Episcopal Bishop of Central New York in 1869.
Location: CU.

B21   IMPERIAL DICTIONARY OF UNIVERSAL BIOGRAPHY, REVISED PRINTING (1866)

Within outer single rule frame, and inner double rule frame:
THE | IMPERIAL DICTIONARY | OF | UNIVERSAL BIOGRAPHY: | A SERIES OF | ORIGINAL MEMOIRS OF DISTINGUISHED MEN, | OF ALL AGES AND ALL NATIONS. | BY | WRITERS OF EMINENCE IN THE VARIOUS BRANCHES OF LITERATURE, | SCIENCE, AND ART. | CONDUCTED BY | [the next three lines are in two columns, separated by a vertical rule, represented as ||] PROFESSOR

JOHN EADIE, D.D., LL.D. ‖ EDWIN LANKESTER, M.D., F.R.S. | JOHN FRANCIS WALLER, LL.D., M.R.I.A. ‖ PROFESSOR FRANCIS BOWEN, M.A., United States, | PROFESSOR W. J. M. RANKINE, LL.D. ‖ Late Editor of "North American Review." [end text in columns] | JOHN FRANCIS WALLER, LL.D., M.R.I.A., Editor. | VOL. II. | DAA-GAY. | LONDON: | WILLIAM MACKENZIE, 22 PATERNOSTER ROW; | HOWARD STREET, GLASGOW; SOUTH BRIDGE, EDINBURGH. | [next line outside of rule frames, brackets in original] [THE PUBLISHER RESERVES THE RIGHT OF TRANSLATION.]

New contributions (see *Note*):
In Volume II, Part 2 (GAY-JUX):
"INGEGNERI, Angiolo," 1002, column 2. Signed 'C. G. R."

In Volume III, Part 1 (KAA-POM):
"LAMI, Giovanni," 92, col. 2; "LAMPRIDIO, Benedetto," 94, column 2; "LAPO (diminutive of Jacopo)," 108, column 2; "LATINI, Latino," 115, column 2; "LEOPARDI, Giacomo," 157, column 2 – 158, column 1; "LETI, Gregorio," 167, column 2; "LICETO, Fortunio," 176, column 2; "LITTA, Pompeo," 194, column 2; "LOREDANO, Leonardo," 214, columns 1-2; "LORENZINI (called also Laurentini), Francecso Maria," 214, column 2; "LORIA or LAURIA, Roger De, Admiral," 215, column 1; "LUCA, Giovanni Battista Di," 233, column 2; "MELI, Giovanni," 372, column 2; "MELZI D'ERIL or D'ELRIL, Francesco," 376, column 1; "MELZI, Gaetano," 376, column 1-column 2; "MERULA, Giogio," 387, column 1; "MINUZIANO, Alessandro," 414, column 2; "MINZONI, Onofrio," 414, column 2; "MOCENIGO or MOCENINGO," 420, column 1; "MORCELLI, Stefano Antonio," 448, columns 1-2; "MORELLI, Jacopo," 452, columns 1-2; "MUSONIUS, Caius," 488, column 2; "MUZIO, Giolamo," 489, column 2; "NESTOR, Dionysius," 517, column 1; "NIFO, Agostino (Niphus)," 538, column 1; "ODORICO da Pordenone (Oderico di Portenan)," 556, column 2 – 557, column 1; "ORSINI," 572, column 2; "ORSINI, Felice," 572, column 2; "ORSINO, Fulvio," 572, column 2 – 573, column 1; "PALMIERI, Matteo," 599, column 1; "PANCIROLI, Guido," 600, column 1; "PASSERONI, Gian Carlo," 617, column 1; "PATRIZI, Francesco (Patricius)," 619, column 1; "PECCHIO, Giuseppe," 624, column 2 – 625, column 1; "PESCE (Fish)," 648, column 1; "PIGNOTTI, Lorenzo," 680, column 2; "PINELLI, Maffeo," 683, column 1. All signed "C. G. R."

In Volume III, Part 2 (POM-ZWI):
"RAIMONDI, Giambattista," 768, column 1; "REDI, Francesco," 783, column 2; "RICCI, Lorenzo," 803, columns 1-2; "RICCI, Matteo," 803, column 2; "RICCOBONI, Luigi," 804, column 1; "RINALDI, Odorico," 816, column 1; "ROBORTELLO, Francesco," 830 column 1; "ROLANDINO," 837, column 2; "ROLLI, Paulo," 837, column 2; "ROMAGNOSI, Gian Domenico," 838, columns 1-2; "RUFFO, Dionigi Fabrizio," 864, column 2 – 865, column 1; "SACCHETTI, Franco," 877, column 2; "SAMONICUS, Quintus Serenus," 892, column 1; "SASSI or SAXI, Giuseppe Antonio," 900, columns 1-2; "SCALA, Della," 907, column 2 – 908, column 1; "SELLON, Priscilla Lydia," 947, column 2; "SERASSI, Pietro Antonio," 950, column 2; "SETTALA, Lodovico," 953, column 2; "SIGONIO or SIGONE, Carlo," 985, column 2; "STROZZI," 1077, column 2 – 1078, column 1; "TAMBURINI, Pietro," 1105, columns 1-2; "TANSILLO, Luigi," 1106, column 1; "TANUCCI, Bernardo," 1106, column 1; "TARGIONI TOZZETTI, Giovanni," 1106, column 1; "TASSONI, Alessandro," 1108, column 2; "TICOZZI, Stefano," 1150, column 1; "TOALDO, Giuseppe," 1159, column 1; "TOLOMEI or TOLOMMEI, Claudio," 1161, column 2; "TOMMASEO, Niccolo," 1161, column 2 – 1162, column 1; "TOMMASI, Giuseppe Maria," 1162, column 1; "TORELLI, Lelio or Laelio," 1163, column 2; "TORRE, Filippo del," 1165, column 1; "TRISSINO, Giovanni Giorgio," 1175, column 2; "TRIVULZIO," 1175, column 2 – 1176, column 1; "UBERTI, Bonifacio," 1193, column 1; "VALLE, Pietro Della," 1210, columns 1-2; "VARCHI, Benedetto," 1218, column 2; "VENANTIUS, Honorius," 1226, column 2; "VERGERIO, Pier Paolo," 1232, column 1; "VERGERIO, Pier Paolo, the younger," 1232, column 1; "VERRI, Alessandro," 1234, column 2; "VERRI, Pietro," 1234, column 2; "VETTORI, Pietro," 1237, column 1; "VIDA, Marco Girolamo," 1243, column

1; "VILLANI, Filippo," 1247, column 1; "VILLANI, Giovanni," 1247, column 1; "VISCONTI, Ennio Qirino," 1259, column 1; "ZANCHI, Girolamo," 1412, column 1. All signed "C. G. R."

Note: A (mostly) undated reprinting of the 1857 *Dictionary*, largely though not entirely reset. One of the title pages bound in to a volume of the Baylor copy (volume 2, part 2), is dated 1866, but the date of the other volumes in the set remains uncertain, as does the relationship of the various parts, as it is not possible to determine whether, or to what extent, the Baylor copy is a collection of separately issued parts. All of CGR's entries in the earlier printing are retained except for "Ughelli, Ferdinando."

The entry on Priscilla Sellon constitutes CGR's only published commentary on Anglican sisterhoods (see Ives, "'The Din of Controversy': Christina Rossetti, Priscilla Lydia Sellon, and the Sisterhood Debate in Maude").
Location: Baylor.

B22   PRACTICAL HINTS ON THE ART OF ILLUMINATION (1867)

PRACTICAL HINTS | ON THE | ART OF ILLUMINATION. | BY | ALICE DONLEVY. | [short rule] | NEW YORK: | A. D. F. RANDOLPH, 770 BROADWAY. | 1867.

"Consider," 74-78. Signed "Christina G Rossetti" on 74.

Note: A textbook on illuminating. CGR's poem is presented within a set of designs, created by Donlevy, which combine calligraphic text, ornamental borders, and other decorative elements. Also printed and sold separately; see A6. See Ives, "Teaching Women's Art in America: Alice Donlevy's Designs for Christina Rossetti's Consider."
Locations: AzU; TxCM.

B23   GOLDEN THOUGHTS FROM GOLDEN FOUNTAINS (1867)

Engraved title page within ornamental gilt frame; printed in gilt and sepia; some text in black letter, other fonts as noted:
[(first three lines in sepia outline, gilt fill)] [first line with ornamental G, T] GOLDEN THOUGHTS | FROM | GOLDEN FOUNTAINS. | [next three lines in sepia ink] Arranged in Fifty-two Divisions. | ILLUSTRATED BY EMINENT ARTISTS, | ENGRAVED BY THE BROTHERS DALZIEL. | [ornament, rose with rule, black outline and gilt fill] | [this line gilt] LONDON: | [this line sepia] FREDERICK WARNE AND COMPANY, | [this line gilt] BEDFORD STREET, COVENT GARDEN. | [this line black] NEW YORK: SCRIBNER, WELFORD, AND CO.

"'A bruised Reed shall He not break'," 98; "'The Love of Christ which Passeth Knowledge,'" 194-195; "A Testimony," 243-244; "Advent" ("This Advent moon shines cold and clear"), 280. Signed "Christina G. Rossetti."

Note: Advertised as a "choice selection of sacred songs" for the 1867-1868 holiday season, "printed on a beautiful sepia tint, by the Brothers Dalziel" (*American Literary Gazette*, 1 November 1867: 21); according to White, editions after the first were printed in black (*English Illustration*, 134).
Location: WU.

B24   ILLUSTRATED BOOK OF SACRED POEMS (1867)

Within double rule frame; some text in black letter:
THE | ILLUSTRATED BOOK | OF | SACRED POEMS. | EDITED BY | REV. ROBERT H. BAYNES, M. A., | *Vicar of S. Michael, Coventry; Editor of "Lyra Anglicana," &c.* | Illustrated by | J. D. WATSON, H. C. SELOUS, E. M. WIMPERIS, H. PIXIS, M. E. EDWARDS, R. P. LEITCH, | W. SMALL, R. T.

PRITCHETT, T MACQUOID, J. W. NORTH, &c. &c. | [device] | LONDON AND NEW YORK: | CASELL, PETTER, AND GALPIN

"After Communion," 8; "Advent" ("This Advent moon shines cold and clear"), 46-47; "Good Friday," 346. Signed "Christina G. Rossetti."

Note: Engraved title page also present.
Location: University of Western Ontario.

B25   TOUCHES OF NATURE (1867)

Within compartment with ornamented corners, outer rule frame and inner wavy rule frame:
TOUCHES OF NATURE | BY EMINENT ARTISTS AND AUTHORS | [illustration of two boys] | PHILADELPHIA: J. B. LIPPINCOTT AND CO. | LONDON: ALEXANDER STRAHAN | 1867

"Hoping Against Hope," n.pag. Signed "Christina G. Rossetti."

Note: Rossetti's poem illustrated by F. Sandys; however, the illustrations had previously appeared in various Strahan magazines (White, *English Illustration*, 130). Printed by Dalziel. Reprinted in 1869, 1871, and1872.
Location: KWiU (via photocopy).

B26   TWO CENTURIES OF SONG (1867)

Within brown ornamental compartment:
TWO CENTURIES | OF SONG; | OR, | LYRICS, MADRIGALS, SONNETS, | AND OTHER OCCASIONAL VERSES OF THE ENGLISH POETS | OF THE LAST TWO HUNDRED YEARS. | *WITH CRITICAL AND BIOGRAPHICAL NOTES* | BY | WALTER THORNBURY. | *Author of "Haunted London," "Greatheart," "Tales for the Marines," &c.* | ILLUSTRATED BY ORIGINAL PICTURES OF EMINENT ARTISTS, | DRAWN AND ENGRAVED ESPECIALLY FOR THIS WORK. | WITH COLOURED BORDERS, DESIGNED BY HENRY SHAW, F. S. A., ETC. ETC. | LONDON: | SAMPSON LOW, SON, AND MARSTON, | MILTON HOUSE, LUDGATE HILL. | 1867.

"When I am Dead, My Dearest" ("Song"), 258. Signed "Christina Rossetti."

Location: NjP.

B27   THE GOLDEN SHEAF (1868)

THE | GOLDEN SHEAF | POEMS | CONTRIBUTED BY | LIVING AUTHORS | EDITED BY THE | Rev. CHARLES ROGERS, LL.D., F.S.A. Scot.; | EDITOR OF "LYRA BRITTANICA," "THE MODERN SCOTTISH | MINSTREL," ETC. | "The poet in a golden cline was born, | With golden stars above; | Dowered with the hate of hate, the scorn of scorn, | The love of love."–Tennyson. | LONDON | HOULSTON AND WRIGHT | 65, PATERNOSTER ROW | MDCCCLXVIII.

"Once for All," 192.

Location: NjP.

B28   LIVING THOUGHTS (1869)

Within single rule frame; rule frame and first line in red ink:
LIVING THOUGHTS. | Think truly, and thy thoughts | Shall the world's famine feed; | Speak truly, and

each word of thine | Shall be a fruitful seed; | Live truly, and thy life shall be | A great and noble creed. | H. BONAR. | [ornament, cross, 34 x 22] | BOSTON: | LEE AND SHEPARD. | 1869.

"Thou who didst hang upon a barren tree" ("Long Barren"), 128. Signed "Christina Rossetti."

Note: Preface signed C. A. Means. "Mrs. C. A. Means" is identified as the compiler in various reviews and publisher's advertisements.
Location: MH (via Google Books).

B29   **A MANUAL FOR HOLY COMMUNION (1869)**

Within double rule frame, inner frame red, with ornamented corners; additional ink as noted:
[this line in red] MANUAL | For | ['H' in red] HOLY | [this line in red] COMMUNION | BY | REV. R. H. BAYNES. M.A. | VICAR OF S.MICHAEL AND ALL ANGELS, COVENTRY, | AUTHOR OF "THE MANUAL OF FAMILY PRAYERS." | LONDON: | [this line in red] WHITTAKER AND CO., | AVE MARIA LANE. | [this line in red] MDCCCLXIX

Untitled, numbered: "13" ("The Love of Christ Which Passeth Knowledge"), 87-88; "24" ("After Communion"), 100; "40" ("Good Friday"), 117. Variously signed: "Christina Rossetti" (88), "Christina G. Rossetti" (100), "C. Rossetti" (117).

Note: Nonfirsts. The first, and possibly only, appearance of CGR's writing within such a manual, which includes the order of worship for communion in the Church of England, along with "Questions for Self-Examination," "Directions to Communicants," and several ancillary sections for prayer and meditation. CGR's poems are in the final section ("Hymns on Holy Communion"). A new edition, retitled *At The Communion Time*, was published by C. Kegan Paul in 1878.
Location: Bodleian (via Google Books).

B30   **CHRIST IN SONG (1870)**

Within a compartment:
ΙΧΘΥΣ | [small ornament] | CHRIST IN SONG | HYMNS OF IMMANUEL | SELECTED FROM ALL AGES | WITH NOTES | BY PHILIP SCHAFF D.D. | *Author of "History of the Apostolic | Church," "History of Ancient | Christianity," &c.* | [triangular ornament, foliage] | LONDON | SAMPSON LOW, SON, AND MARSTON | CROWN BUILDINS, FLEET STREET | 1870

"Thou Who Didst Hang Upon A Tree" ("Long Barren"), 218; "I Bore With Thee" ("The Love of Christ Which Passeth Knowledge"), 443-444.

Note: Preface notes "the Collection is intended for private devotion, and hence includes many poems which would be out of place in a hymn-book for public worship" (viii). Also published in New York by Anson D. F. Randolph.
Location: MH (via Google Books).

B31   **A LIBRARY OF POETRY AND SONG (1870)**

Within red ornamented rule frame; some text in black letter:
A LIBRARY | OF | [red and black ornamented P, S] POETRY AND SONG | BEING | Choice Selections from the Best Poets | WITH AN INTRODUCTION | BY | WILLIAM CULLEN BRYANT | [red and black device, J B F & CO] | [this line in red] NEW YORK | J. B. FORD AND COMPANY.

"The Milking-Maid" ("A Farm Walk"), 44; "Up Hill," 261-262. First poem signed "Christina Georgina

Rossetti," second signed "Christina G. Rossetti."

Note: Copyright date 1870 (ii). Title page of 1871 printing is identical to 1870 except for date. The preface in the TxU copy includes an "Advertisement to the Twentieth Edition," said "edition having been called for in little more than six months from the publication of the first." Although later printings are not listed here, this book was frequently reprinted by multiple publishers.
Location: 1870: TxU; 1871: CLU (via Internet Archive).

B32   SONGS OF LIFE (1870)

Some text in <u>black letter</u>:
<u>Songs of Life</u> | SELECTED FROM MANY SOURCES, | WITH NUMEROUS ILLUSTRATIONS FROM ORIGINAL DESIGNS. | BY | HENNESSY, DARLEY, GRISWOLD, FENN, EYTINGE, HERRICK, | WARD, HOPPIN, &c., &c. | [ornament, cherubs and scroll with musical notes] | NEW YORK: | CHARLES SCRIBNER & COMPANY. | 1870.

"Song" ("She sat and sang alway"), 97. Signed "Christina G. Rossetti."

Location: NjP.

B33   PROGRESSIVE EXERCISES IN LATIN ELEGIAC VERSE (1871)

PROGRESSIVE EXERCISES IN | LATIN ELEGIAC VERSE | BY | C. G. GEPP, B. A. | LATE JUNIOR STUDENT OF CHRIST CHURCH, OXFORD, AND ASSISTANT | MASTER AT TONBRIDGE SCHOOL | RIVINGTONS, | London, Oxford and Cambridge | 1871

"Bitter for Sweet," 20. Signed "C. Rossetti."

Location: Bodleian library (via Google Books).

B34   THE NEW POETICAL READER (1872)

THE | NEW POETICAL READER. | EDITED BY | J. C. CURTIS, B.A., | PRINCIPAL OF THE TRAINING COLLEGE, BOROUGH ROAD, LONDON. | *Author of a "School and College History of England," "Chronological | and Genealogical Tables, illustrative of English History," | "Outlines of English History," "Outlines of Scripture History," | "Outlines of Grammar," "Outlines of Geography," etc., | and Editor of "The Poetical Reader" and | Curtis's Junior Reader."* | [short rule] | LONDON: | SIMPKIN, MARSHALL, & CO. | Stationers' Hall Court. | 1872.

"Sound Sleep," 53-54; "Spring," 94-95; "Up-Hill," 105. Signed "Miss Rossetti."

Location: Bodleian library (via Google Books).

B35   ILLUSTRATED LIBRARY OF FAVORITE SONG (1873)

ILLUSTRATED LIBRARY | OF | FAVORITE SONG. | BASED UPON FOLK SONGS, AND COMPRISING SONGS OF THE HEART, | SONGS OF HOME, | SONGS OF LIFE, | AND SONGS OF NATURE. | WITH AN INTRODUCTION, | AND EDITED BY | J. G. HOLLAND, | AUTHOR OF "BITTER SWEET," "KATHRINA," ETC., ETC. | ILLUSTRATED WITH ONE HUNDRED AND TWENTY-FIVE ENGRAVINGS, | AFTER DESIGNS BY CHURCH, JOHNSON, DARLEY, HOPPIN, NAST, HENNESSY, MOAN, GRISWOLD, ETC. | AND WITH TWENTY AUTOGRAPHS IN FACSIMILE. | [short rule] | *Sold only by subscription.* | [short rule] | [engraving, group of figures, woman in foreground with folio book] | NEW YORK: | SCRIBNER, ARMSTRONG, AND COMPANY, | CHICAGO: HADLEY BROTHERS & KANE.

"Marian's Song" (excerpt, "Songs in a Cornfield"), 118-119; "Up-Hill," 492-493; "If All Were Rain And Never Sun," 493; "Song" ("O roses for the flush of youth"), 524; "Song" ("She sat and sang alway"), 617. All signed "Christina G. Rossetti."

Note: Date from copyright page.
Location: NbOU.

B36   LIVING VOICES (1873)

Some text in <u>black letter</u>:
LIVING VOICES | <u>Selections chiefly from Recent Poetry</u> | WITH A PREFACE | By His Grace the ARCHBISHOP OF CANTERBURY | STRAHAN & CO. | 56, LUDGATE HILL, LONDON | 1873

"A Lament" ("Death's Chill Between"), 23-24; "Mother and Child," 158; "Up-Hill," 340; "From House to Home," 368-376. Variously signed: "C. Rossetti," 24; "Christina Rosetti," 158; "Christina Rossetti," 340, 376.

Note: Bodleian library catalog record identifies the compiler as Elizabeth Spooner.
Location: Bodleian library (via Google Books).

B37   SONGS OF NATURE (1873)

Some text in <u>black letter</u>:
<u>Songs of Nature</u> | SELECTED FROM MANY SOURCES, | WITH MANY ILLUSTRATIONS FROM ORIGINAL DESIGNS | BY | T. MORAN, MISS HALLOCK, CHURCH, FENN, PARSONS, KENSETT, JOHNSON, BOLLES, Etc. | [ornament, cherubs and scroll with musical notes] | NEW YORK: | SCRIBNER, ARMSTRONG, AND COMPANY, | SUCCESSORS TO | CHARLES SCRIBNER AND COMPANY. | 1873.

"Up-Hill," 129-130; "If All Were Rain And Never Sun," 130. All signed "Christina G. Rossetti."

Note: Up-Hill" illustrated (129).
Location: MH (via Google Books).

B38   STUDENT'S TREASURY OF ENGLISH SONG (1873)

Within double and single rule frame; some text in <u>black letter</u>:
THE | STUDENT'S TREASURY | OF | ENGLISH SONG. | CONTAINING | <u>Choice Selections from the Principal Poets of</u> | <u>the Present Century.</u> | EDITED, | WITH BIOGRAPHICAL AND CRITICAL NOTICES, PARALLEL PASSAGES, | INDEX OF CRITICAL AUTHORITIES, AND NEARLY FIFTEEN | HUNDRED MARGINAL QUOTATIONS, | *By* | *W. H. DAVENPORT ADAMS.* | [short rule] | The poet in a golden clime was born, | With golden stars above; | Dowered with the hate of hate, the scorn of scorn, | The love of love. | Tennyson. | [short rule] | LONDON: | T. NELSON AND SONS, PATERNOSTER ROW; | EDINBURGH; AND NEW YORK. | [short rule] | 1873.

"The Bourne," 366; "Summer" ("Winter is cold-hearted") 366-367; "Gone For Ever," 368-369. Individual poems not signed, but attributed to "Christina Rossetti" in the contents. Also, each page is surrounded by a triple rule frame, and on each page, four additional lines (attributed to Rossetti, but not otherwise identified) printed horizontally and vertically in the space between the inner single and outer double rule frames, as follows:

366: Across top: "To-day is still the same as yesterday" and across bottom "To-morrow also even as one of them" (from "The One Certainty"); vertically, at left "Does the road wind up-hill all the way? Yes, to the very end" and at right "Will the day's journey take the whole long day? from morn to night, my friend" (from "Up-Hill").

367: Across top: "Watch with me, blessed spirits, who delight" and across bottom "all through the long night to walk in white" (from "Old and New Year Ditties"); vertically, at left "Look up, rise up; for far above our palms are grown, our place is set;" and at right "there we shall meet, as once we met, and love with old familiar love" (from "The Convent Threshold").

368: Across top: "Watch with me, Jesus, in my loneliness" and at bottom "though others say me nay, yet say Thou yes" (from "Old and New Year Ditties"); vertically, at left "There is no time like spring, when life's alive in every thing," and at right "before deft swallows speed their journey back along the trackless track" (from "Spring").

369: Across top: "One cried, 'How long? yet founded on the rock" and at bottom "She shall do battle, suffer, and attain'" (from "From House to Home"); vertically, at left "I looked for that which is not, nor can be, and hope deferred made my heart sick in truth;" and at right "but years must pass before a hope of youth is resigned utterly" (from "A Pause of Thought").

Note: Engraved title page in addition to letterpress; illustrated.
Location: DeU.

B39   VOICES OF COMFORT (1873)

Some text in <u>black letter</u>:
VOICES OF COMFORT | EDITED BY | THOMAS VINCENT FOSBERY, M.A. | HON. CHAPLAIN TO THE LORD BISHOP OF WINCHESTER, | AND SOMETIME VICAR OF ST. GILES'S, READING. | RIVINGTONS | <u>London, Oxford, and Cambridge</u> | MDCCCLXXIII

"These thorns are sharp, yet I can tread on them" ("From House to Home"), 8; "Watch with me, Jesus, in my loneliness" ("Old and New Year Ditties"), 25; "I bore with thee long weary days and nights" ("The Love of Christ Which Passeth Knowledge"), 56; "I love and love not: Lord, it breaks my heart" ("Dost Thou Not Care?"), 93; "I have no wit, no words, no tears" ("A Better Resurrection"), 183-184; "I will accept thy will to do and be," ("A Bruised Reed Shall He Not Break"), 184-185. All signed "Christina Rossetti."

Note: Rossetti's poems included with her permission (xxvii). Frequently reprinted, with "second edition" 1876, "third edition" 1877, "fourth edition" 1878, and a "new edition" in 1885; "A Better Resurrection" was omitted sometime before the 1885 edition, which was reprinted after Fosbery's death.
Locations: 1873, 1885: Bodleian library (via Google Books).

B40   DAY AFTER DAY (1874)

Within rule frame with ornamented corners; some text in <u>black letter</u>:
[ornament, cross] | Day after Day: | A. T. C. | [ornamented rule] | <u>OXFORD:</u> | W. R. BOWDEN, 35, HOLYWELL-STREET. | <u>LONDON:</u> | W. WELLS GARDNER, 2, PATERNOSTER BUILDINGS. | [ornamented rule] | 1874.

Excerpts from "From House to Home" (January 14, October 21); "The Love of Christ Which Passeth Knowledge" (March 8); "Dost Thou Not Care?" (August 6); "Christian and Jew" (November 8); "Advent" ("This Advent moon shines cold and clear") (December 4, 30). Unsigned, but attributed in "Index to the Poetry."

Note: CGR's first appearance in a devotional calendar, in which daily Biblical texts are paired with quotations from poems and hymns. Unpaginated. Reprinted by the Society for Promoting Christian Knowledge in 1883.
Location: 1874, 1883: Bodleian library (via Google Books).

B41   HEAVEN IN SONG (1874)

HEAVEN IN SONG: | COMPRISING THE | GEMS OF ALL AGES | ON | THE BETTER LAND. | BY | HENRY C. FISH, D.D., | AUTHOR OF "HISTORY AND REPOSITORY OF PULPIT ELOQUENCE," "HANDBOOK OF | REVIVALS," "THE HOUR FOR ACTION," "PRIMITIVE PIETY REVIVED," ETC. | NEW YORK: | SHELDON & CO., PUBLISHERS. | 1874.

"Paradise: In a Dream" ("Paradise"), 59-61; "Martyrs' Song," 85-88; "Give Me the Lowest Place" ("The Lowest Place"), 274-275; "Heart-Sick with Hope Deferred" ("Advent," first line "This Advent moon"), 562-564; "As Eager Traveller To The Goal" ("After This The Judgment"), 673-675; "Does the Road Wind Up-Hill All The Way?" ("Up-Hill"), 688; "Paradise in a Symbol" ("Birds of Paradise"), 715-716. All signed "Christina G. Rossetti" except. 274, "Christina Rossetti."

Location: TxU.

B42   PHILIPS' SERIES OF READING BOOKS (1874)

PHILIPS' SERIES OF READING BOOKS | FOR | PUBLIC ELEMENTARY SCHOOLS. | EDITED BY | JOHN G. CROMWELL, M.A. | PRINCIPAL OF ST MARK'S COLLEGE, CHELSEA. | [short rule] | THIRD BOOK. | [short rule] | LONDON: | GEORGE PHILIP & SON, 32 FLEET STREET; | LIVERPOOL: CAXTON BUILDINGS, SOUTH JOHN STREET, and | 49 & 51 SOUTH CASTLE STREET. | 1874.

"Winter Rain," 74.

Note: Rossetti's poem included with her permission ("Advertisement," iii).
Location: Bodleian library (via Google Books).

B43   HYMNS AND RHYMES (1875)

Some text in <u>black letter</u>:
Hymns AND Rhymes | FOR | <u>Home and School.</u> | COLLECTED BY | MRS. C. S. GUILD, | COMPILER OF "HYMNS FOR MOTHERS AND CHILDREN," | AND "HYMNS OF THE AGES." | [floral ornament] | BOSTON: | NICHOLS AND HALL, | 32 Bromfield Street. | 1875.

"Queer" ("A pin has a head, but has no hair"), 139; "Kookoorookoo!" ("Kookoorookoo! kookoorookoo!"), 139-140; "The Difference" ("A toadstool comes up in a night"), 141-142; "Flowers" ("Hope is like a harebell, trembling from its birth"), 143; "How many?" ("How many seconds in a minute?"), 143-144. All signed "Christina G. Rossetti"
Location: OO.

B44   LYRICS OF LIGHT AND LIFE (1875)

LYRICS OF LIGHT AND LIFE: | XLIII. *Original Poems by* | Dr. John Henry Newman, *William Alexander, Bp. of Derry,* | *Christina G. Rossetti, Aubrey de Vere, J. C. Earle, W. Chatterton* | *Dix, Rev. Gerard Moultrie, Rev. Henry Nutcombe* | *Oxenham, H. W. Mozley, Rev. Edward* | *Caswall, B.*

Montgomerie Ranking, Rev. R. | S. Hawker, Rev. John Purchas, Rev. W. | J. Blew, Rev. Dr. Monsell, Capt. | Hedley Vicars, &c. Edited | by the Rev. Frederick | George Lee, D. C. L. | [orn, anchor with fish; text to left and right] | [to left] ALDI | [to right] DISCIP• | [to left] ANGLVS | LONDON: BASIL MONTAGU PICKERING, | 196, PICCADILLY. | 1875.

"A Rose Plant in Jericho," 11-12. Signed "Christina G. Rossetti."

Note: A "second edition, revised and enlarged" was published in 1878.
Locations: 1875: NjP, MWH; 1878: NjP, TxLT (large paper issue).

B45   HEART AND HOME SONGS (1876)

HEART AND HOME SONGS. ORIGINAL AND SELECTED. ARRANGED BY | M. E. TOWNSEND. | [ornament] | LONDON: | HATCHARDS, PICCADILLY. | 1876.

"King and Queen" ("If I were a queen"), 64; "Faith, Hope and Charity" ("Hope is like a harebell, trembling from its birth"), 64; "A Crown" ("Twist me a crown of wind flowers"), 65. All signed "C. Rossetti."

Note: Published with Rossetti's permission (xii).
Location: Bodleian library (via Google Books).

B46   LITTLE GRAVES (1876)

[ornamented L, G] LITTLE GRAVES | CHOICE SELECTIONS | OF | POETRY AND PROSE. | WITH AN INTRODUCTION BY J. G. HOLLAND. | [rule] | "O when my days are ended, | I would rest | Where little children keep | Their slumbers long and deep; | My grave be near the little mounds | I know that God hath blest." | [rule] | NEW YORK: | NELSON & PHILLIPS. | CINCINNATI: | HITCHCOCK & WALDEN. | 1876.

"Sweet Death," 226-227. Signed "Christina G. Rosetti" (misspelled).

Location: OU.

B47   TRANSLATIONS LITERAL AND FREE OF THE DYING HADRIAN'S ADDRESS
        (1876)

TRANSLATIONS, | LITERAL AND FREE, | OF THE | DYING HADRIANS | ADDRESS TO HIS SOUL. | [short rule] | Quo vadam nescio. | *Appian—Pagan Epitaph.* | [short rule] | COLLECTED AND ARRANGED BY DAVID JOHNSTON. | [rule] | *For private circulation only.* | BATH: | PRINTED AT THE "CHRONICLE" OFFICE, KINGSTON BUILDINGS. | [rule, 8 mm] | MDCCCLXXVI

"Soul rudderless, unbraced" ("Hadrian's Death-Song Translated") and "Animuccia, vagantuccia, morbiduccia," ("Adriano"), 49. Both signed "Christina G. Rossetti."

Location: NjP.

B48   WORKS OF THE BRITISH POETS (1876)

WORKS | OF | THE BRITISH POETS, | FROM CHAUCER TO MORRIS, | WITH BIOGRAPHICAL SKETCHES. | EDITED BY | ROSSITER JOHNSON. | IN THREE VOLUMES. | VOL. III. – KEATS TO MORRIS. | *ILLUSTRATED WITH FINE STEEL ENGRAVINGS.* | NEW YORK: | D. APPLETON AND COMPANY, | 549 AND 551 BROADWAY. | 1876.

"Dream-Land," 647; "At Home," 647; "A Triad," 647; "Cousin Kate," 648; "Noble Sisters," 648; "A Birthday," 648-649; "Remember," 649; "An Apple-Gathering," 649; "The Love of Christ Which Passeth Knowledge," 649; "Advent" ("This Advent moon shines cold and clear"), 650; "The Three Enemies," 650. Not individually signed, but attributed to "Christina G. Rossetti" in table of contents and section heading.

Note: Biographical note, with name given as "Christina Gabriella Rossetti" (647).
Location: University of California, Berkeley (via Google Books).

B49   BABY DAYS (1877)

Within single rule frame:
BABY DAYS | A SELECTION OF | SONGS, STORIES, AND PICTURES, | FOR | VERY LITTLE FOLKS. | WITH AN INTRODUCTION | BY THE EDITOR OF ST. NICHOLAS. | [short rule] | 300 ILLUSTRATIONS | [short rule] | SCRIBNER & CO., NEW-YORK.

"An Alphabet from England" ("An Alphabet"), 46-49. Signed "Christina G. Rossetti."

Note: Date from copyright page. Illustrated. A selection of materials from the periodical *St. Nicholas*, which published Rossetti's poem in 1875 (see **C92**); the text and illustrations seem to be printed from the *St. Nicholas* plates.
Location: Center for Research Libraries.

B50   THE POETICAL BIRTHDAY BOOK (1877)

Within single rule frame; some text in black letter:
THE | POETICAL | BIRTHDAY BOOK; | OR, | Characters from the Poets. | EDITED BY | THE COUNTESS OF PORTSMOUTH. | Illustrated Edition. | LONDON: | HATCHARDS, PICCADILLY. | 1877.

Excerpts from "Enrica, 1865," 4; "Songs in a Cornfield," 108; "Noble Sisters," 140; "Love From the North," 192; "'The iniquity of the fathers upon the children" ("Under the Rose"), 212.

Note: Compiler's full name is Eveline Alicia Juliana Herbert. This is the only anthology appearance of "Under the Rose."
Location: Bodleian library (via Google Books).

B51   LATTER-DAY LYRICS (1878)

Some text in black letter:
LATTER-DAY LYRICS | BEING | *Poems of Sentiment and Reflection* | By Living Writers | Selected and Arranged with Notes | By W. DAVENPORT ADAMS | [ornament, floral] | *WITH A NOTE ON SOME FOREIGN FORMS OF VERSE* | *BY AUSTIN DOBSON* | London | CHATTO AND WINDUS, PICCADILLY | 1878 | [*All rights reserved*]

"Somewhere Or Other," 54; "If" ("Hoping against Hope"), 58; "A Smile and a Sigh," 60; "Oh roses for the flush of youth" ("Song"), 187; "Passing away" ("Old and New Year Ditties"), 209; "After Death," 254. All signed "Christina Rossetti."

Locations: No location (microfilm); MH (via Google Books).

B52   A MASQUE OF POETS (1878)

Two issues were published, priority undetermined:
Issue a: [within red single rule frame] A | MASQUE OF POETS. | INCLUDING | GUY VERNON, A

NOVELETTE IN VERSE. | BOSTON: | ROBERTS BROTHERS. | 1878.

Issue b: NO NAME SERIES. | "Is the Gentleman Anonymous? Is he a Great Unknown?" | Daniel Deronda. | [ornamented rule]' | A | MASQUE OF POETS. | INCLUDING | GUY VERNON, A NOVELETTE IN VERSE. | BOSTON: | ROBERTS BROTHERS. | 1878.

"Husband and Wife," 42-44. Unsigned.

Note: Edited by George Parsons Lathrop.
Locations: Issue a: NjP; Issue b: IXA, NjP.

B53   ROUTLEDGE'S EVERY GIRL'S ANNUAL (1878)

Engraved title; text within compartment with outer yellow single rule, inner black single rule; some text in red and orange ink as noted:
['R' in black outline with red within] Routledge's | [all letters black outline; large caps red, small caps orange within] Every Girl's [swash Rs] | [all letters black outline; large caps red, small caps orange within] Annual | Edited by | Miss Alicia A. Leith | Illustrated | GEORGE ROUTLEDGE & SONS. | K. C.

"Freaks of Fashion," 326-328. Signed "Christina G. Rossetti."

Location: CaBVaU.

B54   A POETRY-BOOK OF MODERN POETS (1878)

A POETRY-BOOK | OF MODERN POETS | CONSISTING OF | SONGS & SONNETS, ODES & LYRICS | SELECTED AND ARRANGED, WITH NOTES, | FROM THE WORKS OF THE MODERN ENGLISH | AND AMERICAN POETS, | DATING FROM THE MIDDLE | OF THE EIGHTEENTH CENTURY TO THE PRESENT TIME; | BY | AMELIA B. EDWARDS. | *COPYRIGHT EDITION.* | LEIPZIG | BERNHARD TAUCHNITZ | 1878.

"Up-Hill," 288.

Note: First (and apparently only) CGR publication in a Tauchnitz edition. CGR gave permission for the publication in 1873, and received copies in January 1879 (*Letters* 1: 429; 2:197). Reprinted in London by Longmans, Green & Co. in 1879 (not seen).
Location: Cooper Union Library; 1879: copy located at NjP.

B55   SONGS OF REST (1878)

Some text in black letter:
[rectangular ornament] | Songs of Rest. | EDITED BY | W. R. NICOLL, M.A., | MINISTER OF THE FREE CHURCH, KELSO. | "And Moses drew near unto the thick darkness | Where God was." | Edinburgh: | MACNIVEN & WALLACE.

"Passing Away," ("Old and New Year Ditties"), 75-76; "Paradise" ("Saints and Angels"), 82-83; "I will lift up mine eyes unto the hills" (first line "I am pale with sick desire"), 85-86. All signed "Christina G. Rossetti."

Note: Reset second edition published in 1879; frequently reprinted, with a "Fifth edition" published in 1885. The "Second Series" (B81, 1886) includes additional Rossetti poems. BL depository copy: '21 JY 79'.
Locations: BL; 1879 ("second edition"): BL; 1886 (title page: "First Series," "Fifth Edition"): BL.

B56   RESURGIT (1879)

Within double rule frame, outer rule in red; some text in <u>black letter</u>; red ink as noted:
['R' in red ink] Resurgit: | A COLLECTION OF | [this line in red] <u>Hymns and Songs of the Resurrection.</u> | *EDITED, WITH NOTES,* | By FRANK FOXCROFT. | *WITH AN INTRODUCTION* | By ANDREW PRESTON PEABODY, D.D. | [ornamented rule with cross in center] | [this line in red] <u>Boston:</u> | LEE AND SHEPARD, PUBLISHERS. | [this line in red] <u>New York:</u> | CHARLES T. DILLINGHAM, | 1879.

"I have no wit, no words, no Tears" ("A Better Resurrection"), 281-282. Not signed, but attributed to "Christina Georgina Rossetti" in prefatory biographical note.

Location: VtU.

B57   SONGS OF THE SOUL (1880)

Songs of the Soul | GATHERED OUT OF | MANY LANDS AND AGES. | BY | SAMUEL IRENÆUS PRIME, | AUTHOR OF "THE ALHAMBRA AND THE KREMLIN," "THE POWER OF PRAYER," | ETC., ETC. | NEW YORK: | ROBERT CARTER AND BROTHERS, | 530 Broadway. | 1880.

"Advent Hymn" ("Advent," first line "This Advent moon"), 82-84; "Christmas Carol" ("Before the paling of the stars"), 88-89; "Long Barren," 168; "I Bore With Thee Long, Weary Days" ("The Love Of Christ Which Passeth Knowledge"), 169-170; "Am I a Stone" ("Good Friday"), 257; "A City That Hath Foundations" ("From House to Home"). Signed "Christina G. Rossetti" except 170, "Christina Rossetti."

Location: RPB.

B58   HE GIVETH SONGS (1880)

HE GIVETH SONGS | A Collection of Religious Lyrics | BY | W. M. L. JAY, A. E. HAMILTON | AND OTHERS | With Illustrations by Miss L. B. Humphrey | [vignette, portrait of girl and boy reading, girl holding book, 44 x 52] | NEW YORK | E. P. DUTTON & COMPANY | 713 Broadway | 1881

"Paradise," 5-7; "That Day" (excerpt, "From House to Home"), 23-25; "The Lowest Place" (excerpt, "The Lowest Room"), 71; "Who Shall Deliver Me?," 175-176; "A Better Resurrection," 189-190. Individual poems not signed, but attributed in table of contents to "Christina G. Rossetti."

Note: On verso of title: "Copyright 1880 by E. P. Dutton & Co"; printed in late 1880 with 1881 as title page date (see notice in *Publishers' Weekly* September 25 1880: 403). Advertised as "A companion to our edition of Faber's Hymns." (*American Bookseller*, 1 November 1880: 365). Reprinted in 1885, and, with new title *At the Evening-time: And Other Poems*, in 1892.
Locations: 1881: Ives; 1885: GEU; 1892: University of California, Berkeley (via Google Books).

B59   CHRISTMAS CAROLS AND MIDSUMMER SONGS (1881)

CHRISTMAS CAROLS | AND | MIDSUMMER SONGS. | BY | AMERICAN POETS. | ILLUSTRATIONS BY | AMERICAN ARTISTS. | BOSTON: | D. LOTHROP & COMPANY, | FRANKLIN STREET.

"A Christmas Carol" ("A holy, heavenly chime"), 3 pages (unpaginated). Attributed to "Christina G. Rossetti" in the table of contents.

Note: Copyright date 1881, and advertised in the *Literary World* (Boston) for 3 December (436). Illustrated, using the same woodcuts (but not the same layout) that would subsequently appear in the

December, 1882 number of *Wide Awake* (Boston) Rossetti's extant correspondence with Ella Farman Pratt, editor of *Wide Awake*, makes no reference to this earlier printing (*Letters* 3: 63). Despite the title page's identification of the contributors as "American Poets," both Rossetti and Dinah Craik are included. In 1884, Rossetti's poem appeared in Lothrop's *Yule Tide*, using the same plates as *Wide Awake*.
Locations: MH (via Google Books); 1884: AU.

B60   SELECTIONS IN VERSE (1881)

SELECTIONS | IN VERSE. | [rule] | "As in the meadow the wheat is growing, | So, sprouting and waving, in mortal souls | Thoughts are growing. | Aye! but the soft inspirations of poets | Are like the blue and crimson flowers | Blossoming amid them." | LELAND'S HEINE. | [rule] | PHILADELPHIA: | J. B. LIPPINCOTT & CO. | 1881.

"Roadside Grasses" ("Consider the Lilies of the Field," first line "Flowers preach to us if we will hear"), 56; "One Day," 109; "Rest," 131. All signed "Christina G. Rossetti."

Note: Preface signed "R. J. A. H."
Location: NjP.

B61   ENGLISH SONNETS BY LIVING WRITERS (1881)

ENGLISH SONNETS | BY | LIVING WRITERS | SELECTED AND ARRANGED, WITH A NOTE ON THE | HISTORY OF THE 'SONNET' BY | SAMUEL WADDINGTON | [oval device, lyre with owl] | 'Laborum dulce lenimen.'–HOR. | LONDON: GEORGE BELL AND SONS | YORK STREET COVENT GARDEN | 1881

"If Only," 30; "Rest," 31; "The World," 53; "Autumn Violets," 83; "After Communion," 100; "On the Wing," 123; "After Death," 143. All signed 'Christina Rossetti.

Note: First publication of "If Only," "The World," "Autumn Violets," "On the Wing."
Location: IDeKN.

B62   HOUSEHOLD LIBRARY OF CATHOLIC POETS (1881)

THE HOUSEHOLD LIBRARY | OF | [ornamented first letters C, P] CATHOLIC POETS | FROM CHAUCER TO THE PRESENT DAY. | (1350-1881). | EDITED BY | [ornament] ELIOT [small maltese cross orn] RYDER. [ornament] | [short rule] | "THE POETRY OF EARTH IS NEVER DEAD." | *Keats*. | [short rule] | JOSEPH A. LYONS. | THE UNIVERSITY OF NOTRE DAME: | NOTRE DAME, INDIANA. | 1881.

"When I am Dead" ("Song"), 87; "Husband and Wife," 87; "Weary in Well Doing," 87-88.

Note: First publication of "Weary in Well Doing." Biographical paragraph on 87.
Location: InND.

B63   CAMBRIDGE BOOK OF POETRY AND SONG (1882)

Within red compartment; some text in black letter:
CAMBRIDGE BOOK | OF | POETRY AND SONG. | SELECTED FROM | ENGLISH AND AMERICAN AUTHORS. | BY | CHARLOTTE FISKE BATES, | AUTHOR OF "RISK, AND OTHER POEMS." | COMPILER OF "THE LONGFELLOW BIRTHDAY BOOK," "SEVEN | VOICES OF SYMPATHY." | *ILLUSTRATED* | BY FREDERICKS, CHURCH, DIELMAN, TAYLOR, HARRY FENN, GIFFORD, |

AND OTHER EMINENT ARTISTS. | <u>With Indexes of Authors, Titles, and First Lines.</u> | NEW YORK: | THOMAS Y. CROWELL & CO., | No. 13 Astor Place.

"Up-Hill," 464; "Remember," 465; "The First Spring Day," 465; "Song" ("When I am dead, my dearest,") 465; "Sound Sleep," 465-466; "Wife to Husband," 466; "At Home," 466. Signed "Christina Georgina Rossetti."

Note: First publication of "The First Spring Day," "Sound Sleep," "Wife to Husband."
Location: NjP.

B64 FIVE MINUTES DAILY READINGS OF POETRY (1882)

Some text in <u>black letter</u>:
FIVE | MINUTES | <u>Daily Readings of Poetry</u> | SELECTED BY | H. L. SIDNEY LEAR | AUTHOR OF 'FOR DAYS AND YEARS,' 'CHRISTIAN BIOGRAPHIES,' | ETC. | RIVINGTONS | WATERLOO PLACE, LONDON | MDCCCLXXXII

"By the Sea," 105; "Dream Land," 116-117; "Flowers preach to us if we will hear" ("Consider the Lilies of the Field"), 146; "A Green Cornfield," 153-154; "Sound Sleep," 191-192; "Memory," 195; "Twice," 217-218; "Rest," 263; "Life and Death," 326; "They scarcely waked before they slept" ("Holy Innocents"), 377. Signed "Christina Rossetti" except misspelled as "Rosetti" on 105, 117.

Note: Compiled by Henrietta Louisa Farrer Lear. Frequently reprinted ("second edition," 1884; "third edition," 1885; "fourth edition," 1887 and a "new edition" in 1896). The misspelling of Rossetti's name was corrected in the 1884 printing. A US edition was published in New York by Thomas Whittaker in 1883.
Locations: BL; 1884: Bodleian library (via Google Books); US edition (1883): MH (via Internet Archive). Later printings not seen: 1885, copy located at BL; 1887: copy located at National Library of Scotland; 1896: copy located at National Library of Wales.

B65 IN THE SHADOW OF HIS HAND (1882)

Within red rule frame with ornament at upper right corner:
IN THE SHADOW OF HIS HAND: | THOUGHTS FOR LONELY HOURS. | BY | ROSE PORTER, | *Author of "Our Saints," "Charity, Sweet Charity," etc.* | NEW YORK: | ANSON D. F. RANDOLPH & COMPANY, | 900 BROADWAY, COR. 20TH STREET.

"Light is our sorrow, for it ends to-morrow," 28-29. Signed "Christina Rossetti."

Location: CtY.

B66 POETRY FOR CHILDREN (1882)

POETRY FOR CHILDREN. | FIRST BOOK. | SELECTED AND ARRANGED, WITH NOTES, | BY EDMUND ARTHUR HELPS. | [triangular ornament, foliage, pointing down] | LONDON | GEORGE BELL AND SONS, YORK STREET, | COVENT GARDEN. | 1882.

"Little Alice" ("Dancing on the hill-tops"), 7; "Out in the Country" ("Minnie and Mattie"), 8; "The Wind" ("Who has seen the wind"), 16; "The Rainbow" ("Boats sail on the rivers"), 16; "Birds' Nesting" ("Hear what the mournful linnets say"), 51; "Hope, Faith and Love" ("Hope is like a harebell trembling from its birth"), 102. All signed "Christina G. Rossetti" except "Birds Nesting," which is unsigned and unattributed.

Another poem, "The Sparrows" ("Sparrows in a nest") is a misattribution. The author of "The Sparrows" is Alexander J. Ellis, who included it in *Original Nursery Rhymes, For Girls and Boys* (London: F. Pitman, 1865).

Note: Although no copies of an 1887 printing have been located, a review in the *Practical Teacher* (May, 1887: 137) of "Poetry for Children. For Infants and Standard I." indicates that the two volume set includes CGR poems.
Locations: Bodleian (via Google Books).

B67   SONNETS OF THREE CENTURIES (1882)

With red ink as noted:
[Capital S in red] Sonnets | OF | [capital T, C in red] Three Centuries: | A SELECTION | *INCLUDING* | *MANY EXAMPLES HITHERTO UNPUBLISHED.* | Edited by T. HALL CAINE. | [this line in red] London: | ELLIOT STOCK, 62 PATERNOSTER ROV. | [this line in red] 1882.

"Rest," 186; "After Death," 187; "If there be any one can take my place" (sonnet twelve in "Monna Innominata"), 188; "After Communion," 189; "To-Day's Burden," 190. Individual poems unsigned, but attributed to Rossetti in the list of authors and titles.

Note: The NjP copy is a presentation copy from the editor to Dante Gabriel Rossetti, inscribed 1882. Both copies examined on large paper. First printing of "To-Day's Burden."
Locations: NjP, TxHR.

B68   INTIMATIONS OF IMMORTALITY (1883)

Some text in black letter:
Intimations of Immortality: | Thoughts for the Perplexed and Troubled. | BY | W. GARRETT HORDER, | *Editor of "The Poets' Bible," etc.* | ". . . . . Truths that wake, | To perish never; | Which neither listless-ness, nor mad endeavour, | Nor Man, nor Boy, | Nor all that is at enmity with joy, | Can utterly abolish or destroy! | Hence in a season of calm weather | Though inland far we be, | Our Souls have sight of that immortal sea | Which brought us hither, | Can in a moment travel thither, | And see the Children sport upon the shore, | And hear the mighty waters rolling evermore." | William Wordsworth. | LONDON: | ELLIOT STOCK, 62, PATERNOSTER ROW. | [short rule] | 1883.

"If I could trust mine own self with your fate" (sonnet thirteen from "Monna Innominata"), 48-49; "Does the road wind up-hill all the way?" ("Up-Hill"), 50; "The wise do send their hearts before them" (sonnet 24 from "Later Life"), 156. Variously signed: first poem unsigned but attributed in text (48); second signed "Christina Georgina Rossetti"(50); third signed "Christina G. Rossetti." (156).

Note: CGR's permission to publish her poems is mentioned in the preface (xiii) and referenced in CGR's correspondence with Horder (*Letters* 3: 56; Ives, "The Letters of Christina Rossetti," 23).
Location: Meadville Lombard Theological School.

B69   ENGLISH POETESSES (1883)

Last line brackets in original:
English Poetesses: | *A SERIES OF CRITICAL BIOGRAPHIES,* | WITH | *ILLUSTRATIVE EXTRACTS.* | BY | ERIC S. ROBERTSON, M. A. | [ornamented rule] | CASSELL & COMPANY, Limited: | *LONDON, PARIS & NEW YORK.* | 1883. | [ALL RIGHTS RESERVED.]

"She dropped a tear more rare than pearl" ("Goblin Market"), 341; "Dream Land," 343-344; "A Farm

Walk," 344-346; "Remember," 346; "After Death," 346-347; "Rest," 347; "Maude Clare," 347-348. Unsigned, but attributed via a prefatory biographical essay (338-343).

Note: First British anthology publication of "A Farm Walk." CGR reviewed the proof of Robertson's essay and made several corrections (*Letters* 3: 156-157).
Location: AzTeS.

B70   LIVING ENGLISH POETS (1883)

LIVING | ENGLISH POETS | MDCCCLXXXII | [device, two trees with banner and text 'ARBOR SCIENTIAE ARBOR VITAE | BOSTON | ROBERTS BROTHERS | LONDON: KEGAN PAUL, TRENCH, & CO. | 1 Paternoster Square | 1883

"Amor Mundi," 181-182; "Up-Hill" 183; "Song" ("When I am dead, my dearest,") 184; "Bird Raptures," 185; "Noble Sisters," 185; "At Home," 188; "Dream Land," 189; "After Death" 191. Individual poems not signed, but section is headed "Christina Georgina Rossetti."

Note: Also published in England by Kegan Paul, Trench & Co. In 1893 Kegan Paul, Trench, Trübner & Co. published an expanded edition including an additional Rossetti poem; see B115.
Location: NjP.

B71   THE POETS' BIBLE, NEW TESTAMENT (1883)

Some text in black letter:
The Poets' Bible | *SELECTED AND EDITED BY* | W. GARRETT HORDER, | AUTHOR OF 'INTIMATIONS OF IMMORTALITY.' | New Testament Section. | *NEW AND REVISED EDITION.* | LONDON: | Wm. ISBISTER, Limited | 56 LUDGATE HILL | 1883

"A Prodigal Son," 269-270; "The Descent From The Cross," 372. Both signed "Christina G. Rossetti."

Note: The first edition (1881) did not include Rossetti. Reprinted 1895 ("Third Edition," published by Ward, Lock & Bowden).
Locations: 1883: CLavC; 1895: IaAS.

B72   SPICES FOR EASTER INCENSE (1883)

SPICES | FOR | Easter Incense. | COLLECTED AND EDITED | BY | ALICE L. WILLIAMS. | [rule] | "Break through my bonds, whate'er it cost; | What is not Thine within me slay; | Give me the lot I covet most, | To rise as Thou hast risen to-day." | [rule] | CHICAGO: | BELFORD, CLARKE & CO.

"An Easter Carol," 12-13; "Weep not; O friends, we should not weep" ("My Friend"), 62. Signed "Christina G. Rossetti."

Note: Announced in "New Publications," the *Literary World* (Boston) (24 March 1883: 98).
Location: Ives (disbound).

B73   THE TABLETS OF THE HEART (1883)

Some text in black letter:
THE | TABLETS OF THE HEART: | Poems, Rhymes, and Aphorisms, | DOMESTIC, SOCIAL, COMPLIMENTARY, AND AMATORY. | *CHRISTMAS, NEW YEAR, EASTER, BIRTHDAYS, FRIENDSHIP, LOVE,* | *MARRIAGE, BIRTH, BEREAVEMENT.* | SELECTED AND ARRANGED BY |

THE REV. FREDERICK LANGBRIDGE, M.A. | AUTHOR OF "SONGS IN SUNSHINE," "GASLIGHT AND STARS," ETC. | WITH TEN COLOURED ILLUSTRATIONS BY | J. R. HERBERT, R.A., ALICE SQUIRE, BARONESS MARIE VON BECKENDORFF, | HERBERT J. ALLCHIN, J. McINTYRE, ETC. | [device, easel displaying "R T & S" and text "LONDON REGISTERED" on palette, with "TRADEMARK" below] | LONDON: | RAPHAEL TUCK AND SONS, | COLEMAN STREET, E.C. | 1883.

"New Year left me somewhat sad" ("Old and New Year Ditties"), 62; "While roses are so red," ("Beauty is Vain"), 95; "Stop Thief!" 101; "Song" ("When I am dead"), 104; "My heart is like a singing bird" ("A Birthday"), 118; "Let us strike hands as hearty friends" ("No, Thank You, John"), 161; "One Day," 163; "Better by far you should forget and smile" ("Remember"), 171; "Watch with me, Jesus, in my loneliness" ("Old and New Year Ditties"), 366. All signed "Christina Rossetti" except 95, "Christina G. Rossetti."

Note: The Preface explains that the book includes "little pieces written with the sole object of their being made to do duty on Christmas, New Year, Valentine, Easter, Birthday, Wedding, and Condolence cards" (v). CGR's "Stop Thief!" appears on the list of "Original and Copyright Poems" written specifically for the volume and copyrighted by Tuck and Sons, and CGR is listed among writers thanked in the Preface for contributing "poems hitherto unpublished" (vii). CGR's contribution was not included in any of her collected volumes, perhaps because Tuck would not allow it, but it did appear in another 1883 Tuck volume edited by Langbridge, *Love-Knots and Bridal Bands* (which includes all of the CGR entries from *Tablets* except the extracts from "Old and New Year Ditties."

Text of "Stop Thief!":

My heart is yours. What can you want with *two*
Hearts? oh you traitor, you!
What can you keep a second heart to do?

Location: Bodleian library (via Google Books).

B74   THOUGHTS FOR HOLY DAYS AND VIGILS (1883)

Some text in <u>black letter</u>:
THOUGHTS FOR HOLY | DAYS AND VIGILS | <u>Original and Selected</u> | *WITH A PREFACE BY* | THE LORD BISHOP OF DERRY | "*Meanwhile with every son and Saint of Thine | Along the glorious line, | Sitting by turns beneath Thy sacred feet, | We'll hold communion sweet, | Know them by look and voice, and thank them all | For helping us in thrall, | For words of hope and bright examples given, | To show through moonless skies that there is | light in heaven.*" | RIVINGTONS | WATERLOO PLACE, LONDON | MDCCCLXXXIII

"Not to be first" ("The Lowest Room"), 143; "God be with you" (sonnet five, "Monna Innominata"), 173; "Does the Road Wind Uphill all the way" ("Up-Hill"), 182. All signed "Christina Rosetti" (sic).
Location: Bodleian library (via Google Books).

Note: The author of the preface, signed "William Derry and Raphoe" (x) is William Alexander, Bishop of Derry and Raphoe and husband of Cecil Frances Alexander; the introduction is signed "J. D. M." (xii).

B75 NF   DAILY STRENGTH FOR DAILY NEEDS (1884)

Some text in <u>black letter</u>:
DAILY STRENGTH | FOR | DAILY NEEDS. | "*As thy days, so shall they strength be.*"| <u>Selected by the Editor of "Quiet Hours."</u> | [ornament, leaf pointing down] | BOSTON: | ROBERTS BROTHERS. | 1884.

Prose excerpts: "O Lord, who art our Guide even unto death" ("Annus Domini"), 23, signed "C. G.

Rossetti"; "O Lord, who art as the Shadow of a great Rock" (unidentified), 166, signed "Christina G. Rossetti"; "O Lord God gracious and merciful"("Annus Domini"), 213, signed "C. G. Rossetti."

Note: Compiled by Mary Wilder Tileston. An extremely popular book, frequently reprinted and still available. Excerpts from Rossetti also appear in Tileston's 1897 compilation, *Prayers Ancient and Modern*.
Locations: 1884: Ives; 1885: MH (via Google Books); 1896: TxDN.

B76   FOREGLEAMS OF IMMORTALITY (1884)

FOREGLEAMS OF IMMORTALITY, | AND AN | IN MEMORIAM. | BY | ROSE PORTER, | *Author of "In the Shadow of His Hand," etc.* | NEW YORK: ANSON D. F. RANDOLPH & COMPANY, | 900 BROADWAY, COR. 20th STREET.

"Death may bring our friend exceeding near" (sonnet 28 from "Later Life"), 60; "Does the road wind up-hill all the way?" ("Up-Hill"), 73-74; "Sparks fly upward toward their fount of fire" ("An Immurata Sister"), 89.

Note: date from copyright page (verso of title).
Location: Andrews University (damaged, pages missing).

B77   A CHRISTMAS GARLAND: CAROLS AND POEMS (1885)

Within red ornamental rule frame; some text in black letter:
[this line underlined] A Christmas Garland | CAROLS AND POEMS | FROM | THE FIFTEENTH CENTURY TO | THE PRESENT TIME | EDITED BY | A. H. BULLEN | With Seven Illustrations newly designed | by Henry G. Wells | LONDON | JOHN C. NIMMO | 14, KING WILLIAM STREET, STRAND, W.C. | 1885

"A Christmas Carol" ("In the bleak mid-winter"), 78-79.

Note: Bullen acknowledges permission from the SPCK to publish CGR's poem (xii). Although no prior publication of "A Christmas Carol" with the SPCK has yet been located, CGR also refers to the poem having appeared in a SPCK periodical (see Ives, "The Letters of Christina Rossetti: Two New Letters"). The 1885 printing included a limited large paper issue. Reprinted by Nimmo, retitled *Carols and Poems*, in 1886.
Locations: MiU, Bodleian (via Google Books); 1886: OkU.

B78   ROS ROSARUM (1885)

Title in red ink, within intersecting single rule frame, except as noted:
[ornamental large capitals] Ros Rosarum | EX HORTO POETARUM | [rule] | [small leaf ornament, pointing down] | DEW OF THE EVER-LIVING ROSE | Gathered from | The Poets' Gardens of many Lands | BY | "E. V. B." | [ornament, roses in basket] | [rule] | LONDON | ELLIOT STOCK, 62, PATERNOSTER Row, E.C. | 1885 | [below rule frame] *All rights reserved*

"Unmindful of the roses" ("One Sea-Side Grave"), 237-238. Signed "Christina Rossetti."

Note: Compiled by Eleanor Vere Boyle. Reprinted: 1896 ("Second Edition", London: Stock; Chicago: A C. McClurg; not seen); 1897 ("Third Edition"), with CGR contribution on 239-240.
Locations: MH (via Google Books); 1897: MH (via Google Books). Not seen: 1896, (London): copy located at NjP; 1986 (McClurg): copy located at Washington State University.

B79   THE CHILDREN OF THE POETS (1886)

Within red rule frame; with red ink as noted; some text in <u>black letter</u>:
<u>The</u> | [this line in red] <u>Children of the Poets</u> | *AN ANTHOLOGY* | FROM | [this line in red] ᴇɴɢʟɪꜱʜ ᴀɴᴅ ᴀᴍᴇʀɪᴄᴀɴ Wʀɪᴛᴇʀꜱ ᴏꜰ | [this line in red] Tʜʀᴇᴇ Cᴇɴᴛᴜʀɪᴇꜱ | *Edited, with Introduction* | BY | ᴇʀɪᴄ S. ʀᴏʙᴇʀᴛꜱᴏɴ. | [ornament in red ink] | LONDON: | [this line in red] Walter Scott, 24 Warwick Lane, Paternoster Row, | AND NEWCASTLE-ON-TYNE. | 1886.

"Johnny," 211-213; "Buds and Babies," 213. Both signed "Christina Rossetti."

Note: Printed with Rossetti's permission (see *Letters* 3: 272; Ives, "The Letters of Christina Rossetti," 24).
Location: VtU.

B80   REPRESENTATIVE POEMS OF LIVING POETS (1886)

American issue:
ʀᴇᴘʀᴇꜱᴇɴᴛᴀᴛɪᴠᴇ Pᴏᴇᴍꜱ | OF | LIVING POETS | AMERICAN AND ENGLISH | SELECTED BY THE POETS THEMSELVES | WITH AN INTRODUCTION BY | GEORGE PARSONS LATHROP | [rule, 11 mm] | CASSELL & COMPANY, Lɪᴍɪᴛᴇᴅ | 739 & 741 Broadway, New York | [rule. 4 mm] | 1886.

British issue:
ʀᴇᴘʀᴇꜱᴇɴᴛᴀᴛɪᴠᴇ Pᴏᴇᴍꜱ | OF | LIVING POETS | AMERICAN AND ENGLISH | SELECTED BY THE POETS THEMSELVES | WITH AN INTRODUCTION BY | GEORGE PARSONS LATHROP | [rule, 11 mm] | CASSELL & COMPANY, Lɪᴍɪᴛᴇᴅ | *LONDON, PARIS, NEW YORK & MELBOURNE* | [rule. 4 mm] | 1886

"A Christmas Carol" ("In the bleak mid-winter"), 540-541; "An Apple Gathering," 541-542; "'No, Thank You, John," 542-543; "Jessie Cameron," 543-547. Not individually signed, but attributed in the table of contents to "Rossetti, Christina G."; a facsimile of Rossetti's signature also appears on 540.

Note: Compiled by Jeanette Gilder, and published with Rossetti's permission. An extra-illustrated copy at Yale includes CGR's correspondence with Gilder (see Ives, "The Letters of Christina Rossetti").
Location: AzTeS.

B81   SONGS OF REST, SECOND SERIES (1886)

Some text in <u>black letter</u>:
[floral ornament] | <u>Songs of Rest.</u> | *SECOND SERIES.* | EDITED BY THE REV. W. ROBERTSON NICOLL, M. A. | Mors ultra non erit, neque luctus, neque clamor, | neque dolor erit ultra *quia prima abierunt.* | <u>London:</u> | HODDER AND STOUGHTON, | 27, PATERNOSTER ROW. | MDCCCLXXXVI.

"Paradise" (first line: "Once in a dream I saw the flowers"), 31-32; "Sweet Death," 33; "Mother Country," 34-36; "Remember," 79; "Sound Sleep," 80. All signed "Christina G. Rossetti."

Note: An extremely popular collection, frequently reprinted and expanded after its initial publication in 1878. Three Rossetti poems appeared in the first edition (see B55); in 1893, another edition was printed, combining the Rossetti poems from 1878 and 1886.
Locations: BL; 1893: BL, NjP.

B82 L   ANNE GILCHRIST HER LIFE AND WRITINGS (1887)

ANNE GILCHRIST | HER LIFE AND WRITINGS | EDITED BY | HERBERT HARLAKENDEN

GILCHRIST | With a Prefatory Notice by | William Michael | Rossetti. | LONDON: | T. FISHER UNWIN | 1887

Eight letters from CGR: 147-148, 154-158, 160-161, 173, 175-177.

Location: TxCM.

B83–B90   THROUGH THE YEAR WITH THE POETS (1887)

A series of volumes, one for each month of the year, sold in boxed sets of three (Winter, Spring, Summer, Autumn) or individually. Rossetti's poems appear in the following volumes:

(B83)   JANUARY

JANUARY | EDITED BY | OSCAR FAY ADAMS | The wave is breaking on the shore, | The echo fading from the chime, | Again the shadow moveth o'er | The dial-plate of time! | JOHN GREENLEAF WHITTIER. | *The New Year*. | BOSTON | D. LOTHROP AND COMPANY | FRANKLIN AND HAWLEY STREETS

"Tempus Fugit," 10; "On the Wind of January" ("A Year's Windfalls"; Rossetti's title is printed beneath her signature at the end of the poem) 112; "Where Are The Songs I Used To Know?" ("The Key Note"), 115; "A Wintry Sonnet," 119-120. All signed "Christina Georgina Rossetti."

Note: Copyright statement on verso of title: "COPYRIGHT, 1885, BY | D. LOTHROP AND COMPANY.'; Preface dated "December 21, 1885."
Location: TxU.

(B84)   FEBRUARY

FEBRUARY | EDITED BY | OSCAR FAY ADAMS | Slowly, with shaking staff and snowy stole, | His frosty-bearded lips wild muttering, | Gaunt dying Winter grimly plods along; | What sound has thus disturbed his peace of soul? | Ah! he has caught a presage of the Spring, | The faint far echo of a throstle's song! | CLINTON SCOLLARD. | BOSTON | D. LOTHROP AND COMPANY | FRANKLIN AND HAWLEY STREETS

"On the Wind in February."(excerpt from "A Year's Windfalls"; Rossetti's title is printed beneath her signature at the end of the poem), 65; "Winter Rain," 89-90. Both signed "Christina Georgina Rossetti."

Note: On verso of title, 'COPYRIGHT, 1886, BY | D. LOTHROP AND COMPANY.'; Preface is dated "January 14, 1886." (iv).
Location: NjMD.

(B85)   MARCH

MARCH | EDITED BY | OSCAR FAY ADAMS | On these debatable borders of the year | Spring's foot half falters; scarce she yet may know | The leafless blackthorn blossom from the snow; | And through her bowers the wind's way still is clear. | DANTE GABRIEL ROSSETTI. | *The House of Life*. | BOSTON | D. LOTHROP AND COMPANY | FRANKLIN AND HAWLEY STREETS

"Spring," 2-83. Signed "Christina Georgina Rossetti."

Note: Briefly reviewed in the *Literary News* (April 1886: 117).
Location: NBuU (via photocopy).

(B86)   **JULY**

JULY | EDITED BY | OSCAR FAY ADAMS | High midsummer has come, midsummer mute | Of song, but rich to scent and sight. | The sun is high in heaven, the skies are bright | And full to blessedness. | Lewis Morris. | *The Ode of Life.* | BOSTON | D. LOTHROP AND COMPANY | FRANKLIN AND HAWLEY STREETS

"Summer," 131. Signed "Christina Georgina Rossetti."

Note: On verso of title, 'Copyright, 1886, by | D. LOTHROP AND COMPANY.'
Location: CUS (via Internet Archive).

(B87)   **AUGUST**

AUGUST | EDITED BY | OSCAR FAY ADAMS | Loud pulses of the field are heard to leap | Now all night long; all day the birds are mute. | The month hangs heavy, like a perfect fruit | That holds the opiate seeds of winter sleep. | Helen Gray Cone. | BOSTON | D. LOTHROP AND COMPANY | FRANKLIN AND HAWLEY STREETS

"The August Wind" ("A Year's Windfalls"; Rossetti's title is printed beneath her signature at the end of the poem), 98. Signed "Christina Georgina Rossetti."

Note: On verso of title, 'Copyright, 1886, by | D. LOTHROP AND COMPANY.' Preface dated "July 23, 1886" (iv).
Location: CUS (via Internet Archive).

(B88)   **SEPTEMBER**

SEPTEMBER | EDITED BY | OSCAR FAY ADAMS | . . . The ripe fruits rattle from the boughs, | Peaches and sweetings, and the leaves grow red, | And the torn rushes with the water-soughs | Go floating by where fruit's ingarnerèd | To fill the press with luscious pulp and scent | Of pines and cloves. | Theophile Marzials. | *The Angel of God in the Garden of Phantasy.* | BOSTON | D. LOTHROP AND COMPANY | FRANKLIN AND HAWLEY STREETS

"Summer is Ended," 101. Signed "Christina Georgina Rossetti."

Note: On verso of title, 'Copyright, 1886, by | D. LOTHROP AND COMPANY.' Preface dated "August 19, 1886." (iv).
Location: TxU.

(B89)   **OCTOBER**

OCTOBER | EDITED BY | OSCAR FAY ADAMS | Shorter and shorter now the twilight clips | The days, as through the sunset gate they crowd, | And summer from her golden collar slips | And strays through stubblefields, and moans aloud, | Save when by fits the warmer air deceives, | And, stealing hopeful to some sheltered bower, | She lies on pillows of the faded leaves, | And tries the old tunes over for an hour. | Alice Cary. | *Autumn.* | BOSTON | D. LOTHROP AND COMPANY | Franklin and Hawley Streets

"An October Garden," 77; "Autumn Violets," 88. Signed "Christina Georgina Rossetti."

Location: NbuU.

(B90)   **NOVEMBER**

NOVEMBER | EDITED BY | OSCAR FAY ADAMS | For now the wind-beat twigs had lost their hold | Of the faint yellow leaves, and thin and light | The forest grew, and colder night by night, | Or soaked with rain, and swept with bitter wind, | Or with white creeping mist made deaf and blind. | William Morris. | *The Life and Death of Jason.* | BOSTON | D. LOTHROP AND COMPANY | Franklin and Hawley Streets

"November Wind" (excerpt from "A Year's Windfalls"; Rossetti's title is printed beneath her signature at the end of the poem), 48; "So Late in Autumn" (number 18 in Rossetti's sonnet sequence "Later Life"), 124. Signed "Christina Georgina Rossetti."

Note: On verso of title, 'Copyright, 1886, by | D. LOTHROP AND COMPANY.' Preface dated "October 19, 1886." (iv).
Locations: CUY (via Internet Archive); OClW (via photocopy); PSC (email correspondence).

B91   **FIFTY YEARS OF ENGLISH SONG (1887)**

FIFTY YEARS | OF | English Song. | SELECTIONS FROM THE POETS | OF | THE REIGN OF VICTORIA. | EDITED AND ARRANGED BY | HENRY F-RANDOLPH. | *** | The Poets of the Second Half of the Reign. | The Writers of Vers de Société. | NEW YORK: | ANSON D. F. RANDOLPH & CO.

"Dream-Land," 250-51; "Bird Raptures," 251; "Amor Mundi," 251-252; "After Death," 252-253; "Song" ("When I am dead, my dearest"), 253; "Consider," 253-254; "Up-Hill," 254. Individual poems not signed, but section is headed "Christina Georgina Rossetti."

Note: On verso of title, '*Copyright, 1887,* | By Anson D. F. Randolph & Co.'; edited by Henry Fitz-Randolph. Biographical note on Rossetti appears on xxiii.
Location: TxHR.

B92   **A SECOND SCHOOL POETRY BOOK (1887)**

Some text in <u>black letter</u>:
A SECOND SCHOOL | POETRY BOOK | COMPILED BY | M. A WOODS | HEAD MISTRESS OF THE CLIFTON HIGH SCHOOL | FOR GIRLS | <u>London</u> | MACMILLAN AND CO. | AND NEW YORK | 1887 | All rights reserved

"Goblin Market," 392-409. Signed "C G Rossetti."

Note: Copy viewed lacks period after the middle initial "A" in author's name on title page. Reprinted in *A Second Poetry Book*, Part II, 1890.
Location: University of Allahabad (via Digital Library of India).

B93   **VICTORIAN HYMNS (1887)**

Red ink <u>underlined</u>:
VICTORIAN HYMNS | ENGLISH SACRED SONGS | OF FIFTY YEARS | [ornament, two trees with scroll and text 'ARBOR SCIENTIAE | ARBOR VITAE'] | <u>LONDON</u> | KEGAN PAUL, TRENCH & CO., 1 PATERNOSTER SQUARE | <u>MDCCCLXXXVII</u>

"Am I a stone and not a sheep" ("Good Friday"), 8-9; "I bore with thee long weary days and nights" ("The Love of Christ Which Passeth Knowledge"), 51-52; "I would have gone; God bade me stay" ("Weary in Well-Doing"), 67-68. All signed "Christina Georgina Rossetti."

Location: MH (via Google Books).

B94   WOMEN'S VOICES (1887)

Red ink <u>underlined</u>:
<u>Women's</u> | <u>Voices</u> | *AN ANTHOLOGY* | *OF THE MOST CHARACTERISTIC POEMS* | *BY* | *ENGLISH, SCOTCH, AND IRISH WOMEN* | <u>SELECTED, ARRANGED, AND EDITED</u> | <u>BY</u> | <u>MRS. WILLIAM SHARP</u> | [ornamented rule] | LONDON | WALTER SCOTT, 24 WARWICK LANE | 1887

"Dream-Land," 208-209; "A Birthday," 210; "Confluents," 211-212; "Echo," 213; "The Hour and the Ghost," 214-216; "Rest," 217; "Love Lies Bleeding," 218; "The World," 219; "Later Life. VI" (sonnet six of "Later Life"), 220; "Later Life. XXVI" (sonnet 26 of "Later Life"), 221. Individual poems not signed, but attributed to "Christina G. Rossetti" in running title and table of contents.

Note: Biographical note on 416. US edition published by White and Allen.
Locations: British edition: OrCS; US edition: NjP.

B95   BOOK OF LATTER-DAY BALLADS (1888)

THE BOOK | OF | LATTER-DAY BALLADS. | (1858-1888.) | SELECTED AND ARRANGED BY | HENRY F-RANDOLPH, | EDITOR OF 'FIFTY YEARS OF ENGLISH SONG.' | [ornament, leaf pointing down] | NEW YORK: | ANSON D. F. RANDOLPH & CO.

"Jessie Cameron," 59-63. Signed "Christina Georgina Rossetti."

Location: NjP.

B96   IDEAL ENTERTAINMENTS (1888)

Underlining in original:
[ornament] IDEAL [ornament] | ENTERTAINMENTS | [three rules; middle rule is dotted line] | FOR | Parlor, Church and Platform, | CONSISTING OF | [ornament] Elocutionary Gems [ornament] | <u>P</u>oetry, <u>P</u>rose, <u>D</u>ialogues <u>and</u> <u>D</u>ramas, | BY | GEORGE M. VICKERS, | AUTHOR OF | *"The Lightkeeper's Daughter," Nora "Flogeo," "The Secret," | "The Little Gypsy," | "The Public Worrier," "The Two | Lives," "The Cobbler of Lynn," "Only a Word | at Parting," "For Goodness Sake Don't | Say I Told You," Etc.* | [rule] | 1888: | THAYER, MERRIAM & CO., LIMITED, | PHILADELPHIA.

"Maiden Song," 201-206; "The Months. A Pageant," 238-254. Both signed "Christina G. Rossetti."

Note: Later, enlarged edition published under the title *The Speaker's Ideal Entertainments* (Philadelphia, Chicago: J. H. Moore), undated but with 1892 copyright. Other copies with 1892 copyright but different Philadelphia publishers identified but not seen.
Locations: Ives; 1892 edition: Franciscan University of Steubenville. Other 1892 copies not seen: Bell Publishing: copy located at OU; Columbia Publishing: copy located at TxDN; Stanton: copy located at SUNY Binghamton.

B97   THE STORY OF MARY THE MOTHER (1888)

THE STORY OF | MARY THE MOTHER | COMPILED BY ROSE PORTER | [vignette, Madonna with two children] | BOSTON | D LOTHROP COMPANY | FRANKLIN AND HAWLEY STREETS

"Herself a rose, who bore the Rose," 65. Unsigned, attributed to Christina Rossetti in the text.

Note: Date from copyright statement.
Location: GAT

B98   SACRED SONG (1888)

Some text in <u>black letter</u>:

Sᴀᴄʀᴇᴅ Sᴏɴɢ | <u>A Volume of Religious Verse</u> | *SELECTED AND ARRANGED WITH NOTES* | BY | SAMUEL WADDINGTON | NEW YORK AND LONDON | WHITE AND ALLEN

"Weary in Well-Doing," 29; "After Communion," 79; "Dost Thou Not Care?," 85; "Despised and Rejected," 130-132; "Advent" ("This Advent moon shines cold and clear"), 301-303.

Note: Biographical note (331). Listed in "Weekly Record of New Publications," *Publishers' Weekly*, 6 October 1888: 508. Also published in London by Walter Scott (not seen).
Location: IEG. Not seen: 1888 (London): copy located at BL.

B99   ABOUT ROBINS (1889)

Engraved title page, within single rule frame; all text script except last line:

ABOUT ROBINS | [first two lines in two columns, represented by ||; at top left, a curved bracket connects 'Songs' and 'Facts'; lines three through five form a single right hand column; between the left and right columns, a full page illustration of woman feeding birds:] Songs, || Legends, | Facts, & || collected & illustrated | by | Lady Lindsay, | R. I. | [at bottom, within frame but beneath illustration:] GEORGE ROUTLEDGE & SONS, LONDON, GLASGOW, MANCHESTER AND NEW YORK

"The Months: A Pageant," 82; "The Key-Note," 83. Signed "Christina Rossetti."

Note: Illustrated. Compiled and illustrated by Lady Caroline Blanche Elizabeth Lindsay, co-founder of the Grosvenor Gallery. Date inferred from reviews and notices published in late 1889 (including *Punch*, 16 November 1889: 237). Reprinted by Frederick Warne, n.d.
Location: WU.

B100   FROM QUEENS' GARDENS (1889)

Some text in <u>black letter</u>:

Fʀᴏᴍ Qᴜᴇᴇɴs' Gᴀʀᴅᴇɴs | <u>Selected Poems</u> | OF | ELIZABETH BARRETT BROWNING | JEAN INGELOW ADEAIDE A. PROCTER | CHRISTINA ROSSETTI | AND OTHERS | *GATHERED BY ROSE PORTER* | TROY, N. Y. | NIMS AND KNIGHT | 1889

"Another Day" ("Then Shall Ye Shout"), 141; "Our Heaven," ("Our heaven must be within ourselves"), 142; "Sooner or Later" ("Sooner or later: yet at last"), 142-143; "The Power of Love" ("Every one that is perfect shall be as his master"), 144; "A Life's Parallels," 145; "The Weary" ("Through burden and heat of the day"), 145; "Our Dead," ("Who would wish back the saints upon our rough"), 146; "One step more, and the race is ended" ("Septuagesima"), 146; "Maiden May," 147; "Pleasure" ("Lay up for yourselves treasures in heaven"), 150; "Love Understands" ("Judge nothing before the time"), 151; "Sow and Reap," ("But Thy commandment is exceeding broad"), 152; "Who scatters tares shall reap no wheat" ("Rogationtide"), 152; "We sow to reap" ("That which hath been is named already, and it is known that it is man"), 152; "Roses" ("Roses and Roses"), 153; "Through coldness and through keenness" ("Endure hardness"), 153; "Homeward Bound" ("The end is not yet"), 154; "An "Immurata" Sister," 155; "Heartsease" ("Balm in Gilead"), 156; "Where Love Is" ("Where love is, there comes sorrow"), 157; "Love recognizes love's own cry" ("As a king . . . unto the King"), 157; "Tempus Fugit," 157; "To-morrow Blots Out Sorrow" ("Parting after parting"), 158; "Saints are like roses when they flush rarest" ("I gave a sweet smell"), 158-159; "De Profundis,"159; "Double" ("Sorrow hath a double voice"), 160; "The Voice of the Wind" ("Hollow-sounding and Mysterious"), 160-161; "Flowers" ("The flowers appear on the earth"), 162; "Briefness" ("Whither the Tribes go up, even the Tribes of the

Lord"), 163; "The Lily and the Lamb" ("Thy lilies drink the dew"), 163-164; "Passing and Glassing," 164-165; "Golden Glories," 165; "If Love is Not" ("If love is not worth loving, then life is not worth living"), 165-166; "Love's Light" ("O ye, who are not dead and fit"), 166; "Yet a Little While," 167; "Summer Will Come" ("One swallow does not make a summer"), 167-168; "Wait" ("What is that to thee? follow thou me"), 168; "Show Pity" ("Vanity of Vanities," first line "Of all the downfalls in the world"), 168-169; "One by the Clock" ("Praying always"), 169; "Grief is not grievous to a soul that knows" ("Surely he hath borne our griefs"), 169; "In the Willow Shade," 170-172; "Golden Silences," 173; "What's in a Name," 173-175; "An October Garden," 175-176; "Joy and Pain" ("Joy is but sorrow"), 176; "Until the Day Break," 176-177; "A Day of Days," (sonnet two of "Monna Innominata"), 178; "Christmas Eve," 178-179; "Christmas Day," 179-180; "Ash Wednesday," 180; "Good Friday" ("Lord Jesus Christ, grown faint upon the Cross"), 181; "Easter Even," 181-182; "Easter Day," 182; "Question and Answer" ("Up-hill"), 183. Individual poems not signed, but section is headed "Christina G. Rossetti."

Note: Reprinted from same plates under title *Love's Thread of Gold* (New York, Boston: H. M. Caldwell, no date).
Location: TxHU.

B101   OPEN SESAME (1889)

Some text in <u>black letter</u>:
OPEN SESAME! | POETRY AND PROSE FOR SCHOOL-DAYS. | EDITED BY | BLANCHE WILDER BELLAMY | AND | MAUD WILDER GOODWIN. | <u>Volume I.</u> | ARRANGED FOR CHILDREN FROM FOUR TO | TWELVE YEARS OLD. | [ornamented rule] | GINN & COMPANY | BOSTON • NEW YORK • CHICAGO • LONDON

"Consider," 54; "A Christmas Carol" ("In the bleak mid-winter"), 216-217; "A Chill," 289-290; "Milking Time" ("When the cows come home the milk is coming"), 298.

Note: First publication of "A Chill." Date from copyright page.
Location: MH (via Google Books).

B102   POPULAR POETS OF THE PERIOD (1889)

Within double rule frame; some text in <u>black letter</u>:
"– *HE SINGS OF WHAT THE WORLD WILL BE* | *WHEN THE YEARS HAVE DIED AWAY.*" | –TENNYSON. | [short double rule] | [floral ornament surrounding first P] <u>Popular Poets</u> | OF THE | <u>Period:</u> | BEING A VOLUME CONTAINING | BIOGRAPHICAL & CRITICAL SKETCHES | OF THE CAREERS OF | <u>Poets of our own Time and Country</u>, | TOGETHER WITH | CHOICE SELECTIONS FROM THEIR WORKS. | [short rule] | *EDITED BY* | F. A. H. EYLES. | [short rule] | LONDON: | GRIFFITH, FARRAN, OKEDEN, AND WELSH. | And Sydney, N.S.W. | [short rule] | 1889.

"Sonnet from "Later Life" (sonnet 21 of "Later Life"), 236; "After Communion," 236; "Dream-Land," 237; "The Fifth of March" ("Roses and Roses"), 238; "The Sixteenth of May" ("If love is not worth loving, then life is not worth living"), 238-239; "After Death" 239; "Song" ("When I am dead, my dearest"), 239; "To-Day for Me" ("The German-French Campaign"), 240.

Note: With prefatory essay "Some Aspects of Contemporary Poetry" by CGR's biographer Mackenzie Bell (xvii-xxiii), and biographical note on CGR by John Walker (234-235).
Location: NBiSU.

B103   THE POETS' BIBLE, OLD TESTAMENT (1890)

Some text in <u>black letter</u>:
THE POETS' BIBLE | *SELECTED AND EDITED BY* | W. GARRETT HORDER | *Author of "Is There a Future Life?" and "The Hymn-Lover,"* | *Editor of "Congregational Hymns," etc.* | <u>Old Testament Section</u> | LONDON | Wm ISBISTER, Limited | *56 LUDGATE HILL* | 1889

"Adam and Eve" (sonnet 14, "Monna Innominata"), 84; "Did any bird come flying" ("Bird or Beast"), 89; "A king dwelt in Jerusalem" ("A Testimony"), 439-440; "'The half was not told me,' said Sheba's queen," ("She came from the uttermost part of the earth"), 453; "By the Waters of Babylon" ("By the Waters of Babylon. B.C. 570"), 498-501; "Esther" (sonnet eight, "Monna Innominata"), 526-527. All signed "Christina Georgina Rossetti."

Note: CGR's permission (and that of SPCK) noted in Preface (x). "Second edition" published in 1895 by Ward, Lock and Bowden.
Locations: MsJRT; 1895: IaAS.

B104   AN ENGLISH ANTHOLOGY FROM CHAUCER TO THE PRESENT TIME (1891)

AN | ENGLISH ANTHOLOGY | FROM CHAUCER TO THE PRESENT TIME | SELECTED AND EDITED | BY | JOHN BRADSHAW, M.A., LL.D. | *Inspector of Schools, Madras.* | EDITOR OF MILTON'S POETICAL WORKS AND OF GRAY'S POEMS. | *THIRD EDITION.* | London: GEORGE BELL AND SONS, YORK STREET, | COVENT GARDEN. | MADRAS: V. KALIANARAM AIYAR. | 1891.

"If Only," 524.

Note: Description is of the 1891 third edition, as no earlier copies have been located. However, according to a notice of the second edition in the *Calcutta Review* (April 1888: 15), the earlier printing also includes "one sonnet by Christina Rossetti."
Location: Newberry Library.

B105   TREASURY OF SACRED SONG (1891)

Within red ornamented compartment, some text in <u>black letter</u>:
THE | TREASURY OF | SACRED SONG | SELECTED FROM THE | ENGLISH LYRICAL POETRY | OF FOUR CENTURIES | WITH NOTES EXPLANATORY AND BIOGRAPHICAL | BY | FRANCIS T. PALGRAVE | PROFESSOR OF POETRY IN THE UNIVERSITY OF OXFORD | <u>Er Ipso et per Ipsum et in Ipso</u> | [shield] | <u>Oxford</u> | AT THE CLARENDON PRESS | MDCCCLXXXIX

"This Advent moon shines cold and clear" ("Advent"), 270-272; "A Christmas Carol" ("In the bleak mid-winter"), 273; "Despised and Rejected," 273; "Give me the lowest place: not that I dare" ("The Lowest Place"), 274. First poem signed "C. G. Rossetti" on 272; rest unsigned, but all attributed in the "Index of Writers."

Note: Nonfirsts. A limited edition was also published.
Location: NjP; limited edition: AAP.

B106 L   THE ART OF AUTHORSHIP (1890)

Some text in <u>black letter</u>:
THE | ART OF AUTHORSHIP | *Literary Reminiscences,* | *Methods Of Work* | *And Advice To Young Beginners.* | PERSONALLY CONTRIBUTED BY | LEADING AUTHORS OF THE DAY. | COMPILED AND

EDITED BY | GEORGE BAINTON | <u>London:</u> | JAMES CLARKE & CO., 13 & 14, FLEET STREET. | [short rule] | 1890.

Two CGR letters quoted, 150-152.

Note: Bainton contacted writers and quotes from their responses. The CGR letters Bainton quotes are reprinted, without identification of Bainton as the recipient, in *Letters* 4 (65-66, numbers 1547 and 1549). Printed in the United States by D. Appleton in 1891.
Location: 1890: OrU; 1891: University of Michigan (via Google Books).

B107   THE CHILDREN'S CASKET (1891)

THE | CHILDREN'S CASKET | *Favourite Poems for Recitation* | BY | LADY HAWKSHAW LADY FLORA HASTINGS | MRS BROWNING CHRISTINA G. ROSSETTI | JEAN INGELOW MARY HOWITT | FANNY FORRESTER 'SABINA'| W. H. LONGFELLOW D. HENRY, JUN. | J. C. PRINCE, ETC., ETC., ETC. | COMPILED BY | ANNIE M. HONE | AUTHOR OF | 'WOMAN'S ENTERPRISE AND GENIUS,' 'SELF-HELP | FOR WOMEN,' ETC. | LONDON: | GRIFFITH FARRAN OKEDEN & WELSH | NEWBERY HOUSE, CHARING CROSS ROAD | AND SYDNEY | 1891

"A Prodigal Son," 4-5. Signed "Christina G. Rossetti."
Location: FU.

B108 NF   A GIFT OF LOVE (1891)

A GIFT OF LOVE | Loving | Greetings | for | 365 Days | Chosen and arranged by | Rose Porter | FLEMING H. REVELL COMPANY | [remaining text in two columns:]

NEW YORK	PUBLISHERS
CHICAGO	OF EVANGELICAL
TORONTO	LITERATURE

Poetry and prose excerpts: "Love is more potent to breed faith" (*Time Flies*), 10; "Charity or Love includes all graces" (*Time Flies*), 33; "O Thou Who seest what I cannot see," ("O Christ My God Who seest the unseen"), 35; "Watch yet a while, weep till that day" ("The Day is at Hand"), 43; "Where love is, there comes sorrow," 44; "Love is all happiness, Love is all beauty," 50; "Love understands the mystery" ("Judge nothing before the time"), 52-53; "As long as time is" ("Piteous my rhyme is"), 86; "O, my soul spread wings of Love to fly" ("Everything that is born must die"), 94; "Our heaven must be within ourselves," 94-95; "Jesus, Lord God from all eternity," ("The Name of Jesus"), 112; "There is a time for all things, saith" ("I will lift up mine eyes unto the hills," first line "When sick of life and all the world"), 120; "Among the duties which are characteristically Christian" (*Time Flies*), 122-123; "As grains of sand, as stars" ("All Saints"), 123; "In that world we weary to attain" ("His Banner over me was Love"), 129; "God makes our service Love" (combination of "All Thy Works Praise Thee, O Lord" and "If love is not worth loving, then life is not worth living"), 169; "A friend Loveth at all times" (*Time Flies*), 176; "God is Love" ("Lord, grant me grace to love thee in my pain"), 180; "Love doth so grace and dignify" ("As a king . . . unto the King"), 186; "Hast thou that hope which fainting doth pursue?" ("Mid-Lent"), 198; "The gospel tells us little specially of St. Philip" (*Time Flies*), 198-199; "O Christ, our All in each, our All in all" 211; "'Beloved, let us Love one another'," 223; "Love can make us like St. Peter" ("Every one that is perfect shall be as his master"), 228; "It is worth while to live!" ("What good shall my life do me?"), 229; "Love came down at Christmas" ("Christmastide"), 230; "O ye who taste that Love is sweet" ("O ye who are not dead and fit"), 231. Variously signed "Christina Rossetti" (33, 112, 120, 123, 129, 176 180, 198, 199, 211, 223, 228, 229) or "Christina G. Rossetti" (10, 35, 43, 44, 50, 52-53, 186) or "C. G. Rossetti" (86, 94, 95 230) or "Christiana G. Rossetti" (169) or "Christina J. Rossetti" (231).

Note: date from copyright statement (6).
Location: Dallas Theological Seminary.

B109   THROUGH WOODLAND AND MEADOW (1891)

Engraved title page:
(To left of illustration of branch with leaves and a ribbon bow tied at top center): Through | Woodland and | Meadow | & other poems | with sketches from nature | by | Marie Low | and | Maud West | [publisher names and addresses in two columns] London: [column two] New York: | ERNEST NISTER [column two] E. P. DUTTON & Cº | 24 St. Bride Street E. C. [column two] 31 West Twenty Third Street. | *Printed by E. Nister at Nuremberg (Bavaria)*

"Winter: My Secret," no pagination. Signed "Christina Rosetti" (sic).

Note: Advertised in *New York Times*, "E. P. Dutton & Co's List of New Holiday Books"(8 December 1891: 5).
Locations: Ives; PSt (photocopy).

B110   THE CLOUD OF WITNESS (1891)

Within red ornamental border; some text in <u>black letter</u>; red ink as noted:
[T, C, W in red] <u>The Cloud of Witness</u> | *A DAILY SEQUENCE* | OF | [this line in red] <u>Great Thoughts from Many Minds</u> | *FOLLOWING THE CHRISTIAN SEASONS* | BY THE | [this line in red] HON. MRS. LYTTELTON GELL | "Certain even of your own poets have said, For we are | also His offspring." | "Every good gift and every perfect gift is from above, | and cometh down from the Father of lights." | [this line in red] <u>London</u> | HENRY FROWDE | OXFORD UNIVERSITY PRESS WAREHOUSE | AMEN CORNER, E.C.

"Watch with me, Jesus, in my loneliness" ("Old and New Year Ditties"), 224. Signed "C. Rossetti."

Note: An extremely popular anthology, with over 80 thousand sold by 1899 (*Publishers' Weekly* 1 October 1898: 536).
Location: InND.

B111   WOMEN'S THOUGHTS FOR WOMEN (1891, 1899)

Some text in <u>black letter</u>:
<u>Women's Thoughts</u> | FOR WOMEN | Chosen and Arranged | By ROSE PORTER | [device, three-sectioned leaf pointing to right within circular vine, 5 x 5] | DAVID C. COOK PUBLISHING COMPANY | ELGIN, ILLINOIS.

Poetry and prose excerpts: "God makes our sorrow love" (misquoted from "All Thy Works Praise Thee, O God"), 115; "Tact is a gift; it is likewise a grace" (*Time Flies*), 117; "Lie still, my restive heart" ("What is that to thee? Follow thou Me"), 117; "Let to-day suffice to-day" ("Maiden May"), 117; "Hope afresh, for hope shall not be vain" ("But Thy commandment is exceeding broad"), 117; "Sing notes of love, that some who hear" ("O ye, who are not dead and fit," 118; "Can anything be sadder than work left unfinished?" (*Time Flies*), 118; "Love understands the mystery, whereof" ("Judge nothing before the time"), 118; "Yet a little while" ("Vigil of All Saints"), 118; "Holy scripture bids us 'run with patience the race'" (*Time Flies*), 119; "If any man do his will, he shall know" (*Time Flies*), 119; "'Beloved, let us love one another,' says Saint John," 119; "Stars, like Christians" (*Time Flies*), 119; "Our Heaven must be within ourselves," 120; "The wise do send their hearts before them to" ("Later Life" sonnet 24), 120;

"When will the day bring its pleasure?" ("Until the day break"), 120; "Here life is the beginning of our death" ("'Behold a Shaking'"), 121; "In life our absent friend is far away" ("Later Life" sonnet 28), 121; "Home by different ways. Yet all" ("The end is not yet"), 122; "Through burden and heat of the day," 122; "'Friend, go up higher,' to one; to one" ("What is that to thee? Follow thou Me"), 123; "Love lights the sun. Love through the dark" ("O ye, who are not dead and fit"), 123; "Thou who hast borne all burdens, bear our" ("'If Thou Sayest, Behold, We Knew It Not'"), 123; "Grief is not grievous to a soul that knows" ("Surely he hath borne our griefs"), 124; "Love came down at Christmas" ("Christmastide"), 124; "Rest remains when all is done," ("There remaineth therefore a Rest to the people of God"), 124; "Now is winter and now is sorrow" ("Roses and Roses"), 125; "Life is but a working day" ("Man's life is but a working day"), 125; "Who scatters tares shall reap no wheat" ("Rogationtide"), 125; "One step more, and the race is ended" ("Septuagesima"), 126; "Looking back along life's trodden way," 126.

Note: Each month of the year features a different woman writer; "December" consists of "Selections from the Writings of Christina G. Rossetti." Description from 1899 reprint.
Location: 1891: not seen, copy located at Southwestern College (Winfield, KS). 1899: Ives.

B112   AUTOBIOGRAPHICAL NOTES OF THE LIFE OF WILLIAM BELL SCOTT (1892)

Red ink as noted:
[Red initial A] AUTOBIOGRAPHICAL NOTES | OF THE LIFE OF | [this line in red] WILLIAM BELL SCOTT | H. R. S. A., LL.D. | And Notices of his Artistic and Poetic Circle of Friends | 1830 to 1882 | [this line in red] EDITED BY W. MINTO | Illustrated by Etchings by Himself | and Reproductions of Sketches by Himself and Friends | [this line in red] VOL. II | [round vignette] | LONDON | [this line in red] JAMES R. OSGOOD, MᶜILVAINE & CO. | 45 ALBEMARLE STREET, W. | MDCCCXCII | *All rights reserved*

"My old admiration before I was twenty" ("To William Bell Scott"), 314. Signed "C. G. R." and attributed in the text.

Location: NjP (2).

B113   A BOOK OF THE HEAVENLY BIRTHDAYS (1892)

Red ink as noted:
[Red A, B] A Book | of the | [red H, B] Heavenly Birthdays. | BY | E. V. B., | *Author of "Days and Hours in a Garden,"* | *"Ros Rosarum," etc., etc.* | [ornament] | [this line in red] CHICAGO: | A. C. McCLURG & CO. | ELLIOT STOCK, 62, PATERNOSTER ROW, LONDON.

Excerpts from "Underneath the growing grass" ("The Bourne"), 14; "Grief hears a funeral knell," ("Death of a Firstborn"), 23; "At midnight, at morning, one certain day," ("Old and New Year Ditties"), 25; "Yet one pang, searching and sore," ("Martyrs' Song"), 104; "Remember me when I am gone away," ("Remember"), 117; "Indeed I loved you, my chosen friend" ("The Poor Ghost"), 118; "Shall I forget in peace of Paradise?" ("Shall I Forget?"), 123. Signed "Christina Rossetti."

Note: Edited by Eleanor Vere Boyle. Date from *English Catalogue* listing. Reprinted in 1894 and 1896.
Location: NjP. Not seen: 1894: copy located at Washington State University, 1896: copy located at Baylor University.

B114   THE POETS AND THE POETRY OF THE CENTURY (1892)

Red ink as noted:
The | [this line in red] POETS | and the | [this line in red] POETRY | of the | [this line in red] CENTURY | [rule] | Joanna Baillie | to | Mathilde Blind | [rule] | [rule] | [this line in red] Edited by | [this line in red]

ALFRED H. MILES | [rule] | HUTCHINSON & CO. | 25, PATERNOSTER SQUARE, LONDON

Excerpts from "Goblin Market," 420; "The Prince's Progress," 421-422; "Despised and Rejected," 424; "A Testimony," 425; "The Convent Threshold," 427-429.

"Miscellaneous poems" (quoted in entirety): "Yea, I Have A Goodly Heritage," 433; "An Echo from Willowwood," 433; "Cardinal Newman," 434; "A Death of a Firstborn," 435; "Lord Babe, if Thou art He" ("Epiphany"), 435-436; "Laughing Life cries at the feast," 436; "Where shall I find a white rose blowing?" ("Roses and Roses"), 437; "Weigh all my faults and follies righteously," 437-438; "Piteous my rhyme is," 438; "Young girls wear flowers" ("The Flowers appear on the Earth"), 439; "Golden haired, lily white" ("As cold waters to a thirsty soul, so is good news from a far country"), 439-440; "Innocent eyes not ours" ("These all wait upon Thee"), 440; "Man's life is but a working day," 441; "Have I not striven, my God, and watched and prayed?" 441; "Through burden and heat of the day," 441-442; "Sorrow hath a double voice," 442; "Who is this that cometh up not alone," 442-443; "The goal in sight! Look up and sing," 443; "Bury Hope out of sight," 443-444; "Behold, the Bridegroom cometh:–go ye out" ("Advent Sunday"), 444-445; "The tempest over and gone, the calm begun" ("Easter Even"), 445; "Love me, – I love you," 446; "Heartsease in my garden bed," 446; "What are heavy? Sea-sand and sorrow," 446; "The days are clear," 446-447; "Twist me a crown of wind-flowers," 447; "I planted a hand," 447; "Roses blushing red and white," 448; "When a mounting skylark sings," 448; "Goodbye in fear, good bye in sorrow," 448.

Note: First published in 1892 as the seventh volume in Miles's survey of the century's poetical production. Copy examined is undated, but prior to 1894, as Rossetti's death is not referenced. The CGR extracts are included in a biocritical essay by Arthur Symons, (417-432).
Location: CLU (via Internet Archive).

B115   LIVING ENGLISH POETS (1893)

Red ink as noted:
[this line in red] *LIVING* | [this line in red] *ENGLISH POETS* | *MDCCCXCIII* | [device, two trees with banner and text 'ARBOR SCIENTIAE ARBOR VITAE] | *LONDON* | [this line in red] *KEGAN PAUL, TRENCH, TRÜBNER & CO., Ltd.* | *MDCCCXCIII*

A section of poems from *Time Flies* is added to poems included in the 1883 printing (B70): "My love whose heart is tender said to me" ("Doeth well . . . doeth better"), 55; "Where shall I find a white rose blowing?" ("Roses and Roses"), 55-56; "If love is not worth loving, then life is not worth living" 57; "Of all the downfalls in the world" ("Vanity of vanities"), 57-58. Individual poems not signed, but section is headed "Christina G. Rossetti."

Location: Victoria University, University of Toronto (via Internet archive).

B116   BECAUSE I LOVE YOU (1894)

Some text in black letter:
BECAUSE I LOVE YOU | Poems of Love | SELECTED AND ARRANGED BY | ANNA E. MACK | "Love is too precious to be named | Save with a reverence deep and high." | LEE AND SHEPARD Publishers | 10 MILK STREET | BOSTON

"Sonnet" (sonnet 6 from "Monna Innominata"), 34; "Sonnet" (sonnet 5 from "Monna Innominata"), 75. Both signed "Christina G. Rossetti."

Location: NN (via Google Books).

B117 NF   A GIFT OF PEACE (1894)

A Gift | of Peace | LOVING | GREETINGS | FOR | 365 DAYS | CHOSEN AND ARRANGED BY | ROSE PORTER | FLEMING H. REVELL COMPANY | [remaining text in two columns:]
NEW YORK   PUBLISHERS
CHICAGO   OF EVANGELICAL
TORONTO   LITERATURE

"It is also written, '"A just man falleth' (*Time Flies*), 16. Signed "Christina Rossetti."

Note: date from copyright statement (6).
Location: CtMW.

B118   MACMILLAN'S NEW LITERARY READERS (1894)

MACMILLAN'S | NEW | LITERARY READERS | London | MACMILLAN AND CO. | AND NEW YORK | 1894

"Goblin Market" abridged, in three sections: 129-133; 143-147; 156-160. Signed "C. G. Rossetti" on 160.

Note: Two illustrations by Laurence Housman (130, 146), reprinted from Macmillan's 1893 *Goblin Market* (see A25). CGR agreed to publish the "extracts" and was paid £5 (*Letters* 4: 385). The copyright page of the 1925 printing lists nine subsequent reprintings from 1896 through 1925.
Locations: 1894: (via Digital Library of India); 1925: Ives.

B119   PHILLIPS BROOKS YEAR BOOK (1894)

PHILLIPS BROOKS YEAR BOOK | SELECTIONS FROM THE WRITINGS | OF THE | RT. REV. PHILLIPS BROOKS, D.D. | BY | H.L.S. AND L.H.S. | "The thought is stronger for us because he has thought it. The feeling is more | vivid because he has felt it. And always he leads us to God by a way along | which he has gone himself." – PREACHING, p. 119. | NEW YORK | E. P. DUTTON & COMPANY | 31 WEST TWENTY-THIRD STREET | 1894

"I saw a Saint" ("Embertide"), 11; "And thither thou, beloved" ("Beautiful for Situation"), 17; "Alone Lord God, in whom our trust," 35; "We know the way" ("Easter Tuesday"), 40; "A Song for the Least of All Saints," 55; "We lift to Thee our failing eyes" ("As dying, and behold we live"), 59; "I peered within, and saw a world of sin" ("Escape to the Mountain"), 63; "Love is alone the worthy law of love" ("Quinquagesima"), 64; "I lift mine eyes, and see" ("Palm Sunday"), 69; "Thou who wast Centre of the whole earth" ("Thou Who wast Centre of a stable"), 83; "I lift mine eyes to see: earth vanisheth," 111; "O mine enemy," 118; "Little lamb, who lost thee?" ("Rejoice with Me"), 127; "O God the Holy Ghost Who art Light unto Thine elect," 134; "The twig sprouteth" ("Are ye not much better than they?"), 154; "Thou Who wast Centre of all Heights" ("Thou Who wast Centre of a stable"), 162; "I think of the saints I have known" ("So great a cloud of Witnesses"), 181; "None other Lamb, none other Name," 223; "Lord, carry me," 232; "As flames that consume the mountains" ("Love is strong as Death"), 244; "O Lord, fulfil Thy Will" ("The Will of the Lord be done"), 252; "Trembling before Thee" ("Epiphanytide"), 267; "Up, my drowsing eyes!" ("Vigil of all saints"), 287; "Mother she is and cradle" ("Sexagesima"), 296; "O Jesus, Who lovest us all" ("God is our hope and Strength"), 300; "Lord, grant us eyes to see and ears to hear," 307; "Light is our sorrow for it ends tomorrow" ("Whither the Tribes go up, even the Tribes of the Lord"), 309; "Shadows to-day, while shadows show God's Will," 320; "Lord, make me one with Thine own faithful ones," 324; "Who knows? God knows" ("Take no thought for the morrow"), 332; "Beside Thy Cross I hang" ("Ready to Perish"), 342; "Long and dark the nights," ("Vigil of the Presentation"), 345; "It is not death, O Christ, to die for Thee," 361.

Note: A strong seller; announced to be in its "thirty-first thousand" in December 1894. Also published in London (R. D. Dickinson, 1894), with a later printing by Macmillan in 1903 (not seen).
Location: MH (via Google Books). Not seen: 1903: copy located at National Library of Scotland.

B120   POPULAR BRITISH BALLADS (1894)

Engraved title, red ink as noted:
POPULAR | [this line in red] BRITISH BALLADS | ANCIENT AND MODERN | chosen by | R BRIMLEY JOHNSON | ILLUSTRATED BY | W CUBITT COOKE | [short rule] | IN FOUR VOLUMES | VOL: III | [illustration of singing man, seated, holding harp, with wreath at lower left, and text on pillar at right: 'I NEVER HEARD | THE OLD SONG | OF PERCY AND | DOUGLAS THAT | I FOUND NOT | MY HEART MOVED MORE | THAN WITH A | TRUMPET | SIR PHILIP | SIDNEY'] | LONDON [leaf ornament] J. M. DENT & CO. ALDINE HOUSE | 69 Great Easter Street E.C. | PHILADELPHIA [leaf ornament] J. B. LIPPINCOTT COMPANY | MDCCCXCIV

"Maiden-Song," 269-277; "Love from the North," 277-278; "Maude Clare," 279. All signed "Christina Rossetti."

Note: Illustrated.
Location: Victoria University (via Internet Archive).

B121 L   A BRIEF MEMOIR OF CHRISTINA G. ROSSETTI (1895)

A BRIEF MEMOIR | OF | Christina G. Rossetti. | BY | ELLEN A. PROCTOR. | WITH A PREFACE BY | W. M. ROSSETTI. | S.P.C.K., | LONDON: NORTHUMBERLAND AVENUE, W.C. | 1895

Ten letters from CGR: 47-48; 50-66; 70-73.

Note: Includes several untraceable quotations (51, 53-54, 55, 61, 62) that may or may not be from CGR's correspondence; Harrison notes several instances in which Proctor adds material not in the original letters (see *Letters* 4: 367).
Location: CU (via Google Books).

B122   DANTE GABRIEL ROSSETTI: HIS FAMILY-LETTERS (1895)

DANTE GABRIEL ROSSETTI | HIS FAMILY-LETTERS | WITH A MEMOIR | BY | WILLIAM MICHAEL ROSSETTI | MANUS ANIMAM PINXIT | *VOL. I* | LONDON | ELLIS AND ELVEY | 1895

"The Chinaman," 79; "The P.R.B." ("The P.R.B. is in its decadence"), 138. Unsigned, attributed in the text.

Location: University of Toronto (via Internet Archive).

B123 NF   FARRAR YEAR BOOK (1895)

FARRAR YEAR BOOK | SELECTIONS FROM THE WRITINGS | OF THE | REV. FREDERIC W. FARRAR. D.D. | ARCHDEACON AND CANON OF WESTMINSTER | BY | W. M. L. JAY | "Rich gift of God! a year of time!" | NEW YORK | E. P. DUTTON & COMPANY | 31 WEST TWENTY-THIRD STREET | 1895

Poetry and prose excerpts: "Bring me to see, Lord, bring me yet to see" ("The General Assembly and Church of the Firstborn"), 7; "Love, thine own Bride, with all her might" ("Love, to be love, must walk Thy way"), 19; "Lord, make me pure," 33; "Feed my hungry brethren for My sake" ("Because He First Loved Us"), 35; "O Lord, seek us, O Lord, find us" ("Lord, Save Us, We Perish"), 42; "Whiteness most white! Ah, to be clean again" ("They Shall be White as Snow"), 60; "If we can forget the Tree" (*The Face of the Deep*), 79; "In Thee God's promise is Amen and Yea" ("Thy Name, O Christ, is incense streaming forth"), 89; "Patience must dwell with Love, for Love and Sorrow," 90; "Tune me, O Lord, into one harmony," 110; "From building on the sand and not on the rock" ("From worshipping and serving the creature more than the Creator"), 115; "Lord, give me grace" ("Sit Down in the Lowest Room"), 123; "What will it be, O my soul, what will it be," 127; "Grant us, O Lord, that patience and that faith" ("Lord, it is Good for Us to Be Here"), 134; "O Lord, I cannot plead my love of Thee," 155; "What is the beginning? Love," 159; "Where light dwells, pleasure dwells" ("Truly the Light is Sweet"), 165; "O Thou the Life of living and of dead" ("Ascension Eve"), 177; "Content to come, content to go" ("Do this, and he doeth it"), 206; "From worshipping the creature more than the Creator," 225; "Lord, bring me low" ("Lord, make me pure"), 237; "My God, wilt Thou accept, and will not we," 242; "From cleaving to anything apart from Thee" ("From worshipping and serving the creature more than the Creator"), 246; "There dwells in this wide world" (*The Face of the Deep*), 272; "Thy lovely saints to bring Thee love" ("The ransomed of the Lord"), 302; "Lord, make us all love all," 313; "From lamps going out, gone out" ("From all kinds of music which worship an idol in Thy stead"), 339; "Grant, O Lord," 356; "Hath he gone up to glory?" (*The Face of the Deep*), 363; "Unspotted lambs to follow the one Lamb," 363. All signed "Christina Rossetti."

Location: WaPS.

B124   LYRA SACRA (1895)

Red ink as noted:
[this line in red] LYRA SACRA | A BOOK OF RELIGIOUS VERSE | SELECTED AND ARRANGED BY | H. C. BEECHING, M.A. | METHUEN & CO. | 36 ESSEX STREET, W.C. | LONDON | 1895

"A New and Old Year Song" ("Old and New Year Ditties," section 3) 295-296; "A Bruised Reed" ("A Bruised Reed Shall He Not Break"), 296-297; "From House to Home" (excerpt) 297-299; "'The Will Of The Lord Be Done'," 299; "'That Where I Am, There Ye May Be Also'," 299-300; "Sooner or Later, Yet at Last," 300-302; "A Chill Blank World. Yet Over The Utmost Sea," 302-302; "O Foolish Soul! To Make Thy Count," 303; "'Vain Shadow'," 302. Signed "Christina Rossetti" on 302.

Note: Published with CGR's permission (353). Reprinted, with same CGR poems, in 1903.
Locations: AzU. 1903: MH (via Google Books).

B125 L   CRITICAL KIT-KATS (1896)

CRITICAL KIT-KATS | BY | EDMUND GOSSE | HON. M.A. OF TRINITY COLLEGE, CAMBRIDGE | [oval publisher's device, "WH" with text 'SCRIPTA MANENT'] | LONDON: WILLIAM HEINEMANN | 1896

Letters from CGR, 140-141, 159-160; excerpts from "The Dead City,"142; "Divine and Human Pleading," 143-144; "The Convent Threshold," 148; "The Prince's Progress," 150-151; "A Birthday," 151-152; "Song" ("Oh, roses for the flush of youth"), 153. Unsigned, attributed in text.

Unsigned, attributed in text.

Location: MH (via Google Books).

B126 NF   GOOD CHEER FOR A YEAR (1896)

GOOD CHEER | FOR A YEAR | SELECTIONS FROM THE WRITINGS OF THE | Rt. Rev. PHILLIPS BROOKS, D.D. | BY | W. M. L. JAY | All life which would not grow stale and monotonous must feed itself upon | God. . . . All life which would make To-day the transmutation place | where Yesterday shall give its power to Forever, must be full of the felt | presence of Him in whom yesterday, to-day and forever are one. – vi. 344. | NEW YORK | E. P. DUTTON AND COMPANY | 31 WEST TWENTY-THIRD STREET | 1896

Poetry and prose excerpts: "Lord, we are rivers running to thy sea," 22; "O only Lord God" (*Face of the Deep*), 29; "Because thy love had sought me," 37; "Earth holds heaven in the bud," (*Face of the Deep*), 87; "Lord, make me one with Thine own faithful ones," 99; "O Jesus who lovest us all" ("God is our hope and strength"), 122; "So when the times of restitution come" ("Who Have a Form of Godliness"), 148; "Beyond this shadow and this turbulent sea" ("Faint, Yet Pursuing"), 149; "Safe as a hidden brooding dove" ("A Burden"), 151; "Wisest of spirits that spirit which dwelleth"("Yea, the sparrow hath found her an house"), 161; "The subtlest and profoundest of men" (*Face of the Deep*), 166; "Fear ballasts hope," ("Hope is the counterpoise of fear"), 180; "Turn all to love, poor soul" ("If not with hope of life"), 181; "O Lord God, hear the silence of each soul" ("I will come and heal him"), 198; "What is the flame of their fire" ("Love is Strong as Death"), 206; "But we would be of those who do thy will" (source unidentified), 218; "Evil knowledge acquired in one wilful moment" (*Face of the Deep*), 239; "O, if our brother's blood cry out at us," ("Lord, make us all love all"), 263; "Grant us, O Lord, that patience and that faith" ("Lord, it is good for us to be here"), 288; "Whiteness most white. Ah, to be clean again" ("They shall be as white as snow"), 312; "If thou be dead, forgive and thou shalt live," 318; "My faith burns low, my hope burns low" ("None other Lamb, none other name"), 348; "Lord, if Thou grant me grace to hear and see" ("Lord, I am feeble and of mean account"), 357; "Yet shall I envy blessed John?" ("Hymn after Gabriele Rossetti"), 361; "Thou Who wast Centre of all heights" ("Thou who wast Centre of a stable"), 370. Signed "Christina G. Rossetti" except "Christina Rossetti" (29, 37).

Note: Complied by Julia Louisa Matilda Woodruff. Reprinted 1907.
Location: KU; 1907: NN (via Google Books).

B127 A TREASURY OF MINOR BRITISH POETRY (1896)

A TREASURY | OF | MINOR BRITISH POETRY | SELECTED AND ARRANGED WITH NOTES | BY | J. CHURTON COLLINS, M.A. | [two lines of Greek] | EDWARD ARNOLD | LONDON NEW YORK | 37 BEDFORD STREET 70 FIFTH AVENUE | 1896

"Maiden May," 285-287. Signed "Christina G. Rossetti."

Note: Includes a brief commentary on 407.
Location: MiU (via Google Books).

B128 A CHARM OF BIRDS (1897)

A CHARM | OF BIRDS | [small ornament, leaf] | CHOSEN AND ARRANGED | BY | ROSE PORTER | [publisher's device] | NEW YORK | E. R. HERRICK & COMPANY | 70 FIFTH AVENUE

Within section titled "Christina Rossetti's Birds": "May" ("The Months: A Pageant"), 72; "Sparrows" ("The Months: A Pageant"), 72-73; "The Lark" ("Maiden May"), 73-74; "Eagle and Dove" ("All Thy Works Praise Thee, O Lord"), 74; "One Solitary Bird" (sonnet 20 from "Later Life"), 74; "Freaks of Fashion," 75-78; "A Melody of Birds" ("In the Willow Shade"), 79; "Birds" ("All Thy Works Praise Thee, O Lord"), 79. Not individually signed.

Note: Copyright date is 1897 (2).
Location: OrU.

B129   **FIFTY SONGS OF LOVE (1897)**

Fifty Songs of Love | [ornament] | Dodge Stationery Company | Art Publishers | 317 Broadway, New York

"If now you saw me you would say" ("The Convent Threshold"), 21; "Dear Lord, let me recount to Thee" ("It is Finished"), 56-57. Author's name precedes each poem, in place of title: "Christina Georgina Rossetti."

Note: Copyright date is 1897 (verso of title).
Location: Ives.

B130   **THE GOLDEN TREASURY (1897)**

Some text in <u>black letter</u>:
THE | GOLDEN TREASURY | SELECTED FROM THE BEST SONGS AND LYRICAL | POEMS IN THE ENGLISH LANGUAGE | AND ARRANGED WITH NOTES | BY | FRANCIS T. PALGRAVE | LATE PROFESSOR OF POETRY IN THE UNIVERSITY OF OXFORD | *SECOND SERIES* | [vignette, woman reading book, child holding torch] | <u>London |</u> MACMILLAN AND CO., Limited | NEW YORK: THE MACMILLAN COMPANY | 1897

"Listening," 52; "Somewhere Or Other," 53; "A Pause," 62; "Next of Kin," 72-73; "Sleep at Sea," 95-97; "Heaven overarches earth and sea" ("Heaven Overarches"), 105; "Up-Hill," 108; "Mother Country," 108-109; "Italia, Io Ti Saluto!" 148-149; "Three Seasons," 197-198; "Echo," 207; "To The End," 224; "The Summer Is Ended," 227; "The Bourne," 229; "Song" ("When I am dead, my dearest"), 229-230. All signed "C. G. Rossetti."

Note: One of the century's most well known anthologies, frequently reprinted through the 20th century. As Palgrave's preface explains, previous editions of the *Treasury* had excluded living poets.
Location: MiU (via Google Books).

B131 NF   **THE PILGRIM'S STAFF (1897)**

The Pilgrim's Staff | or | Daily Steps Heavenward | by The Pathway of Faith | Chosen and arranged | by Rose Porter | [small ornament] | CHICAGO NEW YORK TORONTO | FLEMING H. REVELL COMPANY | *Publishers of Evangelical Literature.*

Poetry and prose excerpts: "Watch yet awhile" ("The day is at hand"), 49; "Time flies, hope flags, life flies on wearied wing" (sonnet 10 from "Monna Innominata"), 60; "He — our Lord — perfect in wisdom, power, love" (*Time Flies*), 107; "If we are spirit-broken" (*Time Flies*), 167-168; "These lovely graces are "fruits" not flowers" (*Time Flies*), 200; "Watch with me, Jesus, in my loneliness," ("Old and New Year Ditties"), 214; "Our heaven must be within ourselves," 226; "Earth strike up your music!" ("Christmas Eve"), 241. Variously signed: Christina G. Rossetti (49, 60, 107), Christina Rossetti (168, 214); "C. G. Rossetti" (200, 226, 241).

Note: Date from copyright page (verso of title).
Location: Point Loma Nazarene University.

B132 NF   **PRAYERS ANCIENT AND MODERN (1897)**

Within single rule frame; all text black letter:
[ornament] Prayers [ornament] | Ancient and Modern | Selected and arranged | for Daily Reading | by the | Editor of | Daily Strength for | Daily Needs | [ornament] | New York: Doubleday and | McClure Co. 1897

Prose excerpts from *Annus Domini* unless otherwise noted: "O Lord, who callest Thine own sheep by name," 16; "O Lord, in Whom is our hope," 23; "O Lord, Who seest that all hearts are empty," 28; "O Lord, begin, we beseech Thee," 34; "O Lord, make us, we implore Thee," 36; "O Lord, with Whom is the Fountain of Life," 40; "O Lord, Whom all Thy good creatures bless," 48; "O Lord, our Refuge from the storm," 55; "O Lord, make Thy law, I entreat Thee," 58; "O God, Gracious and Merciful," 63; "O Lord, the Portion of our inheritance," 66; "O Lord, perfect, we beseech Thee," 70; "O Lord, give us all, we beseech Thee," 81; "O Thou who chastenest whom Thou lovest," 89; "O Lord, whose way is perfect," 92; "O Lord, fill us, we beseech Thee," 94; "Give us grace, O Lord, to work while it is day," 99; "O Lord, the Lord whose ways are right," 111; "O Lord, who lovest the stranger," 199; "O Lord, because being compassed with infirmities," 125; "O Lord, help us by prayer to hold Thee fast," 128; "O Lord, with whom are Strength and Wisdom," 133; "O faithful Lord, grant to us," 142; O king of Glory, bring us all home," 146; "O Lord, grant us grace never to parley with temptation," 151; "O Lord, move us by Thine example," 159; "O Lord, faithful Creator, give us grace," 164; "O Lord, God of our fathers," 168; "Give, I pray thee, to all children," 169; "O Lord, long-suffering and abundant in Goodness and Truth," 171; "O Lord, our Guide even unto death," 177; "O Lord, give us all grace," 182; "O Lord, who delightest in mercy," 184; "Grant, O Lord, that we may carefully watch," 191; "O Lord, help us, we entreat Thee," 195; "O Lord, shew forth Thy loving-kindness," 207; "O Lord, Shield of our help," 218; "O Lord, our hiding-place," 225; "O Lord, who spreadest out the heavens," 231; "O Lord, Strength of our life," 237; "O Lord, who art as the shadow," 240; "O Lord, give us grace, I pray Thee," 246; "O Lord, give us grace, we beseech Thee," 253; "O Lord, strengthen and support," 269; "Open wide the window or our spirits," 281; "O Lord, in whom is the Truth," 289; "O Lord, who dost promise a crown of life," 305; "O Gracious Lord God, who deignest to make of man Thy mirror" (*The Face of the Deep*), 309; "O my God, by whose loving Providence" (*The Face of the Deep*), 315; "O Merciful Lord God" (*The Face of the Deep*) 321; "O Lord, Creator of all things," 329; "Speak, Lord, for Thy servant heareth" (*The Face of the Deep*), 340; "O God Almighty, who to them that have no might" (*The Face of the Deep*), 345; "O God of patience and consolation," 351; "O my God, bestow upon us such confidence," 355; O Lord my God, perfect us" (*The Face of the Deep*), 363.

Note: Compiled by Mary Tileston. Frequently reprinted. Rossetti is the author most frequently quoted in the volume (57 separate quotations).
Location: MH (via Google Books).

B133 L   CHRISTINA ROSSETTI: A BIOGRAPHICAL AND CRITICAL STUDY (1898)

Christina Rossetti | A BIOGRAPHICAL AND CRITICAL STUDY | BY | MACKENZIE BELL | AUTHOR OF 'SPRING'S IMMORTALITY, AND OTHER POEMS' | AND 'CHARLES WHITEHEAD, A BIOGRAPHICAL | AND CRITICAL MONOGRAPH' | *WITH SIX PORTRAITS AND SIX FACSIMILES* | BOSTON | ROBERTS BROTHERS | 1898

"Heart's Chill Between," 222-223, and "Death's Chill Between," 224-225. Letters from CGR to DGR, WMR, and various correspondents passim.

Note: Published in the UK by Hurst and Blackett (not seen), and later by Thomas Burleigh.
Location: Ives.

B134   THE MORE EXCELLENT WAY (1898)

Within green acantus border; all text in blue ink, some text in black letter:
The | More Excellent Way | WORDS OF THE WISE | ON | The Life of Love | *A SEQUENCE OF MEDITATIONS* | COMPILED BY THE | HON. MRS. LYTTELTON GELL | 'Though I speak with the tongues of men and of angels, and | have not LOVE, I am become as sounding brass.' – St. Paul. | TWENTIETH THOUSAND | London | HENRY FROWDE

"Love understands the mystery" ("Judge nothing before the time"), 25; "O ye, who taste that love is sweet" ("O ye who are not dead and fit"), 28; "Ah! poor man, befooled and slow" (excerpt, "What is this above thy head"), 55; "Is it worth while to live?" ("What good shall my life do me?"), 64; "Grant us, O Lord, that patience and that faith" ("Lord, it is good for us to be here"), 68; "Our heaven must be within ourselves," 103; "Lord, whomsoever Thou shalt send to me" ("Are they not all ministering spirits?"), 113; "Bleed on beneath the rod" ("If not with hope of life"), 120; "A lovely city in a lovely land" ("Beautiful for situation"), 163; "Shall I forget in peace of Paradise?" ("Shall I Forget?"), 204; "To every living soul that same He saith" ("That no man take thy Crown"), 205; "Beloved, yield thy time to God! for he," 243; "The shout of a King is among them" ("What hath God wrought?"), 254; "Lift up thine eyes to seek the Invisible," 282; "So brief a life, – and then! an endless grief"("All flesh is grass"), 299. Signed "Christina Rossetti."

Note: Compiled by Edith Mary Lyttelton Gell. Originally published December 1898 (*English Catalogue*); copy examined is undated. Printed entirely in green and blue ink.
Location: CoDI.

B135   AN APPRECIATION OF THE LATE CHRISTINA GEORGINA ROSSETTI (1899)

AN APPRECIATION | OF THE LATE | CHRISTINA GEORGINA ROSSETTI | BY THE | Right Rev. B. F. Westcott, D.D., D.C.L., | LORD BISHOP OF DURHAM. | WITH A PREFACE | BY THE REV. | PREBENDARY GLENDENNING NASH, M.A. | PREBENDARY OF ST. PAUL'S CATHEDRAL, | AND INCUMBENT OF CHRIST CHURCH, WOBURN SQUARE. | [short rule] | PUBLISHED UNDER THE DIRECTION OF THE TRACT COMMITTEE. | [short rule] | LONDON: | SOCIETY FOR PROMOTING CHRISTIAN KNOWLEDGE, | NORTHUMBERLAND AVENUE, W.C.; 43, QUEEN VICTORIA STREET, E.C. | BRIGHTON: 129, North Street. | New York: E. & J. B. Young & Co. | 1899.

Brief quotations from numerous CGR poems on 14-22.

Note: The Bishop of Durham dedicated CGR's memorial in Christ Church, Woburn Square, on 1 November 1898; as Nash's preface explains, "His Lordship has consented to publish in the following pages the eloquent appreciation he delivered on that occasion" (8).
Location: CLU (via Google Books).

B136   THE LISTENING CHILD (1899)

Some text in <u>black letter</u>:
THE LISTENING CHILD | A SELECTION FROM THE STORES OF ENGLISH | VERSE, MADE FOR THE YOUNGEST | READERS AND HEARERS | BY | LUCY W. THACHER | *WITH AN INTRODUCTORY NOTE* | BY | THOMAS WENTWORTH HIGGINSON | <u>New York</u> | THE MACMILLAN COMPANY | LONDON: MACMILLAN & CO., Ltd., | 1899 | *All rights reserved*

"Milking Time" ("When the cows come home the milk is coming"), 332; "Twist Me A Crown" ("Twist me a crown of wind-flowers"), 332.

Note: Frequently reprinted. The copyright statement from 1900 states that the book was "Set up and electrotyped October, 1899. Reprinted July, 1900."
*Location*s: 1899: University of Louisiana at Monroe (via photocopy); 1900: CSt (via Google Books).

B137 NF L   RUSKIN ROSSETTI PRERAPHAELITISM (1899)

RUSKIN: ROSSETTI: | PRERAPHAELITISM | PAPERS 1854 TO 1862 | ARRANGED AND EDITED BY | WILLIAM MICHAEL ROSSETTI | "Then by her summoning art | Shall memory conjure back the sere | Autumnal springs from many a dying year." | –D. G. R. | WITH ILLUSTRATIONS | NEW YORK: DODD, MEAD AND COMPANY | LONDON: GEORGE ALLEN | 1899

"Note by Christina Rossetti – A Dream," 48-49; Letter from CGR to WMR, 207.

Location: CUBANC (via Internet Archive).

B138 L   THE LIFE OF CHARLES TOMLINSON (1900)

London: Elliot Stock, 1900.

Note: Letter from CGR cited by Harrison as source in *Letters* 2: 273.
Location: not seen; copy located at King's College, London.

B139 L   ROSSETTI PAPERS (1903)

RossETTI PAPERS | 1862 to 1870 | A COMPILATION BY | WILLIAM MICHAEL ROSSETTI | C'est par là qu'ont passé des hommes disparus | Victor Hugo | NEW YORK | CHARLES SCRIBNER'S SONS | 1903

Letters of CGR to DGR: 50; 67-70; 72-73; 74-78; 80-84; 87-89; 93-95; 96-97; 97-100.

Location: TxCM.

B140   THE NATIVITY IN SONG (1910)

With ornamental dashes indicated by = :
The = | Nativity | In = = | Song = | [small trefoil ornament] | S. P. C. K., London

"Christmas Day" ("A baby is a harmless thing"), 7-8.

Location: Ives.

B141 L   WILLIAM SHARP A MEMOIR (1910)

Red ink as noted:
[This line in red] WILLIAM SHARP | (FIONA MACLEOD) | A MEMOIR | COMPILED BY HIS WIFE | ELIZABETH A. SHARP | [device, D & Co] | NEW YORK | [this line in red] DUFFIELD & COMPANY | 1910

Letters to Sharp: 67, 100.

Location: TxCM.

B142 L   THE LIFE AND LETTERS OF FREDERIC SHIELDS (1912)

THE LIFE | AND LETTERS OF | FREDERIC SHIELDS | EDITED BY | ERNESTINE MILLS | WITH PHOTOGRAVURE PORTRAIT AND | 41 OTHER ILLUSTRATIONS | LONGMANS, GREEN AND CO. | 39 PATERNOSTER ROW, LONDON | NEW YORK, BOMBAY, AND CALCUTTA | 1912 | All rights reserved

Letters to Shields: 267; 269-270; 270; 271-272; 280-281; 283.

Location: MiU (via Google Books).

B143 L   TWENTY-FIVE YEARS: REMINISCENCES (1913)

Within triple-rule border:
Twenty-five Years: | Reminiscences | BY | KATHARINE TYNAN | Author of "Her Ladyship," "Mary Gray," "Men and Maids," etc. | [device, rose and crescent moon] | NEW YORK | THE DEVIN-ADAIR COMPANY | 437 Fifth Avenue

Letter to Tynan: 172-173.

Location: NjP (via Google Books).

B144 L   THE LIBRARY OF JEROME KERN (1929)

Brackets in original:
SALE NUMBER 2311 | ON PUBLIC EXHIBITION FROM SUNDAY, JANUARY THIRTEENTH | [WEEK DAYS 9-6 P.M. – SUNDAYS 2-5 P.M.] | THE LIBRARY OF | JEROME KERN | NEW YORK CITY | [PART TWO] | J-Z | TO BE SOLD BY HIS ORDER | AT UNRESERVED PUBLIC SALE | MONDAY EVENING, TUESDAY AFTERNOON & EVENING | WEDNESDAY & THURSDAY EVENINGS | JANUARY TWENTY-FIRST, TWENTY-SECOND | TWENTY-THIRD, TWENTY-FOURTH | AT TWO O'CLOCK AND EIGHT-FIFTEEN | THE ANDERSON GALLERIES | [MITCHELL KENNERLEY, PRESIDENT] | 489 PARK AVENUE AT FIFTY-NINTH STREET, NEW YORK | 1929

"Common Holly bears a berry" ("Golden Holly"), and letter from CGR to Holman Stephens, 326.

Note: Full text of letter published in Baker and Kingery, "Some New Christina Rossetti Materials" (C164).
Location: IcarbS.

B145 L   STUDIES IN STRANGE SOULS (1929)

Red ink as noted:
[this line in red] STUDIES IN | [this line in red] STRANGE SOULS | BY | ARTHUR SYMONS | *Author of* | 'A Study in Thomas Hardy," 'Studies in Seven Arts.' | With Three Portraits | LONDON | CHARLES J. SAWYER | GRAFTON HOUSE, GRAFTON STREET W. I | *MCMXXIX*

Letter to Lucy Madox Rossetti, 37-38. Excerpted in *Letters* 4: 402.

Location: TxCM.

B146 L   THE LIFE OF CHRISTINA ROSSETTI (1930)

THE LIFE OF | CHRISTINA ROSSETTI | *By* | MARY F. SANDARS | WITH EIGHTEEN ILLUSTRATIONS | HUTCHINSON & CO. (Publishers) LIMITED | 34-36 PATERNOSTER ROW, LONDON, E.C.

Letters to WMR, 228; William Aytoun, 85-86; Edmund Gosse, 209; Miss Newsham, 256-257, 263-264; Frederic Shields, 231-232; 267; "unknown correspondent" (probably William J. Bryant), 232.

Location: TxLT.

B147 L   THREE ROSSETTIS (1937)

THREE ROSSETTIS | UNPUBLISHED LETTERS | TO AND FROM | DANTE GABRIEL, CHRISTINA, WILLIAM | COLLECTED AND EDITED | BY | JANET CAMP TROXELL [publisher's device, shield with text "VE RI TAS"] | CAMBRIDGE | HARVARD UNIVERSITY PRESS | 1937

Letters to DGR: 142-144; 145; 146-147; 161; 161-162; to WMR: 190-191, 191-192, 195, 196-197; to various correspondents: 149-150; 150; 150-151; 152; 153; 153-154; 155; 155-157; 157; 158; 159; 159-160; 162-164; 164-165; 166-167; 168-169; 169; 170-171; 171-172; 172-173; 173; 173-174; 174-175; 175-176; 177-178; 178; 179; 197-198.

Location: MoSW.

B148 L   THE ROSSETTI-MACMILLAN LETTERS (1963)

THE | ROSSETTI-MACMILLAN | LETTERS | [ornament] | *Some 133 Unpublished Letters Written to | Alexander Macmillan, F. S. Ellis, and Others, | by Dante Gabriel, Christina, and William | Michael Rossetti, 1861-1889 |* [ornament] | EDITED, WITH AN INTRODUCTION AND NOTES | *by Lona Mosk Packer |* UNIVERSITY OF CALIFORNIA PRESS | BERKELEY AND LOS ANGELES 1963

Ninety-six letters to various correspondents, primarily Alexander Macmillan:13-15, 19-20, 22-24, 31-32, 33-35, 37, 39, 44-47, 51-52, 55-56, 58-60, 64, 69-70, 74-80, 81-86, 88-91, 92-94, 96, 98-102, 103-108, 111-115, 117-118, 120-124, 125-128, 133-141, 144-150, 152-157.

Location: TxCM.

B149 L   THE OWL AND THE ROSSETTIS (1978)

THE OWL | AND THE | ROSSETTIS | Letters of Charles A. Howell | and Dante Gabriel, | Christina, and | William Michael Rossetti | Edited, with an Introduction, | by C. L. Cline | The Pennsylvania State University Press | University Park and London

Six letters, numbered 42, 45, 122, 123, 124, and 133. Not paginated.

Note: Publication date (1978) from copyright statement.
Location: TxCM.

B150 L   A PRE-RAPHAELITE CIRCLE (1978)

A | PRE-RAPHAELITE | CIRCLE | By | RALEIGH TREVELYAN | Rowman and Littlefield | Totowa, New Jersey

Letters to Pauline Trevelyan: 140; 146; 161.

Location: TxCM.

B151 L   THE LETTERS OF LEWIS CARROLL (1979)

THE LETTERS OF | LEWIS CARROLL | *Edited by* | Morton N. Cohen | *with the assistance of* | Roger Lancelyn Green | VOLUME ONE | ca. 1837-1885 | New York | OXFORD UNIVERSITY PRESS | 1979

Two letters to Carroll: 81; 464.

Location: TxCM.

B152 L   CHRISTINA ROSSETTI: A DIVIDED LIFE (1981)

Georgina Battiscombe | [in script] Christina | [in script] Rossetti | [thin-thick rule] | A DIVIDED LIFE | [publisher's device, owl within square] | HOLT, RINEHART AND WINSTON | NEW YORK

Letters to WMR, 86, 202; Letter to Henry Buxton Forman, 200.

Location: Ives.

B153 L   THE ACHIEVEMENT OF CHRISTINA ROSSETTI (1987)

The Achievement of | CHRISTINA | ROSSETTI | EDITED BY | David A. Kent | Cornell University Press | Ithaca and London

Antony Harrison, "Eighteen Early Letters by Christina Rossetti," 192-207. Summaries and brief quotations of eighteen letters between 1845 and 1854.

Location: Ives.

B154 L   CHRISTINA ROSSETTI IN THE MASER COLLECTION (1991)

CHRISTINA ROSSETTI | in the Maser Collection | *With essays by* | Mary Louise Jarden Maser | *and* | Frederick E. Maser | *Including a Group of Christina's Letters* | FOREWORD BY | James Tanis | [ornament, flower] | BRYN MAWR COLLEGE LIBRARY | 1991

Forty-five letters to various correspondents: 63-103.

Location: NPV.

B155 L   CHRISTINA ROSSETTI (1992)

[ornamented rule] | *Christina* | *Rossetti* | FRANCES THOMAS | [ornamented rule]

Letters to DGR, 303; Lucy Madox Brown, 325: Rose D. Donne, 339-340.

Note: Publisher given on verso of title as "The Self Publishing Association Ltd" "in conjunction with Frances Thomas" (4). Reprinted by Virago Press in 1994.

Locations: 1992: Ives; 1994 Virago reprint: CoU.

B156 L   CHRISTINA ROSSETTI: A WRITER'S LIFE (1995)

CHRISTINA | ROSSETTI | [long dash] *a writer's life* [long dash] | JAN MARSH | [Viking publisher's device]

Letters to WMR, 136-137, 146; Barbara Leigh Smith Bodichon, 297, 308; Lewis Carroll, 345; Caroline Maria Gemmer, 488; Rose Donne Hake, 525.

Location: Ives.

MISATTRIBUTIONS

See B66, *Poetry for Children* (1882).

C: APPEARANCES IN PERIODICALS

This section includes all first appearances of Rossetti's work in periodicals. Books in series and annuals are included in Section B: Book and Pamphlet Appearances. This section is arranged in chronological order; within a given month, monthly periodicals are listed before periodicals issued more frequently. All contributions are poems unless otherwise identified in the heading by inclusion of the sigla 'NF' (nonfiction prose), 'F' (fiction), or 'L' (letter), after the entry letter and number. CGR's correspondence is reprinted in *Letters* unless otherwise indicated.

Each entry includes: A genre symbol if needed; the title of the item; the title of the periodical or newspaper (and place of publication; volume and/or issue numbers if known); inclusive page numbers of the Rossetti material; indication of whether and how Rossetti's name appears with the text (e.g., unsigned or signed, "C. G. Rossetti"); notes; and location(s) of copies examined or other sources of information. When Rossetti's contribution was published without a title, or appears with a title different from that which appears in Rossetti's collected publications, the title or first line as printed in the periodical is given first, followed by the title or first line given by Rossetti when the contribution appeared in a collection, with Rossetti's title or first line appearing within parentheses: ("Up-Hill"). London is the place of publication for periodicals and newspapers unless otherwise specified; dual publication (for periodicals published in Britain and the United States) is indicated if known.

It should be assumed that copies examined are in aggregated form (that is, within a bound volume) unless otherwise indicated. Given the increasing difficulty of access to original documents, I have of necessity made use of copies obtained either through interlibrary loan, or through various media, including microfilm, full text databases such as *APS Online* and *Harpweek*, and electronic archives such as *The Making of America* collections at Cornell and the University of Michigan. Whenever possible, I have noted the microfilm series or name of the database or archive consulted.

The term "First appearance" is difficult to define for works that appear in multiple versions. In such cases, each version is considered a first appearance of that version.

~

C1　"Death's Chill Between." *The Athenaeum* No. 1094 (14 October 1848): 1032. Signed "C. G. R." *Note*: Reprinted in *Beautiful Poetry* I (1853): 248-249.
Location: University of Wyoming.

C2　"Heart's Chill Between." *The Athenaeum* No. 1095 (21 October 1848): 1056. Signed "C. G. R." *Location*: Johns Hopkins University.

C3–C9　*The Germ*

(C3)　"Dream-Land." *The Germ: Thoughts Towards Nature in Poetry, Literature and Art* No. 1 (January 1850): 20. Unsigned. Reprinted in *Dwight's Journal of Music* (Boston), 13.13 (26 June 1858:97), with no attribution ("From the pages of an English Magazine, where it appeared anonymously").

(C4) "An End." *The Germ: Thoughts Towards Nature in Poetry, Literature and Art* No. 1 (January 1850): 48. Unsigned.

(C5) "A Pause of Thought." *The Germ: Thoughts Towards Nature in Poetry, Literature and Art* No. 2 (February 1850): 57. Signed "Ellen Alleyn" in "Contents" (inside front wrapper).

(C6) "Song." ("Oh Roses for the Flush of Youth") *The Germ: Thoughts Towards Nature in Poetry, Literature and Art* No. 2 (February 1850): 64. Signed "Ellen Alleyn" in "Contents" (inside front wrapper).

(C7) "A Testimony." *The Germ: Thoughts Towards Nature in Poetry, Literature and Art* No. 2 (February 1850): 73-75. Signed "Ellen Alleyn" in "Contents" (inside front wrapper).

(C8) "Repining." *Art and Poetry: Being Thoughts Towards Nature* No. 3 (March 1850): 111-117. Signed "Ellen Alleyn" in "Contents" (inside front wrapper).

(C9) "Sweet Death." *Art and Poetry: Being Thoughts Towards Nature* No. 3 (March 1850): 117. Signed "Ellen Alleyn" in "Contents" (inside front wrapper).

Initiated by DGR as a platform for the Pre-Raphaelite aesthetic, and largely the result of his efforts along with those of its editor, WMR, *The Germ* (retitled *Art and Poetry* with the March number) was a commercial failure, discontinued after four numbers due to poor sales. Its undisputed importance as a document of the Pre-Raphaelite movement, and as an outlet for the publication of work by key figures in the Pre-Raphaelite circle including CGR, prompted Thomas Mosher to reprint it in 1898, followed by a 1901 facsimile reprint by Elliot Stock, with a preface by WMR.
Location: *The Germ*: NjP; BL (via *Rossetti Archive*). *Dwight's Journal of Music*: Texas A&M, Commerce.

C10 "Versi." *The Bouquet, Culled from Marylebone Gardens* No. 5 (October 1851): 175.
Note: The journal's title also appears as *The Bouquet, From Marylebone Gardens* within the volume.
Location: NN (via Google Books).

C11 "L'Incognita." *The Bouquet, Culled from Marylebone Gardens* No.7 (December 1851): 216.
Note: Presentation of the journal's title varies; see C10.
Location: NN (via Google Books).

C12-C13

(C12) "'Purpurea Rosa'" ("Nigella"). *The Bouquet, culled from Marylebone Gardens* 15.8 (1852): 56. Within "Correspondenza . . ." below.

(C13 F) "Correspondenza famigliare." *The Bouquet, culled from Marylebone Gardens* (January to July, 1852): 120-121, 218-219; (July to December 1852): 14-15, 55-57.

Note: Reprinted as *Familiar Correspondence*, translated by Stanford Dindley (Np: The Mill House Press, 1962).
Location: MnU.

C14 "The Dead Bride." *Our Paper, Being a Monthly Serial for Private Circulation* No. 1 (January 1855): 21.
Location: not seen: NjP.

C15–C16

(C15) "'Giani My Friend and I both Strove to Excel.'" In "The Lost Titan," 202.

(C16 F) "The Lost Titan." *The Crayon* (New York) (1856): 200-202.
Note: CGR was paid £1.16.0 for the story (*SWMR* 70). Journal reprinted, New York: AMS Press, 1970.
Location: TxCM (AMS reprint).

C17 F "Nick: A Child's Story." *The National Magazine* 2 (October 1857): 375-376. Signed "Christina G. Rossetti."
Location: microfilm, *English Literary Periodical Series*.

C18 "The Round Tower at Jhansi: June 8, 1857" ("In the Round Tower at Jhansi, June 8, 1857"). *Once a Week* 1 (13 August 1859): 140. Signed "Caroline G. Rossetti."
Location: UPB.

C19 "Maude Clare." *Once a Week* 11 (5 November 1859): 381-382. Signed "Christina G. Rossetti." Illustration by John Millais of tall woman (presumably Maude Clare) in crowd (of wedding guests?) (382).
Location: microfilm, *Early British Periodicals*.

C20 "Up-Hill." *Macmillan's Magazine* 3 (February 1861): 325. Signed "Christina G. Rossetti."
Note: Rpt. in *English Woman's Journal* (May 1862): 207. Unsigned. Within an unsigned review of *Goblin Market and Other Poems*.
Location: microfilm, *Focus on English Literature*; *English Woman's Journal*: *Gerritsen Collection*.

C21 "A Birthday." *Macmillan's Magazine* 3 (April 1861): 498. Signed "Christina G. Rossetti."
Location: microfilm, *Focus on English Literature*.

C22 "An Apple Gathering." *Macmillan's Magazine* 4 (August 1861): 329. Signed "Christina G. Rossetti."
Note: reprinted in the *Living Age* (Boston; volume title, *Littell's Living Age*) 961(1 November 1862): 240.
Location: microfilm, *Focus on English Literature*.

C23 "XLII. "'Behold, I Stand at the door and Knock'." *The English Woman's Journal* 9.46 (December 1861): 245. Signed "Christina G. Rossetti."
Note: See D'Amico, "Christina Rossetti and *The English Woman's Journal*," *Journal of Pre-Raphaelite Studies* (Spring 1994: 20-24).
Location: *Gerritsen Collection*.

C24 "'A Bruised Reed Shall He Not Break'." *The English Woman's Journal* 9.51 (May 1862): 207-208. Unsigned, but within a review of *Goblin Market and Other Poems*.
Location: *Gerritsen Collection*.

C25 "Seeing, Unseen" ("At Home"). *The Albion, A Journal of News, Politics and Literature* (New York) (14 June 1862): 277. Signed "Christina Rossetti."
Note: Also reprinted in the *Independent* (New York) (19 June 1862): 7.
Location: APS Online.

C26 "Light Love." *Macmillan's Magazine* 7 (February 1863): 287. Signed "Christina G. Rossetti."
Location: microfilm, *Focus on English Literature*.

C27 "The Bourne." *Macmillan's Magazine* 7 (March 1863): 382. Signed "Christina G. Rossetti."
Location: microfilm, *Focus on English Literature*.

C28 "L. E. L." *The Victoria Magazine* 1.5 (1863): 40-41. Signed "Christina G. Rossetti."
Location: microfilm, Library of Congress.

C29 L "Prayer for the Church Militant." *Notes and Queries* 3rd series 3 (16 May 1863): 397. Signed "Christina G. Rossetti."
Location: TxCM.

C30 "The Fairy Prince Who Arrived Too Late" ("The Prince's Progress"). *Macmillan's Magazine* 8 (May 1863): 36. Signed "Christina G. Rossetti."
Note: Only lines 481-540.
Location: microfilm, *Focus on English Literature*.

C31 "A Bird's Eye View." *Macmillan's Magazine* 8 (July 1863): 207. Signed "Christina G. Rossetti."
Note: Reprinted in the *New York Times*, 8 July 1866: 2.
Location: microfilm, *Focus on English Literature*; *New York Times*: ProQuest Historical Newspapers.

C32 "The Queen of Hearts." *Macmillan's Magazine* 8 (October 1863): 457. Signed "Christina G. Rossetti."
Location: microfilm, *Focus on English Literature*.

C33 "XV. Gone Before." *The English Woman's Journal* 12.68 (October 1863): 91. Signed "Christina G. Rossetti."
Location: *Gerritsen Collection*.

C34 "One Day." *Macmillan's Magazine* 9 (December 1863): 159. Signed "Christina G. Rossetti."
Location: microfilm, *Focus on English Literature*.

C35 "Bitter for Sweet." *College Rhymes* (Oxford, Cambridge): 4 (1863): 131. Signed "Christina Rossetti."
Note: English text appears as epigraph to its translation in Latin by "G." Copy consulted is reissue, original issue number and date unknown.
Location: TxU.

C36 "The Eleventh Hour." *The Victoria Magazine* 2.2 (1864): 317-18. Signed "Christina G. Rossetti."
Location: NcU.

C37 "Sit Down in the Lowest Room" ("The Lowest Room"). *Macmillan's Magazine* 9 (March 1864): 436-439. Signed "Christina G. Rossetti."
Location: microfilm, *Focus on English Literature*.

C38 "Song" ("When I am dead, my dearest"), "Song" ("She sat and sang alway"), "Three Seasons," "An Apple Gathering," "Dream Land," "Rest." In "A Campaigner at Home." *Fraser's Magazine for Town and Country* 70 (August 1864): 210-212. Unsigned, but attributed in text.
Note: Included in a discussion of contemporary poetry by women (Browning, Procter, Rossetti, Ingelow). Article unsigned but attributed to John Skelton in *Wellesley Index*.
Location: *British Periodicals*.

C39 "My Friend." *Macmillan's Magazine* 11 (December 1864): 155. Signed "Christina G. Rossetti."
Location: microfilm, *Focus on English Literature*.

C40 "Books in the Running Brooks." *The Englishman's Magazine of Literature, Religion, Science, and Art* (January 1865): 20-21. Signed "Christina G. Rossetti."
Location: NjR (photocopy).

C41 "Paradise" in two parts, "I. In a Dream" ("Paradise") and "II. In a Symbol" ("Birds of Paradise"). *The Englishman's Magazine of Literature, Religion, Science, and Art* July 1865: 82-83. Signed "Christina G. Rossetti."
Location: Bodleian (via Google Books).

C42 "Spring Fancies" ("Spring Quiet"). *Macmillan's Magazine* 11 (April 1865): 460. Signed "Christina G. Rossetti."
Location: microfilm, *Focus on English Literature.*

C43 "'Last Night'." *Macmillan's Magazine* 12 (May 1865): 48. Signed "Christina G. Rossetti."
Location: microfilm, *Focus on English Literature.*

C44 "Amor Mundi." *The Shilling Magazine* 2 (June 1865): 193.
Note: With an illustration by Anthony Frederick Sandys. Forrest Reid, who identified the illustration as Sandy's "favourite among his wood engravings," described it as "a beautiful, slightly unpleasant, and extraordinarily suggestive drawing, depicting two lovers strolling down the easy path of sensuality to the hidden hollow where death lies waiting" (60).
   Later quoted within a story by "Johnny Ludlow" (pseudonym of Ellen "Mrs. Henry" Wood), "A Crisis in His Life," *Argosy* (February 1873): 125-126; and reprinted in *Argosy* 15 (May 1873): 350.
Location: Not seen; copy located at BL; *Argosy:* MiU (via Google Books).

C45 "Consider." *Macmillan's Magazine* 13 (January 1866): 232. Signed "Christina G. Rossetti."
Note: Reprinted in *Littell's Living Age* 88 (3 February 1866): 399.
Location: microfilm, *Focus on English Literature*; *Littell's: Making of America* archive, Cornell.

C46–C48

(C46) "Peter Grump," in "Hero: A Metamorphosis," 164.

(C47) "Forss," in "Hero: A Metamorphosis," 164.

(C48 F) "Hero: A Metamorphosis." *The Argosy* 1.2 (January 1866): 156-165. Signed "Christina G. Rossetti."
Location: MiU (via Google Books).

C49 "Who Shall Deliver Me?" *The Argosy* 1.3 (February 1866): 288. Signed "Christina G. Rossetti."
Location: MiU (via Google Books).

C50 "Helen Grey." *Macmillan's Magazine* 13 (March 1866): 375. Signed "Christina G. Rossetti."
Location: microfilm, *Focus on English Literature.*

C51 "If." *The Argosy* 1.4 (March 1866): 336. Signed "Christina G. Rossetti."
Location: MiU (via Google Books).

C52 "Summer" ("Winter is cold-hearted"). *Our Own Fireside* 3 (September 1866): 517. Signed "Christina Rossetti."
Note: A sixpenny monthly edited by Rev. Charles Bullock, Rector of St. Nicolas, Worcester.
Location: Bodleian (via Google Books).

C53 "By the Waters of Babylon. B. C. 570." *Macmillan's Magazine* 14 (October 1866): 424-426. Signed "Christina G. Rossetti.

Note: Reprinted in *Every Saturday* (Boston) (27 October 1866): 508.
Location: microfilm, *Focus on English Literature*; *Every Saturday*: *APS Online*.

C54 "Seasons" ("Oh the Cheerful Budding-Time"). *Macmillan's Magazine* 25 (December 1866): 168-169. Signed "Christina G. Rossetti.
Location: microfilm, *Focus on English Literature*.

C55 F "The Waves of this Troublesome World. A Tale of Hastings Ten Years Ago." *The Churchman's Shilling Magazine and Family Treasury* 1.2 (April 1867): 182-193; 1.3 (May 1867): 291-304.
Location: not seen; information from Trinity College Library, Dublin.

C56 F "Some Pros and Cons about Pews" (Pros and Cons"). *The Churchman's Shilling Magazine and Family Treasury* 1.5 (July 1867): 496-500.
Location: not seen; information from Trinity College Library, Dublin.

C57 NF "Dante: An English Classic." *The Churchman's Shilling Magazine and Family Treasury* 2.8 (October 1867): 200-205.
Location: not seen; information from Trinity College Library, Dublin.

C58 F "A Safe Investment." *The Churchman's Shilling Magazine and Family Treasury* 2.9 (November 1867): 287-292.
Location: not seen; information from Trinity College Library, Dublin.

C59 "Twilight Night." *The Argosy* 5.1 (January 1868): 103. Signed "Christina G. Rossetti."
Location: MiU (via Google Books).

C60 "Mother Country." *Macmillan's Magazine* 18 (March 1868): 403-404. Signed "Christina G. Rossetti."
Location: microfilm, *Focus on English Literature*.

C61-C62 "A Smile and A Sigh" and "Dead Hope." *Macmillan's Magazine* 18 (May 1868): 86. Each signed "Christina G. Rossetti.
Note: Both rpt. in *Littell's Living Age* (6 June 1868): 595 ("Dead Hope"), 618 ("A Smile and a Sigh").
Location: microfilm, *Focus on English Literature*; *Littell's*: *Making of America* archive, Cornell.

C63 L Untitled letter, "Perhaps the following allegories may be worth adding to your list." *Notes and Queries* 4th ser. 2 (14 November 1868): 457. Signed "Christina G. Rossetti."
Note: not in *Letters*.
Location: TxCM.

C64 "Autumn Violets." *Macmillan's Magazine* 19 (November 1868): 84. Signed "Christina G. Rossetti."
Note: Rpt. in *Littell's Living Age* (Boston) (12 December 1868): 671.
Location: microfilm, *Focus on English Literature*; *Littell's*: *Making of America* archive, Cornell.

C65 "They Desire a Better Country." *Macmillan's Magazine* 19 (March 1869): 422-423. Signed "Christina G. Rossetti."
Note: Rpt. in the *Ladies' Repository* 4.6 (New York) (December 1869): 418.
Location: microfilm, *Focus on English Literature*; *Ladies' Repository*: *Making of America* archive, Michigan.

C66 "Thy Brother's Blood Crieth." ("The German-French Campaign. 1870-1871. I."). *The Graphic* (5 November, 1870: 450. Signed "Christina G. Rossetti."
Note: Reprinted in at least two American periodicals: *Every Saturday* (Boston) New series 1.49 (December 3, 1870): 786; and Supplement to *Harper's Weekly* 14. 727 (December 3, 1870): (unpaginated, supplement page 1).
Location: TxHR; *Every Saturday*: APS Online; *Harper's Weekly*: Harpweek.

C67 "A Nursery Rhyme." ("Fly away, fly away, over the sea"). *Old and New* (Boston) 4 (1871): 410. Signed "Christine G. Rossetti."
Location: OClW (photocopy).

C68 "Sing-Song." Two poems, numbered I ("Oh, fair to see") and II ("There is one that has a head without an eye"). *Old and New* (Boston) 4 (1871): 418. Signed "Christina G. Rossetti."
Location: OClW (photocopy).

C69 "Sing-Song." ("Seldom 'can't' "). *Old and New* (Boston) 4 (1871): 424. Signed "Christina G. Rossetti."
Location: OClW (photocopy).

C70 "Three Seasons." Supplement to *Harper's Weekly* 25.746 (15 April 1871): 347. Signed "Christina G. Rossetti."
Location: Harpweek.

C71 "A Summer Wish." Supplement to *Harper's Weekly* 25.751 (20 May 1871): 470. Signed "Christina G. Rossetti."
Location: Harpweek.

C72 "Consider the Lilies of the Field" ("Flowers preach to us if we will hear"). *Arthur's Lady's Home Magazine* (Philadelphia) 38.3 (September 1871): 177. Signed "Christina Rossetti."
Location: APS Online.

C73 "The One Certainty." Supplement to *Harper's Weekly* 25.769 (Saturday, September 23, 1871): 898. Signed "Christina G. Rossetti."
Location: Harpweek.

C74 "A Christmas Carol." ("In the bleak mid-winter"). *Scribner's Monthly* 3.3 (January 1872): 278.
Note: Illustrated by John Leighton, featuring a vignette of the infant Jesus in the manger with Mary, Joseph and the three shepherds.
The forthcoming poem was described as "a little poem [. . .] wise in a sort of child-wisdom, sweet and clear and musical" in 3.2 (November 1871): 239. WMR noted that CGR was paid £10 for the poem, which she sent to *Scribner's* "at Stillman's request" (*Diary* 122); in later correspondence, CGR did not remember the Scribner publication and instead thought the poem had been published in the *People's Magazine* (see Ives, "The Letters of Christina Rossetti: Two New Letters," 21-22). Reprinted in the *Reformed Church Messenger* (Philadelphia) (December 27, 1871: 1) with note "Scribner's for January," and the *New York Times* (25 December 1872: 1).
Location: *Scribner's* 1872: Ives. *Reformed Church*: APS Online. *New York Times*: ProQuest Historical Newspapers.

C75 "A Nursery Rhyme." ("Hope is like a harebell, trembling from its birth"). *Old and New* (Boston)

5.2 (February 1872): 169. Signed "Christina G. Rossetti."
Location: MiU (via Google Books).

C76   "Sing-Song." ("What does the bee do?"). *Harper's New Monthly Magazine* 44.261 (February 1872): 476. Attributed to "Christina Rossetti" but not signed.
Location: *Making of America* archive, Cornell.

C77   "A Nursery Rhyme." ("Hear what the mournful sparrows say:"). *Old and New* (Boston) 5.3 (March 1872): 278. Signed "Christina G. Rossetti."
Location: MiU (via Google Books).

C78   "Days of Vanity." *Scribner's Monthly* 5.1 (November 1872): 21. Not signed.
Location: OkU.

C79, 80   "Two Sonnets. I. Venus's Looking-Glass. II. Love Lies Bleeding." *The Argosy* 15.1 (January 1873): 31. Signed "Christina G. Rossetti."
Note: Rpt. in *Littell's Living Age* (Boston) 165.1497 = 5th ser., 1) (February 15, 1873): 386.
Location: MiU (via Google Books); *Littell's: Making of America* archive, Cornell.

C81   "A Bird Song." *Scribner's Monthly* 5.3 (January 1873): 336. Not signed.
Location: OkU.

C82 L   "Artemus Ward." *Notes and Queries* 4th ser. 11 (29 March 1873): 253.
Location: TxCM.

C83   "Rest." *The Woman's Journal* (Boston) 5.1 (31 January 1874): 38. Signed "Christina G. Rossetti."
Location: WaU (photocopy).

C84   "A Peal of Bells." *The Woman's Journal* (Boston) 5.23 (6 June 1874): 182. Signed "Christina G. Rossetti."
Location: Gerritsen Collection.

C85   "Autumn" ("I dwell alone"). *The Woman's Journal* (Boston) 5.26 (27 June 1874): 208. Signed "Christina G. Rossetti."
Location: Gerritsen Collection.

C86   "Three Seasons." *The Woman's Journal* (Boston) 5.27 (4 July 1874): 216. Signed "Christina G. Rossetti."
Location: Gerritsen Collection.

C87   "Sound Sleep."*The Woman's Journal* (Boston) 5.28 (11 July 1874): 224. Signed "Christina G. Rossetti."
Location: Gerritsen Collection.

C88   "Sleep at Sea." *The Woman's Journal* (Boston) 5.32 (8 August 1874): 251. Signed "Christina G. Rossetti."
Location: Gerritsen Collection.

C89   "A Dirge" ("Why were you born when the snow was falling?"). *The Argosy* 17.1 (1874): 25. Signed "Christina G. Rossetti."
Location: Ives.

C90   "A Bride Song." *The Argosy* 19 (1875): 25. Signed "Christina G. Rossetti."
Location: MiU (via Google Books).

C91   "Dost Thou Not Care?" *The British Friend* (Glasgow) 33 (1 5ᵗʰ Month 1875): 115.
Note: Excerpt, titled "To-Morrow."
Location: Oxford University Library (via Google Books).

C92   "An Alphabet from England." *St. Nicholas: an Illustrated Magazine for Young Folks* (New York)
3.1 (November 1875): 56-59.
Note: Illustrated with eight vignettes, often comic.
Location: APS Online.

C93   "Johnny." *Friendly Leaves* 1.3 (July 1876): 97-98. Signed "Christina G. Rossetti."
Location: Oxford University Library (via Google Books).

C94   "Mirrors of Life and Death." *The Athenaeum* (17 March 1877): 350.
Note: CGR was paid £10 for a "general contribution" to the magazine (*Letters* 2: 130). Rpt. in *Harper's
Weekly*, 21. 1061 (Saturday, April 28, 1877): 326.
Location: CtMW; *Harper's*: Harpweek.

C95   "An October Garden." *The Athenaeum* No. 2609 (27 October 1877) 532.
Note: CGR received £5 for the poem (*Letters* 2: 161). Reprinted in the *Eclectic Magazine of Foreign
Literature, Science and Art* New ser. 27 (January 1878): 128.
Location: CtMW.

C96   "Yet a Little While" ("I dreamed and did not seek"). *(Dublin) University Magazine* 1 new ser.
(January 1878): 104. Signed "Christina G. Rossetti."
Note: Journal title appears as *The University Magazine* on volume title page and first page of January
number.
Location: MiU (via Google Books).

C97   "Weary in Well-Doing." *Frank Leslie's Sunday Magazine* 4.2 (August 1878): 206. Signed "Christina
G. Rossetti."
Location: NN (via Google Books).

C98 NF   "A Harmony on First Corinthians XIII." *New and Old: For Seed-Time and Harvest* 7 (January
1879): 34-39. Signed "Christina G. Rossetti."
Note: The parish magazine of St. Cyprians, Marylebone, edited by the Rev. Charles Gutch. A paragraph
titled "Noah's Sacrifice" appears above Rossetti's text on 34, and an accompanying full page illustration
of Noah's burnt offering after the flood appears on 35. Reprinted in Mary Arseneau and Jan Marsh,
"Intertextuality and intratextuality: the full text of Christina Rossetti's Harmony on First Corinthians
XIII rediscovered." *Victorian Newsletter* 88 (1995): 17-26.
Location: BL (photocopy).

C99   "A Royal Princess." *The Quarterly Elocutionist* (New York) 5.18 (April 1879): 75-80. Signed
"Christina G. Rosetti."
Note: Rpt. in *The Reading Club and Handy Speaker*, (Boston, New York) no. 7 (1879): 1- 4; also included
in *One Hundred Choice Selections* (Philadelphia, Chicago), No. 17 (28-31).
Location: NjP. Bound in wrappers.

C100 "Jessie Cameron." *One Hundred Choice Selections* (Philadelphia, Chicago) no. 18 (1880): 99-101. Signed "Christina G. Rossetti."
Location: NjP (via Google Books).

C101 "Somewhere or Other." *The Woman's Journal* (Boston) 12.46 (12 November 1881): 362. Signed "Christina G. Rossetti."
Location: *Gerritsen Collection.*

C102 "The irresponsive silence of the land." (first stanza of "The Thread of Life."). *Littell's Living Age* (Boston) (November 19, 1881): 386. Signed "Christina Rossetti."
Location: *Making of America* archive, Cornell.

C103 "Fluttered Wings." *The Saturday Evening Post* 61.19 (November 26, 1881): 11. Signed "Christina Rossetti."
Location: *APS Online.*

C104 "Old and New Year" ("Old and New Year Ditties"). *The Woman's Journal* (Boston) 12.53 (Saturday, December 31, 1881): 422. Signed "Christina G. Rossetti."
Note: Excerpt (section 1 only).
Location: *Gerritsen Collection.*

C105 "A Christmas Carol" ("Christmas Carols" 2. "A holy, heavenly chime"). *Wide Awake* (Boston) 16.1 (December 1882): 102-103.
Note: See **B59**.
Location: OrU.

C106 F "True in the Main: Two Sketches." *The Dawn of Day* (May 1882):57-59; (June 1882): 69-70.
Note: Citation from Arseneau (215).
Location: not seen; copy located at BL.

C107 "Resurgam." *The Athenaeum* No. 2831 (28 January 1882): 124. Signed "Christina G. Rossetti."
Location: MCM.

C108 "Birchington Churchyard." *The Athenaeum* No. 2844 (29 April 1882): 538. Signed "Christina G. Rossetti."
Location: MCM.

C109 L Letter to the editor. *The Athenaeum* No. 2959 (12 August 1882): 207.
Note: Rpt. in *Letters* 3:57 (but with an incorrect citation of the periodical appearance).
Location: microfilm, *Early British Periodicals.*

C110 "The Key Note." *Church's Musical Visitor* (Cincinnati). 12.1 (January 1883): 9. Signed "Christina Rossetti."
Location: *APS Online.*

C111 "Michael F. M. Rossetti." *The Athenaeum* 2886 (17 February 1883): 214. Signed "Christina G. Rossetti."
Location: microfilm, *Early British Periodicals.*

C112 "A Wintry Sonnet." *Macmillan's Magazine* 47 (April 1883): 498. Signed "Christina G. Rossetti."
Location: microfilm, *Focus on English Literature*.

C113 L "A Memoir of Mrs. Radcliffe." *The Athenaeum* 2906 (7 July 1883): 15. Signed "Christina G. Rossetti."
Location: Washington State University.

C114 "At Home." *Frank Leslie's Popular Monthly* 16 (September 1883): 318. Signed "Christina Rossetti."
Location: TxCM.

C115 "Remember." In Edward B. Aveling, "Shakespeare the Dramatist." *Our Corner* 2.5 (November 1883): 268-269. Unsigned, but attributed in text.
Location: *British Periodicals*.

C116 NF "Dante. The Poet illustrated out of the Poem." *The Century Magazine* 27.4 (February 1884): 566-573. Signed "Christina G. Rossetti."
Note: The journal's title also appears as *Century Magazine* within the volume. CGR accepted Edmund Gosse's invitation to write the article in January 1883 (*Letters* 3: 83), for which she was paid 20 guineas (*Letters* 3: 118).
Location: APS Online.

C117 "Oh Lady Moon." *St. Nicholas* 12.2 (December 1884): 125. Signed "Christina G. Rossetti."
Note: Illustrated, with two circular vignettes of the moon, and with the text of poem incorporated into the illustration. Illustration signed "JWL," identified in table of contents as Julia W. Lee.
Location: Washington State University.

C118 "One Sea-side Grave." *The Century Magazine* 28.1 (May 1884): 134. Signed "Christina G. Rossetti."
Note: See **C116** regarding journal title.
Location: APS Online.

C119 "Brother Bruin." *Wide Awake* (Boston) 22.1 (December 1885): 11-12.
Note: Illustrated with four vignettes of the bear and/or his master. CGR was paid £5.2.8.
Location: TxU.

C120 "Laughing life cries at the feast." *Littell's Living Age* (Boston) 167.2162 (= 5th ser., 52) (28 November 1885): 514. Signed "Christina Rossetti."
Location: *Making of America* archive, Cornell.

C121 "A Christmas Carol." ("Christmas Carols. 1. Whoso hears a chiming"). *The Century Guild Hobby Horse* 2 (1887): 1. Signed "Christina G. Rossetti."
Note: Facing volume's frontispiece, "The Angel of Death Crowning Innocence" by G. F. Watts.
Location: MH (via Google Books).

C122 "A Christmas Carol." ("Christmas Carols 3. Lo! Newborn Jesus"). *Atalanta* 1.3 (December 1887): 154. Signed "Christina G. Rossetti."
Note: A facsimile of CGR's signature appears beneath the title, and the poem's text appears within three-sided rectangular compartments, with an evergreen branch and stars in the background. The poem faces

a full page illustration of painting by Raphael, captioned "Madonna Della Granduca."
Location: Chicago Public Library.

C123 "A Helpmeet for Him." *New and Old: For Seed-Time and Harvest* 16 (January 1888): 22.
Location: not seen; copy located in BL.

C124 "A Candlemas Dialogue." *Atalanta* 1 (February 1888): 264. Signed "Christina G. Rossetti."
Location: InU (photocopy).

C125 "Exultate Deo." *Atalanta* 2 (October 1888): 3. Signed "Christina G. Rossetti."
Note: The poem's title appears in an ornamented rectangle that also contains a lamp and flowers; a facsimile of CGR's signature appears below the text. Also, the poem faces the issue's frontispiece, an untitled illustration by E. J. Poynter of an androgynous face looking upward; captioned "Exultate Deo."
Location: Chicago Public Library.

C126 "A Hope Carol." *The Century Guild Hobby Horse* 3.10 (April 1888), 41. Signed "Christina G. Rossetti."
Note: Facing full-page illustration, identified in "Contents" as "Miranda. Frederick Sandys. By the kind permission of J. Anderson Rose, Esq."
Location: MH (via Google Books).

C127 "Golden Silences." *The Magazine of Poetry* 1.2 (1889): 236. Signed "Christina Georgina Rossetti."
Location: MiU (via Google Books).

C128 "On Sea and Shore." ("One Foot on Sea, And One on Shore"). *The Washington Post* (21 September 1889): 4.
Location: APS Online.

C129 "Lazarus Loquitur" ("Son, Remember"). *New and Old: For Seed-Time and Harvest* 17 (October 1889): 274.
Note: Citation from Crump (III: 582).
Location: not seen; copy located in BL.

C130 "There is a Budding Morrow in Midnight." *Century Guild Hobby Horse* NS 4 (1889): 81.
Note: Facing full-page illustration, identified in "Contents" as "A Study of a Head: Being a Reproduction In Photogravure of the Drawing by E. Burne-Jones. From a negative by Mr. Hollyer."
Location: MH (via Google Books).

C131 "Mary Magdalene and the Other Mary." *New and Old: a parochial magazine for all readers* April 1890: 95.
Location: not seen; copy located at NNC.

C132 "Cardinal Newman." *The Athenaeum* No. 3277 (16 August 1890): 225. Signed "Christina G. Rossetti."
Location: MCM.

C133 "An Echo from Willowwood." *The Magazine of Art* 13 (September 1890): 385.
Note: Within illustrated compartment by Charles Ricketts (see Kooistra, 53-54). In August 1888, CGR responded to an invitation from the editor, Marion Spielmann, with a poem "capable of illustration" (*Letters* 4: 87); CGR responded positively to the illustrated version, "interpreted by the delicate fanciful-

ness of Mr. Ricketts" (*Letters* 4: 212). CGR received £4.4.0 for the poem, and granted Cassell "the right to publish it in the subsequent issue of "Poems & Pictures" in Book form" (*Letters* 4: 214). I have not traced a subsequent publication by Cassell, but the poem and illustration were reprinted in *Frank Leslie's Popular Monthly* 34.5 (November 1892): 528.
Location: *British Periodicals*; *Frank Leslie's*: Indiana UL (via Google Books).

C134 "Yea, I Have a Goodly Heritage." *Atalanta* 4.37 (October 1890): [3]. Signed "Christina G. Rossetti."
Note: Rossetti's poem appears on the first page of the issue, and a facsimile of her signature appears below the poem title.
Location: Cornell.

C135 "A Death of a First-born." *Literary Opinion* (February 1892): 227.
Note: CGR was paid three guineas for this sonnet, which she wrote at the request of the journal's editor, Arthur Patchett Martin (*Letters* 4: 261).
Location: not seen; National Library of Scotland.

C136 "'Faint, Yet Pursuing." *Literary Opinion* 2 (May 1892): 67.
Note: CGR read (and corrected an error) in proof (*Letters* 4: 273). A facsimile of the corrected proof is reprinted in Bell, 147.
Location: not seen; National Library of Scotland.

C137 NF "The House of Dante Gabriel Rossetti." *Literary Opinion* 2 (June 1892): 127-129.
Note: CGR offered to write down her "reminiscences" of DGR's residence at Cheyne Walk, "in case you should care for such text to accompany Miss Thomas's drawing" (*Letters* 4: 276). "Miss Thomas" is Margaret Thomas, whose woodcut was published along with CGR's text.
Location: not seen; National Library of Scotland.

C138 "The Way of the World." *The Magazine of Art* 17 (July 1894): 304. Signed "Christina G. Rossetti."
Note: Facing full page illustration, captioned "The Way of the World. (Drawn by W. E. F. Britten. For Miss Rossetti's Poem see opposite Page)."
Location: ABAU.

C139-C141 "Ash Wednesday" ("My God, my God, have mercy on my sin"); "Good Lord, to-day"; "Lent." *The Dawn of Day* New ser. No. 194 (February 1894): 40. Signed "Christina Rossetti."
Location: Ives.

C142 "If Thou Sayest, Behold We Knew it Not." *Heathen Woman's Friend* (Boston) 26.3 (September 1894): 63. Signed "Christina G. Rossetti."
Location: WU (via Google Books).

C143 L Sharp, William. "Some Reminiscences of Christina Rossetti." *The Atlantic Monthly* 75 (June 1895): 736-749.
Three letters to Sharp, 744-745.
Location: *Making of America* archive, Cornell.

C144 "In Patience." *The Wesleyan-Methodist Magazine* 111 (July 1896): 558. Signed "Christina G. Rossetti."
Location: *British Periodicals*.

C145 L W., I. M. "Some Autograph Letters and Their Associations." *Good Words* 37 (April 1896): 232-236.
Note: Month unidentifiable from source. Includes a facsimile of a letter from CGR to an unidentified journal editor. Not in *Letters*.
Location: British Periodicals.

C146 L Gilchrist, Grace. "Christina Rossetti." *Good Words* 37 (December 1896): 822-826.
Note: "The Convent Threshold" (excerpt), "After Death," "Dream Land," 826. Also includes seven letters to Anne Gilchrist, one of which, probably from 1867, is not in *Letters*.
Location: British Periodicals.

C147 "Goblin Market." *Werner's Magazine* 19.3 (March 1897): 231-232. Signed "Christina B. Rossetti."
Note: An abridged version. *Werner's Magazine*, published by Edgar S. Werner, focused on elocution and recitation.
Location: University of Michigan (via Google Books).

C148 L "A Poetic Trio and Their Needlework." *The Athenaeum* No. 3641 (7 August 1897): 193-194.
Note: CGR to Dora Greenwell, 193.
Location: Washington State University.

C149 NF Paragraph from *The Face of the Deep*, beginning "Strength attaches to union, resource to multiplicity." *The Church of Scotland Home & Foreign Mission Record, with which is combined News of Female Missions* (Edinburgh) 24 (January 1899): 20.
Note: Same passage, slightly longer, reprinted within "The Present Crisis in the Church of England," the *Nineteenth Century* 45 (February 1899): 187.
Location: MH (via Google Books); *Nineteenth Century*: NjP (via Google Books).

C150 L *Literature* 7.10 (8 September, 1900): 167.
Note: Excerpt "from an unpublished letter written [. . .] in 1893" to an unidentified recipient. The excerpt concerns childhood pets, including a tabby cat, a dormouse that hibernated in a drawer, two squirrels, a bluebird, and a bullfinch, and included a sketch of a cat (not reproduced). Not in *Letters*.
Location: InU (via Google Books).

C151 L J., A. H. (Adrian Hoffman Joline) "Meditations of an Autograph Collector." *The Literary Collector* (New York) 2.3 (June 1901): 71-78.
Note: CGR to "Mrs. G. Linneaus Banks," 72. Rpt. in Joline, *Meditations of an Autograph Collector* (New York: Harper & Bros, 1902), 96. Not in *Letters*.
Location: MiU (via Google Books).

C152 L Purvis, John. "Dante Gabriel Rossetti: Letters to Miss Alice Boyd." *The Fortnightly Review* 123 N.S. (1 May 1928): 594.
Note: CGR to Alice Boyd.
Location: British Periodicals.

C153 L Curti, Merle Eugene. "A Letter of Christina Rossetti." *Modern Language Notes* (Baltimore) 51.7 (November 1936): 439.
Note: CGR to Elihu Burritt.
Location: JSTOR.

C154 L   Packer, Lona Mosk, "Speaking Likenesses." *The Times Literary Supplement* (5 June 1959): 337.
Note: Quotations from five letters from CGR to Macmillan.
Location: TxCM.

C155 L   Packer, Lona Mosk, "Christina Rossetti and Alice Boyd of Penkill Castle." *The Times Literary Supplement* (26 June 1959): 389.
Note: Two poems, "Gone to his rest," and "Hail, noble face of noble friend!" ("To my Fior-di-Lisa")
reprinted Crump 3: 335, 347, and three letters to Alice Boyd.
Location: TxCM.

C156 L   Packer, Lona Mosk. "Christina Rossetti's Correspondence with her Nephew: Some Unpublished
Letters." *Notes and Queries*, New ser. 6 (December 1959): 425-32.
Note: Thirteen letters from CGR to Gabriel Arthur Rossetti.
Location: TxCM.

C157 L   Putt, S. Gorley. "Christina Rossetti, Alms-Giver." *English* 13.78 (Autumn 1961): 222-23.
Note: Quotations from nine letters from CGR to William Bryant.
Location: WU.

C158 L   Packer, Lona Mosk. "F. S. Ellis and the Rossettis: A Publishing Venture and Misadventure."
The Western Humanities Review (Salt Lake City). 16.3 (Summer 1962): 243-253.
Note: Quotations from eleven letters from CGR to F. E. Ellis, one to Macmillan.
Location: TxCM.

C159 L   Standley, Fred L. "Christina Georgina to Dante Gabriel: An Unpublished Letter."
English Language Notes (Boulder). 5 (June 1968): 283-5.
Note: CGR to DGR, circa 1873-1875. Not in *Letters*.
Location: TxCM.

C160 L   Lasner, Mark Samuels. "Christina Rossetti's 'Common Looking Booklet': A New Letter about
her *Verses* of 1847." *Notes and Queries* New ser. 28 (October 1981): 420.
Note: CGR to William Bryant, circa 1886, accompanying a copy of *Verses*. Not in *Letters*.
Location: TxCM.

C161 L   Gardner, Kevin J. "A New letter by Christina Rossetti." *Notes and Queries* 40.1 (March
1993): 59.
Note: CGR to WMR, circa 17 April 1893. Not in *Letters*.
Location: TxCM.

C162 NF   D'Amico, Diane, and David A. Kent. "Christina Rossetti's Notes on Genesis and Exodus."
The Journal of Pre-Raphaelite Studies (Toronto) 13 (Spring 2004): 49-98.
Location: TxCM.

C163 L   Ives, Maura. "The Letters of Christina Rossetti: Two New Letters." *The Journal of Pre-
Raphaelite Studies* (Toronto). 15 (Spring 2006) 19-26.
Note: CGR to Mary Mapes Dodge, 5 July 1875; and Jeannette Gilder, 20 April 1885. Not in *Letters*.
Location: Ives.

C164 L   Baker, William and Emily Kingery. "Some New Christina Rossetti Materials." *Notes and
Queries* 56 (September 2009): 394-396.

Note: Transcript of "Golden Holly" and full text of letter from CGR to Holman and Holly Stephens. A partial transcript appeared in *Letters* 1: 390-391.
Location: *Oxford Journals online*.

C165 L   Baker, William. "Christina Rossetti: An Unpublished Letter and An Unrecorded Copy of Verses." *Notes and Queries* 57 (June 2010): 221-223.
Note: Reports corrections in a copy of *Verses* (A2) owned by Dr. G. N. Wachs, and includes transcript of letter from CGR to Charles Howell.
Location: *Oxford Journals online*.

MISATTRIBUTIONS

C166   "The Common Offering." *The Woman's Journal* (Boston) 21.17 (26 April 1890): 134. Signed "Christina G. Rossetti."
Note: This poem (first line "It is not the deed we do") is by Harriett McEwen Kimball, published in her volume *Swallow-Flights* (New York: E. P. Dutton, 1874). Rpt., attributed to Rossetti, in *Heathen Woman's Friend* (Boston). 26.8 (February 1895): 227.
Location: *Gerritsen Collection*.

C167   "A Place For Me." *Heathen Woman's Friend* (Boston). 27.1 (July 1895): 3 Signed "Christina G. Rossetti."
Note: First line "Use me, God, in thy great harvest field"; author unidentified. Subsequently reprinted in additional religious periodicals and anthologies, under various titles.
Location: WU (via Google Books).

D: HYMNALS AND POEMS SET TO MUSIC

This section is divided into two subsections: Hymnals, with or without music (DH); and all other music (DM).

~

HYMNALS (DH)

This subsection is limited to hymnals published through 1900, along with a few significant post-1900 publications. Although works listed in this subsection were intended to be used in public singing, they do not include music unless noted, and even those that include music generally do not include many of the features commonly found in other forms of printed music (see subsection DM).

Books in this subsection are listed in chronological order. Each entry includes a title page transcription in quasi-facsimile; first line or titles and inclusive page numbers of Rossetti material; an indication of whether and how Rossetti's name appears with the text (e.g., unsigned or signed, "C. G. Rossetti"); tune designation (if any); notes; and the location(s) of copies examined. For entries that include music, the name of the composer, the tune name or other identification (if any), and the key signature, plate number and instrumentation (if any) are indicated.

Entries for hymn texts or settings that appeared with a title different from that which appears in Rossetti's collected publications include both the title or first line as printed in the hymnal, and the title or first line given by Rossetti when the contribution appeared in a collection, with Rossetti's first lines or titles in parentheses. For untitled texts or settings, Rossetti's first line or title is given in parentheses.

The term "signed" indicates that Rossetti's name appeared with the text either as a heading or a byline; if Rossetti's name appears elsewhere, its location is noted.

Information about publication in multiple issues (such as simultaneous British and American publication) and reprintings is provided if known.

Cross Listed items:

The following collections, listed in Section B, were not primarily intended for use as hymnals, but often include hymn texts as well as poems that were used as hymns.

B7 POEMS OF RELIGIOUS SORROW (1863)

B8 LYRA EUCHARISTICA (1863)

B11 LYRA EUCHARISTICA (SECOND EDITION) (1864)

B13 LYRA MESSIANICA (1864)

B16 LYRA MESSIANICA, SECOND EDITION (1869)

B17 LYRA MYSTICA (1865)

B18 POEMS OF THE INNER LIFE (1866)

B20 ELIM; OR HYMNS OF HOLY REFRESHMENT (1866)

B23 GOLDEN THOUGHTS FROM GOLDEN FOUNTAINS (1867)

B24 ILLUSTRATED BOOK OF SACRED POEMS (1867)

B30 CHRIST IN SONG (1870)

B43 HYMNS AND RHYMES (1875)

B44 LYRICS OF LIGHT AND LIFE (1875)

B56 RESURGIT (1875)

B57 SONGS OF THE SOUL (1880)

B58 HE GIVETH SONGS (1880)

B93 VICTORIAN HYMNS (1887)

B98 SACRED SONG (1888)

B105 TREASURY OF SACRED SONG (1889)

The following separately issued hymns are listed in section DM:

DM126/DM127 "Advent" ("This Advent moon shines cold and clear"); "And Now Why Tarriest Thou?"

DM142 "All Thy Works Praise Thee" Frank T. Lowden, 1897

DM164 "A Song for the Least of all Saints." [Frank T. Lowden], 1898

DH1   HYMNS OF THE AGES (1865)

HYMNS OF THE AGES. | *THIRD SERIES.* | [device, "TF" in shield] | BOSTON: | TICKNOR AND FIELDS. | 1865.

"A City That Hath Foundations" ("From House to Home"), 70-71. Signed "Christina Rossetti."

Note: Previously printed in *Poems of Religious Sorrow* (B7). Preface signed C. S. W. and A. E. G. (Caroline Snowden Whitmarsh and Anne E. Guild).
Location: InNd.

DH2   THE PEOPLE'S HYMNAL (1867)

THE PEOPLE'S HYMNAL. | [rule] | He set singers also before the altar, that by their voices they might | make sweet melody, and daily sing praises in their songs. He beautified | their feasts, and set in order the solemn times until the end, that they | might praise His holy Name, and that the temple might sound from the morn- | ing." -*Ecclus.* xlvii. 9, 10. | [rule] | LONDON: | JOSEPH MASTERS, ALDERGATE STREET, | AND NEW BOND STREET. | 1867.

"What are these that glow from afar," 207, no title, numbered 579. Unsigned; index attributes to C. Rossetti.

Note: Editorship attributed to Richard F. Littledale.
Location: Lutheran Theological Seminary at Philadelphia.

DH3   SONGS OF GLADNESS (1869)

Songs of Gladness | FOR THE SABBATH-SCHOOL. | CONTAINING MUSIC AND HYMNS SUITED TO OVER | THIRTY PURELY SABBATH-SCHOOL OCCASIONS. | ALSO A CHOICE SELECTION OF | PRAYER-MEETING AND CHOIR TUNES, | WITH OVER | [with ornamental capitals] ONE HUNDRED OF THE CHOICEST OLD STANDARD HYMNS. | BY J. E. GOULD, | AUTHOR OF "SACRED CHORUS BOOK," "MODERN HARP," "TYROLEAN LYRE," "AMPHION," ETC. | [ornamented rule] | PHILADELPHIA: | PUBLISHED BY J. C. GARRIGUES & CO., 608 ARCH STREET. |

FOR SALE BY BOOKSELLERS THROUGHOUT THE COUNTRY.

"Consider the Lilies" ("Consider"), 190. Signed: "Words by Rossetti."

Music: No composer identified (Gould?). Key signature F (1 flat), no time signature.
Note: Includes minor textual alterations. Copyright date 1869.
Locations: Ives; ViU.

DH4   SAVOY HYMNARY (1880)

No title; transcription from wrapper; text within single rule frame intersecting at corners:
SAVOY HYMNARY. | [coat of arms ornament between these words] CHAPEL ROYAL, | SAVOY.

"God the Father give us grace" (three stanzas drawn from "Martyr's Song"), no pagination, numbered 9.
Attribution "Adapted from Christina Rossetti." Tune: "Vesper Chant."

Note: For use in the Queen's Chapel Royal. No date or publication information; post-1865; dated 1880 in
British Library catalogue listing. In 1889, CGR referred to "a Doxology based on words of mine in [. . .]
"Martyrs' Song" in "the collection in use at the Savoy Chapel" (*Letters* 4: 110).
Location: GEU.

DH5   THE CHILDREN'S HYMN BOOK (1881)

Some text in <u>black letter</u>:
THE | CHILDREN'S HYMN BOOK | FOR USE IN | CHILDREN'S SERVICES, SUNDAY SCHOOLS |
AND FAMILIES | <u>Arranged in Order of the Church's Year</u> | PUBLISHED UNDER THE REVISION
OF | The Right Rev. W. WALSHAM HOW, D.D. | *Bishop Suffragan for East London* | The Right Rev.
ASHTON OXENDEN, D.D. | *Late Bishop of Montreal, and Metropolitan of Canada* | AND | The Rev.
JOHN ELLERTON, M.A. | *Rector of Barnes* | <u>With Accompanying Tunes</u> | LONDON | RIVINGTONS,
WATERLOO PLACE, PALL MALL | SEELEY & Co., 54, FLEET STREET

"Thou art the same, and Thy years shall not fail" ("Patience of Hope"), 289. Not signed.

Music: "Grasmere," hymn meter "8.6.4.D," composer Cameron W. H. Brock. Key signature E flat (3
flats), time signature 3/4.
Note: First published by Rivington in 1881, and (after 1888) by the Society for Promoting Christian
Knowledge. Rivington offered the book in at least three forms, two without music (not seen).
Locations: 1881: CtMW; 1888: Southwestern Baptist Theological Seminary.

DH6   CONGREGATIONAL HYMNS (1884)

CONGREGATIONAL HYMNS. | [short rule] | "God is the King of all the earth: sing ye praises with under- |
standing." PSALM xlvii. 7. | "Speaking to yourself in psalms and hymns and spiritual | songs, singing and
making melody in your hearts to the Lord." | Eph. v. 16. | [short rule] | LONDON: | ELLIOT STOCK,
62, PATERNOSTER ROW, E.C. | 1884.

"I would have gone; God bade me stay" ("Weary in Well-Doing"), no pagination, numbered 807.

Note: Compiled by W. Garrett Horder. Apparently Horder did not ask Rossetti's permission to be included
in the hymnal, as she wrote to him after publication: "It really gratifies me to see my few lines in your
Hymnal: so the result is exactly the same as if you had applied betimes" (20 May 1885; *Letters* 3: 264).
Reprinted in the second volume of Horder's *The Treasury of Hymns* (London: Elliot Stock, [1896]).
Locations: BL. *Treasury of Hymns*: Allen County Public Library.

DH7   CHRISTIAN CHORALS FOR THE CHAPEL AND FIRESIDE (1885)

Within double rule frame:
CHRISTIAN CHORALS, | FOR THE | CHAPEL & FIRESIDE. | EDITED BY | Melancthon Woolsey Stryker. | [rule] | "THOU SHALT COMPASS ME ABOUT WITH SONGS OF DELIVERANCE." | [rule] | NEW YORK AND CHICAGO, | BIGLOW & MAIN. | 1885.

"The flowers that bloom in the sun and shade" ("Patience of Hope"), no pagination, numbered 206. Signed "Christina G. Rossetti."

Music: "Cayuga," meter "8.6.4.8.6.4."; composer Max Piutti. Key signature E flat (3 flats), time signature 4/4.
Location: St. Olaf's College.

DH8   SOUGHT-OUT SONGS FOR CHRISTIAN WORKERS (1889)

SOUGHT-OUT | SONGS | FOR | CHRISTIAN WORKERS. | [rule] | COMPILED BY | Rev. A. B. Earle, D.D. | [rule] | BOSTON: | JAMES H. EARLE, Publisher, | 178 WASHINGTON STREET, | 1888. | [RULE] | Single copies, 25 cts. (Postage, 5 cts. Extra); $2.50 per dozen; $20.00 per hundred. | Copyright, 1887, by James H. Earle.

"Submission" ("Weary in Well-Doing" with alterations; see *Note*), no pagination, numbered 97. Signed "CHRISTINA GEORGIANNA ROSETTI."

Music: Composer C. B. J. Root. Key signature: F (1 flat), time signature 3/4.
Note: Text presented as numbered verses between the treble and bass staves. The first three "verses" are attributed to CGR; two additional verses are attributed to C. B. J. Root.
Location: Ives.

DH9   WINTERSDORF HYMNAL (1893)

WINTERSDORF HYMNAL | COMPILED BY | MARY S. SIMON | *"With his whole heart he sang songs and loved Him that | made him."* –Ecclesiasticus xlvii. 8 | LONDON | ISBISTER AND COMPANY Limited | 15 & 16 TAVISTOCK STREET W.C. | 1893

"Grant us such grace that we may work Thy Will" (numbered 141), 189; "How know I that it looms lovely that land I have never seen" ("That where I am, there ye may be also") (numbered 142), 189-190; "I was hungry, and Thou feddest me" ("Because He first loved us") (numbered 143), 190-191; "Lord, grant us grace to rest upon Thy word" (numbered 144), 191; "Who knows? God knows: and what He knows" ("Take no thought for the morrow") (numbered 145), 192. All signed "Christina G. Rossetti."

Note: "The Society for Promoting Christian Knowledge requests me to emphasize the fact that it has granted me permission to use the five hymns of Miss Rossetti (141-5), in consideration only of the Wintersdorf Hymnal being for private circulation" (7-8). The Preface also promises "an accompanying Tune Book is in process of completion" by "Miss M. E. Greaves" (11), but no such book has been located.
Location: MH (via Google Books).

DH10   HYMNS OF FAITH AND LIFE (1896)

HYMNS OF | FAITH AND LIFE | INCLUDING | PSALMS, CANTICLES AND ANTHEMS | COLLECTED AND EDITED | BY THE | Rev. JOHN HUNTER, D.D. | TRINITY CHURCH, GLASGOW | NEW EDITION | I will sing with the spirit, and I will sing with the | understanding also.—I. *Cor.* xiv. 15 | GLASGOW | JAMES MACLEHOSE AND SONS | Publishers to the University | 1896

"Lord, grant us grace to mount, by steps of grace" (numbered 541), 407-408. Signed "Christina G. Rossetti."

Music: No score; hymn meter "10.10.7.7.4.4."
Note: CGR's poem was used with permission from the SPCK (vi).
Location: MH (via Google Books).

DH11   CHURCH HYMNS WITH TUNES (1893)

CHURCH HYMNS | WITH TUNES. | The Music Edited by | CHARLES H. LLOYD, | M.A., Mus. Doc. Oxon. | The Plain Song Tunes Selected and Harmonized by | BASIL HARWOOD, M.A., Mus. Doc. Oxon. | NEW EDITION. | London: | SOCIETY FOR PROMOTING CHRISTIAN KNOWLEDGE. | 1903. | [short rule] | (*Published under the direction of the Church Hymn-Book Committee.*). | [Edition F.]

"A burdened heart that bleeds and bears" ("When I was in trouble I called upon the Lord") (numbered 123), 193, words as text on 193; "None other Lamb, none other Name" (numbered 479), 748, words as text on 748; "We know not a voice of that River" ("Whitsun Monday") (numbered 583), 898, words as text on 898. Not signed, but attributed in the "Index of Authors and Sources" to "Rossetti, Christina Georgina" (xxxi).

Music:
For "A burdened heart": "Wreford," meter "8.6.8.4."; composer E. S. Carter. Key signature E (4 sharps), time signature 4/2, tempo half note equals 92.
For "None other lamb": "In Te, Domine, speravi," meter "8.10.10.4."; composer C. H. Lloyd. Key signature F (1 flat), time signature 3/2, tempo: half note equals 60.
For "We know not": "Achnasheen," meter "9.8.10.5."; composer C. H. Lloyd. Key signature F (1 flat), time signature 4/2, tempo: halfnote equals 76.

Note: Published in various forms, including words only, words only bound with prayer-book, and words and music, with each form available in multiple sizes and bindings. Copy examined, "Edition F," is identified in an advertisement as "Long Primer, Imperial 16mo."
Locations: words and music: CtY. Other formats: not seen.

SELECTED HYMNALS AFTER 1900

DH12   THE SUNDAY SCHOOL HYMNARY (1905)

THE | SUNDAY SCHOOL | HYMNARY | A TWENTIETH CENTURY HYMNAL | FOR YOUNG PEOPLE | WORDS AND MUSIC EDITED BY | CAREY BONNER. | Published at 57 & 59 Ludgate Hill, London | By The Sunday School Union . . . . mdcccv.

("A Christmas Carol" ("The shepherds had an angel")) (numbered 16), 15. Signed "Christina Rossetti."

Music: "Agatha," meter "8.6., 6 lines," composer R. Y. Harding. Key signature G (1 sharp), time signature 4/4. Note at bottom of page "This hymn may also be sung to tune "Rhineland," No. 12."
Note: Published in words only and music and words formats, in various bindings.
Location: MH (via Google Books).

DH13   THE ENGLISH HYMNAL (1906)

1. Without music:

THE | ENGLISH HYNMNAL | OXFORD | PRINTED AT THE UNIVERSITY PRESS | LONDON: HENRY FROWDE | AMEN CORNER | 1906

"In the bleak mid winter" ("A Christmas Carol") (numbered 25), 21; "What are these that glow from afar" ("Martyrs' Song") (numbered 203), 169-170. Signed "Christina G. Rossetti."

2. With music; see *Note*:

THE | ENGLISH HYMNAL | WITH TUNES | OXFORD | PRINTED AT THE UNIVERSITY PRESS | LONDON: HENRY FROWDE | AMEN CORNER | 1906

("A Christmas Carol") (numbered 25), 44, words as text on 45; ("Martyrs' Song") (numbered 203), 292-293, words not presented separately. Both signed "Christina G. Rossetti."

Music:
For "A Christmas Carol": "Cranham," composer Gustav Holst; key signature F (1 flat), no time signature but notation "In moderate time [quarter note] = 100." Also "The metre of this hymn is peculiar. The music as printed is that of the first verse, and it can easily be adapted to the others" (44).
For "Martyrs Song": "Ymdaith Mwngc," no composer ("Welsh Traditional Melody"). For voices in unison and organ. Key signature E flat (3 flats), no time signature but "In moderate time [quarter note] = 96."

Note: Published with and without music; frequently reprinted. Later printings list Humphrey Milford rather than Henry Frowde on the title page. Subsequently reprinted in *Songs of Praise* (DH 14) and the *Oxford Book of Carols*, where it is titled "Mid-winter" (London: Humphrey Milford, 1928: 408-409).

The *English Hymnal* was a cultural and musical landmark, intended by general editor Percy Dearmer and its other Church of England compilers to "redress defects in popular hymnody," namely, that of *Hymns Ancient and Modern*, the Church's standard hymnal. The new Hymnal incorporated new hymn texts by CGR and other literary figures, as well as new hymn tunes under the guidance of musical editor Ralph Vaughan Williams, who enlisted Gustav Holst to compose "Cranham" for "A Christmas Carol." While Holst's remains one of the most well known settings for this poem, it was not the first; see DM173.
Locations: Without music: MH (via Google Books). With music: 1906: MoSW; not seen: 1909, copy located at GEU.

DH14   SONGS OF PRAISE (1925)

SONGS OF | PRAISE | [triangular grouping of ten leaf ornaments] | OXFORD UNIVERSITY PRESS | LONDON: HUMPHREY MILFORD

("A Christmas Carol") (numbered 50), 68, words as text on 69. Signed "Christina G. Rossetti."

Music: same as D10, but note terms meter "irregular" rather than "peculiar" (68).
Note: Published with and without music. Edited by Percy Dearmer, Ralph Vaughan Williams and Martin Shaw, and intended as an ecumenical "national collection of hymns" representing "that faith which is common to the English-speaking peoples to-day, both in the British Commonwealth and in the United States" (iii).
Location: With music: CU. Without music: not seen.

DH15   HYMNS ANCIENT AND MODERN REVISED (1950)

HYMNS | ANCIENT & MODERN | REVISED | 1950 | PRINTED FOR THE PROPRIETORS BY | WILLIAM CLOWES AND SONS, LTD. | PUBLISHING OFFICE | LITTLE NEW STREET, LONDON, E.C.4.

("A Christmas Carol") (numbered "Hymn 67"), 79. Signed "Christina Rossetti."

Music: Tune name given as "Cranham – Irregular."
Note: CGR's first appearance in the Church of England's oldest standard hymnal, described in the Preface as "something of a national institution" (vi).
Location: TxHR.

∼

MUSICAL SETTINGS OTHER THAN HYMNALS (DM)

This subsection includes all known published musical settings of Christina Rossetti's work through 1900, as well as a handful of significant settings published through 1950. A few works likely (but not known) to have been published are included. Settings are arranged in chronological order. Those published within the same year are arranged alphabetically by poem title.

For each entry, the title of the Rossetti poem, the name of the composer, and the publication date are given in the entry heading. If the identification of the Rossetti title is unconfirmed, the probable title appears in square brackets. All entries also include the title of the setting, publication information (including plate or publisher's numbers), and locations of extant copies (or citations of sources that reference settings that cannot be located). All entries are for separately published sheet music unless otherwise indicated.

For sheet music, a brief description or a transcription of the front cover or other title page equivalent is provided when possible. Given the complex graphic design of many sheet music wrappers from this period, most of the entries do not include full transcription in quasi-facsimile. Instead, any images on the cover are briefly described, and the following information is provided if present: dedication; song title; Rossetti's name as given on the wrapper; the price; publishing information (publishers, cities of publication, copyright information and dates), and publisher's numbers.

All settings are for voice and piano unless otherwise indicated. The length of the score in printed pages, and the initial key signature notation (expressed as numbers of sharps or flats), time signature, and tempo notations (such as "andante") are included.

Some settings were frequently reprinted by various publishers. Information about reprintings is provided when known. Many published settings from this period are undated, or retain early publication or copyright dates long after the initial printing. Approximate dates for items that are undated are derived from external sources, including advertisements, reviews, British Library stamps, and library catalog listings. It should be assumed that items marked "not seen" are dated from catalog listings if no other information is given.

DM1   "Song" ("When I am dead, my dearest"). Alice Mary Smith, 1864

Note: No copies located. In December 1864, Rossetti wrote that "A Miss Smith has asked and obtained Mac's leave to melodize one of my things, I know not which" (*Letters* 1: 211). Malcolm Lawson's discussion of settings of "Song" in *Notes and Queries* (17 March 1917: 214) references Smith's setting as having preceded his own (DM31).

DM2   "The Bourne." Alice Macdonald, 1865

Note: No copies located. DGR suggested that this poem be removed from *The Prince's Progress and Other Poems*, but CGR kept it "partly because it has been set to music very prettily by Alice Macdonald" (*Letters* 1: 243). Macdonald was the mother of Rudyard Kipling.

DM3   "Song" ("When I am dead, my dearest"). William Pinney, 1865

Remember or forget: ballad. London: Cramer & Co.
Note: Not in Gooch & Thatcher.
Location: not seen: copy located at UkCU.

DM4   **"A Birthday." Henry F. Schroeder, 1866**

My Heart is like a singing bird. Part song. London: Dearle & Co.
Note: BL depository copy dated 25 Oct 1866.
Location: not seen: BL.

DM5   **"Up-Hill." Charles W. Ewing, 1867**

Uphill. London: Augener and Co.
Note: Not in Gooch & Thatcher. Reviewed in the *Musical Standard* (7 December 1867): 354.
Location: not seen: copy located at UkCU.

DM6   **"Gone For Ever." Agnes Zimmerman, 1867**

Gone for ever. No. 120. Novello's Part-Song Book. Second Series. Book 14. London: Novello & Co.
Note: Indentified in British Library catalogue as a four-part song. Dated from advertisement in the *Musical Times* (1 December 1867: 239). Available in a set of six songs, price 1s. 6d, or as vocal score (octavo, 3d, folio, 1s) or vocal parts, 6d.
Location: not seen: copy located at BL.

DM7   **"A Birthday." A. L. Traventi, 1868**

My Love is Come to Me. London: Duncan Davison & Co.
Note: Not in Gooch & Thatcher. No copies located. Two "New Songs by Signor Traventi," including this setting and "If Thou Wilt Remember," were advertised in the *Musical World* (22 February 1868: 118; also 14 and 21 March).

"Signor Traventi" is probably A. L. Traventi. CGR commented upon a performance of "my song" at "Traventi's concert" in July 1866 (*Letters* 1: 277); this may or may not have been "A Birthday," which Traventi was (still?) working on in November, when "Traventi called at Albany Street, wishing Christina to make some verbal alterations in the Birthday, to make it more intelligible when set to music . . ." (*RP* 197).

Earlier published settings have not been traced, but in 1867, CGR mentions Traventi settings, apparently in print, in a letter to Thomas Niles: "I am glad the music (one song, at least) has come to hand" (*Letters* 1: 304).

DM8   **"Dream Land." Karl Reden (pseudonym of Charles Crozat Converse), 1868**

St. Louis: Balmer & Weber.
Cover description: Engraved ornamented text, with abstract, foliage-shaped designs in background.
Cover lists two songs, under the heading "Two Beautiful Ballads with Chorus ad lib": "No 1. Silent Land" and "No. 2 Dream Land."
Names on cover: "Christina Rossetti" and "Carl Reden."
Prices: for "Silent Land": 3; "Dream Land": 3 ½.
Publisher: Balmer & Weber, 206 N.Fifth St., St. Louis. "Entered according to act of Congress 1868 by Balmer and Weber in the Clerk's office of the U. S. Dist. Court for the East. dist. of M⁰."

Signed above score "Christina Rossetti."

Music: Composer's name is given as "Karl Reden" above the score. Key signature A flat (4 flats), time signature common time. Plate number 1799 = 4.
Note: Converse, a lawyer and composer, is best known for composing the tune for Joseph Scrivern's "What a Friend We Have in Jesus."
Location: MoSW.

DM9   "Echo." Mary Ann Virginia Gabriel, 1868

Echoes, Song. Virginia Gabriel. *Hanover Square; a Magazine of Pianoforte and Vocal Music.* 1.6 (April 1868): 160-165.

Music: Periodical; score 160-165. Key signature F (one flat), time signature common time.

Note: CGR was aware of the setting as early as December 1864: "I hear that my "Echo" is likely to be published, set to music by a Miss Gabriel" (*Letters* 1: 206, 222). In 1868, WMR noted that it had been published and dedicated to him (RP 340). The *Hanover Square* number containing "Echoes" was reviewed in the *Musical World* (4 April 1868: 231).

The British Library holds an undated separate publication by Ashdown & Parry (publishers of Hanover Square): BL depository copy dated 25 Nov. 1868, plate number A & P No. 5538, dual key signature for F and D (one flat and two sharps).

Locations: Hanover Square: Boston Public Library; Ashdown & Parry: BL.

DM10   ["Remember"]. Karl Reden (pseudonym of Charles Crozat Converse), 1868

Silent land. "No. 1" of "Two beautiful ballads with chorus ad lib." St. Louis: Balmer & Weber.

Note: no copies located. Identified via DM 8.

DM11   "Song" ("When I am dead, my dearest"). A. L. Traventi, 1868

If thou wilt remember. London: Duncan Davison & Co. Price 3s.

Location: no copies located; see *Note*.

Later printing:

Cover with ornamented engraved text, design of foliage and branches at left beneath "I" of "If" and encircling words beneath song title.

Song title: "If Thou Wilt Remember."

Names on cover: "C. G. Rossetti" and "A. L. Traventi."

Price: number "3 ½" within star.

Publishers: Oliver Ditson & Co, 277 Washington St., Boston; J. G. Haynes & Co., Boston; Lyon & Healy, Chicago; J. Church Jr., Cincinnati, C. H. Ditson & Co., New York; C. W. A. Trumpler, Philadelphia.

Signed above score "C. G. Rossetti." Words in English and German.

Music: Sheet music, score 2-5. Key signature: F (1 flat), time signature: common time, tempo "Andantino." Plate number 24066.

Locations: IN; NjP.

Note: The Duncan Davison printing was advertised, along with "My Love is Come to Me," in the *Musical World* (22 February 1868: 118; also 14 and 21 March). Performance noted in the *Musical World* (4 January 1868: 12). The date of the Ditson printing is uncertain (circa 1880s).

DM12   "Songs in a Cornfield." G. A. (George Alexander) Macfarren, 1869

Songs in a Corn-field. London: Hutchings and Romer.

Title page transcription:

Songs in a Corn-Field. | [short ornamented rule] | A CANTATA | FOR FEMALE VOICES, | WITH | ACCOMPANIMENT FOR PIANOFORTE | [short wavy rule] | THE POETRY BY CHRISTINA ROSSETTI. | *The Music Composed, and Dedicated to* | MISS E. D' O. JAMES, | BY | G. A. MACFARREN. | [short wavy rule] | *Price 3s. Net.* | LONDON: | HUTCHINGS AND ROMER, 9, CONDUIT STREET, REGENT STREET.

Rossetti's name appears above the score as "Christina Rosetti" with note below score "Words by permission." Words as text (3-4).

Music: Cantata, score 1-68. Solo voice, chorus, choral recitative, trio and piano. Plate number H & R. 3085. Ten numbers, as follows:

1. "Introduction and Choral Recitative." Key signature B flat (2 flats), time signature 6/8, tempo "Allegretto pastorale."
2. "Where is he gone to?" Chorus. [Not seen]
3. "May sang with Rachel." Choral Recitative (14). Key signature C (no sharps, flats), time signature common time.
4. "Take the wheat in your arm." Trio (soprano, mezzo-soprano and contralto) (14-26). Key signature E (4 sharps), time signature 3/4 time, tempo "Moderato."
5. "A silence of full noontide heat." Chorus (27-35). Key signature A (3 sharps), time signature 6/8, tempo "Andante quasi allegretto."
6. "While the reapers took their ease." Choral recitative (36) Key signature C (no sharps, flats), time signature common time, tempo "Andante."
7. "There goes the swallow." Song (contralto) (37-41). Key signature F (1 flat), time signature common time, tempo "Moderato."
8. "Then listless Marian raised her head" Chorus (42-47). Key signature A flat (4 flats), time signature 12/8, tempo "Andante."
9. "Deeper than the hail can smite." Song (soprano)(48-53). Key signature D flat (5 flats), time signature 3/4, tempo "Adagio."
10. "If he comes to-day" Chorus (54-68). Key signature B flat (2 flats), time signature 2/2, tempo "Allegro agitato."

Note: The cantata was "performed for the first time in 1868, by Mr. Henry Leslie's Choir" (Banister: 207). WMR, with FLR and MFR, attended a performance at St. James's Hall in February 1869 (RP 384). The 1869 performance was reviewed in the *Athenaeum* (27 February 1869: 316). Although CGR apparently did not attend, she wrote to Leslie to give him permission to "reprint my "Songs in a Cornfield" in your book of words for next Thursday," asking that he make sure that "the text is correctly printed" and "the spelling of my name set right" (*Letters* 1: 316). The cantata was still being performed in 1899 (*Musical News*, 15 April 1899: 396). CGR received a copy of the published score from Macfarren (*RP*: 338). "There Goes the Swallow" and "Deeper than the Hail can Smite" were also published separately.

WMR commented that "to me, the music appeared truly beautiful; but I believe it did not take much with the public" (*Poetical Works*: 485). The subsequent publication history of the cantata argues otherwise. By July 1881, it was available in a tonic sol-fa edition (advertised in the *Tonic Sol-fa Reporter*, 1 July 1881: 1). It was still in print in 1894 (the *Musical Times*, 1 September 1894: 631), and in 1885, Novello offered another version with harmonium and harp ad libitum (reviewed in the *Musical Times*, 1 September 1885: 550).

Locations: 1869: BL, Koninklijke Bibliotheek; not seen: Tonic Sol-Fa edition: BL (with 1882 depository stamp): copy located in BL; 1885: copy located at BL.

DM13   "Sound Sleep." Maria Tiddeman, 1869

London: J. B. Cramer & Co.
Note: Reviewed in the *Musical Times* (1 May 1869: 87).
Location: not seen: copy located at BL.

DM14–DM15   "Song" ("When I am dead, my dearest"); "Up-Hill." Sibyl, 1870

Two Songs. London: A. Weekes & Co. Ltd.
Note: Reviewed in the *Musical World* (30 July 1870: 513).
Location: not seen: copy located at BL.

DM16 "Song" ("When I am dead, my dearest"). T. Walton Gillibrand, 1871

When I am Dead. Manchester: Hime & Addison.
Note: No copies located. Reviewed in the *Monthly Musical Record* (1 July 1871: 93).

DM17 "Song" ("When I am dead, my dearest"). Emily Sophia, Lady Jenkinson, 1871

When I am dead my dearest: song. London: C. Lonsdale.
Note: Not in Gooch & Thatcher. Plate number 3410.
Locations: not seen: copies located at BL, UkCM.

DM18 "Song" ("When I am dead, my dearest"). Wilhelm Schulthes, 1871

Remember or Forget. London: Duncan Davison & Co.
Note: No copies located. Not in Gooch & Thatcher. Advertised as "Published this day" in the *Musical World* (8 April 1871: 202).

DM19 "A Birthday." Francis Edward Gladstone, 1872

London: Lamborn Cock & Co.
Note: Reviewed in the *Musical Standard* (27 July 1872: 47) and also the *Musical Times* (1 October 1872: 636): "The theme of this song is excellently adapted to the words, which are re-printed by permission of Messrs. Macmillan and Co., and are admirably suited for a musical setting."
Location: not seen: copy located at BL.

DM20 "Mirage." Karl Reden (pseudonym of Charles Crozat Converse), 1872

New York: Wm. A Pond.
Cover description: Ornamented engraved text within scroll decorated with ribbons and floral foliage.
Song title: "Mirage."
Names on cover: "Christina Rossetti" and "Karl Reden."
Price: number "3 ½" within star.
Publishers: Wm. A. Pond & Co, 547 Broadway and 39 Union Square; additional publication and copyright information not legible in digital image.

Signed above score "Christina Rossetti" and "Karl Reden."

Music: Sheet music, score 2-5. Key signature D flat (5 flats), time signature common time, tempo "Moderato." Plate number 8205.
Location: DLC (via *Music for the Nation: American Sheet Music*).

DM21 "Song" ("When I am dead, my dearest"). Francis Hueffer, 1872

Remember. London.
Note: Francis Hueffer became music critic of the London *Times* in 1878. WMR attended a performance of the setting on December 15, 1870: "Dined at Brown's–partly in order to hear Hueffer's music, which I like much, to Christina's song, "When I am dead, my dearest" (*Diary* 36). In 1872, he noted "Hueffer called with Brown, and asked Christina's authority for setting to music, and so publishing, two of her poems–'When I am dead' and another. Christina of course consented." (*Diary* 163). Presumably the other song was "Twist me a Crown of Wind-Flowers"; both appear in Hueffer's collection, *Seven Songs* (1873).
Location: not seen: copy located at BL.

DM22   "Song" ("When I am dead, my dearest"). W. H. J. Graham, 1873

And if thou wilt, remember. New York: Wm. A Pond.
Cover description: Engraved text within ornate compartment, with foliage and flowers in background of text and framing the song title.
Dedication: "To Miss Mary Callender."
Song title: "And if thou wilt, remember."
Names on cover: "Christina C. Rossetti," "W. H. J. Graham."
Price: number "3 ½" within star.
Publishers: New York: Wm. A Pond & Co., 25 Union Square; Chicago: Chicago Music Company 152 State Street; Boston: Carl Prufer; Philadelphia: E. D. Freeman; San Francisco: M. Gray; Detroit: C. J. Whitney & Co; New Orleans: L. Grunewald. At bottom of page, "Copyright 1873 by Wm. A. Pond & Co."

Signed "Christina G. Rossetti" above score.

Music: Sheet music, score 3-5. Key signature D flat (5 flats), time signature ¾. At bottom of first page of score "Copyright, 1873, by Wm. A. Pond & Co." Plate number 9697.
Note: Not in Gooch & Thatcher.
Location: DLC (via *Music for the Nation: American Sheet Music*).

DM23–DM24   "Song" ("When I am dead, my dearest"); "Twist me a Crown of Wind-Flowers." **Francis Hueffer, 1873**

Seven Songs. No. 1: "When I am Dead, My Dearest" (DM23); No. 6, "Windflowers" (DM24). London: Stanley, Lucas, Weber & Co.
Note: Reviewed (negatively) in the *Examiner* (8 November 1873: 1127-1128) and the *Musical Times* (1 December 1873: 329, with composer's name as Franz Hüffer).
Location: not seen: copy located at BL.

DM25   "Up-Hill." Elizabeth Jane Caulfeild, Countess of Charlemont, 1873

London: J. B. Cramer.
Cover transcription (some text in <u>black letter</u>; first and fifth line in ornamental font):
UP-HILL, | WORDS BY | <u>Christina Rossetti</u>, | MUSIC BY | THE COUNTESS OF CHARLEMONT. | *Ent. Sta.Hall.* [swelled rule] *Price 4ˢ/=* | London, | J. B. CRAMER & Cº 201, REGENT STREET.

Signed "Christina Rossetti" above score.

Music: Sheet music, score 1-5. Key signature B flat, time signature common time. Plate number C. & Cº. 6743.
Note: Not in Gooch & Thatcher. Library catalogs (Michigan and British Library) list 1874 publication date, but reviewed in the *Orchestra* (21 November 1873: 119).
Location: MiU.

DM26   "Hoping Against Hope." Augusta Catherine Baker (Lady Baker), 1874

If. Klein & Co.
Note: No copies located. Not in Gooch & Thatcher. Reviewed in the *Musical Standard* (13 June 1874: 391), as one of six songs, presumably published together.

DM27   "Song" ("When I am dead, my dearest"). S. M. Downs, 1874

Request. Boston: G. D. Russell & Co.
Note: Not in Gooch & Thatcher. Reviewed twice in *Old and New,* with different titles: "When I am

Dead" (June 1873: 758) and "Request" (July 1874: 143), the latter review including CGR's poem to demonstrate that the sad melody "befits the words."
Location: DLC (via *Music for the Nation: American Sheet Music*).

DM28   **"Song" ("When I am dead, my dearest"). Oscar Weil, 1874**
When I am Dead. San Francisco: M. Gray.
Cover description: Engraved text within linear frame, with dedication and song title within scrolls.
Dedication: "To Wm. B. Young Esq. Of Selina Alabama."
Song title: "When I Am Dead."
Names on cover: "Oscar Weil."
Price: 35 cents.
Publisher: M. Gray, 623 & 625 Clay St., San Francsico. Copyright statement at bottom of cover not legible in digital image.
Music: Sheet music, score 2-5. Key signature E flat (3 flats), time signature common time. Tempo notes "Con molto espressione" and "Poco lento." At bottom of first page of score "Entered according to Act of Congress A. D. 1874 by M.GRAY in the Office of the Librarian of Congress at Washington." Plate number M.G. 959.
Note: Not in Gooch & Thatcher.
Location: DLC (via *Music for the Nation: American Sheet Music*).

DM29   **"May." Geraldine Fitz Gerald, 1875**
One May. London: Augener & Co.
Cover description: Text in various ornamented fonts, subtitle "SONG" within scroll.
Dedication: "To Paul Naftel."
Song title: "One May."
Names on cover: "Christina Rossetti," "Geraldine Fitz Gerald."
Price: 3/.
Publisher: Augener & Co., 86. Newgate St.

Signed "Christina Rossetti" above score.

Music: Sheet music, score 2-5. Key signature G (1 sharp), time signature common time.
Location: UPB.

DM30   **"Hope is like a harebell." Georgina Schuyler, 1877**
New York: William A Pond.
Cover description: Engraved ornamented text, a spray of harebells at top of the page (slightly left of center), with Rossetti poem printed in the foreground:
'Hope is like a harebell trembling from its birth, | Love is like a rose the joy of all the earth; | Faith is like a lily lifted high and white | Love is like a lovely rose the world's delight | Harebells and sweet lilies show a thornless growth | But the rose with all its thorns excels them both.'
Song title: "Hope is like a Harebell" (printed diagonally across center of page).
Names on cover: beneath poem, "Christina G. Rossetti"; "Georgina Schuyler."
Price: the number "3" appears on the cover within a small star.
Publisher: New York: William A. Pond & Co., 547 Broadway and 39 Union Square; Milwaukee: H. N. Hempsted; San Francisco: M. Gray; Savannah, Ludden & Bates; New Orleans, L. Grunewald. Copyright statement at bottom of cover: "ENT^D ACCRDING TO ACT OF CONGRESS, IN THE YEAR 1877 BY W^M A. POND & C^O IN THE OFFICE OF THE LIBRARIAN OF CONGRESS AT WASHINGTON"
Signed "Christina Rossetti" above score. Words as text on cover.

Music: Sheet music, score 3-5. Key signature D (2 flats), time signature 2/4. At top of score "Song for Contralto or Baritone." Note above score: "N. B. The words should be distinctly enunciated." At bottom of first page of score, "Copyright, 1877, by Wm. A. Pond & Co." Plate number 9267.

Note: Not in Gooch & Thatcher. Announced in the *American Bookseller* (1 June 1877: 349).

Location: DLC (via *Performing Arts Encyclopedia*).

DM31   "Song" ("When I am dead, my dearest"). Malcolm Leonard Lawson, 1877

When I Am Dead. People's Song No. 10 (Op. 8). E flat major. London: Stanley Lucas, Weber & Co. Plate number SLW834.

Note: Apparently a separate issue, although bound with Lawson's setting of John Suckling's "Love's Resolves," both of which were also collected in *People's Songs and Ballads* (see below).

Location: not seen: copy located at Royal Academy of Music.

1) Sheet music:

Hereafter: (When I am dead). Op. 8, No. 10. No. 2 in G. London: Stanley Lucas, Weber & Co., [1886]. Plate number SLW 1383.

Note: Cambridge catalog record notes "Sung by Miss Wakefeld" on the wrapper.

Location: not seen: copy located at UkCM.

2) Periodical:

"Hereafter." The *Strand Musical Magazine*. 1 (June 1895): 421-423.

Signed "Christina Rossetti" above score. A small vignette of couple walking, and with portrait of Lawson also appear above the score.

Music: key signature E flat (3 flats), time signature 3/4, tempo "Slow and Sad."

Location: NN (via Google Books).

3) Song collections:

A) "When I am Dead, my Dearest." *People's Songs and Ballads*. London: Stanley Lucas, Weber & Co., 1877.

Note: Reviewed in the *Examiner* (1 September 1877): 1112.

B) "Hereafter ("When I am Dead"). *First Album of People's Songs and Ballads*. London: S. Lucas & Co, [1893].

Later published by Joseph Williams, date not established.

Location: not seen: copy located at BL.

General note: Lawson contributed a note about the publication and performance of the setting to *Notes and Queries* (17 March 1917: 214), in which he recounts CGR's response to a performance by Lawson's sister Kate at the home of William B. Scott.

DM32   "Song" ("When I am dead, my dearest"). Mrs. John P. Morgan, 1877

And if thou wilt, remember, and if thou wilt, forget. Boston: Oliver Ditson & Co.

Cover description: Within engraved frame, with foliage.

Song title: "And if thou wilt, remember, and if thou wilt, forget."

Names on cover: "As sung by Miss Annie Louise Cary, words by Christine Rosetti. Music by Mrs. John P. Morgan."

Price: number "3 ½" within star.

Publishers: Boston: Oliver Ditson & Co, 452 Washington St.; New York, C. H. Ditson & Co; San Francisco, Sherman Hyde & Co; Philadelphia, J. E. Ditson & Co.; Savannah, Ludden & Bates; Chicago, Lyon & Healy. At bottom of cover, "Copyright 1877 by O. Ditson & Co."

Signed "Christine Rossetti" above score.

Music: Sheet music, score 2-5. Key signature G (1 sharp), time signature common time, tempo note "Agitato con moto." Plate number 46163.

Note: Not in Gooch & Thatcher.

Location: DLC (via *Music for the Nation: American Sheet Music*).

DM33–DM35   "The First Spring Day"; "Song" ("When I am dead, my dearest"); "A Birthday."
A. C. (Alexander Campbell) Mackenzie, 1878

Issued separately, and together in at least two song collections, including:

1) Separate issues:

(DM33)   "The First Spring Day." Alexander Mackenzie

No. 1, *Three Songs*, op. 17. E-flat major. London: Novello, 1878. Plate number 5622 Novello.

Note: The manuscript, with some engraver's pencil markings, is at Royal Academy of Music.

Location: Not seen: copy located at Royal Academy of Music.

(DM34)   "Song" ("When I am dead, my dearest"). Alexander Mackenzie

When I Am Dead. No. 2, *Three Songs*, op. 17. A major. London: Novello, 1878. Plate number 5623 Novello.

Note: The manuscript, including the notation "One of my best songs ACM 1927" and with engraver's pencil markings, is held by the Royal Academy of Music.

Location: Not seen: copy located at Royal Academy of Music.

(DM35)   "A Birthday." Alexander Mackenzie

No. 3, *Three Songs*, op 17. F major. London: Novello, 1878. Plate number 5624 Novello.

Note: The manuscript, with engraver's pencil markings, is at Royal Academy of Music.

Location: Not seen. copy located at Royal Academy of Music.

2) Song collections:

A) Three Songs. Op. 17. London: Novello & Co., 1878.

Note: Advertised in the *Musical Times* (1 March 1878): 167.

Location: not seen: copy located at BL.

B) Eighteen Songs.
Op. 18 and 31. London: Novello, Ewer and Co., 1885.

Title page transcription:
TO | SIGNORINA ADELAIDA PLACCI, | FLORENCE. [short rule]| Eighteen Songs | COMPOSED BY | A. C. MACKENZIE. | (Op. 17 and 31.) | Ent. Sta. Hall. [short rule] Price 7s. 6d. | *LONDON & NEW YORK* | NOVELLO, EWER AND CO. | [short rule] | *Also separately, in Three Books, 2s. 6d. Each.*

Subdivided into three books, with the CGR settings in Book III. Both signed "Christina Rossetti" above score (61, 66).

Music: All songs in Book III with plate number 6933.
1. "The First Spring Day" (61-67). Op. 12 No. I. Key signature E flat (3 flats), time signature common time, tempo "Allegro moderato."
2. "When I am Dead" (66-70). Key signature A (3 sharps), time signature common time, tempo "Adagio molto."
3. "A Birthday" (71-76.). Key signature F (1 flat), time signature 3/4, tempo "Vivace molto."

Note: Advertised in the *Musical Times* (1 August 1885: 448). Ives copy is undated.

Location: Ives.

DM36   **"Dream Land." Jacques Blumenthal, 1878**

Dreamland. London: Boosey, Patey, & Co.

In two keys, A flat (4 flats) and C (no sharps, flats).

Note: The C printing has plate number P & Co. 415. BL depository copy dated 19 December 1878. Blumenthal was pianist to Queen Victoria, and possibly the "Blumenthal" mentioned by CGR in a letter to WMR in March 1878 (*Letters* 2: 161).

Location: Not seen: copy located at BL.

DM37   **"Song" ("When I am dead, my dearest"). Harrison Millard, 1878**

Remember or Forget! New York: Spear & Denhoff.

In two keys, G and E flat.

1) In G (soprano), 1878

Cover transcription: engraved ornamented text, within oval compartment; in foreground, at top of compartment, lilies and at bottom, roses.

TO | MRS. E. L. LANDON. | N.Y. | Remember or Forget! | (LE SOUVENIR OU L'OUBLI.) | BALLAD | WORDS BY | MISS C. G. ROSSETTI. | MUSIC BY | Harrison Millard | CONTRALTO. SOPRANO. | NEW YORK, | PUBLISHED BY | SPEAR & DENHOFF. | 717 BROADWAY. | COPYRIGHT, 1878 BY HARRISON MILLARD. | [within star] 4 | [below engraved design] *R. TELLER, 116 E.11.ST.N.Y.*

Signed "Miss C. G. Rossetti" above score. Also "French translation by E. Pottier."

Music: Sheet music, score 3-6 (see *Note*). Soprano version. Key signature G (1 sharp), time signature common time, tempo "Moderato e con espressione."

Locations: TmurS (Center for Popular Music); InU.

2) In E flat (contralto), 1879

Same cover. Signed "Miss C. G. Rossetti" above score, no translator's name.

Music: Sheet music, score 3-6. Contralto version. Key signature E flat (3 flats), same time signature, tempo as version in G. At bottom of first page of score "Copyright, 1879, by Harrison Millard."

Note: Middle Tennessee State copy lacks cover. At bottom of first page of score "Copyright, 1878, by Harrison Millard."

Location: UPB.

DM38   **"Twist me a Crown of Wind-Flowers." Theo (Théophile-Jules-Henri) Marzials, 1879**

Windflowers. Op. 6, No.2. London: Stanley Lucas, Weber & Co. In English and German. Plate number SL.W. 213a.

Location: not seen: copy located at UkCM.

DM39   **"Goblin Market." Emanuel Abraham Aguilar, 1880**

Goblin Market, Cantata.

London: Hutchings & Romer.

Cover description (ornamented engraved text within compartment shaped as classical entry with two columns and lyre at top center):

Goblin Market, | CANTATA, | E. Aguilar.

Title page transcription (within ornamented compartment; ornamented text, some in <u>black letter</u>):

GOBLIN MARKET, | Cantata, | FOR | TREBLE VOICES. | *The words adapted by permission of the Authoress* | <u>Christina Rossetti</u>, | The Music by | EMANUEL AGUILAR. | [short double rule] | *All Applications respecting the Libretto* | *and Performance of this Work to be made* | *to the Publishers*. | [short double rule] | Ent. Sta. Hall. [short ornamented rule] Price 3/= net. | *Published by* | HUTCHINGS & ROMER, |

LONDON, W.

Rossetti's name appears on the score as "Christian Rossetti." Words as text printed separately; see *Note*.

Music: Cantata, score 1-57. Solo voice, chorus and piano.

"Introduction" and seven numbers, as follows:

"Introduction" (1). Key signature F (1 flat), time signature 2/4, tempo "Allegreto," quarter note = 132.

1. Chorus with Solos "Come Buy, Come Buy" (2-17). Same key and time signature, no tempo note.
2. Duet. "Dear, You Should Not Stay So Late" (18-22). Key signature E flat (3 flats), time signature 3/4, tempo "Andante con moto."
3. Chorus, "Sleep Song" (23-25). Key signature A flat (4 flats), time signature 2/4, tempo "Andante sostenuto," eighth note=104.
4. Solo "Early In the Morning" (26-29). Key signature C (no sharps, flats), time signature common time, tempo "Moderato," quarter note = 104.
5. Solo "'Woe is Me.' (A week later.)" (30-32). Key signature D (2 sharps), time signature common time, tempo "Moderato Affettuoso," quarter note = 100.
6. A – Appearance of the Goblins. B – Chorus with Solo. "Look at our apples." subtitled "Lizzie's Interview With The Goblins" (33-44). Key signature G (1 sharp), time signature 6/8, tempo "Allegro," quarter note = 132.
7. Finale. "Laura! Come now in the Garden" (45-58). Key signature A (3 sharps), time signature common time, tempo "Allo. Agitato," half note = 92.

Note: Date from the Bodleian stamp (October 1880). Aguilar (1824-1904), a composer and pianist, was the brother of novelist Grace Aguilar. CGR "made an agreement" to allow Aguilar the exclusive right to set the poem (*Letters* 4: 107); no further musical settings appear until Ricci in 1901 (DM 174).

In 1879, WMR noted in his diary that "Christina is now engaged with a Mr. Aguilar in *settling* a text of Goblin Market wh. he has set to music. He is looking out for a publisher, & I believe with a fair prospect of success" (WMRD). Aguilar's is one of the few settings in which CGR participated. Aguilar's completion of the setting, and its pending publication, were announced in the *Athenaeum* in December 1879 (13 December: 772), and a private performance for the Rossetti family took place on January 10, 1880, at Aguilar's home. WMR "thought it bright, spirited, & tuneful, & not in the least tedious: in fact, I enjoyed it considerably–& the same feeling seemed very general among the small audience," but went on to lament that Aguilar's "Publishers require A. to cut his work short by just about a half–wh. will certainly, I think, be no advantage to it artistically, but the contrary" (WMRD). A public performance sponsored by the Musical Artists Society took place at the Royal Academy on April 1, 1882 (London *Times*, 29 March 1882: 1), and received a brief but positive review in the *Musical World* (8 April 1882: 213).

An "index" of the "Introduction" and seven numbers of the cantata appears on the page before the score proper, and includes the notation "Books of the words 6d. each"; unfortunately, no copies of the librettos have surfaced.

In 1893, Mathias & Strickland advertised *Goblin Market* for sale as number 10 in a series of "Cantatas for schools and classes" (the *Musical Times*, 1 Feb. 1893: 120). No copies of this publication have been located.

Location: Oxford University; NjP (inscribed by WMR "From Christina - 1887").

DM40   "Your Brother Has a Falcon." Francis Hueffer, 1880

A Nursery Rhyme. Duet. London: Novello & Co.

Note: On January 1, 1880, WMR attended a dinner party at the Hueffers, at which Hueffer and Cathy Brown Hueffer (WMR's sister-in-law) performed the setting (WMRD). Reviewed in the *Musical Times* (1 April 1880: 190).

Location: not seen: copy located at BL.

DM41   **"A Birthday." Theo (Théophile-Jules-Henri) Marzials, 1881**

In two keys, C and D.

In C:
My Love is come. In C major. London: Boosey & Co, [1882].
Location: not seen: copy located at BL.

In D:
My love is come. No. 2 in D. London: Boosey & Co., [1882].
Location: not seen: copy located at UkCM.

Note: Among the most popular Rossetti settings, frequently reprinted in Britain, the United States, and Australia, and frequently performed. Announcements or reviews of public performances appeared in the *Academy* (7 July 1883: 17); the *Musical Standard* (7 April 1883: 207); the *Musical World* (30 June 1888: 516); and the London *Times* (4 October 1897: 1).

Composition and initial publication circa 1881, the date assigned by Gooch & Thatcher (4225). In September 1881, Marizals and "Mrs. Moncrieff" had apparently written to CGR regarding a setting of the poem. However, it is unclear from CGR's response whether Marzials was setting the poem by himself, or with (or for), Moncrieff, herself a singer and composer who published her own setting in 1882.

Since the chronology of later printings is unclear, all printings identified through 1901 are listed here.

Additional printings in C (with variant presentations of the opening, as noted; publication dates uncertain):

A) In C, without introduction
Cover description: text in compartment within design with cottage roofs at top, meadow at bottom, songbirds grouped throughout:
Song title "My Love is Come" appears as the fifth in a list of eight titles under the heading "Select Songs." Composer's name on wrapper given as "Marzails."; names of other composers also listed, but Rossetti's name does not appear.
Price: 35.

Signed above score "Christina G. Rosetti."

Music: sheet music, 3-5. Key signature C (no sharps, flats), no time signature. No tempo. Plate number 638.–3. First note is vocal, with piano accompaniment following; contrast with other scores in which begin with piano.
Note: Undated, with no publisher information other than plate number.
Location: IU.

B) In C, with introduction, Boosey
My Love is Come. London: Boosey & Co.
Cover description: ornamented engraved text
Dedication: "To Edward Morton."
Song title: "My Love is Come."
Names on cover: "Theo. Marzials," "Christina G. Rossetti."
Publisher: London, Boosey & Co, 295, Regent Street, W.
Price: 2/= net.

Signed "Christina G. Rosetti" above score.

Music: sheet music, score 1-5. Key signature C (no sharps, flats), time signature common time, tempo "Allegro appassionato."
Note: Possibly pre-1892 (when Boosey's New York branch opened). As I have not seen the British Library's copy of the setting in C, I cannot say whether this is the same version as the first setting in C listed above.
Location: Ives.

C) In C, with introduction, Boosey/Paling

My Love is Come. London, New York: Boosey & Co.; [Sydney], W. H. Paling & Co.

Cover description: ornamented engraved text; same as C except additional address "9 East Seventeenth Street, New York" and additional publisher, "W. H. Paling & Co."

"My Love is Come." Signed "Christina G. Rossetti" above score.

Music: sheet music, score 1-5. Same key, time, tempo as A.

Note: Similar to A, but with some alterations in the design and punctuation of the front cover (double underline under key designation, no comma after "Rossetti") and the first page of the score (on which Rossetti's name is corrected). Library's copy is cropped; text is presumed to be missing from bottom of wrapper. Post 1892 (when Boosey's New York branch opened). Paling's city of publication is given in the National Library of Australia catalog listing but not printed on score.

Location: National Library of Australia (via NLA Digital Collections).

D) In C, with introduction, Ditson

My Love is Come. New York: C. H. Ditson & Co.

Cover description: ornamented engraved text.

Song title: "My Love is Come."

Names on cover: "Theo. Marzials."

Price: the number 3 ½ appears within a small star.

Publishers: New York: C. H. Ditson & Co, 843 Broadway; Boston, O. Ditson & Co.; Chicago, Lyon & Healy; Philadelphia, J. E. Ditson & Co; St. Louis: J. L. Peters; Galveston: Goggan & Bro.; S. Francisco: Sherman Clay & Co.

Signed above score "Christina G. Rosetti".

Music: Sheet music, score 2-5. Key signature C (no sharps, flats), time signature common time, tempo "Allegro appassionato." Plate number 48782.

Note: This version includes several measures of piano introduction before the vocal part begins.

Location: CU (via California Sheet Music Project).

E) In C, with introduction, A. P. Schmidt (1884?)

My Love is Come. Boston: A. P Schmidt & Co.

Cover description: At top of page: "X. L. C. R. EDITION. COPYRIGHTED 1884 BY W. F. SHAW"; below this, in large letters: "Theo. Marzials" above (at left) image of man and woman in front of fireplace and (at right) list of 29 songs with prices, including "MY LOVE IS COME" priced at 35 cents. Below image: "HOFSTETTER BROS LITH. PHILA."

Publishers: Boston: A. P. Schmidt & Co., 13 & 15 West St."

Signed "Christina G. Rosetti" above score.

Music: Sheet music, score 2-5. Same key, time, tempo as B (but not the same typesetting). No plate number.

Location: Ives.

F) In C, with introduction, newspaper supplement

My Love is Come. New York: Richard A. Saalfield.

Cover description: Printed in blue and black ink, with oval vignette photograph of woman in center. At top of page: "Musical Supplement to the NEW YORK SUNDAY PRESS Sunday September 22d, 1901."

Song title: "My Love is Come."

Names on cover: "Christina G. Rosetti"; "Theo Marzials."

Publisher: Richard A. Saalfield, New York. Name "P. B. Nash" also appears on cover (illustrator?).

Signed "Christina G. Rosetti" above score.

Music: score unpaginated (3 pages). Same key and time signature as B (but not the same setting), tempo "Allego Appassionata."
Location: Ives.

Additional printing in D:

A) In D, with introduction, Boosey/Glen

My Love is Come. London: Boosey & Co.; Melbourne: W. H. Glen.
Cover description: ornamented engraved text.
Dedication: "To Edward Morton."
Song title: "My Love Is Come."
Names: "Christina G. Rossetti," "Theo Marzials."
Price: 2/= net.
Publishers: London, Boosey & Co., 295 Regent Street. W.; Melbourne: W. H. Glen & Co., 272 & 274 Collins Street.

Signed "Christina G. Rosetti" above score.

Music: sheet music, score 1-5. Key signature D (2 sharps), time signature common time, tempo "Allegro appassionata."
Note: With piano introduction preceding voice.
Location: National Library of Australia (via NLA Digital Collections).

DM42   **"Song" ("When I am dead, my dearest"). Caroline Reinagle, 1881**

"Two Songs." No. 2, *When I am Dead*. London: Stanley Lucas & Co.
Note: Not in Gooch & Thatcher. Reviewed in the *Monthly Musical Record* (1 April 1881): 74.
Location: not seen: copy located at BL.

DM43   **"Twilight Calm." Theo (Théophile-Jules-Henri) Marzials, 1882**

Eventide. Two-part song for ladies voices. London : Stanley Lucas, Weber & Co.
Note: Not in Gooch & Thatcher. Reviewed in the *Monthly Musical Record* (1 March 1882: 64), *Literary World* (7 July 1882: 12).
Location: not seen: copy located at UkCM.

DM44   **"A Birthday." Nita Gaetano Moncrieff, 1882**

My Heart is like a singing bird. London: Boosey & Co.
Cover description: Engraved text, in various fonts.
Dedication: "The Music Composed & Dedicated to Miss Louise Johnston."
Song title: "My Heart is Like a Singing Bird."
Names on cover: "Christina Rosetti," "Mrs. L. Moncrieff," "Sung by Miss Wakefield."
Price: "2/ net."
Publishers: Boosey & Co, 295 Regent Street W.

Signed above score "Christina Rosetti"and "Mrs. L. Moncrieff."

Music: Sheet music, score 1-5. Key signature F (one flat), time signature common time, tempo "Allegro grazioso."
Note: Available in two keys: "No 1 in F" and "No 2 in G" are both printed on the cover, with "No 1 in F" underlined. A contemporary inscription – "J. J. Pringle 1883" – is written in ink on the upper right corner of the front cover; the signature "Nita Moncrieff" is written in another hand at the lower right corner. See also Marzials' setting, DM42.
Location: In F: PBm.

DM45　　"It is Finished." George L. Osgood, 1882

"A Christmas Carol." *Wide Awake* (Boston) 14.1 (January 1882): 74.

Signed "Christina Rossetti" above score.

Music: Periodical. Key signature G (1 sharp), time signature common time, tempo "Joyfully," "With rythmic swing" [sic]. Note below score "Copyright, 1881, by D. Lothrop & Co."
Note: Not in Gooch & Thatcher. Osgood adapts the poem for use as a Christmas carol by retaining only stanzas 1-4 and 10 (so as to omit references to the Crucifixion as well as to Judgment Day).
Location: Ives.

DM46　　"Song" ("When I am dead, my dearest"). Frederic H. Cowen, 1882

Six songs. London: Joseph Williams.
Note: No copies located. Reviewed in the *Musical Standard* (6 May 1882): 279. Cowen released several sets of six and twelve songs, of which this is the earliest to contain a Rossetti setting. Although Rossetti settings included within Cowen's collections were often published separately, I have not located a separate publication of this setting.

DM47　　"The Months: A Pageant." Catharine Adelaide Ranken, 1882

Twelve Songs: from The Months, A Pageant. London: Duncan Davison & Co.
Note: Not in Gooch & Thatcher. Composer's name given as "C. A. Ranken." Reviewed in the *Musical World* (30 December 1882: 819).
Location: not seen: copy located at UkCM.

DM48　　"Song" ("Two doves upon the selfsame branch"). Robert Brydges Addison, 1882

Two Doves. London: Stanley Lucas, Weber, & Co.
Note: Not in Gooch & Thatcher. According to review in the *Literary World* (6 October 1882: 219), for contralto voice, in E. Advertised as "Sung by Miss Spenser Jones" (the *Musical Times* 1 August 1884: 487). Performed at the Charterhouse School in 1886 (the *Carthusian* March 1886: 163). The British Library also has an 1886 printing.
Location: not seen: copy located at BL.

DM49　　"Bird Raptures." Louis Maas, 1883

Wide Awake (Boston) 16.6 (May 1883): 455-456.

Signed "Christina G. Rossetti" above score.

Music: Periodical. Key signature F (1 flat), time signature 3/4, tempo "Allegro." Beneath score, "Copyright, 1883, by D. Lothrop & Co."
Note: Not in Gooch & Thatcher. Note on first page of score "Music composed for WIDE AWAKE by LOUIS MAAS." A copy with WMR's signature is in the Janet Camp Troxell collection at Princeton University Library. Separate printing (Boston: Arthur P. Schmidt, copyright 1886) not seen.
Location: Ives. Separate printing: not seen; copy located at the Free Library of Philadelphia.

DM50　　"A Summer Wish." Clara Daniel, 1883

London: Lamborn Cock.
Locations: not seen: copies located at BL, UkCM.

DM51   "Somewhere or Other." Theo (Théophile-Jules-Henri) Marzials, 1883
Vocal duet. London: Metzler & Co.
Note: Advertised in the *Musical Times* (1 August 1883: 467), price 2s.
Location: not seen: copy located at BL.

DM52   "Somewhere or Other." Alice Millais, 1884
London: Stanley Lucas, Weber & Co. Two numbers:
No. 1. Music plate: S.L.W. & Co. 2223.
No. 2. Music plate: S.L.W. & Co. 2251.

Note: Library catalog holdings indicate 1884 as publication date. Reviewed in the *Saturday Review* (11 April 1885: 487), the *Academy* (15 August 1885: 110), and the *Theatre* (2 February 1885: 101).
Locations: not seen: copies located at UkCM (numbers 1 and 2); BL (number not given in catalog listing).

DM53   "A Birthday." Ferencz Sandor Korbay, 1885
Printed in Britain and in the United States.
1) British printing:
Two versions located, chronology unknown.
A) London: Schott, copyright 1895. Key: F major (high). Plate number 1672 Schott.
Location: not seen: copy located at Royal Academy of Music.
B) London & Leipzig: Stanley Lucas & Co, 1895.
Location: not seen: copy located at BL.

2) United States printing:
Birthday Song. New York: Wm. A. Pond & Co.
Cover description: Ornamented engraved text, within ornamental border with hearts at the corners.
Dedication: "To Miss Emma Schenck."
Song title: "Birthday Song."
Names: "Christina Rosetti," "F. Korbay."
Price: number 5 appears within a round compartment centered in an ornamental rule.
Publishers: New York: Wm. A. Pond & Co., 25 Union Sq., Chicago; Chicago Music Co., 52 State St." At bottom of page, "Copyright 1884 by Wm. A. Pond & Co."

Signed above score "Christina Rosetti."

Music: sheet music, score 2-7. Key signature F (1 flat), time signature common time, tempo "Allegro con molto spirituo" and "impetuoso." Plate number 11171. At bottom of first page of score "Copyright 1884 by Wm A Pond & Co."
Location: IU.

DM54–DM80 *Sing-Song* (various). Mary Grant Carmichael, 1884
1) 1884 printing:
Singsong. London: Stanley Lucas, Weber & Co. Plate number S. L. W. & Co. 1901.
Note: BL depository copy dated 10 April 1884. Same titles, in same order, as undated copy.
Location: not seen: copy located at BL.
2) Undated later copy:
London: Augener Ltd.

Cover description: Text in black ink, within green decorative compartment featuring vignettes of children, and a group of eight doves at the lower edge of the text opening.

Title: "Sing-Song," subtitled "27 Nursery Rhymes selected from the volume by Christina Rossetti."

Names on cover: "Christina Rossetti," "Mary Carmichael."

Publishers: Augener Ltd., London: 63, Conduit Street, W; 16, Newgate Street, E.C.; 57, High St. Marylebone; 18 Gt. Marlborough Street, W.; Max Eshig, Paris; Boston Music Co., Boston.

Publisher number "Augener's Edition No. 8887."

Signed above score "Christina Rossetti."

Music: songs, score 1-27. Plate number 11785. Songs separately numbered but not titled, as follows:

(DM54) 1. ("Ferry me across the water") (1). Key signature E flat (3 flats), time signature 2/4, tempo "Moderato."

(DM55) 2. ("What will you give me for my pound") (2). Key signature C (no sharps, flats), time signature 6/8, tempo "Allegro."

(DM56) 3. ("Mix a Pancake") (3). Key signature D (2 sharps), time signature 2/4, tempo "Andantino."

(DM57) 4. ("Growing in the vale") (4). Key signature F (1 flat), time signature common time, tempo "Andantino."

(DM58) 5. ("Wrens and robins in the hedge") (5). Key signature B flat (2 flats), time signature 2/4, tempo "Allegretto."

(DM59) 6. ("Hopping frog, hop here and be seen") (6). Key signature E flat (3 flats), time signature common time, tempo "Con moto."

(DM60) 7. ("The days are clear") (7). Key signature B flat (2 flats), time signature 6/8, tempo "Andantino."

(DM61) 8. ("Mother shake the cherry-tree") (8). Key signature G (1 sharp), time signature 2/4, tempo "Allegro."

(DM62) 9. ("Three plum buns") (9). Key signature D (2 sharps), time signature 3/4, tempo "Allegro."

(DM63) 10. ("A white hen sitting") (10). Key signature A (3 sharps), time signature 2/4, tempo "Allegretto."

(DM64) 11. ("Who has seen the wind?") (11). Key signature F (1 flat), time signature common time, tempo "Allegretto con moto."

(DM65) 12. ("O sailor, come ashore") (12). Key signature C (no sharps, flats), time signature common time, tempo "Allegro."

(DM66) 13. ("A peach for brothers, one for each") (13). Key signature G (1 sharp), time signature 6/8, tempo "Andantino."

(DM67) 14. ("If the moon came from heaven") (14). Key signature E flat (3 flats), time signature common time, tempo "Con moto."

(DM68) 15. ("Lullaby, oh lullaby!") (15). Key signature A flat (4 flats), time signature 6/8, tempo "Andantino."

(DM69) 16. ("Fly away, fly away over the sea") (16). Key signature E (4 sharps), time signature common time, tempo "Allegretto."

(DM70) 17. ("All the bells were ringing") (17). Key signature G (1 sharp), time signature common time, tempo "Allegro."

(DM71) 18. ("A pocket handkerchief to hem") (18). Key signature A (3 sharps), time signature 6/8, tempo "Allegretto."

(DM72) 19. ("Love me! I love you") (19). Key signature E (4 sharps), time signature common time, tempo "Andante con moto."

(DM73) 20. ("Wee, wee husband") (20). Key signature G (1 sharp), time signature 6/8, tempo "Allegro."

(DM74) 21. ("If I were a Queen") (21). Key signature B flat (2 flats), time signature common time, tempo "Allegretto con moto."

(DM75) 22. ("Eight o'clock") (22). Key signature F (1 flat), time signature 6/8, tempo "Allegro."

(DM76) 23. ("A house of cards") (23). Key signature E flat (3 flats), time signature 2/4, tempo "Allegro."

(DM77) 24. ("If a pig wore a wig") (24). Key signature C (no sharps, flats), time signature 6/8, tempo "Allegretto."

(DM78) 25. ("Pussy has a whiskered face") (25). Key signature A (3 sharps), time signature 3/4, tempo "Andantino."

(DM79) 26. ("A diamond or a coal?") (26). Key signature F (1 flat), time signature 2/4, tempo "Allegretto."

(DM80) 27. ("Dancing on the hill-tops") (27). Key signature C (no sharps, flats), time signature 2/4, tempo "Con moto."

Location: BL.

Note: In December 1877, Carmichael, introduced to the Rossettis by Theo Marzials, had "borrowed of us, with a view to musical setting, Christina's Combined Poems, & Singsong" (WMRD). In June 1878, WMR recorded another visit, at which Carmichael brought with her a "Miss Green" who sang four of Carmichael's settings from *Sing-Song*: "The Ferry, Shillings in Pound &c, Wind, & Lullaby: the latter 2 I liked particularly"; later that month, WMR gave Carmichael "a note to Edmund Routledge" to assist her in securing publication of the settings, apparently to no avail.

Reviewed in the *Monthly Musical Record* (1 March 1884: 66), the *Athenaeum* (23 August 1884: 251), and the *Musical Times* (1 September 1885: 550). In 1886 the London *Times* termed the setting "as appropriate as it is charming" (17 February 1886:4). Reprinted in 1900.

DM81 **"The First Spring Day." John More Smieton, 1885**

London: Weekes & Co.

Note: Not in Gooch & Thatcher. Reviewed in *Magazine of Music* (August 1885): 127.

Location: not seen: copy located at BL.

DM82 **"Song" (When I am dead, my dearest"). Louisa H. Grant, 1885**

When I am dead, my dearest. Song, with Violin obbligato. Edinburgh: Paterson & Sons.

Note: Reviewed in the *Athenaeum* (21 August 1886): 250.

Location: not seen: copy located at BL.

DM83 **"Echo." Theo (Théophile-Jules-Henri) Marzials, 1886**

Come back in dreams. Milan, London: Tito di Gio. Ricordi.

Note: According to the University of Melborne catalog listing, score includes words printed as text. The Melborne copy is also "2 in E flat," with publisher's number 50242 Ricordi.

Location: not seen: copies located at BL; University of Melborne.

DM84 **"One Foot on Sea, and One on Shore." Henri Logé, 1886**

London: C. Jefferys.

Location: not seen: copy located at BL.

DM85   "Song" (When I am dead, my dearest"). Henri Logé, 1886
When I am dead, my dearest. London: C. Jefferys.
Location: not seen: copy located at BL.

DM86   "Echo." Nita Gaetano Moncrieff, 1886
Come to me in Dreams. London: Enoch & Sons.
Location: not seen: copy located at BL.

DM87   "Bird Raptures." Moir Clark, 1887
London: Stanley Lucas, Weber & Co.
Note: Reviewed in the *Orchestra Musical Review* (December 1887): 6, and advertised as a "Song (for soprano)" in the *Musical World* (25 February 1888: 142), with quotations from reviews dated June and December 1887.
Location: not seen: copy located at BL.

DM88   "Lord God of Hosts, most Holy and most High." C. A. Macirone, 1887
"O Lord of Hosts." *The Sunday at Home* (29 October 1887): 696-697.

Signed "Christina G. Rosetti" above score.

Music: periodical, score 696-697. Key signature F (one flat), time signature common time, tempo "Allegro con grazia," half note = 84.
Note: Not in Gooch & Thatcher.
Location: *British Periodicals*.

DM89   "Song" ("When I am dead, my dearest"). John More Smieton, 1887
E. Ascherberg and Co.
Note: City of publication presumably London. No copies located. Not in Gooch & Thatcher. Reviewed in *Musical World* (15 October 1887: 811).

DM90   "Long Barren." Alexander Thomson, 1888
"Easter Song." *The Magazine of Music* (April 1888): 6-8.

Signed "Christina Rosetti" above score.

Music: periodical, score 6-8. For violin, voice and piano. Key signature F (one flat), time signature common time, tempo "Lento con espress"; quarter note = 72.
Note: Not in Gooch & Thatcher.
Location: *British Periodicals*.

DM91   "Memory." Charles C. Bethune, 1888
London: Reid Brothers.
Note: No copies located. Listed in the weekly list of new music, the *Musical World* (28 April 1888: 336) and reviewed a few weeks later in the same periodical (12 May 1888: 368).

DM92   "Shall I forget?" Helen Matilda Chaplin Pleydell-Bouverie, Countess of Radnor, 1888
London: R. Mills & Sons.
Location: not seen: copy located at BL.

DM93   **"Song" (When I am dead, my dearest"). Frederic Augustus Packer, 1888**

"When I am Dead, My Dearest." Hobart: J. Walch & Sons; Launceston: Walch Bros. & Birchall, no date.

Cover description: Ornamented text within rectangular frame.

Title: "When I am Dead, My Dearest."

Names on cover: "Fred. A. Packer."

Price: 4/.

Publishers: Hobart: J Walch & Sons; Launceston: Walch Bros. & Birchall.

Music: sheet music, score 3-6. Key signature E flat (3 flats), time signature common time, tempo "Moderato con espressione." "Words and Music by Fred. A. Packer" appears above the score. Plate number L.M. 615 P.Co.

Note: The publication date is uncertain. The only extant copies, at The National Library of Australia and the State Library of Tasmania, are undated, with the catalog listing estimating a date between 1880 and 1899. Presumably also printed in London, although the only evidence of this printing is an advertisement bound within an 1888 printing of *Sims Reeves: His Life and Recollections* (London: Simpkin Marshall & Co. and The London Music Publishing Company) and the letters "L. M." in the plate number of the Tasmanian printing, which suggests that the Australian printing derived from London plates. The London Music Publishing Company was in business from 1883 through 1896.

Location: State Library of Tasmania (via *Tasmania's Memory* digital collections).

DM94   **"Song" (When I am dead, my dearest"). Sir Arthur Somervell, 1888**

When I am dead, my dearest. London : J.& J. Hopkinson.

Locations: not seen: copies located at BL; Royal Academy of Music.

DM95   **"Twilight Calm." Charles King Hall, 1888**

Three-part song. St. Cecilia. Fourth Series. No. 14. London: Joseph Williams.

Note: Williams' St. Cecilia series was advertised as "A Selection of Two, Three, and Four Part-Songs for Ladies' Voices, by the best composers, both Ancient and Modern" (the *Journal of Education*, 1 June 1894: 354).

Location: not seen: copy located at BL.

DM96   **"Song" ("When I am dead, my dearest"). C. A. Lee, 1890**

Mocatta and Co., 1890.

Note: No copies located. Reviewed in the *Musical World* (16 August 1890: 657) with comment "The tender but sad poetry is set to an unconventional and expressive melody suitable to a baritone."

DM97   **"Remember." Amy Woodforde Finden, 1890**

Remember me. London: Chappell & Co.

In two keys, E flat and F.

Note: The composer's name as it appears on the score is "Amy Ward." Finden may be the person who asked CGR for permission "to set Remember (sonnet) to music" in December 1889 (*Letters* 4: 166).

Location: not seen: copy located at BL (E flat and F).

DM98   **"Bird Raptures." Isabel Hearne, 1891**

Bird Raptures. 3 Songs with pianoforte accompaniment. London: Augener & Co.

Note: British Library catalog date is 1891, but reviewed in the *Monthly Musical Record* (1 March 1892: 57) and among "New Songs," London *Times* (3 March 1893: 3). British Library catalog also lists a 1910 "revised edition" in A and G published by Schott & Co.
Locations: not seen: 1891, 1910: copies located at BL.

DM99   **"Bird Raptures." Lucy March, 1891**
London: Boosey & Co.
Location: not seen: copy located at BL.

DM100   **"A Birthday." Adrienne Ardenne, 1891**
London: Weekes & Co.
Note: British Library catalog identifies the author's name as pseudonym. Reviewed in the *Musical Standard* (29 August 1891): 174.
Location: not seen: copy located at BL.

DM101   **"Christmas Carols" ("Whoso hears a chiming"). Reginald B. Clarke, 1891**
A Christmas Chime. London: Novello, Ewer & Co.
Note: Announced as "published during the last month" in the *Musical Times* (1 July 1891).
Location: not seen: copy located at BL.

DM102   **"Mirage." W.P. Collins, 1891**
Dundee: Methven Simpson & Co.
Note: No copies located. Not in Gooch & Thatcher. Reviewed in the *Monthly Musical Record* (1 February 1891: 40) and the *Musical Standard* (21 March 1896: 191).

DM103   **"Remember." Herbert Bedford, 1891**
If thou wilt. London: J. B. Cramer & Co.
Note: Not in Gooch & Thatcher. Bedford contacted CGR, who granted permission for the setting to be published (*Letters* 4: 1890); Bedford also invited CGR to a performance of the setting (*Letters* 4: 254). Reviewed in the *Musical Standard* (27 May 1893: 409).
Location: not seen: copy located at BL.

DM104   **"Song" (When I am dead, my dearest"). Anne Jane Finch-Hatton, Countess of Winchilsea and Nottingham, 1891**
When I am dead, my dearest. London: Moutrie & Son.
Note: Not in Gooch & Thatcher.
Location: not seen: copy located at BL.

DM105   **"A Birthday." Frederic H. Cowen, 1892**
In two keys, D flat and B flat.

1. In D flat:
A Birthday: My Heart is Like a Singing Bird. With words in English, German (translated by L. G. Sturm) and Italian. London: Joseph Williams, Limited, 1892. In D flat major. Plate number JW15506e Williams.
Location: not seen: copy located at Royal Academy of Music.

2. *In B flat:*
Cover description: with engraved text, no images.
Song title: both setting title and CGR's first line are given: 'A Birthday ("MY HEART IS LIKE A SINGING BIRD").'
Names on cover: "Christina Rossetti," "Frederic H. Cowen" and performers (see *Note*).
Price: "2/=."
Publishers: London: Joseph Williams, Limited, 32, Great Portland Street, W; New York: Edward Schuberth & Co.

Signed above score "Christina Rossetti."

Music: score 1-4. Key signature B flat (2 flats), time signature 2/4, tempo "Poco Allegretto ma appassionato," quarter note = 72. Plate number N. 9776. At bottom of first page of score, "By permission of Messrs. Macmillan & Co," and "Copyright 1893 by Joseph Williams."
Locations: 1893: not seen: copy located at BL; post-1900: TxCM.

3. *Anthology, key unknown:* see DM66.
Note: In the early 1890s, Cowen released various sets of six and twelve songs. Settings of several Rossetti poems were included within these collections and published separately.

The music description for the B flat setting is from the Texas A&M copy, a post-1900 printing (inscribed '1909') with the same plate number as the British Library 1893 copy. The cover of the Texas A&M copy testifies to the setting's popularity by featuring a list of the singers who had performed it, including "Mr Ffrangcon Davies, Mesdames, Kirkby Lunn, Sobrino, Hortense Paulsen, Miss Gleeson-White, Miss Perceval Allen, Madame Elvey, Madame Emily Squire, Madame Mallia, Madame H. Spalding, Miss Lillie Wormald, Miss Euneta Truscott, Miss Marguerite Cooper, Miss Hilda de Angelis, Mr. Ben Johnson, Philip Ritte and Mr. Herbert Grover."

DM106　　"A Bride Song." Frederic H. Cowen, 1892

Seventh Set of Six Songs. Trans. L. G. Sturm. High voice. English and German. London: Joseph Williams, circa 1892. Plate number 9776 Williams.
Note: Also included in *Third Set of Twelve Songs* (see DM46).
Location: Not seen: copy located at Royal Academy of Music.

DM107　　"Dream Land." Charles Legh Naylor, 1892

Where sunless rivers weep. The *Orpheus*, New Series No. 250. London: Novello & Co. Setting for four part male chorus, a capella.
Note: Advertised in the *Musical Times* (1 December 1892: 748), and reviewed in the same journal(1 August 1893: 488)
Location: not seen: copy located at BL.

DM108　　"Love is Strong as Death" ("I have not sought Thee"). Alexander Thompson, 1892

[London]: Reid Brothers.
Note: No copies located. Reviewed in *Magazine of Music* (March 1892: 47).

DM109　　"May" ("I cannot tell you how it was"). Amy Elise Horrocks, 1892

"I cannot tell you how it was." *Six Songs*, op 10. London: Joseph Williams. Plate number N9215 Williams.
Location: not seen: copy located at Royal Academy of Music.

DM110 "Mirage." Frederic H. Cowen, 1892

For a dream's sake. London: Williams.
Note: In English and German. British Library catalog describes as "For low voice and piano, in C." Also published in song collections (see DM115).
Location: not seen: copy located at BL.

DM111 "Song" ("When I am dead, my dearest"). Frank V. Van der Stucken, 1892

Gedenken-Vergessen = Remember-Forget. Trans. Helen D. Tretbar. Berlin: Friedrich Luckhardt; New York: G. Schirmer, 1892. Text in English and German.
Note: No copies located. Citation from WorldCat. Gooch & Thatcher list a "pre-1940," presumably English only, publication by Luckhardt & Belder.

DM112 "Somewhere." Frederic H. Cowen, 1892

With "A Bride Song," and "A Birthday." *Third Set of Twelve Songs.* Trans. L. G. Sturm. Soprano edition. London: Joseph Williams, circa 1892. Plate number 9370 Williams.
Note: May have been published later; the same title is listed in the *Literary World* among "New Music" in 1893 (16 June 1893: 565).
Location: not seen: copy located at Royal Academy of Music.

DM113 "The summer nights are short." G. W. (George Whitefield) Chadwick, 1892

1) Two Folk Songs
"The Northern Days." Boston: Arthur P. Schmidt.
Cover description: In blue ink. Text within decorative compartment composed of multiple rules and a Greek key pattern with rosettes at corners. Heading "Songs by G. W. Chadwick" features ornate, illuminated capitals with a musical staff in the background.
Song title: List of 30 titles beneath heading "Songs by G. W. Chadwick." The last title listed is "Two Folk Songs" including the separate titles "O Love and Joy" and "The northern Days"
Names on wrapper: Only the composer's name appears.
Price: .40.
Publisher: Arthur P. Schmidt, Boston: 140 Boylston St.; Leipzig; New York: 136 Fifth Avenue.

Signed "Words by Christina Rosetti" on first page of "II" (first line: "The northern days are short") (4). Note also on first page of score, dedication "To Mrs. G. H. Stoddard."
Music: sheet music, score 3-4. For song II: Key signature G (1 sharp), time signature 3/4, tempo "Con moto," quarter note equals 80.
Locations: 1892: Manhattan School of Music. Post-1900: Ives.

2) Song Album
No. 10, "The Northern Days are short." *Song Album.* 17 Songs for alto or baritone with pianoforte accompaniment. Edition Schmidt, no. 38. Boston: A. P. Schmidt, [1920].
Music: score 32-33. Title above score "Northern Days." Key signature, time signature, tempo same as "Two Songs." At bottom of first page of score, "Copyright 1892 by A. P. Schmidt. Copyright 1920 by G. W. Chadwick."
Location: NN (via Internet Archive).

Note: Chadwick heavily revised Rossetti's text. Gooch & Thatcher list a separate issue of "The Northern Days" by Schmidt in 1893 (Gooch & Thatcher 4812); I have not located any copies.

DM114   "Remember." Harriet Kendall, 1892

A Song of Remembrance. London: Beal & Co.
Note: Key signature C (no sharps, flats). Plate number B & Co. 1274. BL depository copy dated 16 Aug 1892.
Location: not seen: copy located at BL.

DM115   "Bird Raptures." Frederic H. Cowen, 1893

Separate publications (priority unknown):
1. Sheet music:
A) National Music Company
Chicago: National Music Company.
Cover description: Center vignette portrait of woman, with birds in background; linear ornamentation around the vignette and at the upper left and lower right corner.
Song title: "Bird Raptures."
Names on cover: "Christina Rossetti" and "Frederic H. Cowen."
Price: 40 cents.
Publishers: National Music Company 215 to 221 Wabash Ave, Chicago; Benj. W. Hitchcock, 385 Sixth Ave New York.
Signed "Christina Rossetti" above score.
Music: sheet music, score 1-4. "Mezzo Soprano or Baritone." Key signature A (3 sharps), time signature 3/4, tempo "Allegro vivace," quarter note = 112. Plate number 3312. Date from notice on back wrapper "Copyrighted 1893, by National Music Company"
Location: DLC (via Performing Arts Encyclopedia).

B) Oliver Ditson
Bird raptures. Soprano or tenor in C. Boston: Oliver Ditson Co., [189-?].
Plate number 53052 Oliver Ditson Co.
Location: not seen: copy located at University of South Florida.

2. Song collections (priority uncertain):
A) With "Mirage" (titled "For a dream's sake"). *Fifth Set of Six songs.* English and German. London: Joseph Williams. Plate number 8162 Williams.
Location: not seen: copy located at Royal Academy of Music.

B) With "Mirage" (titled "For a dream's sake"). *Album of twelve songs.* Soprano edition. London: Joseph Williams. Plate number 8162 Williams.
Note: Also distributed in the United States by H. B. Stevens for Williams, plate number N. 8162 Williams.
Locations: not seen: copy located at Royal Academy of Music; Stevens/Williams: not seen: copy located at MoSW.

DM116   "Boats sail on the rivers." Howard Orsmond Anderton, 1893

"Boats." Number 5 in *12 Children's Songs.* London: Charles & Dible. 10-11.
Note: Key signature E (4 sharps). BL depository copy dated 16 February 1893.
Location: not seen: copy located at BL.

DM117   "Echo." Marie W. Fobert, 1893

In the Silence of the Night. Boston: O. Ditson Company.

Note: Plate number 70-57080-4. BL depository copy dated 10 Nov. 1893. Advertised among Ditson's "Choice Sheet Music Publications for January," *Musical Record* (January 1894: 17).
Location: not seen: copy located at BL.

DM118   "He and She." Frederic H. Cowen, 1893
Published in several anthologies, priority uncertain.

1) Fourth Set of Six Songs
London: Joseph Williams, [n.d.]. Plate number 15277 Williams. For low voice.
Words in English and German.
Location: not seen: copy located at Royal Academy of Music.

2) Twelve Songs
Twelve songs: for voice and piano. London: Joseph Williams, 1887.
Plate number 7437 Williams.
Note: Reviewed in the *Musical World* (2 April 1887): 253. Also available in German and English, with translation by A. M. Von Blomberg.
Locations: not seen: copy located at Royal Academy of Music; German and English: National Library of New Zealand.

3) Frederic H. Cowen's Album of Twelve Songs.
Boston: Oliver Ditson, circa 1890. For high voice and piano. Plate number 53363-53374.
Location: not seen: copy located at MoSW.

4) Cowen Vocal Album
Vol I. London: Joseph Williams, [circa 1893?].
Note: Gooch & Thatcher 4451; no copies located.

5) Vocal Album
New York: Schirmer, circa 1915.
Music: Score 31-33. For high voice and piano. Key signature B flat (2 flats), time signature 3/4, tempo "Andante con moto," quarter note = 63. Plate number 7792.
Note: A two volume song collection, with "He and She" in No. 1017, Volume 1, *Twelve Songs*, high voice, and (presumably) also in No. 1018 (low voice).
Location: MoKU.

DM119   "May" ("I cannot tell you how it was"). Charles Rawlings, 1893
"May." A Collection of Four-Part Songs. No. 9. London: J. Williams.
Note: Published under the name "Ed. Sachs"; British Library catalog lists Rawlings as the composer. British library depository copy dated 11 May 1893. Plate number N. 9386. At bottom of first page "By permission of Messrs. Macmillan and Co. Copyright 1892 by Joseph Williams." Reviewed in *Magazine of Music* (April 1893: 80).
Location: not seen: copy located at BL.

DM120   "Three Seasons." Charles Rawlings, 1893
A Collection of Four-Part Songs. No. 10. London: J. Williams.
Note: Published under the name "Ed. Sachs"; British Library catalog lists Rawlings as the composer. Key signature E flat (3 flats). Reviewed in *Magazine of Music* (April 1893: 80).
Location: not seen: copy located at BL.

DM121   "A Chill." Cecil Forsyth, 1894

Anthology, title unknown. London: Marriott and Williams.
Note: No copies located. Not in Gooch & Thatcher. Mentioned among "New Songs" in the London *Times* (28 August 1894: 10): "Six songs by Cecil Forsyth are apparently the work of a clever amateur [. . .] the best numbers in the album are Shelley's "To Music" and Christina Rossetti's "A Chill." Possibly Forsyth's first published setting of CGR; several additional settings were published after 1900.

DM122   "Song" ("When I am dead, my dearest"). Alexander Edward Fynes Clinton Davenport, 1894

Remember or forget. London: R. Cocks & Co.
Note: Key signature G (1 sharp). BL depository copy dated 28 Feb 1894. Plate number 1475a.
Location: not seen: copy located at BL

DM123   "Moonshine." Edward Alexander MacDowell, 1894

Four Little Poems. New York: NY: Breitkopf & Hartel, 1894. Revised edition, in German and English *Vier kleine Poesien* / Four little poems, Leipzig, New York: Breitkopf & Hartel, c1906.
Note: No copies located of 1894 (Gooch & Thatcher 4643).
Locations: 1894: no copies located; 1906: not seen: copy located at NjP.

DM124   "Song" (When I am dead, my dearest"). Mrs. Walter Creyke, 1894

"When I am dead, my dearest." *Six Songs*. London: Weekes & Co.
Location: not seen: BL.

DM125   "Song" (When I am dead, my dearest"). D. Magill Rogers, 1894

Wilt thou remember?. London: Swan & Co.
Note: Key signature G (1 sharp). BL depository copy dated 21 Mar 1894. Plate number S. & Co. 70a.
Location: not seen: copy located at BL.

DM126   "Up-Hill." Lady Barrett Lennard, 1894

London; Novello & Co.
Note: Advertised as published "During the last month" in the *Musical Times* (1 August 1894: 559).
Location: not seen: copy located at BL.

DM127–DM128   "Advent" ("This Advent moon shines cold and clear"); "And Now Why Tarriest Thou?" Frank T. Lowden, 1895

"The Porter Watches at the Gate," "Lord, Grant us Grace to Mount." London: Skeffington and Son.
Cover transcription:
[within ornamental rule frame] Two Hymns | By the late | Christina G. Rossetti | Set to Music by | Frank T. Lowden | Organist and Choir Director, Christ Church, Woburn Square | London | Skeffington and Son, Piccadilly, W. | Publishers to H. R. H. the Prince of Wales | MDCCCXCV | [beneath frame] *Price Two Pence*.

Signed "Christina G. Rossetti" above both scores.

Music: sheet music, unpaginated (4 pages; music on 2-3).
(**DM127**) "The Porter Watches At The Gate." Key signature D (2 sharps), time signature common time.
(**DM128**) "Lord, Grant us Grace to Mount." Key signature E flat (3 flats), time signature common time.
Note: Folio, with music of first hymn printed on verso of cover. The same poems were included in a

printed leaflet distributed at CGR's memorial service; in both the leaflet and the music, "Advent" appears without the first stanza. Both sung at the dedication of the memorial to CGR at Christ Church in 1898 (London *Times*, 2 November 1898: 10).
Location: Ives.

DM129   **"A Birthday." Henry Richard Charles, Lord Somerset, 1895**

A Birthday. London: Chappell & Co.
Note: Probably composed much earlier. Somerset (not named in CGR's correspondence, but identified in WMR's diary) had contacted CGR in 1880 for permission to publish settings of one or more of her songs. CGR initially assented, but DGR convinced her to withdraw her consent because (as WMR wrote in his diary) "there was not long ago a terrible scandal (but G. did not give C. any details of this) regarding Lord H. & a son of Mrs.Dalrymple" (WMRD 9 September 1880; see also *Letters* 2: 248)
    British Library lists holdings in E flat and F.
Location: not seen: copy located at BL.

DM130   **"Bitter for sweet." Amy Elise Horrocks, 1895**

Two-part song. Op. 18. No. 3. St. Cecilia. Sixth Series. No. 8. London: Joseph Williams.
Note: See DM95 re. the St. Cecelia series.
Location: not seen: copy located at BL.

DM131   **"Echo." Henry Richard Charles, Lord Somerset, 1895**

1) Sheet Music:

A) No. 1 in F, Chappell

Ai) London: Chappell, 1895.
Cover with engraved, lightly ornamented text, with various decorative lines, spirals, and small ornaments. Song title: "Echo."
Names on cover: "Christina Rossetti," "Lord Henry Somerset"
Price: 4 shillings.
Publishers: Chappell & Co., 50, New Bond Street, London. At bottom of cover, "The words printed by kind permission of Messrs. Macmillan and Co"
Signed about score "Christina Rossetti."
Music: sheet music, score 1-5. Key signature F (one flat), time signature common time, tempo "Adagio con espressione." Plate number 19867.
Location: University of Colorado at Boulder.

Aii) London, New York, Melbourne: Chappell & Co., [post-1896]
Cover: same as Ai.
Price: 2 shillings/60 cents.
Publishers: Chappell & Co., Ltd, 50 New Bond St., London, W; 37 W. Seventeenth St., New York; 11 and 12, The Rialto, Collins Street, Melbourne.
At bottom of cover, "The words printed by kind permission of Messrs. Macmillan and Co" and publisher's number 4372.
Signed above score "Christina Rossetti."
Music: same as Ai.
Note: Copies with publisher "Chappell & Co., Ltd" were printed sometime after Chappell became a limited company in 1896.
Location: National Library of Australia (via NLA Digital Collections).

B) No 2 In G, Chappell

Bi) London: Chappell & Co.
Note: Plate number 19858. BL depository copy dated 27 March 1893.
Location: not seen: BL.

Bii) London, New York, and Melbourne: Chappell & Co. (post-1896).
Cover nearly identical to A (same song title, names, and publishers number), except:
Price: 1/6, presented with differences in punctuation and lineation.
Publisher's addresses: same as A except New York address changed to 41 East 34th Street; Melbourne changed to 235 Flinders Lane.
Note: Plate number same as Bi.
Location: Ives (post-1896).

C) No. 3 in A, Chappell

Ci) London: Chappell & Co.
Note: Plate number 19875. BL depository copy dated 27 March 1893.
Location: not seen: BL.

Cii): London, New York, Melbourne: Chappell & Co., Ltd. [post-1896].
Cover nearly identical to A (same text and design, except for the price which now appears with different punctuation and lineation). Same song title, names, price, publishers and publisher's number (4372).
Music: sheet music, score 1-5. Key signature A (3 sharps), time signature common time, tempo "Adagio con espressione." Plate number same as BL.
Location: National Library of Australia (via NLA Digital Collections).

2) Song Collection:

A) Famous songs.
New York: The University Society, 1908.
Location: not seen: copy located at MoSW.

DM132   **"The First Spring Day." Lord Henry Richard Charles Somerset, 1895**
London: Chappell & Co.
Location: not seen: BL.

DM133   **"Mariana." Frederic H. Cowen, 1895**
Fourth Set of Twelve songs. High Voice. In English and German. London: Joseph Williams. Plate number 10122 Williams.
Note: Listed in "New Music," the *Literary World* (25 November 1895: 443).
Location: not seen: copy located at Royal Academy of Music.

DM134   **["Memory."] Reginald B. Clarke, 1895**
A Memory. London: Weekes & Co.
Location: not seen: copy located at BL.

DM135   **"Monna Innominata" (2. "I wish I could remember that first day"). Maude Valerie White, 1895**
Did One but Know. In D and F. London, New York: Chappell & Co., Ltd..
In two keys:
F major (high), plate number 20219 Chappell.

D major (low), plate number 19951.
Location: not seen: copy located at Royal Academy of Music (D and F).

DM136 **"Song" ("When I am dead, my dearest"). Mrs. M. Gould Del Castillo, 1895**

Remember or Forget. Song. Boston: H. B. Stevens Co.
Note: Key signature D flat (5 flats). Plate number H. B. S. Co. 618. BL depository copy dated 6 Dec 1895.
"Copyright 1895 by H. B. Stevens Co."
Location: not seen: copy located at BL.

DM137 **"Song" (When I am dead, my dearest"). Beroald Innes, 1895**

When I am dead my Dearest. London & New York: Novello, Ewer & Co.
Note: Name given as "Bewald Innes" in Novello catalog.
Location: not seen: copy located at BL.

DM138 **"Summer." Amy Elise Horrocks, 1895**

Two-part song. St. Cecilia. Sixth Series. London: Joseph Williams.
Note: No copies located. Mentioned in "Secular Choral Music," the London *Times*, 19 November 1895: 4):
"The sixth series of "Saint Cecilia," [. . .] consists of two-part songs for ladies' voices. A. E. Horrocks's
"Summer," to words by the late Christina Rossetti, is a charming little composition." See also DM94 on
the St. Cecilia series.

DM139 **["Confluents"]. Henri Logé, 1895**

Thee at Last. London: Chappell & Co. Ltd.
Note: No copies located. Identified from bookseller's listing.

DM140 **"Another Spring." Amy Elise Horrocks, 1896**

Another Spring. Two-part song.. Op. 18. No. 5. St. Cecilia. Seventh Series. No. 7. London: Joseph Williams.
Note: See DM95 re. the St. Cecilia series.
Location: not seen: copy located at BL.

DM141 **"In the Round Tower at Jhansi." Stanley Hawley, 1896**

"In the Round Tower at Jhansi." Recitation-Music Series, number 13. London: Bosworth.
Note: Gooch & Thatcher lists for 1895, with Cocks as publisher (4497). Mentioned in "New Songs,"
London *Times* (30 July 1896: 10). Advertised in the *Musical Times* (1 February 1896: 123).
Location: not seen: copy located at Royal Academy of Music.

DM142 **"Song" ("When I am dead, my dearest") W. H (William Henry) Pommer, 1896**

Remember or Forget. *Four Songs*, Op 8, no 2. St. Louis: Thiebes-Stierlin Music Co.
Cover description: Scroll design across top, with foliage at upper left and ornamental vertical designs
extending down left and right sides of the page.
Dedication: "To Miss Halsey C. Ives."
Cover lists four numbered songs, under the heading "Four Songs," including "2. Remember or Forget";
the set of songs identified as "Opus 8."
Names on cover: "W. H. Pommer."

Price: 40 cents.
Publisher: Thiebes-Stierlin Music Co. St. Louis
Signed above score "Christina Rossetti"
Music: Key signature A (3 sharps), time signature 2/4, tempo "Andante espressivo." Plate number 3172-3.
Note: "Copyright MDCCCXCVI by Theibes_Sterilin Music Co" at bottom of first page of score.
Location: MoSW (Gaylord Music Library Special Collections, Washington University in St. Louis).

DM143   "All Thy Works Praise Thee" Frank T. Lowden, 1897

"A Processional of Creation." Cantata.
Note: Publication presumed, but none located. WMR reports that "In 1897 Prebendary Glendenning Nash, the Incumbent of Christ Church, Woburn Square (the church frequented by Christina Rossetti in all her closing years), adapted a portion of this poem for a harvest festival under the name "A Processional of Creation." It was set to music by Mr. Frank T. Lowden, and sung at the evening service in that church, 21 October" (*PW* 463). The Harvest Festival performance was reviewed in *Musical News* (30 October 1897): 384.

DM144   "Echo." Francis Boehr, 1897

Come back in Dreams. London: R. Cocks & Co.
Note: Key signature B flat (2 flats). Plate number 1599a. BL depository copy dated 30 Dec 1897.
Location: not seen: copy located at BL.

**DM145–DM147   "He and She"; "The Key Note," "Song" ("Oh roses for the flush of youth").
Lance Smith, 1897**

Four Songs. 1. "He and She" (**DM145**); 2. "The Key Note" (**DM146**); 3. "Song" (**DM147**). London: Weekes & Co.
Note: The collection's fourth song has words by K. Mann. British Library catalogue identifies "Lance Smith" as a pseudonym. Reviewed in *Musical News* (October 1897): 384.
Location: not seen: copy located at BL.

DM148   "Mariana." A. M. Rough, 1897

London: Robert Cocks & Co.
Location: not seen: copy located at BL.

DM149   "May" ("I cannot tell you how it was"). Beatrice Ramsay Hallowes, 1897

When May was young! London: Robert Cocks & Co.
Note: Key signature G (1 sharp). Plate number 1594a. BL depository copy dated 30 Dec 1897.
Location: not seen: copy located at BL.

DM150   "Parting after parting." Hermann Loehr, 1897

Love's Parting. London: Chappell & Co.
Note: Key signature F (1 flat). Plate number 20,327. BL depository copy dated 17 December 1897. Composer's name appears as "Hermann Löhr" in Chappell's advertisements (*Musical News*, 4 December 1897: 512). Reviewed in the *Musical Standard* (11 December 1897: 381).
Location: not seen: copy located at BL.

DM151   "Song" ("Two doves upon the selfsame branch") Henry Richard Charles, Lord Somerset, 1897

Two Songs. London: Chappell & Co.
Note: Gooch & Thatcher dates 1896.
Location: not seen: copy located at BL.

DM152   "Song" (When I am dead, my dearest"). Philip Harker, 1897

When I am dead, my Dearest. London : Phillips & Page.
Location: not seen: copy located at BL.

DM153   "Song" (When I am dead, my dearest"). Percy Pitt, 1897

When I am dead, my dearest. An English Series of Original Songs. No. 6. London: Weekes.
Note: The "English Series of Original Songs" was edited by J. R. Courtenay Gale and Charlton T. Speer. Reviewed in *Musical News* (30 June 1896: 589).
Location: not seen: copy located at BL.

DM154   "Song" ("When I am dead, my dearest"). Arthur Edmund Grimshaw, 1897

"Remember or Forget." *Two Songs.* London: R. Cocks & Co.
Note: Not in Gooch & Thatcher. "Copyright MSCCCXCVII by Robert Cocks & Co." Plate number 20,577.
Location: not seen: copy located at BL.

DM155   "Song" ("When I am dead, my dearest"). M. Oakley, 1897

"When I am dead, my Dearest." *Two Songs.* With "Crocus Gathering." London: Office of "The Organist."
Note: Not in Gooch & Thatcher.
Location: not seen: copy located at BL.

DM156   "Song" (When I am dead, my dearest"). Richard Henry Walthew, 1897

When I am dead, my Dearest. London & New York: Boosey & Co.
Note: Not in Gooch & Thatcher.
Location: not seen: copy located at BL.

DM157   "Bird Raptures." G. F. Huntley, 1898

A two-part song. No. 109. Novello's Octavo Edition of Two-part Songs for Female Voices. London: Novello & Co.
Note: Announced as published "During the last month" in *The Musical Times* (1 May 1898: 345).
Location: not seen: copy located at BL.

DM158   "A Birthday." Henry Thacker Burleigh, 1898

"A Birthday Song." *Three Songs.* New York: G. Schirmer.
Cover transcription: within thick-thin-thick rule frame:
To A. M. Perry | [rule] | Three Songs | for | Baritone of Mezzo-Soprano | with | Piano Accompaniment | by | H. T. Burleigh | [double rule] | If you but know | (Translated from the French) | A Birthday Song (Christina Rossetti) | Life (John Boyle O'Reilly) | [double rule] | Pr [illegible]c each | [rule] New York: G. Schirmer
Signed "Christina Rossetti" above score.

Music: score 3-5. Key signature A (3 sharps), time signature 2/4, tempo "Fervently, with joy." Plate number 14093 C. At bottom of first page of score, "Copyright, 1898, by G. Schirmer."
Note: Price on cover scratched out. Tim Brooks identifies Burleigh as "perhaps the most prominent figure in the world of black concert music in America during the early 20th century"; "A Birthday Song" was one of his first published compositions (Brooks, 475).
Location: Los Angeles Public Library.

DM159   "Dream Land." P. J. Haydn Mulholland, 1898

"Dreamland." Four-Part Song for S. A. T. B. London & New York: Novello, Ewer & Co.
Note: Advertised in the *Musical Times* (1 February 1898: 125).
Location: not seen: copy located at BL.

DM160   "Golden Glories." Frederic Hymen Cowen, 1898

No 4. *Third Set of Six Songs*. London: J. Williams.
Note: Reviewed in the *Musical Times* (1 February 1901: 113).
Location: not seen: copy located at BL.

DM161   "Golden Silences." G. F. Huntley, 1898

A Two-Part song. No. 108. Novello's Octavo Edition of Two-part Songs for Female Voices. London: Novello & Co., 1898
Note: Not in Gooch & Thatcher. Announced as published "During the last month" in *Musical Times* (1 May 1898: 345); reviewed in the *Musical Times* (1 October 1898: 675).
Location: not seen: copy located at BL.

DM162   "Mirage." Harold Thorp, 1898

The Dome 1 (1898) 125-127. London: Novello & Co, 1898.

Signed "Christina Rossetti" above score.

Music: periodical, score 125-127. Key signature C (no sharps, flats), time signature 3/4, tempo "Andante Sustenuso"; quarter note = 54.
Note: Not in Gooch & Thatcher.
Location: NjP (via Google Books).

DM163   "Song" (When I am dead, my dearest"). Reginald W. Craddock, 1898

No. 2. "When I am dead my dearest." *Three Songs for Medium Voice*. London: R. Cocks & Co, 1898.
Note: Not in Gooch & Thatcher.
Location: not seen: copy located at BL.

DM164   "Song" ("When I am dead, my dearest"). Frederick Barry, 1898

Boston: Boston Music Company.
Note: No locations identified. Listed in Gooch & Thatcher.

DM165   "A Song for the Least of all Saints." [Frank T. Lowden], 1898

"Love is the key of life and death."
Note: Publication presumed, but none located. A hymn with this title was sung at the conclusion of the dedication of the memorial to CGR at Christ Church in 1898 (London *Times*, 2 November 1898: 10).

Lowden is presumed to have composed the setting, as the service also included the two hymns composed by him and sung at CGR's memorial service (see DM 102).

DM166   **"Twice." Lita Jarratt, 1898**
My Heart. London: Chappell & Co.
Location: not seen: copy located at BL.

DM167   **"Remember." Dorothy Whale, 1898**
Remember. London: Dinham, Blythe & Co.
Note: Key signature E flat (3 flats). British Library copy is signed, presumably by the composer, "Dorothy Whale" with date 28.7.98.
Location: not seen: copy located at BL.

DM168   **"Old and New Year Ditties." Isabella Caroline Somerset (Lady Henry Somerset), 1898**
Song of the New Year. London: J. Curwen & Sons.
Note: Not in Gooch & Thatcher. Key signature D (2 sharps). Plate number C. & S. 1624. BL depository copy dated 7 Sept 1898. Advertised as "Now Ready," the *Musical Herald (*1 November 1898: i)
Location: not seen: copy located at BL.

DM169   **"A Birthday." Walter J. Lockitt, 1899**
London: Weekes & Co.
Note: Not in Gooch & Thatcher. Reviewed in *Musical News* (4 March 1899: 233).
Location: not seen: copy located at BL.

DM170   **"Song" ("When I am dead, my dearest"). Edward J. Napier, 1899**
Pittsburgh, Pa: E. J. Napier.
Note: Not in Gooch & Thatcher.
Location: not seen: copy located at BL.

DM171   **"Song" ("When I am dead, my dearest"). John W. Metcalf, 1899**
Wilt Thou Forget? Boston: Arthur P. Schmidt.
Cover description: Text in green ink within dark green and brownish-orange art nouveau compartment formed of flowers, stems and leaves. "Des. By F. G. Hale" appears beneath the frame.
Song title: Heading "Songs by John W. Metcalf" above a list of 20 titles; "Wilt Thou Forget?" is second in the list.
Names on cover: only Metcalf's name is listed.
Price: .40.
Publisher: Arthur P. Schmidt, Boston: 120 Boylston St.; Leipzig; New York: 136 Fifth Ave.

Signed "Words by Christina G. Rossetti" above score.

Music: score 3-5. Cover specifies "For medium voice." Key signature A flat (4 flats), time signature ¾, tempo "Andante moderato," quarter note = 80. Plate number A. P. S. 5116-3. At bottom of first page of score "Copyright 1899 by Arthur P. Schmidt."
Note: Not in Gooch & Thatcher. Reviewed in *Music* (February 1900: 442-443).
Location: ABAU.

DM172   **"Up-Hill." Mabel Saumarez Smith, 1899**
Part-song. London: C. Vincent.
Location: copy located at BL.

SELECTED SETTINGS AFTER 1900

DM173   **"A Christmas Carol" ("In the bleak mid-winter"). Henry Bird Collins, 1900**
"A Christmas Carol." *Six Songs*. Op. 14, No 2. London: Houghton & Co.
Note: Although Gustav Holst's setting in *The English Hymnal* (1906; DH13) is often assumed to be the first setting of this poem, Holst was preceded by Collins, whose setting was also published in the *Vocalist* (December 1903).

DM174   **"Goblin Market." Vittorio Ricci, 1901**
London: Joseph Williams.
Cover and title page: with engraved ornamented text above, within, and below an art nouveau-designed floral compartment.
Dedication: "To John Kirkhope, Esq."
Title: "Goblin Market (Der Gnomen Markt)."
Names on cover: "Christine Rosetti"; "Vittorio Ricci"; text adapted by "M. C. Gillingham."
No price.
Publisher: Joseph Williams, 32, Great Portland Street, W; Edw. Schuberth & Co (J. F. H. Meyer), New York; Breitkopf & Haertel, Leipzig; "Copyright 1901 by Joseph Williams"; "by kind permission of Messrs. Macmillan & Co"; engraver "Oscar Brandstetter, Leipzig."
Publisher number "N. 13237."

Signed "Christina Rossetti" above score. With English words as text on 1-2; abridged.

Music: cantata, score 3- 95. For solo voice (soprano and contralto), either two or three-part chorus, and piano.
In two parts, with individual numbers not separately titled, first lines provided after page numbers:
Part I:
1. Chorus (3-15; "Morning and evening"). Key signature F (1 flat), time signature 6/8, tempo "allegro leggiero," quarter note = 116.
2. Duet and chorus (Laura and Lizzie) (16-24; "Look, Lizzie"). Key signature F (1 flat), time signature common time. Tempo "Recitativo."
3. Solo and chorus (25-37; "Good folk, I have no coin"). Key signature C (no sharps, flats), time signature common time, tempo "Recitativo."
4. Solo (Lizzie) (38-40; "Dear, you should not stay so late"). Key signature G (1 sharp), time signature common time, tempo "Recitat," quarter note = 63.
5. Chorus. Slumber song (41-44; "Golden head by golden head"). Key signature B flat (2 flats), time signature common time.
Part II:
6. Chorus (45-53; "Day after day, night after night'). Key signature F (1 flat), time signature 3/4, tempo "Andante molto moderato," quarter note = 69-76.
7. Chorus (54-59; "Laugh'd then every goblin"). Key signature E flat (3 flats), time signature 6/8, tempo "Allegro spiritoso," quarter note = 160.
8. Solo (Lizzie) and chorus (60-72; "Good folk, good folk, now give me much and many"). Key signature D (2 sharps), time signature common time, tempo "Piuttosto largamente."

9. Laura, Lizzie and chorus (73-81; "Laura, Laura, did you miss me?"). Key signature D (2 sharps), time signature common time, tempo "Recitativo."

10. Finale. Duet and chorus (Laura, Lizzie and chorus; "But when the first birds chirped") (82-95). Key signature D (2 sharps), time signature common time, tempo "Allegro gioioso," quarter note = 160.

Note: In German and English. Copy examined inscribed by the composer.

Location: NBuU.

DM175-DM182   **"Sing-Song" (various poems). Felix Swinstead, 1907**

Sing-Song Cycle. Leipzig: Charles Avison.

Cover transcription (underlines in original):

SING-SONG CYCLE | WORDS BY | <u>CHRISTINA ROSSETTI</u> *) | [rectangular publisher's device, text 'CH. AVISON EDITION' above seated musician with lute and score, and in lower corner, 'J. G. WITHYCOMBE'] | MUSIC BY | <u>FELIX SWINSTEAD</u> | CHARLES AVISON, ltd. | AGENTS: BREITKOPF & HÄRTEL | LEIPZIG • BRUSSELS • LONDON • NEW YORK | PRINTED BY BREITKOPF & HÄRTEL, LEIPZIG. | *) by permission of Messrs Macmillan & Co., Ltd.

Music: songbook, score 2-15. Plate number Avison Ed. 23. At bottom of first page, "Copyright 1907, by Charles Avison, Ltd. Printed by Breitkopf & Härtel, Leipzig." Songs separately numbered and titled, with separate dedications, as follows:

(DM175) 1. "Love me, -- I love you." (2-3). Key signature B flat (2 flats), time signature 2/4, tempo "Allegro moderato, con brio," quarter note = 150. Dedicated "To Nora Meredith."

(DM176) 2. "I caught a little ladybird" Song title: "The Ladybird." (4-5). Key signature B flat (2 flats), time signature 2/4, tempo "Allegretto," quarter note = 160. Dedicated "To Zelpa Mullett."

(DM177) 3. "Ferry me across the water." Song title: "The Maid and the Ferry." (6-7). Key signature D (2 sharps), time signature 2/4, tempo "Allegro moderato," quarter note = 144. Dedicated "To Margaret Cooper."

(DM178) 4. "Is the moon tired?" (8). Key signature G (one sharp), time signature common time, tempo "Andante tranquillo," quarter note = 60. Dedicated "To Bessie Cartwright."

(DM179) 5. "When a mounting skylark sings." (9-10). Key signature C (no sharps, flats), time signature cut time; tempo "Allegretto grazioso," quarter note = 72. Dedicated "To Katie Moss."

(DM180) 6. "The wind has such a rainy sound" Song title: "Will the ships go down?" (11). Key signature C (no sharps or flats), time signature common time, tempo "Misterioso," quarter note = 63. Dedicated "To Olive Turner."

(DM181) 7. "If I were a Queen." (12-13). Key signature B flat (2 flats), time signature common time, tempo "Allegro con spirito." Dedicated "To Mrs. Tobias Matthay."

(DM182) 8. "Minnie and Mattie and quaint little May." Song title: "Minnie and Mattie and May." (14-15). Key signature B flat (2 flats), time signature 6/8, tempo "Molto allegro e giocoso," dotted quarter note = 150-160. Dedicated "To Ada Marie Thomas."

Note: The first known setting of *Sing-Song* after Mary Carmichael (DM54-80); see also settings by Sidney Homer (DM183-199), Mabel Watson (DM201), John Ireland (DM 228-35) and the collections *Kookoorookoo* (DM202-DM227) **and** *Kikirikee: a sequel to Kookoorookoo* (DM 236-269).

Location: IU.

DM183–DM199   *Sing-Song* **(various). Sidney Homer, 1908**

Seventeen lyrics: from Sing-song. New York: G. Schirmer.

Cover and title page transcription:

[this line above a rule] *To my Wife and Children* | *Seventeen Lyrics* | from | *Sing-Song* | By Christina

Rossetti | Set to Music by | *Sidney Homer* | *Op.* 19 | [ornament, small bouquet of flowers] | *High Low* | Price, $1.25 *net* | *New York : G. Schirmer* | *Boston : Boston Music Co.*

Signed "Christina Rossetti" above score on first page of numbers (in part I) 1, 3,5, 7, 9 and (in part II) 1, 3, 5, 7. Words as text on iv-vi.

Music: score 2-32. Plate number 21870C on 2, 21870 on remaining pages.

In two parts, separately numbered, as follows:

Part I:

(**DM183**) 1. "Eight o'clock; the postman's knock!" (2). Key signature A flat (4 flats), time signature common time, tempo "Allegro," "gaily," quarter note = 104. Note at bottom of page "All metronome-marks merely approximate."

(**DM184**) 2. "Baby cry – Oh fie!" (3). Key signature A flat (4 flats), time signature common time, tempo "Allegro," quarter note = 116.

(**DM185**) 3. "Dead in the cold, a song-singing thrush." (4). Key signature E flat (3 flats), time signature common time, tempo "Lento," "simply," quarter note = 84.

(**DM186**) 4. "Love me, I love you." (5, mispaginated '7'; see *Note*). Key signature F (1 flat), time signature common time, tempo "Lento," quarter note = 66.

(**DM187**) 5. "Kookoorookoo! Kookoorookoo!" (6-7, with 6 mispaginated '4'). Key signature D (2 sharps), time signature 12/8, tempo "Vivace," "with spirit and imagination," quarter note = 138.

(**DM188**) 6. "Boats sail on the rivers" (8-9). Key signature A flat, time signature common time, tempo "Lento," "with breadth and elevation," quarter note = 58.

(**DM189**) 7. "In the meadow – what in the meadow?" (10-11). Key signature A (3 sharps), time signature 2/2, tempo "Vivace," "with delicacy and sentiment," half note = 104.

(**DM190**) 8. "The dog lies in his kennel" (12-13). Key signature B flat (2 flats), time signature common time, tempo "Allegro," "with mingled humor and love," quarter note = 144.

(**DM191**) 9. "Lie abed, sleepy head" (14). Key signature B flat (2 flats), time signature common time, tempo "Lento," "with great tenderness," quarter note = 60.

(**DM192**) 10. "Mix a pancake, stir a pancake" (15). Key signature G (1 sharp), time signature 2/4, tempo "Vivace," "with spirit and humor," quarter note = 144.

Part II

(**DM193**) 1. "Who has seen the wind?" (18-19, 19 misnumbered '21'). Key signature B flat (2 flats), time signature 2/2, tempo "Andante con moto," "with imagination," half note = 58.

(**DM194**) 2. "Dancing on the hilltops" (20-21, 20 misnumbered 18). Key signature A (3 sharps), time signature 3/4, tempo "Animato," "with grace and affection," dotted half note = 56.

(**DM195**) 3. "A pocket handkerchief to hem"– (22-23). Key signature C (no sharps, flats), time signature common time, tempo "Allego molto, con amore," "tearfully," quarter note = 138.

(**DM196**) 4. "A motherless soft lambkin" (24-25). Key signature F (1 flat), time signature common time, tempo "Molto lento," "very tenderly," quarter note = 60.

(**DM197**) 5. "Lullaby, oh lullaby!" (26-27). Key signature E flat (3 flats), time signature common time, tempo "Molto lento," "sustained, with deep feeling," quarter note = 52.

(**DM198**) 6. "Hurt no living thing" (28). Key signature A flat (4 flats), time signature common time, tempo "Allegretto," "simply," quarter note = 106.

(**DM199**) 7. "Minnie and Mattie and fat little May" (29-32). Key signature F (1 flat), time signature 6/8, tempo "Allegro," "with humor and affection," quarter note = 76.

Note: Pages 4-6, 19-20 incorrectly paginated. Copy examined for high voice.

Location: NN (via Internet Archive).

DM200 "A Christmas Carol" (In the bleak midwinter). Harold Darke, 1911

In the Bleak Mid-Winter. Stainer & Bell's Carols No. 8. Reigate, Surrey: Stainer & Bell.
Note: Plate number St. & B. Ltd. 852.
Location: not seen: copy located at BL.

DM201 Sing-Song (various). Mabel Madison Watson, 1915

Over the bridge to sing song: twenty-eight little piano sketches. London, New York: G. Schirmer.
Note: Includes drawings by Ada Budell.
Location: Not seen; copy located at Free Library of Philadelphia.

DM202–DM227 Sing-Song (various). Walter Alcock et al, 1916

Kookoorookoo and Other Songs. Year book press series of unison and part songs.
London : A & C Black Ltd.
Title page transcription:
THE YEAR BOOK PRESS MUSIC SERIES | KOOKOOROOKOO | AND OTHER SONGS | Words by | CHRISTINA ROSSETTI | Music by | VARIOUS COMPOSERS | A. & C. BLACK LTD | 4, 5 & 6 SOHO SQUARE LONDON W. I

Signed "Christina Rossetti" on first page of each song.

Music: 26 songs, score 4-48. For voice and piano, including sol-fa notation for voice. By various composers; unnumbered, minor keys noted if designated above score:

(**DM202**) 1. "Kookoorookoo! Kookoorookoo!" (4-5). Composer Thomas F. Dunhill. Key signature C (no sharps, flats), time signature 3/4.

(**DM203**) 2. "Brown and Furry" (6-7). Composer C. Hubert H. Parry. Key signature C (no sharps, flats), time signature 2/4, tempo "Dainty."

(**DM204**) 3. "A White Hen Sitting" (8). Composer P. C. Buck. Key signature E flat (3 flats), time signature 2/4, tempo "Comodo." Note at bottom of page "The long words must be interpreted by the grown-up."

(**DM205**) 4. "Growing in the Vale" (9). Composer Alfred J. Silver. Key signature G (1 sharp), time signature 2/4, tempo "Allegretto grazioso."

(**DM206**) 5. "Boats Sail On the Rivers" (10-11). Composer Charles Wood. Key signature "G minor" (2 flats), time signature 6/8, tempo "Moderato."

(**DM207**) 6. "The Summer Nights are Short" (12-13). Composer C. V. Stanford. Key signature E flat (3 flats), time signature 6/8, tempo "Allegretto."

(**DM208**) 7. "Rosy Maiden Winifred" (14). Composer Walter Parratt. Key signature C (no sharps, flats), time signature 3/4, tempo "Allegretto."

(**DM209**) 8. "Fly Away, Fly Away Over The Sea" (15). Composer H. Walford Davies. Key signature G (1 sharp), time signature 3/4.

(**DM210**) 9. "The Peacock" (16-17). Composer C. Hubert H. Parry. Key signature B flat (2 flats), time signature 3/4, tempo "Moderato giocoso."

(**DM211**) 10. "Hope is like a Harebell" (18-19). Composer Sir Frederick Bridge, C. V. O. Key signature E (4 sharps), time signature 3/4, tempo "Lightly and not too fast."

(**DM212**) 11. "A Mother less Soft Lambkin" (20-21). Composer A. C. Mackenzie. Key signature G (1 sharp), time signature common time, tempo "Andantino semplice."

(**DM213**) 12. "I Dug and Dug Amongst The Snow" (22-23). Composer Walter G. Alcock. Key signature

D (2 sharps), time signature common time, tempo "Allegretto scherzando."

(DM214) 13. "The Horses Of The Sea" (24-25). Composer C. V. Stanford. Key signature "A minor" (no sharps, flats), time signature 6/8, tempo "Allegro."

(DM215) 14. "If Hope Grew On A Bush" (26-27). Composer Thomas F. Dunhill. Key signature C (no sharps, flats), time signature 6/8, tempo "Andantino."

(DM216) 15. "What is Pink?" (28-29). Composer Charles Wood. Key signature B flat (2 flats), time signature common time, tempo "Allegro."

(DM217) 16. "Is the Moon Tired?" (30-31). Composer A. C. Mackenzie. Key signature A (3 sharps), time signature 6/8, tempo "Andante moderato."

(DM218) 17. "If a Pig Wore a Wig" (32). Composer Walter Parratt. Key signature F (1 flat), time signature common time, tempo "Giocoso, leggiero."

(DM219) 18. "A Rose Has Thorns as Well as Honey" (33-35). Composer Charles H. Lloyd. Key signature G (1 sharp), time signature 3/4, tempo "Moderato." Note at the bottom of the second page of the score (34) "Here the singers may join hands and dance in a ring."

(DM220) 19. "The Wind Has Such a Rainy Sound" (36-37). Composer C. Hubert H. Parry. Key signature G (1 sharp), time signature common time, tempo "Rather slow."

(DM221) 20. "What Do The Stars Do?" (38-39). Composer Donald Francis Tovey. Key signature A flat (4 flats), time signature 3/4, tempo "Calmly, without dragging, but well sustained."

(DM222) 21. "A Pin Has A Head, But Has No Hair" (40-41). Composer Charles H. Lloyd. Key signature C (no sharps, flats), time signature 6/8, tempo "Not too quickly."

(DM223) 22. "Who Has Seen The Wind?" (42-43). Composer Sir Frederick Bridge, C. V. O. Key signature C (no sharps, flats), time signature 6/8, tempo "Allegro."

(DM224) 23. "Ferry Me Across The Water" (44-45). Composer C. V. Stanford. Key signature F (1 flat), time signature 2/4, tempo "Andante."

(DM225) 24. "Sing Me A Song" (46). Composer Walter Parratt. Key signature D (2 sharps), time signature 2/4, tempo "Vivace." Note at bottom of page "The voice should linger on the last letter in bell."

(DM226) 25. "Mix A Pancake" (47). Composer Charles Wood. Key signature G (1 sharp), time signature common time, tempo "Con moto."

(DM227) 26. "Lullaby" (48). Composer H. Walford Davies. Key signature F (1 flat), time signature 6/8.

Note: The idea for this collection originated with Martin Ackerman, editor of the Year Book Press Music Series. As the "Preface" explains, Ackerman approached "composers who had already shown through their sound work that there are men in England competent to help our children in forming a native musical appreciation based on contemporary English musical thought" (2). The "Contents" page (3) groups the settings by composer, with each composer's signature in facsimile on the right side of the page.
Location: University of Maryland.

DM228–DM235   Sing-Song (seven poems). John Ireland, 1918

Mother and Child: Nursery Rhymes. London: Winthrop Rogers.
(DM228) 1. "Newborn" ("Your brother has a falcon"); **(DM229)** 2. "The Only Child" ("Crying, my little one"); **(DM230)** 3. "Hope" ("I dug and dug amongst the snow"); **(DM231)** 4. "Skylark and Nightingale" ("When a mounting skylark sings"); **(DM232)** 5. "The Blind Boy" ("Blind from my birth"); **(DM233)** 6. "Baby" ("Love me- I love you"); **(DM234)** 7. "Death-Parting" ("Good-bye in fear, good-bye in sorrow"); **(DM235)** 8. "The Garland" ("Roses blushing red and white").

Note: For medium voice. "Newborn" published separately in the same year as "Your Brother has a falcon." Plate number M30 Winthrop Rogers.

Location: not seen: copy located at Royal Academy of Music; "Your brother has a falcon": copy located at BL.

DM236–DM269   Sing-Song (34 poems). Charles Wood et al., 1925

Kikirikee: a sequel to Kookoorookoo. London: A. & C. Black, Ltd; H.F.W. Deane & Sons.

Thirty-four songs by various composers, as follows:

(DM236) 1. "All the bells were ringing," Charles Wood; (DM237) 2. "Margaret has a milking pail," George Dyson; (DM238) 3. "Wee wee husband," C.S. Lang; (DM239) 4. "Pussy has a whiskered face," Hubert S. Middleton; (DM240) 5. "A linnet in a gilded cage," Hilda M. Grieveson; (DM241) 6. "O wind, where have you been?," Emily Daymond; (DM242) 7. "Eight o'clock, the postman's knock," Herbert Howells; (DM243) 8. "A diamond or a coal?," Henry G. Ley; (DM244) 9. "There's snow on the fields," Hilda M. Grieveson; (DM245) 10. "Three plum buns," J.F. Read; (DM246) 11. "When the cows come home," E.L. Bainton; (DM247) 12. "Your brother has a falcon," D. Wauchope Stewart; (DM248) 13. "If a mouse could fly," Thomas F. Dunhill; (DM249) 14. "If all were rain," R.F. Martin Akerman; (DM250) 15. "I know a baby," William H. Harris; (DM251) 16. "An emerald is as green as grass," Charles Wood; (DM252) 17. "Oh fair to see," J.F. Read; (DM253) 18. "Rushes in a watery place," Alan Palmer; (DM254) 19. "If I were a queen," Charles MacPherson; (DM255) 20. "Mother, shake the cherry-tree," Herbert Howells; (DM256) 21. "Love me, I love you," Thomas F. Dunhill; (DM257) 22. "Heat's-ease in my garden bed," Robert T. White; (DM258) 23. "When a mounting skylark sings," Edgar L. Bainton; (DM259) 24. "I am a king," C. S. Lang; (DM260) 25. "If the sun could tell us half," William H. Harris; (DM261) 26. "The days are clear," Herbert Howells; (DM262) 27. "On the grassy banks," Alan Palmer; (DM263) 28. "Hear what the mournful linnets say," Emily Daymond; (DM264) 29. "O wind, why do you never rest?," Martin Akerman; (DM265) 30. "Dancing on the hilltops," C. S. Lang; (DM266) 31. "Twist me a crown of wind-flowers," Basil Harwood; (DM267) 32. "Hopping frog," Charles MacPherson; (DM268) 33. "Lie a-bed, sleepy head" Charles Wood; (DM269) 34. "Angels at the foot," Charles Wood.

Locations: not seen: Black: copy located at National Library of New Zealand; Deane: copy located at UkCM.

DM270   "Goblin Market." Ruth Gipps, 1954

Title page transcription:

RUTH GIPPS | GOBLIN MARKET | CANTATA FOR TWO SOPRANO SOLOISTS | S.S.A CHORUS AND STRING ORCHESTRA | (OR PIANO) | Words by | CHRISTINA ROSSETTI | 6S 6D | (1951) | NOVELLO | AND COMPANY LIMITED | 160 WARDOUR STREET | LONDON W1

Music: score 1-78. Arranged as a continuous performance, without divisions into separate numbers. Initial key signature C (no sharps or flats), time signature 5/8. Note text on [6]: 'TIME OF PERFORMANCE ABOUT 30 MINUTES | FULL SCORE AND STRING PARTS ARE AVAILABLE ON HIRE' Plate number 18023.

Note: The price and date on the title page of copy examined are covered by a small sticker, with "NOVELLO & COMPANY, LIMITED" printed on it and a new price, "7/=" written by hand in blue ink. Signed "Christina Rossetti" above score. At bottom of first page of score, "Copyright, 1954, by Novello & Company, Limited." Words as text on unpaginated leaves [2]-[5], beginning on verso of title.

Location: IU.

DM271   "Goblin Market." Polly Pen and Peggy Harmon, 1987

New York: Dramatists Play Service.

Location: not seen: copy located at Sam Houston State University.

DM272   **"Goblin Market." Aaron Jay Kernis, 1995**

New York: Associated Music Publishers.

Note: Sinfonietta for solo narrator and large ensemble. Commissioned by the Birmingham Contemporary Music Group.

Location: not seen: copy located at DLC.

MISATTRIBUTIONS

DM273   **Misattribution. Jacques Blumenthal, 1899**

"When the grass." *In memoriam: book of ten songs.* Op. 102. London: Boosey & Co. Plate number H 2258

Note: The words to "When the Grass" are attributed to CGR in the table of contents and above the score, with the notation "By kind permission of Messrs. Macmillan & Co." The poem, "When The Grass Shall Cover Me," is actually by the American poet Ina Donna Coolbrith. Apparently the mistake was not noticed even by the London *Times*, which reported a performance by Blanche Marchesi of "A plaintive setting by Blumenthal of Christina Rossetti's poem, beginning "When the grass shall cover me" (28 March 1900: 6).

Location: National Library of New Zealand.

E: TRANSLATIONS, PRINTED EPHEMERA, AND ROSSETTIANA

This section is numbered consecutively but divided into the following subsections: translations; printed ephemera; and other Rossettiana, including memorials, plaques, and commercially produced items incorporating text by Rossetti.

Some printed material could be variously (and multiply) classified. For the purposes of this bibliography, printed ephemera includes materials not authorized by Rossetti that were not intended to be kept.

~

TRANSLATIONS

See also C12-13; DM11, DM37, DM38, DM105, DM106, DM110, DM111, DM115, DM118, DM123, DM132, DM174.

TRANSLATIONS BY CHRISTINA ROSSETTI

E1 *Memoirs and correspondence of Mallet du Pan illustrative of the history of the French Revolution.* Collected and arranged by A. Sayous. 2 Volumes. London: Richard Bentley, New Burlington Street, 1852.

Note: According to WMR, all of the Rossetti siblings, including CGR, assisted Benjamin Paul in translating this work (Bell, 33; see also WMR's comments in *Dante Gabriel Rossetti: His Family Letters* 2: 87; and *Some Reminiscences*, 168).
Location: not seen: copy located at University of Nebraska, Lincoln.

E2 *Il Nuovo Testamento* ("Diodati's Italian New Testament"). 1858.

Note: WMR told Bell that near, or before, her work on *The Terra-Cotta Architecture of North Italy*, CGR "revised an edition (may have been [that of the] S. P. C. K. [. . .] of Diodati's Italian New Testament, in very small print" (Bell, 36).

Rossetti's cousin, Teodorico Pietrocola Rossetti, worked on the Society's 1855 edition of Diodati's translation of the Bible (*La Sacra Bibbia, contenente l'Antico ed il Nuovo Testamento, secondo la traduzione di Giovanni Diodati*, Londra: Gilbert e Rivington, Stampatori, 1850; also Londra : Bagster e Figliuoli, Stampatori, 1855; see Darlow and Moule, 5641 and 5647). The Italian New Testament based on the 1850 and 1855 translation was published in 1858 (*Il Nuovo Testamento del nostro Signore Gesu Cristo*, Cambridge: Alla Stamperia dell'Universita per C.J. Clay, 1858); according to Darlow and Moule, "A similar edition in smaller size was issued by the S. P. C. K. in the same year" (828). Presumably CGR was involved in the latter work.
Location: University of Lausanne (via Google books); copy also located at Cambridge University.

E3 *The Terra-Cotta Architecture of North Italy, (XIIth-XVth centuries), pourtrayed as examples for imitation in other countries, from careful drawings and restorations by Federigo Lose.* London: John Murray, 1867.

Note: CGR translated from Italian, and received payment for the work in 1867 (*RP* 214, 229).
Location: University of Colorado at Boulder.

E4   "Ninna-Nanna."

Note: Both CGR and Teodorico Rossetti translated but did not publish some of CGR's poems from *Sing-Song* (*Letters* 2: 183-185, 186, 195). WMR included CGR's translations in *New Poems* (A26). Some translations from *Sing-Song*, preserved in a commonplace book owned by Dora Browning Dick, may be by Teodorico Rossetti.

Location: Not seen; commonplace book, NjP.

TRANSLATIONS OF CHRISTINA ROSSETTI'S WORK THROUGH 1900

E5   *Il Mercato de' Folletti* (Goblin Market). Trans. T. P. Rossetti. Firenze: 1867.

Note: Teodorico Rossetti also translated *Alice in Wonderland* in 1872.

Location: not seen: copy located in BL.

E6   Latin translation of "Bitter for Sweet." by "G." *College Rhymes* (Oxford, Cambridge): 4 (1863): 131. Signed "Christina Rossetti." See C35.

E7   Latin translation of "Bitter for Sweet." "Exercise XXVIII." *Key to Progressive Exercises in Latin Elegiac Verse*. Trans. C. G. Gepp. London, Oxford and Cambridge: Rivingtons, 1871.

Note: Companion volume to Gepp's *Progressive Exercises in Latin Elegiac Verse* (B31). Gepp may be the "G" who had previously translated this poem, but the two translations are not identical. Reprinted in 1879 and in a revised edition, 1887.

Location: 1871: Bodleian Library, Oxford (via Google books). 1879, 1887: not seen: Bodleian Library, Oxford.

E8   *Poeti Inglesi e Tedeschi, Moderni o comtemporanei*. Trans. Luigi Gamberale. Firenze, Tipographia de G. Barbera. 1881.

Note: Contains "Ricordo" ("Remember"), "Maggio" ("May", first line "I cannot tell you how it was"), "Sulla collina" ("Up-Hill"), "Miraggio" ("Mirage"), 227-231. Also contains poems by DGR. Gamberale's translations of "May" and "Up-Hill" were reprinted in Florilegio Lirico, edited by Angelo de Gubernatis (Milano: Ulrico Hoepli, 1883).

Location: not seen: CtY (photocopy); Gubernatis: NjP (via Google books).

PRINTED EPHEMERA

See also **A1**, "To My Mother on the Anniversary of her Birth"; **A6**, "Consider"; **A19**, "Roses and Roses."

E9   Morse, Anne G. *Christmas Offerings*. Louis Prang Prize Christmas Card.

Card, printed by chromolithography on both sides (127 x 190).

Front: Within an ornamental border in gilt with an ornamental band of blue, red and lavender hearts and green leaves, a rectangular vignette, printed in various colors, of four kneeling children holding holly and mistletoe, with six doves. To the right of the vignette is a branch of holly. To the left of the vignette, the first stanza of "A Christmas Carol" ("In the bleak mid-winter") is printed in gold and red; beneath the vignette, the fifth stanza is printed, also in gold and red, and signed 'Christina G. Rossetti."

Back: In green ink, in upper left, within decorative compartments, "Prang's American 4th Prize Christmas Card by Anne G. Morse" and prize amount "$200"; at the bottom right, "Judges in the competition of 1880" and facsimile signatures of "Saml Coleman," "R. M. Hunt" and "E.C. Moore." In lower left corner, "Copyright 1880 by L. Prang & Co Boston."

Note: In late spring 1880, the Louis Prang company offered a total of $2000 in an open competition for Christmas card designs. The first through fourth place winners received cash awards and publication of their designs by Prang. Sample sets of the four winning card designs were advertised to be available in October 1880 (*Publishers' Weekly*, 25 September 1880: 415).

In 1885, the Boston Terra Cotta Company designed a "handsome and unique mantlepiece" based on the children and doves in Morse's card design ("Art Notes," *New York Times*, 5 July 1885: 4).
Location: Ives.

E10   *Children From The Poets*. London, Raphael Tuck, 1893.

Note: Includes first six lines of "Johnny" with an illustration of a child and a dog. Described in *Publishers' Weekly* as "a series of twelve highly artistic plates representing children of the poets, after original paintings by Ellen Welby, with interleaves containing appropriate quotations and pen-and-ink sketches by J. Pauline Sunter. This set is in a cloth portfolio, with gold stamping, and tied with ribbon" (30 September 1893: 407).
Location: not seen: Bodleian Library, Oxford.

E11   World's Woman's Christian Temperance Union. *Our Portrait Album*. London: World's Woman's Christian Temperance Union British Head-quarters, nd [circa 1893].

Note: Pamphlet, advertised as "a dainty and most artistically arranged "Portrait Album," containing photographs and brief biographies of some of the most notable women on each side of the Atlantic" (the *Woman's Herald*, 28 January 1893: ii). Contains photograph of CGR ("From a Copyright Photography by Elliott and Fry, Baker Street, W.") and a one-page biography of CGR (not paginated).
Location: DLC.

E12   Leaflet distributed at memorial service, January , 1895, Christ Church, Woburn Square.

Printed in blue ink on one side of folded sheet (165 x 208).

Contents:
Left page opening, headed 'CHRIST CHURCH, WOBURN SQUARE | [short rule] | HYMNS | TO BE SUNG IN THE MORNING SERVICE, ON THE | Festival of the Epiphany, | (Sunday, January 6th, 1895.)' with stanzas 2-5 of "Advent" ("This Advent moon shines cold and clear"), untitled, but identified as "Hymn by the late Christina G. Rossetti."

Right page opening, headed 'MEMORIAL SERMON, | For the late Christina Georgina Rossetti,| BY THE | REV. J. J. GLENDENNING NASH, M.A.,' and including 'HYMN AFTER THE SERMON, | *by the late Christina G. Rossetti. | to Music composed by Frank T. Lowden, Organist | of Christ Church, Woburn Square.*' Followed by "And now why tarriest thou?"

Note: Nash's sermon was published as *A memorial sermon preached at Christ Church, Woburn Square on the festival of the Epiphany, 1895 for the late Christina Rossetti* (London: Skeffington and Son, 1895).
Location: Ives.

E13   Leaflet, *In memory of Christina G. Rossetti: Pierce Hall, January 10, 1895*. No publisher.
Note: Leaflet from a memorial service in Boston.
Location: not seen: NjP.

E14   *Vitae Aeterna: In Memoriam Christinae G. Rossetti*.
Note: Separate publication of poem by John Walker, published (under pseudonym Rowland Thirlmere) in the *Manchester Quarterly* 15 (January 1897): 39-45.
Location: not seen: NjP.

E15 Leaflet, *Dedication of the memorial to the late Christina Georgina Rossetti, on All Saints' Day, November 1st, by the Lord Bishop of Durham*. No publisher. 4 pages.
Location: not seen: NjP.

E16 *A Lesson from the Flowers*. International Art Publishing Company, Ltd., no date (late 1800s – early 1900s). No. 2318.
Note: CGR's name misspelled as "Christine Rossetti" on the front wrapper. Contains text of "Consider The Lilies Of The Field." An illustrated booklet with die-cut edges (perforated on the front and back wrapper), and bound by a pink ribbon. Undated; the International Art Publishing Company was founded in 1895 (*Publishers' Weekly*, 28 December 1895: 1245).
Location: Ives.

E17 *Snowflakes and Holly Wreaths*. New York, Berlin: International Art Publishing Company, no date. No. 6670.
Note: Illustrated booklet. Includes text of "Christmastide."
Location: not seen: RPB.

E18 "A Bright and Happy Christmas to You." Divided back postcard. London: Ernest Nister; New York: E. P. Dutton, no date (circa 1907-1915).
Contents:
Front: Printed in black, red, blue, and gilt; text in black, except ornamented capitals in red, blue, and/or gilt, "Start and Goal" in gilt, and the word "Love" printed in red throughout; text decorated by ornamented rules in blue, red and gilt. Headings 'A Bright and Happy Christmas to you. | Start and Goal.' above poem "What is the Beginning ? Love. What the course? Love still."
Back: Printed in green ink, 'POST CARD.' centered at top, above short double horizontal lines and double vertical dividing lines; at left, printed vertically at edge, 'Ernest Nister, London. No. 1253. E. P Dutton & Cº. New York. | PRINTED IN BAVARIA.'; at right, blank rectangle for stamp in upper corner; text 'THE ADDRESS ONLY TO BE | WRITTEN HERE.'
Note: Postcard, printed by chromolithography on both sides, 89 x 140.
Location: Ives.

E19 "Spring Bursts Today." Divided back postcard. No publisher, date (circa 1907-1915).
Contents:
Front: Printed in multiple colors; at top, rural scene of road leading to horizon; at either side, a stalk of lilies; in center, text printed in red and green, lines 1-2 of "An Easter Carol" signed "Christina Rossetti."
Back: Printed in black ink; "Post Card" centered at top, above vertical dividing line; at left, 'THIS SIDE FOR CORRESPONDENCE'; at right, 'THE ADDRESS TO BE WRITTEN/ ON THIS SIDE' and rectangle with text 'PLACE STAMP | HERE. | UNITED STATES | AND CANADA | ONE CENT. | FOREIGN | TWO CENTS'
Note: Postcard, printed by chromolithography on both sides, 85 x 137. Number '7213' appears on front of card.
Location: Ives.

E20 Patricia Andrle, Halloween cross stitch pattern, "Goblin Market" (1990).
Note: Folded card stock sheet with cross stitch chart, published by Counted Illuminations (no place or date). On one side of the sheet is the cross stitch chart with instructions. The other side of the folded sheet includes the front and back covers.

The front cover features a photograph of the framed, completed cross stitch design of a goblin behind a fruit stand and lines 42-45 of "Goblin Market" ("We must not look at goblin men, [...] Their hungry, thirsty roots"), signed "C. G. Rossetti"; the background of the design includes a spider in a web and outlines of goblins. The designer's name, "P. Andrle," appears on a box beneath the fruit stand, and the date "1990" is incorporated in the lower right corner of the border design.

The back cover includes a brief biography of Rossetti and a summary of "Goblin Market."

Copyright Registration Number / Date: VA0000488715 / 1991-10-28.

Location: Ives.

E21 "Christina Rossetti (1830-1894)." Postcards.

"Christina Rossetti (1830-1894)." London : National Portrait Gallery, 1994. Printed by the Beacon Press.

Note: Consists of a folded sheet with eight pages of text and images, including "Christina Rossetti: An Introduction" by Frances Thomas, and contextual information about the eight postcard images by Peter Funnell. The postcards include reproductions of a pencil drawing of CGR by DGR, circa 1850; two paintings by DGR for which CGR modeled ("The Girlhood of Mary Virgin" and "Ecce Ancilla Domini"); the frontispiece to *Goblin Market and Other Poems*; an 1865 caricature, "Christina Rossetti in a Tantrum," by DGR; one of Lewis Carroll's photographs of the Rossetti family; a 1877 chalk drawing of CGR by DGR; and the Edward Burne-Jones memorial panels (see E22).

Location: not seen: Courtauld Institute of Art Library; information courtesy of Erica Foden-Lenahan.

ROSSETTIANA

MEMORIALS AND PLAQUES

E22 Reredos and memorial, Christ Church, Woburn Square.

Note: Dedicated on All Saints Day, 1898, by B. F. Westcott, Bishop of Durham.

Subscriptions for the memorial, organized by Glendenning Nash, were solicited via letters published in various periodicals in Britain and the United States beginning in May 1896 (the *Critic*, 16 May 1896: 357; the *Nation*, 21 May 1896: 394; the *Academy* 27 June 1896: 534).

The memorial consisted of a reredos with five painted panels depicting Christ and the four evangelists. The panels were designed by Edward Burne-Jones and executed by Burne-Jones's assistant T. M. Rooke. An inscription carved in a marble slab beneath the reredos included the opening line of "The Lowest Place" ("Give me the lowest place"). The church was demolished in the 1960s, but the painted panels survived to be displayed in CGR exhibition in National Portrait Gallery in 1995 and are now in the Parish Room of All Saints, Margaret Street, London, W1W 8JG.

The original memorial is described in some detail, with two photographs, in the *Magazine of Art* (22: 1899, 88-90), and also mentioned in *An Appreciation of the Late Christina Georgina Rossetti*, which features a photograph of the reredos as the frontispiece.

Christ Church was also home to two other Rossetti items: "a silver communion service set with the names of Mrs. Rossetti, the Misses Polidori, and Christina" (Thomas, 119), and a jeweled cross, which Eliza Polidori had received from the Sultan of Turkey in recognition of her work as a nurse in the Crimea. The fate of the communion service is unknown; the cross was stolen in 1901. A description of the cross, and a report of its theft, appear in a note by "N. S. S." in *Notes and Queries* (2 November 1901: 361).

E23 Plaque, 30 Torrington Square.

Contents:

Text "ROSSETTI, Christina Georgina (1830-1894), Poetess, lived and died here."

Note: A bronze plaque erected by the Duke of Bedford at Rossetti's former home.

E24 Plaque, Brunswick Villa, Fromefield, Frome.
Contents:
Text "Christina Georgina | Rossetti (1830-1894) | Poet and pre-Rapahelite model, | ran a school in this building | from April 1853 until March 1854 | when the Rossetti family returned | to London. | ERECTED BY FROME SOCIETY FOR LOCAL STUDY A.D. 2000'.
Note: Round green plaque with white text, erected by The Frome Society for Local Study.

OTHER ROSSETTIANA

E25 Halcyon Days Enamel Box, "A Christmas Carol" (1974).

Note: Small, oval enamel box manufactured by Bilston & Battersea for Halcyon Days Enamels. On exterior (including lid), winter scenes in black on white background. Inside lid, musical staves and text "Gustav Holst 1874-1934"; within box, first four lines of "A Christmas Carol" ("In the bleak midwinter").

Produced in 1974, in a limited edition of 250, to mark the centenary of Holst's birth. The artist was Moira Hodell.
Location: not seen; description from Ebay auction listing; production details courtesy of Jan Duff, researcher at Halcyon Days Enamels.

E26 Hallmark Betsey Clark ornament, "Christmastide" (1980).

Note: Round blue plastic disc with silver metal edge. Both sides of the disc feature an embossed wreath border of holly with a bow at the top, and four embossed stars scattered within the wreath. In the center of one side of the disc is a Wedgewood-style, raised white plastic image of a cherub kneeling in prayer. The wreath design on this side also features a scroll at the bottom, upon which 'CHRISTMAS 1980' is printed in white ink. In the center of the other side of the disc is printed 'LOVE CAME DOWN | AT CHRISTMAS, | LOVE ALL LOVELY, LOVE DIVINE; | LOVE WAS BORN AT CHRISTMAS, | STAR AND ANGELS | GAVE THS SIGN. | C ROSSETTI'; beneath this text is embossed ' [copyright] 1979 Hallmark Cards'.

In rectangular clear plastic packaging with paper inserts to hold the ornament. Text printed on top insert: (on top) "Tree-Trimmer Collection" and (on front) "Hallmark Cameo Keepsake Ornament". Text printed on bottom insert: (on front) "Betsey Clark" First in a series" (on bottom) "Tree-Trimmer Collection" and (on back): [copyright symbol] 2980 Hallmark Cards, Inc., K. C., Mo. 64141 Made in U.S.A. QX307-4."
Location: Ives.

E27 "The Poetry of Love" series collectable plate, "Monna Innominata" (1882).

Note: Porcelain collector's plate manufactured in 1982 by the Franklin Mint; artwork by John Speirs. Front of plate features decorative blue border with yellow and pink flowers, and central image of a social gathering, with a woman and a man seated at a piano, and with text from "Monna Innominata," sonnet 2 (lines 1-2, "I wish I could remember that first day, / First hour, first moment of your meeting me").
Location: not seen; description from Ebay auction and retail listings.

E28 Celestial Seasonings Tea Canister, "Another Spring" (1986, 1989).

Notes: Metal box with removable lid, 75 (height with lid) x 122 x 98. Enamel on gold colored metal (interior, bottom, edges of lid and bottom), with metal showing through to form dotted background and other design elements. Background very pale violet (Centroid 213), with text and images in deep yellowish green (Centroid 132) and other colors on the lid and sides. The lid includes an image of a girl and boy gathering berries and the text "Celestial Seasonings Herb Teas Wild Forest Blackberry." The four sides of the tin each feature a rectangular compartment; three compartments contain images (of trees, small animals, and berry gathering); the remaining compartment includes an oval medallion with an image of a robin, and lines 20-24 of "Another Spring" ("If I might see another Spring" through "Be glad today and sing"). Copyright information appears beneath the Rossetti lines: "@ 1989 Celestial Seasonings, Inc., 4600 Sleepytime Drive, Boulder, CO 80301-3292 U.S.A."

Artwork registered in the U. S. Copyright office in 1986 and 1989 (Registration number VA-381-266).

Location: Ives.

E29   Boyds Yesterday's Child figurine, "A Birthday" (1996-2000).

Note: Cast resin figurine of a girl with a birthday cake and teddy bear, manufactured by The Boyds Collection, style #3509, "Rebecca with Elliot ... Birthday!" No. 2 of the Celebration Series within the Dollstone Series; produced from 1996 through 2000 (Phillips 233, 321).

On the bottom of the figurine, text from "A Birthday": "The birthday of my life has come, my love has come to me."

Boyds also issued a "Rebecca with Elliot" doll in 2000-2001 (number 4927); I am unable to determine if a Rossetti quotation was included with it.

Location: not seen; details from Ebay auction and retail listings.

E30   Boyds Bearstone figurine, "Goblin Market" (2006-).

Note: Cast resin figurine of two bears playing checkers, manufactured by The Boyds Collection, style #2277983, "Ava & Rae Ann...Rainy Afternoon." Introduced in 2006 in the Bearstone collection; still in production.

On the bottom of the figurine, text from "Goblin Market": "There is no friend like a sister," signed "Christina Rossetti."

Location: not seen, description from Ebay auction and retail listings.

E31   Seraphim Classics Angel figurine, "Spring" (1999-2002).

Note: Cast resin angel figurine manufactured by Roman, No. 81517, "April–Spring's Blossom." Designed by Gaylord Ho for Roman's Seraphim Angels series, Four Seasons Collection. Introduced 1999, retired 2002.

Includes quotation from "Spring" (lines 19-20, "There is no time like Spring, | When life's alive in every thing") signed "Christina Rossetti."

Location: not seen, description from retail listing.

E32   Boyd's Faerie Frost Collection, "Who has seen the wind" (2003).

Note: Cold cast resin figurine manufactured by The Boyds Collection, No. 36025, "Freesia Faeriechill... First Frost." Winged female figure seated on tree stump. Introduced October 2003, 6000 produced.

Includes second stanza of "Who has seen the wind," signed "Christina Rossetti."

Location: not seen; description from retail listing.

E33   Halcyon Days Enamel Box, "A Birthday" (2004-2006).

Note: Small, heart-shaped enamel box manufactured by Halcyon Days Enamels. On lid, bird on rose branch, within border composed of ribbon and bow. Inside lid, quotation from "A Birthday" ("My heart is like a singing bird"), signed "Christina Rossetti." Rose and foliage design on outside of box.

The box was introduced in 2004 and remained in production for two years.

Location: not seen; description from auction listing; production details courtesy of Jan Duff, researcher at Halcyon Days Enamels.

E34   Mary Englebreit Christmas tea box, "Christmastide" (2004).

Note: Tea in decorative box, manufactured by Brownlow Gifts Inc. Produced in 2004 as part of a collection called "A Mary Little Christmas" designed by artist Mary Engelbreit. The box, printed in red, green, brown, white, and yellow, includes an image of a teapot and the text "Mary Engelbreit: A Mary Little Christmas Tea Gourmet Snowberry Blend"; the first stanza of "Christmastide" (retitled "Love Came Down") is printed on one side of the box.
Location: not seen; design and production information courtesy of Tammy Zook, Executive Sales Manager at Brownlow Gifts.

E35   Halcyon Days Enamel Box, "Goblin Market" (2005).

Note: In 2005, Halcyon Days produced a square box designed by Patricia Chitolie incorporating text from "Goblin Market," "For there is no friend like a sister."
Location: not seen; information courtesy of Jan Duff, researcher at Halcyon Days Enamels.

E36   TreeFeathers miniature book, *The Prince's Progress*.

Note: A blank miniature (1:12 scale) book for dollhouses and collectors, produced by TreeFeathers Miniatures. The binding reproduces that of *The Prince's Progress and Other Poems*.
Location: Ives.

E37   DLTK's Crafts for Kids, Holiday Activities, "To My Mother"; "Sonnets are full of love, and this my tome."

Note: "Poem poster/coloring pages" at the DLTK Crafts for Kids website. Two Rossetti poems, as follows:

1) "To My Mother": CGR's poem, signed "Christina Rossetti," and illustration of a hyacinth and foliage. Users can select a black and white template to color themselves, or can print the poem and illustration in color (purple text and flower with green foliage).
Location: http://www.dltk-holidays.com/mom/songs/mrossetti-tomymother.htm.

2) "Sonnets are full of love, and this my tome": CGR's poem, signed "Christina Rossetti," above a row of flowers. Users can select a black and white template to color themselves, or can print the poem and illustration in color (text in light and dark blue, floral design in light blue, pink and yellow).
Location: http://www.dltk-holidays.com/mom/songs/mrossetti-sonnets.htm.

E38   Halcyon Days Enamel Medallion, "A Christmas Carol" (2009).

Note: An oval medallion of yellow metal, 2 1/8 inches high, manufactured in 2009. At the top of the medallion is a bail through which a chain can be inserted. The front of the medallion features an enameled oval, bezel set. The enamel's design is of a rural landscape; in the foreground, a man, woman and dog walk through the snow; in the background is a cottage (to the left) and the steeple of a church (to the right, behind a wooden fence). At the center top of the enamel are lines 1-4 of "A Christmas Carol" ("In the bleak mid-winter"); Rossetti's name does not appear. The year '2009' is engraved on the back of the medallion. Limited edition of 365. According to the Halcyon Days website, the medallion's price was £95.
Location: not seen; information from the Halcyon Days website, www.halcyondaysonline.com.

WORKS CITED

MANUSCRIPTS AND ARCHIVES

Specific materials from library collections are identified in the text.

Angeli-Dennis Collection, The Library of the University of British Columbia, Special Collections Division.

Christina Georgina Rossetti Collection, Special Collections Department, Bryn Mawr College Library.

Janet Camp Troxell Collection of Rossetti Manuscripts, Department of Rare Books and Special Collections, Princeton University Library.

Macmillan Archives, Basingstoke, England.

Mark Samuels Lasner Collection, Special Collections, University of Delaware Library.

PUBLISHED SOURCES

APS (American Periodical Series) Online. Full text database. ProQuest/Chadwyck-Healey. www.proquest.com.

Arseneau, Mary. *Recovering Christina Rossetti: Female Community and Incarnational Poetics.* Basingstoke: Palgrave Macmillan, 2004.

Arseneau, Mary, and Jan Marsh. "Intertextuality and Intratextuality: the Full Text of Christina Rossetti's Harmony on First Corinthians XIII Rediscovered." *Victorian Newsletter* 88 (1995): 17-26.

Baker, William. "Christina Rossetti: An Unpublished Letter and an Unrecorded Copy of Verses." *Notes and Queries* (June 2010): 221-223.

Banister, Henry C. *George Alexander Macfarren: His Life, Works and Influence.* London: George Bell and Sons, 1891.

Battiscombe, Georgina. *Christina Rossetti: A Divided Life.* New York: Holt, Rinehart and Winston, 1981.

Bell, Mackenzie. *Christina Rossetti: A Biographical and Critical Study.* Boston: Roberts Brothers, 1898.

Bishop, Philip R. *Thomas Bird Mosher, Pirate Prince of Publishers.* New Castle and London: Oak Knoll Books and The British Library, 1998.

Bowers, Fredson. *Principles of Bibliographical Description.* 1949. Winchester, UK: St. Paul's Bibliographies, 1986.

Brooks, Tim. *Lost Sounds: Blacks and the Birth of the Recording Industry, 1890-1919.* Chicago: University of Illinois Press, 2005.

C19: The Nineteenth Century Index. Database. ProQuest/Chadwyck-Healey. http://c19index.chadwyck.com/home.do.

Carman, W Judith E.; William K. Gaeddert, Rita M. Resch, and Gordon Myers. *Art song in the United States, 1759-1999* Third edition. Lanham, MD: Scarecrow Press, 2001.

Carter, John. *Binding Variants with More Binding Variants.* New Castle, DE: Oak Knoll Books, 1989.

Cassell's History of the War Between France and Germany. 2 Vols. London: Cassell and Company Limited, 1894.

Colbeck, Norman, comp. *A Bookman's Catalogue: The Norman Colbeck Collection of Nineteenth-Century and Edwardian Poetry and Belles Lettres in the Special Collections of the University of British Columbia.* Vancouver: University of British Columbia Press, 1987.

Crump, R. W., ed. *The Complete Poems of Christina Rossetti.* 3 vols. Baton Rouge: Louisiana State University Press, 1979-90.

D'Amico, Diane. "Christina Rossetti and *The English Woman's Journal*," *Journal of Pre-Raphaelite Studies* n. s. 3 (Spring 1994): 20-24.

Darlow, T. H., and H. R. Moule. *Historical Catalogue of the Printed Editions of Holy Scriptures in the Library of The British and Foreign Bible Society.* Vol.2, Polyglots and Languages Other Than English. 1903. Rpt. New York: Kraus Reprint, 1963.

Dictionary of British Portraiture. Vol. 3. New York: Oxford University Press, 1981.

Early British Periodicals. Microfilm. Ann Arbor, MI: University Microfilms, 1972–1979.

English Catalogue of Books. London: Sampson Low, 1878–1898.

English Literary Periodical Series. Microfilm. Ann Arbor, MI : University Microfilms, 1951–1976.

"E. P. Dutton & Co's List of New Holiday Books." *New York Times* 8 December 1891: 5.

Evans, Clifford. "A Botanist Who Painted: Emily Stackhouse." *A Passion for Nature.* Ed. Deirdre Dare and Melissa Hardie. Cornwall: Hypatia Press, 2008. 173-185.

Focus on English Literature. Microfilm. Ann Arbor, MI: Xerox University Microfilms, 1974.

Fredeman, William. *Pre-Raphaelitism: A Bibliocritical Study.* Cambridge: Harvard UP, 1965.

Genz, Marcella. *A History of the Eragny Press, 1894–1914.* New Castle and London: Oak Knoll Press and The British Library, 2004.

The Gerritsen Collection: Women's History Online, 1543–1945. Full text database. ProQuest/Chadwyck-Healey. http://gerritsen.chadwyck.com.

Gooch, Bryan N. S and David S. Thatcher. *Musical Settings of Early and Mid Victorian Literature: A Catalogue.* New York: Garland, 1979.

Google Books. www.google.com/books.

Gosse, Edmund. "Christina Rossetti." *Century Illustrated Monthly Magazine* 46 (June 1893): 211-217.

—. *The Life of Algernon Charles Swinburne.* London: Macmillan, 1917.

Hardie-Budden, Melissa. 'Stackhouse, Emily (1811–1870).' *Oxford Dictionary of National Biography*, online ed. Oxford University Press, May 2009. http://www.oxforddnb.com/view/article/98100, accessed 19 Nov 2009.

Harpweek. Full text database. Alexander Street Press. http://alexanderstreet.com.

Internet Archive. Brewster Kahle, Director and Co-Founder. www.archive.org.

Ives, Maura. "'The Din of Controversy': Christina Rossetti, Priscilla Lydia Sellon, and the Sisterhood Debate in Maude." *Journal of Pre-Raphaelite Studies* 17 n.s., Spring 2008: 73-94.)

—. "The Letters of Christina Rossetti: Two New Letters." *Journal of Pre-Raphaelite Studies* 15 (Spring 2006): 19-26.

—. "Teaching Women's Art in America: Alice Donlevy's Designs for Christina Rossetti's Consider." *Textual Cultures* 4.1 (Spring 2009): 26-54.

—. "A Stop-Press Correction in Christina Rossetti's *Goblin Market*." *PBSA* (Papers of the Bibliographical Society of America) 94 (2000): 35-48.

Jones, Kathleen. *Learning Not to be First: The Life of Christina Rossetti*. Oxford: Oxford University Press, 1981.

Kent, David A., ed. *The Achievement of Christina Rossetti*. Ithaca: Cornell University Press, 1987.

Kooistra, Lorraine Jantzen. *Christina Rossetti and Illustration*. Athens: Ohio University Press, 2002.

Kramer, Sidney. *A History of Stone & Kimball and Herbert S. Stone & Co: with a Bibliography of their Publications, 1893-1905*. Chicago: Norman W. Forgue, 1940.

Lasner, Mark Samuels. "Christina Rossetti's 'Common Looking Booklet': A New Letter About Her Verses of 1847," *Notes and Queries* (October 1981): 420-421.

Letter Books, 1854-1940. R. & R. Clark. Macmillan Archives. Microfilm. Part 2: Publishing Records. Cambridge: Chadwyck-Healey, 1982. Reel 27.

Library of Congress. Music for the Nation: American Sheet Music. Digital archive. http://memory.loc.gov/ammem/mussmhtml/mussmhome.html.

Library of Congress. Performing Arts Encylopedia. Digital archive. http://www.loc.gov/performingarts.

Macmillan, George, ed. *Letters of Alexander Macmillan*. Glasgow: privately printed, 1908.

Making of America at Cornell University Library. Digital archive. http://digital.library.cornell.edu/m/moa.

Making of America at University of Michigan. Digital archive. http://quod.lib.umich.edu/m/moagrp.

Marsh, Jan. *Christina Rossetti: A Writer's Life*. New York: Viking Penguin, 1995.

Maser, Mary Louise Jarden and Frederick E. *Christina Rossetti in the Maser Collection*. Bryn Mawr: Bryn Mawr College Library, 1991.

Nowell-Smith, Simon, ed. *Letters to Macmillan*. London: Macmillan; New York, St. Martin's Press, 1967.

"Our American Letter." *Athenaeum*, No. 2240 (1 October 1870): 430.

Packer, Lona Mosk. *Christina Rossetti*. Berkeley: University of California Press, 1963.

—. "Christina Rossetti's "Songs in a Cornfield": A Misprint Uncorrected," *Notes and Queries* n.s. 9 (March 1962): 97-100.

Peattie, Roger W. "William Michael Rossetti and the Making of Christina Rossetti's Reputation." *Haunted Texts: Studies in Pre-Raphaelitism in Honour of William E. Fredeman*. Ed. David Latham. Toronto: University of Toronto Press, 2003.

ProQuest Historical Newspapers. Full text database. http://www.proquest.com.

Phillips, Beth. *Boyds Tracker Resin*, 2. Braintree, MA: Bangzoom Publishers, 2004.

Reid, Forrest. *Illustrators of the Eighteen Sixties*. Originally published as Illustrators of the Sixties (London: Faber & Gwyer, 1928). Rpt. New York: Dover, 1975.

Roberts Brothers advertisement, *New York Times* (10 July1866): 5.

Rossetti Archive. Ed. Jerome McGann et al. www.rossettiarchive.org.

Rossetti, Christina Georgina. *The Family Letters of Christina Georgina Rossetti*. Ed. William Michael Rossetti. London: Brown, Langham, 1908.

—. *The Letters of Christina Rossetti*. 4 vols. Ed. Antony Harrison. Charlottesville: University Press of Virginia, 1997-2004.

—. *The Poetical Works of Christina Rossetti*. Ed. William Michael Rossetti. London: Macmillan, 1904.

—. *Selected Prose of Christina Rossetti*. Ed. David A. Kent and P. G. Stanwood. New York: St. Martin's, 1998.

Rossetti, Dante Gabriel. *The Correspondence of Dante Gabriel Rossetti*. 3 vols. to date. Ed.William E. Fredeman. Cambridge: D. S. Brewer, 2002-.

Rossetti, William Michael. *Dante Gabriel Rossetti: His Family Letters*. 2 vols. London: Ellis and Elvey, 1895.

—. *The Diary of W. M. Rossetti 1870-1873*. Ed. Odette Bornand. Oxford: Clarendon, 1977.

—. Diary (unpublished). Angeli-Dennis Collection, University of British Columbia.

—. *Rossetti Papers 1862 to 1870*. New York: Charles Scribner's Sons, 1903.

—. *Selected Letters of William Michael Rossetti*. Ed. Roger W. Peattie. University Park: Penn State University Press, 1990.

—. *Some Reminiscences of William Michael Rossetti*. 2 vols. New York: Charles Scribner's Sons, 1906.

Smith, Timothy L. *Revivalism and Social Reform: American Protestantism on the eve of the Civil War*. 1957. Baltimore: Johns Hopkins University Press, 1980.

Surtees, Virginia. *The Paintings and Drawings of Dante Gabriel Rossetti (1828-1882). A Catalogue Raisonné*. Oxford: Oxford University Press, 1971.

Stanley, Susie Cunningham. *Holy Boldness: Women Preachers' Autobiographies and the Sanctified Self*. Knoxville: University of Tennessee Press, 2002.

Tanselle, G. Thomas. "The Bibliographical Concepts of Issue and State." *PBSA* (*Papers of the Bibliographical Society of America*) 69:1 (1975): 17-66.

—. "The Bibliographical Description of Patterns." *Selected Studies in Bibliography*. Charlottesville: U Press of Virginia, 1979. 171-202.

—. "A Sample Bibliographical Description with Commentary." *Studies in Bibliography* 40 (1997): 1-30.
Thomas, Eleanor Walter. *Christina Georgina Rossetti*. New York: Columbia University Press, 1931. Rpt. New York: AMS Press, 1966.

Tobin, Thomas J. *Pre-Raphaelitism in the Nineteenth-Century Press: A Bibliography*. No 87 ELS Monograph Series. Victoria, British Columbia: University of Victoria, 2002.

Wakeling, Edward and Roger Taylor. *Lewis Carroll Photographer: The Princeton University Library Albums*. Princeton: Princeton University Press, 2002.

The Wellesley Index to Victorian Periodicals, 1824-1900 (Online). Chadwyck-Healey. http://wellesley. chadwyck.com.

White, Gleeson. *English Illustration 'The Sixties': 1877-1870*. Westminster: Constable, 1897.

INDEX OF POEMS

Poems are indexed under the latest title given by CGR. Alternate titles of first lines of poems retitled by CGR, as well as of poems given titles by WMR, are included, with a "see" reference to CGR's title. Former titles appear in brackets; first line references appear in parentheses.

To avoid confusion and multiple crosslistings, ambiguous titles in *Time Flies* (such as section headings that also function as titles) are retained only if there is no conflict with later titles given by CGR. When CGR has retitled poems from *Time Flies*, the first line of the poem, rather than the *Time Flies* title, is included here with a "see" reference. Poems sequentially numbered in *Time Flies* are also treated as a single poem, since CGR invariably reprinted them in that form.

Posthumous collections of poetry excerpts are not indexed here.

INDEX OF PROSE

Excerpts from Rossetti's books of devotional prose are indexed under the book title. Short fiction and nonfiction prose is indexed under the last title given by Rossetti. Entries in the *Imperial Dictionary of Universal Biography* are not separately indexed.

GENERAL INDEX

Note: The publication history of individual works by Rossetti is presented in the Indexes of Poems and Prose.